D1480473

Old Fields

Only rarely do color, light, and form combine to flatten perspective. Here the artist Suzanne Jevne casts almost no shadow, appears to float, and seems to have just thrown the rock embedded in the clay cliff ten feet behind her.

JOHN R. STILGOE

Old Fields

Photography, Glamour,
and Fantasy Landscape

UNIVERSITY OF VIRGINIA PRESS

CHARLOTTESVILLE AND LONDON

University of Virginia Press
© 2014 by the Rector and Visitors
of the University of Virginia
All rights reserved
Printed in the United States of America on acid-free paper

First published 2014

1 3 5 7 9 8 6 4 2

Library of Congress Cataloging-in-Publication Data
Stilgoe, John R., 1949–.
Old fields : photography, glamour, and fantasy landscape /
John R. Stilgoe.
pages   cm
Includes bibliographical references and index.
ISBN 978-0-8139-3515-7 (cloth : alk. paper) —
ISBN 978-0-8139-3516-4 (e-book)
1. Photography—Philosophy. 2. Landscape photography.
3. Vernacular photography. 4. Photography, Artistic.
I. Title.
TR183.S755 2014
778.3—dc23
2013024097

All illustrations unless otherwise noted from the author's collection. Page 31, Keystone View Co. Inc. of N.Y.; page 187, courtesy Houghton Library, Harvard University.

for Suzanne Jevne

CONTENTS

PREFACE

LANDSCAPE GLIMMERS IN FANTASY FICTION AND IN GLAMOUR PHOTOGraphy. Both subvert contemporary convention and postmodern ideology. They herald the end of traditional ecosystem concern and the imminent arrival of designed life forms, and they offer innovative views of traditional landscape, especially of devalued and abandoned terrain.

They assert that some people, especially some women, are gifted in ways that transform landscape and shatter brittle meritocracies. Fantasy fiction emphasizes unnerving novelty in space and in seeing, and in the magic of visual magic, glamour itself. In the twilight of film photography it appeals to young people and adults no longer adept at deliberate and accidental image making. Glamour photography slithers among photographic genres definitely not art, deftly separating itself from erotica, pornography, fashion imagery, from pinup, cheesecake, and formal portraiture, and from casual and candid picture making of landscape and people. Almost always, its critics focus on its models, not its settings. In the first years of the twenty-first century, glamour photography still embraces barbed definitions of visual magic and disused landscape that suffuse contemporary fantasy fiction written ostensibly for children and teenagers but now read by adults. Together, fantasy fiction and glamour photography inaugurate something glimpsed just around the curve of time.

Glamour itself creates tension. Always the tension allures. It snares the eye, skews the consciousness, and sometimes evokes physical action. It halts walking adults, stills conversation, now and then produces goose bumps, often despite will power marshaled against it. All kissing cousins of the erotic feelings pornography often stimulates, the physical responses suggest that glamour is power only slightly refined from raw energy. Children glimpse it rarely and fleetingly and want to know it intimately, but formal education trains their eyes from it. Anthropologists once wrote of animal magnetism and political commentators still gush over charisma, but schoolteachers and scholars shun glamour and glamour photography especially. Some children descry the organized avoidance and veer toward the power that scares so many self-styled responsible adults.

Visual magic—glammyre or glamour—warns discerning people that words and numbers prove less than comprehensive, but only photographers, often idiosyncratic amateurs long estranged from mainstream art but now on the cusp of discovery, routinely embrace it. Fantasy fiction introduces glamour to wider audiences: its preoccupation with faerie, what young scholars define as some place other than the everyday, emphasizes visual acuity. Apparition and appearance order the best of fantasy, especially that written for adolescents. Glamour structures much of J. R. R. Tolkien's 1937 *The Hobbit* and subsequent books, but in the 1970s it focused fantasy authors already dismissing kinetic media. As most children and adults forsook looking around for gazing at cinema and television screens, fantasy writers followed the lead of a handful of early twentieth-century photographers whose images contradicted cinema views. Later photographers clashed with the makers of Hollywood and television imagery and ideology, then diverged from the main-traveled roads media studies scholars trudge. Art historians ignore the deviants, as do almost everyone else: academics dismiss their work as sexist or worse. Post-1970s fantasy fiction, especially that directed at very smart adolescents in well-nigh subversive ways, dismisses ordinary landscape and visual media. It maps a scarcely discernible path away from mere consumption of images, a faint, overgrown path meandering into the ruins and lone-lands of glamour photography. It populates new landscape with new genii loci in ways glamour photographers approve.

Glamour is power its makers scarcely control. Visually produced magic frightens the timid: they condemn it as delusive or compulsively alluring. Women and photographers who wield its power understand its relation to place and to an elitist acuity that grows stronger by the year. They know that genuine glamour originates often in accident, frequently slips free of stricture, and sometimes harms. The timid fear glamour, but they fear more the ways it empowers children bored with school and mass media alike.

Modern fantasy fiction recognizes glamour as elucidating secularization and worries about planetary climate transformation, social realignment, and the imminence and potential preeminence of biological engineering. It prepares readers for inchoate change heralded by visual force. It warns of danger, difference, and opportunity, while savoring all; it champions hard looking, seeing shadows of transparent or invisible things and forces. It gradually replaces the photography that establishment critics still dismiss as illustration enterprise neither art nor advertising. Indeed, except among cognoscenti it supplants almost all but cellphone snapshot photography. Despite the proliferation of digital cameras and camera-fitted cell phones, few young people know much about photographic technique, and almost none know glamour photography. Many women equate it with pornography and scorn it or pretend to scorn it even as they feel its allure. Many men know it as something distinct from pornography but rarely mentioned aloud since the middle 1970s. Nowadays they accept it as power imbued with chance, an emblem of imminent change fitfully traced in the best fantasy fiction.

A camera can make anyone, even a child or other novice, momentarily a gifted photographer. While pencils, paints, and paper cannot make a neophyte a superb artist any more than a saxophone or violin can make their holders instantly musicians, it is possible for a first-time photographer to make a superb image. It is possible, if unlikely, because it is technically feasible.

What cameras do independently makes meditative photographers wary. Photographers often forget the mischief latent in cameras, but a few know the intermittent, sometimes intransigent independence of their instruments. So long as he clicks away thoughtlessly, or with only a little regard for exposure and composition, the typical image maker almost never discovers surprise. Only when he begins making better than average images in other than average light and surroundings may he encounter excellence by chance. Glamour thrives in traditional photography now alien to an electronics-addicted, image-consuming generation. It suffuses quality fantasy fiction because glamour is raw, often erratic visual power a few photographers understood by 1925 but which disappeared from Hollywood film soon after. But ten years later, 35 mm photography, itself a product of the Hollywood industry using 35 mm cine film, almost obliterated a photographic effort mainstream critics by then derided. Only a few photographers persevered. Their success shaped a new genre of edgy fiction emphasizing special people making abandoned or unfrequented landscape special.

As an undergraduate I glimpsed a young woman rising from sitting tailor-fashion on the floor, her hands touching nothing but air. Many of the men at the party unconsciously glanced at her and then away, and a handful of women stared momentarily, not at the woman but at the men turning their heads. I saw this in a mirror hung on an open door partially separating two rooms. The mirror enabled my noticing something I have noted regularly since. Any woman who rises to her feet without touching her hands to the floor draws the eyes of men, and always a few women half-consciously notice the eye movement. Haphazard inquiry indicates that no one recalls anything: they remember neither looking nor noticing looking. Their attention wavered but they do not recollect the wavering. But unrecollected wavering of attention orders *The Dark Is Rising, Greenwitch,* and other 1970s adolescent-focused books by Susan Cooper that my undergraduates reread to unwind. Only the now-rare student devoted to traditional photography grasps the link between such fiction and the making of photographs. All others vaguely glimpse a message about glimpsing.

In the late 1980s women students arrived in my office hours: few had enrolled in my courses, and most I had never met. Most carried images clipped or torn from fashion magazines. They found the images not disturbing but intriguing, often fascinating and seductive, yet somehow subversive, almost illicit; they kept the images close but under notebook covers, out of sight and private, but near. They understood the advertisements as somehow connected to fantasy fiction they cherished in girlhood, and contradicting feminist theory enunciated in the 1970s and later. They designated the images *glamour* or *fantasy*. None knew much of the technologies involved in making them: none of the women made more than the rare snapshot. By the late 1990s I listened to a woman a week and recognized the framework merging juvenile-adult fantasy literature and upscale, women-focused advertising imagery, almost of it set in outdoor, mysterious, shadowy, ruined landscape. The women spoke still of glamour and fantasy, but more frequently of power: after the September 2001 terrorist attacks they spoke of power constantly.

Then one afternoon at my local gas station a young customer showed a young mechanic a photograph of his curvaceous girlfriend wearing an exiguous bikini at the edge of the nearby estuary. The eighty-year-old proprietor of the gas station overheard the conversation, stared at the image, then reached for his billfold and extracted a faded photograph of a woman wearing much less and smiling far more provocatively in meadow running down to salt marsh. He compared the two images, squinting through his reading glasses. When asked the identity of the woman in his picture, he replied, "My girlfriend, 1942." One of the twenty-something men asked why he still carried his girlfriend's photograph despite his long-term marriage, and the owner replied, "My wife, you idiot. Married her in '45." A few days later I mentioned the incident to my father, who stared at me a moment, then pulled out his wallet and withdrew a faded photograph. I stared at the smiling, wide-eyed, scantily clad woman standing in a wash of sunlight; he chuckled and said, "Got it at mail call, June 1942." When I asked my mother about the image, she blushed, then explained that she had sewn the outfit herself, built a self-timer for her camera, and photographed herself, then developed and printed the images so that no one but she and her sweetheart might see them. In the next few years I inquired about the images aged veterans carried in their billfolds and their hearts, discovering a fragment about the glamour and female power that heartened the war effort, especially overseas. In many of the images, landscape flowed and shaped itself around the women.

Not for several years did I probe how cameras and determined amateur photography linked glamour and fantasy. For decades I had peered down the dark well of top-viewfinder cameras, especially my beloved Rolleiflexes, but workaday 35 mm photography distracted me from the medium-format cameras that welded glamour and fantasy just before World War II. In the twilight of film photography I began experimenting with period cameras, rummaging in the mass of photography instruction magazines, books, and manuals I have assembled over decades, and asking undergraduates what caused them to reread a handful of fantasy novels they first read between ages ten and twelve. A few authors transcended the mass, and their transcendence often opposed ordinary educational enterprise. I wondered especially at Philip Pullman's masterful *The Golden Compass,* and the glamour of Mrs. Coulter, which transforms an alternate-world Oxford University.

In the autumn of 1997 I sheared a bearing on the plow assembly that attaches to my old John Deere farm tractor. One frosty Saturday afternoon, as I knelt next to the fifty-year-old implement, I realized that my monkey wrench grasped a bolt holding a huge coulter wheel. When the tractor moves forward, the coulter wheel cuts sod and tangles of vegetation and rides over large rocks, easing the thrust of the plowshare and moldboard behind it. I leaned against one of the rear tires of the tractor, glanced again at the coulter wheel, then stared across the field into the shadowed woodlot, wondering why Pullman named his glamorous woman Coulter. In the end, her glamour cuts more sharply than any knife, even the subtle knife that orders another of his books.

Glamour photography rewards sustained analysis, but here I focus chiefly on its outdoor, typically ruined rural setting. Ideology proves useless in analyzing individual images, let alone their contexts. Feminism, even radical feminism, shifted its gaze from fashion advertising, especially upscale fashion advertising, circa 1990, just as powerful, aggressive models supplanted the frail. Until about 2000, women's studies academics advanced little beyond earlier notions of such illustrations as demeaning women and destroying the body images of little girls. The pictures sell clothing, cosmetics, and accessories to the women who view them: the images work, especially among wealthy women. Only rarely do men page through *Vogue* and similar magazines, let alone the holiday catalogs published by the Boca Raton Bal Moral shops and other extremely expensive boutiques too thoughtlessly designated *exclusive.* Few women who view most magazine images can afford the advertised items, but enough buy them to support an industry capable of developing products and arresting images year after year. The imagery reveals a great class divide otherwise infrequently apparent in a self-styled middle-class nation: some women buy the advertised products and have places to wear them. Critics typically address the models and the clothing and rarely ponder the meaning of the settings, most of which emphasize mystery and might be the habitat of sprites, elves, and creatures yet to be.

Many Harvard undergraduate women aspire to the wealth that enables women to purchase the advertised items and access the rare places. Most of the women who arrive in my attic office understand, often in inchoate ways, that the images tap a source of power their mothers abandoned to film stars, supermodels, and a small coterie of other women who enjoy landscapes most women see only in advertising. They want that power back. And they fear that that it now lies in the hands of men camouflaged in realms typical scholarship derides. They realize that their formal education never addresses the power of certain types of photographic image making, a power they understand as fundamentally male and fundamentally mysterious, let alone the powers that shape certain sorts of landscape.

The images prove almost visceral. Few of the women know much about making photographs other than snapshots, and none has been photographed by a glamourist. As they speak I smile to myself. Long ago I considered glamour photography as a career. In the late 1960s I found Peter Gowland's *How to Photograph Women* and read that "he photographs beautiful women, clothed and unclothed, and he gets paid for it." Along with Peter Basch's *Glamour Photography* and Carl Bakal's *How to Shoot for Glamour,* the book made clear how photographers produced fashion magazine images and others they understood as pure glamour. Graduate school restricted my forays into glamour imagery, and a scholarly career terminated it: 100,000 35 mm slides of the built environment later, I realize that I rarely make a photograph. But decades ago I knew that photography sometimes connects setting and person in ways that evoke glamour, especially when the camera acts independently. Glamour can empower a woman, especially if she understands it, her surroundings, and a bit of photographic technique. What she does with the power lies beyond the scope of this book. The study of glamour empowers not only some women but some photographers intent on making glamour manifest, on facilitating the very happening of glamour.

Two themes order this very personal book: the setting of fantasy glamour and the creation of the glamorous genii loci who people it. "When man cannot conquer his environment in actuality, he inevitably does so symbolically," mused the photographer Clarence John Laughlin in "Surrealism in New Orleans." His 1941 *Harper's Bazaar* photographic essay addresses objects and landscapes "that are moving because their appeal is not to the intelligence" but instead they "embody surrealistic elements and attain a hyper-reality." His grasp of "singular and bitter beauty" only now begins to intrigue historians of photography, but in 1941 it fitted perfectly into an edgy aesthetic. Wartime fashion and cheesecake photography obscure the more creative, idiosyncratic personal enthusiast effort almost swamped by cinema and television after World War II. Glamour photographers, especially the dedicated amateurs critics routinely condemned, not so long ago toyed with concentrated power. Some do so still.

All that follows here concerns that power, not its commercial manifestations. Something fragmented in the 1910s as the bulk of the American population drifted into viewership, consuming print images, then cinema, then television and video and Internet-based pictures, the latter all programmed, the last by software few viewers understand or even realize. While experts in visual culture studies focus on the flood of imagery intended for mass or large-cohort consumption, I do not. This book examines not the makers of public imagery nor its consumers, but the cognoscenti who made and make images, usually for themselves. What they make illuminates the longing for the glamour fantasy writers explicate.

Bilbo Baggins is fifty years old when *The Hobbit* opens. In 1968 I promised myself that I would reread the story when I turned fifty. I did. My square-format cameras are at least a half-century old now and in their viewing wells I see the conjunctions that follow here.

Over decades many friends have enabled my old photography, old camera, old glamour enterprise. I thank first Cynthia Buck, Suzanne Jevne, Jacquelyn Paradise, and Marcia Zottoli Stone, all patient models from high-school days. Anthony Ferranti, owner of the now-vanished Ferranti-Dege camera store in Harvard Square, deserves special thanks too. I thank also Robert Belyea, April Cottini, Dana Cushing, Babette Haley, David Marsden, Joseph McGuire, Laura Nowosielski, and Harold Tuttle. I honor the memory of Loring Jacobs, Harry Merritt, and Eleanor Norris, who shared my deep love of the abandoned agricultural landscape. And I thank my editors at the University of Virginia Press, Ruth Melville, Ellen Satrom, and Boyd Zenner. Suzanne Jevne shaped and still shapes my thinking about light itself: I am especially indebted to her.

Old Fields

Introduction

Beyond the ground glass of the nineteenth-century view cameras few photographers still cherish, images shimmer in ways that once caused thoughtful observers to imagine that each camera enclosed a fantasy world.

GLAMOUR GOVERNS EVERYTHING THAT FOLLOWS
here. Descrying anything in haze or twilight, especially the shadows and
shimmering of long-marginalized subjects, demands sustained scrutiny
of what is there, might be there, and seems not to be there but nonetheless casts shadows. Scrutiny often begins in glimpse. Viewing itself
changes in the glimmer, and always involves lenses that reflect and re-
fract observer bias. Three topics shape this inquiry: old-road abandoned
landscapes fraught with imaginative potential, genii loci powerful in
ways most intellectuals dismiss or ignore, and traditional glamour photography, particularly the square-image, medium-format photography
designated 2¼ and still known by the brand name of a German twin-lens
reflex camera, *Rolleiflex*. None of these topics much concerns academics
nowadays.

All concern me first because I live down the road from where I grew
up. What I see around my barn and henhouse, across my fields, and inside
the margin of the woods shapes a view most urban academics find obsolescent.[1] I live in an old-fields landscape not so much historical in textbook ways as antique enough to enable the merging of times before with
an always-undesignated something else.[2] However quintessentially New
England visitors find my acres and their setting, the structures and fields
make up pieces of an old-fields landscape still visually rural but no longer agricultural.[3] In an urban, media-fixated age, Brookside Farm offers a
portal on something slipping into the past but slewing sideways too.[4]

This book began in my boyhood. I was six before I saw television,
and early rural reception proved so erratic I never developed the habit
of watching. My town lacked a cinema and the nearest lay beyond bicycle range. My closest friends and I roamed the outdoors, especially
the old fields, swamps, cart paths, and salt marshes, and never bonded
with electronic media in ways our younger siblings did.[5] They consumed
televised images, especially when winter days found us outside playing
hockey on frozen mill ponds or indoors in woodstove-warmed basements
and workshops building model railroads, small boats, and other things.[6]
I liked making images rather than only looking at them and by age ten I
liked fixing old cameras.[7] A succession of hand-me-down square-format
cameras facilitated my efforts and haphazardly connected me with outdated photographic technology. I never worried about endangering the
clunkers along the windblown beach or in rain and fog.[8] Throughout my
school years I made photographs, shifted from one square-format camera to another, cheerfully eschewed 35 mm cameras I could not afford,

and repaired or modified the square-format ones adults abandoned. By my middle teens I knew that some men made careers photographing women, I had acquired a few books on glamour photography, and I had begun to study the importance of landscape in outdoor photography of women.[9] Finding subjects presented no difficulties in college, where I discovered fast-deepening divisions between undergraduates male and female who consumed images and those who made them, and between women who wanted to be photographed and women who did not.[10] There too I first discerned the long-wildered landscape sheltering fantasy and glamour in fiction and in photography, and have been wondering at it—especially its crypto-British rural foundations—ever since.

Glamour gleams everywhere in the contemporary fantasy landscape. Light, shadow, sparkle, shimmer, glimmer, shape-shifting, and reflection swirl throughout a genre now and then tracing visual acuity evolving into visual power in ways that draw energy from place or energize place.[11] Fantasy fiction gains readers as metropolitan sprawl overwhelms traditional landscape and as traditional image making declines in popularity and nuance. Most young people consume programmed imagery rather than make their own, and as digital technique makes esoteric almost all traditional knowledge of cameras, film, processing, sensitized paper, and dark-chamber accident, they forget the force of photographic accident.[12] In an age when spectators bound to cinema and television screens, video games, and hypertext-language protocols wax fat and sluggish and academics fear the obsolescence of word printed on paper and their comfortable positions both, novelists imagine long-mislaid wisdom—religious and otherwise—hidden in paintings or stashed in volumes unknown to librarians.[13] Fantasy fiction offers thoughtful adolescents a portal on alternative universes and worldviews different from those espoused in most unionized public-school classrooms, but seductively and sometimes salaciously beckoning in high-fashion magazines.[14] It offers more to adults, perhaps especially to those sensing that difficult times may grow worse.[15] Even those only astonished by the merchandising success of J. K. Rowling's Harry Potter series or wondering why bookstores shelve Anne Rice's New Orleans–centric vampire dynasty novels outside the fantasy section find real-world revelations in fantasy writing.[16] The genre offers most to young and middle-aged adults who reread the fantasy novels that entranced them as adolescents. They discover that fantasy often concerns an alternative immediate nearness.

Fantasy writing prepares its readers for the imminent arrival of genetically engineered life forms, for the open, perhaps promiscuous intersection of near-parallel universes, and for post-ecological ways of envisioning designed nature.[17] Always it suggests that some people have or momentarily wield immense power, sometimes power beyond their ability, and typically it insinuates that visual magic creates alternative realities.[18] Topography and plant species remain as usual, but the color of everything acquires new luster and vibrancy: the protagonist might be looking into the shielded ground-glass finder of a Rolleiflex camera.[19]

Glamour occasionally invests devalued, usually disused or abandoned and nearly always unnoticed, landscape with something special, but only certain people will notice.[20] While glamour typically involves the fall of light on a place, mist in the air, moonlight obscured by clouds, or perhaps an obtuse view into shadows, it involves too the sensitive observer with time and space to notice.[21] "It is most remarkable that the ancient track leading to the southwestern gate, shown so clearly on the air-photograph, should at midday be absolutely invisible and untraceable on the ground," wrote the archaeologist-topographers G. S. Crawford and Alexander Keiller in their 1928 *Wessex from the Air*, "but gradually, as evening approaches, an observer resting on the southern rampart will see its whole line and course mysteriously emerge, take form, and rise into view as the setting sun strikes it with its slanting rays."[22] They understood aerial photography as revealing the remnants of henges, alignments, and other prehistoric landscape features hitherto seen only by a handful of people. Sometimes the fall of light turns a place momentarily glamorous for those who notice: thus light becomes a protagonist.[23]

Fantasy writing offers readers, especially young ones, a portal on what some acute observers occasionally experience in specific places. Contemporary fantasy fiction, especially that aimed at juvenile readers, invariably concerns place, especially marginal zones; most descends directly from stories of faerie, what Tolkien called the perilous realm. Such places, typically rural, long abandoned, and almost overwhelmed by nature, figure subtly in British and American (especially New England and Southern) thinking about landscape. Most faerie-tradition fantasy authors premise their work in glamour, in visual magic, and in esotery, especially alternative ways of seeing, and of fixing the seen. People raised away from cinema, television, and other programmed electronic media sometimes notice in ways that shock and threaten those narrowed by media.[24] Most "alerts" or "sensitives" learn to keep silent, indeed to observe inconspicuously, sometimes almost invisibly: they dislike jeers and fear condemnation.[25] Fantasy writers use them as prototypes: the authors build on what the scryers discern, at the edges of specific places and then within them, and in so doing create entire alternative landscapes and worlds.

Trolls, dwarfs, elves, and other creatures enliven fictional woods out back, vacant lots, and portals opening on faerie. Fantasy writers create protagonists most unlike contemporary media celebrities: often underdogs, they discover powers within and around themselves, stumble into adventures, and frequently help others less fortunate than themselves. Invariably they confront the locals, the genii loci of places washed by glamour. The genii loci reward scrutiny: they illuminate and fuel a deepening twenty-first century desire to people landscape and wilderness with something other than ordinary animals.[26] Their popularity in fantasy fiction suggests that readers have lost what an earlier generation at least surmised: that some people belong in and to some places, draw energy from place, and shape place about them.

No one photographs a gnome or nymph. Critics praise or revile fantasy fiction in part for its book-jacket illustrations. The genre supports an entire cohort of artists versed in depicting humanoids, dragons, and other creatures of authorial imaginings. It supports no photographers.[27]

But some photographers discern glamour and enhance it; sometimes they create it. Nowadays tainted by forced association with pinup, cheesecake, and pornographic photography, glamour photography flourishes away from its more respectable and accepted partner, fashion photography.[28] In *Vanity Fair* and similar magazines, readers typically encounter photographs of women modeling clothes in very improbable settings indeed: the women are the professional, employed genii loci of a new era.[29] For more than seventy years such images have successfully sold clothing and built brand loyalty.[30] If such images can alter the body images of girls and women and cause eating disorders, for example, they may do more.[31] Certainly they stimulate a desire for consumerist glitz: they conflate glamour with attire in ways feminists identified in the early 1970s as leading to the objectification of the female body and of women themselves.[32]

Fashion magazine imagery and now *Second Life* and other Internet massively multiplayer online role-playing games (in which most players craft gorgeous or handsome avatars) mask a long-standing effort by advanced amateur photographers to photograph the glamour they find or create in places most people ignore.[33] Typically the amateur effort involves the photography of women as the genii loci of particular places.[34]

If not exactly a class-identifiable avocation, glamour photography as I define it in the pages following ordinarily requires high-quality cameras and experience purchased by way of hundreds of rolls of film. In the late 1920s glamour photography diverged from most advertising imagery and from 35 mm photography, especially so-called candid photography. At the beginning of World War II its practitioners favored square-format, medium-format, ground-glass focused cameras, especially the Rolleiflex built by Franke and Heidecke in Braunschweig. Many still do, for reasons subsequent chapters elucidate.

I see in squares. I acknowledge my peripheral vision and the assertions of experts that the closest photographic format to human vision is 6×12 or 6×17 centimeters.[35] But I see in squares.[36] The most venerable medium-format image size is 6×6 centimeters, still called 2¼ × 2¼, the view and film size of my aging, recently rebuilt Rolleiflex twin-lens reflex cameras. Square-image medium-format photography strikes me as more versatile than the 35 mm format derived from cinema film: the larger negative produces a far sharper negative or color transparency (cropping images for printing on standard-size sensitized paper means losing only a tiny amount of film area), and medium-format transparencies produce sumptuous projected images.[37] But the square format itself militates against the totalitarian rectangular rule of automobile windshields, cinema screens, 35 mm camera viewfinders, wide-screen televisions, laptop computer screens, and other high-tech gadgets.[38] Fringe vision proves exactly that: marginal. The walker, the horseback rider, the cyclist and motorcyclist, even the farmer high atop an old farm tractor looks ahead largely by square.[39] Artists know configurations other than rectangles sometimes charge their creations in part because the configurations differ from the accustomed: artists work with age-old formulas too easily dismissed as golden-section derivatives.[40]

Into the 1930s the square view seemed natural, and the rectangular one forced. "From the technical point of view it is therefore established that the square surpasses the oblong, because it brings more into the picture," Walther Heering asserted in *The Rolleiflex Book*. "But also the square is more beautiful than the oblong. It is created organically by the circular form of the objective and is optically realistic, corresponding to the field of vision of the human eye." Newtonian optics demonstrates that the round lens and aperture indeed produce an image best suited to square-format film; only experience and personal preference confirm the correctness of Heering's insistence that "the weighty mass of the square is modern, all concentrated realism, calm, and serene."[41] His understanding of serenity and related emotional states parallels what Ansel Adams concluded in a 1934 *Camera Craft* article: the photographic effort involves an effort to "*emotionally* represent" the tonalities of the subject itself by approaching "the full tonal scale of eye vision."[42] Heering scorned the rectangle he saw framing everything from windshields to cinema screens, and he understood the deepening nuances of emotional response to images. Few cinematographers agreed.[43]

Sergei Eisenstein, however, championed square-format cinematography in a 1930 speech before the Technicians Branch of the Academy of Motion Picture Arts and Sciences in Hollywood. In "The Dynamic Square," published a year later in the Swiss magazine *Close Up,* he insisted that "for thirty years we have been content to see excluded 50 per cent of compositional possibilities, in consequence of the *horizontal shape* of the frame." In 1889 Edison had invented what became the de facto rectangular cinema graphic aspect ratio, what everyone called "Edison-size film."[44] Eisenstein argued that standardizing cinema screen proportions at approximately a 3:5 ratio in a moment when sound technology innovation roiled the entire industry originated solely in corporate greed. Nothing intellectual, no awareness of the square-format images "available to the cheapest magazine yet debarred for thirty years from the screen," and not even something as popular as the Kodak snapshot camera figured in the corporate effort to standardize screen proportions globally. Eisenstein admitted that his "desire to chant the hymn of the male, the strong, the virile, active, *vertical* composition" led to sexual issues "possibly too offensive for many a sensitive hearer," but he nonetheless angled attention at the fundamental femininity of the rectangular cinema screen. While largely unread today, "The Dynamic Square" avers that "no matter what the theoretic premises, only the square will afford us the real opportunity at last to give decent shots of so many things banished from the screen." In noting that twisting medieval streets and Gothic cathedrals defeated cinematographers, Eisenstein unwittingly cited exactly the sort of subject Heering and other Rolleiflex users reproduced in defense of the square. "Why the hell should we drag behind us in these days of triumph the melancholy memory of the unfulfilled desire of the static rectangle striving to become dynamic?" Eisenstein asked of an art form increasingly constricted by corporate technology and mandate.[45] But he knew that cinema-industry moguls around the world understood the profit in architecture dictated by optics: rectangular screens enabled architects to build balconies roughly a third as long as the main floors of cinema houses, thus packing in even more paying customers.[46]

Now and then when I visit a cinema house I amuse myself by comparing screen size and proportion against the main-floor footprint.[47] Elsewhere I realize the enduring force of the square view and the square image and the bulky Rolleiflex camera that moves liner-like among the small-craft 35 mm film and digital cameras almost everyone else holds. Heering and Eisenstein may be wrong about the weighty mass of the square, but I know well the weighty mass of the Rolleiflex medium-format camera and at least some of the encoded messages implicit in that mass.[48] Some of those messages whisper from smaller square-format cameras still.

My 1967 Kodak Instamatic S-10 still nestles in my hand as it did throughout my college and graduate-school days. Lightweight and far thinner than earlier brick-like Instamatics, the S-10 epitomizes Eastman Kodak box camera innovation. Its lens and shutter release pop out of its aluminum body at the touch of a button. The Instamatic S-10 produces crisp images within a broad range of ambient lighting conditions: fast film and battery-powered Magicube flashbulbs enable it to make quality images indoors, in shade, and in dark New England winters that caused me to keep it loaded with ISO 400 film. Once I knew the seven-and-a-halffoot distance intuitively, the casual images (almost all black-and-white) pleased most subjects.[49] That the S-10 always made square images occasionally prompted friends to ask why the square format satisfied me in ways boyhood hand-me-down cameras had satisfied me. I found the square strong, stark, and stable. And the square glowing at the bottom of the dark well of the Rolleiflex light well makes color vibrant in ways that resemble accounts of sorcerers scrying in black bowls of oil-covered water.[50]

People pantomiming a fashion photographer at work still make squares from thumbs and raised forefingers brought together, then mime hands holding a large camera at waist level. For fifty years the square-format Rolleiflex made most fashion magazine images, and it lurks still in the recesses of cultural memory. My decades-old Rolleiflexes attract the attention of women, often at the beach, but elsewhere too; fashion magazines intermittently if subtly still depict the camera, usually in retrospective articles.[51]

In the 1940s glamour became a mystery itself. Already distinct from pinup and cheesecake photography, glamour photography swerved from fashion imagery and pornography too.[52] In his 1950 *A Rhetoric of Motives,* Kenneth Burke admitted, "'Glamour' is now a term, in the world of publicity, for mystery." But he acknowledged that part of the mystery originated in the root meanings of the word, especially their connotations of a haze in the air which makes things appear different than usual or anything else through which something "appears delusively magnified or glorified."[53] Hollywood and Madison Avenue alike feared glamour as something sliding beyond corporate control, and perhaps already gone into the hands of private makers.[54]

Glamour and its children's fantasy framework have become the mysterious, risky portal through which children and many adults now view alternative presents and futures.[55] Late nineteenth- and early twentieth-century fantasy writers discerned depths of European history absent from schoolbooks, and by the late 1920s American fantasy writers bemoaned not so much a perceived shallowness of American history but the prudery of its written record. Many pulp magazine fantasy writers peopled the New World with medieval explorers, Norse conquerors, and other deeper-past characters, and such effort continues sporadically. But by 1948, when Randall Jarrell published "The Märchen," a long poem elucidating the sumptuous richness of the European folk past, fantasy writers had punched into the pasts of colonial New England, the antebellum South, and similar places as proper locales for glamour. In his 2001 *American Gods*, Neil Gaiman depicts deities arriving as cargo aboard Phoenician ships trading near present-day St. Louis: his novel continues the 1920s tradition. Faerie now blossoms as pre-, proto-, or a-industrial but essentially ahistorical and apart; perhaps Philip Pullman's Dark Materials series proves the most powerful recent example of faerie existing as an elsewhere magical present reaching into alternative futures presenting more unsettling themes than biological morphing alone, especially the making and glimpsing of glamour in hazy landscape.[56] Much fantasy writing endures not as the first outpost of new social Darwinism, but as a fast-moving field force just now harrying well-established academic bastions.[57] The best of it involves glamour, landscape, genii loci, and seeing in ways some amateur photographers accepted in the 1920s (and many more by 1940) as fundamentally opposed to advertising and cinema imagery, and subsequently to television, video, and computer imagery.[58]

At the near-parallel-universe Oxford University, the chief character of Pullman's *The Golden Compass* spies on an event becoming rare in this continuum. The novel opens with the magisterial Lord Asriel projecting transparencies before a collection of scholars. The first "circular photogram in sharp black and white" depicts an Arctic hut by moonlight: Lord Asriel explains that the "photogram was taken with a standard silver nitrate emulsion," but the next with a "new specially prepared emulsion." The much darker slide "was as if the moonlight had been filtered out," but the man discernible in the hut doorway stands bathed in light with a "fountain of glowing particles" streaming downward toward his hand. Slide follows slide, ordinary emulsion ones of the northern lights preceding ones made with the special emulsion. Finally Lord Asriel projects an image of a city in the night sky: the special emulsion has caught something behind the shimmering of the Aurora.[59] The image is not a simulacrum exactly, but something more mysterious and in the beginning less well defined and designated: it is glamorous and instantly and immediately powerful.[60] On a screen of stretched white linen the image projected by the white-hot flame of the hissing lantern—what the 1900 era knew as a "magic lantern"—transfixes the scholars.[61] Lord Asriel has been in the Arctic in part to test the new emulsion that records a radiant energy otherwise unseen.

Nowadays projecting transparencies, especially the color ones Lord Asriel apologizes for not having made, grows obsolescent. I teach still with slide projectors, utterly reliable Kodak Carousel machines silent in a glass-fronted oak box at the rear of my classroom. My students find projected 35 mm transparencies effective, and lately serene when compared to the grainy digital images other faculty prefer.[62] But in my attic office, on a great rolling stand I built for it, slumbers the immense German-built Lucent 2¼ projector. The ancient cannon-like monster specially ordered for projection of medium-format transparencies in large lecture halls serves mostly to instill curiosity among students who have never seen images projected by a technology obsolescent by 1960 and terminated as too costly by 1980.[63] Only when it comes to life once a year do the students murmur their amazement at the exquisite detail visible in the gigantic images. Lately they mention the magic lantern of Pullman's Dark Materials novels.[64]

It is rewarding to watch young men and women confront a technological dinosaur throwing images vastly better than those the 35 mm slide projectors produce and extraordinarily sharper and richer in color saturation than anything digital.[65] It is satisfying to make it perform tricks, as when I insert two medium-format transparencies simultaneously, demonstrating what Susanna Clarke describes in her fantasy novel *Jonathan Strange and Mr. Norrell*. "It was as if two transparencies had been put into a magic lantern at the same time, so that one picture overlaid the other," she writes of an ephemeral vision of two houses mingled into one that means more to readers familiar with the resolving power of antique long-lens projectors throwing large transparencies than it might to younger ones familiar only with Adobe Photoshop manipulation.[66] A generation of students inured to technological invention and especially to cinema murmurs, then wonders aloud at a machine whose visions make 35 mm projection pale.

Photographic technique can produce a visual pleasure nowadays missing from critical theory centered on photography and cinematography as art forms.[67] The film scholar David Rodowick emphasizes that "political modernism" necessarily means feeling an "endlessly deferred, unsatisfiable desire" but never joy.[68] Much of the near-visceral visual pleasure of cinema disappeared from movie houses more than a generation ago when cost-cutting measures diminished Edison-size cine-film formats already shaped to maximize profit.[69] But much photography still flourishes beyond the purview of art and documentary image making: much of it is square, medium format, and angled into glamour. It gives joy to its makers, few of whom strive for or achieve the level of art, but who know technical mastery as part of the mystery of fusing photography and glamour.

"The more adept the photographer, the more likely he is to intrude between object and viewer," warned Oscar Handlin in 1979. In *Truth and History*, he urged historians to evaluate comic books, Hollywood films, television commercials, and magazine advertisements as simple storytelling creations that "demanded little attention or understanding from their audiences" and as inventions sometimes more nuanced than most prose. He worried acutely about images produced by genius. "The work of the especially talented is both specially rewarding and specially dangerous," he concluded of photographs made by Matthew Brady, Lewis Hine, Jack Delano, and Dorothea Lange.[70] Such images rarely provide anything in the way of glamour, and they overshadow entire genres of photographs, including that intimately related to fantasy.

Critics assume photographers are adults, often ones in middle age, and not children or teenagers. Virilio, Flusser, and Barthes—who admits in his 1982 *Camera Lucida* that he is not a photographer—all published their seminal works on photography in their middle sixties. In *The Poetics of Space,* Gaston Bachelard insists that "it is not until late in life that we really revere an image, when we discover that its roots plunge well beyond the history that is fixed in our memories. In the realm of absolute imagination, we remain young late in life."[71] Undergraduates, themselves young and, despite ostentatious skepticism, inclined to trust middle-age faculty who champion texts above images, rarely realize how much contemporary technical image making belongs to the young, and how much theoretical writing about images exists merely as new text for the middle-aged to deconstruct. All too often their teachers forget the fantasy they read as adolescents, or denigrate it when it comes to mind: only a few connect fantasy fiction with contemporary imagery and image making and set about making images themselves.[72]

I am younger than Flusser, Virilio, and Barthes, but I too sense the youthfulness that suffuses so many images which lie outside the confines of art but which please young photographers and subjects intrigued with landscape, genii loci, and glamour. I wonder sometimes at my undergraduates reading dense theoretical texts about photography rather than making photographs of their own. If they made photographs they might realize, perhaps accidentally, perhaps in half-lit woods, the supernatural power of light trapped momentarily in a box of dark glass.

1 Fantasy

Nineteenth-century fantasy illustration often focused on flight that gave transformed humans the aerial view of raptors.

FANTASY OPENS ON FAERIE. BRITONS LONG IMAG-
ined faerie as the place of enchantment, sorcery, and illusion, the ground
itself of visual magic, of glamour. Well into the eighteenth century, rural
Britons knew it sometimes as a place and sometimes as pure illusion itself.[1] Early nineteenth-century novelists reshaped rural tradition into the
foundation of contemporary fantasy fiction; always they emphasized the
visual portal between the mundane world and faerie.

In Charlotte Brontë's 1847 novel *Jane Eyre,* her protagonist tells
Rochester that the men in green forsook England a hundred years before
she encountered him in Hay Lane one moonlit night, and that no longer
will summer, harvest, or winter moon shine on their revels. Unnerved by
"fairy tales" and injured from his fall on the ice-covered lane, Rochester
remains unconvinced, and wonders if Jane Eyre is not of faerie herself.[2]
Thirteen years earlier, Walter Scott assured readers of his *Demonology
and Witchcraft* that some noble families traced their ancestry back to
the goblins and nymphs still emblazoned on coats of arms.[3] Rural, traditional faerie of the sort *Jane Eyre* alludes to no more embraces the fairies
who trick Shakespeare's Falstaff than it does the elfin or insect-winged
creatures of late-Victorian and Edwardian children's book illustration.
Faerie is precisely what Tolkien called it, the perilous realm.[4] Just off the
woods or moorland path, especially after dark, faerie is another realm
altogether and its ruler is the visual.[5] Nowadays fantasy fiction offers the
most popular portal opening into it, but glamour photography offers another, one intimately connected with Brontëan glamour.

In college I first glimpsed some tracery connecting Edmund Spenser's
late sixteenth-century *The Faerie Queen* and *The Vision of Piers Plowman*
with my own glamour photography avocation. In a blaze of light a thousand times the brilliance of the sun, the nature goddess emerges from the
woods near the end of *The Faerie Queen:* Spenser likens her splendor,
even the bright and wondrous shining of her attire, to an image seen
in a glass or mirror.[6] "For thy it round and hollow shaped was,/Like to
the world it self, and seem'd a world of glas," Spenser says of Merlin's
wondrous looking glass in which Britomart scrys afar.[7] Britomart is not
the wizard, only a first-time scryer, but she uses the glass acutely, and her
momentary control intrigued me, the photographer fancying himself in
control of planes and arcs of glass.

Other glass made me wonder about the Spenserian vision.[8] Colonial-
era windowpanes sometimes vary in thickness: the waviness warps seeing.[9] Along the Massachusetts coast, centuries-old panes made on Cape

Cod now turn yellowish or lavender. At dawn or evening, often when snow covers the ground and the sky is clear, the tints skew ordinary seeing in ways that struck me as peculiarly if elusively evoked in *The Faerie Queen*.[10] Spenser concerned himself with faerie, illusion, and glamour, with what Tolkien calls "sub-creation," the making of visions beautiful and terrible. Glamour photography seemed a sub-creation akin to the view through the wavy, lavender glass in my old house surrounded by fields.[11] Shoved against oblivion by microchips and pixels, this old way of looking at the world along with glass and film cameras, film, paper, and darkrooms now strike almost everyone as obsolete.[12] But something lingers in the farewell glimmer.

This book examines those who are not "almost everyone."[13] Such individuals remain sensitive to the glamour implicit in faerie and in traditional photographic image making, see that glamour gaining power unnoticed, and value the images sometimes produced in image making now and then skewed by technical accident.[14] Some image makers possess a sort of second sight, and sometimes a film camera records gleams of the vitreous Spenserian world.[15]

Technique and equipment facilitate accident. In 1953 Franke & Heidecke introduced a graduated filter designed only for black-and-white photography. In distancing the filter from the lens, it makes the Rolleiflex camera even more versatile by acting upon direct and reflected sunlight before the rays reach the vicinity of the lens itself. A glass rectangle, one half dyed yellow, slides up and down through a square frame that fits onto the lens hood. With the Rolleiflex mounted on a tripod, the photographer slips the unit onto the finding lens, moves the yellow area of the glass until its lower edge aligns with the horizon, locks the set screw, then shifts the filter to the taking lens. The yellow zone accentuates clouds but enables full exposure of the landscape below. Given the great sensitivity of orthochromatic film to the blue-violet end of the spectrum, the gradient filter holds back the intense blue of mountain skies while enabling greater (and more precise) exposure of landscape browns and greens. With panchromatic film, the photographer reverses the position of the yellow zone, especially in springtime when high-altitude landscapes are light green against deep blue skies.[16] Most Rolleiflex owners contented themselves with one of several ordinary yellow filters, but the expensive Verlauf filter still makes possible the extremely nuanced landscape work implicit in the meaning of its name: it scatters light over time and distance.[17] It enables Rolleiflex users to record differences of light above and below horizon lines, and to experiment with optical effects unknown to photographers who simply screw circular filters immediately in front of lenses.[18] It makes the Rolleiflex to which it is attached even more likely to well-nigh accidentally record something through glass.[19]

Despite the best efforts of photographic equipment manufacturers, art school instructors, and above all, mainstream critics of photography-as-art, throughout the twentieth century a minority of photographers savored the risky magic implicit in glamour- or fantasy-based image making.[20] Almost never noticed by critics except when scorned or condemned, their efforts skirt the boundaries of propriety, pornography, and the aesthetic and moral standards espoused by corporate visual media, especially those producing images under government license.[21] Minority-created images evolve from opposition to establishment standards and find scant place in histories of art, photographic illustration, advertising, even amateur image-making manuals.[22] As traditional photography now seems time-consuming, risky, and expensive to people who want to see their electronic images instantly, otherwise self-effacing people, particularly young people condemned by their peers as traditionalist or nerdy, find fantasy fiction addressing issues that fascinate some photographers.[23]

Most fantasy fiction is trash. Shopping-mall bookstores retail it by the yard, and anyone who delves into it almost always discovers formulaic, awkward prose battered by science-fiction competition. Badly written and worse edited, the bulk of it builds on the late-1950s popularity of Tolkien's *The Lord of the Rings* or older work by Lord Dunsany and H. P. Lovecraft. Castles, ruins, thatched-roof villages, greenways, and windblown seaports materialize in vaguely medieval settings; goblins, dwarfs, trolls, orcs, elves, and humans converge in plots featuring quests, coming-of-age tribulations, erroneous succession to thrones, and, frequently, large dragons guarding treasure. Protagonists often leave humdrum real-world lives by accident: they find the woods out back, the disused commuter train station, the overgrown cart path, the abandoned gas station, the thicket behind the playground as gateways to the perilous realm.[24]

Place-names, old roads, temples, barrows, standing stones, and assorted other landscape constituents figure largely in Tolkien's fantasy writing but also in his scholarly work because they help archaic words and concepts endure.[25] *The Hobbit* and *The Lord of the Rings* introduce even young readers to the significance of words, especially those applied to place. "Real names tell you the story of the things they belong to in my language, in the Old Entish as you might say," Treebeard insists to the Hobbits; he then speaks in his own tongue before asking their pardon. "That is part of my name for it; I do not know what the word is in the outside languages."[26] Once noticed, often by adults rereading the books, Tolkien's philological didacticism intrigues not least because it typically parallels acute scrutiny of the visual environment.[27]

Tolkien's finely developed visual capabilities manifested themselves in his watercolors and the maps he made for his books, but his lifelong commitment to archaic northern language explains his fascination with concepts ranging from how twisting produces both wreaths and wraiths to glimpses of things seen in shadowed woods.[28] *The Hobbit* and *The Lord of the Rings* describe landscape topographically from a pedestrian viewpoint: in many ways, both books work as travel narratives and adventures alike.[29] Roads and paths preoccupied Tolkien, who continuously wondered at perceptions of them; the ways Hobbits and others discern paths at twilight or in different seasons of the year order much of the plots.[30] One daybreak in October, the Hobbits and Strider discern a military-made path in the foothills of mountains: "It ran cunningly, taking a line that seemed chosen so as to keep as much hidden as possible from view, both of the hilltops above and of the flats to the west." Strider the ranger eventually explains the reason for the path leading to Amon Sûl, the hill called Weathertop in Common Speech where Elendil watched for Gil-galad returning from Faerie in the West.[31] But the path, archaic place-name, and local history in time lead, not only to misadventure away from easily discerned paths and old roads and other greenways long untrodden by long-distance wayfarers and even paths scarcely descried from hilltops at noonday, but to another way of seeing altogether.[32]

Glimpses open on glamour, especially in dim light, and words often corroborate what the sensitive see, perhaps particularly those sensitives free of advertising-industry goggles and able to descry auras.[33]

In the late 1960s and early 1970s a handful of writers moved along a slender gray path away from Tolkien's emphasis on philology toward more than fleeting glimpses of glamour. Susan Cooper published *Over Sea, Under Stone*, the first book in The Dark Is Rising series, in 1965; three years later Ursula K. Le Guin published the first volume of her Earthsea series, *A Wizard of Earthsea*. Cooper and Le Guin seconded Tolkien's exploration of evil and confronted subjects that became dangerous, almost taboo, by the late 1970s, especially the place of individuals capable of making glamour (particularly from nature), the "natural" role of so-called gifted people, and the responsibilities and tribulations of sensitive people who now and then glimpse glamour and its making although they cannot make it themselves.[34]

Visual realms, faerie, fantasy, and the ways some people make glamour or descry people making glamour order the work of Cooper, Le Guin,

Ende, and Pullman. All perhaps owe a debt to the English painter and novelist Mervyn Peake, who began his Gormenghast series with *Titus Groan* in 1946, followed by *Titus Alone* thirteen years later, and *Gormenghast* in 1967.[35] Peake's work and that of the others emphasize envisioning and re-envisioning as their protagonists reach adulthood in sumptuously sub-created landscape.[36] It deserves separation from the trash that surrounds it in bookstores, and placement in a larger critical framework that embraces both painting and sophisticated photography of the sort employing Verlauf filters.[37]

The best of fantasy deserves an old-fashioned encyclopedic historical analysis emphasizing which authors read whose work, especially the short stories that appeared in now-obscure pulp magazines.[38] The role of these, especially *Weird Tales* (founded in 1923), in linking fantasy-minded authors, readers, and photographers was to open a portal on sub-creation or making.[39]

Making things designates activity fast becoming almost as mysterious as making things *happen*. "Mage and sailor are not so far apart," asserts Le Guin in *The Farthest Shore*. "Both work with the powers of sky and sea, and bend great winds to the uses of their hands, bringing near what was remote."[40] Experienced seamen, especially those who sail, may know nothing of spell weaving, but they know the power of sea and sky to inform and shape their passages.[41] In many ways, making a thing corresponds to making an ocean passage or other event. After about 1900 engineers and factory superintendents and foremen used "shop theory" to designate the creative thinking that follows design, especially in unforeseen manufacturing problems. It delineates the welding of making things and making things happen.[42] Anyone who makes things, especially things important to happiness, career, or personal advancement, possesses the power and the chance of making something better than most others can buy.[43] But the act of making itself shapes context, and spectators frequently find themselves aliens in complex events in which makers rule and spectators look but do not see.[44] Living-history museums display blacksmithing, for example, but only rarely do spectators realize that the dim ambient light in the smithy enables the smith to gauge the color of hot iron. Things happen when people make things, and often what happens transcends or violates intention and mandates alternative technique; shop theory embraces too the alternatives used only when intention goes awry.[45] "The weaving of spells is itself interwoven with the earth and the water, the winds and the fall of light of the place where it is cast," a mage tells his apprentice during a long open-boat passage in *The Farthest Shore*.[46] But like the seaman, Le Guin's wizard must first see the fall of light before it can be used: without that accomplished, neither navigation nor glamour goes well.[47] In much fantasy, what proves powerful exists in the borderlands of dark light, and only makers discern, reveal, and shape it, sometimes by shaping the dark light—or dark materials—itself.

Yet however serious the making—and perhaps the corollary finding of raw materials, equipment, and other components in the unmediated environment—sometimes whimsy shapes glamour. *Whimsy* properly designates a small, hand-powered crane. Typically whimsies work in barn-loft doorways, and a handful still grace the narrow gables of Dutch, British, and New England harbor warehouses and older barns across rural New England and upstate New York. Whimsies lift, more or less intentionally, but their operators expect to muscle cargos and hoisting gear and to have cargoes go momentarily astray. Whimsy operators expect intermittent if short-lived loss of control. Whimsy infuses fantasy and glamour, not art.[48]

Art lies beyond this book. Here glamour and fantasy enable a glimpse of forces that might well shape a future in which academics and other intellectuals lose power to Web-based inquiry or other venues and forces.[49]

Whimsy once characterized much small-camera photographic enterprise.[50] Between about 1900 and the beginning of World War I, the Eastman Kodak Company advertised its roll-film box cameras as instruments of spontaneity, playfulness, and creativity. The firm illustrated its dry-plate cameras in landscapes of leisure, especially vacation locales including beaches, mountains, and hotel porches conducive to relaxation, serendipity, and whimsy. It marketed its first Brownie roll-film box cameras to children and their parents, but quickly discovered that the low-cost cameras sold at least as well to adults who used them in childlike ways. Its advertising implied that "the camera can see what the human eye cannot, that it can open onto a larger, preternatural world—in this case, a world to which children seemingly have sole access." By 1900, however, an outpouring of complaints against the use of handheld cameras on beaches and elsewhere made clear that many American adults found others using cameras to be rude or risqué. In the first years of the twentieth century, George Eastman himself began to reshape advertising policies toward respectability. By 1917 his firm hammered away at a single theme: amateur photographers made serious, useful records of the present which grew more valuable as time passed. Seriousness overwhelmed whimsy by design. While the company never activated its planned campaign to urge American adults to photograph children so that images might exist following untimely death, it did make clear that men entering the armed services ought to be "Kodaked." World war definitively curtailed the earlier childlike gleefulness and especially its risqué strains. By 1925 most Americans expected photography to become ever more serious and ever more proper.

While Brownie cameras sold well through the 1950s, children never embraced photography as George Eastman originally envisioned.[51] The inexpensive cameras proved simple enough for any child of seven to operate and for almost any parent to afford. Eastman Kodak advertising suggested that children carry cameras outdoors, on everyday and special adventures, and certainly the firm provided masses of instructional material aimed at different cohorts of children. In 1930 the company offered every twelve-year-old American child a free Brownie, but the extraordinary effort did nothing to curtail a deepening lack of interest.[52] After 1917 an almost sinister gravity overwhelmed the early playfulness, then accidentally strengthened the consumerist attitude Hollywood encouraged after 1920.[53] Evolving from the effort to make photography serious enough for all adults, the gravity combined with Depression-era grimness and poverty to curtail whimsical photography, and not only on the part of children.[54]

In 1932 one amateur photographer essayed a theory about the lack of interest. In "A Peter Pan of the Camera," David Kennedy distinguished in *Photo-Era* between those adults who made a few snapshots as children and those who made many photographs. "Somehow we all seem to have become enthusiasts in about the same way and about the same time," he asserted of adults devoted to photography of all types. "Strange, isn't it?" Kennedy knew that something had happened twenty years earlier. He recalled his excitement at receiving a subscription-offer free pinhole camera from *Youth's Companion,* and his excited ignoring of instructions, "everything ruined, negative, print, and youthful ardor." Slowly he mastered the camera and the darkroom processes, and eventually he learned to make photographs that satisfied his intentions and impressed others. "Although the more serious things of life have, at times, interfered with camera work, the boyhood love for it has persisted," he admitted, before explaining that he still photographed the same sorts of subjects. Odd jobs first gave him the funds to buy an adult camera, and with a friend who owned another, Kennedy "tramped all over the surrounding country, making pictures of old cement quarries, steamboats, bridges, and anything else that took my fancy." In looking at photographs from his boyhood, Kennedy felt like Peter Pan. In a way, he had not grown up. "They were wonderful days, and I was happy."[55] Happiness and a sort of Spenserian light if not technical expertise gleamed in his early teenage-years photographs. Kennedy understood that he had bought a camera equal to his hoped-for photographic efforts and that his original angle of vision extended far in adulthood. But he knew something changed around World War I that killed photographic whimsy.

Brownie box cameras often failed children. They worked poorly indoors in daytime, even when light conditions seemed favorable and children erected reflection screens, usually made of bed sheets. They functioned worse in shadow and at twilight, and never after dark: not for decades did their manufacturer supply flash attachments. Close-up photography defied success, although "portrait attachment" lenses made some facial work possible. Distance photography seemed almost unattainable, and even candid shooting meant using commendable guile to bring the bulky cameras near unsuspecting subjects. Kennedy thought that amateurs who remained enthusiast photographers had moved as children from simple cameras that could not meet both childlike and rising expectations to sophisticated ones that could.[56] But everything depended on the expectations, and perhaps on expectations remaining fairly specific over time. Kennedy photographed steamboats and other landscape constituents, but he knew photographers who aimed chiefly at people, often to record or create glamour.

Americans still speak in early twentieth-century photography jargon. They remark an idea coming to them in a flash, or note that something clicked. While lightning flashes and telegraph sounders click, popular terminology originates in pre-1917 photographic playfulness, when cameras made things happen. But now adults do as children did beginning in the 1970s: when they relate seeing something exciting, perhaps a gunfight on a city street or a massive automobile collision, they exclaim that "it was just like in the movies" or "on television." Manufactured imagery becomes the standard by which they measure even extraordinary reality. For most people, image making becomes prosaic, a momentary cellphone sizzle, and traditional photography seems ever more cumbersome and expensive, and still not completely controllable.[57] In a 2006 *Wall Street Journal* article entitled "Fade to Black: The Twilight of Film Photography," Douglas Gantenbein lamented the end of the "film-as-magic era."[58] But Gantenbein was wrong. Traditional photography remains magic, and not only because film-and-paper images last far longer than anything digital, as couples now learn when they find their 1980s wedding videos disintegrated.[59] And "fade to black" remains cinema jargon. Language now evidences deepening confusion about fantasy, traditional photography, cinema, and glamour, the last a most dangerous topic indeed, one Tolkien the philologer-visualist scrutinized constantly.

Glamour is visual magic. Most fantasy writing seems at first reading focused on low-tech alternate worlds: unlike science fiction, few machines hum through its pages. Fantasy fiction often depends on magic, and especially the seeming magic of altered physical-universe rules. But then again, nowadays almost no one reads Newton's 1704 opus, *Opticks*, and so most modern readers find their understanding of some physical-universe rules, let alone the history of the camera obscura and other vision-enhancing devices, rather fuzzy.[60] "In one person he combined the experimenter, the theorist, the mechanic and, not least, the artist in exposition," Einstein wrote of Newton in the foreword to a 1952 edition of *Opticks*.[61] Einstein valued Newton as a theorist and as a discoverer whose shop-theory expertise enabled both experiments and the elucidation of laws that ought to intrigue the present, self-styled visual generation. Newton described his experiments precisely: one demonstrating facets of the prism placed "so that its Axis might be parallel to the Axis of the world" on sunny summer days also demonstrates that the earth rotates.[62] Newtonian optics underlie Vaughan Cornish's *Scenery and the Sense of Sight,* Paul Schultze-Naumburg's *Die Gestaltung der Landschaft durch den Menschen,* M. G. J. Minnaert's *Light and Color in the Outdoors,* and other pre–World War II books that sharpened the visual acuity of readers willing to experiment with cameras in fields, woods, mountains, and alongshore.[63]

Cinema, and perhaps especially television, demolished much shop theory, Newton's included, and edged children and adults away from science, rationality, and sustained scrutiny of seeing acutely and making images, including the ephemeral ones that fixed Newton's attention, and from effects that enable glamour.[64] As late as the 1970s, readers of *Scientific American* and similar journals regularly encountered articles describing firsthand experiments involving mirrors, frost-covered windowpanes, and other objects that produced nuanced visual phenomena. Many involved cameras and accessories, say placing polarizing filters on either side of windowpanes covered in frost.[65] But Hollywood and television had changed attitudes, something films sometimes announced explicitly.[66] When Luke Skywalker pilots his spacecraft deep into the canyons of the 1977 *Star Wars* Death Star, a vague voice-over directs his attention away from digital readouts. "Trust the force," it whispers in what might well be the mantra of Hollywood turning away from the envelope-pushing films of the early 1970s toward an older, simpler, more profitable formula.[67]

Makers tend to acquire shop theory from other makers and by trial and error, rather than from published sources only, and much shop theory involves disused or unvalued techniques and materials scrutinized and reemployed.[68] In the 1970s much optical and photographic shop theory disappeared into near oblivion as apprenticeship, especially volunteer, intergenerational apprenticeship, ended.[69] Only determined searchers now find paths leading toward subject-specific photography studios and darkrooms, into what is still called glamour photography, itself a sort of visual magic melding shadow, reflection, cast image, distance, and accidental making with a force most photographers consider essentially feminine.[70] Glamour imagery attests that the photographer recorded the existence of the tangible: someone was there, and the someone and the there existed however momentarily before the camera lens, Verlauf filter equipped or not.[71]

Glamour photography, along with cheesecake and some fashion photography, exists beyond the shadow lands of contemporary cinema and television.[72] Persistent rumor suggests that MTV originated in 1979 when a reader of trash novels showed a videographer a 1950s men's magazine photo sequence illustrating a strip-tease act.[73] Like many girlie and pseudo-photography magazines, the photo layout perhaps presented a visual concept forbidden to cinema and airwave-licensed television producers, but nonetheless sequential in format. Comic-book imagery, which works as sequential narrative as readers turn pages and randomly as reader eyes move haphazardly among the different cells encapsulated in each two-page spread, resembles the Microsoft Corporation Windows operating system.[74] It is likely that nowadays few Windows users think much about the graphic background of the software, why conifers dominate the wallpaper called "forest," or why blue, the dominant and default operating-window color, morphs to green on Microsoft Money screens.[75] It is likely that few computer users notice the screens that appear and disappear in milliseconds when programs load or shift, or consider the gendered nature of the screens themselves.[76] It is likely that few wonder at the skin tones and other palette constituents of digital-photography alteration software: Adobe Photoshop still lacks a glamorize-portrait menu.[77] It is likely that few ponder the precisely sited horizon line characterizing so many computer games: the line causes the gazer to gaze upward at the action.[78] Girlie magazines, comic books, and other pulp-paper productions, including some eventually distributed on glossy paper, facilitate the post-1985 corporate-based, high-tech programming now eroding academic strongholds.[79] Personal photography enables something more positively glamorous but equally dangerous to academic comfort.[80]

Radical feminism and then women's studies academics denigrated glamour and glamour photography after the late 1970s, even as glamour photography reshaped portraiture, advertising photography, and computer-generated imagery.[81] I read Kathrin Perutz's *Beyond the Looking Glass: America's Beauty Culture* in 1970, the year it appeared, in part because *looking glass* made me think of my camera lens as the glass through which I looked, and into which my models sometimes glimpsed themselves reflected.[82] Thereafter anthropologists, feminists, and anti-feminists debated fiercely about beauty and fashion, some seeing both as possible evidence of natural inequality and some understanding them as crafted exploitation of innate biological advantage.[83] Forgotten was the wisdom Margaret Mitchell voiced on the first page of her 1936 novel, *Gone with the Wind:* "Scarlet O'Hara was not beautiful, but men seldom realized it."[84] Glamour originates in something other than biological beauty; in World War II and throughout the 1950s, some women (and some photographers) understood that implicitly.[85] But by the late 1960s *Cosmopolitan Magazine,* Terry Garrity's *Sensuous Woman,* and related popular-media sources had conflated it with sexuality.

Into the 1980s women demonstrated against institutionalized glamour each winter in Harvard Square: they picketed news kiosks selling the swimsuit issue of *Sports Illustrated.*[86] By the late 1980s the protests ended in spectator snickering, heckling, and scorn; the 1983 congressional vote exempting women from draft registration tainted the protests with hypocrisy, and by 1990 they ended.[87] After that only the most radical of feminists condemned *Vanity Fair* imagery or linked bikinied women with pornographers. By 2000 obesity and worries about sun exposure only accentuated the glamour of trim, fit, strong women.[88] Commercialized glamour triumphed, exactly as Margery Wilson insisted it would in *Charm,* a 1928 tour de force book inspired by her years as a Hollywood actress and film director.[89] As was the custom of the time, Wilson insisted that any woman might be charming and that most might be glamorous if they made focused effort. "You are not asked to believe in fairies or mystery or magic—but simply to believe in yourself and the workable laws of charm," she asserted at the beginning of the first edition of a book that passed through many revised editions. "He who truly has *savoir-faire* may be said to have a magic power which blends, harmonizes and transmutes all the little roughness and awkwardness that touch him, into a smoother, more graceful, higher atmosphere." Wilson used the male pronoun easily, but she directed her books to women, writing out of much experience on the stage and in silent-picture Hollywood. "Well-bred people are almost entirely free from physical mannerisms," she averred. In arguing that charm parallels glamour, she explicated her core understanding that "it is nearer the truth to regard charm as a force, as electricity is a force, expressing itself now in a locomotive and now in a festive little red bulb of joy on a Christmas tree."[90] Glamour works silently, as Wilson learned in Hollywood, the "land of shadow shapes" that consumed genuine glamour in manufacturing glitz.[91] D. W. Griffiths used Leonardo's painting *Mona Lisa* to explain how he wanted Wilson to portray the character Brown Eyes in his film *Intolerance*. Wilson knew cinema as lower-grade imagery than painting, and charm as less powerful but more accessible than glamour.[92] The last involved visual transformation.

"The body is our tool of expression rather than being in itself the aim and end of our effort," she explained. In the 1928 edition, *Charm* divides roughly between suggestions for improving posture, placement of hands while sitting, walking, ascending stairs, and so on, and directions for mental and psychological readjustments which make individual women better listeners, more able executives, and, especially, better contenders in the scrabble for genuinely good husbands. Wilson insisted that any woman might break bad habits, create new good ones, and use the energy and time freed by good habits to advance her personal agenda. Every woman ought to have "dove-colored" as well as white or pink stationery on hand, since every woman sooner or later must write sympathy notes, and having somber stationery on hand helps eliminate procrastination and eliminates one special errand.[93] Along with advice on improving personal appearance, eliminating nervous gestures and slouching, and other visual cues, Wilson explained how women should listen acutely and speak precisely in social and business situations alike.

Charm passed through multiple editions, many entitled *Margery Wilson's Book of Charm or The Woman You Want to Be,* all insisting that "beauty is far less important to charm than is well-being. A clean body, refreshed and smoothly functioning, not only gives off the vibrations that make one's physical presence felt and admired, but gives speed and accuracy to thought." No edition offered much advice about clothing or cosmetics or indeed about anything else that might be purchased in a store; instead all focused on physical presence and simple but effective habits of mind and behavior. Over decades Wilson advised readers to stand nude before a full-length mirror, inspect posture and correct failings as dictated, then practice walking toward and away from the mirror, moving arms, sitting down and standing up, and so on. "If you are well-groomed, move with efficient grace, and have one better-than-ordinary feature, you can be handsome in the beholder's eye," Wilson explained in 1942. No one needed special beauty, especially the sort Hollywood retailed, to succeed as Wilson specified: to make visual magic a woman required only will, practice, and experience, not fine clothes.[94]

A glamorous woman *"creates her own environment."*[95] Genuine glamour enables a woman to do so silently. Most women must do so with words too, and the right words spoken correctly at the proper moment makes the speaker charming or enchanting. But Wilson emphasized that silence might prove more powerful. *"It is possible to sit silently and gradually have everyone who is talking address his remarks to you,"* she insisted. Such women possess and may sometimes use a force "like a dynamic magnet." They attract and wield other powers Wilson thought so dangerous that she cautioned her readers not to experiment until they had attained a high level of word-based achievement.[96]

It is difficult to evaluate the impact of Wilson's books on American women.[97] While entangled in cinema imagery, the books transcend it: their arguments anticipate the social transformations they helped shape. In the midst of World War II, readers learned that "the fashionable attitude of the future will be an even more conscious recognition of our responsibility to others." Edition after edition warns women to not drop their voices at the end of sentences.[98] In an age when American college deans routinely caution faculty that many women undergraduates drop their voices at the end of sentences or make statements in a questioning tone, Wilson's shop-theory advice remains important. Anyone familiar with it now and then encounters a young woman who has clearly studied it carefully, practiced its exercises for years, and enjoys the success the books describe.[99] Any reader of photography magazines published after the early 1930s finds evidence of Wilson's thinking too, especially her insistence that clothes and cosmetics matter very little.[100]

Some women are glamorous. Most are not, or at least are rarely so. Wilson would argue that they choose to be unglamorous. While journalists frequently mention the charisma of political figures, they rarely consider glamour as anything other than a celebrity-connected concept. Robert B. Ray and a few other film historians admit what Ray notes in *The Avant-Garde Finds Andy Hardy*—"inadvertently the movies glamorized everything: faces, clothes, furniture, trains, landscapes"—but even fewer examine how the medium accomplished virtual-reality glamorization by accident.[101] Real glamour raises intractable but subtle issues of social Darwinism: fate endows some women with beauty, some with brains, some with physical strength, and some with glamour—and some with the ability to descry glamour around them.[102] Professional photographers frequently work with women wearing formal evening attire and cosmetics intended for artificial light.[103] Amateur photographers often work with models wearing almost nothing, in part because they follow the argument Wilson advanced in the late 1920s, one that photographers advising amateurs accepted after World War II.[104] The photographers associate pure glamour with a healthy naturalness disassociated from cosmetics, gowns, jewelry, and other accessories, in part because swimsuits are daytime apparel. Available light means much to amateur photographers, and while many learn to manipulate artificial light, few find models, including girlfriends and wives, willing to pose in makeup and formal clothing under hot lights for long.[105] Too many women and photographers correctly associate such lighting and attire with the 1930s cinema aesthetics against which Margery Wilson rebelled.[106] Exiguous attire and nudity, however, only subject photographers and models to the excoriations of religious fundamentalists and many feminist ideologues even as they unnerve advocates of Hollywood-centric glitz.

Depression-era Hollywood cinema fascinates contemporary undergraduates who want glamour and glamour-making codified, then preserved in amber. Period cinema produces confusion about a shimmering past and about something seemingly missing now; for many contemporary undergraduates ignorant of Spenser and faerie, cinema is enough a world of glass or, literally, films. But some undergraduates scorn cinematic imagery and its kin.[107] *Cosmopolitan* "is exactly the sort of publication the conservative matriarchs of my family shun, and yet the magazine itself reinforces some of those old-fashioned values," noted one perplexed undergraduate woman in the Harvard student newspaper.[108] Often my students gaze at period Hollywood films, muse on the seeming grace and suavity of the 1930s and 1940s beautiful people, and arrive in my office to ask what went wrong.[109] They—especially the women—speak of period actors, actresses, and especially settings as *glamorous*.[110] In the kinetic images they perceive a larger vision that clashes with what many modern academics teach, and sometimes they understand it as a portal to a perilous realm. But they no more know the glamour that reigned outside cinema houses than they realize the rectangular screen on which their savored images move.[111] They keep arriving, typically with pages torn from upscale fashion magazines, and now and then with photographs made of their mothers or grandmothers.[112] They ask especially about the 1960s in ways European undergraduates, especially Dutch, German, and British design students, began asking about in the late 1980s.[113] I applaud their determination to discover fault lines demarcating recent epochs in ideology, imagery, and image making, and ponder their deepening insistence that the early 1980s marked the collapse of creative openness.[114]

But I can suggest little to read concerning what so many now call "real glamour."

"It is far easier to be sensible in cities than in many country places I could tell you of," William Butler Yeats asserted in his 1893 *The Celtic Twilight: Myth, Fantasy, and Folklore.* "When one walks on those grey roads at evening by the scented elder-bushes of the white cottages, watching the faint mountains gather the clouds upon their heads, one all too readily discovers beyond the thin cobweb veil of the sense, those creatures, the goblins, hurrying from the white square stone door to the north, or from the Heart Lake in the south."[115] Only gradually have I understood that what focuses the attention of so many fashion magazine–gazing women is the background of the models. The models might be charming or fashionable or heroin-chic skinny or glamorous, but my women undergraduates look past them to their settings, remarking ruins, stone steps and benches, casement windows, and other details.

All too often, the settings remind both men and women undergraduates of locales in fantasy fiction they read as adolescents or in the adolescent-focused fantasy they read for recreation. The graveyard-become-nature preserve of Neil Gaiman's 2008 *The Graveyard Book* strikes many as the perfect setting for fashion photography.[116] Many undergraduates have seen fashion photographs made among tombs, derelict and otherwise, but lately more than a few begin to trace the links between fantasy fiction aimed at adolescents and fashion-magazine imagery aimed at adults, especially well-off women. Such tracery often bypasses cinema and television imagery, and while it now and then pauses before computer-game illustration, it tends to delineate visual effort made outside of mainstream for-profit mass media. Often my students ask me shop-theory questions about the making of the fashion-magazine images: only rarely am I of much help. But when they probe into the enduring power of glamour in folklore, linguistics, and independent enthusiast photography they return again and again to the power of the best juvenile-oriented fantasy writing, all of which sketches power outside the ordinary forces taught by schoolteachers and purveyed by mass media.

Fantasy fiction assures smart, savvy adolescents that power exists secretly within the ordinary just as everyday words mask the old languages Tolkien revered. It insists too on the power of beyond-words glamour, the power Margery Wilson warned lay beyond charm. It essays the trial-and-error approach of shop theory and very frequently asserts the primacy of seeing uniquely, often whimsically but always in ways transcending the programming of for-profit mass media. Always it contradicts the mass-media message and inveigles some readers away from cinema and television. It insists on the sub-creation Tolkien championed. To young people increasingly divorced from the whimsy and staggering power of traditional photography, ignorant of the Verlauf filter and other majesties, the best juvenile fantasy fiction introduces worlds of glass and amphitheaters of making.

2 Media

Many teenagers quickly developed a fanatical attachment to radio. Here a girl demonstrates her homemade radio receiver, antenna, and earphones that made haying more palatable.

Belly BUTTONS ATTRACTED MY ATTENTION IN 1966.
I Dream of Jeannie debuted as a prime-time television situation comedy
the previous year. I dismissed it: the syrupy actress in harem pants and
the improbable plots seemed beyond stupidity. In the early winter of 1966
I heard on overseas radio that "the American film production code" governing television content drew United States culture downward. The
commentator explained that the code reflected the biases of Catholics,
poor southerners, and second-generation urban immigrants. He argued
that middle- and upper-middle-class people watched little television in
part because they understood the origins and skewing power of the code
and scorned its products.[1] Mostly I recall his example. The code prevented the producers of *I Dream of Jeannie* from displaying the navel,
which was always just hidden by the harem pants waistband.[2]

I said nothing about what I heard. My parents gave me a Hallicraft-
ers short-wave receiver at Christmas in 1963, knowing of my growing
interest in amateur radio. I stretched a copper wire far from my bedroom window to an old white pine, put on the headphones my dad had
kept from his amateur radio days, and listened not to ham operators but
to foreign-service broadcasts, then mostly to Die Deutsche Welle, the
German waves, the state broadcasting service of West Germany. I had
begun studying German in high school, and quickly learned the pleasure of hearing it outside a language lab. Soon I realized that often I
heard news absent from United States media. I expected different interpretations of events from Radio Moscow, even from the BBC, but I
quickly learned that European journalists analyzed entire components
of American culture unmentioned in United States news media and in
my schoolrooms.[3] English-language broadcasts from The Netherlands to
Australia and New Zealand turned out to be tricky to tune, but extremely
intriguing. A Dutch journalist intermittently reported on his travels in
the darkest High Plains, noting in one segment that supermarket automatic doors might diminish chivalry in Nebraska. Die Deutsche Welle
programs in German aimed at Germans proved more incisive about the
United States. One commentator spoke about the long-term pedagogical
dangers implicit in the unionization of American public-school teachers.
Another reviewed a French opinion that the civil rights movement would
founder on class issues originating in the incipient decline in industrial
jobs. After two unsettling moments in civics class, I learned to keep overseas viewpoints to myself.[4]

Hiding belly buttons seemed nonsensical. At the time many women and girls wore swimsuits that exposed their navels. In a small, close-knit, quasi-rural coastal New England town, I knew religious affiliation (or agnosticism) as well as automobile ownership or road address: very definitely, Catholic girls and women displayed their belly buttons. From my teachers I learned little about any code governing television broadcasting, let alone about why a German radio commentator thought it related to Catholics or immigrants. A ripple of irritation caused me to inquire circumspectly.

A close Catholic friend had been warned in his church youth group in 1964 against seeing the James Bond thriller *Goldfinger*. My mother had thought the film might be slightly racy, but my parents offered no more objection to my seeing it than his. He and I concluded afterward that we had seen nothing risqué in the film, and as usual we joked about the continuity mistakes we noticed. When I asked him what he knew of the code, he said only that the film rating system had evolved from prohibitions encouraged by the Catholic Church. He thought that as children some people the age of his parents had been told in church that they might be eternally damned if they saw certain films. I more or less dropped the subject of the code, whatever it was, since I cared little for movies or television, and since any mention of the code made teachers and other adults uneasy and sometimes angry.[5] But I did think more about belly buttons.

As sunbathing evolved into creating the perfect tan, something tricky to achieve in New England, especially by July 4th, bikinis became briefer by the summer: tan lines signified tackiness by 1968. Exposed skin seemed everywhere in private space, although it surprised teenaged boys visiting from cities.[6] Women and teenage girls wore abbreviated suits around local teenage boys and did so casually, in part because boys wore very little too.[7] For such women and girls, brief bikinis were clothes, albeit clothes unfit for the public realm: never did I hear a woman or girl wearing a brief suit say that she needed "to put on clothes."[8] Sunbathing and gardening in very little continued a rural Yankee tolerance originating in part in spatial privacy, and—at least among fishermen and other men working in inshore waters and alongshore—in a pre–World War II attitude that only effeminate men wore bathing suits.[9] Barking dogs and crunching gravel nonetheless sometimes prompted women and girls to cover themselves. Many women kept men's shirts hanging on garden fence posts or on sundeck hooks, and pulled them on when rare strangers intruded.[10] As early as 1955, Anne Morrow Lindbergh argued that when wearing little or nothing, "one finds one is shedding not only clothes— but vanity."[11] Near nudity and sometimes nudity, as I mention in chapter 15, had become accepted among a cohort of socially secure people far less wealthy than the few that had swum and sunned in nothing since the 1930s.[12] While some of the behavior developed from Margaret Mead's writing, both her 1928 *Coming of Age in Samoa* and many subsequent women's magazine columns, Desmond Morris's 1967 *The Naked Ape*, and René Dubos's 1968 *So Human an Animal,* much of it appears to have originated in social mores relaxation prompted by tanning.[13] By 1970 some parents may have advanced it as a way of countering illicit drug use by encouraging pride in the body: by that year a few mothers had noted that some high-school and college-age children, especially girls, who prided themselves on their bodies seemed to avoid drugs, alcohol, and junk food.[14] Bikinis and G-strings made of soft, braided fishing line and hosiery nylon, what a handful of older women called thrions, passed for backyard and back-garden attire on teenage girls and boys alike.[15] Exiguous, home-sewn bikinis displaying belly buttons seemed modest to women who sometimes sunned nude, and many mothers found home-made thrions forestalled decisions about teenage nudity.

Hollywood confronted serious difficulties with the alongshore private display of skin. "Those Swinging Beach Movies," a July 1965 *Saturday Evening Post* article by Richard Warren Lewis, interpreted the films as shaping teenager and parental tolerance of displayed skin, along with music and dance.[16] Deepening regional-, class-, and education-based division concerning adultness and teenager sexuality confused both local behavior and thinking and national literature.[17] Herman Raucher's 1971 bestselling novel *The Summer of '42* revolves around a young widow having sex with a fifteen-year-old boy. No contemporaneous reviewer noted what now would be condemned as rape of a child, nor did any find significance in its casual juxtaposition of what skin its protagonist sees in films and how much more he sees on the half-deserted beach of a New England island.[18] Ann Oakley averred bluntly in her 1972 *Sex, Gender, and Society* that "women are psychologically, no less than anatomically, incapable of rape."[19] Not for decades did fashion historians discern that the bikini reflected bottom-up revolution and the potential for powerful glamour, and that private attire often provided far less coverage than anything Hollywood could show under the code.[20] Even today, few scholars study the links between casual, private near nudity and aversion to tobacco, alcohol, illicit drugs, junk food, and sedentary behavior, and even avoidance of breast cancer.[21] Most too quickly dismiss exiguous attire as brazen or sexy, not as one envelope that enables glamour.[22] "I think people should be what they are visually: they should simply enhance with clothing what they are naturally," declares the British dress designer Jean Muir. "You should like yourself, not disguise or hide it."[23] Too many academics forget that *suit* designates not only the uniform-like envelopes in which white-collar men and women work but the wisps women wear outdoors, in the sun.[24]

Nowadays belly buttons take all sorts of shapes, as they did in 1966, but only in the flesh. Roughly half are vertical, the other half horizontal; many are quite circular, but many deviate into trapezoids and other shapes, and while many are concave, some are convex.[25] A walk down any beach confirms this. But scrutiny of any fashion magazine published after 1970 implies that almost all belly buttons are vertical and concave. Women photographed modeling bikinis, lingerie, and skin-care products almost invariably display vertical belly buttons. If an anthropologist two centuries hence used only fashion magazine images as source materials, his study would be hopelessly biased in favor of vertical belly buttons. In advertising imagery, the vertical belly button serves a role in sexual innuendo, suggesting the shape of the opening below. I am not sure when I noticed the disjunction between belly buttons on the beach or behind the house and belly buttons in fashion magazines, but I know that I had begun noticing such visual nuance by the time I went to college in 1967.

As a boy I watched little television: I found too many better things to do, especially on winter nights and rainy days.[26] My family bought its first television when I was six, perhaps too late for me to adjust to its presence or programming.[27] Although I found television choppy, stupid, and dull, I did not dislike movies, but I lived in a town without a cinema house, so my best friends and I generally spent our money on something other than viewing a film.[28] Rainy Saturday afternoons, especially in winter, found me doing something other than watching old movies on television: commercials diced them in a way that irritated me deeply.[29] I graduated from high school realizing that I paid kinetic imagery much less attention than did my friends, especially almost all of the girls.[30]

Rather than watch television, I far preferred to examine the pages of *Life* or *Look* or some other magazine featuring photographs prominently. My junior-high-school librarian made clear her opinion of boys who sat with an issue of *Life* spread on the table, even a boy who turned the pages deliberately, even one doing well academically. Only gazing at the fields and woods beyond the third-floor windows struck her as more wasteful of intellectual energy. But even as I pored over the images, I realized that she permitted far more latitude to girls. In high school I decided that staring at photographs in any sort of magazine that might be girlish meant sitting at tables surrounded by girls. Beyond hearing what girls whispered when they pointed out photograph details to one another, I valued being able to return to images I had seen before. I could sift through the stacks of magazines and look again at images I had noticed a year or so before. Elderly relatives began giving me old magazines long ago put "up the top of the house," and slowly I started comparing not only photographic styles but the ways so many magazine images anticipated cinema and television ones. *National Geographic*s from the 1930s soon stood stacked against 1880s copies of *McClures, Century,* and *Harper's Weekly.* Not many decades earlier, ordinary people valued magazines highly enough to put them aside. Whatever had prompted them to lug them up to the attic, the stacks of magazines enabled me to return again and again to images in a way television did not.

In the summer of 1968, after my college freshman year, a handful of older people—mostly women who had attended Smith, Vassar, and similar colleges before World War II and a few men who had attended first-rate universities—suggested that my avoidance of television might prove empowering. As I helped one fifty-something woman fix her garden shed, for the first time I heard what I had begun to suspect. People who consume mass-media images differ greatly from people who do not, and perhaps also from those who make such images especially well. She argued that the difference involved social class, educational level, religious denomination, and a social security unlike anything offered by the Social Security Administration.[31]

That day I heard briefly and matter-of-factly what graduate-school coursework later confirmed obliquely, but the conversation began in remarks about how entertainment media considered bikinis, no matter how brief, more innocent than one-piece cutout suits. In 1954 the Catholic Church and its Legion of Decency organized opposition to any showing of the RKO film *The French Line,* starring Jane Russell. Archbishop Joseph E. Ritter of St. Louis told his 473,000 parishioners that any who saw the film would fall "under penalty of mortal sin."[32] I had never heard of the film, let alone seen it, but that day in 1968 I learned that in it Russell danced in a strapless one-piece suit featuring large cutouts, but with fabric strategically covering her navel. Her décolletage worried the hierarchy of the Catholic Church: the suit apparently scarcely covered her aureoles and her gyrations threatened to dislodge her breasts.

That discussion eventually shaped my graduate-school work in American studies and much subsequent inquiry into how people look around at the world. In 1968 I knew that manufacturers of film and television worked under restrictions unknown to writers, scholars, and photographers, and that the restrictions opened on significant if rarely mentioned issues in modern culture. As I helped my friend fix her garden shed I thought her analysis likely to be right: her facts aligned with those cited by other well-educated, wealthy, tiny bikini–wearing middle-aged women who understood the rising power of visual media on some cohorts of American society.

After about 1972 I examined belly buttons more and more warily, especially in summers when home from college and graduate school. Revealed skin had begun to annoy some people and nudity began to strike others as wrong rather than different or natural, yet others seemed more relaxed than ever in their bikinis, and almost determined to shock or irritate the already annoyed. As some women began arguing that men should not wear extremely brief, tight swimsuits, I detected their genuine confusion about period photographs in which men and women casually exposed navels to camera lenses, men posed bare chested and in skimpy briefs, and women posed nude or nearly so. Well-to-do people appeared in 1930s and 1940s photographs that might have been made in 1970: their attire or exposed skin resembled that beginning to vex a new kind of social conservative. One day in 1974 the middle-aged woman friend who had argued so clearly about mass-audience visual media remarked that people offended by scanty attire might be suffering from the collapse of cinema and television as infallible arbiters of fashion, morals, and behavior. Neither medium had embraced nudity, let alone homosexuality and other contemporaneous issues, and so had forced many devoted fans to seek elsewhere for knowledge, even how to think.[33] I reported her remarks to a girlfriend later that day, who while tying on her bikini top retorted that self-appointed champions of modesty lacked the money to subscribe to *Vanity Fair* or *Glamour* or were fat.[34] A few days later I realized that people frightened of illicit drug use and unable to stop it might deflect their energy into condemning brief swimsuits and nudity.[35]

In the 1930s many photographers abandoned Hollywood studio work since they could no longer stomach the rule of lower-class public taste.[36] Twenty years earlier, reform-minded New Yorkers had worried that motion pictures would corrupt the poor, and especially the immigrant poor making up the bulk of cinemagoers, and so shaped the People's Institute, hitherto a sort of settlement-house project, into a censorship bureau. As Jacob Riis smugly noted in a 1910 *Century* article, with the connivance of the Moving-Picture Trust the institute censored more than three-fourths of the films made in the country and imported from abroad, "determining what twelve million children and adults shall see, and what they shall not see, from week to week."[37] Censorship grew more powerful by the decade. Photographers escaping the onerous restrictions of the 1930s Production Code, which Hollywood filmmakers adopted to head off federal censorship, excoriated the deepening prudishness forced on the industry by national distributors aware that relatively few well-educated, tolerant people attended cinema houses anyway.[38] As Frank Walsh demonstrates in *Sin and Censorship: The Catholic Church and the Motion Picture Industry,* Hollywood film producers struggled to produce films that might titillate while selling widely in the most conservative parts of the country, specifically East Coast cities with large immigrant, Catholic populations and across the South.[39] The struggle diluted artistic quality and crippled artistic license.[40] By 1935 Hollywood had lost its edge, something lower-class, often second-generation immigrant American film audiences failed to recognize, since they often used films as tutorials on "American" behavior.[41] But photographers—often middle class and higher on the economic ladder, socially secure, usually mainstream Protestant and rural or suburban, and often although certainly not always male—smoothly sidestepped a stagnant film industry they shrugged off as corporate, prudish, feminized, and corroded by the declining expectations of its lower-class audiences.

Nowadays academics obsessed with the auteur approach to film history simply ignore the corporate-industrial filmmaking context many photographers despised after the 1920s.[42] From the first days following its 1908 incorporation, the Motion Pictures Patents Company—known as "The Trust" to cinematographers who refused to submit to its demands—sued, sabotaged, and otherwise ruined any firm manufacturing cinema cameras, projectors, film, and flickers, as people called the first entertainment films. Violence characterized an industry dependent on Edison patents, especially those covering sprocket film. Trust-instigated intimidation and violence, including gunfire, on New York streets drove many non-Trust cinematographers to Florida and Cuba, then to California.[43] Cecil B. De Mille routinely received anonymous threats on his life, was shot at twice in his first months in Hollywood, and always carried a Colt .45 revolver, as did many other directors and producers.[44]

In *At the Picture Show: Small-Town Audiences and the Creation of Movie Fan Culture,* Kathryn Fuller details how Hollywood studios, publicity agents, and fan magazines deliberately shifted post–World War I spectator interest toward stars, love lives, and personal quirks of the people now called celebrities.[45] *Motion Picture Story Magazine,* then *Motion Picture Magazine,* and, after 1917, especially *Photoplay* feared the growing power of male fans interested in the technical details of filmmaking and the financial tentacles, especially in advertising, of cinema consumption. Their fear built on the mounting terror of widespread, wildcat competition suffusing the new, undercapitalized filmmaking industry. The magazines deliberately replaced articles on the technique of making films with ones focused on the star system, and quickly eliminated most male readership, Fuller avers.[46] Just as the studios quashed the careers of prominent women directors after 1920, so fan magazines emphasized anything but shop theory.[47] The magazines and the film industry wanted a female readership unlikely to produce competition, especially innovative competition, to an industry neither well capitalized nor fitted with equipment beyond what any determined or inspired tinkerer might buy or build.[48] The filmmaking industry wanted a largely female audience ignorant of cinematography technicalities, and hoped that such an audience might deflect male thinking away from targeted technical experimentation.[49] It knew too well the success of amateurs like Walt Disney, who started Laugh-O-Gram Films in his parents' Kansas City garage at age nineteen.[50]

By the end of the 1920s, fan magazines and studio publicity offices had accomplished an extraordinary transformation of lower- and middle-income American culture, especially visual culture. Fuller claims the magazines became the chief promoters of the understanding of women as the dominant cinema fans. But studios had orchestrated the sexual segregation on-screen since at least 1920, when Cecil B. De Mille's *Why Change Your Wife?* depicted a woman, played by Gloria Swanson, disgusted at her husband's habitual reading of fan magazines. The film is only one nonmagazine effort the industry made to emphasize that fascination with the star system, the personal lives of Hollywood celebrities, and anything from costuming to the themes of individual films is feminine, unworthy of male attention.[51] As men became only a third of the audience for Hollywood films (women, teenagers, and children constitute the other two-thirds), fan magazines continued on a trajectory that produced the current academic discipline of film studies.

When Anne Hollander, a costume designer the editors of *American Scholar* described in 1973 as "at work on *The Clothed Image,* a book about the nude, drapery and dress in art," explicated the nuanced connections between operatic and cinema costume in a path-making article, she shaped my subsequent film viewing and reading of film criticism and theory but shifted my view of the body instantly. "The importance of what actors actually wear is singularly unrecognized by critics or audience," she asserted, directing reader attention to actresses wearing uplift bras and intricate eye makeup while portraying desperate castaways. "American cinematic convention demands that all movie actresses wear the face and torso of the current moment, whatever the century in which the film is set, presumably so that they are believable as real women to a contemporary audience."[52] The article hit hard as I walked in from my parents' sundeck, saw my nudity reflected in the glass door, and realized that nudity clashes with all the intricate costuming conventions on which corporate cinema marketing depends to reach its largely female audience.[53] That day Hollander's article caused me to realize that Hollywood eschewed nudity not only because of the code but because nudity might well destroy many very profitable conventions carefully guarded since the 1930s.

Pre–World War II filmmaking occupies an amorphous realm between photography and amateur radio. In a year or so after 1917, filmmaking became almost wholly corporate: "home movies" still designates almost all amateur filmmaking into the home-video era. The invention of the 35 mm still camera designed to use corporate-industrial motion-picture film rather than 16 mm certainly connected the Hollywood industry with amateur photographers. But amateur filmmakers almost never acquired the 35 mm motion-picture cameras and editing equipment studios used, and even "independent" filmmaking remained mired in the 16 mm format. Technology and cost limited the creativity of almost all skilled amateur filmmakers, while the Production Code self-censoring of Hollywood films paralleled the licensing of all radio broadcasters by the federal government. After the Radio Act of 1912 passed, ostensibly to eliminate the amateur broadcasting which perhaps interfered with Titanic distress signals, amateur radio devotees worked only with so-called short waves, and soon found themselves in a situation resembling that of amateur cinematographers.[54] Radio equipment became better, but after about 1925 manufacturers produced two sorts—corporate-professional and amateur. Only enthusiast photographers, many of whom abandoned their interest in motion-picture making in the late 1920s as top-quality cinema cameras proved far too expensive for amateurs, continued to enjoy cameras, film, chemicals, and paper identical to those used by professionals. Moreover, they enjoyed utter freedom from corporate censorship, licensing, and even the public gaze, so long as they did not publish their images or send them via less than first-class mail.

In 1936 Rudolf Arnheim, already a formidable visual arts critic, published *Radio,* a book that insists on the primacy of vision over hearing, that insists almost frantically that radio can only guide the listener toward the visual.[55] Worry drove Arnheim. By 1936 European radio carried the voice of fascism and elevated gramophone music above almost all sound other than Hitler's voice.[56] American radio threatened to destroy American popular film, in part because it reached men, especially men at work, and in part because it blasted apart the contrived vision of film fan magazines aimed at women.[57]

But after 1928 RCA shaped Hollywood filmmaking as it amalgamated the Keith Orpheum Theater Circuit and the Film Booking Office created by Joseph P. Kennedy in 1917 into RKO, the film production studio known for its logo of an Eiffel Tower–like antenna shooting a distinct, jagged spark atop the world. The firm continuously threatened the stability of the Hollywood film industry, in part because it remained fundamentally a radio business morphing into monopoly.[58] Its spark-centric logo emphasized the primacy of radio.

Broadcast radio almost killed cinema around 1923. Sound films, immediately dubbed "talkies," proved a direct response to the explosive power of radio in an era when the Hollywood industry suffered from ongoing scandals involving stars and directors, outcries about immoral behavior in films, and massive overinvestment in real estate, particularly in the form of palatial cinema houses. Most importantly, however, talkies deflected attention from the perceived degradation of filmmaking after about 1920.[59] As the cinema industry emphasized formulaic films often crippled by poor technical quality which packed in lower- and middle-income viewers, especially women, many Americans stopped attending films.[60]

A few noted the devastating damage talkies did to cinema enthusiasts who expected high-quality films. "We could plainly hear a nasal chant out of a Californian tin. In one of the shabby music-halls of the past the soloist would have 'got the bird' for making such a noise," growled a prominent British novelist, H. M. Tomlinson, in 1925. "I used to think that the producers of the Movies had learned, after many trials, the limitations of their art. They knew the best use to make of their material. They had almost reached the point—Charlie Chaplin reached it very quickly—where they would have seen the power of the cinematograph was in the allegorical presentation of life." Tomlinson argued explicitly that cinema might have excelled poetry: "that it was silent was the secret of its power."[61] They left behind a downscale following, young, uneducated, and often poor, that did not exactly attend films; Tomlinson said it merely gaped.[62]

In 1916 *Motion Picture Magazine* rhapsodized over an eighteen-year-old Ohio girl who saw thirty films a week, covered her bedroom walls with hundreds of images of Hollywood stars, and preferred watching films to enjoying the company of young men. As an exemplar of the new fan, the girl devoted little attention to discriminating among films: she simply viewed one after another.[63] But by the end of the 1920s even teenagers tended to avoid the cinema on the nights when radios broadcast their favorite shows; for a short while, radio seemed poised to accomplish what reformers had urged for a decade.[64] In 1930 *Parents Magazine* summarized the anticinema argument and advised against letting any child under eleven years of age attend films. The magazine urged that all children should have the opportunities routinely enjoyed by upper-class ones, especially access to traditional folk and fairy tales, and to books they chose themselves from vast assortments. Broadcast radio kept many children home, and often their hands busy with making things. Moreover, it enabled children to save money that they then ought to spend on books, sporting goods, and hand tools.[65]

Throughout the Depression, the war years, and well into the 1950s, most Americans easily and unhesitatingly accepted the programmed radio smorgasbord and the sequence of films emanating from Hollywood, but devoted more daily attention to radio, often while doing something beyond listening.[66] At the start of World War II, many urban, suburban, small-town, and rural listeners accepted broadcast radio almost uncritically.[67] Broadcast radio indeed meant broadcast, the way farmers once seeded fields to grain. Most people heard the same programs sponsored by the same advertisers, and even if they did not listen regularly or at all, they lived among people who did and who believed what they heard.[68] In the war years, for example, the Liberty Broadcasting System used canned noises and other special effects to fake major league baseball broadcasts for its vast audience across the South and Southwest. Working in studios and following the games via tickertape, LBS announcers pretended to describe games unfolding before them. But short-wave radio listeners discovered that the Armed Forces Radio Service broadcast the games in real time from ballparks. Nevertheless, when alerted to the deception, which sometimes involved errors of fact, most listeners, especially men, preferred the colorful LBS broadcasts.[69] Even after Orson Welles tricked many listeners into believing Martians had landed in New Jersey, audiences wanted to believe.[70] And as a result, almost no one doubted the first news bulletins about the attack on Pearl Harbor, except those who thought Welles had attempted another trick.[71]

A handful of older, well-educated, wealthy people, almost all women, who spoke with me in the late 1960s about my dislike of film and television understood a lower-class addiction to film and television, and especially to radio, as potentially crippling to American culture.[72] Some alluded to the power of Nazi cinema and radio propaganda in the late 1930s.[73] A handful had experienced that power firsthand: two had visited Germany in the early 1930s, immediately distrusted its advertising, and thought Nazi propaganda grew from it; another had attended the 1936

Olympics in Munich and returned wary of state-controlled radio.[74] Several thought Nazism had stained American media by 1938. They spoke of Charles E. Coughlin, a Catholic priest who published a weekly magazine, *Social Justice,* and hosted a nationwide radio show they condemned as unnervingly anti-Semitic and pro-Fascist. "In the documentary history of the rise of the Third Reich very little allusion is made to radio," McLuhan wrote in 1970. "Without radio there would have been no Hitler," he continued, and "no world of jazz." His *Understanding Media* shaped my graduate-school efforts and caused me to pay close attention to the people I visited when home in summer.[75]

In the late 1980s, when I discovered that a preeminent American art critic, Clement Greenberg, had anonymously translated a 1936 exposé of Nazi foreign activities, *The Brown Network: The Activities of the Nazis in Foreign Countries,* I remembered the jumble of allusion and echoes I first heard two decades earlier. Until I read *The Brown Network* I had not known that the Nazi Party had an office on West Fourth Street in Los Angeles from which it distributed anti-Semitic leaflets and posted anti-Semitic broadsides in beach bathhouses.[76] Perhaps his translation effort made Greenberg acutely wary of weaknesses underlying leftist critical thinking, especially the "high-brow" culture identified by H. L. Mencken, Van Wyck Brooks, and other critics in the early 1920s.[77] His 1939 *Partisan Review* essay "Avant-Garde and Kitsch," so seminal in aesthetic criticism a quarter-century later, recognizes the power of something neither avant-garde nor kitsch, perhaps akin to 1920s Brazilian "cultural cannibalism" or to subsequent European cutting-edge propaganda, but perhaps simply the might of Bernarr Macfadden's publishing empire grounded in *Physical Culture, Sport, True Story,* and especially *Liberty,* a news magazine that regularly flirted with fascism.[78] In July 1940 E. B. White noted in *Harper's* that *Mein Kampf* makes explicit Hitler's understanding of radio.[79] The Nazis learned from the Italian Fascists. As early as 1919 Giovanni Papini, an academic and well-known social commentator, confided to a friend that the diverse, fiercely independent Italian intellectual class had begun to collapse. What he termed the talkative or discursive class found itself marginalized by cinema and radio while squeezed between the power of wealthy industrialists and the poor.[80] As it withered in the new-media blast, liberty of thought disappeared in the impending collision of fascism and communism: the rich co-opted many once-independent intellectuals, while the poor distrusted all intellectuals as bribed.[81] Italian Fascism emphasized the primacy of the state in ways race-centric, anti-Semitic Nazism thereafter eclipsed, but the Fascists immediately recognized the way cinema and radio might convince middle-class people to join with the rich against the rapidly organizing proletariat.[82]

Few postwar Italian critics analyzed the smooth absorption of Papini and so many other intellectuals into Fascism, let alone the role of cinema and radio in the Fascist triumph. Elémire Zolla made a determined if indirect effort in a 1956 book translated into English twelve years later as *The Eclipse of the Intellectual*. "The profusion of reproduced images from movies, magazines and television shows man the world in order to hide it from him: the interpretive function of reality is suffocated, and perception is transformed from an active into a receptive detail," he argued of something Fascists understood long before the invention of television. "We are afflicted by blindness before the unrepeatable detail; the aura surrounding things has vanished, and the things begin to coincide with their mechanical reproduction: reality becomes photographic."[83] Zolla understood actual aura as something that cinema especially made virtual, and he distrusted the crowds of individuals who watched the virtual aura of cinema stars in dark theaters and felt somehow ashamed as they left.

Italian intellectuals succumbed to Fascism in part because they succumbed to modern media, and few contemporary media historians analyze the Bernarr Macfadden publishing empire that eventually subsidized a weekly radio show and at least eight nonstudio films while championing Italian Fascism.[84] The critical effort still centers in Europe, far from New York and Hollywood.

Mariners knew the power of film and radio, in large part because long cruises meant no access to films and almost none to radio. In 1955 the master mariner J. R. Stenhouse mused on the changes cinema and radio brought to the isolated British rural families he intermittently visited when briefly home on leave. He asserted that both media destroyed a steadfast calmness while shifting attention to frivolous subjects, and making attention itself fleeting and shallow.[85] Five years earlier, in her 1950 novel of the Maine coast before World War II, *Candlemas Bay,* Ruth Moore traced the generational gap widening between people who stayed calm in crisis and those who acted as cinema characters did when terrified. Too much cinemagoing might make a man unfit for the sea just as it might blind men and women to the nuances of glamour everywhere along the coast.[86] In 1982 Tristan Jones looked back on his 1930s boyhood aboard British sailing vessels and concluded that modern people "whose view of life and the world has been distorted by the false values ground out daily by the 'modern' media" could not begin to imagine the mind-set of mariners almost always away from cinema and radio. In the late Depression, Jones served aboard one sailing vessel whose master refused to carry a wireless because it transmitted too much disturbing material, some of it Nazi.[87]

In 1924 the critic Gilbert Seldes published *The Seven Lively Arts,* one of the first monographs championing cinema and other new media as perfectly equivalent to any so-called fine art.[88] Deftly and courageously, he ranged over ragtime and jazz, the Ziegfeld Follies, comic strips, and above all cinema, especially the cinema of Chaplin. In the Keystone comedies, Seldes asserted, Chaplin "first detached himself from life and began to live in another world, with a specific rhythm of his own, as if the pulse-beat in him changed and was twice or half as fast as that of those who surrounded him."[89] The year 1914 made the Chaplin reputation, and established cinema as something special, especially in comedy and spectacle. That it heralded the start of World War I meant nothing to Seldes, who swept across innovative media and reinvented media with a near-boyish enthusiasm and an exceptionally mature disdain for cheap failure. *The Seven Lively Arts* endures as incisive cultural criticism and a nearly unique portal on criticism in time.[90] Within five years of its publication, Hollywood cinema had collapsed in upon itself; within ten, the Production Code had destroyed the innovation Seldes extolled.[91]

In 1950 Seldes published *The Great Audience,* in which he declared his earlier optimism mistaken and misplaced. Having worked in Hollywood, in magazines, and in broadcasting, Seldes argued forthrightly that two forces destroyed the immense creative potential and profitability of Hollywood cinema. In the middle 1920s the industry confronted broadcast radio by emphasizing formulaic "mythmaking" over originality and by adding sound to films. After a fitful few years, Seldes asserted, the Catholic Church imposed the Production Code on the studios, thereafter twisting not only the portrayal of thighs and other subjects but also the treatment of divorce, adultery, homosexuality, nudity, and a host of other topics in mythmaking frames. Then, according to Seldes, the Production Code strangled cinema creativity because of "the special circumstances of the movies." Films communicate through emotion, not reason, and do so in an "atmosphere of relaxed enjoyment"; films have already dulled filmgoer perception of "present events" and continue to "make their impressions slowly" by working on the "subconscious, through images, and their effects are long-lasting."[92] But midway through his enumeration Seldes hit upon something that shapes my thinking here.

"The interaction of the Production Code and the system of distribution has eliminated from this audience the mature and the thoughtful," he declared. At the beginning of the consumer-economy era defined by the economist John Kenneth Galbraith in *The Affluent Society* in 1958, Seldes insisted that a whole cohort of people no longer attended films.[93] Exactly as Murrow, Frank Stanton, and a handful of other television insiders argued at roughly the same time about the loss of many Americans as television viewers, Seldes delineated a striking division between the bulk of people who consumed mass-media images and those who did something else. Between 1937 and 1945 Seldes worked as director of television programs for CBS: not only did he specify how his earlier enthusiasm for cinema eroded as the Production Code stymied possibilities, he linked the Production Code directly to the poverty of television programming. In 1956 he published another indictment, *The Public Arts,* which opens with further analysis of modern media deserted by people with something better to do.[94]

Cinema and radio presaged the staggering impact of television after about 1952, and the equally staggering but unremarked avoidance of it by many Americans. After 1934, as the motion-picture industry struggled under guidelines it created under pressure from a Congress fearing the Catholic Church and southern fundamentalists, most remaining viewers soon unthinkingly accepted what industry insiders called "the code." Since no "proper" motion-picture manufacturer produced a film showing the inside of a woman's thigh, viewers never saw the inside of a thigh on screen. What cinema and then television failed to depict frequently vanished from other elements of popular culture, comic books included, produced by firms anxious to appear moral.[95] Most viewers rarely knew the strictures of the code or studied how they reshaped subsequent regulation of television by the Federal Communications Commission.[96] People who scorned the code and products made under its auspices simply eschewed the products.[97]

Just as most children easily accepted the formulaic underpinning of so many made-for-children films, so most abandoned 1950s Saturday afternoon cinema visits as television proved increasingly attractive.[98] When television journalist Edward R. Murrow lambasted fellow broadcast executives in his keynote address at the 1958 Radio-Television News Directors Association conference, he made televised entertainment congruent with film. Changing the entire basis of programming remained possible, he argued, despite the raw power of prime-time sitcoms. "There might ensue a most exciting adventure—exposure to ideas and the bringing of reality into the homes of the nation," he argued. If "this instrument is good for nothing but to entertain, amuse, and insulate, then the tube is flickering now and we will soon see that the whole struggle is lost."[99] Only four years later, when Frank Stanton, president of the Columbia Broadcasting System, presented a lecture entitled "Mass Media and Mass Culture" at Dartmouth College, the tube had flickered into dimness.

Stanton expressed not just frustration at what his and other networks offered and puzzlement at the paucity of viewers for the very programming Murrow envisioned, but wondered at the growing willingness of experts to believe that "the intellectual and cultural tastes of the majority are relatively limited."[100] Film and television satisfied many viewers, he argued; at least many watched and many seemed satisfied to visit the movie theater again or tune in the following day.[101] Stanton could neither define nor number those who did something other than view film or television, nor did he think that cohort willing to embrace television if it changed only slightly. In the years when television refused to aim cameras at Elvis Presley's gyrating hips, a small segment of the American public dismissed the medium.[102] Two years after Stanton grimly admitted that film and television lurched down the path Murrow condemned, Marshall McLuhan published *Understanding Media: The Extensions of Man.*[103] By then many of those who eschewed cinema and television, and very often radio when away from their automobiles, had become deeply entrenched in private making—often in the making of glamour and fantasy.[104]

High-quality fantasy writing stresses power and magic, and emphasizes the raw strength of the visual, especially the terrible power that accompanies the remaking of the visual realm. It addresses themes largely absent from public-school curricula while snaring the attention of independent-school students who are taught to suspect the programmed visual realm and in fact are kept from it.[105] It emphasizes class, family, sexuality, physicality, and visual competency in ways that illustrate the power of glamour and defy the silence of many educators, especially university faculty threatened by glamour itself. "Mrs. Coulter, on the other hand, was not like any female Scholar Lyra had seen, certainly not like the two serious elderly ladies who were the other female guests," writes Philip Pullman of a young girl raised in an alternate-world Oxford University. "Mrs. Coulter had such an air of glamour that Lyra was entranced. She could hardly take her eyes off her." The last of the afternoon sun pours into the room, illuminating the pictures and the "glum silver the Master collected," and it charges Mrs. Coulter with something that thrusts Dame Hannah Relf, "head of one of the women's colleges" into obscurity.[106] In *The Golden Compass* and subsequent Dark Materials novels, Pullman presents Mrs. Coulter as a glamorous woman whose glamour overwhelms the senior women scholars. His series mocks not only organized religion but also organized higher education, especially education established for women on 1970s principles. Mrs. Coulter's glamour overwhelms professorial intelligence, self-discipline, and learning.

Beginning in the 1920s, a handful of fantasy writers explored glamour as it empowered women. "She had nothing, absolutely nothing on but a transparent white chiffony sort of dressing-gown. She was trying to undo it," writes May Sinclair in a 1923 tale concerning wraiths and paranormal experience. "He was fascinated by her, by the sheer glamour of her body, gleaming white through the thin stuff, and by the movement of her fingers. I think I've said she was a beautiful woman, and her beauty at that moment was overpowering."[107] *Uncanny Stories* originates in Freudian distinctions concerning the real, the surreal, and the in-between, the uncanny, and in the growing awareness among some 1920s women that their visual selves might work an overwhelming glamour—perhaps after sustained practice. It originates too in photography, as young women and men realized their visual appearance as increasingly important in the creation and protection of self.[108]

In the 1930s many expert professional and amateur photographers saw genuine glamour as a threat to the organized glitziness of Hollywood, just as Hollywood glitz threatened the traditional educational establishment. Glamour thrust beyond the self-censorship the industry imposed on its employees and contractors. The desire for something more daring than stylized glitter drove many professional photographers away from Hollywood and from the people J. B. Priestley called "born to achieve reality in a photograph."[109] These adventurous professionals and expert amateurs realized that glamour transcended the economic downturn and would build upon itself. Given the right equipment and materials, some photographers ignored the limits under which filmmakers and radio broadcasters worked, then transcended them.

Glamour photography became a powerful corporate genre before World War II. By 1938 it shaped the private enterprise of many expert photographers and their models. It fueled an escapist, girly magazine industry that funded the cheesecake photographs dear to the hearts of GIs, and the aircraft art that so strikingly resembles contemporary fantasy illustration of scantily clad or nude women.[110] It produced too a wealth of private, often eyes-only photographs made not only by sophisticated male and female enthusiasts but by equally sophisticated women models utterly relaxed around cameras. After Pearl Harbor, many young American women viewed glamour photography as a sort of fantasy magic with which they might experiment and might indeed control. As boyfriends went into the armed forces, thousands of girlfriends sewed swimsuits and other abbreviated costumes they might never wear in public, but wore in photographs their mothers and other relatives made, or they made themselves using camera self-timers. Many created suits that emphasized their belly buttons. Fifteen years before the Catholic Church condemned the one-piece suit in which Jane Russell danced in *The French Line,* many young women delighted in revealing the belly buttons Hollywood hid. Despite media protestations to the contrary, the bikini is an American invention, circa 1936, not a postwar French innovation: it evolved simultaneously with, not from, the brief swimsuits actresses wore in *Palmy Days, The Kid from Spain, Dancing Lady, Birds of Paradise,* and other early 1930s films.[111] But it is not "good-girl" apparel.[112] In bikinis, G-strings, and less, American women supported the war effort in ways perhaps equally effective as anything Rosie the Riveter accomplished, and GIs arrived home to delights more racy than tract homes surrounded by rose-covered picket fences. Hollywood ignored the glamour-based war effort and peacetime aftermath. It still does.

Much late 1940s and early 1950s amateur glamour photography remains as private today as it was then, but fragments drift into the public realm as people die and photographs turn up in secondhand stores or on Internet auctions. Postwar expert amateurs photographed their girlfriends following the instructions of Peter Gowland, whose 1953 *How to Photograph Women* emphasized the bikini-and-beach formats he and a competitor, Bunny Yeager, created beyond the edge of mainstream visual media. Yeager moved rapidly and ruthlessly from model to photographer-model, and her many books, perhaps especially *How to Photograph the Figure* and *Tropical Nudes,* shaped the efforts of men and women discovering the symbiotic magic implicit in the relationship between photographer and model. Fritz Henle's 1954 *Figure Studies* offered finer direction to amateurs. Shot on the Virgin Islands beach along which he and his wife lived, Henle's images of Marguerite reinforced the efforts of many men and women exploring the making of glamour free of lower-class restriction and prudery.[113] In a 1961 volume of sample images, *Figure Study Photos,* Peter Basch distinguished precisely between American and foreign glamour and glamour photography techniques, building on his 1956 how-to-do-it manual, *Glamour Photography.*[114] Always subverting or ignoring the standards of Hollywood cinema and then television, the private images made by amateur photographers and their models and the near simultaneous work by professionals illustrated an effort that defied prudishness and mass-culture standards.

Women models sewed their own bikinis in the late 1930s, but by the late 1940s they ordered exiguous suits from the ads in the back pages of photography magazines. While photographers sometimes focused cameras on women in evening dresses and other formal attire, the bulk of the fantasy photography enterprise centered on bikinis, G-strings, and nudity.[115]

Glamour photography is all too frequently ignored or dismissed with snorts about the objectification of female bodies. Glamour too often collides with narrow-minded critics scornful and frightened of commercial advertising imagery and terrified by the imminent collapse of 1970s word-centric ideologies.[116] Speaking the word "fantasy" often elicits quips or snide remarks about "sexual fantasy" before the speaker completes the sentence, or explains his meaning. In many ways, glamour photography and the varieties of expert amateur nude photography remain intensely illustrative not only of private fantasy but of the little-known path skirting the enormous bulk of mass-media, corporate-made visuals. Devotees of mass-culture theory, especially those academics who used cinema and television as forms of acculturation in the 1970s, recoil when they glimpse the winding path so different from their own broad highway.[117] Part of the recoil originates in simple jealousy, perhaps: in an age of obesity and scruffy frumpiness, many women might envy the power of Mrs. Coulter, especially when it effortlessly pierces university walls. But much of it stems from the fear that much 1970s theory has become obsolete or lower-class or both. Fewer and fewer educated Americans can use a camera. The fact is that much image making since the 1930s has been private. Glamour photographs of wives and grown daughters together, especially nudes, for example, ring alarm bells in the heads of the prudish, who are suspicious of the husband-father photographers. Other glamour images, especially those involving explicit fantasy tropes, shake entire bell towers, especially ivory ones.

In his 1957 poem "The Naked and the Nude," the poet Robert Graves addressed the growing power of the nude. He warned that the "sly" nudes gathered strength because they knew something secret, or at least something neither noticed nor realized by the naked. He traced the deepening division I saw in the late 1960s, in a rural place where skinny-dipping in the ocean and from small boats, sunbathing in the nude, and swimming nude in backyard pools was, if not ordinary, at least acceptable—and perhaps empowering. Appearing a year after Kenneth Clark's *The Nude: A Study in Ideal Form*, Grave's poem raised precisely the point Tomlinson raised in 1925 and my self-appointed, middle-aged tutors raised in the summer of 1968. When cinema and television eschewed belly buttons and nudity, the two media might shape popular standards but empower a tiny minority comfortable in skin and tans.

Hollywood films, especially the beach films popular in the late 1960s, shaped men's swimwear. The films extolled cut-off jeans and made them stylish even along the New England coast of my boyhood, where the slow-drying heavy cloth proved cold and uncomfortable. In the early 1970s few boys and almost no men swam on public beaches in brief-style suits, let alone extremely exiguous ones that dried instantly.[118] As women's swimsuits, especially bikinis, became briefer by the year, most men's swimwear became more and more voluminous, inhibiting swimming and provoking Europeans "either to helpless mirth or serious compassion."[119] Americans educated by restricted and restrictive popular media had begun to fear the outline of male genitals, and by the mid-1980s had become embarrassed by European men swimming and sunning at Caribbean resorts attired in the briefest of briefs, even sunning nude.[120] In the first years of the twenty-first century, even the most daring American publications aimed at readers in their early twenties feared the tiny suits that emphasized anatomy designated "package" in a new, women's magazine euphemism.[121] In *The Vice Guide to Sex and Drugs and Rock and Roll,* Suroosh Alvi, Gavin McInnes, and Shane Smith caution young twenty-first-century male readers against wearing such package-delineating suits. But while they recognize their prudishness, and admit "it's not Nazi Germany," they nonetheless emphasize their conformist recommendation.[122] They say nothing about class or locale or indeed anything about men who swim in private in such suits or in the nude.

As Europeans assert, in overseas radio programs and elsewhere but especially in private conversation, most Americans still fear nudity.[123] Many accept gross violence in films and on television, but most still recoil from the nudity that figured in so much glamour photography after the middle 1930s and that today discomfits even university undergraduates looking at postwar images of skin divers, sunbathers, and boaters.[124] So long as violence excites and sexuality and nudity titillate filmgoers and watchers of television, mass-media vendors will continue to emphasize such within larger frameworks of race and gender orientation: the formula sells.[125] Exactly as Seldes, by then no longer director of television programming for CBS, asserted in his 1950 *The Great Audience,* those producers ignore the minority of Americans who reject their products.[126] They focused and still focus their products at an audience dulled by long-term consumption of formulaic imagery.[127] Manufacturers of Hollywood film and both broadcast and cable television ignore the minority that ignores them.[128]

In the 1960s I became one of the ignored. A close friend and I watched *Goldfinger* attentively, and we noticed that the 1964 Lincoln Continental supposedly crushed in the junkyard compactor is a 1963 model. In the sequence when Bond stops Goldfinger's cheating at cards, the dead girl is first shown lying on her stomach; in the next shot she lies on her back. Nowadays such issues are mere trivia intriguing film aficionados concerned about continuity lapse. But at the time they annoyed us. We liked the film, but neither of us understood the media-based high-school buzz about it, nor did we appreciate being told repeatedly that we should not think about the films as we watched, but simply enjoy them.[129] We had failed to understand the uproar over the Beatles appearance on television the previous year, especially the emotional response of many girls, and we disliked being told we should not think about such things but join in. Our friends liked us well enough but did not understand why we mulled over the images they simply consumed.[130]

My friend drowned in the estuary a few days before our high-school graduation in 1967. He might have been the scientist-astronaut he intended to be when he graduated from MIT, but he might have become a photographer too. He discovered 35mm photography in his senior year, and the secondhand camera did wonders in his hands. Perhaps he composed shots so well because he noticed the jarring discontinuities in mass-market cinema. Perhaps he made such fine images because he consumed very few mass-market ones.[131]

The following summer, looking out at the estuary, listening to a woman wearing a bikini briefer by far than any Sean Connery examined in the James Bond films, I wondered how many Americans my age shared my lack of interest in cinema and television and my deepening suspicion that mass-media fascination camouflaged the activity of a small minority of image makers unremarked almost everywhere.[132] Two summers later I read Agatha Christie's new novel *Passenger from Frankfurt,* mistaking it for a mystery and discovering an incisive if idiosyncratic assault on the ease with which neo-fascists might use modern media.[133] Thirty years later, when I regularly encountered film-studies scholars writing glibly that "the world according to Hollywood is an exotic, sensual cousin of the realm outside the cinema," I found myself no longer wondering why film-studies scholars conjure the simulacrum of Hollywood motion-picture glamour against a pasteboard one of reality, but rather at the eerie willingness of so many students to accept their assertion that the media create something exotic.[134] By then I knew other people who viewed the Hollywood-centric world as essentially sterile, a sort of cardboard mockup deflecting the masses from glimpsing something genuinely glamorous.[135]

Booksellers and advertising specialists deftly place Anne Rice's novels beyond the fantasy shelves, but not only because they revolve more about armatures of sex, power, race, region, and family than they do about vampirism, voodoo, and glamour. Unlike so many fantasy authors, Rice grapples directly with what she calls "popular movies" and the music flowing from radios and disc players.[136] Unwittingly or knowingly, she taps into the potency of modern media programming and the unsettling ability of some to negate or ignore it.

In 1938 Sergei Eisenstein equated viewing cinema with following a path. As the projector displays the film, the viewer moves along an "imaginary" path from perception to perception. But to him the word "path" meant something more as well. "Nowadays it may also be the path followed by the mind across a multiplicity of phenomena, far apart in time and space, gathered in a certain sequence into a single meaningful concept, and these diverse impressions pass in front of an immobile spectator."[137] Around the immobility of the viewer revolves contemporary critical interest. But in "Montage and Architecture" Eisenstein avers that only rarely is the cinematographer immobile. Most of the time he moves about constantly, stopping only to set up his camera to film a specific concatenation of figures, objects, and movements in ways that both mimic and transcend what a child attempts to depict in drawings most adults typically dismiss. He would be surprised to encounter a generation of children inured to the programmed imagery in which he delighted, a generation wary of belly buttons and the insides of women's thighs, but not of violence.

3 Shop Theory

Tinkering with radio equipment quickly supplanted the early nineteenth-century effort of modifying cameras, but both enterprises attracted mostly boys and men intrigued with signals and images.

In THE TOWN WHERE I GREW UP, MOST LOCAL
women and girls refused point-blank to be photographed in homemade
bikinis briefer than those they wore on the beach and aboard boats. The
quasi-public gaze of far-off photo processing plant employees and the possibility that clerks at the one local drugstore might open envelopes inhib-
ited image making.[1] At-home processing freed photographer and subject:
the tentative use of new Polaroid instant cameras accelerated easiness in
front of cameras. Images of private behavior—mother or sister sunbathing or playing badminton in wisps so brief they scarcely stayed in place;
mom and dad sharing a beer while curled up in the stern of a boat; mom
savoring her coffee while sun-drying her hair and reading a racy novel;
teenage siblings sunning or swimming nude in the pool; friends jumping
into the estuary on a blistering hot summer day—all existed because the
photographer controlled image making. The sixty-second camera gave
absolute privacy of image to many photographers unwilling to process
film and prints at home and by 1975 produced a plethora of images only
infrequently put into albums.[2] But in the late 1960s and early 1970s Polaroid equipment remained novel, expensive, and often tricky to use. Local
photography enthusiasts stuck with traditional cameras and film.

Out of fascination or financial need, photographers modified obsolescent equipment and made do with homemade equipment.[3] They developed their own negatives and prints, learning by intent and by accident the shop theory of what magazines addressing professionals and
advanced amateurs designated "glamour photography." The deep red filter that makes any sky turn sumptuously dark on black-and-white film
makes rouged lips appear ghastly fish-belly pale.[4] Lenses distort the size
of feet, especially when sitting subjects thrust feet at cameras. Blondes
photograph especially well because blonde hair is finer than brown or
black, and because blonde-headed people typically have about a fifth more
strands of hair than others. Disparate filters fitted into homemade holders and simple sunlight reflectors worked wonders: subjects smiled at
the contrivances but the contrivances worked. Composition and lighting often frustrated, but many images pleased photographer and subject
both, now and then by accident.

Old cameras worked a peculiar magic in the old fields of my boyhood.
From grandparents and great-uncles I acquired a variety of cameras with
better lenses and other features than the Brownie box camera my parents
gave me on my seventh Christmas. Aperture settings fascinated me: suddenly I could make better images in dimmer light or achieve far greater

depth of field. By the time I turned twelve I understood the old cameras as extremely versatile and, while not quite expendable, fine to take into harm's way. Two folding Kodaks refused to remain folded. Around both I wrapped rubber bands, and on one I stuck black electrician's tape to repair a tiny light-leaking hole in the fabric bellows. Kodak vest-pocket models from the 1930s made me wonder why adults gave children bulky box cameras: the compact cameras fit in no vest pocket, but folded flat enough to slide easily into a jacket pocket or bicycle saddlebag. Only film-manufacturing changes irritated me. Eastman Kodak began phasing out 127- and 620-size film, and as two general stores and one drugstore re-tailed the only film in town, I started shifting to 120-size film and then the 126-size cassette film developed for square-format Kodak Instamatic cameras.[5]

I accepted the first Instamatic hopefully, but it seemed boxy. But the unique aluminum-frame S-10 Instamatic my parents gave me at Christmas in 1967 partially collapsed, fit in my jacket pocket easily, did well in all weather, and best of all, made the square-format images I treasured.[6] In 1968 Eastman Kodak introduced a variety of Instamatic accessories, especially the rugged but now forgotten Ektagraphic Visualmaker. Essentially a stand coupled with close-up lenses and parallax-corrected framing accessories, the Visualmaker enabled even the cheapest Instamatic to make high-quality photographs and transparencies of postage stamps and other very small items. Aftermarket manufacturers produced similar items, one with an f/32 aperture offering the great depth of field needed by dentists; entomologists, jewelers, and others quickly adapted such accessories to their own needs.[7] The Oceanic Equipment Corporation built inexpensive Instamatic underwater housings, which pleased the glamour photographer Peter Gowland, who found he could make four to six underwater shots while holding his breath, something impossible with his homemade plywood-and-Plexiglas Rolleiflex housing.[8] In the spring of 1968 *Popular Photography* announced that Kodak had made available its ISO 400 Tri-X black-and-white film in 126 size; it demonstrated how well Instamatics made rainy night Tri-X images in Times Square.[9] In June the magazine asserted that 126 film had become a "major-league" size likely to equal or surpass 35 mm film in popularity.[10] For about ten years, roughly the decade spanning my undergraduate and graduate student years, Eastman Kodak supported its Instamatic line and 126-size film in ways that confirmed my square-format view of things.

In high school I learned to ignore yard-sale cameras using obsolescent film. I did not know that local retailers no longer carried some sizes of film because distributors insisted they buy more than one or two rolls at a time. Rural demand had dropped too low to justify maintaining stock. Two storekeepers told me rather brusquely that they could no longer get the film I used: I never suspected they lied. Before I acquired my S-10 I thought Kodak had stopped manufacturing 616, 620, and 828 film. I passed up a variety of single-lens and twin-lens reflex cameras, especially several near-pristine Kodak Retinas, some of the finest cameras ever manufactured in the United States, because I thought they used discontinued film. Their sellers thought so too, and priced them almost as junk.

College subsequently involved exploring Boston camera stores selling all sizes of film, and while I delighted in the ruggedness and small size of my S-10, I dreamed of owning a Rolleiflex using 120 film and building a large-format camera. In summertime I bought more old cameras at barn sales, acquired the parts of two view cameras, and kept on modifying cameras no one wanted. I tried altering several to accept new film sizes. Reducing the diameter of 120-size film-spool ends to 620 proved a bit frustrating, since I first tried to turn down the ends with unexposed film attached to the spindle. Only when that experiment failed did I try re-shaping camera interiors, discovering the mysterious pleasure of rebuilding the dark chambers.

Reworking a camera involved hit-or-miss shop activity. I had almost no shop theory to guide my efforts. I knew no one even slightly interested in modifying fifty-year-old cameras, and many people who learned of my attempts thought my time wasted. Older people told me to enjoy a modern camera, and friends my age dismissed my efforts as quirky in an era when advertisers extolled new 35 mm camera systems boasting interchangeable lenses. *Popular Photography* offered almost no guidance, nor did similar magazines. I considered tinkering with cameras as relaxation likely to produce visual revelation: altered cameras behaved unexpectedly, making every exposure a risk.

In high school I discovered dusty books on early twentieth-century photography in the James Library, a private athenaeum facing our town common.[11] Even then I wanted to build a large-format camera, and knew I had the woodworking tools and skills to do so, and that my boat-builder father had the carefully dried hardwood. But I could find no information, and after I started college I moved on to other interests, intoxicated with a surfeit of information on other subjects.[12] Only when I stumbled into junk-store collections of Depression-era photography magazines did I find the shop-theory advice that made sense of the long-ignored books in the tiny library. In my college years I began to scrutinize photographs to understand how photographers had made them, and with what sort of camera, stock or modified.

I discovered too the oddities of family photograph albums, including those of my own family, and the photographs somehow unfit for albums. Curiosity involving hand-me-down cameras made me notice images made to test photographer judgment of lighting rather than record any ostensible subject. I saw my great-grandparents, grandparents, parents, and other adults staring outward from childhood, from wartime, from boats and convertibles, from newlywed status. Some discoveries seemed unimportant—I knew my dad had had a convertible—but others struck sparks: an aunt had been a showgirl, my bachelor great-uncle had vacationed with an unmarried woman for forty years, and so on. I watched my dad grin when he saw a photograph of my mom, then his girlfriend, wearing his army Eisenhower jacket in a way that implied she wore nothing else. I saw the faces of my aged great-uncles change as they stared at photographs of trains long gone from tracks only recently torn up, and of farms grown up in pine trees. The pictures led aged people to remember buying a specific camera or being around a relative smitten with a new camera. Sometimes they led my oldest relatives to show me images long ago deemed unsuited to family albums.

I compared family photographs against those in the albums of other families. Old people, especially elderly women who lived alone, frequently knew stories associated with images in their albums, and told some of them, usually the second or third time I visited. As my interest in history deepened in college, then in graduate school, I glimpsed possibilities implicit in studying family albums. When I encountered Michael Lesy's *Wisconsin Death Trip* in 1974 my interest quickened: Lesy had rummaged in a state historical society archive and turned up treasure. I might rummage in the private albums of my town. I might understand the snort that accompanied one elderly female comment about the time a summer visitor used a Leica to make candid photographs. I might understand why some amateur photographers favored some cameras and formats over others. I might understand why so few photographers realized the power accompanying total control of film and paper processing. In the end, I thought I might learn how cameras and film and inclination shaped my own scholarly efforts in the last years when I weighed an academic career against others.

I revaluated photography as it had shaped my boyhood, and I shelved my projected photographic history projects. I liked making photographs, but I especially enjoyed making ones of women. In high school several of my friends had purchased 35 mm cameras and begun teaching themselves composition, knowing that photography might make art. I stuck to my square-format cameras and carried a Kodak S-10 square-format camera every day in college and most days in graduate school. In graduate-school summers I played with a massive if clunky Polaroid camera, shoved into license by a family friend who provided boxes of film free. But I spent little time reading about how to make better photographs, except for directions involving glamour photography. I knew by the end of high school that however girls claimed to dislike being photographed, they prized images of themselves that revealed them as special, not so much sexy or beautiful as alluring or mysterious or, in the words of one, "worth getting to know." In college I read more seriously on glamour photography. Simple shop-theory directions proved immediately effective. Never did I think about my photography as art, but through my graduate-school years I watched academics grudgingly accept some photography as art.

In the early 1970s photography and photographic history emerged as academic subjects controlled by art history faculty. The photography that intrigued me did not intrigue them, either as a subject of study or as something to do. They considered glamour photography beneath contempt, almost on a par with pornography, a hallmark of everything feminists loathed. I separated my glamour photography from the landscape photography that consumed so much of my graduate-school training, and indeed from my public biography. By the mid-1970s I knew enough about glamour photography to realize that it required opportunity, daring, luck, and a serious, long-term effort that conflicted with an academic career. I read on it as recreation, but found almost nothing in Harvard University libraries: secondhand bookstores and the back room of a camera store proved my main source of material. In a camera store across the street from Widener Library I found not only a hodgepodge of ever-changing written material but the company of amateur and professional photographers.[13] There too I met the agents of foreign camera and film manufacturers who connected me with overseas publications offering viewpoints as critical of much American popular culture, mass media, and ideology as anything I heard on short-wave radio.[14] Acquaintances who championed the study of cinema and even television found the books, tattered photography magazines, and glossy European technical leaflets subversive.[15] I found them intriguing because they dealt occasionally with the visual power of some women in some settings: that power fascinated a few photographers who conceived of glamour as something worth knowing intimately. In the shop-theory literature of glamour photography I glimpsed a force growing stronger as feminism grew stronger, a force feminists rarely noticed, and tended to underestimate and condemn when they did.

Some people read and follow directions, learning from success and failure and discovering knowledge implicit in instructions but revealed only in the following of them. Back in 1975, when I was tinkering with cameras from the 1930s, *Popular Electronics* heralded the coming of the personal computer age in a cover story announcing the Altair 8800, a computer kit selling for just under $400.[16] Enthusiasts skilled at soldering, circuit-board wiring, and other tasks could not only own a powerful computer but upgrade it at will. The machine ran the first Microsoft language, Altair BASIC, and proved revolutionary.[17] Nowadays such enthusiasts are considered "nerds," and many people dislike the simplest of system assembly directions. Favorable attention accrues to almost anyone but those who read directions: Americans appreciate "intuitive" approaches to anything.

High-tech devices once arrived with sophisticated instruction manuals that rewarded sustained attention and gave a sense of accomplishment to readers who followed their leads, especially beyond introductory procedures. Such manuals existed within frameworks of periodicals and stand-alone volumes offering more nuanced instructions for beginners and experts alike, detailing modifications and uses that voided product warranties immediately. Many adults and older children shifted original-equipment manufacturer instructions into larger, often idiosyncratic frameworks, then proceeded to build or modify equipment accordingly. "A fair camera can be made from two or three old cigar-boxes by boys and girls who are reasonably expert in carpentry," one children's magazine writer, Arthur Loring Bruce, opined in 1910. "The writer once saw one made in such a way by a boy of fourteen for a total cost of fifty cents." The camera made of cigar-box wood and candy-wrapper tinfoil facilitated the making of long-distance landscape views impossible with Kodak Brownie cameras: for his preferred purpose, the boy had a better camera than most other children. Bruce then explained how to modify a discarded camera using brass shim stock and a no. 11 sewing needle. The pinhole camera would make superb long-distance images and vignette views of houses and other nearer structures.[18] At the close of the first decade of the twentieth century, children and adults from middle- and upper-income families experienced a new thrill: in suddenly obsolescent cameras, they found the components of idiosyncratic innovation.

Instruction and trial-and-error learning facilitated the fracturing of photography in the 1920s.[19] New cameras, film, and paper caused many photographers to abandon older equipment and techniques, but many others altered older cameras to accomplish specific goals. Modified cameras proved useful in environments known to harm photographic equipment: on beaches, in small boats, and elsewhere around salt water, photographers often carried second- or third-best cameras adapted to harsh conditions. Other altered cameras furthered the goals of photographers dedicated to very specific interests ranging from glamour imagery to the photography of skyscrapers. During the Depression, photographers lacking money to buy new cameras often had the time to modify obsolescent ones. Such shop work shaped the American photographic enterprise for decades.

In 1932 *The Camera* published detailed instructions on converting an Eastman Kodak 3A Autographic Camera into a pinhole camera capable of extraordinary depth-of-field image making. Nowadays any would-be photographer equipped with a micrometer and other simple machine tools, some sewing needles, shim brass from an auto parts store, and a 3A can still apply John Parker's instructions and own a versatile camera. With high-school Algebra 2 skills, he can use Parker's equations to calculate exposure times and depth-of-field settings rather than expose in hit-or-miss ways.[20] Kodak never explained how to dismantle, alter, and reassemble its 3A, but Parker and other experts did, and they and other authors addressed a dedicated readership. Well into the 1950s, *Popular Mechanics* and photography magazines routinely published articles on photographic techniques. *Popular Mechanics* produced an annual, *Photokinks,* aimed at professionals and advanced amateurs anxious to push the limits of equipment, technology, and expertise, often by making devices or altering factory-built products.[21] Through the 1980s, photographic magazines published instructions on photographic techniques involving owner-altered equipment, materials, and subjects, especially models, but the articles diminished in number after the 1970s.[22] Suburbanization fragmented camera-store camaraderie amounting to informal apprenticeship programs. The shift of much camera manufacturing to Japan limited accessibility to repair manuals and other manufacturer-produced literature. American photographers had read German-language technical literature for decades, but few read Japanese. More sophisticated cameras proved awkward to modify, too. In the final analysis, however, many photographers lacked the time, tools, and risk-taking attitude to modify equipment built after 1970. By 1980 they also lacked directions written by successful experimenters.

Not reading directions once meant accepting terrific risk. Selecting or changing the 1/500 of a second shutter speed of a 1950s Rolleiflex 2.8C medium-format camera after cocking the shutter meant jamming the mechanism, something that necessitated expensive professional repair. The manufacturer issued a warning both in the text of the instruction booklet and in a black-bordered box printed lower on the page, and subsequent nonmanufacturer book-length manuals dedicated to the camera and its uses emphasized the possibility of error.[23] Blurred and overexposed negatives evolved from lack of attention to instructions, producing irritation and sometimes dejection. A jammed shutter meant shipping the Rolleiflex to New York, and perhaps on to Germany.[24]

Reading seemingly innocuous directions presented risks, too. A 1951 *Photokinks* article, "How to Pose a Pretty Girl," explained how to make wholesome girl-next-door images. But it offered discreet suggestions for making cheesecake and pornography also, chiefly by emphasizing errors that destroyed wholesomeness.[25] By the end of World War II such veiled instructions had become obsolete. In an article innocuously entitled "The Paper Negative Process Is Simple," readers of the 1939 annual *Good Photography* learned how to pose a bare-breasted woman in ways that made her look like an odalisque, as exotic as any female imagined by a pulp-fiction fantasy writer and posed in opposition to Hollywood standards.[26] A few years earlier William Mortensen had reoriented professional and enthusiast viewpoint with a series of monographs, most importantly *Monsters and Madonnas* in 1936, probing experimental techniques involving the photography of people, chiefly women, costumed, lighted, and posed in ways and settings Hays Code–era Hollywood rejected.[27] The *Photokinks* article aimed at far less knowing amateurs fifteen years after Mortensen and others had pioneered a daring shop-theory approach to glamour that subverted anything Hollywood attempted.

In *Outdoor Portraiture* and *The Model*, Mortensen explored not only the power of the male photographer interested in glamour but the often greater power of the female model able to wrest control of the sitting.[28] His *How to Pose the Model* details not only the use of cosmetics but the risk that a confident model may usurp the photographer in part because of her cosmetics knowledge.[29] Throughout the 1930s he asserted that photographic directions often led even expert amateur photographers into the moral quicksand that strengthened the Production Code, and that only tough-minded directions and courageous experimentation would lead them out. Hollywood feared full-frontal nudity and especially pubic hair, but Mortensen abjured this squeamishness. "Let us take leave of public morals and get back to matters of private taste," he proclaimed. "It is essential to the healthy presentation of the nude that it carry the implication that this is the normal condition of the body."[30] By the late 1930s it was—at least for some prosperous rural, suburban, and vacationing urban women luxuriating in summer sunlight, lonely beaches, and old-fields freedom.[31] Mortensen and other professional photographers abandoned Hollywood studio work in the early 1930s because they could no longer stomach the rule of lower-class cinema-house public taste.[32] Their work, especially the directions they aimed at advanced amateurs and younger professionals, reflects what Seldes and subsequent authors recognized as the deflective power of the Production Code. A cohort of cinema audiences abandoned movies, many photographers left Hollywood, and many amateur and professional photographers and subjects embarked on image making beyond the strictures of mass-culture entertainment.

Mortensen and other photographers taught classes (Mortensen opened his own school adjacent to a California beach) and published books denouncing Hollywood prudery. They attacked the fan magazine–driven shift from acute technical scrutiny of films to single-minded devotion to star-system glitziness. While these photographers—and manufacturers of sophisticated cameras and related products—skewed upscale photography magazines toward more sophisticated how-to-do-it articles, film magazines emphasized escapist fluff.

Motion Picture Story Magazine, then *Motion Picture Magazine,* and after 1917 especially *Photoplay* initially catered to the growing power of male fans interested in the technical details of filmmaking and cinema consumption, including advertising. But after 1920, such fan magazines emphasized anything but technical shop theory.[33] They and the film industry wanted a female readership unlikely to introduce competition, especially innovative competition, to a fledgling industry outfitted with equipment any determined or inspired tinkerer might buy or build. The filmmaking industry was fearful of well-to-do rural and suburban men who had the space and visual privacy in which to make outdoor films, and was made particularly uneasy by the idea that women cinemagoers might want male friends to make movies starring them.[34] The industry and fan magazines consequently worked to deflect interest from filmmaking itself and to make the process seem impossibly difficult.[35]

In the 1910s *Scientific American, Popular Mechanics,* and similar magazines devoted regular attention to technical issues in photography, filmmaking, and radio at both corporate and private levels. Historians who contend that such magazines created and fostered a culture of masculinity ignore an important moment in broader American social history.[36] Magazines grounded in science and technology proved the catalyst for shop-theory innovation and fostered high-tech adventure novels like Allen Chapman's Radio Boys series.[37] Photography, cinematography, and shortwave radio became almost entirely middle- and upper-class male avocations threatening the hegemony of corporate filmmaking and broadcast radio.[38] Shop-theory-driven technical experimentation kept experimenters, most of them male, from becoming mere consumers of imagery and broadcasts, and connected experimenters with each other. "Only the creative mind can really comprehend the expressions of the creative mind," Van Wyck Brooks asserted in a 1918 essay entitled "The Culture of Industrialism," an essay probing the energy of innovation outside the arts and humanities.[39] Inventors grew powerful and even more creative when they communicated with each other via circular letters (which often included photographs and diagrams), magazines, and amateur radio. Several patented their discoveries and grew rich, sometimes by selling their innovations to Hollywood studios.

As male experimenters grew sophisticated, organized, and linked through shared resources, film industry investors, executives, and technical experts gradually opened their eyes to the potential of amateur photography, telephone, and radio innovation to move silent-film production beyond corporate control.[40] The commercial film industry—both the entertainment sector and the educational one serving manufacturing and public education—feared not only innovation thrust upon it from experimenters everywhere in the country but potential competition from thousands, if not tens of thousands, of independent cinematographers hellbent on power and profit.[41] The catalyst for their fear was a small cadre of American enthusiasts in regular short-wave radio contact with foreign film critics owing nothing to the American filmmaking industry.[42]

At the end of the 1920s, fan magazines and studio publicity offices had accomplished a transformation of mass-media-centered American culture, especially media-centered visual culture. Fascination with the star system, the personal lives of Hollywood celebrities, and anything from costuming to the moral themes of individual films became feminized and therefore unworthy of male attention, in the eyes of filmmakers themselves.[43] Fan magazines and newspaper columnists emphasized the glitzy realm of Hollywood, and so deliberately obscured the technology rapidly becoming available to advanced amateurs, almost all male and often anxious to grasp film-making power.[44]

In a 1932 *Camera* reprint of an *American Cinematographer* article detailing his experiences with a 16 mm motion-picture camera aboard a coastal liner steaming from California to Cuba and Florida, Walt Disney implied that the superb camera offered startling potential to modify his already innovative animation techniques. "The 16mm. user of today," he observed, "is certainly a far luckier fellow than even the best-equipped professional of a few years ago." He realized that animation "can be done with an amateur camera—and patience."[45] Concern that wealthy, dedicated amateurs equipped with the latest in personal-use motion-picture cameras might supplant his animation monopoly simmers throughout his article. Disney connected radio-enthusiast shop theory and at-home radio-wave experimentation with the fast-growing readership of a fifteen-year-old shop-theory cinematographer magazine, *Ciné Miniature*.[46] Perhaps he reasoned that an effort akin to that energizing amateur radio enthusiasts might overwhelm the corporate production of animated films.

The Radio Club of America (RCA to its members and friends) organized in 1909, and sent its first transatlantic signal in 1921. In the booming 1920s it benefited enormously from the commercial and home-use technology showcased at the annual New York "radio fairs." In 1929 *Photo-Era* magazine reviewed the visual components of fair-displayed radio technology, and opined that what came to be known as television seemed imminent. It insisted that the merging of cinema and radio firms "will result in the production of new devices and equipment which will be of the greatest benefit to the amateur."[47] Throughout the Depression the club prospered in a symbiotic relationship with the Radio Corporation of America (RCA), the parent firm of the National Broadcasting Company (NBC), which transmitted video imagery by television before World War II.[48]

So many issues that now fix the attention of cinema historians seem grounded in radio history, especially the concept of the viewer (or in radio, the auditor), the role of government control (or after about 1930, the motion-picture association self-policing effort contrived to forestall government censorship), and the internationalizing of technology. In one 1925 issue of *The Experimenter* enthusiasts learned how to transmit pictures by radio, a hobbyist activity whose history lengthens the long foreground of television and emphasizes the symbiotic relationship of amateur radio innovation and engineering and sophisticated amateur photography.[49]

In the 1920s men—and teenage and even younger boys—indeed moved away from what became feminized fandom.[50] But many moved not toward amateur radio but deeper into still photography, and within a decade created a culture of masculinity, technology, photography, and fantasy that presaged and shaped the contemporary high-tech culture of video games and digitized imagery, especially in its military simulation and scenario applications.[51] Those photographers centered their efforts on birds, ships, sports, sunsets, and children; many worked on fantasy themes then shaping so much pulp fiction. A handful focused on glamour.[52] Whatever their ostensible subjects, shop theory guided most of their efforts, misadventures, and creative successes.

Unlike its prestigious scientific and younger humanist cousins, shop theory originates and prospers in the midst of making, not retrospective analysis. Around 1901 the Popular Mechanics Company began aiming dense annuals entitled *Shop Notes: Easy Ways to Do Hard Things* at expert machinists and factory superintendents.[53] By the 1930s *shop theory* began to designate both an increasingly formalized approach to making things, especially to solving factory-floor problems and embracing opportunities for spur-of-the-moment innovation, and an informal, experimental way of proceeding, often under difficulties.[54] Largely owing to the publication of *Shop Theory* by the Henry Ford Trade School in Dearborn, the term entered United States English through the national network of Ford Company dealerships, then through World War II military training.[55]

While somewhat formalized in technical colleges and vocational high schools by 1950, shop theory remains bifurcated: the term itself still connotes knowledge more frequently acquired in actual out-of-the-ordinary creative activity than in the classroom. Shop theory is seldom mentioned by commentators on high-tech innovation, especially the handheld digital devices invented by Apple, Inc.[56] Never is it mere practice, the run-of-the-mill activity that informs a smooth-running machine shop or factory.[57]

Shop-theory projects boomed in the Depression, when many photographers had little hobby cash but lots of spare time.[58] "My facilities were limited to five and ten cent store tools and materials, with the kitchen as my workshop," wrote one builder of a sophisticated horizontal negative enlarger, who admitted having a carpenter cut several boards to measure.[59] Mary E. Hopkins explained to readers of *American Photography* not only why she mounted her enlarger upside down in a manner that did not damage the ceiling but also how to plumb the support rack so that negatives would print without distortion.[60] Every month *Popular Science* published a few brief articles on photography tinkering; about every three months it featured longer pieces. Usually facing full-page advertisements for Kodak cameras, film, and paper, General Electric flashbulbs, and other photo-related products, often announcing reduced prices for top-quality equipment, the articles were aimed at mechanically sophisticated, determined readers able to interpret plans and usually having some prior experience with photographic equipment experimentation. Perhaps more importantly, the articles were aimed at photographers with peculiar needs, who were either unable to afford specialist off-the-shelf equipment and other products or to find exactly what they needed to accomplish personal agendas. After its debut in 1934, *Popular Photography* published dozens of such shop-theory articles, most written by creative, determined, but financially battered photographers.[61]

Around 1930 radio tinkering surpassed photographic tinkering. *Popular Science* ran a regular column, called "Helpful Hints for Radio Fans," with "hints" divided between neophytes reading "ABC's of Radio" and experienced amateurs anxious to understand how novel inventions and components worked.[62] In the February 1930 issue it described in detail how to reduce humming in well-built dynamic speakers; in another, much longer article aimed at advanced readers, it explained that a loose connection on a filter condenser will produce "a severe increase in hum."[63]

Popular Science, Popular Mechanics, Mechanix Illustrated, and similar magazines provided a wide portal on technological development and shop theory alike, which appealed especially to adolescent and teenage boys.[64] As some readers developed acute interest in one technology, they often abandoned the general magazines for *Popular Photography, Electrical Experimenter,* or other specialized periodicals. But others acquired interdisciplinary interests deeply rooted in specific technologies. Television produced the most nuanced overlap. In January 1937 *Popular Science* reported on the new television studio in Radio City, the new transmitter atop the Empire State Building, and the two hundred viewers who "recently enjoyed the city's first complete television program of speeches, news films, and entertainment originating in the new studio."[65] By then the magazine and Paramount Pictures had succeeded in a joint venture, weekly cinema newsreels entitled *Popular Science.*[66]

For more than a decade, *Popular Science* had routinely analyzed Hollywood special effects, detailing how ground-up chicken feathers represented snow, how studio experts had begun to use mirrors to seemingly enlarge studio space to conserve production costs, and so on.[67] By 1940 its photographic shop-theory articles often involved using flashbulbs to simulate the flames in fireplace shots, and similar tricks involving the camera shutter as electric switch.[68] Before World War II *Popular Science* had presented still photography as nuanced and sometimes vexingly troublesome, but by 1930 it saw amateur cinema photography as straightforward and highly likely to produce good results from the beginning. The manufacturers of cine cameras had learned from decades of trial-and-error effort involving the design, engineering, and manufacture of still cameras; the magazine argued too that magic lantern technology had solved many optical problems inherent in cine projectors.[69] The 150,000 Americans already using cine cameras in 1930 seemed the vanguard of a revolution.[70] Television cast shadows over photography, radio, and cinematography twenty years before it became commercially viable.

A lengthy 1933 article in *Popular Science* analyzed a top-of-the-line Kodak amateur cine camera that "now places the professional's bag of tricks in the hands of the amateur." The camera made "fade-outs, double exposures, animations, and enlarged close-ups" relatively simple, often when its holder merely pushed one of its many buttons or used removable masks to produce double exposures. Additionally, "dolls and other toys can be brought to life with the animator button on the camera." Amateur cinematographers tended toward playfulness, perhaps because most of them valued films made for entertainment rather than documentation, and many treated their expensive cinema cameras as near-magical toys making near-magical images, often by accident.[71] *Popular Science* maintained a strong technical interest in newsreels, noting in 1930 how sound newsreels had matured since their debut three years earlier, but writers were leery about the use of special effects in distorting nonentertainment film and television in an era when many well-to-do Americans had acquired cinema cameras, editing devices, and movie projectors, along with record players, radios, and other sound-producing devices.[72] Television threatened to produce all sorts of crises, some perforce shaping magazine content, but deeper ones influencing American understanding of visual technology.[73]

Television united people interested in radio and sound recording with those interested in photography and filmmaking. In September 1930 a brief article appeared noting that the skimpier dresses worn by flappers absorbed far less sound inside auditoriums than pre-1920s wool attire, something that had perplexed acoustics engineers and radio enthusiasts alike.[74] The following month, General Electric began purchasing full-page, densely argued advertisements, the first entitled "This Thing Called Ultra-Violet": television had concentrated interest in novel types of light, some recorded on special photographic film.[75] Throughout the 1930s *Popular Science* and its competitors reported on newly important sorts of light and other radiation, often in the context of photography: "mercury arc tubes which are made to produce intense flashes of a bluish-white light" enabled MIT electrical engineers to photograph splattering drops of milk at 1/500,000 of a second.[76]

Popular Science provided readers with television-based shop-theory articles as well, among the most sophisticated one entitled "Weird Lights and Cold Flames," detailing how to produce special effects using phosphorus.[77] Others explained how to use a neon darkroom light in developing novel films and a potentially dangerous experiment using batteries producing a hundred volts of direct current, moist newspaper, and a neon tube connected to a radio condenser.[78] While the magazine routinely published articles warning about electricity causing serious injury or harm, it understood television experimentation as fundamentally more dangerous than radio and photography enterprise.[79] Television rays themselves might prove lethal: in 1930 one article reported that a Berlin laboratory was experimenting with ultraviolet and other rays on living tissue, and another revealed that the Naval Research Laboratory had discovered massive atmospheric electric tides.[80]

By February 1939, when *Popular Photography* published a feature article entitled "Television Needs Cameramen," television had merged "a complete mastery of elementary physics and a working acquaintance with the theories of radio and electronics" with traditional and novel photographic techniques, many grounded in subliminal print-media advertising shop theory.[81] In five years the nascent industry had accomplished a shop-theory revolution that transformed photography and cinematography but is now largely ignored by film-studies scholars.

Through the shop-theory portal vanished tens of thousands of American males in the 1920s and later, but almost all disappeared into individual or quasi-solitary creativity, not into corporate or even large-scale cooperative effort. After the late 1930s those intrigued by glamour photography and fantasy followed paths blazed by William Mortensen, Clarence John Laughlin, Peter Gowland, and other now-ignored photographers whose personal aesthetic visions irritated many critics loyal to Hollywood-based standards but whose peculiar techniques proved applicable to a range of individual agendas. Mortensen and Laughlin explained how to make inexpensive, specialized equipment, choose settings based on the characteristics of models, and use props to accentuate lighting.[82] In the early 1950s, at the start of his career, Gowland published articles on photography and on furniture making, shop machinery, and the building of studios. His shop-theory effort in time produced the Gowlandflex, his home-built camera intended chiefly for glamour photography and sold to hundreds of professionals and enthusiasts, and a range of articles about cameras modified for underwater and surf use.[83] He wrote at the very end of the shop-theory era. Like the magic doorways in Pullman's Dark Materials series, the shop-theory portal opened onto a realm similar to the everyday one, but subtly and sometimes brutally different too. For the men—and the few women and girls—who moved through it, the photographic shop-theory portal opened on the visual magic or fantasy known after the late 1950s as glamour photography.

Shop theory grew increasingly sophisticated but narrower in the 1960s, enabling fortunate photographers to advance along photographic back roads and overgrown paths unvisited by contemporary critics and historians. In *Camera Lucida*, Roland Barthes distinguishes between the "*Spectator's* Photograph" and the "*Operator's* Photograph," postulates that he and other nonphotographer critics can never understand any photograph through the prisms photographers know, and suggests that nonphotographers consequently feel none of the creative emotion any photograph engenders.[84] Barthes identifies explicitly the duality that so weakens Susan Sontag's nearly contemporaneous *On Photography.* Not only do nonphotographers confront photographs differently from photographers, they may never fathom the depths of creativity and range of vision that drive any one photographer, especially one using shop-theory-based techniques and equipment.[85]

Making images, and especially making images according to personalized shop-theory practice and invention, changes the way anyone sees.[86] "As I never throw anything away, recently I decided to try one for my nudes," Forman Hanna told *Camera Craft* readers in 1935 of some old-fashioned, soft-focus lenses he tried outdoors in rural Arizona. "Finally I tried stopping down the lens and when I reached f11 my problem was solved. There is a feeling of luminosity in negatives made with my old Pinkham & Smith semi-achromatic ten-inch lens, that I have been unable to get any other way." But luminosity derived too from additional experiment: he made his 11 x 14–inch prints by enlarging negatives in a holder masked by one layer of fine chiffon cloth producing "shimmery lighting," which won Hanna, an isolated mining-town pharmacist, prizes in European competitions and made him a fellow of the Royal Photographic Society. "Doesn't sound sensible, a contrast film developed for softness and a normal paper with a contrast developer, but if one were sensible he wouldn't be a photographer," Hanna concluded.[87] His thinking dovetails with that of contemporary photographers using antique equipment, home-coated glass negatives, and personalized film chemistry.[88]

Manuals as straightforward as Tom Branch's *The Photographer's Build-It-Yourself Book* and as sophisticated as Christopher James's *Book of Alternative Photographic Processes* presume not only dedicated interest and advanced technical competence but a fierce willingness to accomplish the making of photographs in individual ways using customized equipment and processes.[89] After about 1920 many expert amateurs followed a path deviating year by year from the standardized imagery of Hollywood cinema and American advertising, then from television. First they abandoned the movie-house rectangular format, then they eschewed much of the cinema aesthetic, especially its prudery.[90] Shop theory facilitated deviation: by 1970 it facilitated subtle but determined rebellion against mass-media norms that vexed and deflected critics.[91]

Early 1960s photographers found glamour by glimpsing something in the haze, and then defining the glimpse, often by making or modifying cameras, but sometimes by accepting photographic accident. By the late 1960s an elite grounded in shop theory used simple hand tools to modify Diana cameras to make images predicated on accident and idiosyncrasy. At first available only as a carnival prize, the Hong Kong–made medium-format cameras manufactured for Republic of China peasants slowly entranced a handful of American photographers willing to accept their bizarre features—especially a shutter that operates erratically and a plastic lens that distorts everything it records (and that varies from camera to camera).[92] The inexpensive Diana and its successors, especially the Holga 120S, still startle photographers accustomed to 35 mm cameras. They are bulky but extremely lightweight, and prone to technical difficulties making every negative a surprise. But their very low price, often under twelve dollars, enables determined enthusiasts to disassemble them and then modify them by changing aperture settings, converting them into pinhole cameras, sawing out partitions to change format from 120-film rectangles to squares or even to ones accepting 35 mm film, painting interiors to eliminate or alter reflection, electrifying contacts to activate flash units, and concocting filters emphasizing or otherwise distorting the vignetted images made by plastic lenses most photographers scorn.[93] Tinkering, trial and error, and the efforts of organization-minded Holga enthusiasts energize a global network devoted to photography via surprise, a way of photographing grounded in shop theory, guesswork, skill, and glamour.[94] Few Holga cameras, even the newer, glass-lens models designed to capitalize on the widening antidigital enthusiasm, make snapshots pleasing to anyone expecting ordinary box-camera quality. But with simple tools, skilled shop-theory adventurers alter the cameras to make arresting images, especially when negatives are printed in out-of-the-ordinary ways.[95] Nowadays constituting only one sliver of a global revolt against digital image making, the aficionados of shop-theory built or modified inexpensive cameras savor accident, risk, and glamour predicated on do-it-yourself technology.[96]

Some people follow oral or written instructions, read between the lines, and glimpse something more in the midst of the shop-theory process, just as alchemists once valued the haphazard discoveries punctuating their experiments.[97] Sometimes they stride or tiptoe or blunder into discovery and misadventure, perhaps into faerie itself.[98] Most people do not.[99]

Most people play little part in this book.[100] By 1900 the Eastman Kodak Company understood the deepening division between snapshot photography and serious photography, the last embracing professional photographers and determined, educated, often affluent amateurs of all ages.[101] It classified people satisfied with making snapshots as part of a larger group casually and voraciously consuming all sorts of images, especially print-media advertising.[102] Within fifteen years, the firm found itself caught in an immediately profitable but confusing situation threatening to become difficult over the longer term. Its cinema-industry sales skyrocketed as Edison's sprocketed-film technology drove an entire industry that pulled many people away from activities in which they used Kodak cameras loaded with Kodak film. Scholars have not examined the firm's response to the situation: they instead analyze the marketing research and advertising campaigns aimed at individual users of Kodak film.[103] But the Eastman Kodak Company recognized that cinemagoers constituted something other than a cross-section of the American public and acted accordingly.[104]

By the early 1930s it produced massive amounts of cine film aimed at its corporate market, and a range of cameras and film aimed at two groups: people satisfied with snapshots and people who demanded far more from Kodak film and from cameras the firm found difficult to produce at moderate cost, including cine cameras amateurs used. Perhaps nowhere else in twentieth-century cultural history is the split between consumers and makers of images more manifest than in the range of Eastman Kodak advertising and products, but nowhere is it less closely studied. At the start of World War II the company had long advertised to three groups, snapshooters, dedicated amateurs and professionals, and corporations, but it saw the latter two groups as driving the bulk of its research-and-development effort.[105]

While Gilbert Seldes and a handful of other critics scrutinized the impact of cinema and television after 1950, only the appearance of Marshall McLuhan's *Understanding Media: The Extensions of Man* in 1964 precipitated serious study of the so-called new media and its consumption.[106] By then only a few students from independent schools and a few well-heeled public high schools arrived in college knowing how to sketch, how to make photographs or maps, and how to analyze, if only in rudimentary ways, a film or television show or magazine advertisement or topographical map.[107] But many other freshmen arrived poorly prepared in making anything visual. Shop theory seemed the province of well-heeled students, not working-class ones, and college faculty and administrators confronted the class divide that cripples so much well-intentioned liberal arts curricula.

College faculty and administrators rarely studied the long-term impacts of the Sputnik-inspired curricular changes in high schools across the country. Shop-theory thinking vanished from public high schools when few college-bound students took woodworking, metalworking, and similar classes. The enhanced public-school focus on physical science, especially chemistry, biology, and physics, prompted the near elimination of art and geography, especially for high-achieving students in homogeneous-grouping public high schools. Abandoning geography proved disastrous by 1980. If nothing else, the old grades 1 through 12 public-school geography curriculum taught students that however they looked at paintings and advertising, they could read a map. What some inquirers identified in the early 1960s as the enduring harm class division caused college undergraduates and curricula, especially in elite colleges and universities, became by the early 1980s a well-nigh taboo topic and remains so.[108] Independent-school students ordinarily watch little television as children and teenagers, often less than two hours a week, including news broadcasts, but public-school students watch upward of fourteen hours a week. In some of my classes, independent-school students, especially those who boarded at school, note that they watched no television for months at a time but enjoyed fully equipped woodworking and other shops. The pattern has remained essentially stable since 1969.[109] Even today, independent-school-educated students have watched far fewer films than public-high-school-educated students, whether in video format or otherwise, and they tend to have spent far more hours reading than public-school ones. As a group, they have spent vastly more time making things.[110]

Only rarely does the pervasive and subtle influence of cinema and television on public-school graduates receive attention in the larger context of university teaching and research. Harrison G. Pope is a professor of psychology now convinced that no science demonstrates the existence of repressed memory, which he argues must henceforth be discredited in legal cases. He notes that "Hollywood may be partly responsible for the persistence of this notion because film is perfectly suited to the whole concept of memory. . . . An entire storyline can be resolved by a flashback of a repressed memory."[111] Pope's twenty-five-year-long study indirectly illuminates the stark division between young people with minds shaped by cinema and television-show flashbacks and young people far less sanguine about a psychological disorder lacking scientific basis.[112] In elite colleges and universities the cohort distinction Murrow, Stanton, Seldes, and other broadcasting industry executives noted in the late 1950s and early 1960s remains striking.[113]

The summertime advice I got from my older woman friend in 1968 alerted me to awkward topics about the chasm separating two segments of high-school graduates. In 1972, as a teaching fellow at Purdue University asked to evaluate potential readings for freshman-level expository writing classes, I read T. J. Ross's anthology *Film and the Liberal Arts*. The collection of essays struck me as biased toward freshmen who had watched a lot of television; two other teaching fellows, neither of whom had watched much television before attending graduate school, agreed.[114] But our classification of the anthology as a special-interest one irked our colleagues, who explained that freshmen not intimately familiar with film and television must be socially maladjusted.[115] A few years later, I noticed a new divide between academics who filed film and television (and radio and popular music) as components of American popular culture certainly worth study and those who understood film (but never television) as a subject around which entire departments might be built. The latter had little interest in the technology of cinema making, but expressed fierce interest in the subject matter of the films themselves.

In the very early 1970s I realized a slight discontinuity in language, something I first marked when I read *Film and the Liberal Arts*. To me, *film* designated Kodak products I used in my cameras, the contents of the rows of yellow-and-red boxes on the shelves behind the general-store cash register or lining half a wall of the Ferranti-Dege store in Harvard Square. To many of my friends and acquaintances, *film* sometimes meant *movie,* especially when they argued for the artistic value of a particular motion picture. As I entered graduate school at Harvard in 1973 the distinction sharpened, and I discovered I alone carried a camera and used it. Around 1973 I noticed no one said "motion picture," but people my age increasingly said "still photographer." *Film* no longer designated something one used but something one watched.

When I arrived at Harvard to begin my Ph.D. work, John Brinckerhoff Jackson told me to get a good 35 mm camera with interchangeable lenses. He growled that I must begin creating my own slide collection of the visual environment. I pointed out that I owned perfectly good square-format cameras capable of making slides, and he retorted that the era of 2¼ slide projectors had almost ended and that 35 mm slide projectors would shape my teaching. He thought little of the 35 mm square-format slides I made with the S-10: while satisfactory, I had to learn to make slides in rain and other low-light conditions, and for such I needed a more versatile camera. All through that year I resisted the purchase, partly for financial reasons, and I resisted it throughout the summer I spent at my parents' home and in the old fields along the estuary. The middle-aged woman friend who had cautioned me about media talked with me one day about my graduate studies, and our talk swung around to cameras. She told me that after so many summers of helping her repair her decrepit buildings she might as well see me on the road to *production* image making. I still use the all-mechanical 35 mm camera she gave me. More than one hundred thousand slides of the North American built environment later, I realize how few photographs I have made since I shifted format from square to rectangle and began making images chiefly to show to students learning to look around them, away from screens.[116]

My formal education, then my teaching and research, skated away from my shop-theory pleasures. Only now and then did the two approach each other. I used shop-theory techniques to photograph railroad landscapes and trains for my *Metropolitan Corridor: Railroads and the American Scene.*[117] Years later I spoke about the work of David Plowden when he donated his negatives to Yale University, and I surprised him and my audience by mentioning his work in pulp railroad-enthusiast magazines in the early 1960s.[118] As boys we shared a love of trains, and as men we share some understanding of railroad-photography shop theory.[119] When I did *Borderland: Origins of the American Suburb,* I used a bit of tree-top photography shop theory to tease out the meanings of period photographs. When I wrote *Alongshore* I found myself so involved with seacoast photographic kinks that I subsequently wrote specifically on the changes in beach photograph making over time.[120] But most of my time, my teaching and research involve making slides to show to students: it is straightforward pedagogical effort, definitely not art.

But in the course of my teaching I realize repeatedly that some undergraduates arrive knowing what the old-fields women told me in 1968 and the years immediately following. They know of visual matters beyond the mass-media output evident in film, radio, television, and now video games and computer imagery. Often high-school summer jobs have opened portals as secret as any Philip Pullman describes in his Dark Materials series.[121] In ever-growing numbers they arrive at my office, sometimes holding fashion magazine pages or old family photos that intrigue them. Often they express suspicions about divisions implicit in image watching vs. image making, and articulate hunches about the 1970s as some kind of turning point and about the visual forces accompanying nuanced class and other cohort divisions.[122]

As did the girls I knew in 1970, they suspect photo-processing employees of looking at photographs; they prefer digital photography in part because they control it, especially the printing of digitized images, within software parameters. I tell them that by 1977 the way processing-plant employees examined images had become shop-theory knowledge among working photographers. Too many amateur and professional photographers did not process color film themselves, but instead sent it to places called "labs."

The year I joined the Harvard faculty, Michael Lesy published "Fame and Fortune: A Snapshot Chronicle" in *Afterimage.* The autobiographical statement confirmed rumors circulating in camera stores. Lesy explained that in 1965 he had removed five thousand snapshots a week for two months from the discard piles of a large urban photo-processing plant. His experience shaped his art and his scholarship: he published *Wisconsin Death Trip* in 1973 and *Real Life: Louisville in the 1920s* three years later. His 1977 *Afterimage* article emphasized implicitly that processing-plant voyeurism caused many photographers to prefer black-and-white film they processed themselves, or to splurge on expensive color-film processing equipment. Freedom from commercial processing produced images unlike those Lesy analyzed three years later in *Time Frame: The Meaning of Family Pictures* and that only now surface as late 1960s and early 1970s period pieces in Lenny Gottlieb's *Lost and Found in America: The Homefront, Fall 1968: Family Photos during the Vietnam War* and similar books. Gottlieb collected his images from the quality-control discard pile of a Boston photo-processing plant, and his book delineates the division Lesy discovered in 1965. Employees did collect images, exactly as women feared then and fear now, but they typically collected from a very narrow range: prudent photographers process much work privately.

In 1972 a woman I had known since first grade stopped at my parents' home with enlarged color photographs. She had taken a summer quality-control job in a photo-processing plant and made the enlargements for free.[123] The 8 × 10 prints of a bikinied woman aboard my parents' boat made me smile: my friend winked and told me she thought I might like the enlargements. I had no way of processing color film at home, but after that sent my exposed film to an out-of-state plant. I began paying closer attention to camera- and film-manufacturer advertising innuendo concerning the benefits of home darkroom processing. In the early 1970s photographic shop theory involved privacy; within ten years it emphasized it.

Technological innovation skewed professional and amateur photography when 1920s manufacturers developed still cameras using 35 mm cinema film. Today few photographers know the resistance following the debut of the Leica, let alone the anger expert amateurs directed toward candid photography. When I use my fifty-year-old medium-format Rolleiflexes I luxuriate in the square viewfinder that shaped my boyhood. Then and now, making images intrigued me in ways viewing images does not. I enjoy visiting museums as much as anyone, but I cannot stomach watching reruns of *I Dream of Jeannie*. And just as long ago I noticed the discontinuities in *Goldfinger*, I notice now the vertical belly buttons still characterizing fashion-magazine photography. But what I notice most is that a different-shaped camera, a playful attitude toward making a photograph, a bit of smiling notice directed at a belly button well above a bikini bottom all irritate most of my colleagues. They find some image making or some attitudes about some image-making effort discomforting; they prefer to study photographs, especially published or exhibited ones guaranteed to be fine art, not the making of photographs. They analyze some genres of images but denigrate others, and shy from making almost any images of their own. They shy too from women intimate with glamour if not anxious to wield it, women who understand the power of glamour and of photographic technique alike, the women who understood the symbiosis of photographic shop theory and the shop theory of glamour, and perhaps a good deal about the making of exiguous costumes more effective than anything for sale in stores.[124]

Perhaps academics fear the camera as a sometimes-sentient machine. As early as 1951 Dorothea Lange insisted to readers of the new magazine *Aperture* that "for better or worse, the destiny of the photographer is bound up with the destinies of a machine." Lange argued that every photographer must prove that passion and humanity can endow the machine; she assumed her readers understood that such proof arrived only in using the machine, not in talking to it or about it.[125] Academics enamored of ideas favor pens and keyboards, which record the words expressing their ideas. Cameras make images, do not always behave, and implicitly call the bluff of so many academics.

Many academics distrust their ability to hold a camera or a paintbrush or even a pencil and begin to make an image.[126] I am almost certain that they distrust students to do so, and not because they fear the students will stumble: they realize some students may produce superb images that catapult their makers to fame.[127] And I am certain that they insist on studying images they consider art because they distrust the power of images that are not art, and at the shop-theory ways such images come to exist.[128] One of my younger colleagues calls their attitude "iconophobia."[129] Uncertainty, perhaps especially mechanical uncertainty, offends them.[130] "Alternative and non-silver processes are somewhat mercurial in nature and full of surprises; enjoy their quirks and see them as opportunities," counsels Christopher James in his magisterial *Book of Alternative Photographic Processes,* perhaps the quintessential contemporary photographic shop-theory grimoire. Until one has experimented with silver albuminate, gold alkaline and sodium bicarbonate toners, and what James calls "hot and humid image development," a process involving refilled spice bottles, pantyhose toes, and honey emulsion, one cannot begin to know intimately the accidental and seemingly possessed strangenesses of photographic processes long forgotten, or the way a handful of contemporary photographers, perhaps especially Sally Mann in making the images collected in her *Deep South,* embrace them.[131]

Until one has explored a bit of shop theory one cannot realize the limitations of electronic image-altering software.

James embraces a shop theory wholly in the tradition of that explicated by L. P. Clerc in his 1926 *Photography: Theory and Practice.* Clerc told photographers how to hold scenery negatives "sky downwards, during the local application of the bromide, thus preventing the bromide from running on to the image of the landscape part," an admittedly risky darkroom development procedure that obtained, sometimes, "the correct tone value of the sky in landscapes photographed without special precautions."[132] Clerc—and James eighty years later—accept risk and accident, the hazard Lange avers accompanies photography and lion taming alike.[133] A handful of books, perhaps especially Kenneth Mees's 1937 *Photography* (which explains *as a detail* which type of film with which filter produce images of antique furniture that emphasize grain and make scratches almost invisible), Otto Litzel's 1967 *Darkroom Magic,* and the 1974 manual produced by the Amphoto Editorial Board, *Photographic Tricks Simplified,* bridge the thinking of Clerc and James by assuming technical competence, and a willingness to accept risk and accident by embracing fitful loss of control over technological process and glamorous subject alike.[134]

Paul Valéry observes that "light and shade form very particular systems, present very individual questions which depend upon no knowledge and are derived from no practice, but get their existence and value exclusively from a certain accord of the soul, the eye, and the hand of someone who was born to perceive them and evoke them in his own inner self." His thinking profoundly shaped that of Walter Benjamin, who noted in a 1937 essay, "With these words, soul, eye, and hand are brought into connection. Interacting with one another, they determine a practice. We are no longer familiar with this practice. The role of the hand in production has become more modest, and the place it filled in storytelling lies waste."[135] But traditional photographic practice still weds soul, eye, and hand, and the realm of the traditional photographer merges into the realm fantasy authors descry. It is anything but a wasteland. It is every bit as sumptuous as drawing and painting.

"He worked fast then, pleased with the drawing, absorbed in its detail, sensing the awareness—still new, this spring—that something of himself was going out through his fingers," writes Susan Cooper in *Green-*

witch of a young boy discovering a talent for sketching. "It was a kind of magic."[136]

In the 1970s seeing glamour and making images oriented much first-rate fantasy writing aimed at children.[137] All of Ursula K. Le Guin's magisterial *Farthest Shore* involves a wizard and a teenage boy sailing a small boat in search of the place where magic drains from their world. As magic runs out the dark hole of immortality, wizards and village witches can no longer make magic, even minor spells. Shop theory no longer works. Out of the mass-media hole now flows the magic of shop-theory-based making, leaving only the mass of children and adults washed by the bluish-gray light of flickering screens.[138]

4 Brownies

Portable cameras figured in many outdoor adventure stories published before World War I: the wilderness offered surprises, as did the cameras.

Excited but determined to stay calm, the boy Scouts hurry to develop the film just removed from one of their cameras. Huddled in a tent atop a West Virginia mountain, they unpack their small developing tank, decide to speed the processing of the film, and mix in double the amount of developer. A few minutes later they shift the large negatives to the printing frame, and begin contact printing, placing each negative atop a piece of sensitized paper. "The developer had worked perfectly, notwithstanding the haste, and the printing was well advanced in the soft light of the tent," writes the author of the thriller. "Directly he had the picture taken in the cave under view—the snapshot of the wall showing the entrance to the secret passage." The Scouts gather around their processing expert and his print, determined to confirm or scrap a hunch.

The still-wet image reveals a face accidentally caught spying on the subterranean photographic effort made hours earlier. All the while the Scouts explored and photographed the small cave, a whiskered man had watched through a small crevice. But while the Scouts had sensed and laughed off an eerie presence underground, later they realized that their photographs might offer some verification about something one Scout had half-noticed.

Developing and printing the image reshapes their attitude toward their surroundings and predicament. "The camera see things the human eye does not see," asserts one solemnly, before suggesting that they develop and print other negatives to learn if they had been observed at other times. Eventually they print a negative revealing fragments of a face and legs hidden by trees and shrubs. One Scout thinks the face "may be caused by some odd arrangement of the leaves" because it is "very indistinct," but another contradicts him. "Sure, because it is in the shade. It is almost a miracle that we see it at all. I'll get a better print of it soon and enlarge it." When they examine the next printed negative they find what may be a coat shoved between rocks; another on the roll, after the closest scrutiny, reveals a boulder wedged in place by small stones placed against its bottom, and what might be the booted feet of a standing man. The Scouts compare prints, especially those made from the compact "baby camera" one prefers to use for candid photographs, and agree that the boots in two photographs might be identical. "The camera caught the same man twice," one exclaims. The Scouts had never noticed him.

After a few more moments of scrutiny, they realize that one negative shows a young boy riding on a man's shoulders, both boy and man carefully hidden in vegetation and spying on the picture-taking Scouts. "All this means," one concludes, is "that we were watched when we were taking the pictures that afternoon. Those people were looking at us! We might as well have been walking through an open street."[1]

G. Harvey Ralphson's *The Boy Scout Camera Club, or, The Confessions of a Photograph,* appeared in 1913, two years after the Boy Scouts of America issued what subsequently became known as the first edition of the merit-badge booklet entitled *Photography.* Despite its improbable plot, Ralphson's juvenile thriller taught readers that spies easily observe even the most vigilant unless the subjects of observation consciously seek out the voyeurs. More importantly, it taught readers not only that photography offered ways of honing already acute observational skills but also that now and then cameras seemed possessed of jarring willfulness.

Cameras sometimes record what photographers never noticed. Very rarely photography might be near-magical, the camera well-nigh haunted, if not by demons, perhaps by brownies.

Haunted machinery informs much American fiction—for example, that of Nathaniel Hawthorne. In his notebooks he outlined a tale in which a machine rips off a man's arm, drags another by his coattails "and almost grapples him bodily," snares a girl by her hair and scalps her, and finally "draws in a man and crushes him to death."[2] He speculated that while some objects might behave as if possessed, similar behavior might originate in the essence of particular devices. He scrutinized mirrors, knowing that they sometimes momentarily reveal quirks of character, and imagined a short story in which someone learns the secret of making all the images reflected in an old looking glass "pass back again across its surface." He imagined a process that might enable viewers of a magic-lantern show to focus attention on minute parts of a scene rather than on the large projected image.[3] His fascination with optical instruments showing more than their designers and operators ever imagined shaped several of his tales and a romance, *The House of the Seven Gables.*

In "Fancy's Showbox," an old man sipping wine sees through his wine-glass the appearance of Memory, Conscience, and Fancy. The last "had assumed the garb and aspect of an itinerant [magic-lantern] showman, with a box of pictures on her back," and Fancy orders the tale. The old man pulls the string shifting the hand-painted miniature pictures within the box, then stares through a magnifying glass at image after image. While the magnifying glass, "which made the objects start out from the canvas with magical deception," serves only to advance the scathing visual indictment of a smug, self-satisfied, and outwardly reputable elderly man, it indicates Hawthorne's enduring interest in closed-box pictorial displays. Another such box appears incisively in "Ethan Brand," when an "old German Jew traveling with a diorama on his back" blunders into the emotion-charged crowd assembled at a lime burner's remote home. The pictures "were worn out, moreover, tattered, full of cracks and wrinkles, dingy with tobacco-smoke, and otherwise in a most pitiable condition," but the view becomes grisly when the showman encourages a young boy to put his head inside the box, behind the twin magnifying lenses. The boy's cheerful expression turns to horror when Ethan Brand looks through the lenses, then when the showman asks Brand to look again, Brand himself is horrified at what a "curious youth, who had peeped in almost at the same moment, beheld only as a vacant space of canvas."[4] Brand had glimpsed what Hawthorne designates the Unpardonable Sin, not as the old man glimpsed a series of misdeeds in Fancy's show box, but in a way skewed by the show box mechanism itself. The show box did something on its own, although the showman suspected it might.

In a similar way, Holgrave the daguerreotypist scarcely shapes what his camera does. Throughout *The House of the Seven Gables* he remains a minor character, albeit one who "never lost his identity." The simple phrase implies that Hawthorne knew that some people do lose their identities, often through callous or deep-seated wickedness. Too, it implies that Holgrave, who makes daguerreotypes for a living and insists he will abandon the art form for anything more intriguing and remunerative, is almost independent—and innocent—of the effects his camera occasionally produces. He works as a sort of mediator or facilitator of accident. When young, innocent, and virtuous Phoebe tells him that she does not "much like pictures of that sort—they are so hard and stern; besides dodging away from the eye, and trying to escape altogether," Holgrave tells her that most subjects look unamiable in daguerreotypes because they are indeed unamiable people, and that sunshine properly angled, as in a camera, "brings out the secret character with a truth that no painter would ever venture upon, even could he detect it." Of course, some painters do sometimes detect the secret character, and Holgrave offers a daguerreotype of the living Judge Pyncheon as proof. Phoebe thinks it an altered image of a portrait painted in late Puritan days.[5]

In the heyday of the daguerreotype, not only Hawthorne wondered at sunlit images fixed permanently beneath glass. He and his contemporaries confidently believed that portrait cameras frequently caught the essence of sitters' characters, sometimes revealing character traits and political allegiances sitters kept hidden. While Hawthorne toyed with the idea of fixing mirror images—in "The Hall of Fantasy" he created an inventor who knew "the secret of fixing images reflected in pools of water"—he wondered at the real-world wisdom of making permanent records of faces. In "The Old Apple Dealer," one character praises the fact that images of faces cannot be fixed, but instead vanish like mist on a sunny morning. But once daguerreotypy became fashionable, then common, Hawthorne, Emerson, and others began realizing that every now and then the camera snared something neither daguerreotypist nor sitter intended.

In 1857 Emerson wrote that "I learn from the photograph & daguerreotype men, that almost all faces & forms which come to their shops to be copied, are irregular & unsymmetrical, have one eye blue & one grey, one the nose is not straight, & one shoulder is higher than the other," that most sitters are "shreds and patches, borrowed unequally from his good & bad ancestors."[6] He suspected to be true what Hawthorne insinuates in *The House of the Seven Gables:* that daguerreotypists—and analyzers of daguerreotypes—sometimes learned from likenesses thoughts that their subjects wished to conceal. Indeed Emerson wondered if daguerreotypy might not unmask closet abolitionists.

In the early years of the movement, abolitionists were viewed as half-crazed, amoral people who might be identified by wild looks in their eyes. Something about daguerreotypes of abolitionists, especially of John Brown, suggested that cameras, if not daguerreotypists, routinely fixed glimpses of character molded by something other than altruism.[7] Abolitionists and others might lie, but now and then cameras might catch them out in ways beyond the control or intention of photographers.

As daguerreotypy morphed into photography, and the novelty of photography devolved into the prosaic, often dutiful visit to the photographer's studio and the routine viewing of professionally made images of people, landscape, historic spots, and important events, the educated general public increasingly accepted the photographer as a maker of crisp, objective, and certain images of reality. In the late nineteenth century professional photographers reveled in their control of camera and developing and printing processes, and in their control of the people who entered their studios and became their subjects. What they could not control, especially fast-moving objects cameras recorded as blurs, they tended to avoid. Historians of photography as fine art or social documentation routinely emphasize the professional dedication to realism and to technical perfection, and recently literary scholars have demonstrated the profound impact of professional photography upon novelists and poets of the period.[8] All too often, however, scholars ignore the simple fact that until the 1870s photography existed as an almost wholly professionalized technology, and that not until 1900 did it become a quite common avocation. While scholars embroider the already rich fabric of photography, especially the crucial shift from realist to pictorial to realist epochs, not even historians of popular culture devote much attention to the technological changes that made photography an upper-class, then a mass-culture hobby.

Gelatine dry-plate technology perfected between 1874 and 1880 changed photography permanently. Instead of dealing with cumbersome glass negatives coated with emulsion that failed if dry and always had to be developed immediately following exposure, professional photographers began using dry-coated glass negatives that might be stored before and after exposure. Almost immediately professionals realized that dry-plate technology permitted the development of long-awaited miniature "vest pocket" or "detective" cameras equipped with postage-stamp-size plates smaller than frames of contemporary 35 mm film. Equally quickly, however, amateurs discovered that the technology allowed them to dispense with a great deal of worrisome, uncertain chemistry and very large cameras: suddenly they could buy boxes of unexposed, long-lived negative plates fitted to ever smaller, more user-friendly cameras that might be taken anywhere.[9]

By the late 1880s dry-plate photography had energized well-to-do Americans as no other technological fad had done: one *Century* author called it "a gentle madness" that spread by "the curious contagion of the camera." Cameras especially, but related equipment too, came in great variety, although most remained expensive by any standards. Enthusiasts found themselves equipped with cameras offering shutter speeds of 1/200 of a second, boasting fast, distortion-free lenses, producing negatives of about 5 × 8 or 6½ × 8½ inches, and fitting snugly under the arm on long rambles. In his 1887 *Century* article "The Amateur Photographer," Alexander Black commented that amateurs had themselves produced most of the recent innovations in photography, simply because they accepted the risk of failure.[10] Professionals, especially portraitists, avoided such risk because their living depended on the certain production of technically accomplished images. Professionals could not afford regular failure and so knew little of serendipity.

Amateur blunders advanced photography on several fronts. Enthusiasts experimented with color photography, candid photography (especially on city streets), and innovative darkroom technique. Black noted that larger dry plates had "become somewhat expensive playthings," but cost deflected few well-to-do hobbyists. Especially popular with physicians, photography seemed likely to become the hobby of attorneys, engineers, and other well-educated, well-remunerated professionals—and their wives. As women embraced the hobby, men found less and less opposition to temporary and permanent home darkrooms, even to the bathroom being converted night after night.[11] Amateurs found themselves anxious to see what their cameras might do, almost as though cameras had wills of their own.

Black wrote seven years following the introduction of George Eastman's Kodak roll-film camera. When the Eastman Kodak Company introduced its No. 1 camera using smaller roll film, change transcended the limits heretofore imagined. Loaded with a 100-frame roll of film, the No. 1 produced images of about 2¾ inches in diameter. It shifted Edison's attention to the possibilities of motion pictures, skewed amateur photographers toward making narrative sequences, and transformed amateur photography into a national, if still upscale, hobby. But the No. 1 worked too as a prototype. Kodak soon introduced roll-film cameras making thirty-two to fifty-four exposures of 4 × 5 and 5 × 7 inches.[12] By 1890 most United States cities boasted camera clubs, usually organized groups of white-collar men, which not only sponsored lectures and demonstrations by experts but organized competitions and shows and operated photographic field trips.[13] At the turn of the century, amateurs using roll-film technology shaped the photographic equipment industry.

But Ralphson makes clear that photography is not an inexpensive hobby. His Scouts live in upper-class families, and have a dedicated meeting room "on the top floor of the handsome residence" in which one lives in Manhattan. Among the group are "the son of a ship builder" who "has a launch and a yacht of his own," the son of "a famous corporation lawyer," and the son of a New York daily newspaper publisher. "His letters to his father's newspaper were usually addressed to the financial department, upon which he had permission to draw at will!," Ralphson exclaims of the Scout who subsidizes the lone nonmillionaire of the patrol, one "who had never had a home except that provided by himself, and this, in the early days of his life, had as often been a box or barrel in an alley as anything else." However improbable, *The Boy Scout Camera Club* explicitly emphasizes that the Scouts' entire adventure originates in wealth, and that their photographic effort consumes capital rapidly. Not only do the Scouts shoot a lot of film, they shoot it with abandon, and often produce excellent results along with surprising images.

The "baby camera" one Scout carries, often beneath his jacket, might be a Kodak No. 2 Folding Pocket Brownie camera.[14] Between 1904 and 1907 Eastman Kodak produced about 76,000 of that model before starting production of an improved version, the No. 2 Model B, which it manufactured for the next eight years. The No. 2 used 120-size film and produced eight 2¼ × 3¼–inch negatives per roll; its excellent lens, variable aperture openings, precise focusing, and adjustable shutter speeds made it a favorite almost at once. By contemporaneous standards its size made it miniature: it was 6½ inches long, 3½ inches tall, and 2 inches deep, scarcely pocket-sized but easily carried beneath a coat, as one Scout does, partly to the annoyance of the others, who carry larger cameras in cases.[15] But however the one-pound No. 2 Folding Pocket Brownie transformed amateur photography, it stretched pockets in more ways than one.

In 1904 it retailed for $5. In contemporary terms, it cost about $110 based on the Consumer Price Index, about $538 using the unskilled wage indicator, and about $770 based on the per capita distribution of the Gross Domestic Product.[16] Ralphson describes the baby camera just vaguely enough to make precise identification difficult. The camera might be the No. 2 Folding Pocket Kodak, introduced in 1899 priced at $15.[17] It seems too small to be a No. 4 Folding Kodak, introduced in 1890 and retailing for $50, or the successor camera, the No. 4 Folding Pocket introduced in 1912 at $59.[18] As the novel unfolds, any thoughtful reader muses about the equipment on which the plot turns. Perhaps some of the Scouts have ten-year-old cameras, but all or most of the adventurers use fairly new ones. However the reader decides, Ralphson suggests that at least one Scout roams the West Virginia hills with a camera retailing for about $1,350 today.

Film itself proved expensive in 1913. Before 1920 Eastman Kodak manufactured film in several sizes, and aimed it at box camera and folding camera users owning a range of Kodak cameras. By 1912 the company understood that financial gain lay in maximizing profit from roll-film sales, not squeezing profit from the manufacture of cameras. Its entry-level box cameras existed chiefly to encourage adults and children to become photographers, and thereafter use roll film, hopefully Kodak film sized to fit specific Kodak cameras. Under perfect conditions, the box cameras made extremely satisfactory images.[19] Very frequently they "caught" fleeting expressions and other subjects simply because their users were not busy adjusting shutters, bellows, and other components of expensive cameras.

Given the abandon with which the Scouts expose film, no reader wonders that now and then the cameras record what their users missed.[20] All of the cameras seem now and then possessed of autonomous will. But the baby camera, whose owner exposes film almost as a machine gun sprays bullets, frequently photographs details its photographer missed. Not only is he often surprised at the high quality of his images, he is surprised at the constituents of many images.

George Eastman named his company Kodak because he liked the letter K, and he called many of his cameras "Brownies" to emphasize their near-magical ability to record images. Through the first fifty years of advertising, the Eastman Kodak Company subtly changed its advertising slogans. In the beginning, it told would-be buyers, "You press the button, we do the rest."[21] By the 1930s the company had shifted its emphasis to the sale of film, with a slogan explaining, "You push the button, it does the rest." The company appears to have retreated a bit from its first slogan, and the camera itself had become the "it" that did things in conjunction with the photographer and film. Brownies did things on their own, often with no regard for consequences.

Kodak appears to have used the verbal and visual concept of brownies without acknowledging or paying Palmer Cox, the late nineteenth-century reinventor of the creatures of Scottish folklore. Perhaps Cox accepted the pirating of his signature creations simply because Kodak advertising only enhanced their popularity, especially among parents and children. But without a doubt, George Eastman successfully snatched something from faerie that energized the sale of an industrial product by attributing magical powers to mass-produced cameras.

Brownies long enlivened the folklore of Scotland. Named for their tawny or swarthy skin, the miniature humanoids did mostly good, usually by night. They churned milk into butter, threshed grain, and swept floors, and rarely performed mischief. In the larger hierarchy of supernatural creatures, they skipped about the cellar, and even King James I, a devoted scourge of witches, spirits, and other beings he categorized as evil, could find scant reason to condemn them. In his view they served the Devil, "and haunted divers houses, without doing any evil, but doing as it were necessary turns up and down the house." In his 1597 *Daemonologie,* he wrote of "this spirit they called *Brownie* in our language," meaning a "rough man" with the complexion of one who lived outdoors, that "some were so blinded, as to believe that their house was all the sonsier, as they called it, that such spirits resorted there."[22] He understood that his Scottish subjects, especially the poorest, accepted brownies as both indicator and provider of health, happiness, tentative prosperity, and luck, and that they rarely if ever associated them with the malignant spirits he thought conspired against him, the English throne, and Protestantism.

Brownies lingered in Scottish folklore for centuries, and mid-nineteenth-century British writers eventually employed them in children's books.[23] In her 1871 *The Brownies and Other Tales,* Juliana Horatia Ewing depicted one as "a dwarf with largish head" apt to help around the cottage and then cause mischief.[24] For a handful of other writers, *brownie* denoted the powers of the imagination working behind the conscious mind. "For the most part, it will be seen, my Brownies are somewhat fantastic, like their stories hot and hot, full of passion and the picturesque, alive with animating incident; and they have no prejudice against the supernatural," maintained Robert Louis Stevenson in "A Chapter on Dreams." He claimed that brownies suggested the plot of his 1884 novel *The Strange Case of Dr. Jekyll and Mr. Hyde* as he slept, and that they intervened during his writing.[25] For Stevenson, *brownies* seemed merely a convenient term for whatever unconscious and undirected energy drove his art, an energy perhaps connected to faerie. By the 1880s the term had become familiar in many ways.[26]

Stories of brownies crossed the Atlantic much earlier, with emigrants to Canada. Palmer Cox recalled tales of them long after he left his Granby, Quebec, home in the early 1860s for a career as a newspaperman-cartoonist in San Francisco. Fourteen years after beginning that career he left California for New York, and in 1881 published his first brownie sketches. Two years later the children's magazine *St. Nicholas* published his first complete brownie tale, a mix of doggerel and sketches. Success in the magazine fired his career. His brownies quickly appeared in *Harper's Young People, Scribner's, Ladies' Home Journal,* and other magazines. The first of his sixteen brownie books debuted in 1887; punctuating his *Queer People with Claws and Paws* and other books, the brownie books became his signature product. His meteoric rise continued until his death at eighty-four in 1924: he died with eleven books in print, new sketches on his desk, and a host of admirers and imitators.

In an 1892 issue of *Ladies' Home Journal* Cox explained the origin of his spectacularly successful cartoon creatures. He understood mid-nineteenth-century Scottish folklore as containing traces of pre-Christian religion. Brownies endured from pagan times, doing good deeds and small household tasks, always at night; in return, rural people left out a few drops of milk or cream. Some villages quietly accepted the enduring existence of a "brownie stone" usually located near the local church: onto the stone every Sunday someone poured a tiny bit of milk to honor the tiny wild people. Away from the hearth and stable, brownies redirected lost travelers and performed other good deeds, including showing people where to sit to win at board and card games, and so on. In the Hebrides and other islands, wholly illiterate cottagers knew the brownies as helpers against modern ills inaugurated by literate off-islanders.[27] As Cox told the readers of the *Journal,* King James I misjudged the tiny people. Superstitious Scots were correct in having "absolute faith in the 'Brownies'' wisdom or judgment."[28]

Cox's brownies are the first creatures of faerie to embrace industrialization.[29] He snatched them from the deep past when the Old Religion clashed with Christianity, molded them to personify cultural traits from nations around the world, and set them to work and mischief in modern, usually urban and suburban settings energized with mechanism. Children from well-to-do families found them in *St. Nicholas* after 1883, and instantly embraced them.[30] In Cox's first brownie book, the tiny creatures experiment with bicycles, lawn tennis, gymnasium equipment, hot-air balloons, canoes, roller skates, and the contents of a modern toy shop. While several chapters focus on the brownies doing good deeds, visiting the seaside, and ordering a feast, most involve the brownies toying with the latest in fashion, fad, and machinery, often with catastrophic if hilarious results.[31]

Cox produced a monthly feature for *Ladies' Home Journal*. In a series entitled The Brownies through the Year, the tiny creatures are not only more complexly developed but more likely to invade the nighttime urban scene. Some of the tiny characters are definitely not American: one wears silk robes and a Chinese pigtail, and another Russian furs. Others are distinguished by occupation and class: a tough urban cop in long blue coat and helmet keeps order by chasing miscreant brownies with upraised nightstick, several dressed as sailors provoke the cop, and a millionaire in monocle and top hat intermittently causes trouble by claiming ownership and shouting commands. In the February feature, the brownies enjoy Valentine's Day by assisting in the delivery of love letters, then get tangled up in urban telephone lines while climbing ladders to upper windows.[32] In "The Brownies in June," the band approaches the new Brooklyn Bridge and begins scampering along its great cables, then racing in teams. Soon a few brownies trip, nearly fall, and require rescue, not only by intrepid colleagues from above but by others maneuvering rowboats below.[33] The August adventure involves more rowboats and canoes, a southern landscape of "Where sweet the white magnolia smiled,/Where sugar-cane and cotton grew," the "Crescent City" of New Orleans, and excruciating encounters with alligators, then a glimpse of Caribbean shipping.[34] While undoubtedly written on one level for children, on another the series comments acerbically on cross-cultural confusion, class division, modern technology, and regional identity. Brownies always set off at nightfall intending the best, but accident invariably shoves them into difficult situations. Month after month, the brownies plunge into situations involving industrial sites, inventions, and mechanism, then triumph over the most modern, intractable problems.[35]

Cox's success prompted many imitators. John Barton Gruelle is especially known today for his Raggedy Ann doll, which he patented in in 1915, but the doll, and especially its face, evolved from his work as a newspaper cartoonist. He began publishing cartoons in small-town Indiana newspapers when a teenager, and by 1904 worked in St. Louis for the World Color Printing Company producing comics pages for local newspapers nationwide. While maintaining his weekly output of some ten comic strips for his employer, over the name Johnny Gruelle he published his own cartoons in *Ladies' World, McCall's, Good Housekeeping, Life,* and *Physical Culture.* He moved deliberately into book publishing, beginning with *My Very Own Fairy Stories* and capitalizing on that success—and the success of his doll business—with *Friendly Fairies.*

Gruelle depicts a wide range of fairies, elves, and other diminutive creatures in his own ways, but he shows brownies essentially as Cox depicts those in the background of his cartoons, tiny male creatures with vertical eyebrows and wide mouths, round heads too large for thin bodies, and always wearing a sort of beanie cap. The beanie cap proves a stable indicator of Cox influence: while some juvenile authors emphasize the "peaked cap" worn by the British coal-bin brownie, almost every post-1900 illustrator depicts brownies wearing beanies.[36]

Gruelle illustrated his books in full color, and the images drive rather than decorate his stories lifted from traditional British tale-telling. His work sits squarely within the larger context of other circa-1900 Midwest fantasy writers, a context cultural historians still piece together from ephemeral evidence. While nowadays far less well known than L. Frank Baum, the creator of *The Wizard of Oz* and similar works, in his heyday Gruelle proved almost as popular as Cox, but in a gentler way. Gruelle emphasized that no child reading his works would find anything disturbing, remotely sinister, or even tangentially wicked. While not overtly moralistic in the way of Miss Mulock's *The Adventures of a Brownie,* the plots of his tales revolve around accidents made good, not mischief for the sake of mischief. Gruelle children and fantasy creatures rarely misbehave, never take chances, and often find adventure beginning in simple misunderstanding, not mischief, let alone meditated wickedness. The stories typically occur in vaguely European lands long ago, places characterized by nobles, thatched cottages, and, less frequently, Dickens-like cities, all clearly far removed from the United States at the beginning of the twentieth century.[37] Despite intermittent disjunctions—his period interiors often depict eighteenth-century rural New England more than anything foreign, and mosquitoes and other North American insects inhabit foreign lands—his sumptuously illustrated books enable children and adult readers to move effortlessly into realms disconnected from their modern surroundings.[38] They are more ventures into the past than into faerie.

Gruelle and other writers emphasized the vaguely medieval settings Cox eschewed, not brownies and other creatures from an often-harsh faerie.[39] After his 1903 compendium *Brownies and Other Stories,* Cox avoided castles, unhappy princes and princesses, and other stock items he argued characterized "long-ago and far-away" fairy tales.[40] The following year he published *The Brownies in the Philippines,* a multilayered examination of cross-cultural collision in a neo-imperialist age.[41] A handful of competitors struggled to reconfigure Cox's brownies as slightly different creatures, perhaps just different enough to skirt copyright-infringement suits. Nathaniel Moore Banta tried in 1905 in his *Brownie Primer,* and he was still trying in the early 1920s (perhaps because Cox had by then greatly reduced his output of sketches and tales) when he published *Ten Little Brownie Men* in 1922, and *Busy Little Brownies* and *The Little Brown Man,* both in 1923. He followed Cox in having his tiny men appear only after dark.[42]

Cruelty suffuses many brownie illustrations produced by Cox imitators, especially anonymous ones working after 1910. Illustrators of fairies depicted the long-standing cruelty of fairies to small animals as early as the 1860s; into the twentieth century, M. R. James and other writers delineated the nastiness of fairies toward birds, especially owls.[43] But the shift in attitude toward brownies after the first decade of the twentieth century seems utterly disconnected from fairy-illustration tradition, and may originate in artists' irritation at being unable to match Cox's worldwide success. In many illustrations after 1910, brownies work no nastiness on children or animals. Instead they coerce fairies into serving them, or punish fairies for perceived misdeeds, especially spying. Brownies attack winged fairies, beating them with sticks or sticking them with harpoon-like lances. Individual postcards and other unsigned ephemera combined to produce a subgenre that endured into the 1930s, one implying the superiority of modern, outdoor, rough-and-ready brownies over the ephemeral, insipid, elegant, and sometimes sinister fairies of Victorian fairy tales.[44] In it brownies do things exactly as Cox drew them doing things: in the dark, with mechanism.

In one important way Gruelle wrenches early twentieth-century readers away from temporal and spatial settings into modernity as twisted as anything Cox inked. His books include stories of dolls becoming alive. Almost certainly the motif originates in his boyhood, when he cheered his dying sister with adventure tales of her rag doll, the prototype of Raggedy Ann. While children, and perhaps especially little girls, have imagined for centuries that their dolls and puppets might live and adventure, Gruelle emphasizes that dolls becoming live involves as much fantasy and magic as any tale set in some distant time and place. "My, how the dolls laughed and giggled, now that Marcella was not in the room," he writes in "Uncle Clem" of a doll mauled by the family dog. They laugh even more when, days after its owner removes it from her doll cupboard, the mauled doll returns wearing a police uniform, a gift from the owner's father. Everything about the tale is modern, including the uniform and Marcella's own wardrobe, and everything hinges on what Marcella sees and misses.[45] Marcella cannot see her dolls alive. She has no camera with which to capture their image, either.

While scholars have long studied living-doll folktales from Japan and Europe (and lately from the Inuit regions), and the nuanced contexts of Pinocchio, E. T. A. Hoffmann's circa 1816 tale "The Sandman," which features a full-size mechanical woman; a wealth of toy soldier tales including those by Hans Christian Andersen; and—far less rarely, simply owing to lack of familiarity with it and its old rural heritage—Hawthorne's "Feathertop," none emphasizes the important divide between Cox's brownies and the contemporaneous creatures of Gruelle and others.[46] Cox's living brownies deal unsettlingly easily with modern technology, but in his books only the acute descry them and their nocturnal activities. Gruelle and other early twentieth-century author-illustrators set their fantasy tales in bygone eras and remote places where kings, witches, dwarfs, and talking birds mingle promiscuously for any character to see and imagine. In their works, only come-alive dolls having adventures beyond the scrutiny of their owners jerk readers into contemporary places. Gruelle's books imply intermittently but continually that girls dislike something in the present, especially after dark, and are far happier reading about the fairy-tale past. But the doll-come-alive motif enabled him and other Cox competitors to suggest that fantasy might occur as forcefully in early twentieth-century American cities as it might in fabricated pseudo-medieval castles, and that it might delight girls as fully as Cox's mechanism-minded brownies delighted boys.

Cox rejected sappy juvenile-literature moralizing and the reluctance of Gruelle and others to place fantasy squarely at the center of the nighttime modern city. Clearly he reveled in presenting brownies to both girls and boys. In his chunky 1888 *Juvenile Budget: Containing Queer People with Paws, Claws, Wings, Stings, and Others Without Either: Goblins, Giants, Merrymen and Monarchs: Stories of their Mischievous Pranks and Humorous Doings,* Cox explicitly merged traditional folktale and modern technology. Sometimes his brownies appear in far-off medieval settings, and once they incite the livestock of a cruel modern farmer and guide a farmyard revolt; in another chapter the brownies steal farm horses and ride them along well-maintained if empty rural roads. The letters of the alphabet take humanoid form and dispute about priority, giants go fishing, and a wicked Chinese mandarin forces his slaves to slide down a stairway banister and laughs when they fall. Children who pelt a young goat with stones each day as they walk to and from school discover the following spring that the goat has matured and terrifies them. Cox depicts the children almost as brownies, and the goat as a maddened satyr, perhaps as Satan himself.[47] Mischief, cruelty, and misadventure exist for their own sakes, especially after dark when bats, brownies, and mice collide beyond the gaze of all but the acute. In all his subsequent work, Cox focused on faerie and fantasy as integral parts of modern life, not fairy-tale long ago and far away, and he dealt fluently with brownies manipulating machines, and other subjects his competitors distrusted or mishandled.

Brownies prosper in risky, often treacherous places and in accident and misadventure, and their capacity to snatch surprise and delight from ordinary and tricky environments and situations fitted perfectly with Eastman Kodak advertising needs. In *The Book of the Brownies* the firm emphasized that "to start the children along the delightful road of photography, the Brownies, by their simplicity, low cost, and substantial construction, stand supreme." Brownie cameras soon came to be seen as part of a larger system of photograph making. "There is not one of the seven models which any boy or girl of average intelligence cannot easily use," Kodak advertising material boasted in 1913 of cameras manufactured to use film that might be processed away from darkrooms, in either the Kodak Film Tank or the Brownie Developing Box. Then it could be simply contact printed full size or enlarged in the Brownie Enlarging Camera, again with no need of darkrooms.[48] The Eastman Kodak Company had created a graduated hierarchy of entry-level cameras advertised not only to adults wishing to embrace simple, low-cost photography but to children eager to make photographs too. The bulk of Kodak advertising between 1890 and 1920 suggested that within the black boxes of Kodak box, folding, and other Brownie cameras now and then occurred near-magical glimpses of seemingly ordinary subjects.[49] Intermittently any Brownie camera worked its own in-the-dark magic or mischief, and by the early 1890s that dark power focused the attention of parents wanting the best opportunities for children growing up in a technological age.

All of Cox's monthly *Ladies' Home Journal* features ran against an evolving backdrop of camera advertising. Subscribers to the magazine could purchase toys, sporting equipment, and other items at special discounts, in part by using points accrued through length of subscription and by encouraging other women to subscribe. The magazine touted expensive, high-quality goods, especially those not available in small-town and even small-city stores. The Cox features not only led women to subscribe and to maintain subscriptions, and to urge friends to subscribe, but also subtly empowered the women by enabling them to learn about and order items. In the first 1892 issues, for example, subscribers might purchase a "breech-loading spring gun" and a very handsome wood "historical panorama," much like the one Hawthorne describes in "Ethan Brand." Along with lesser "premiums" like carved-oak bookcases and a plethora of novels, "a splendid fishing outfit for the boys," the "three-draw, 12-line achromatic telescope," and two large steam-powered toy boats (one a paddle-steamer and the other a screw-propeller vessel) aim largely at males: only advertisements for hammocks and hammock chairs show women relaxing.[50] Illustrations for the other premiums show boys using the equipment, always outdoors, with now and then a girl patiently watching.

Premium imagery and advertising changed in the July 1892 issue. Thereafter *Ladies' Home Journal* no longer advertised "camera outfits" showing boys and men, and sometimes a girl, using tripod-mounted, dry-plate cameras. Instead a girl still looks through the viewfinder of "Outfit No. 2," while a man holds the newly advertised "Outfit No. 3 'Snap-Shot' Camera." The new camera uses roll film, not individual plates, and while the outfit comes with all the necessary processing supplies, it is clearly aimed at men. "To Catch the Figure You Touch the Trigger," one ad proclaimed month after month, and the man standing beside or behind a fence mostly definitely engages in an operation as chancy as any boy holding the spring gun. Amateur photography had begun to change extremely rapidly in the early 1890s, as Kodak roll-film and box cameras revolutionized photograph making, and the advertising traces the changes.

Kodak's *Book of the Brownies* depicts a Huck Finn–like boy on its cover: tanned, barefoot, and carrying fishing pole, lunch pail, and Brownie camera, the overall-wearing boy stands on a dirt road. Inside illustrations depict Boy Scouts using Brownie cameras, but nowhere does the firm show a girl using them. The lone girl appears as the subject of a photograph: she might as well be the lone goat appearing in another. Despite the text, the illustrations imply that photography suits boys rather than girls, and that it involves an element of risk. Not all photographs "turn out," but sometimes the photographer makes more than a good shot. The photographer gets lucky.

By the end of the nineteenth century it had become clear that roll-film cameras had forever changed photography, but in ways yet to be defined. On the one hand, many would-be photographers, especially men and boys, wanted the snapshot camera that "took" pictures as a bandit might take valuables with a firearm. On the other, some would-be photographers prized cameras that made finer photographs, often from negatives manipulated during the printing process. The Kodak slogan "You Take the Picture" had already changed photography by 1892, but the split remarked by so many observant adults, especially prosperous parents, had already become a class divide. Within a few years, the Eastman Kodak Company had published *Picture Taking and Picture Making* and other books acknowledging the divide between snapshooters and those who made photographs. Palmer Cox's brownies advertised Brownie cameras, including snapshot ones, and the Eastman Kodak Company implied that brownies worked far more magic in sophisticated Brownie cameras and in its cameras not carrying the Brownie label than in cameras used by fuddy-duddy professional photographers self-incarcerated in studios.

In the pages of *Ladies' Home Journal* readers found not only Cox's modern view of faerie but advertisements for cameras whose dark chambers enabled a second sight utterly up-to-date and utterly unlike anything Gruelle and his cronies depicted. The Eastman Kodak Company used Cox brownies to infuse its ultramodern black boxes with the potential of faerie.

As the booming popularity of photography caused the *Ladies' Home Journal* to replace premiums involving telescopes and panorama boxes with multiple "camera outfits," Cox's understanding of fantasy in modern urban settings fused with the visualization tradition of Hawthorne and his contemporaries to create an aura of mystery, and often mischief, around the new amateur photography. That photography deflected attention from the sumptuous illustrations of Gruelle and other early twentieth-century authors of fairy tales. Many children, especially many wealthy children, no longer preferred to turn the pages of gorgeously printed books. Instead they wanted to make their own photographs.

Those children, almost all photographing outdoors, typically carried Brownies, and all became a sort of brownie themselves.[51] Tanned, learning to see differently from ordinary children, able to search negatives and prints in second-sight ways, they edged toward the portal of faerie and sometimes glimpsed things beyond. Throughout her 1913 *Outdoor Girls of Deepdale: or, Camping and Tramping for Fun and Health,* Laura Lee Hope thrusts her fifteen-year-old girl hikers into confrontations with women who despise them as militant suffragettes. The girls grow wiry and tanned on their summer-long rural walking tour, and they are never without a camera; in time they accomplish things they had hitherto thought only boys capable of doing.[52] While Banta and other Cox competitors struggled to delineate "the brown man," some children became brownies, the tanned, outdoor barefoot boy of the Brownie advertising booklet, the privileged teenage Boy Scouts in Ralphson's thriller, the young girls photographing cows in Hope's novel, all young people adventuring and misadventuring in seeing and making images.[53]

The long relationship between American children and photography begs to be written, and its bare outline must necessarily include the four million Boy Scouts who had learned photography through the Merit Badge course. In 1937, when 27,232 Scouts encamped near Washington, D.C., boys overwhelmed the do-it-yourself temporary darkrooms. The film-processing concessionaire produced 25,000 prints daily from the 300 rolls of film it developed every hour for Scouts unable to process their own, and one newspaper reported that more than half the Scouts always carried a camera. "Most Scouts had simple box and folding cameras which cost but a few dollars," reported James E. West, chief Scout executive and editor of *Boys' Life*. "However, there were hundreds of expensive miniature cameras and motion picture cameras very much in evidence."[54] Eastman Kodak produced Brownie cameras, and more sophisticated ones, specially painted for the Boy Scouts, and for the Girl Scouts too: the firm realized the life-long branding potential in the symbiotic relationship between the organizations and itself.[55]

As early as 1902 Charles King experimented with camera accident in "A Camera Capture," a short story detailing the misadventures of a young American woman traveling in Germany. She clandestinely photographs several handsome Imperial Army lieutenants and accidentally photographs an innovative cannon, a secret weapon. The simplicity of the Brownie camera viewfinder reinforces her inability to notice all that the viewfinder encompasses.[56] Many subsequent writers toyed with accidental image making, particularly images made by children with Brownie cameras or adults with Brownies or slightly more sophisticated cameras.[57] In a 1922 *Strand Magazine* short story, "The Prophetic Camera," L. De Giberne Sieveking teases out the unsettling potential in a large old box camera, almost certainly a very early Kodak product, left in a pawn shop. The pawnbroker's very young nephew makes snapshots with the camera: the developed prints depict details from some aberrant future. As in Ralphson's novel, much of the action turns on darkroom excitement. In the drugstore across from the pawnshop, the pharmacist, the nephew, and the pawnbroker and his wife cluster about the developing trays as unnerving negatives slowly develop. "Of course the camera cannot lie," sniffs the wife as she struggles to maintain her faith in the accuracy of photographic reproduction.[58] But by the early twenties, mass-culture cinematography featuring special effects had shaken such obdurate faith in photographic honesty. People realized that complex cameras might lie, especially in the hands of cinematographers and other professionals.

Photographs that misled, especially those of seemingly accidental but actually faked images, ordered much pulp fiction within a few years of Ralphson's novel and Cox's death. By the late 1920s enough photographers had made images that produced details unnoticed in viewfinders that pulp-fiction authors had begun musing on deliberate but seemingly accidental images.

"The Photograph," a 1928 *Detective Fiction Weekly* short story by J. Jefferson Farjeon, hinges on a photography-savvy detective investigating a love-triangle murder at a vacation resort. Two men vying for the heart of a young woman grow increasingly belligerent and one suddenly disappears. An amateur photographer making "tree studies" in a nearby forest approaches the detective with a negative. He claims that only after developing the film did he spot what must be a body nearly hidden in undergrowth. After visiting the spot and finding only a handkerchief belonging to one of the vying men, the photographer and detective return to the hotel, where the photographer develops his other plates. The detective meanwhile ascertains that one of the rivals has disappeared, ostensibly to London, and that the handkerchief belongs to the other. He then visits the photographer, and learns that another negative shows the handkerchief owner in the woods, albeit as a minute background figure. Without waiting for the washed negative to dry, the detective carries it back to the woods, finds the spot where the photographer had held his camera to make it, and scrutinizes the shadows. He returns to arrest the photographer.

"The Photograph" revolves around two lies, each supported by a photograph. The first involves the supposedly accidental nature of the image depicting the body: the photographer had made it after murdering the man, composing it to make it appear that the body appears by accident. The second is more contrived. The photograph of the other man walking in the woods dates to the previous day, but the photographer claims he made it shortly after he made the image showing the obscured body. "You were facing north, as in the case of the first picture," the detective tells the photographer at the close of the story. "But whereas the sun was almost behind you, and the shadows pointed practically northward in the first picture, the sun was on your right and the shadows pointed westward in the second picture."[59] The detective understands that the photographer also desires the young woman, and has killed one rival and framed the other for murder.

Farjeon later experimented further with the idea in this story. His screenplay for the 1933 British film *The Ghost Camera* creates a simple accident-within-an-accident embroiling a dull chemist in a murder-robbery investigation. En route home from a boring vacation, the protagonist finds a camera tossed in the rear seat of his open automobile. He develops the film, attempts to interpret the disconcerting images, and then finds his home burgled and both camera and negatives gone. In an amateur, sometimes quirkily humorous way, he becomes a rather efficient detective, having finally realized the import of the shapes captured accidentally on the film of the camera dropped from the window of an upper room, the scene of a murder. Simple, stark, and now forgotten, *The Ghost Camera* emphasizes the haphazardly independent way cameras occasionally work, and the surprises implicit in developed film.

Depression-era fantasy authors embroidered accidental image making in ways that shaped wartime and 1950s science-fiction writing and detective fiction alike. In "The God-Box," a 1934 *Astounding Stories* tale, Howard Wandrei juxtaposes an archaeologist and an engineer probing a found device similar to Sieveking's box camera. What the men designate a camera makes holograms existing in two places simultaneously and enables people remote from each other to communicate through some kind of visual wave. "Pence never fully understood the working of the camera," Wandrei notes near the close of the tale. "Thorn could have given a great deal of information if he were asked for it, but Pence was increasingly independent." As the archaeologist becomes more skilled with the camera, he stops considering how it works and how its technology might produce unanticipated effects. But the engineer keeps thinking and worrying, and in time attempts to block the growing electrical field flowing from ordinary household outlets into the camera. The holograms increase in size, and suddenly one cube expands to fill the room in which the two men stand; the hologram merges with another, and they think themselves in Egypt until they see two suns in the sky.[60] "The God-Box" is prescient, anticipating the postwar impact of the television technology primitive in 1934 but already seductive. But it is also blunt about the possibilities inherent in any camera, even the simplest Brownie.

In the 1950s sophisticated cameras give way to homemade or prototypical cameras sometimes working independently of builders and operators. Basil Copper's 1965 short story "Camera Obscura" perhaps best represents the shift: it delineates a homemade camera that produces an eerie image on a horizontal ground-glass screen. "The picture was of enormous clarity: it was like looking into an old cheval glass which had a faint distorting quality. There was something oblique and elliptical about the sprawl of alleys and roads that spread about the foot of the hill," Copper writes of a square image vignetted with mauve, violet, and "the blood red of the dying sun." Unlike Wandrei's God-box, Copper's camera obscura opens on scenes from the past, but spatially accessible by the hapless viewer, who turns from the image and runs down the wrong staircase from the attic studio. It offers real-time images of people walking along streets in a setting temporally twisted.[61] Copper wrote both fantasy and detective fiction, exploring parallel universes in his *Great White Space* and nonsilvered reflections in a mystery, *The Dark Mirror*. Seeing, especially through camera viewfinders attached to simple or sophisticated cameras that now and then behaved independently of photographers, attracted both fantasy and mystery writers, one seeking glimpses of visions and the other interpreting the discovery of clues. Many of the tales revolve around the shop-theory-based techniques enthusiasts use when struggling to build cameras which act independently of photographers.

While the 1960s witnessed an outpouring of fantasy and science fiction writing about accidental photography, the decade also marked a deepening interest in photographic negatives and prints in which sensitive observers saw forms others did not. In his 1966 "Proof Positive," Alexander Malec detailed a curious three-dimensional photographic image and the camera that made it in a place other than earth.[62]

In her 1965 short story "Girl Bathing," Olivia Davis, already widely published in the *Virginia Quarterly Review*, the *Kenyon Review*, and similar periodicals, explored the problems implicit in a photograph discovered a generation after its making. A teenage girl finds a carefully composed photograph of her mother nude, kneeling in shadow water and contemplating her own reflection. A ne'er-do-well male friend had made the photograph with a camera belonging to the man the girl knows as her father.[63] But the photograph suggests more the longer Nina gazes at it in the brilliant sunlight filling the room above the floor in which her parents and their friends party, and even more when a young man photographs her along a river filled with swans.

Disturbance by camera-willed photography figures in postwar short stories, perhaps most pointedly in "Sun and Shadow," a 1953 tale by the science-fiction writer Ray Bradbury. An American fashion photographer on location in Central America encounters a peasant determined to stop his enterprise. Angered that his house and his family and neighbors have become mere backdrop, not even actors, in the mind of the photographer, the peasant drops his pants. Even after the photographer sends for the police, the man refuses to move on, and the police officer champions his nudity, concluding that the peasant is "naked, yes, but doing nothing with this nakedness in any way to offend the community." The gringo photographer and his scantily clad models are not part of the community, and after they disturb the locals, the man disturbs them: but the displayed skin of the models annoys the locals not at all. It is the camera, clicking like some "great fat beetle" in the hands of the photographer, which makes locals and landscape into backdrop only.[64]

In some of his stories, John Buchan explored issues of light, vision, and imagination. "The Far Islands" traces the maturation of two visions vexing a young Scot since boyhood. On some days when the light hits exactly right, the sea "seemed to him a solid pathway" running west through the location where a far-off island ordinarily broke the horizon. At other times he wonders how he had imagined so perfectly the topography of the coast visible from crest of a headland he had been forbidden to climb until just before he departed for boarding school. In the delirium of a long illness he dreams repeatedly of something beyond the island but not visible from the ridge of the headland, and in time tries to understand his visions as either pathological or evidence of some occult phenomenon. In "The Watcher by the Threshold," the narrator visits close friends living in an unfrequented part of England, summoned by a wife who sees her healthy, secular husband increasingly troubled by a religious mania occasioned by an apparition strongest "in the early dawning, in the twilight, and in the first hours of the morning," a "kind of amorphous shadow." In "The Outgoing of the Tide," the merest glimpse of a sixty-year-old woman "cast a cold grue, not to be remembered without terror" even by rational people. "I am aggressively healthy and wholly Philistine," asserts the narrator of "The House of More." "I love clear outlines and strong colours, and More, with its half-tints and hazy distances, depressed me miserably."[65] Buchan intuited the power of the visual to unsettle and even destroy the equilibrium of modern, educated people accustomed to word-based understanding and communication.[66] In Buchan's fantasy writing, "tone" designates, not sounds, but half-tints that mock clear confrontation and subsequent relation, typically in places away from well-traveled roads.

Money buys the enthusiast photographic technology and, typically, the often-expensive travel to remote, abandoned locations that facilitate happenings curving into faerie. Throughout the twentieth century almost every author addressing the willfulness of cameras brushes against the deliberate acquisition of the camera and its regular, not rare use, then addresses the fundamental connection between camera willfulness and particular place. Some locales facilitate or evoke dark-chamber willfulness, almost as though cameras act as compasses, finding not north but faerie, or perhaps some force at the extreme edge of human optics.

5 Od

Well into the 1910s, Eastman Kodak advertising suggested the enduring mysteries suffusing photography. Here a catalog cover hints at connections with Od and Oda, and with paganism.

SHE STANDS FACING THE OBSERVER IN A ROBE, NOT diaphanous but not opaque, and in a headdress glorifying the tree of life. Hair up, hands down, she holds a No. 3A Autographic Kodak Special, offering what the Eastman Kodak Company called "the highest type of hand-camera efficiency." The No. 3A could boast not only the novel autographic feature, in which the photographer might write with a stylus directly on one edge of every negative before development, but also a German-made Zeiss lens. "With this equipment it is possible to get well-timed pictures under light conditions that would be fatal to good results with the ordinary camera," an advertisement proclaimed in 1915. To the Eastman Kodak Company, the camera is exquisite, and exquisitely special. Its body is made of aluminum, "light, strong, and durable," and "it is richly finished in genuine Persian Morocco" leather. It is more than an astonishingly versatile camera fitted with a superb lens and shutter. It is a gorgeous object, one seemingly exotic, transported from afar. The triptych cover of the 1915 camera catalog not only isolates the first and final letters of the word *Kodak* but makes a word between them that changes headdress into antenna.

Oda designates either a room in a harem, or an occupant of the room. The woman in the photograph might be a harem girl, then, suitably Americanized against a white-painted Federal-era wall paneled high enough to accentuate her shoulders and waist.

But *oda* might also refer to the life forces which Karl Freiherr von Reichenbach discovered in the middle of the nineteenth century and which vexed scientists and laymen into the 1930s. Headdress might be antenna. Von Reichenbach named the forces Od, creating a word he derived from the classical Greek term for road, *odos;* Od, the abbreviated name for the Norse god Odin; and *voda,* an Old Norse expression meaning "I flow forth." Historians of photography routinely note that company tradition credits George Eastman's love of the letter *k* to his playing anagrams with his mother when a boy.[1] They ignore the letters the *k*'s bracket. But Od subtly shaped photographic technology and sometimes seemed to explain the eerie visual effects at which amateurs photographers wondered.

Von Reichenbach began his career in basic research on coal tar and coal-tar derivatives. He developed paraffin in 1830, the antiseptic Eupion a year later, and in 1832 creosota or creotsote, which he understood as both an antiseptic and a preservative, especially of wood. In the next years he discovered the indigo colorant Pittical, a red dye he called Cidreret, and Picomer, a perfume base. His discoveries not only shaped the foundation of the German synthetic dye and chemical industries, out of which grew the German photographic industry, but made him a very wealthy young man able to shift his attention to other research.

While he studied aeroliths well before some astronomers even accepted meteorites as fact, and analyzed exotic types of lightning and other atmospheric electrical energy, he interested himself especially in somnambulism and related psychophysiological conditions. Grouping sleepwalking, night cramp, and what he loosely termed "emotional hysteria" under the larger heading of neurasthenias, Von Reichenbach focused not only on pure research but also on helping those whom many peasants from remote areas still considered possessed or intrinsically evil. Eventually he determined that some individuals are more sensitive than most to something (perhaps forces particularly strong when the moon is full) and that some of the sensitives suffer terribly. The sick sensitives perhaps endured illnesses Franz Anton Mesmer had begun treating with electric current—not shock—from a homemade battery.[2] Mesmer treated mostly upper-class people, some of whom merely wanted the frisson of touching the battery posts, and while better known for his hypnosis work, pioneered in the fields of psychology and neurobiology. Through a colleague and successor, Jean-Martin Charcot, who combined Mesmer's work with electricity and hypnosis, his early research eventually brought Sigmund Freud to Paris. But years before the research attracted Freud, it shaped Von Reichenbach's evolving hypothesis that some sort of external force impaired some people peculiarly sensitive to it.

In an effort to locate the force or forces, Von Reichenbach turned to photography. He photographed the energy flowing through the bodies of sick sensitives exposed to sunlight and moonlight, and to antennae connected to the roof of a laboratory otherwise lightproof. In a dark laboratory, sensitives saw the probes attached to their fingertips emit white light: depending on the metal used in the probes, solar light tended to produce green light from copper and white light from gold. Scientifically, Von Reichenbach tried to demonstrate that the light seen by sensitives existed outside their imagination—and outside the imagination of laboratory workers too. In 1861 he produced his first *odograph,* a photograph of the energy field emitted from the probes on human fingertips. Photography itself interested him very little: he asked the help of professional photographers, and struggled to make certain that nothing contaminated his negatives.[3]

A New York firm published his *Somnambulism and Cramp* in translation in 1860 and some of his books remained in print until at least 1920;

his work interested scholars researching perception and apparent hallucination. In 1895 the psychologist-philosopher William James acquired an 1851 English edition of Von Reichenbach's *Physico-physiological Researches: On the Dynamics of Magnetism, Electricity, Heat, Light, Crystallization, and Chemism in their Relations to Vital Force.* Albert de Rochas d'Aiglun published *Le fluide des magnetseuis* in 1891, which contained a translation of some of Von Reichenbach's work along with a bibliography of articles on Od. As late as 1910 a Leipzig publisher brought out an edition of *Der sensitive Mensch und sein Verhalten zum Ode,* and ten years later published a new edition of *Wer ist sensitiv, wer nicht? Kurze Anleitung, sensitive Menschen mit Leichtigkeit zu finden.* In 1889 the *Century Dictionary* defined *od* as designating a life force produced by research that "rests upon no scientific foundation." The 1934 *Webster's New International Dictionary* defined it as an "alleged" force rather than dismissing it out of hand.[4] By then enough scientists, medical practitioners, and amateur inventors knew just enough about force fields to value Von Reichenbach's thinking. But in the late nineteenth century, Od seemed mysterious, real, and approachable through photography.

As a young man, George Eastman may well have known of Von Reichenbach's research. Upstate New York pulsed with all sorts of religious, spiritual, and psychological energy: there the Latter Day Saints had discovered the principles of a new denomination of Christianity; there spiritualism had evolved through Mesmerism; and there theosophy expanded, intersecting a variety of small-scale scientific and technological industries, among them the manufacture of photographic equipment and supplies.[5] While many scientists derided Von Reichenbach's research into *od* or *oda,* especially after his death, others were more ambivalent, particularly following the discovery by Wilhelm Conrad Roentgen in 1895 of the mysterious force he called *X-rays.* To illustrate his first journal article on the unknown force, he photographed his wife's hands, and these images are now known as the first X-ray photographs. He speculated that a photograph might be the dispassionate witness Von Reichenbach sought. Roentgen had been studying the properties of light when he blundered into X-rays by watching a barium-coated screen light up across his laboratory. He might have discovered the rays had he placed unexposed photograph plates next to his equipment. After the discovery of radium by Pierre and Marie Curie in 1897, Americans began experimenting with a force similar to light, but in some ways far less obvious even though it affected photographic film.[6] George Eastman hit upon Palmer Cox's Brownies as a splendid way of advertising inexpensive cameras to children and adults, but he may also have glimpsed in his cameras the potential to facilitate scientific discovery and breakthrough. *Oda* floats bracketed in the name of the firm he established at a time when the world wondered at electricity, light, and energy the eye might see only in specific places under certain conditions.

In 1880, when Eastman patented his dry-plate chemistry, leased the third floor of a building, and began his manufacturing enterprise, no scientist used the term *force field,* but at least a few recognized the long-term difficulties posed by the Von Reichenbach research. The physician, neurologist, and author of psychology-based novels S. Weir Mitchell argued that weather affected the daily health of everyone, and perhaps adversely affected wounded Civil War veterans more than anyone admitted. He averred especially that it affected women sensitive to humidity and barometric pressure, and perhaps to the electrical field that flowed in advance of oncoming thunderstorms. Working long hours as a Civil War hospital surgeon, Mitchell had begun a lifelong study of the impact of physical wounds upon the nervous system. He and other medical researchers worried that something external to the body might produce emotions, pain, and other effects still beyond the reach of medicine and definitely not imaginary.[7]

Dedicated amateur radio hobbyists have long probed not only defense-related signals but other forces readable by simple receivers and antennae built with parts purchased from hardware, radio, and photography stores.[8] Anyone who buys two five-foot copper grounding rods, several hundred feet of twelve-gauge wire, and a hundred-dollar electrical meter at an electrical-supply house can perform a simple but unnerving experiment in large-lot suburbs or rural areas. The experimenter drives one grounding rod into the ground, preferably near the roots of a mature tree, firmly attaches one end of the wire to it, and then stretches out the wire, drives in the second rod, and connects the meter between the end of the wire and the second rod. Almost invariably the meter will record some current, and as the second rod is driven in at different spots, the current will vary in intensity. Radio enthusiasts still build underground antennae named after James Harris Rogers, an amateur who published his findings in a 1919 *Electrical Experimenter* article, and experiment with sending and receiving signals through the earth. They quickly learn that they can receive signals from around the world, but that transmission varies with lunar phases over the sending regions.[9] Some enthusiasts re-create experiments that Nikolai Tesla, the great electrical genius of the late nineteenth century, cautioned would produce more questions than answers.[10]

Amateur radio research gradually moved away from urban areas simply because too much manufactured current strayed into the ground. Trolley car company electricity flowed along gas and water mains rather than returning along rails to power station dynamos. Resulting electrolysis eroded pipes and produced numerous lawsuits. As street-railway firms refined their current flow, many began to worry about stray current harming family health, especially that of children.[11] Minuscule ground faults saturated early twentieth-century cities with subterranean electrical fields, and vexed amateur radio operators, who learned that they could not use the Rogers underground wireless antennae. By the summer of 1919, when thousands of enthusiasts had written magazines begging for data about such antennae, Rogers explained a simplified version of his system.

Following his directions, a rural amateur might build an underground antenna from ordinary household copper wire. Rogers specified that the antenna be in the form of an X, each leg extending a hundred to five hundred feet from the intersection; the antenna worked best if buried about three feet deep in damp soil. He had other designs, not all of which needed such depth; to speed construction of buried antennae, he told readers to hire a farmer with a good plow. Enthusiasts fortunate enough to own ponds or brooks might lay wire along their beds. Rogers also suggested lowering loop antennae into dug wells.[12] As amateurs followed his advice, they learned the truth of his assertions: not only could they send and receive signals at least as well as they could in the air, their buried antennae eliminated static and interference from surface-situated radios, motors, and other electrically powered devices. Tesla and his contemporaries spoke accurately: whatever fields carried the radio signals were not themselves radio fields.[13]

Moreover, no one knew how to depict these fields, in line drawings and otherwise, in ways that might further the understanding of them. Mapping unknown territory always challenges cartographers, but mapping territory that moves around or shifts in and out of multiple existences or planes according to lunar phases or sunspots or forces unknown defeats traditional mapmaking. If the unknown territory shelters threats, however, mapping becomes a necessary adjunct to defense, especially if the threats intensify as seemingly innocuous forces strengthen. In the first years of the twentieth century, experts, enthusiasts, and the general public found themselves surrounded by mysterious force fields suddenly measurable and even useful, if not at all understood. The wary worried that some forces might be harmful.

Ground-wave signaling morphed into its circa-1910 popularity with crystal-set radios hobbyists understood as a distinctly separate component of the larger broadcast radio fascination. With galena crystals and cat whiskers, amateurs received airborne radio signals using no electrical source at all to power their seemingly magical receivers: the *right* crystals mined from the earth focused airborne electricity, along with whiskers yanked from cats.

Crystal listening became the experienced counterpart of the imagined crystal-gazing folklorists and storytellers had long described in ways Andrew Lang summarized in his 1897 *Book of Dreams and Ghosts*.[14] Building crystal radios entranced readers of *Modern Electrics* and similar magazines. Most experimenters, especially those who wrote letters to magazines demonstrating their accomplishments and asking readers to duplicate their findings, realized that they needed loop antennae and perfectly grounded connections, usually to copper water pipes.[15] Their efforts originated in genuine curiosity about radio signals, crystals, and electric fields, but soon the general public anxious to listen to radio broadcasts copied their designs. Depression-stricken Americans built crystal radios from galena crystal and safety pins, erected ungrounded, outdoor linear antennae subject to lightning strikes, and sometimes grounded their contraptions only to bedsprings; others used wire fences as antennae.[16] The crystal set fad produced juvenile fiction, especially the Radio Boys series, but expense and class played only slight roles.[17] Even the poor could afford crystal radios, including the rural poor who lived far beyond dynamo-produced electricity, and while wealthier people quickly shifted from crystal-powered to battery-powered radios, few forgot the eerie impact of unpowered, simple, homemade devices demonstrating the ubiquity of radio signals, manmade and otherwise.[18] Shop theory guided most amateur experimenters, and newspaper make-it-yourself articles directed the efforts of most general-public builders of crystal sets.

Manipulating electricity and similar force fields, especially the magnetic ones so essential in building telegraph sounders, radio speakers, and other devices, worried many, perhaps especially the mothers of boys so fascinated with experimentation that they avoided other activities. In the eyes of many adults, the boys risked not only electric shock but the psychological dangers self-styled experts supposed implicit in aloneness. L. Frank Baum plunged into such issues in his 1901 novel *The Master Key: An Electrical Fairy Tale Founded upon the Mysteries of Electricity and the Optimism of Its Devotees*. Beneath its long title Baum inserted a seductive warning sentence: *It Was Written for Boys, But Others May Read It*. The story begins with a teenage boy experimenting with battery-produced electricity in a small attic room. The wires he strings throughout the house, especially those operating bells and telephones, upset his mother and sister, who "soon came to vote the boy's scientific craze a nuisance," but please his father, who provides ample funds for additional equipment and checks the opposition of the women in the house, including the servants. "So he experimented in a rather haphazard fashion, connecting this and that wire blindly and by guesswork, in the hope that he would strike the right combination," Baum writes of the privileged loner whose experiments culminate in a blinding electrical flash in which a "Being" becomes visible.[19]

Written a year after *The Wizard of Oz*, the novel signals Baum's departure from the fairy-tale formula developed by Gruelle and other midwestern writers, and his determination to confront Cox's Brownies directly. In the 1908 edition of the annual *American Fairy Tales*, Baum embroiders the creature he introduced in the first edition seven years earlier. The Ryl dislikes being mistaken for a fairy. "Do you see any wings growing out of my body? Do you see any golden hair flowing over my shoulders, or any gauzy cobweb skirts floating about my form in graceful folds?" But the Ryl loathes being mistaken for a Brownie. "Do I look like one of those impossible, crawly, mischievous elves? Is my body ten times bigger than it should be? Do my legs look like toothpicks and my eyes like saucers?" The Ryl tells his listeners that only "old nurses" talk about fairies and hobgoblins, and that "fairy tales and goose books and brownie books" are mere "rubbish."[20] Part of what the Ryl denounces Baum had left behind already when he abandoned fairy tales and the tales he published in 1899 in *Father Goose: His Book*, and much of the rest is what fueled Cox's popularity among children and adults alike. Baum had begun to move on, into an energy-charged future most fairy-tale authors scrupulously avoided. He knew the driving force of electricity, both ordinary Edison electricity generated at power plants and in batteries, and the mysterious electromagnetic fields that anyone might discover accidentally in the immediate future, probably in some spot far distant from cities and suburbs. He saw it as something that might well re-energize antique understandings of the world, personality, time, space, and light. Baum understood that electricity in any form might offer a way into other continua, and he insisted on its fundamentally male identity. Girls enjoyed hearing of fairies, but boys understood the power implicit in meeting Ryls and demons, and in controlling them: perhaps they especially enjoyed the idea of seeing via magic glasses that made individual force fields visible.[21]

In the 1900s physicists shifted from studying light to studying rays, forces, and time, and within a decade scientists and engineers discovered that electromagnetic fields other than X-rays might wreak havoc on humans and other living things. In 1929 one engineering firm, puzzled by the illness of employees at high-power broadcast radio stations, deliberately microwaved some of its staff to study fever induced by proximity to powerful shortwave radio transmitters. The results, published in *Science* in 1930, seemed to support anecdotal but confirmed cases of electrically charged force-field behavior noticed in the first years of the twentieth century.[22] Very definitely, man-made forces moved through the air, often in ways that adversely affected some people perhaps especially sensitive to them. Once legislation and lawsuit forced trolley car companies, public transit authorities, and electric utilities to carefully ground and bond their urban electric lines, media and public gaze shifted away from ground-carried fields and then from airborne ones too.[23] Radio proved so seductive almost everyone wanted to believe radio waves safe, far safer than rays so unknown their discoverer called them "X-rays."

By the 1920s underground force-field research had become the province of a few dedicated experts, chiefly electrical engineers working on military-related matters and some physicists, and a determined group of amateurs, usually linked by licensed shortwave radio and often working far from cities. Both groups produced data nowadays difficult to find. One group created material that was secret or at least proprietary at the time, and perhaps still is if it has not been destroyed or lost. The other communicated by amateur radio signal, perhaps the most ephemeral of high-tech messaging: its members apparently kept no records. Both groups worked in the borderlands of science and pseudoscience, as alchemists once had, especially those intrigued by vision, reflections, and images.[24] Both groups tended to adopt alchemical terminology, and kept open minds about many centuries-old arguments.

Alchemists valued several stones, not merely the philosopher's stone that turned base metals into gold, but the "magicall or prospective stone" Elias Ashmole described in his 1652 *Theatrum Chemicum Britannicum*. The prospective stone enabled an astute gazing viewer to "discover any person in what part of the world so ever, although never so secretly concealed." But in another way, the stone enabled the adept to "convey a spirit into an image."[25] Almost no one has grappled with the long-term impact of the Zoroastrian, Cathar, Kabbalistic, and Arab understanding of divine entity and human vision on European alchemy, let alone the ways alchemists challenged and reinterpreted both classical and Christian understanding of vision, the Deity (especially the alchemical trinity of sulfur, mercury, and salt in the alchemical cosmogony of Paracelsus), and the individual human spirit.[26] Alchemy is far more than the threshold to modern chemistry: it is a portal opening on light, vision, catoptrics and pyromancy, astronomy, the human self as envisioned spirit, and the Almighty.[27] Much of it, especially the astrological and catoptrical theorizing of John Dee, who argued for the creative action of light itself, concerns images, especially image making that destroys the human spirit or reduces it to spectacle.[28]

Many alchemists worked in the tradition of Robert Fludd, the early seventeenth-century English scientist and mystic so influenced by Dee and nowadays best known for his *Macrocosm,* a two-volume work published in stages between 1617 and 1621. The mathematician and astronomer Johannes Kepler battled with Fludd immediately upon reading the first fascicle, attacking him for ideas he found "occult and shadowy," dreamlike, and symbolic, not scientific, and for arguing in and with pictures. Kepler holds a secure place in the history of science. Fludd is now almost unknown.

A few scholars nonetheless now insist that Kepler understood philosophical concepts visually and perhaps envied Fludd. "His admirable method of thinking consisted in forming in his mind a diagrammatic or outline representation of the entangled state of things," noted the philosopher Charles Sanders Peirce of Kepler at the close of the nineteenth century, "omitting all that was accidental, observing suggestive relations between the parts of his diagram, performing divers experiments upon it, or upon the natural objects, and noting the results."[29] That Kepler—and Fludd—understood concepts visually rather than in more traditional, mathematical ways piqued the interest of a handful of twentieth-century scholars intent on identifying people, scientists especially, who "think visually" but are not necessarily artists and often invent concepts and create images that predate scientific discovery.[30]

Fludd derived some of his visual philosophy from Dee, and some also from Dürer, whose work he cited approvingly, and some probably from Michael Maier, an alchemist who devoted his life to integrating music, visual analysis, and geometry, but Fludd applied it to issues that confounded scientists and theologians.[31] He probed deeply at the relationship, symbolic and otherwise, between the visible and the invisible, and while his work perhaps influenced Descartes and Hobbes, both of whom worried about the dissonance between visible and invisible things, it also appears to have made an impression on the twentieth-century psychologist Carl Jung.[32] In a 1932 essay on Picasso, Jung stated simply that "for almost twenty years, I have occupied myself with the psychology of the pictorial representation of psychic processes."[33] Jung owned a copy of Maier's 1617 *Atalanta Fugiens,* the work that pushed around the edges of Fludd's enterprise even as it mocked the best efforts of mathematicians.[34]

Fludd—and Maier—asserted that scientists who fail to visualize in complex ways must necessarily know only narrowness. Jung agreed.

Well after the birth of photography, which many contemporaneous pundits analyzed as a sort of alchemy, visualization and mysticism figured in serious works.[35] In 1846 Thomas South's *Early Magnetism in its Higher Relation to Humanity: As Viewed in the Poets and Prophets* appeared, and four years later his daughter, Mary Anne Atwood, published *A Suggestive Inquiry into the Hermetic Mystery with a Dissertation on the More Celebrated of the Alchemical Philosophers: Being an Attempt towards the Recovery of the Ancient Experiment of Nature.* Atwood's massive work shaped discussion for seventy years: publishers reissued it as late as 1920, and contemporary historians of alchemy and science value it today as an early and incisive probing of how some science proceeds.[36] It links alchemy, magnetism, visualization, and, obliquely, photography with the Jungian argument that alchemical practice involved the projection of the unconscious upon the matter held in the alchemical vessels.[37] Moreover, it illuminates the cognitive issues that focus much of the thinking Jung elucidates in *Psychology and Alchemy, Paracelsus as a Spiritual Phenomenon,* and *The Spirit Mercurius.*[38] "Projections repeat themselves whenever man tries to explore an empty darkness and involuntarily fills it with living form," Jung asserts in a section of *Psychology and Alchemy* devoted to "the psychic nature of the alchemical work."[39]

In *The Principles of Psychology,* published in 1890, William James explained that "consciousness does not appear to itself chopped up in bits; it flows. Let us call it the stream of thought, of consciousness, or of subjective life."[40] Here James glimpsed something ancient, certainly already marginalized as obsolete when Fludd argued its importance, and yet nonetheless profoundly modern. "The attempt at introspective analysis" resembles "trying to turn up the light quickly enough to see how the darkness looks," he concluded in a way that suggests he took Von Reichenbach's *Physico-physiological Researches* seriously.[41]

Sensitive film might record what sensitive people see consciously or unconsciously, and might jolt scientific progress forward. So reasoned a handful of photography experts, especially Walther Heering, the author of a number of sophisticated books on medium-format photography, especially that accomplished with Rolleiflex cameras. Well into the 1930s, Von Reichenbach's larger motifs shaped Heering's conceptual framework. In his 1934 *Rolleiflex Book,* Heering argued simply that some people are far more aware of light and shadow, especially in their seasonal variation, than most, just as some can hold a Rolleiflex steady for 1/5 of a second exposures while others can barely manage 1/50 of a second ones. But as film became more sensitive, especially by infusing the manufacturing process with "ultra-short waves" sensitivity, anyone might record and see on a print what only sensitives see around them. Near the end of his book, in a chapter on infrared photography, Heering included a chart relating the visible-light spectrum, infrared photography, Hertzian waves, radio waves, and alternating-current waves. He knew that Kodak had just discovered how to impregnate film with Xenocyanin, making it sensitive to infrared waves up to 1300 Å (the film had to be packed in ice during exposure), and he assumed that further research might enable cameras to record Hertzian waves. Radio waves, roughly a kilometer in length, might always remain beyond the reach of photography, but shorter wave–length electromagnetism might not. "What is the use of it?" Heering asked of Kodak proprietary technology meshing photography with radio and other electromagnetic research. "The control of occult experiments in the dark, particularly secret photography," he concluded. "Of course for most amateurs this field will be of purely theoretical interest, but in any case it is at least interesting and one never knows what may come of it." Whatever came of it, however, would be certain to further discommode many people, even many photographers, who could not perceive that in June and July, at high latitudes, the summer light is about four times as bright as it is in December and January. Heering knew that some people were incredibly sensitive to light in its varying intensity, and that they might well understand uses for the newly invented Kodak film.[42]

The role played by Von Reichenbach in shaping Jamesian, Freudian, and Jungian thought is not known, just as scholars still cannot trace which medieval books the German researcher studied as he moved toward Od. Earlier than most, Von Reichenbach discerned some sort of force field or fields that some people might detect, and by 1861 he understood the need for visualizing such fields in photographs.[43] Throughout the nineteenth century, lexicographers defined Od in reasonably respectful terms, as did Elizabeth Barrett Browning in *Aurora Leigh* in 1864:

> Yet I doubted half
> If that od-force of German Reichenbach
> Which still from female finger-tips burns blue
> Could strike out, as our masculine white hearts
> To quicken a man.[44]

As physiology and psychology moved away from anything Von Reichenbach posited, however, fragments of research kept his concepts from oblivion. From the back of 1920s radio sets flowed an eerie blue light emitted from the tubes that glowed with varying intensity inside cabinets. Beyond the crystal set, radio reception involved apparatus producing blue light.

Mitchell argued that at least some people somehow sensed forces, if only incipient change in weather. Electrical engineers and amateur experimenters, then radio enthusiasts especially, argued that electromagnetic forces encircled the earth and fluctuated constantly in time and space. The midsummer solar magnetic storms of 1894 interrupted telegraph service west of Chicago while affecting submarine cables only slightly; but engineers discovered earth-current seepage of up to 150 volts into some buried lines. Far more importantly, electrical engineers equipped with very sensitive measuring devices found that earth currents fluctuated in magnetic storms in ways indicating a flow along straight lines otherwise unidentified.[45] Gradually psychologists and physicists began to see the synergy of energy flow (especially earth current) and hypersensitivity: some sensitive people might suffer because they accidentally lived along energy-field alignments. Engineers glimpsed the nuances of visual perception altered by force-field sensitivity, and especially such perception as represented in visual imagery made by artists and others unaware of the impact of forces to which they proved sensitive.

"Everything, then, emits light," Von Reichenbach asserted. "Everything. We live in a world filled with shining matter." He understood in 1860 the need to photograph the light emitted from the cables attached to the fingertips of sensitives, and his basic philosophy only heightened the awareness of Browning and other artists that a sharpened gaze might descry light other than ordinary.[46]

Von Reichenbach's work guided many subsequent photographic experimenters, especially in Britain, and some began making full-color images. In 1883 the *British Journal of Photography* published a series of letters and articles on magnetism, the polarization of light, and color photography, the most energetic of which came from W. Harding Warner, a follower of Von Reichenbach. Warner found that some people seemed far more sensitive to nuances of color depicted in prototype color photographs than others, and that much of the difficulty in photographing color involved levels of seeing, not only through the camera but in the darkroom and subsequently. Arthur Conan Doyle, himself an avid photographer, blasted Warner's thinking, calling his entire analysis of Od "gloriously and symmetrically absurd." But Ward insisted that his photographs of silver-leaf geraniums revealed color to some twenty observers, but not to all, and "that we do not all see alike."[47] Five years later, F. E. Ives published a lengthy analysis in the *Journal of the Franklin*

Institute of the material and shape of what Westerners called "the Japanese Magic Mirror," concluding that shape and a copper-based coating produced the reflected illusions that intrigued Westerners.[48] Years later, when Doyle grew fascinated with the photography of illusion, faerie, and fairies, he regretted his earlier attack on Warner while continuing to dismiss the thinking of Ives and other optical-novelty researchers.[49]

Photographers, ground-radio experimenters, crystal-radio enthusiasts, and electrical engineers and physicists had begun to probe the mysteries of force, force fields, energy, and light. Not surprisingly, their ongoing effort attracted the attention of a wide range of pseudoscience-loving fanatics. They struggled to understand how visually acute people perceived the world usually designated *faerie,* and how such people interpreted what they saw to those unable to see it. Some sensitives might see around the curve of time, it seemed, into other continua.

Andrew Lang pushed far into such otherworldly issues in his 1897 work *The Book of Dreams and Ghosts.* His children's fairy-tale books, beginning in 1889 with *The Blue Fairy Book,* used colors in their titles to indicate the range of stories he collected from around the world. In offering British children a graduated rainbow of traditional tales from their own islands and from everywhere else, Lang focused their attention on a sort of intellectual imperialism Barrie refined in his 1904 masterpiece, *Peter Pan.* But unlike Baum, Lang emphasized pretechnological tales, although he did more than collect and arrange them. He wondered at the schematics implicit in world-world patterns, what Jung soon after identified as archetypes. In particular, Lang wondered at the way some especially sensitive people might visualize energy.

In *The Book of Dreams and Ghosts,* Lang asserted that ghosts never actually appear but instead are visualized, usually by people especially sensitive to energy fields, but not always. His preface echoes William James's definition of hallucination as a perception "as good and true a sensation as if there were a real object there. The object happens *not* to be there, that is all."[50] Lang excluded delusions caused by drugs, brain disease, alcohol, and modern urban exhaustion and anxiety, and emphasized that, like James, he knew some people who had some kind of hallucinatory experience only once in a lifetime. While most of his contemporaries assumed that hallucination derived from illness, Lang pushed forward in testing his notions of apparitions. He knew well, perhaps better than most of his contemporaries, the old traditions of ghosts, bizarre creatures, haunted houses, and so on, but he chose to ignore most of them. Instead he interested himself in the way some people see forces, or the physical manifestations of forces, in specific locations.

Visualizing anything challenged Lang personally, just as it did psychologists of his era. He followed test results Francis Galton had published fourteen years earlier in *Inquiries into the Human Faculty and Its Development*. Galton asked fellow scientists to think of their breakfast tables, to create a "mental picture" of them, and then explain as precisely as possible their understanding of the clarity of the picture, emphasizing "illumination," "definition," and "colouring." At once Galton discovered that his scientist friends claimed that "mental imagery was unknown to them," and that most thought he wasted his time in analyzing expressions like "mental image" and "mind's eye." Galton shifted his research to other groups and eventually concluded that the scientists "had a mental deficiency of which they were unaware, and naturally enough supposed that those who affirmed they possessed it, were romancing."[51] Sustained effort at developing the faculty of "retaining a retinal picture" caused some experts to prosper in their professions. "A scene is flashed upon the eye: the memory of it persists, and details, which escaped observation during the brief time when it was actually seen, may be analyzed and studied at leisure in the subsequent vision."[52] Others had learned to visualize numbers, relations of numbers (especially orders of magnitude), and relations of colors. Galton was especially impressed by one respondent who simply visualized parts of his slide rule when doing calculations.[53] He explained how readers might examine their visualization faculties by sitting "in perfect darkness" and studying what visions eventually float across the eye.[54] And he explained at least some of the causes of apparitions, especially those perceived by great men and other visionaries.

Asserting that "the visionary tendency is much more common among sane people than is generally suspected," and that "in early life, it seems to be a hard lesson to an imaginative child to distinguish between the real and the visionary world," Galton decried the willingness of adults to denigrate the fantasies of children: "The seers of vision keep quiet; they do not like to be thought fanciful or mad, and they hide their experiences, which only come to light through inquiries such as these that I have been making."[55] Galton devoted little attention to arguing about the so-called reality of visions, hallucinations, and fantasies: the breadth of human perceptual and imaginative faculties intrigued him far more, as did the power that accrued to visionaries, especially in his own era. "The best workmen are those who visualize the whole of what they propose to do, before they take a tool in their hands. The village smith and the carpenter who are employed on odd jobs employ it less for their work than the mechanician, the engineer, and the architect," he insisted of a sort of high-level practice of shop theory. "The lady's maid who arranges a new dress requires it [the visualization faculty] for the same reason as the decorator employed on a palace, or the agent who lays out great estates." For all such people, the use of the visualization faculty is an "immense" pleasure, and a high proportion of them carry "whole picture galleries in their mind" of past accomplishments and observations.

Galton considered sensitives powerful in their own right, but even more so if they visualized the forces that affected them. He determined that fundamental changes in the physical and cultural environment had begun to awaken a visualization faculty "starved by lazy disuse, instead of being cultivated judiciously," but that educators seemed strangely unwilling to accept that awakening. "I believe that a serious study of the best method of developing and utilizing this faculty, without prejudice to the practice of abstract thought in symbols, is one of the many pressing desiderata in the yet unformed science of education."[56] The new age defined itself largely through scientific breakthrough and technological innovation, both often the product of people caught between traditional thought, especially mathematics, and the fast-growing power of visual imagining, exactly as the physicist Niels Bohr asserted. The images Fludd and Maier so valued and that presaged the fascination Jung had with the mandalas produced by scientists undergoing psychological analysis struck many as capable of producing knowledge, rather than simply transmitting it.[57]

The Society for Psychical Research was founded in 1882 and many physicists became members. Heinrich Hertz, one of the discoverers of radio waves, became a corresponding member from Germany, joining William Crookes, the inventor of the cathode-ray tube Roentgen used to produce X-rays, and J. J. Thomson, the discoverer of the electron in 1897. The society focused on developing understanding of telepathy, clairvoyance, and other often-derided, quasi-scientific phenomena suddenly made more believable compared to ray- or energy-based forces. Energy-field discoveries drove the blossoming of child-focused fantasy writing in late nineteenth-century Britain: Barrie's *Peter Pan*, E. Nesbit's *Five Children and It*, Kenneth Grahame's *Wind in the Willows*, and a host of similar works appeared concurrently with Andrew Lang's twelve color-titled *Fairy Books* as physics was revealing some forces so mysterious that they made fantasy seem as possible as energy-field reality.[58] The forces also drove the fiction of writers aiming far darker fantasy visions at adults.[59] In "The Great God Pan," "The Terror," and other short stories, Arthur Machen explicitly probed the likelihood of more discoveries illuminating the reality of what most educated people dismissed as rural superstition.[60] Machen saw into Welsh landscapes in ways that approximated X-ray vision and that dovetailed with the mystical observation AE (George William Russell) detailed in *The Candle of Vision*. "Formerly the camera merely saw surfaces, now it actually sees through things," mused Wallace Nutting in his 1927 *Photographic Art Secrets*.[61]

"For the best of possible reasons I then believed in ghosts and goblins, because I saw them, both by day and by night," noted Lafcadio Hearn in an unpublished autobiographical fragment Jean Temple quoted in her 1931 *Blue Ghost*.[62] In this, Hearn was not so different from George Sand, who, as Andrew Lang reported in 1897, routinely saw "wonderful moving landscapes in the polished back of a screen" next to her fireplace.[63] Visualizers argued that as-yet unexplicated electromagnetic forces might explain traditional belief in faerie and its inhabitants, prospects glimpsed by alchemists, and a range of apparitions loosely categorized as psychic.[64] "We see objects within the limits which make up our colour spectrum, with infinite vibrations, unseen by us," wrote Arthur Conan Doyle in 1922. His *Coming of the Fairies* deserves better than the opprobrium that descended on it almost immediately. However credulous Doyle may have appeared, and however much he wanted to believe in fairies, his speculation that they might be "separated from ourselves by some difference of vibration" was not entirely unreasonable. In an age struggling not only with unsettling scientific discoveries and the aftermath of world war but with cinema and other new media, differences of vibration might explain the witchery of light that passed in waves through empty space.[65]

Like Von Reichenbach, Doyle thought photography might support his hypothesis, which he explained in terms of utility company transformers converting high-tension electricity into current useful in dwellings. "It is hard to see why something analogous might not occur with the vibration of ether and the waves of light," he insisted at the beginning of his book. Doyle took the negatives of fairies made by the girl photographers to the London office of the Eastman Kodak Company, where two experts examined them. "Neither of them could find any evidence of superposition, or other trick," he reported. "On the other hand, they were of the opinion that if they set to work with all their resources they could produce such pictures by natural means, and therefore they would not undertake to say that these were preternatural." Other photographic experts reached the same conclusion, several by explaining processes involving double-printing or the making of double negatives.[66] Two rural girls possessing superb visual imaginations and a working knowledge of millinery shop theory, especially the use of hat pins, were thus able to trick Doyle and his associates.[67]

But they did not quite trick the Eastman Kodak Company, which refused to provide a certificate of authenticity. By 1922 that firm had become one arbiter of which visual manifestations of unknown forces deserved sustained study and which must be dismissed as self-begotten fantasy. Doyle reported that in Waterville, New Hampshire, an eleven-year-old girl photographing mushrooms "with a 2a Brownie camera, portrait lens attached" had photographed some kind of fairy or elf by accident. Eastman Kodak cameras could not lie, especially in the hands of young children, and perhaps especially in the hands of girls "sweet and incapable of deceit" who in rural, out-of-the-way places accidentally photographed through or into the ether or force fields or variant light currents. Trust in cameras grounded Doyle's argument, and he delighted when a friend loaned the English girls a better camera, a Cameo.[68] Doyle acknowledged contrary ideas, quoting one international authority on radium as stating that "anyone who has studied the extraordinary effects which have from time to time been obtained by cinema operators must be aware that it is possible, given time and opportunity, to produce by means of faked photographs almost anything that can be imagined," but he insisted that ordinary box cameras now and then photographed realms beyond ordinary reality.[69]

Meanwhile, the photographer Paul Strand was asserting that photography existed in the afterglow of alchemy and other occult arts. "In all ages, therefore, we find the empirical thinker, the alchemist and astrologer, mathematician and philosophic experimenter, at work, frequently, as in the early Christian world, at considerable risk of his life, liberty and pursuit of happiness. Now in all of this it should be well understood, that the machine is a passive and an innocent party." But while the camera might now and then do something haphazard, it might also reveal the special powers of its user. "Granting the limitations which all media have in common, it is only when the limitations of *photographers* are under examination, that the discussion becomes realistic."[70] The combination of machine and photographer might now and then produce supernatural images, especially if the photographer proves supernaturally sensitive to anything beyond reality, Od and fairies alike.

But perhaps extrasensitive film would prove even more effective. In 1923 László Moholy-Nagy forecast "various chemical mixtures" in emulsions "which produce light effects imperceptible to the eye (such as electro-magnetic rays, x-rays)." *Broom* magazine readers learned that Moholy-Nagy had made only a few primitive attempts at creating new emulsions, but that soon laboratory science would produce "impressive" results.[71] New candles of vision would soon illuminate new worlds.[72]

Interest in such worlds waxed and waned until midway during World

War II. In several best-selling books, especially *The Road I Know,* which appeared in 1942, Stewart Edward White detailed the spiritualist exploits of his wife, Betty, after about 1919. From some other realm, beings she called "Invisibles" told her to "put your energy and your daring into throwing out to your farthest limits in search of comprehension of the hitherto unknown," to pass beyond intellect. "You must *gain it in imagination first,*" she reported them telling her, "and then work back through slow steps to connect it with observed facts." As a "sensitive" owning "an exquisitely sensitized vision," Betty received "direct impression" from minds in another realm and comprehended whole edifices from thin air and light.[73] She routinely described her psychic voyaging in terms of riding on particular radio waves or of encountering (and later creating) radiance, but her evocation of momentary super realities appears intimately related to the results ordinary photographers now and then discovered in developed film.[74]

The most conservative and respected physicists, perhaps especially those studying radioactivity, found themselves besieged by logical if enthusiastic spiritualists. Isaac K. Funk, the cofounder of the Funk and Wagnalls publishing firm, quoted William Crookes, the renowned British physicist, to the effect that waves of different frequency undoubtedly explained all sorts of activity and visions hitherto dismissed or classed as paranormal.[75] How some people, sensitives and others, visualized such forces in certain places focused the attention of far fewer individuals, but definitely focused that of George Eastman, whose cameras figured in all manner of experiments and trickery.

From the very beginning, Eastman's intent was to produce a camera enabling anyone to make an acceptable snapshot in average natural light. Eastman understood that many people are not sensitive to light; instead they have intractable difficulty in seeing light, even when they apply themselves to the task, as when they begin to make a photograph. Visualizing many elements of the composition they intend to make permanent vexes them; even after sustained and conscious effort, their photographs reveal people with utility poles seemingly sprouting from their heads and other crudities unnoticed at the time of exposure. Nuances of light and shadow defeated amateur photographers in the late nineteenth century and do so even now, well more than a century after Eastman marketed Brownies designed and engineered to accomplish what insensitive photographers would fail to see.

Kodak dry plates and, subsequently, film arrived sensitized from factories. Sensitized film quickened the efforts of sensitive observers and photographers who no longer had to coat glass negatives with homemade solutions. But light itself shaped all Eastman Kodak enterprise. Always the Kodak cameras, even the Brownie models so often used by children and teenagers, opened on the most intractable and arcane concepts imaginable.

Cameras might be willful, especially in the hands of sensitive photographers who somehow arrived at quiet, secluded, often abandoned rural places. Cameras and photographers might record what earlier generations called ghosts. But the same cameras and photographers might record energy fields as mysterious as X-rays, often in prosaic locations. Any film, perhaps especially the multitude of esoteric films Kodak developed for scientific and industrial purposes, might record force fields especially well or at least more often than black-and-white films purchased in drugstores. But the prints from any negative might facilitate envisioning and creativity.

Od or some other force might be the energy of glamour, the visual magic radiating from some individuals and, sometimes, from some landscapes. In an age when most people fixed their attention on cinema, a handful of photographers fixed their attention on what their brownie-like cameras occasionally recorded. The photographers sought a frisson beyond anything Kodak advertised, but within the vast confines of what George Eastman called "oda."

6 Ways

·MOTORING WITH A KODAK·

*Roll-film cameras transformed automobiling by about 1910.
Men drove, but often women used the delicate instruments
that made memory-shaping images of the roadside.*

IN 1910 HILAIRE BELLOC REMARKED "AN ISOLATION which our forefathers never knew" in regions of Great Britain distant from railroads and laced by the overgrown roads and footpaths from which stagecoaches, long-distance wagons, and even oxcarts had long disappeared. Belloc found the great high road along the Pennines and its connectors "utterly deserted" and warned potential hikers that "you will be as completely cut off from men the whole day long as you could be in the West of Canada." Often the desuetude began a mile or so at right angles from a tertiary road: bits of macadamized pavement lay overgrown in bogs and hillsides, undergrowth consumed collapsed bridges, once-prosperous inns stood ruined, and whole swaths of half-worked or abandoned agricultural land announced wrenching post-railroad change. The "novel isolation" enjoyed by the observant walker "is not wholly pleasurable (especially on winter evenings, after a day bereft of human intercourse)" when he begins tracing the economic forces underlying the abandonment and emptiness. Walking far in such abandonment meant embracing dirty inns, sleeping outdoors, and other physical discomfort, and perforce wondering at its causes. Belloc urged people to experiment, knowing well that for every one who tramped into abandonment "there are a thousand who would rather delude themselves into a *simulacrum* of the emotions of travel by reading of them in some book," often written by an author who had not walked far from railroad stations himself or who chose locales half a world away rather than explore regions near home.[1]

Into such regions tramped men and women intrigued with ruin, natural history, oblivion, and antiquities. Many carried cameras, finding the mix of built landscape and encroaching vegetation photogenic but not traditionally scenic or picturesque: the unpopulated places encouraged deliberate, contemplative, time-consuming photography. In regions overtaken by wilderness cameras seemed especially willful.[2]

By the 1930s British and American photographers had appropriated old-road landscape as their own realm, following the grass-grown routes into the quietude that facilitated unhurried photography by refining an aesthetic peculiar to abandonment. They haphazardly discovered the peculiar power of abandoned places. Tolkien had embraced and elaborated upon the power on which so many 1970s fantasy writers eventually centered their novels. The writers, and some photographers, fused traditional folk beliefs about faerie with scrambled notions about Od, force fields, X-rays, and related subjects. Abandoned places, especially overgrown roads and paths, had proved peculiarly attractive to dry-plate photographers in the 1890, then to users of Brownies willing to hike deep into them; in the last decades of the twentieth century they became the ground itself of fantasy fiction.

"Ahead of him, the sun was going down," writes Susan Cooper in *The Dark Is Rising* of a sensitive boy trudging home from Christmas shopping. "It blazed out fat and gold-orange through a gap in the clouds, and all around the snow-silver world glittered with small gold flashes of light." Away from the gray town and a long walk from the rural bus stop, the light-washed English abandonment at first inveigles. The boy turns into woods along "a small, unpaved track, scarcely a road, known as Tramp's Alley, that wandered off from the main road and eventually curled round to join Huntercombe Lane" close to his home.[3] In a few sentences Cooper evokes the English tradition of the Old Way, the disused, narrow path or track limiting longer-distance vision, compressing and stretching the fall of light, and reaching from abandoned landscape toward or into faerie. Huntercombe Lane exposes Will to surreal adventure. It opens on faerie by opening on a seemingly straightforward experience of light only rarely possible in electrically lit, fast-paced cities and towns thronged with people.[4]

Neither the broad highway to Hell nor the crooked, uphill path to Heaven, Huntercombe Lane exists everywhere in the folklore and ballads of the British Isles.[5] It shapes much post-1880 British fairy-tale fiction aimed at children. It is the dark, snowy route along which Ratty and Mole meet Badger in Kenneth Grahame's 1917 *The Wind in the Willows*, the path curving through A. A. Milne's Winnie the Pooh serial stories from 1925 onward, and the route rising uphill from the lakes of Arthur Ransome's Swallows and Amazons books, the first of which appeared in 1930. In *Pigeon Post*, he wrote, "An old track partly brushed over, so that they had to hold the branches out of each other's way, led from the open pitshead into the path by which they had climbed out of the valley.... The old track wound zigzagging to and fro down through the wood."[6]

But this is not much like the old track that the photographer Alfred Watkins described in 1925. Watkins found a path that did not curl round much of anything, but struck straight if almost invisibly across miles of English country. In the right light, he found, one might see a line evident in lanes and paths, edges of fields, walls, churches, and pre-Christian sites, especially those from before the Bronze Age. Only light links Huntercombe Lane and the many other twisting old ways to the old straight track Watkins discovered.

Watkins kept bees. He noted their efficient straight-line flights between flowers and hives, and named the small light meter he invented and manufactured "The Bee." Perhaps beekeeping predisposed him to see straight lines. But more likely, his photographer's eye for light, shadow, and line—but especially for light—prompted his find. His discovery occurred following a quarter century of public fascination with curving, ruin-punctuated old ways, and not until the 1930s did it shape fantasy writing.

In turn-of-the-century Britain, antiquarians and other enthusiasts prompted renewed interest in old ways, and subsequently produced a spate of newspaper and magazine articles and books. Their interest evolved in part from the deepening scholarly interest in the cultural overlays sharp-eyed walkers noticed in abandoned landscapes. Archaeologists had begun assembling a chronology of the peopling of the British Isles which forced many educated adults to stretch imaginations already expanded by Darwinism. Much of the literature evolved from haphazard discerning of landscape-constituent patterns, especially fragments of ruins. Bird-watchers, hikers, and other amateur naturalists discovered that some paths, especially those long ago supplanted by roads, highways, and railroad routes, seemed to organize landscapes older than those through which they passed. While nostalgia for a premodern, especially preindustrial Britain often prompted many men and women to walk far into the countryside or to take hiking vacations, it soon gave way to increasingly sophisticated analysis. Scrutinizing the British rural landscape, especially abandoned landscape, offered casual, low-cost pleasure, but by the early twentieth century it produced entrancing puzzles too, many of which fixated photographers.

"Photography degrades most things, especially open-air things; and in this case, not only had its poor presentments made the scene too familiar, but something of the degradation in the advertising pictures seemed to attach itself to the very scene," wrote W. H. Hudson in 1909 of a small country town heavily advertised in railroad company photographs. Hudson disliked hiking into landscapes he knew from advertising imagery, but he knew too that a bit of poking around might reveal things photographers missed. He was aware that railroad company advertising succeeded in drawing crowds to coastal and other picturesque places which quickly turned into resorts. Hiking away from railroad lines led to unspoiled English countryside and sometimes into the mystery that sharpened awareness. Often he found himself hiking across some prehistoric earthwork, "grown over with oak wood and underwood of holly and thorn and hazel with tangle of ivy and bramble and briar." Hudson emphasized that such unvisited places had little to do with wilderness, which in him produced only a sense of loneliness and desolation. Instead, overgrown ruins reached by disused tracks produce a "peculiar sense of satisfaction, of restfulness, of peace," because in them "it seems good to know, or to imagine, that the men I occasionally meet in my solitary rambles" are "of the same race, and possibly the descendants, of the people who occupied this spot in the remote past—Iberian and Celt, and Roman and Saxon and Dane."[7] Such locals descend from people who knew the original genii loci.[8] He condemned the middle-brow penchant for visiting the pretty scenery depicted in railroad company images as herd-like behavior demonstrating the force of advertising.[9] He urged his countrymen to explore landscapes that forced them to confront the deep past of Britain, along with scenery not immediately beautiful.

Hilaire Belloc too urged educated British outdoorsmen to trace routes more difficult to find than long-abandoned Roman roads. "Of all the relics of antiquity, the prehistoric road is the most difficult to establish," he argued in *The Old Road*. It forces investigators to study "the wild, half-instinctive trail of men who had but just taken on humanity." Formal education might make hikers incapable of noticing, let alone studying the nearly invisible trail: "No mathematical calculation presided at its origin, none can therefore be used to reconstruct it when it has been lost." Much of what Belloc argued he had learned from experience: almost everywhere in England, the old way passes a church building just to the south of the structure. Often the old way is twenty yards broad, lined with hedgerows "guarding land that had been no man's land since public protection first secured the rude communications of the country," but no longer used by anyone except, perhaps, farmers whose land abuts it. Yet the right-of-way endures in law and landscape both.[10]

Not so much the dead hand of the past kept the right-of-way from falling into the hands of private landowners: the cumbersome English legal system made it almost impossible to convert a disused public way into private property. Belloc often had little way of learning much about the old ways he followed, especially when modern towns and cities obscured their junctions. The routes frustrated twentieth-century cartographers, who often ignored them. Often sections of them had multiple names known only locally and not offered promptly to outsiders hiking them or locating their continuations. More than many of his contemporaries, Belloc insisted that hiking the old ways forced hikers to consider the sophistication of pre-Roman Britain. But such consideration proved hard, especially at the end of day when hikers found old ways connecting with modern roads, usually at rural pubs or old coaching inns. "A gramophone fitted with a monstrous trumpet roared out American songs, and to this sound the servants of the inn were holding a ball," he lamented of one such end-of-day effort.[11]

The years just before World War I produced in Britain an outpouring of old-way books. In 1913 Edward Thomas published *The Icknield Way*, a detailed monograph tracing one long-distance prehistoric road across much of England. Thomas argued that disused old ways endure almost as successfully as rivers: in the countryside only abutters use them, and then just often enough to keep them both legal rights-of-way and discernible to probing strangers. "All over England may be found old roads, called Gypsy Lane, Tinker's Lane, or Smuggler's Lane or Beggar's Lane," and "these little-used roads are known to lovers, thieves, smugglers, and ghosts." Almost invariably, as Belloc, Thomas, and his fellow inquirers noted, locals name segments of the roads as though they were dead ends. While *lane* often designates a dead-ended road, the term proved false in many cases. What locals called a lane often linked other segments that made up a wandering whole reaching hundreds of miles.

The antiquarian R. Hippisley Cox worked from maps as well as from personal observation. He focused his efforts on Roman roads and older ways connecting the many ruins archaeologists had begun excavating. He demonstrated that two long-distance road systems overlay each other. In most instances, Roman roads remained wholly abandoned or buried under modern highways, although now and then they were paralleled by modern roads and railroads. The Roman system itself supplanted a sophisticated system of long- and short-distance roads that Cox insisted rewarded far more scrutiny than most experts proved willing to give. The pre-Roman old ways seemed of two sorts—the rambling ones still used just enough by farmers to keep them from utter neglect and vanishing into forest and field, and another, far older type that Cox associated with Stonehenge and other monuments experts thought had been built in part for astronomical observations. "A civilization existed in this country long before the Celtic invasions," Cox insisted. If the ridge roads indeed connected Stonehenge and other sites, themselves "proof that astronomy had advanced beyond the limits of savage outlook"—and Cox insisted that *The Green Roads of England* offers a fair proof that some did—then hikers and amateur inquirers ought to realize the disquieting cultural significance of some old ways. "It is indeed not impossible that the men of the Bronze Age destroyed a civilization more fully developed than their own."[12] Old ways might be pleasant places to ramble on a summer afternoon, but not all originated in the same era, nor did they reflect a continuous improvement in cultural sophistication. Some indicated cultural superiority predating the Bronze Age and destroyed by stronger invaders.

Turn-of-the-century mainstream antiquarianism confounded much old-way analysis and writing. Many history-minded authors produced books about the preceding two centuries of modern English highways. Chapman & Hall published a series of historic-highway books: *The Exeter Road: The Story of the West of England Highway,* published by Charles G. Harper in 1899, endures as one of the strongest. Essentially main-road history, it and the other monographs focus on locales linked by roads; historical events become less narrative than beads on a string. In a time when almost all Britons traveled by railroad, highways quiet since the end of coaching days struck many educated readers as warranting at least backward-glance attention. Many writers dealt with locales a bit distant from mainline railroad routes and their advertised vacation spots, but smack in the center of British historical narrative. Henry James's *English Hours,* a 1905 volume illustrated with drawings by Joseph Pennell, and William Dean Howells's *Certain Delightful English Towns, with Glimpses of the Pleasant Country Between,* which appeared a year later, epitomize collections of essays written by foreigners for upscale American, Canadian, and Australian readers whose English literature–based education produced lifelong interest in British history and countryside.[13] More matter-of-fact volumes appeared in two categories. Henry C. Shelley's *Untrodden English Ways* of 1908 represents one sort, that purporting to deal with the Britain rarely found by foreign tourists, and Thomas D. Murphy's *British Highways and Byways from a Motorcar: Being a Record of a Five-Thousand Mile Tour in England, Wales, and Scotland,* published in the same year, represents the one focused on main roads and automobile touring.[14] Shelley and most of his fellow authors merely kept to secondary roads, and typically concerned themselves with local color and tertiary-level historical events. Murphy made no excuses for his fifty-day high-speed highway tour, and in the end he found no history or historical associations different from those Shelley recorded. Late in the nineteenth century British travel writing became a smooth-road narrative, and a conceptual highway from which most Britons and almost all tourists saw the British countryside.[15]

The smooth-road narrative ignored British railroad corridors. Nineteenth- and early twentieth-century road writing emphasized eras before the heavy industrialization characterized by railroads, shipyards, large-scale mining, and sprawling manufacturing plants. Paradoxically, the industrial-era motorcar swept upper-income Britons and other tourists away from trains onto the best-maintained highways, carrying them and their prejudices against modern industrialism near places that were derelict or had been quaint since the end of the coaching era.[16] Murphy loathed railroad travel: he liked to visit historic sites, but he found train schedules often forced a stay of hours to accomplish a two-hour visit. He praised bicycles, which he counted by the tens of thousands during his summer trip, and he thought motorcycles likely to transform touring for low-income people. "But the bicycle is out of the question for an extended tour by a party which includes ladies," he proclaimed. "The amount of impedimenta which must be carried along, and the many long hills which are encountered on the English roads, will put the cycle out of the question in such cases." So Murphy chose the motorcar, and published a book making clear that his sort of touring "is not at all exorbitant or out of the reach of the average well-to-do citizen."[17] He worried about getting stuck, and he dreaded descending hills not announced as dangerous to bicyclists; he far preferred well-maintained roads over any that might mislead him or damage his car. He never worried about missing anything along the old ways connecting with the country lanes down which he rarely ventured. Given a roomy, powerful, fast car, appropriate maps, and enough forethought to spend every night in a quality urban hotel, anyone might zoom about the British countryside in comfort, much as Toad does in *The Wind in the Willows*.[18]

The Eastman Kodak Company facilitated photography from cars slowing or stopping when near something their occupants deemed historic, quaint, or otherwise photogenic. In 1913 John and Ruth Dobson drove the main and secondary roads of Great Britain, stopping frequently to make photographs. "Ruth jumped from the car and begged to be allowed to take a kodak of them," noted her husband of a pack of hounds being exercised by an old groom on horseback. "The light was good and the promise of a satisfactory picture excellent," and the American Dobsons gloried in discovering something "feudal" along a road just smooth enough for fast motoring. But they shared Murphy's loathing of any picturesque, rutted, hilly road involving downshifting, heavy steering, and getting stuck deep in the backcountry traversed chiefly by farm carts, plowmen, and walkers.[19]

Such motorists are the prototypes of the one who nearly runs down Ratty, Mole, and Toad in *The Wind in the Willows*. "The 'poop-poop' rang with a brazen shout in their ears, they had a moment's glimpse of an interior of glittering plate-glass and rich morocco, and the magnificent motor-car, immense, breath-snatching, passionate, with its pilot tense and hugging his wheel, possessed all earth and air for the fraction of a second, flung an enveloping cloud of dust that blinded and enwrapped them utterly, and then dwindled to a speck in the far distance, changed back into a droning bee once more," wrote Kenneth Grahame in 1908. But the experience enraptures Toad. "The poetry of motion! The real way to travel! Here today—in next week tomorrow! Villages skipped, towns and cities jumped—always somebody else's horizon! O bliss!"[20] Toad acquires a motorcar, begins tearing about the countryside, and becomes the Terror of the Road. His trail of noise, disruption, and destruction irritates everyone, but leaves the old ways in their quiet.

Murphy found rural Britons tolerant of motorcars. He did not assess how tolerant, perhaps because he rarely spoke with them except to ask directions, and when he did walk about a place, he did so after dinner, in the long British summer evening. Grahame knew better. Not only did many rural people dislike and fear the motorcar, they walked away from it, and a few writers followed their retreat from road-based confusion, noise, and danger.

Earlier traveler-authors tended to arrive at some spot by rail and then explore it on foot, often spending days walking out-and-back routes radiating from an inn or private lodging. They noticed details, and they almost always talked with local people, especially the aged, farm women, clergymen, and farmers drinking in pubs where the authors often stayed. Many such writers eschewed guidebooks, and instead read a bit of local history and natural history before venturing to a location. They centered their inquiries on subjects about which they already knew something and which they hoped might lead locals to talk of something more.[21] Pedestrian authors happened into their subjects, and often returned to them in the course of a single visit. Many of them brought cameras on their expeditions, but did not carry them at first or even routinely, as many accounts published in the *British Journal of Photography* reveal.[22] Typically they returned to a spot another day, frequently after rain had stopped and sunlight better illuminated their subjects, with camera and tripod, making an opportunity not only for a photograph but for a second or third look. Railroad schedules did not trap such writers. Instead they found themselves freed by timetable restriction: they had time to explore on foot in part because railroads provided only infrequent service to out-of-the-way places. Pre-motorcar travel writers and determined enthusiast photographers knew that railroads indeed shaped their time in places, but realized that trains easily carried baggage, including cameras. Well into the motorcar era, such travel writers and photographers continued to work on foot.

Bicycles made cameras impedimenta, exactly as Murphy realized. Until about 1900, cameras traveled poorly on bicycles, and long after the East-man Kodak Company perfected its roll-film and box cameras, cameras vexed bicyclists anxious to have them along for the ride. Circa-1900 bi-cycles and roll-film box cameras, though near-simultaneous inventions, coexisted fitfully despite manufacturer efforts. The Eastman Kodak Com-pany made not only cameras fitted with attachments that let bicyclists sling them under seats and strap them to frames but also ones intended to be attached to handlebars. The Bicycle Kodak models remain early twentieth-century manufacturing curiosities: even now the rationale be-hind their creation and their practical, shop-theory use remains mysteri-ous.[23] The Eastman Kodak Company recognized that some people had to choose between buying a bicycle and buying a good camera, but it knew too the potential marketing symbiosis of the two enthusiasms. It found itself trapped by the cyclist's desire for speed.[24] Some bicyclists might stop, unclip the camera, and make a photograph, but others—how many the company never seemed able to estimate—wanted to photograph as they pedaled, looking downward into the viewfinder mounted just over the handlebar yoke. Not surprisingly, the entire Bicycle Kodak effort failed around 1914: bicycle transportation tended to shake cameras, even rugged Kodak Company ones, to pieces.[25]

While automobiling made camera transport more simple and reliable, most motorists did as Murphy did: they refrained from driving along bumpy muddy lanes, especially ones that might dead-end and force long reverse operation. Many cyclists learned that motorists avoided rural back roads, but even the deepening enmity between bicyclists and mo-torists early in the twentieth century could not force cyclists onto the old ways. Bicycles performed so poorly on such tracks that cyclists routinely avoided them, leaving them to locals and dedicated walkers, many carry-ing cameras. Especially in Britain, but also across western Europe and in parts of New England and the old South, old ways became the prov-ince of determined pedestrians who sometimes carried cameras, or who kept cameras nearby and returned with them as needed. By 1924, when Murphy published *New England Highways and Byways from a Motor-car*, most old-road publishing emphasized roads accessible by bicycle and automobile.[26] Only determined walkers knew much about the old ways impassable to motor vehicles and bicycles alike.[27]

In the first decade of the twentieth century, the attention of guide-book writers and explorers wedded to bicycles and automobiles drifted from old ways. Old roads became those passable by determined cyclists and motorists congratulating themselves on venturing from highways. Old ways became the province of abutters, antiquarians, hikers, and sometimes photographers. Writers of ghost and fantasy tales discovered them too.

Between 1894 and 1925 one writer unintentionally chronicled the deepening evocative power of rarely trodden old ways. M. R. James produced a series of remarkable, erudite ghost stories that appeared in *Pall Mall Magazine, National Review, Contemporary Review, Atlantic Monthly,* and other magazines. His plots tended to evolve from bibliographic or ecclesiastical artifacts, and from legal documents tainted by uncertainty, especially conveyances of real estate.[28] James loved railroad travel. "How pleasant it can be, alone in a first-class railway carriage, on the first day of a holiday that is to be fairly long, to dawdle through a bit of English country that is unfamiliar, stopping at every station," begins one story. "You have a map open on your knee, and you pick out the villages that lie to right and left by their church towers." The narrator of "A View from a Hill" quickly learns that ways other than railroads link places deep in the southwest of England, however. After spending some time "looking over the volumes of the County Archaeological Society's transactions" in his host's library, he begins bicycling about, inquiring into places where amateurs had turned up "flint implements, Roman sites, ruins of monastic establishments," and other antiquities. His host hikes the whole countryside and dislikes bicycles. From his hilltop home he shows the narrator points of ancient interest, using binoculars: "Take a line across that big green field, then over the wood beyond it, then over the farm on the knoll," he tells the narrator, Fanshawe. "Do you see a rather sudden knob of a hill with a thick wood on top of it? It's in a dead line with that single tree on the top of the big ridge." Soon Fanshawe rides his bicycle in search of the ruins he sees through the binoculars provided by a determined hiker intimate with old ways.

On one old way, running between a byway and "the top of Gallows Hill" to the "home road on this side," both his tires blow out silently and simultaneously. As he walks his bicycle, Fanshawe feels threatened, almost as if the woods close in on the way: "I know I had all the fancies one least likes: steps crackling over twigs behind me, indistinct people stepping behind trees in front of me, yes, and even a hand laid on my shoulder," he tells his host afterward. He confesses that after he tripped over a block of stone set into the ground and saw it as one of three making a triangle, he felt frightened enough to pick up his bicycle and run. "Everything caught on everything: handles and spokes and carrier and pedals—caught in them viciously, or I fancied so."[29] Eventually his host and an aged local man tell him of the crazed antiquary who once lived in the woods along the old way, and of his rumored discoveries of other-worldly events.

"A View from a Hill" confronts head-on the enmity between bicyclists and motorists, then dismisses it in favor of grappling with something more important but equally technological. The story turns in part on a pair of modern binoculars that reveal different landscape details to different users: the squire loans them to Fanshawe not only to test his own visions but to learn if his guest is a sensitive himself. At first Fanshawe simply misses the point. He carries a camera when he bicycles, and he uses it to make photographs that sometimes reveal what he fails to see firsthand. At one church, he photographs some lettering on stained glass he cannot read, even when he uses the binoculars to look up at it. "I took some sort of a photograph of the window, and I dare say an enlargement would show what I want," he tells his host, as he begins wondering why the binoculars did not work in the church but his camera might.[30] He and the squire learn that the binoculars, obtained from the estate of the half-crazed antiquary, offer a vision of the landscape unlike anything they see with naked eyes. The story turns not so much on the clashes between one sort of modern technology and another as on how cameras and binoculars work slightly differently in a handful of places, especially in the hands of sensitive users.[31] A philologist recognizes ancient roots in modern words; with the binoculars, sensitive observers might see landscape features otherwise faded into near obscurity.[32]

British authors favored the stylistic device of people finding old ways by accident. Elinor Mordaunt's 1923 short story "The Inspired 'Busman" details the bizarre adventures of passengers trapped aboard a London double-deck bus driven fiercely away from the city and far into a dark wood. Determined to see the night sky clearly, its deranged driver plunges his riders into darkness so total that when he stops and urges them to step off "they were like untouched photographic plates, prepared for any impression."[33] By the early 1920s American writers had fully accepted the genre, the device, and a photographic vocabulary that elucidated the experience of seeing anew on old ways unfrequented by automobilists and cyclists.[34]

In the United States the old ways became the "old Indian footpath, which could be plainly seen across the long-unplowed turn of the pastures" and which snaked into "the thick, low-growing spruces of the woods" Sarah Orne Jewett details in her 1896 *The Country of the Pointed Firs*. But the Maine path makes the narrator think of "English landscapes, and of the solemn hills of Scotland, with their lonely cottages," or "the primeval fields of Sicily," not North American wilderness. Her companion explains that the men of the neighborhood never follow strayed cattle into the woods alone, that adults fear forces dating back to Indian and witchcraft days, and that one young woman bewildered overnight while berrying never recovered mentally. "Some folks is born afraid of the woods and all wild places, but I must say they've always been like home to me," remarks the narrator's companion, a vigorous local woman who knows the old way almost no one walks.[35]

In most fiction of the time, old ways lay far beyond the highways and byways described in male-authored travelogues. In 1915 Clifton Johnson condemned automobiles in the first pages of his *Highways and Byways of New England*. He argued that motorcars impoverished their purchasers twice, once financially and then by seducing owners into frenetic weekend trips, often along roads just smooth enough to keep drivers from discovering things a few miles from them.[36] Johnson made a career of travel writing, but his New England book delved scarcely farther into the countryside than his *Highways and Byways of the South,* which appeared eleven years earlier.[37] He traveled by train, and sometimes carriage, and later by motorcar, but he took care to never venture far into regions crossed by bad roads. His books presage Murphy's *New England Highways and Byways from a Motorcar.* Murphy devoted a month to his Toad-like six-state tour, and he avoided most back roads, especially in the three northern states, although detours frequently forced him to drive roads "narrow, dusty, stony and rough as a rule," but rarely muddy. Murphy hated mud. "What a relief it was to feel that, rain or shine, we could still comfortably proceed—that our heavy car would not skid into a ditch or be stalled in mud," he wrote of one road dug into gravel.[38]

From the 1890s onward, Arthur Machen, the pseudonym of Arthur Llewellyn Jones, molded fantasy writing not only in his native Britain but in the United States as he reached a readership wary of all but the very best ghost stories by M. R. James and Henry James. Welding the Celtic legends told to him in boyhood, modern physics, eroticism, and the fierce intellectual interest in psychic research informing the Edwardian era, Machen envisioned the intermittent collision of parallel universes, typically along disued ways. One character in his 1895 "The Great God Pan" wonders if electricity is merely a pebble lying before a mountain, and if old paths might not lead to immense discoveries, not mere technological marvels. Many of his stories revolve around mysterious disappearances and encounters along paths rarely used by anyone except people on abutting farms. "She was seen by some men in the fields making for the old Roman Road, a green causeway which traverses the highest part of the wood, and they were astonished that the girl had taken off her hat, though the heat of the sun was already almost tropical," he notes in "The Great God Pan" of a woman subsequently discovered to have been sacrificed by fairies worshipping Pan.

Machen wandered the Welsh hills continuously as a boy, and his topographical descriptions evoke the deep past infusing scenic beauty. But he wrote equally eloquently about the shifting character of light along the paths, especially when "high mist, grey and luminous," floated in from the Atlantic, and the ease with which twilight bewildered travelers unaccustomed to following paths edging fields and woods rather than connecting houses.[39] He emphasized that examining old ways, especially grassy Roman remnants overlaying older ways, led often to issues of sex, violence, and vision. All anyone had to do was step away from the decrepit towns along the Welsh coast, away from single-line railways traversed by rare trains, away from the Strand and other shining London streets, look a trifle askance, and walk into glamour.[40]

Other writers explored the old-way zone Machen trod. In 1919 Lafcadio Hearn's posthumous essay "Gothic Horror" appeared. The American writer had died fifteen years earlier and, despite his brilliant writing on New Orleans, Caribbean and other Spanish Empire Creoles, and the Japanese suddenly of interest to Western intellectuals, had begun to slip into obscurity. At church, Hearn wrote, "I first learned to know the peculiar horror that certain forms of Gothic architecture can inspire.... I am using the word 'horror' in a classic sense,—in its antique meaning of ghostly fear."[41] Hearn used *horror* precisely: years earlier, the English inventor of photography, H. Fox Talbot, carefully distinguished among terror, dread, and fear in his *English Etymologies*.[42] Talbot's philological work demonstrates the profound visual capabilities of its author: retrospect makes it read as a prologue to his inventing parts of the photographic process.

Darkness and the dark chamber appear repeatedly in works probing at subconscious seeing, especially that which inspires fear, dread, and horror. In another autobiographic fragment published in *Shadowings,* Hearn explained that after his mother died, his guardian locked him into a dark room each night: at age five he knew abandonment and terror. His memories of a high-ceilinged room and pointed window perhaps encouraged his belief in goblins, and his night terrors perhaps skewed his vision of Gothic architecture, but his horror of the Gothic endured long after he grew up, something he worked to understand. Decades later in the Caribbean, confronting two-hundred-foot-tall palm trees swaying gently in the wind, Hearn grasped what prolonged study of architectural histories failed to accomplish. He understood that his horror in a Gothic church stemmed from his feeling *"a horror of monstrous motion"* which seemed "chiefly suggested by the extraordinary angle at which the curves of the arching touched." He saw Gothic interiors slightly differently from other observers and, perhaps because of his childhood night fears, saw "the building stretch itself like a phantasm of sleep."[43] His work suddenly dovetailed with that of William James, Machen, and others trying to understand landscape, sensation, and emotion.

Photography stimulated the energy of sensitive observers struggling with cameras, pen and paper, and architectural renderings, especially those in histories and textbooks; sometimes these observers saw things authorities had failed to notice.[44] In 1926 L. P. Clerc, a leading French photographic expert, confronted the issue head-on in *Photography: Theory and Practice,* in a chapter entitled "Perspective: Monocular and Binocular Vision." He included a sketch "showing in elevation, in plan, and in perspective, a series of identical vertical cylinders, each being surmounted by a sphere," as "an excellent example of anamorphosis." The "perspective which is displeasing, although correct" proves precisely what "the artist, painter, engraver, or draughtsman always modifies" by "means of certain tricks." One alternative produces a "sensation of relief" which "may be so striking that an observer who did not already know would scarcely believe that the solid image which he could see was actually the result of two plane images." Given some shapes of the seemingly solid image, the illusion becomes peculiarly eerie: the observer "might not unnaturally conclude that the solid figure was represented in the act of falling."[45] First translated into English in 1930, Clerc's work addresses the optical conundrums turn-of-the-century photographers realized must affect the operation of cameras having only one lens between subject and film.[46]

For 1920s American fantasy writers, native old ways opened on more than history, in part because the writers accepted the relative shallowness of North American history compared with that of Britain and Europe. Frances Stevens set her 1919 *Argosy* tale "The Elf Trap" in the mountains of North Carolina, miles from the nearest railroad depot, but where out-of-the-ordinary gypsies bring Old World magic to a place abandoned by former slaves.[47] Mountains fixated writers in part because modernization had bypassed them. "On the gentler slopes there are farms, ancient and rocky, with squat, moss-coated cottages brooding eternally over old New England secrets in the lee of great ledges," wrote H. P. Lovecraft in 1927. But two hundred years offered too few secrets compared with those

M. R. James described, and the few Lovecraft imagined fared poorly against those discerned by his British contemporaries.[48]

Lovecraft sited many tales in the half-abandoned, overgrown hill country of rural New England. "There was once a road over the hills and through the valleys, that ran straight where the blasted heath is now," he wrote in "The Colour Out of Space," a story of a blighted valley intended to be flooded as a drinking-water reservoir. "But people ceased to use it and a new road was laid curving far toward the south. Trace of the old one can still be found amidst the weeds of a returning wilderness." The rawness of recently abandoned pastures and arable fields had disconcerted late nineteenth-century United States commentators, who saw the deserted farms as indicating the collapse of Yankee character. Lovecraft understood that Italian and Polish immigrant families often made such farms prosperous, but regions they ignored tended to be ignored by everyone else, until the fad for buying abandoned farms as summer places caused newcomers to arrive around 1910.[49] "The Colour Out of Space" focuses on a valley doubly abandoned, once following the impact of a meteorite in 1882, then again after government agencies purchase it for flooding. Whatever colonial-era secrets it contains, it harbors a late nineteenth-century mystery emblemized in five acres of contaminated ground defying photography. The engineer designing the reservoir discovers his science-biased mind-set shaken by the fifty-year-old site, and after hearing a tale related by a half-mad farmer, decides the whole valley is better flooded. But the engineer resolves to never drink the water.[50]

In the very early 1920s, most American fantasy writers simply sited their tales in Britain or Ireland, often using an American protagonist to connect readers with foreign scenes.[51] By the end of the decade, however, they had cut through the topsoil and subsoil of American history, then dug into imagined "timelessness," which elucidated contemporaneous undercurrents, especially cultural fears.[52] They worked in the British fantasy tradition, but for Lovecraft and other writers connected through *Weird Tales* and other pulp magazines, something had changed. They realized what Von Reichenbach knew in the 1860s. Photography now and then linked unexpectedly with otherworldliness, fusing visioning and sensation in ways that transcended Hollywood glitz.[53]

Belloc had no worries about studying history, especially that underfoot in old ways. "By the recovery of the Past, stuff and being are added to us," he observed, and "our lives which, lived in the present only, are a film or surface, take on body—are lifted into one dimension more." Along with so many other old-way inquirers, Belloc was not much intrigued with mainstream history, or indeed even with history at all. He capitalized the *P* in *past* because he understood the shaping power of historians and the ease with which mainstream history glossed over antiquity.[54] "Visions and intimations are confirmed," he wrote. "Though things are less observable as they are farther away, yet their appeal is directly increased by such a distance in a manner which all know though none can define it."[55] At some point in the inquiry, thinking historically became a near-spiritual experience involving an altered state of mind. Exactly as M. R. James's binoculars produce visions, so does prolonged scrutiny of the deep past produce in sensitive observers an emotional involvement with elemental force, and it most affects those in secluded, abandoned, typically overgrown places.[56]

But it does not always please. Belloc emphasized that modernization and urbanism together drew human activity away from vast reaches of countryside, which quickly went to ruin.[57] He calmly accepted the meanings of ancient ruins, and even of eighteenth-century ones, but recently abandoned industrial sites distressed him. While part of a continuum reaching back for millennia, recent abandonment intimated the narrowness of modern enterprise and forced him to see technological marvel as rickety. Places recently bereft of humanity struck him as indicating that twentieth-century invention and modernization extended across very small regions indeed and might prove as evanescent as disused mills built fifty years before he found their ruins. He worried that too many preferred the simulacrum of travel books, not the edginess of old-way seeing.[58]

Within a few years Belloc's distinctions had become a joke for all but the cognoscenti of wanderers. "You can go to your Junior Proms and your Teas Dansant and your Debutante Parties; you can see Charlie Chaplin and Tom Mix and go to your Ziegfeld Follies, but you will never have half the fun I knew or feel half the thrills that ran down my backbone when I walked with my father in the graveyard on a Sunday afternoon," wrote Charles L. Goodell in 1932. He was seventy-eight when he published *Black Tavern Tales: Stories of Old New England,* and he keenly felt the changes that had swept across rural New England since the beginning of World War I. He worried that cinema would erode children's attachment to place and terminate adult interest in events considered so unimportant that no one recorded them, or so mysterious and significant that knowledge of them was passed on only orally.[59] He acknowledged the fun he had with his father in the decrepit graveyard, but he knew too that subsequent inquiries might lead him to sobering discoveries beyond the stories. Mainstream magazine fiction, radio broadcasts, and Hollywood films might prove as transient as the industrial wreckage Belloc explored, he worried, and what he knew would be forgotten, or else known only to a sparse contingent of old-way explorers and very private photographers who would keep their knowledge to themselves.

In one of his most finely crafted tales, Lovecraft dealt with the intersection of old ways and photography. "The Whisperer in Darkness" emphasizes the edginess characterizing much backcountry folklore research. Now and then old-timers did not want a record made, either a photographic one or a wax-record sound recording, of tales destined to never become ballads. Folklorists studying the "old ones" of backwoods Vermont might find them lurking in tales told by the first white settlers who heard of them from Indians, or the stories might have originated in Celtic ones corrupted by "the Scotch-Irish element of New Hampshire" to the east. The tale concerns something other than "the malign fairies and 'little people' of the bogs and paths," and ways Scottish and Irish immigrants "protected themselves with scraps of incantation handed down through many generations."[60] "The Whisperer in Darkness" aims not at the brownies Palmer Cox learned about from his Scottish grandmother, but at something as troubling as anything Buchan imagined.

"Another photograph—evidently a time-exposure taken in deep shadow—was of the mouth of a woodland cave, with a boulder of rounded regularity choking the aperture. On the bare ground in front of it one could just discern a dense network of curious tracks," the scholar-narrator relates. "When I studied the picture with a magnifier I felt uneasily sure that the tracks were like the one in the other view." He scrutinizes "the Kodak prints" sent by a very unnerved old-way inquirer. "A third picture showed a druid-like circle of standing stones on the summit of a wild hill."[61] Lovecraft offers testimony to the power of the photographs while making an abandoned fragment of Vermont wilderness as eerie as any place in Britain.

"In spite of the vagueness of most of them, they had a damnably suggestive power which was intensified by the fact of their being genuine photographs—actual optical links with what they portrayed, and the product of an impersonal transmitting process without prejudice, fallibility, or mendacity," the scholar determines, having made certain that "no possibility of a tricky double exposure" corrupted the images. Image after image—especially a close-up of a small smooth stone incised with unintelligible markings—demonstrates not only unsettling mystery but superb photography. But when the researchers come together and make an effort to find what lurks along the mountainous old ways, they find serious trouble. "I tried to photograph it for you, but when I developed the film there wasn't anything visible except the woodshed," one tells the other as they struggle to understand what kind of apparition or energy field was capable of tricking Kodak chemistry.[62] In the story, accidental photographs tell more than ones made deliberately, but any of the images developed and printed in the back room of a decrepit Vermont farmhouse seem dangerous. Scientists jeer at them, but the Vermont state police grow very quiet and enterprising. Lovecraft's implication is that the photographs admissible in a court of law and capable of condemning men to death must be equally admissible when folklorists and old-way walkers encounter something that demands scientific investigation.

"The Whisperer in Darkness" marks a watershed in American fantasy writing. No longer did protagonists struggle to induce scientists to visit spots where both reputable people and half-wits reported odd goings-on. Henceforth concerned citizens arrived at universities or state police barracks with photographs in hand. Lovecraft suggests that such images prove dangerous, not only to scientific theory and established scientist reputations but to the photographers as well. A photograph records and may convince. In Ralphson's word, it *confesses*. But it may also seduce or terrify. As an object, a photograph might prove as dangerous as its ostensible subjects, especially when those subjects appear accidentally.

For Lovecraft and his contemporaries, and for most subsequent fantasy writers, photography functions as an unanticipated detour. "When the State highway to Rutland is closed, travelers are forced to take the Stillwater road past Swamp Hollow," begins "The Horror in the Burying Ground," a tale Lovecraft and Hazel Heald published in 1933 in *Weird Tales*. "Motorists feel subtly uncomfortable about the tightly shuttered farmhouse on the knoll just north of the village, and about the white-bearded half-wit who haunts the old burying ground on the south."[63] Half-wits people the nonfiction *Black Tavern Tales* too, and there too they make young people uncomfortable or frightened: they see the invisible and prove sensitive to forces Hollywood distrusts. In his own way, Lovecraft was poking fun at Murphy and other writers of main-traveled-road history: such authors rarely left good roads because they worried about back roads. A detour meant having to take a back road, and perhaps dealing with ruts, washouts, mud, and the possibility that the back road itself had been detoured onto an old way fit only for pedestrians or horsemen.[64] But photography proved as fickle as any back road. It recorded everything in front of the lens, at least usually. Sometimes it recorded things viewers of negatives and prints preferred not to see.

In 1937 the old ways of Britain served up stuff beyond the hopeful dreams of Belloc and other old-way explorers. Tolkien published *The*

Hobbit, or, There and Back Again. It introduces what became (in 1954 and 1955) the evocative imagined terrain of *The Lord of the Rings*. It presents Tolkien's peculiar understanding of roads, cart paths, footpaths, old ways, and "the Lone-lands, where there were no people left, no inns, and the roads grew steadily worse" as components of regions known mostly by rare travelers, including the innocent hobbit protagonists of the books, through both looking and language.[65] Tolkien began writing what appeared as the three-volume *The Lord of the Rings* before *The Hobbit* appeared in print. While the latter books fired the contemporary fantasy genre, readers still undervalue Tolkien's intricate concern with disused roads, older ways of knowing, and obsolescent or dialect ways of speaking as part of a larger twentieth-century British fascination with abandoned landscape, mysteriously named places, and unstudied ruins and forces known chiefly to locals. Tolkien painted and sketched, and his topographical description often exceeds that of Mervyn Peake: far too many readers miss the contextual fabric of his topographical passages just as they miss his philological intent. "Roads go ever ever on," sings the protagonist of *The Hobbit,* and the hobbits of *The Lord of the Rings* know Bilbo Baggins's traveling song well: twice in the novel Tolkien reproduces it, with just enough variation to make it seem a folk song. But the road Tolkien followed led into Faerie, a place he defined as the sub-creation of western European folk imagination but reduced to the setting of moralistic children's literature around 1900.

In "On Fairy Stories," an essay based on an address he gave in 1938 at the University of St. Andrews, Tolkien explains his concept of sub-creation as the making of a Secondary World, philology as one way of approaching much western European folk belief, and at least a bit of the path-pierced landscape awareness lost to his contemporaries. "Faërie contains many things besides elves and fays, and besides dwarfs, witches, trolls, giants, or dragons," Tolkien asserts. "It holds the seas, the sun, the moon, the sky; and the earth, and all things that are in it: tree and bird, water and stone, wine and bread, and ourselves, mortal men, when we are enchanted." Yet if an age or a village or an individual believed or believes that Faerie and elves exist, "elves are not primarily concerned with us, nor we with them," and only those people adventuring "in the Perilous Realm or upon its shadowy marches" can expect to encounter them. "Our fates are sundered and our paths seldom cross," Tolkien concludes. "Even upon the borders of Faërie we encounter them only at some chance crossing of the ways."

Faerie lies somewhere adjacent to wilderness and common landscape and long-deserted places.[66] It possesses marches if not distinct edges, and at least some man-made paths wander into its shadowy frontiers, intersecting, albeit infrequently, with paths ending in mist or darkness or silvery light. Discerning the path or way, especially the unfrequented path nearly hidden by branches and shadow, sometimes enables enchantment: at other times, enchantment enables discernment.[67] "On Fairy Stories" notes magic only in passing, but it distinguishes precisely the permeability of the membrane separating ordinary human landscape and Faerie. The old way often leads into Faerie as well as from it.

Knowing Faerie as place rather than concept necessarily focuses attention on what Josiah Royce termed "provincialism" in a 1902 Phi Beta Kappa address at the University of Iowa. The American philosopher subsequently expanded the lecture into an essay he published six years later. Only recently found by scholars struggling toward a "theory of ecosystem preservation," "Provincialism" has long puzzled historians concerned with modernization in the United States.[68] While its three points antedate concerns John Dewey and other philosophers voiced in the middle 1920s, its idealist solution still strikes readers as vague. Royce saw American intellectuals confronting three "principal evils." They had to assimilate both foreign immigrants and tramps and other displaced native-born citizens in ways that made society as a whole more adaptable to rapid change; they had to counteract a "leveling tendency" evident in homogenized national news, external fashions, and overmastering social forces that discouraged individuality and approached "a dead level of harassed mediocrity"; and they had to eliminate the "mob spirit" that threatened to destroy democratic government. The term "evils" indicates the depth of Royce's concern: he thought much damage had already occurred, some of which might be irrevocable.

Already much localism had disappeared, and with it perhaps the chance for what he designated "wise provincialism." Advocating a modern localism led him at once into the sectional issues that helped produce the Civil War, and he argued at length that he meant something utterly different. He insisted that a county, state, or "even a large section of the country, such as New England, might constitute a province," in which "local independence of spirit" enables thoughtful evaluation of national trends and moods, and especially of national news media.[69] "Provincialism" juxtaposes local attachment and national and global awareness in ways that shaped early twentieth-century environmentalism and still resonate with eco-centric thinkers.[70] But by the early 1920s his argument had shriveled into advocacy of local and regional scenery and ecosystems.[71] Most of what Royce wrote subsequently about national news media, racial clashes, and other thorny twentieth-century issues had been forgotten by the late 1930s, even by New Deal advocates.[72] Localism and regionalism withered in the face of national news and entertainment media exactly as Royce predicted.

Roycean provincialism drifted into the eddies of mainstream American philosophical inquiry, dragged by Roycean insistence that American racial issues originated in capricious, suggestible mental phenomena shaped by forces beyond individuals, families, and provinces. He understood racism to originate in "elemental tendencies" exemplified in "the stage fright of the unskilled, in the emotional disturbances of young people who are finding their way in the world, in the surprises of early love, in the various sorts of anthropophobia which beset nervous patients, in the antipathies of country folk toward strangers, in the excitements of mobs, in countless other cases of social stress or of social novelty." He argued that psychology would soon distinguish among tendencies and illuminate their origins, but he warned repeatedly that greater social forces, especially national media, trained such tendencies and exploited them for their own purposes.[73] Stalwart, subtle, and deep provincialism often provided the positive energy that enabled individuals to rise above both innate, often harmless, tendency and trained antipathy.[74]

"The chance intensity of the passing experience may be alone significant," he argued in a passage that introduced the sensitive observer. "Oddities of feature or of complexion, slight physical variations from the customary, a strange dress, a scar, a too-steady look, a limp, a loud or deep voice, any of these peculiarities, in a stranger, may be, to one child, or nervous subject, or other sensitive observer, an object of fascinated curiosity," only because "we are all instinctively more or less sensitive to such features, simply because we are by heredity doomed to be interested in all facts which may prove to be socially important." Royce shoved hard against forces that trained children and adults, especially ones already slightly unstable, to judge difference of appearance or behavior with "intense irritation," making anyone different an "object of terror, or of violent antipathy." He insisted that racial antipathy itself existed as a mere variant of deeper antipathies that anyone might study, perhaps by observing the way a "tired camper in the forest may readily come to feel whatever racial antipathy you please toward his own brother, if the latter then wounds social susceptibilities which the abnormal situation has made momentarily hyperaesthetic."[75] But given the force of metropolitan newspapers alone, some of which he condemned as having "far too many readers for the good of the social order in which they circulate," fewer educated Americans by the year stepped back from mass-culture thinking to analyze racism and other evils.[76] In 1902 and continuously thereafter,

Royce championed a diversity of thinking grounded in provincialism, but his philosophical framework morphed into one shaping biodiversity.[77]

Indirectly he voiced suspicions that national public education might unwittingly forge alliances with national news and entertainment media. In "Limitations of the Public," a later version of a 1906 Vassar College address, he insisted that "much of the best in human nature simply escapes our present definitions" for it "is known only by its fruits, and prospers best in the forest shade of unconsciousness." Instinct rules the unconscious, and while some instincts link humans with animals, he asserted that "the highest in us is also based on instinct."[78] The province, especially the rural province, engaged Royce because it offered both an observation post from which to view critically mass-media enterprise and because it strengthened those Royce termed "sensitives." Away from cities, suburbs, and large towns awash in mass media, a thoughtful and educated person might connect on many levels not only with the natural environment Royce prized but with nuanced, traditional ways of knowing, feeling, and interpreting. Royce argued not only for prolonged wilderness experience, but also for lengthy visits to rural space.

Post-1970 fantasy fiction heralds a new ecology grounded in the stark awareness that primeval wilderness no longer exists and that ecosystem conservation opens on the Perilous Realm. Fantasy fiction emphasizes peculiar ways of seeing that now and then enable revelation, especially the descrying of paths. "It was only after I'd figured out a safe way in— you can see it if you've been shown what to look for, it's a certain way the light shines off the mud; pretty metaphysical stuff, though I guess there's a perfectly reasonable explanation," a quiet, country-educated nobleman tells a city-based courier mired far from the main-traveled road in K. J. Parker's *Evil for Evil*. "Anyhow, I'd already done all the waiting around for the light to come up so I could see those special reflections."[79]

The rural nobleman understands time exposure. Not only does he have time to look about him, he makes time to watch the sunlight move across the mud. In the novel, and in much fantasy fiction aimed at both children and adults, living in a place with a surfeit of time—let alone having time to look carefully and at length at things, perhaps especially the play of light on a place—elicits all manner of ideas about contemporary metropolitan life, especially the equation of cinema with the view from the too-fast, too-luxurious automobile. Anyone reading fantasy fiction slogs through much trash but nonetheless finds some especially perceptive writing, almost all of it seemingly elucidating Royce, and all of it building on Tolkien's understanding of his predecessors. Lovecraft and Howard struggled with concepts M. R. James, Machen, and Conrad managed far more acutely, but they nonetheless formulated the rough outlines of an old-way ecology now ordering the best of post-Tolkien fantasy writing. A new landscape evolved almost exactly according to that Royce envisioned now orders most fantasy fiction: neither wilderness nor constructed, the abandoned landscape penetrated by old ways entices walkers sensitive to the forces animating it.

7 Light

Photographers frequently juxtaposed nude women and mirrors, typically searching for links between the natural self, light, and reflection.

IN 1911 ALFRED WATKINS REMINISCED ABOUT HIS early photographic efforts along the old ways of Great Britain. Thirty-five years earlier, when he was twenty-one and employed as a brewery salesman, he carried his camera, wet plates, and developing outfit with him in his buggy as he traveled from one rural pub to another. Especially in winter, making photographs proved awkward, particularly in remote, wild areas, but developing the wet plates on the spot taxed his patience and endurance and made him choose subjects thoughtfully. "I remember turning out one cold winter's morning and taking scenes on the little frozen stream with the trees hung with hoar frost, and a lighted spirit lamp required in the tent to thaw needles of ice in bath and developer," he wrote in the preface to *Photography: Its Principles and Applications*. "Those were simple days, when lantern slides and negatives of moving subjects alike were made on one sensitive film—wet collodion—and varying 'speeds of plates' were almost unknown." In 1911 it seemed to him that everyone used a camera, "the schoolboy, snapping his sisters or schoolmates with a Brownie bought yesterday" or "the traveler, seeking records of the people, customs, architecture, and landscape beauties of the country through which he passes." The latter intrigued Watkins, but not as deeply as "the experimenter dipping into the records of early investigators, and eager to be in touch with even small discoveries." As he wrote, the landlady of the inn came in "with the bedroom candle," and he mused on the changes wrought by cinema. In 1890 he had seen "his first moving picture film" and admitted that he "could not predict that the idea would expand until moving photographs would constitute the most widely used form of all entertainment." Photography had moved far from the wet-plate days of 1876, but in the same inn in which he had stopped as a young salesman, the same landlady brought in a candle at nightfall, just as she had years earlier, when he had begun examining the records of early photographic investigators and the walkers of disused pathways.[1]

Watkins explored old ways with as much enthusiasm as he explored photography, but he struggled to make excellent photographs in the deep shadow of so many disused and overgrown places. As years passed, he became owner of a large flour mill and other businesses, but he retained his early love of landscape antiquities, especially standing stones and other cryptic landmarks typically overgrown and hard to locate. Vegetation often masked them in shadow.

By 1890 he had invented the world's first exposure meter measuring relative intensity of light for the purposes of photography. The pocket watch–like instrument used sensitized paper to indicate correct plate exposure settings and times. Essentially it worked as a circular slide rule: the photographer counted the number of seconds that passed before the sensitized paper darkened to the same shade as the fixed reference spot, then used the dials listing aperture settings and speed of plate to assign a numerical value to the ambient light. While technically an actinometer, the meter offered a straightforward way of evaluating light. Experts dismissed his concept, patent, and prototype, and Watkins used his own capital to manufacture the meter in a building attached to the flour mill.

Watkins sold 1,400 meters in his first year of production and quickly produced a smaller, simpler meter he called the "Bee," named not only for its smallness and efficiency but for its straightforward, efficient results. His tiny meters proved a huge success, and for fifty years sold by the tens of thousands around the world. As decades passed, his company improved them in many ways, offering different sets of dials for photographers working with American and other emulsion speeds and camera f-stop numbers, plates—and subsequently roll film—made by manufacturers around the world, and for copying, lantern-slide making, and other specialized activities. His firm made other instruments—Watkins loved pinhole cameras and made his first from a cigar box, then determined that other photographers, perhaps especially children, should have cameras more capable than box cameras if more likely to make unexpected but intriguing results and so manufactured them—but his meters became synonymous with serious photography. The Bee Meter not only worked in the field before the photographer exposed film, it worked in the darkroom too, to guide the photographer in developing the print.

In 1902 Watkins published *The Watkins Manual of Exposure and Development,* offering advice to photographers desperate to know why their expensive cameras made such poor images. Watkins told them that expensive fishing rods often caught no fish. In his manual and subsequent publications, he produced arguments that paralleled Izaak Walton's seventeenth-century *Compleat Angler:* Watkins offered a philosophy of photography based on evaluating light.[2]

He realized that even well-educated photographers knew little of Newton's optics, and that schoolteachers said little about light itself. "The plate is sensitive to different coloured lights in different degrees," he began. "For instance, the yellow reflected by a primrose has a very small effect, while a blue flower reflects light which is very active." Trial and error taught, but Watkins saw it wasting time, plates, and developer. "Such colours as red, orange, yellow and—in a lesser degree—green have a feeble effect on the plate, and are called non-actinic colours, while blue and violet have a vigorous chemical effect on the plate." Such knowledge speeded experiments. Unlike many of his contemporaries, Watkins insisted on the three-dimensional quality of the coated glass plate or roll film: he instructed his readers to henceforth think of the sensitized plate or film "as a *thickness* rather than as a *surface*."[3] Always he assumed readers who developed and printed their own negatives, and from the beginning he explained why manufacturers produced plates less sensitive to the red and orange light that made darkroom work possible. He carried the concept far: he expected readers to learn to print from a negative before ever using a camera. Once they learned how to produce fine prints from different quality negatives, they might move on to making simple cameras, preferably a pinhole one.

A pinhole camera uses a tiny hole made by a pin or needle: the camera lacks a lens. Its use requires long exposures, and as Watkins made clear, ordinarily it is of little use in photographing people. "But for landscapes and buildings the results are usually preferred by artists to the acutely sharp definition given by a lens," he maintained, then admitted he realized most readers either already owned a sophisticated camera or intended to buy one.[4] Such readers needed to know more immediately about light than those who built or bought a simple pinhole camera and learned from shop-theory-based practice.

Watkins concerned himself with a world illuminated according to time of day, clouds and other atmospheric variation, and physical obstructions. He explained that "white fleecy clouds" in summer intensified sunlight, since they bounced back light reflected from the earth. Failing to note clouds as reflectors caused photographers to make poor images. They simply did not see light acutely. "Light which has a yellow tinge (as toward sunset or in fog or east winds) may appear *visually* bright, but is *actinically* (or chemically) feeble," he argued.[5] Moreover, the human eye adapts effortlessly to different qualities of light as ambient light changes, and few photographers make the effort to notice the adaptation as it occurs.

In all of his thinking, one concept remained central: the photographer must measure the light falling on the subject, not that reflected from it. Watkins insisted that the photographer should "test the light which falls upon the shadiest part of the subject in which full detail is required." Much of the *Manual* emphasizes the uses of its author's instruments, but some of it foreshadows a photographic philosophy Watkins emphasized in subsequent writing.

He condemned the lack of slow shutter speeds available in small cameras. Speeds of a ¼ or ⅛ of a second meant that a camera braced "against a fence, wall, or shop front" would produce fine negatives. Too many photographers never learned to hold a camera steady. "Do not presume that as a matter of course you will find it easy to 'press the button' properly," he warned. "It is easy to blunder in this matter and get blurred pictures." By the time the *Manual* appeared, his firm had produced a circular dial indicator that "indicates what shutter speed to use with a certain opening of lens or vice versa" and he had patented a "sliding bar" that connected diaphragm and shutter speed control on most cameras, with the result "that the act of calculating the exposure by setting light value against plate speed automatically adjusts both lens and shutter to make the correct exposure." Repeatedly he instructed readers to understand how "a hand camera can often be placed on an uneven surface such as a heap of stones, a top of a wall, packed level with bits of stone, weighted with a large stone, and a time exposure given."[6]

His personal and corporate philosophy came down to what he called his "golden rule," which he printed in italics: *"Use the slowest speed your subject permits."* Unlike so many of his contemporaries, he insisted that "the proportion of successes you may make with the hand camera will depend on how seldom you use it for snap shooting."[7] He argued consistently that camera manufacturers, and especially the Eastman Kodak Company, skewed photography by striving for fast film and fast shutter speeds that "stopped" speeding trains, bicycles, automobiles, and other fast-moving things and enabled fast-moving photographers to make snapshots, especially in cities and suburbs. Constant advertising of fast film and fast-shutter cameras distorted what he identified as the essential rationale of photography. He knew light as the protagonist and specific landscapes as its theater. He delighted in secluded rural places, especially abandoned landscape threaded by old ways.

His exploration of landscape antiquities shaped his rationale. "I remember a several days walking tour with a hand camera in dull weather when I came back with a number of time exposures but had never used the shutter at all," he remarked of an effort that combined acute seeing, hiking, and photography.[8] He stole time from his many business ventures to probe far along old ways, often in foul weather, and to puzzle at the meaning of prehistoric stones and other ruins, especially at those he found across Herefordshire.

Despite his wealth and his ownership of several automobiles, he walked constantly, and he never forgot children and adult photographers struggling to afford decent equipment. Always he emphasized the homemade pinhole camera as capable of making sumptuous and often surprising images, and he explained that the circular brass tins containing Bee Meter disks of sensitized paper might be converted into fairly accurate exposure meters by anyone willing to drill a ⅜-inch hole in one side and tinker a bit with pieces of cardboard. He considered photography as something people (especially children) ought to do according to their own dictates, not those of advertising, and he routinely insisted that do-it-yourselfers might obtain superb images. He repeatedly cautioned that he intended to provide technical advice only, not artistic suggestion. He stressed the fact that very few individuals could immediately assess ambient light. Evaluating light vexed even experienced photographers, most of whom used a Watkins meter, especially in bad weather or in other conditions where lighting taxed the mind.[9] But the evaluation process itself sometimes revealed mysteries before the camera lens.

A photographer intent on discovering correct exposure might find something more in his viewfinder than what had first attracted his attention.

Nine years after his *Manual* appeared, Watkins published *Photography: Its Principles and Applications,* an exhaustive book which directed many photographers along a conservative track. He argued against the fast-growing fad of collecting accessories, owning multiple cameras, and attempting every new craze in photography. He emphasized simple, high-quality equipment and technical excellence. Certainly serious photographers, amateur or professional, needed proper equipment and materials to make superb images of whatever struck them as worth photographing, but a surfeit of equipment, especially films, paradoxically harmed most photographers, who lugged expensive gear and material which they rarely explored fully and which frequently disappointed them. By 1923 the Bee Meter came not only with a direction manual offering dials for new film types but a sophisticated folder providing numerical values for a wide variety of film produced in Britain, Europe, and the United States. His firm provided data for some 235 different films as a matter of corporate policy, but Watkins himself thought manufacturers had overwhelmed photographers with film, gadgets, and advertising. The last bothered Watkins more each year, since it shoved photographers toward a narrow range of subjects, most of which moved fast or rewarded only snapshot attention in full light. Watkins argued for discrimination and nuance. He claimed that quality photography heightened visual acuity and facilitated serendipity, but people needed solitude to make photographs deliberately.

Calculating exposure taxed and often overtaxed many photographers, especially those determined to record subjects beyond the purview of most photographic manufacturers.[10] While some experts advised making a series of exposures using different shutter speeds and apertures, most photographers countered that the bracketing technique proved exorbitantly expensive. Until the invention of the electronic light meter in the early 1930s, photographers used Watkins sensitized-paper Bee Meter (or one of the less expensive models he manufactured for people determined to make snapshots only, usually at the beach in summer sunlight) or one of three other sorts of devices.[11]

Into the 1930s Zeiss Ikon manufactured the Diaphot. The thin, disk-shaped device smacked of magic. On its front the photographer found a five-sided star; under the pentagram he found an opening, and above it a scale of f-stops and exposure times that varied by types of plates arranged in German Scheiner film-speed notation. On the other side he found an eyepiece. The device worked simply and accurately, once the photographer grew accustomed to reading its scale after looking through the eyepiece at his subject, and rotating the disks until the subject seemed illuminated by the light of the full moon. The Diaphot, named because it "dialed light," proved quicker to use than the sensitized-paper meters Watkins and his competitors manufactured, but it demanded a wary accuracy. Brilliant moonlight meant one thing to one photographer and something else to another. The eerie illumination served to indicate approximate shutter speed and aperture, but Zeiss Ikon made little provision for upgrading the unit as new films appeared. The Diaphot sold well in the United States, but only photographers who read German made sense of the nuanced tables that converted daytime views into sublunar images.[12]

Well into the 1930s other photographers used the expensive Posograph, advertised by its Paris manufacturer as "a simple automatic calculator for solving the problem of correct exposure in photography." About the size of a small paperback book but only a quarter-inch thick, the device contains a series of gears and levers sandwiched between two labeled sides along which pointers move. After setting one pointer along a scale of "Exposure According to Emulsion Speed" (the one thing the manufacturer could assume any photographer would know was the film loaded in the camera) and perhaps next the shutter speed, the photographer set other pointers at his discretion, moving one along a chart labeled "State of the Sky," another along "Month," a third along "Time by the Sun." Each chart offered many choices: "Overcast Grey Sky" and "Blue with White Clouds" or "May–August" or "7 a.m.–5 p.m." On the reverse side, the photographer found other charts and choices, most with pointers. He could make interior estimates according to numbers and kinds of windows, including French doors and oriels, quality of light outside the windows, the distance of his indoor subjects from the windows, and even the color of the flooring, "Dark or Red" through light blue to white. Sometimes the photographer had to flip over the device and reset some pointers in succession, especially when doing close-up portraits indoors adjacent to windows, but in the end the interlocked set of levers moved other pointers until one indicated the correct aperture setting. The thin, elegant Posograph won the Silver Medal at the Turin International Exhibition in 1923.

It remains an astonishingly accurate device, albeit one intended to work best at the approximate latitude of Paris and London. Its tables include one for Autochrome color photography, and its ingenious, hidden mechanism can be recalibrated for emulsion speeds its manufacturer anticipated might be introduced. It endures as the best proof that Watkins estimated correctly how badly so many determined, well-to-do photographers analyzed light. "All that is necessary is to set the pointers to the appropriate positions, and then read the exposure time indicated by the point on the cursor corresponding to the speed of the emulsion used," the directions lie. "The simplicity of this operation prevents those mistakes which so frequently arise when making an exposure, after the photographer has had to concentrate his attention to the adjustments of the camera."[13] The last comment might concern focusing knobs, but the other directions and the device itself suggest otherwise. The Posograph forces a photographer to look at parts of a composition beyond those on which his attention concentrates and in looking systematically analyze direct and reflected light according to angle, intensity, saturation, and even hue. It presumes photographers owning expensive, technically advanced and complicated cameras who see subjects rather than the fall of light on those subjects. Its levers work, but their structured operation indicates a nuanced authoritarianism as accurately as one cursor indicates aperture.[14] It forces operators to distinguish between "Full Sunlight" and "Dazzling," something almost as difficult as evaluating brilliant moonlight.

Into the 1930s manufacturers struggled with the exposure-reckoning issue. In 1931, for example, *Photo-Era* reported on the new Dremo meter, "designed to force proper use." Like many other "picture vision" instruments in which the user viewed the scene while or before measuring the ambient light, the Dremo simplified the calculation problem while complicating the actual viewing problem. Having the image in view while adjusting the meter "presents almost insurmountable difficulties, due to the inability to focus both eye and attention upon two objects simultaneously," commented the reviewer, a problem worsened because the image disappeared as the device calculated the reading.[15] The Dremo engineers indeed tried to force users to use the meter the one correct way, even arranging the viewing lever so that the left hand obscured the view of the left eye and caused users to direct attention at the view through the meter. In the end, the Diaphot, Dremo, and other devices measured only light reflected from the subject, not that falling on the subject, and offered scant provision for measuring what Watkins called "the worst illuminated surfaces."

Other manufacturers created dial calculators intended to train photographers to realize ambient light rather than rely on picture-vision meters. Kodak manufactured a number of plastic "exposure calculators," although the Johnson Company produced some of the most nuanced inexpensive ones. In practiced hands, the Bakelite-plastic calculators worked wonders.

Kodak calculators produced for British photographers came preset for exposures at fifty degrees north latitude: the back of each calculator included a chart that presented Greenwich Mean Time and British Standard Time, time of day according to month, and weather, the last chopped into four segments, "bright sun," "hazy sun," "dull," and "very dull." The photographer dialed the back of the unit to first show the speed of film (measured in the British Standard format) against the month and time of day, then set the derived number against one of the four weather slots, then turned over the device. He then dialed the number obtained on the back against one of eight subject settings ranging from "open sea—clouds" to "normal subjects, streets, groups in the open" to "in heavy shade, in woods, little direct sunlight," and then read in a crescent-shaped window the appropriate combinations of shutter speed and aperture.

Watkins averred that photographers could make superb images in the most shadowy of places, especially along the old ways he frequented in middle and old age. His interest in landscape antiquities often led him to the most overgrown locales, especially places in deep forest or in valleys, and he argued that in such places a tripod might be necessary for the long exposures his Bee Meter indicated.

Far off the ordinary byways explored by so many writers of British travel books, Watkins stumbled into discovery on June 21, 1921. With characteristic diffidence, he acknowledged that coincidence might explain the lines he found in the landscape, but he marshaled much evidence, including many photographs, to the contrary. He published *The Old Straight Track: Its Mounds, Beacons, Moats, Sites, and Mark Stones* in 1925 and stunned academic archaeologists. Unlike W. H. Hudson and R. Hippisley Cox, whose work Watkins knew well and quoted in defense of his own, he failed to defer to recognized experts. He argued in favor of glamour.

Some of his landscape photographs reveal the faintest of near-straight paths running for miles through the English rural landscape. So faint that they appeared only at certain seasons and under certain light and weather conditions, the paths suggested the existence of a prehistoric civilization unknown to experts.

"The outdoor man, away on a cross-country tramp, taking in the uplands, lingering over his midday sandwich on the earthwork of some hilltop camp, will look all round 'to get the lay of the land,'" wrote Watkins. "He will first pick out the hill points: this one bare to the top, another marked by a clump of trees, or less frequently by a single one." Exactly as Fanshawe and the squire in M. R. James's short story look about them, the outdoor man looks around, notices, and then hikes on, often following the oldest of the old ways, barely traceable tracks leading in very straight lines. "A trackway is a path across country for man and horse, often with no more structure than made by the users' feet, but perhaps stoned or 'pitched' in soft places," he asserted in his preface, before warning that his subject "is not that of Roman roads."[16]

In later years Watkins said little about his moment of discovery. However immensely fond of hiking, of locating and studying outdoor antiquities, and of photographing what intrigued him no matter the weather, he seemed to understand the moment in very simple terms. After his death, his son suggested that he may have been studying a topographical map at the time, or perhaps making a photograph of the path ahead of him across open country. He may have had the map in hand to clarify what he saw in the viewfinder of his camera as he adjusted exposure settings. What he saw at first perplexed him mightily, because it contradicted all that he had read, especially in books elucidating the disused roads and ways of Britain.

"My main theme is the alignment across miles of country of a great number of objects, or sites of objects, of prehistoric antiquity," he stated. "Such alignments are either facts beyond the possibility of accidental coincidence or they are not." *The Old Straight Track* offered the strongest imaginable case for design. Before the Bronze Age, ancient Britons laid out what he first called *ley lines* running scores, perhaps hundreds, of miles, and intersecting at Stonehenge and similar sites. Watkins suggested that readers use government topographical maps to check his conclusions, but he insisted on fieldwork. "It is surprising how many mounds, ancient stones, and earthworks are to be found which are not marked, even on the large-scale maps." In the end, in an appendix remarkably like his photography books in precision and tone, he concluded that "it is detective rather than surveying work in the field. But there are plenty of unrecorded finds to be made following a ley." A motorist or cyclist moving along a straight stretch of road should look ahead whenever the road turns: often some trace of a path continues straight into the distance. "A genuine ley hits the crossroads or road junctions as if by magic," and often the examiner finds a mark stone indicating the crossing even if the ley line or disused path is nearly obliterated. "It is almost laughable to find where a ley crosses a road, even if diagonally, how often there is a field gate on each side for it to go through. Field entrances remain unchanged for centuries, and at the first enclosure no doubt the entrance would be at an old track." Unlike archaeologists and other scholars, and most unlike Hudson, Cox, Belloc, Edward Thomas, and the other champions of following old ways, Watkins had descried lines along which no one walked, or had walked for centuries, perhaps for well more than a thousand years.[17]

He found them by looking at light. "Faint traces of ancient track or earthwork are most easily seen when the sun is low on one side—in late evening." Watkins told readers to look especially closely in winter, when leafless trees allow longer views and the sun shines at low angles. "Sun shining on one side and very low down is an ideal condition."[18] Almost certainly, Watkins made his discovery not because of his interest in antiquities or even because of his interest in photography. He found the alignments because for fifty years he had been utterly fascinated with noticing, realizing, and evaluating the fall of light on places and things.

The Old Straight Track appeared at a critical moment in modern British cultural history. In the years following the Great War, many people roved about the countryside, marshaling geographic, linguistic, and historical knowledge to make sense of what they had observed closely.[19] Tolkien's fascination with footpaths, especially ones carrying multiple dialect names, and with archaic designations of barrows and other monuments, thrived within a much larger enterprise.[20] In 1929, having already made a reputation with *Unknown Kent, Unknown Dorset,* and similar books, Donald Maxwell published *A Detective in Kent: Landscape Clues to the Discovery of Lost Seas,* recounting his tramps along the seacoast and explaining his method of analyzing landscape.

Maxwell suggested that the "Royal Academy should have its Landscape Interrogation Department," since anyone who observed the landscape closely in his wandering discovered far more than he might learn about in libraries. Archival research gave Maxwell only more reasons to keep hiking. "Why is the road that leads from Sarre into the centre of Thanet called Gore Street, and why is Birchington in old maps written as Gore End?" asking rhetorically the sort of question that evolved from studying period maps or listening to locals. After looking over the ground very carefully, and finding meadows and farms where ships once sailed, Maxwell concluded that "the wedge-shaped insertion of the sea or marshland into a piece of rising country might be a gore, and Gore Street would be the street that rises from the gore." By using ancient maps and other manuscript sources, by paying very close attention to dialect terminology, and by hiking extremely precisely, Maxwell traced what had once been the harbors Roman ships had used. "In this voyage of discovery on the lost waters of the Wantsum I should like as far as possible to steer not so much by knowledge of the existing charts as by the dead reckoning of landscape observation and nautical place-name clues." Like many of his contemporaries, the well-educated, very precise Maxwell encountered relics. "I have sometimes made valuable finds on account of this unlettered hunger for good things when the rich in archaeology have been sent empty away," he philosophized about his looking-around studies.[21]

Maxwell illustrated his book with sketches and watercolors, and like Watkins he had an acute eye for light, remarking, for example, the way "the slanting light of the morning casting the shadows of small willows across this little cutting made it seem more than ever likely to have been a place of ships."[22] And like Watkins, he argued that some of the ancient earthworks he encountered could not have been built by the Danes, or by locals defending themselves against Danish invasion, or by any other historical population. Maxwell focused on historical ruins, but he seems to have learned the lesson Watkins offered. Just looking around revealed much that archaeologists had somehow ignored or that contradicted what they announced. Listening to locals sometimes raised questions philologists had not yet answered.

Often Maxwell recorded the faint sounds of automobile traffic in the distance, on highways and even byways thronged by summer vacationers only several miles from the old ways he traced. As he walked what he called "ghost roads," he recognized that sometimes he found nearly disused routes diverging from far older straight ways. "The coach-road, however, that entered Sarre a little farther to the north is a deflection of this straight line," he mused. He kept looking, for he realized that in prehistoric times the track lay straight, and that "it would be reasonable therefore to expect a conspicuous landmark of some sort to be placed on the high ground of Sarre as a leading mark."[23] Maxwell had accepted

Watkins's discovery, and had begun to look for straight lines in landscape, especially in early morning and late evening when low-angle sunlight illuminated them.

In *The Old Straight Track* Watkins argued that some prehistoric people had done more than produce straight tracks often punctuated by hilltop standing stones or beacon-fire sites. Along the ley lines they sited their most sacred spots, Stonehenge included. He averred that dialect retained traces of the line making, noting that uneducated farm folk used "dodman" for "snail" in a way suggesting their forebears had seen a resemblance between the snail's antennae and the two staffs carried by dodmen, the surveyors of the ancient alignments.[24] Despite sustained, scornful assault by archaeologists—one journal refused to print a paid advertisement for the book—within a few years *The Old Straight Track* had convinced many readers. Both laymen and scholars began hiking, maps and cameras in hand, looking for the light fitfully illuminating traces of ways long abandoned.

Watkins contented himself with demonstrating that the alignments existed. He mapped them as he hiked, and he photographed them, often returning many times to record the light falling exactly as it must to make the lines discernible. Until his death he refused to speculate about their origin.

Many of his contemporaries realized that the lines linked hills and other rising ground known to antiquarians, philologists, and folklorists as topography important in the old faerie belief systems.[25] *Sithein* denoted a faerie hill of precisely rounded or conical shape and often especially green, even in midsummer. *Tolman* meant a much smaller hummock, and *cnoc* designated a knoll, sometimes called a *knowe* by rural people.[26] In the years immediately following Watkins's first published photographs, philologists and folklorists grudgingly accepted the likelihood that dialect words and local legends concerning faerie might somehow bear on the lines Watkins and others discerned.

Beyond Britain others speculated. By 1929 Wilhelm Teudt had found similar alignments in parts of Germany, but he called them "holy lines," since he found both early churches and pagan sites oriented along them.[27] Others quickly followed his lead, arguing that in Germany, at least, the lines indicated a prehistoric, northern-focused religion based on the sun and stars.[28] Dedicated amateurs attempted to prove that prehistoric people knew techniques to measure both small objects and long distances across uneven country, and that such knowledgeable people must have had even greater knowledge subsequently lost.[29] The concept of lost knowledge from a once-great culture quickly contorted almost all inquiry: enthusiastic amateurs earned only the scorn of archaeologists.

While Watkins continued his work on historic antiquities—in 1930 he published *The Old Standing Crosses of Herefordshire*—he continued to research alignments, publishing *Archaic Tracks round Cambridge* in 1932, shortly before his death. He cheerfully admitted that many prehistoric sites might be aligned purely by coincidence, but he thought not all alignments could be explained so easily. He found alignments based on astronomical patterns and cardinal-point awareness, and while he enjoyed and supported the amateur groups organized to hunt leys, he chose to abandon the term he first used in favor of "straight track." By 1935 research and pseudoresearch had produced an inward-looking hobbyist enterprise: within several years German researchers had linked alignments with the tenets of National Socialism.[30] Much of the old-way looking-around effort, and especially that derived from Watkins's photographic discovery, grew emotional.[31]

In 1936 Violet Mary Firth charged the old straight tracks with magical energy. Writing under the pseudonym Dion Fortune, she produced *The Goat-Foot God*, a sophisticated novel in which an upper-class Englishman decides to re-create pagan rituals to divert his attention from the death of his adulterous wife and best friend, both killed in a motor car accident. What begins as a diffident, hit-or-miss effort by a bookish, well-educated man to buy a house in the country and stage rituals in which he does not believe becomes increasingly tricky when he hires Mona Wilton to help him find a suitable house.

"There are certain places that are more suitable than others for what you want to do, just as there are some places where you can grow rhododendrons, and some where you can grow roses," she tells him, as she shows him a map of southern England and points to "a centre of the old sun-worship." Hugh Paston looks at the map and looks sideways at the beautiful young woman. "Now draw a line from Avebury to any other place where there are the remains of ancient worship, and anywhere along that line will be good for what you want. If you want to wake the Old Gods, then you have to go where the Old Gods are accustomed to be worshipped." Paston asks why he should not go to Stonehenge or some similar ruin, and Wilton says that tourists have spoiled such places, that he would "get no seclusion," and that "the lines of force between the power centres are much better for your purpose." Firth might as well have been speaking of ground radio.[32]

In a few pages Wilton tells Paston that alignments link power centers and that along alignments pulse mysterious but powerful energies. "You see, where people have been in the habit of reaching out towards the Unseen, they wear a kind of track, and it's much easier to go out that way," she explains, before equating the Old Gods with "the Freudian subconscious." All Paston must do is place his ruler on the large-scale ordnance map, "look for standing stones and hammer-pools," and then "sight from one to another, and get a straight line across country." Wilton explains that a prehistoric figure carved in the turf of the chalk downs in southern England holds two staffs because the figure is a dodman, and the staffs are his sightingstaffs for making the alignments. "These lines criss-cross all over England just like a crystalline structure. You can work them out on any large-scale ordnance map by means of the place-names and standing stones and earthworks." The following morning Wilton and Paston drive off to look at houses near old straight tracks, and Wilton quietly watches Paston drive. "One can learn a great deal about a man by watching the way he handles a car," Firth asserts. Wilton learns enough to realize that Paston is capable of being guided into serious energy-tapping effort.[33]

The Goat-Foot God depicts many of the techniques Watkins used: landscape exploration away from byways and old ways, close scrutiny of maps to discern patterns missed by archaeologists, and precise linguistic analysis of place-names. Watkins rummaged deeply in the Oxford English Dictionary, and while he often drew incorrect conclusions from the roots of place-names, he realized the importance of local dialect and small-scale spoken usage in any effort to reveal nearly forgotten alignment information. He repeatedly suggested talking to rural locals, especially elderly people likely to use terms fast disappearing in print-media sources and never recognized in cinema and on radio. Published a year before Tolkien's The Hobbit, The Goat-Foot God reflects a fast-deepening interest not only in the prehistoric enigmas Watkins found and photographed but also in the ways such enigmas might be examined and used by all sorts of inquirers, especially those willing to move off old ways and learn what locals know. But by the time Firth wrote her novel of moral misadventure and decay, alignment hunters had found a technique she ignored.

On the last page of The Old Straight Track Watkins writes simply that "the method in the future is an aeroplane flight along the ley." One researcher, he noted, had already pointed out that "faint tracks are to be seen from the air" which remain "invisible on the ground." The aviator Osbert Guy Stanhope Crawford had flown a fighter plane in the Great War, and the year before Watkins's book appeared had demonstrated in his Air Survey and Archaeology that the air view often revealed much that on-the-ground analysis could not.[34] Watkins extolled the significance of Crawford's work. He knew that aerial photography had begun to reveal military secrets and industrial patterns hitherto unknown, and he assumed that high-level observation and photography would reveal much about alignments.[35]

Aerial photography transformed British archaeology immediately after World War I. Crawford enlisted in the Royal Army Topographical Section in 1914. His undergraduate degree in geography eventually leveraged him into the gunner's seat in Royal Flying Corps airplanes, then into reconnaissance work using hand-held cameras. While at home recuperating from injuries suffered when Germans shot down his plane, he began writing about the depth of human history revealed in reconnaissance images. After the war he entered the British Ordnance Survey, devoted himself to hiking and bicycling around rural Britain, and began revising official maps to show sites of archaeological value. He quickly enlisted the help of outdoorsmen, especially walkers, published *Notes for Beginners* through the Ordnance Survey in 1921, and independently produced a so-called period map of Roman Britain. The map sold out immediately, thus convincing the Ordnance Survey to fund Crawford's Archaeology Office heavily, and spawning an official cooperative agreement with the Royal Air Force, which henceforth forwarded copies of its aerial photographs to Crawford.[36]

In 1922 RAF training photographs revealed the existence of entire ancient systems of field boundaries or lynchets. Crawford reported that the right light enabled photographers to record the visible outlines of communal landscapes 1,500 years old and almost unnoticeable on the ground. A year later other aerial photographs revealed the alignment of the eastern branch of the Stonehenge Avenue leading away from the stone circle to the Avon: in a dry summer, grain grew so slightly differently over the ancient way that it reflected light just differently enough for the emulsion to record the track. In 1928 Crawford produced *Wessex from the Air*, a book of sumptuous photographs he introduced by noting that "on a June morning before breakfast the greater part of Salisbury Plain is seen to be covered with the banks of abandoned Celtic fields, but afterwards they fade into the common light of day." In the Depression amateur aviators aided Crawford. Using a single-shot camera he built on his own from aluminum and aimed more obliquely than military photographers, George Allen recorded the existence of great circles, the remains of prehistoric wood-henge monuments and villages, traceable only in certain wet or dry springs and summers when the light fell perfectly on cereal crops. Image after image recorded the juxtaposition of modern roads, fields, structures, and railroads against Iron Age ditches above which grain turned darker immediately after a light rain and against the ruts of the Icknield Way.

Aerial photography began to show that many Britons lived adjacent to or literally atop landscape constituents nearly invisible on the ground. The residents of suburban villas "cannot see what the aerial viewer can see," Crawford asserted. "It is a disjuncture of perspective that has revealed the ghost. And yet here it is, this ghost; and the uncanny thing is that while it may have been unperceived, it was there all along." In Crawford's mind, the photographs revealed what only a handful of observant walkers had glimpsed: he termed them "heralds of innumerable queer resurrections."[37] But the camera did nothing "simply." Often airborne photographers flew repeatedly over a locale, making image after image as the twilight lengthened above sites just dry or moist enough for crops to signal accurately or lit momentarily just enough for "ancient pack-trails, roads, and hollow-ways" to reveal themselves. Forested land often defeated the best aerial efforts.[38]

On the ground, Crawford struggled to document what aerial reconnaissance located, and he eventually understood how much seasonal light led to success: he learned all the lessons frost, cloudiness, and bright sun taught Watkins. In January in Scotland the cold troubled him, but he argued that "the low, yellow sunlight in midwinter is ample compensation for the slight discomforts endured, and ideal for photography." He avoided much of Wales after May because bracken masked the nuances he sought, and in general he preferred dry afternoons in March before grass and other low-lying vegetation obscured the traces he hoped to discern and photograph.[39]

Unemployment lessened as the Depression ended and the military build-up escalated, and many alignment hunters either devoted themselves to different interests or lacked the time to keep seeking alignments. With Watkins's death in 1935, amateurs lost their central organizing personage. Aerial photography efforts lapsed, and not until the aftermath of World War II did they strengthen Watkins's hypothesis, in part by casting doubt on hitherto accepted topographical-history issues. The Cambridge Air Surveys debuted with a study by David Knowles and J. K. S. St. Joseph, the latter curator in air photography at the University of Cambridge, entitled *Monastic Sites from the Air* in 1952. Six years later appeared the next volume, *Medieval England: An Aerial Survey,* by Maurice Beresford and St. Joseph. A year earlier Beresford had published his seminal *History on the Ground: Six Studies in Maps and Landscapes.* Beresford relied heavily on the growing collection of aerial photographs housed at Cambridge, but he reproduced none in a book "specifically designed for the inquirer without wings." He loved to hike, but suffered from "a chronic inability to drive a car," and he hired a photographer to record some landscape components that illustrated his arguments especially well.[40] All the photographs seem to have been made adjacent to well-surfaced roads, and indeed the book scarcely mentions old ways, except in discussions of field boundaries. It wholly ignores alignments because it focuses on archival-based history, beginning roughly in the tenth century and moving toward the twentieth. Aerial photography did little to advance any post-Watkins-era study of alignments, and only a few amateur inquirers continued hiking, poring over period maps, and making photographs. Experts either laughed or ignored them.

More than a lack of funding may explain the slowness with which landscape historians adapted their research to the evidence available in aerial photographs made during World War II, often by military personnel practicing over England, then by government-funded surveyors. By the middle 1980s aerial surveys revealed a thousand hitherto unknown archaeological sites annually: the rate of discovery simply overwhelmed efforts at interpretation, and sometimes even cataloging.[41] Moreover, many photographs raised troubling issues about the landscape made by prehistoric Britons. Beneath the "ancient" landscape lay others, at least some sophisticated in ways outside accepted chronologies. Not until 1996 did the series publish Timothy Darvill's *Prehistoric Britain from the Air: A Study of Space, Time, and Society.* Yet when Beresford published *History on the Ground,* at least some researchers apparently noticed lines confounding established scholarly understanding. And they had photographs recording what they observed in momentary falls of light.

Aerial photography almost always reveals soil and crop clues. In newly plowed fields, experienced air-photo interpreters discern the slightly darker soil indicating paths buried beneath soil turned over annually for a thousand years after the abandonment of the paths. On hard-packed soil far beneath that disturbed by modern agricultural implements, crops grow shorter and usually lighten in color slightly earlier near harvest. Over ditches filled in a thousand years ago, field crops tend to grow taller and ripen later. Almost never are such subtle changes apparent to anyone on the ground, no matter how experienced. Even many air photos prove useless. The same area—often a very small area—must be photographed repeatedly at different seasons, at different times of day, and under all sorts of weather conditions if researchers are to discern landscape features almost always wreathed in obscurity.[42]

Unfortunately, as Watkins well knew, the same typically proves true for descrying alignments from the ground. He explained that photographing alignments running adjacent to the elevated walls of prehistoric ruins, especially semipermanent fortified encampments, demanded both luck and diligence. "Such camps, with their thickly wooded banks, bring the photographer to despair," he remarked of waypoints along many alignments. "The winter, with its light of low elevation, and with an absence of leaves, is by far the best season, and the lovely December day on which this last photograph was taken gave an opportunity long hoped for." Often Watkins made a photograph of what he suspected might be a fragment of an alignment, knowing full well that the quality of light might change and the view vanish in an instant. Now and then, when the fall of light revealed something ordinarily obscured, educated scoffers apologized. One country squire came to Watkins on November 19, 1924, to "say that he had just seen from the foot of the hill looking up a newly ploughed field, the ancient road as a dark mark going up toward the end mounds." The next morning Watkins hurried to the scene, and the landowner sent a farm boy with him to point out the precise place to stand. By then the harrow had obliterate three-fourths of the line previously discernible against the furrows, but "the dark mark, still to be seen at the top, confirmed the accuracy of the information, and the ploughman at work harrowing on the field had also noticed the dark line." So sometimes Watkins simply photographed the landscape across which he suspected or projected an ancient alignment: he hoped that the image might reveal more than he noticed in the open air, and if it did not, might at least record what could not be seen at some times of the year under certain lighting. He knew that his research irritated many adherents of old-way exploration. He worried that few readers would accept his contention that "few and far between are the fragments remaining of present-day roads or tracks on the leys"; and he worried even more that what he saw one day might not be visible on another, or at another time of day or in another season.[43] Belloc, Cox, and other old-ways writers had no such concern, nor did Maxwell and other sophisticated analysts of historical ruins in larger landscape.

But despite his diffidence and his consistent self-effacement as an amateur inquirer, Watkins irritated everyone. He annoyed old-way experts who saw their subjects as the oldest roads in Britain, and he vexed Maxwell and others by asserting that alignments existed across landscapes where routine examination revealed nothing. Above all, he angered academic archaeologists, who disliked his ability to forecast where ruins might be found.

Predicting the route of alignments made the modest photographer-inquirer into a sort of magician. On several occasions Watkins predicted that cobbled paths ran straight beneath ponds and other bodies of water. Droughts and drainage efforts now and then lowered water levels just enough to reveal the three-foot-wide causeways Watkins insisted must exist. Other times he found waypoint stones buried under debris. Always he talked with farmhands, woodsmen, and children, and invariably he listened to their accounts of what might be alignments. Archaeologists at first scorned him, then announced that his so-called ley lines or old straight tracks must have been Roman built, and finally ignored him and his adherents completely.[44]

Through the 1950s Beresford and the other brilliant and common-sensical scholars who founded the field known now as *landscape history* or *landscape studies* simply ignored Watkins. But long after his death, Watkins's work remained a force, albeit one known mostly by its photographs and the gores it made in scholarship. In his 1955 *The Making of the English Landscape,* W. G. Hoskins devoted only fifteen pages to the pre-Roman landscape and avoided any mention of Watkins's hypotheses. He admitted that people who walked the landscape carefully ("and do not rush in utter blindness through it in a car") now and then encountered "a puzzling feature," that is, "the track, sometimes only a few feet wide, sometimes much broader, which begins suddenly on one side of a field-gate, runs between hedge-banks for several hundred yards, occasionally more, and then stops as suddenly as it began, debouching into a field and losing all identity forthwith." Hoskins insisted that most such "lanes" are not "trackways" but "are in fact ancient boundaries between two estates, sometimes medieval, sometimes Saxon or even Celtic." He ended his brief section on prehistory by asserting that while the explanation does not fit all such ways, "it explains those that appear to go nowhere in particular and to peter out without reason."[45] In his 1973 *English Landscapes* and his 1978 *One Man's England,* Hoskins added nothing to his brief statement of 1955, except to state that "in most parts of England *everything is older than we think.*" He admitted that some landscape elements might be three or four thousand years old, but he passed over them as quickly as he had twenty years earlier. Despite the last line of the preface to *English Landscapes,* a quotation from the eighteenth-century painter Constable he italicized, *"We see nothing till we truly understand it,"* Hoskins might as well have sped over the prehistoric British landscape in a very fast motorcar indeed.[46] Beresford, Hoskins, and other British landscape historians ignored Watkins, his photographs, and the alignments he discerned . . . as well as predicted.

Watkins distinguished between an old way and the vastly older old straight track. He knew very clearly why so many old ways seemed to stop for no reason. He almost certainly knew what a handful of his contemporaries suspected as well. The alignments he found suggested that a culture had destroyed its superior predecessor. As early as 1908, Walter Johnson suggested that scholars should look far deeper into a remote past likely to unsettle academic foundations, one glimpsed in folkloric survivals of ancient beliefs and knowledge best examined in remote rural places. His *Folk-Memory; or, The Continuity of British Archaeology* probed the scruffy edges of oral tradition that might reflect an unconscious "racial memory" which made sense of prehistoric ruins and long-lived beliefs, especially the belief in faerie. The bulk of the book originated in scrutinizing landscape constituents. "Here are set down the results of the spare time of years spent in tramping the country to investigate ancient churches, earthworks, roads, and monuments; in searching for stone implements; in jotting down notes concerning customs and folk-lore," Johnson wrote in his preface. He did not claim to understand much of what he found along the oldest roads and footpaths, but he knew that bits and pieces of landscape often correlated with dialect terms and even human physiognomy.[47] As late as 1973 Hoskins admitted that some prehistoric landscape elements defied description except in very old-fashioned terms. "At one time this was explained by what one called racial history," he wrote of regional differences in the earliest human settlements in Britain.[48] He offered no better term for issues Johnson understood as vital to making sense of what might not be a cheerful and continuous progress toward Victorian and Edwardian modernity, let alone the modern times of the 1970s. Evidence that Bronze Age people destroyed a far finer culture lay within walking distance of most thoughtful rural Britons, but Johnson only hinted at such, and Watkins, a most diffident and traditionally religious inquirer, never pushed the issue.

In the 1960s the issue exploded from its mid-1930s roots in *The Goat-Foot God* and other fantasy fiction. Firth may have known W. Y. Evans-Wentz's monumental *The Fairy Faith in Celtic Countries:* the massive volume appeared in 1911 and shaped the core of early twentieth-century anthropological inquiry. Evans-Wentz devoted much attention to collecting oral tradition; the Oxford University scholar later focused on Central Asia, translated the Tibetan *Book of the Dead,* and emphasized the necessity of hearing nuance precisely. In Ireland he found elderly rural people who still saw the world as opalescent symbol, and from them learned that faerie processions often traveled in straight lines through the nighttime landscape. "An Irish mystic and seer of great power, with whom I have often discussed the Fairy-Faith in its details, regards 'fairy paths' or 'fairy passes' as actual magnetic arteries, so to speak, through which circulates the earth's magnetism," Evans-Wentz noted in a footnote.[49] In 1911 he worked within anthropological frameworks sophisticated enough to order not only traditional material but the ways in which modern concepts interacted with very old ones. Magnetism, electricity, radio-wave transmission, X-rays, and other forces transforming twentieth-century Irish rural life dovetailed in complex ways with extremely old tales, especially about places and alignments. Whether or not Firth knew of *The Fairy Faith in Celtic Countries,* she undoubtedly knew that anthropologists and other academics realized that rural people had always fused tradition and modernity in ways that vexed scholars.

Detecting magnetic or electromagnetic flow using traditional techniques shaped a bit of alignment thinking in the late 1939s, as dowsers claimed to detect force fields running along alignments Watkins had photographed.[50] Reports of Chinese geomancy, particularly that called *feng shui* and especially the concept that vital energy flowed along the so-called dragon paths, had heartened European dowsers beginning in 1873, when E. J. Eitel published *Feng Shui.* Antiquarians and anthropologists tended to place dowsing and feng shui in similar categories.[51] In the late 1890s and after, however, electrical engineers and other technical experts began testing alignments for forces measurable using telegraphic and related metering. The Department of Terrestrial Magnetism at the Carnegie Institution in Washington, D.C., produced a series of studies that sketched patterns of flow across the planet. J. P. Ault's *Ocean Magnetic and Electric Observations* appeared in 1926, and thirteen years later another Carnegie researcher, John Adam Fleming, edited a tome entitled *Terrestrial Magnetism and Electricity.* Read mostly by electrical and radio engineers and by some amateur radio enthusiasts, the reports suggested that ground radio waves moved along specific alignments that varied according to the relative positions of the earth, sun, and moon and that they could sometimes be discerned by examining the plants growing along them. World War II terminated such research, but it produced the advanced aerial photography that changed the minds of archaeologists. Flying saucers changed mind-sets faster.

In 1961 alignment thinking made headlines when a former Royal Air Force pilot, Tony Wedd, argued that along many of the old straight tracks Watkins discerned flew the flying saucers Europeans had noticed throughout the 1950s. Wedd had considerable if sometimes odd supporting material for what he first worked out for himself using maps: he had a bit of background material too.[52] In 1956 an American named Buck Nelson published *My Trip to Mars, the Moon, and Venus* in which he claimed he had been kidnapped by space aliens who cruised above straight magnetic alignments crossing the earth. Two years later Aimé Michel published *Flying Saucers and the Straight Line Mystery,* which traces the routes taken by the UFOs observed across France: the flying saucers moved in straight lines easily plotted on topographical maps. That year too Carl Gustav Jung published his *Flying Saucers: A Modern Myth,* in which he argued that the spaceships reported from about 1947 on represented something neither true nor untrue according to modern science, but symbolized some need suffusing modern industrial societies struggling to comprehend the destructibility of the earth.[53] Other books appeared, sometimes self-published by individuals determined to record and publicize what they themselves had noticed.[54] Hollywood prospered from the fad, producing a number of films about extraterrestrial contact, most notably *The Day the Earth Stood Still,* a 1952 film connecting contact with nuclear weaponry. At least some academics saw the UFO furor as threatening public confidence not only in the military but in modern science, especially physics. As early as 1953 Harvard University Press published a book by Donald Howard Menzel, *Flying Saucers,* but it and similar volumes debunking UFOs accomplished little to reassure the public in the primacy of modern science.

However confused and often idiosyncratic, the first years of the UFO phenomenon focused attention on alignments as sources or conductors of power. No one knew much about UFOs, but anyone might map where observers noticed them. When Wedd published his *Skyways and Landmarks* in 1961, he reacquainted many Britons with Watkins's work and suggested that sensitive people might somehow feel the force fields along which the space aliens cruised. Some people saw UFOs. Others sensed their pathways.

For a decade after the middle 1950s, scientists in several fields made discoveries that profoundly shook popular understanding of modern science, history, and prehistory. In 1957 Derek J. de Solla Price published a seminal *Scientific American* article on the remains of a complex geared device built by the Greeks circa 80 B.C. Retrieved around 1901 from a shipwreck, the machine calculated astronomical movements in sophisticated ways astronomers considered modern.[55] In 1965 Gerald S. Hawkins published *Stonehenge Decoded,* a demonstration that prehistoric Britons worked accurate solar calculations.[56] Two years later, Alexander Thom demonstrated in *Megalithic Sites in Britain* that prehistoric people used not only Stonehenge but other sites for sophisticated astronomical observations.[57] The same year Hans E. Suess demonstrated the flaws marring carbon dating of many artifacts from archaeological sites, arguing that errors worsened over time.[58] Radiocarbon dating of very old artifacts often proved wrong: many artifacts were much older than scholars assumed. Nineteenth-century experts had understood Stonehenge to be the site of some solar observations, eighteenth-century scholars had assumed so, and just before the war one alignment-seeker preempted Hawkins.[59] In a book published in 1939, F. C. Tyler, a retired Royal Army officer, got very close to what scientists discerned twenty years later, but most copies of *The Geometrical Arrangement of Ancient Sites* vanished in the bombing of London. The 1960s discoveries of prehistoric precision calculation ability amazed most conservative researchers and shook the most basic assumptions historians had made about prehistoric Britain. Prehistory suddenly seemed far older and far more sophisticated than academics had dreamed, and Watkins's old-straight-track writing seemed prescient beyond words.

Into the uncertainty John Mitchell moved with immense energy. In 1967 he published *The Flying Saucer Vision* and then shifted from UFO studies to portraying an ancient lost civilization. *The View over Atlantis* galvanized thousands of amateur but educated inquirers even as academics scorned its vision of prehistoric people in touch with cultures beyond earth, and the British government kept secret a Ministry of Defense unit studying UFOs.[60] "The ley system may be actually invisible to those whose previous knowledge tells them that it cannot exist," Mitchell asserted, re-creating the alchemical envisioning framework Fludd and others had championed centuries earlier. He insisted that thoughtful people had to open their minds to potential discoveries that would transform archaeology, history, and above all physical science: they had to see acutely, and utterly differently than schools, cinema, and television suggested. "When Alfred Watkins experienced his extraordinary moment of clairvoyance in which the veins of the countryside appeared to stand out across the plains and hills, he saw or gained knowledge of something beyond the range of normal vision," Mitchell asserted. Perhaps Watkins connected with the force Mitchell insisted flowed along the alignments.[61] Perhaps Watkins proved sensitive to Od or something similar, especially during the moment of seeing light, figuring exposure, and making a photograph.

"We know that the whole surface of the earth is washed by a flow of energy known as the magnetic field. Like all other heavenly bodies, the earth is a great magnet, the strength and direction of its currents influenced by many factors, including the proximity and relative positions of the other spheres in the solar system chiefly the sun and moon," Mitchell insisted, before describing the twenty-seven-day fluctuation cycle of magnetic fields. Prehistoric Britons lived in places almost exactly different from modern centers of British population; perhaps in the hills and on the moors they connected with the magnetic flows they understood. According to Mitchell, when Hawkins revealed that the holes in Stonehenge stones worked as eclipse predictors, his thoughtful readers should have connected eclipses with interruptions in the magnetic energy flow. Bit by bit, Mitchell pieced together a picture of a prehistoric Britain far older than the schoolbook one, and one in which landscape mattered deeply, essentially magically. "Certain trees and plants were held sacred: mistletoe, the yew tree and the thorn, for example," Mitchell averred, and such plants "are invariably to be found growing over a blind spring or at a center of magnetic influence." Watkins's clairvoyance enabled glimpses of glamour that rural people understood in the patterns of bird flight or the distribution of cows in certain fields. "Migrating birds, whose flights were closely observed by the natural magicians of antiquity, follow lines of magnetic current: so do animals and insects."[62] Mitchell did very little more than recount the findings of Ault, Fleming, and other terrestrial-magnetism researchers who corroborated much of what Watkins suggested.

By 1974 magnetic current research seemed to support Mitchell's hypotheses while reinforcing interest in Od.[63] In that year appeared *The Kirlian Aura: Photographing the Galaxies of Life*, a selection of essays focused on the work of Semyon and Valentina Kirlian in the Soviet Union. The Kirlians had developed a technique in which high-voltage spark discharges converted the nonelectrical properties of an object into electrical properties recorded on photographic film. In the early 1970s Kirlian photography struck some scientists as posing problems similar to those of acupuncture. Just as Western physicians did not know whether acupuncture worked or how it worked if indeed it did, neither did scientists understand what the Kirlian process recorded or how exactly the recording process worked.[64] Its findings seemed akin to Von Reichenbach's, recalled questions raised in the years followed the discovery of X-rays, and again tested scientist willingness to envision in ways Fludd and others once argued led to valid discovery.[65] Today's readers of *The Kirlian Aura* typically vacillate between scorn and grudging acceptance that the book foreshadows modern MRI and other diagnostic medical-imaging technology, especially in an era when magnetic therapy seems to alleviate migraine headaches.[66] In the early 1970s, however, some astronomy-archaeology inquirers wondered if the Kirlian process did not record best in certain places, perhaps along specific alignments. Others wondered if some sensitive people might not discern alignments as Watkins had or prove more sensitive to other forces when walking along them.[67]

Readers learned that magicians and animals followed old straight tracks elsewhere than in Britain, perhaps especially in the Andes and in the United States near the Chaco Canyon ruins in New Mexico. A flurry of books on alignments followed, most by amateur field researchers but some by dowsers and other specialists.[68] In the late 1960s the amateurs struggled to shed the unsavory fragments that clung to prewar alignment research, perhaps especially the way Teudt and other Germans slid their research into a focus of the SS-funded German Ancestral Heritage Institute.[69] Watkins himself used a phrase that unnerved post-1960s alignment researchers: he said that his discovery in 1921 came like "a flood of ancestral memory."[70] The phrase evoked notions of what Walter Johnson had called "racial continuity" in his 1908 *Folk-Memory* and what Evans-Wentz termed "subtle forces so strange and mysterious that to know them they must be felt" in *Fairy Faith* three years later.[71]

It irritated many 1960s urban Britons aware that they lacked the lifelong experience with a small section of rural landscape Watkins claimed furthered his discovery.[72] Despite occasional blunt statements like those made in 1976 by one British exorcist that during the 1926 British General Strike the Soviets tried to send psychic energy along some vaguely defined energy line into Britain, alignment research soon shed most of its negative characteristics and much of its perceived zaniness too.[73] Most alignment researchers, even the amateurs intrigued by Mitchell's theses, dismissed the nuttiness of Erich von Däniken's 1968 *Chariots of the Gods: Unsolved Mysteries of the Past,* a convoluted argument that extraterrestrials sometimes originated or shaped human culture in prehistory. By 1980, following the publication of Tony Morrison's *Pathways to the Gods,* interest in alignments had become worldwide. Morrison used photographs made by the Bolivian Air Force a decade earlier to demonstrate the existence of old straight tracks across much of the Bolivian Andes, some running perfectly straight for twenty miles.[74] By then no one doubted the existence of the alignments, but many alignment hunters doubted that UFOs or Od flowed along them: they focused on discerning the alignments and now and then enjoying what might or might not be some frisson of energy, Od or otherwise.[75]

Nowadays line hunters continue to connect the dots, especially in the British landscape, and their efforts suffuse contemporary fantasy writing, as they have since the late 1960s.[76] "His genius was exactly the opposite of whatever kind of genius it was that built earthworks that tapped the secret yet beneficent forces of the leylines," writes Terry Pratchett in the opening of *Interesting Times.*[77] Pratchett's best-selling Discworld series satirizes modern politics, cultural forces, and intellectual positions nowadays unthinkingly accepted. Readers who laugh at the misadventures of the Ankh-Morpork police force in *Guards! Guards!* as it struggles with an affirmative action policy advancing the interests of trolls or the dwarfs in *The Truth* founding a newspaper that offends ruling elites can too easily miss Pratchett's vivisecting of modern scholarship.[78] The vampire photographer retained by the newspaper dwarfs explains that he makes photographs and is inventing *obscurographs* too: the latter are images made with "*true* darkness," the light on the other side of darkness which reveals things powerful entities want hidden.[79] Watkins might just have well have called his alignment images *obscurographs*. They illuminated something on the far side of history, archaeology, and anthropology, endured the scorn of established academics, then gleamed in the findings of electrical engineers, aerial photographers, and others who anticipated the reconceptualization of Stonehenge and its builders.

Shop theory suffused alignment research from its beginning. Watkins and his successors muddled along, noting carefully the fall of light in all seasons and at all times of day, and walking repeatedly along the alignment fragments they momentarily discerned and sometimes photographed. Their enterprise involved almost entirely visual research. They looked, sometimes found, and then followed, typically without any previous training in archaeology, anthropology, or history. Many followed Watkins's example and never cared much about causes and meanings; most found satisfaction in discovering another fragment of alignment, not in discovering why some long-vanished people surveyed the line. They gloried in their ability to predict where alignments might be found and then struggled mightily to record what they found in places they predicted. After the 1960s they walked and photographed knowing their forebears had trumped established academics.

Archaeologists worry that alignment researchers often carry shovels to dig around spots where they think a mark-stone ought to be located. Watkins eventually carried a shovel along with his camera and tripod, and the present-day effort merely extends his. But more than concern for disturbed artifacts echoes in archaeologist voices. Experts condemn shop-theory amateurs who unearth artifacts in places the amateurs call predictable, and they dislike research that proceeds visually in such seemingly casual ways.

Watkins knew that finding alignments in modern British cities proved difficult, so he always watched workmen digging up sewer lines, but he did his best work in rural places, often regions long abandoned. He visualized networks of alignments. Now early twentieth-first-century alignment hunters value the work of Robert Fludd, John Dee, and other mystics who advanced their philosophical arguments visually.[80] Alignment hunters practice their own form of visual magic, although they chuckle at the phrase. They make the landscape answer questions but not speak. They put questions to the landscape and interpret the signs they received in reply.[81] Few know much about semiotics; most do not even know the word. But they understand signs.

Alignment hunters believe (often fiercely) that the fall of light on a place on a given day of the year in particular weather has as much significance as any archival material.[82] They believe in visual magic, in glamour. The fall of light reveals a trace of something almost vanished that challenges photographers, even those using robotic cameras inside Egyptian pyramids, which some researchers think once focused magnetic energy.[83] In the twilight of certain days of the year, sometimes with calendars adjusted for the precession of the equinoxes, and sometimes at noon or moonlit midnights, photographers struggle to record the light that makes place momentarily glamorous. Not only must they identify alignments and nodes, they must also descry the light itself. Sometimes they use old dial calculators that force them to factor in the latitude in which they make exposures. Sometimes they squint and hope the autoexposure sensor records what they see. Often they use period cameras requiring manual setting according to the sort of looking which gave Watkins his visionary glance.

The 1970s 35 mm camera fad floated atop coupled exposure meters. Well-heeled photographers squinted through viewfinders not only to compose scenes but to watch matched needles and circles move in correlation to light-meter indications and f-stop settings.[84] Through-the-lens metering promised freedom from calculating filter factors when setting exposure and perfect exposures both, especially if cameras featured spot-metering capabilities.[85] In the final moment before the 35 mm point-and-shoot era, only a handful of photographers decried coupled metering as dulling photographer sensitivity to light. They argued that photographers who used hand-held electronic meters, the old dial meters, or no meter at all learned more about lighting than those who trusted the new systems.[86] Such photographers found some subjects challenging but certainly not off-putting. In 1938 Israel Holtzman told *Popular Science* readers how to photograph aerial fireworks with Kodak box cameras, and then how to print the negatives.[87] In the 1970s fireworks displays—and lightning—vexed owners of sophisticated 35 mm cameras, who discovered that coupled meters responded too slowly to make quality images.[88] Others found that meters did poorly at twilight, when aimed at the full moon, across snow, sunlit sand, ice, and waves, and through smoke and fog. Exactly as Watkins had warned, another generation of photographers turned away from subjects that intrigued them because they could not analyze the light falling on objects at which they pointed both lenses and internal meters.

By 1980 confirmed skeptics manufactured throwback cardboard exposure calculators that resembled ones from the 1930s. Robert S. Harris explicitly intended his "Memory Meter" to "improve photographic memory" by making a photographer calculate mentally "x-ratings" that help him "gain a mental exposure perspective that will enable you to sense when your meter is 'out to lunch.'" Harris worried that photographers would not realize when failing batteries or cold weather produced inaccurate meter readings, and he insisted that many photographers would be unable to use their cameras when meter batteries failed completely.[89] He argued that coupled exposure meters inveigled photographers away from noticing, even momentarily, exposure and shutter-speed information.[90] As they changed position slightly or as clouds moved before the sun, they ignored the subtle, slow variations of the automatic meter, or the lack of subtle variations, and they failed to learn how to describe light in words to fellow photographers eager to learn about photography in special situations.[91] A half century earlier, other writers argued in the same vein, directing reader attention at the ways cameras caused photographers to see vaguely.

In the middle 1930s experienced photographers warned gadget-happy amateurs that dial calculators worked poorly in bad weather and that the finest photocell electric meters did badly when aimed at predominantly green landscapes or rows of tall red-brick buildings. "I am sixty-five years old, a fact of importance in connection with what follows," begins Henry Thew Stephenson's 1935 *American Photography* article "Meters and How to Use Them." Stephenson insisted that his eyes responded more slowly to fast-changing light than they once did, and that despite his awareness of the change, he found himself tricked by viewfinder extinction meters, except under very low light conditions, at end of day. For Stephenson and many other curmudgeons, bright sunlight on snow dazzled the eye and modern meters alike, and they warned photographers to rely on what they knew of light through experience.[92] Only then might they have the visionary experience of Watkins, the manufacturer of an exposure meter that worked by passage of time.

Realizing light often emerges from trying to calculate it.[93] Simple shop-theory experiments demonstrate how effortlessly the human eye adjusts to changes in light and how a sensitive observer must consciously acknowledge such adjustments. On a sunny day, any camera-carrying walker might set his camera at 125th/sec and f/5.6 and make a series of black-and-white photographs on ISO 125 black-and-white film as he walks from sunlit old fields into second-growth woods, taking perhaps one image every ten paces. When developed and printed, the images reveal not only gradations of darkness inside the frontier of the woods kept from consciousness by the effortlessly adapting eye, but sometimes what the observer notices once aware of the adaptation process itself.[94] Stopping to make a photograph once meant deciding on proper exposure settings.[95] While evaluating the fall of light on a place, the photographer can pick out constituent elements of the views he missed even while noticing closely enough to decide to make the photograph and even after composing the image in his viewfinder.[96] The photographer calculating settings sometimes discovers something hitherto unseen, perhaps the hiding figure Ralphson describes, perhaps an alignment that orders everything else. He sometimes finds glamour or makes it or encourages it, if only momentarily. He finds the armature of a place, the alignment about which energy spins. He finds light.[97]

"Highly desirable is this same diffused light. It is the sort that makes one squint, it is so strong, yet the sun does not shine. This light is as rapid as sunlight," Wallace Nutting cautioned in his 1927 shop-theory manual. "It is caused by a thin haze, as through ground glass. It illuminates effectively every part of an object. A somewhat duller light gives a somewhat less attractive result, yet a good result."[98] In the middle 1920s Nutting addressed professionals and serious, well-to-do amateurs: they understood cameras fitted with ground-glass backs and viewing screens, not the simple viewfinders of Brownies and other box cameras. Nutting knew both the significance of light and the way haze functioned as a sort of glass. He knew too how effortlessly the eye adapts, and how that adaptation tricks the active mind.

Fantasy writers nowadays insist on seeing light and color sensitively in ways Watkins and other photographers emphasized before the invention of coupled exposure meters. "As he stared at the hillside beyond he was sure he could see the line of it, a very slight contrast in color, like an old scar," writes K. J. Parker of a soldier told to find a path sketched on an old map. Captain Eicondoulus plays a very small role in *Devices and Desires*. He fears maps, goes cold when superior officers unroll them and speak confidently, and understands them as sketches of possibility only. "Razor-sharp when it came to faces, but a martyr to names," he sees and understands landscape ever so slightly differently from other soldiers.[99] His frustration with a sloppily drawn map elucidates how sensitivity to landscape color sometimes accentuates acute awareness of light and shadow. Nowhere in Parker's three-volume *Engineer* series does anyone hold a camera, but the novels delineate how the fall of certain light on certain places now and then enables the sensitive to glimpse things mapmakers cannot imagine. None of his superior officers notice the frescoes illuminating the origin of the racial warfare ordering the series, but Captain Eiconodoulus discerns the track, knows the map lies, and realizes his unit is about to collide with people of a skin color different from his.

His is the experience of Will on the snow-covered old way opening on another kind of way altogether, an alignment of forces unknown and fitful. Tolkien emphasized old ways in *The Hobbit* and succeeding books, but Susan Cooper's 1970s series built on the collision of Watkins's alignment hunters and established academics to emphasize lines along which flowed forces energizing those sensitives willing to seek them. Le Guin, Cooper, and their successors all elucidate ways of seeing, especially seeing light, as fundamental to connecting with other forces, and with discovery. In his purely enthusiast way, Watkins glimpsed something while making a photograph of abandoned landscape. That envisioning shaped much pseudoscience writing indeed, but it transformed fantasy writing, especially in the age of semiautomatic 35 mm cameras. Writers of the best fantasy fiction, especially that aimed at young readers, built on Watkins's envisioning in many ways, emphasizing the quietude in abandoned places, especially along old ways, that leads to contemplation and serendipitous discovery that contradicts some tenets of modern science. In the right place, the painstaking photographer might envision. In fantasy fiction, the seer replaces the photographer, but the envisioning, especially the descrying of light that enables the observer to see around the curves of time, remains fundamentally what Watkins experienced.

8 Voodoo

In New Orleans circa 1900 blossomed a literary fascination with race, sexuality, fantasy, photography, and lost landscapes.

BELLE GROVE BURNED ON MARCH 15, 1952. THE GREAT
plantation house blazed into the following morning. "This is the first
picture I made on that Sunday, when the bricks were still hot," wrote
Clarence John Laughlin of one image. "Great cavities had opened in the
walls, and against them moss can be seen dripping against the distant
sky—like a suppuration of doom—the whole scene having much of the
emotional quality of Piranesi's engravings of Roman ruins—and indeed
this house was very much like a palace of antiquity—completely lost in
time and space."[1] For decades Laughlin had been probing the antiquity
of Louisiana, especially among the deserted plantations along the Mississippi and in the oldest neighborhoods of New Orleans. Especially out
in the bayou country, along old ways tourists rarely discovered, he found
obscurities that taxed his photographic skill.

With David L. Cohn he published *New Orleans and Its Living Past*
in 1941, but the limited-edition volume only slightly advanced his reputation. The book emphasizes the peculiarities of a somnolent city dreaming
and intermittently beset by nightmare. Seven years later the editors of
Look published one of his Mardi Gras photographs in *Look at America:
The Country You Know, and Don't Know,* along with three other Laughlin images: one of a cemetery, another of a walled Creole courtyard seen
from above, and one of the filigree of a French Quarter wrought-iron
balcony.[2] The *Look* editors lauded Laughlin's technical brilliance and valued his idiosyncratic aesthetic. Only a few critics had hitherto noticed
his work, and they dismissed it as quirky. In 1948 Laughlin produced
a folio of one hundred photographs, *Ghosts along the Mississippi: An
Essay in the Poetic Interpretation of Louisiana's Plantation Architecture,*
that momentarily captured national attention. Twelve years later, *Life*
featured many of his photographs in a sequence entitled "The Era of
Sentiment and Splendour": "Receding into the distance, shaded rows of
old slave cabins line a long alley on Evergreen Plantation near Edgard,
La.," he wrote in the last caption of the *Life* sequence. "Now empty and
gently dilapidated, the cabins with their square-framed porches create a
haunting perspective of a long-vanished past."[3] By this time obscurity had
well-nigh reclaimed Laughlin. Stung by lack of national notice, he had
retreated into a private realm that rarely admitted publication. Despite
occasional shows, particularly one at the Philadelphia Museum of Art in
1973, critics continued to ignore his work.[4]

Laughlin's images of Belle Grove appeared both in *Life* and in his
Ghosts along the Mississippi. The book emphasizes what Laughlin found

peculiarly expressed in the Belle Grove house, "the dramatic contrast between the grandeur and decay of the great plantation houses." Most of the houses he photographed had been abandoned for decades, or else occupied by caretakers unable to maintain them. The Belle Grove house epitomized the immense wealth made by some sugarcane planters: in 1860 almost all the nation's millionaires were planters living along the Mississippi. The seven thousand acres on which it sat made John Andrews, its creator, one of the wealthiest men in the United States in the 1850s, and the house was one of the most extravagant in the nation when it stood complete in 1857. The Civil War destroyed the Andrews fortune, and the house passed into other hands, then into abandonment in 1924 when imported sugar wrecked domestic sugarcane growing. Laughlin photographed the seventy-five-room mansion over years, documenting the insidious destruction of water and plants, then the collapse of entire sections of façade. It became for him "a doomed and lonely outpost, lost in time, of a pattern of living whose scale can no longer be made to fit into ours." It became something beyond the reach of a national imagination shrinking in cinema houses.

In the 1939 film based on Margaret Mitchell's best-selling 1936 novel *Gone with the Wind,* Hollywood focused public attention on eastern plantation culture just before the Civil War, a culture less sumptuous and nuanced than plantation life in Louisiana and Mississippi.[5] The culture reflected in Belle Grove fit no Hollywood parameters: Belle Grove symbolized the world of an elite still absent from cinema houses. It symbolized an elite obsessed with power, especially glamour.

While photographing the rear wing of Belle Grove in 1939, Laughlin accidentally recorded something to which he drew the viewer's attention. "Near the center of the picture, behind the weeds at the base of the house, a broken plaster area seems like a strange white phantom rising—a note well in keeping with the ruin-haunted majesty of this scene."[6] Laughlin saw most of the ruined architecture as ghosts, and his understanding of the structures as ghosts produced the title of his book. But he called the feature a phantom, not a ghost. The fall of light momentarily revealed something akin to the alignments Watkins discovered. Laughlin knew this phantom as a revenant, unvanquished and undead, something ahistorical, something glamorous stalking modernity, a phantom in a ghost landscape.

Laughlin came of age in a New Orleans writhing in a modernist trap. In the early 1920s modernity shifted across multiple overlaying pasts sliding through one another. "There have been these two things—the speeding up and the standardization of life and thought, the one impulse no doubt the result of the other," argued Sherwood Anderson in a 1922 *Double Dealer* essay. The New Orleans magazine aimed at anything but local color. Its editors and backers hoped it might become a world-class journal, and it published many authors literary historians now honor. But always it reacted against the homogeneity of New York–based media, especially magazines, and Hollywood film. Instead, the *Double Dealer* illuminates the bayou glamour fusing history, fantasy, and modernity.

Anderson lambasted national media. He insisted that "on the cover of each magazine is to be seen the same Broadway New York corruption of womanly beauty" that in turn corrupts national thinking. The New York–based standardization of visual imagery had become "a sort of continual and terrible perversion of life" which ignored the breadth of the American experience. "Where among us live these creatures of the popular magazine short story, the best-selling novel, or the moving picture?" Film provided him with a key to the puzzle that made entertainment and advertising nearly seamless. "The trick when analyzed is very simple. The appearance of life is given by exterior means entirely." As soon as they looked away from the national-circulation magazines and movies, thoughtful adults understood the trick; Anderson thought too few looked away. In New Orleans, however, a peculiar racial juxtaposition made the trick gratingly apparent.

"Almost all of the old city still stands," Anderson mused. "From my window as I sit writing, I see the tangled mass of the roofs of old buildings" and beyond "the old galleries" where locals sat and watched passersby. "What colors in the old walls and doors of these buildings," he exclaimed. "Yellows fade into soft greens. There is a continual shifting interplay of many colors as the sunlight washes over them." As a visitor, Anderson discovered something unnerving. "I am in New Orleans and I am trying to proclaim something I have found here and that I think America wants and needs."[7] If its adherents wanted the modern movement in literature, art, architecture, and morals to endure and prosper, he concluded, they had to acknowledge regional peculiarity, and especially the powerful glamour of southern Louisiana.

In its short life, the *Double Dealer* focused attention on what New Orleans might offer to the world, and especially to modernists. Its 1921 premiere issue denounced the genteel tradition that since Appomattox had romanticized the antebellum South. "We are sick to death of the treacly sentimentalities with which our well-intentioned lady fictioneers regale us," its editors announced. "From the sodden marshes of Southern literature" someone must emerge to shove traditional depictions of the freed slave, the Creole, the happy Negro, and other stock characters into the junk pile and focus on "the soul-awakening of a hardy, torpid race, just becoming re-aware of itself."[8] New Orleans, they maintained, had slithered into the twentieth century, and once analyzed, its peculiarities would transform culture nationwide and in Europe. But by 1925, when the magazine published William Faulkner's "New Orleans," reality had begun to constrain editorial dreams and outbursts. To Faulkner the city seemed a gorgeous but aging courtesan, "who shuns the sunlight that the illusion of her former glory be preserved," lives "in a shadowy house filled with dim mirrors," revels in an "atmosphere of a bygone and more gracious age," and receives few among the many who stand outside her door.[9] So even as the magazine published some of the finest essayists, novelists, and poets anywhere, it could not escape the phantoms of its locale. Anderson suddenly seemed wrong. America neither wanted nor needed what he had found outside his New Orleans window.

Organized vice bankrolled New Orleans politicians and enriched its police. Prostitution boomed in the early nineteenth-century keelboat and flatboat era, returned from steamboat-induced recession in the 1840s, and blossomed after the 1869 legalization of gambling. By 1880 New Orleans had become the national center of legal and quasi-legal vice, its lavish whorehouses visited by hundreds of thousands of men, including many traveling from coast to coast, and many others arriving from the Caribbean on business. Seamen from around the world knew the city as the planetary capital of sexual frolic, and prostitutes gravitated to it from New York, Atlanta, and overseas. The industry grew so feverishly in the late 1880s that New Orleans struggled to zone it: reputable families often found neighborhood houses converted into bordellos overnight. As northern cities curtailed and sometimes almost eliminated prostitution, whores and pimps escaped into the steamy interracial excitement of New Orleans.

Splendid whorehouses provided convenience and opportunity. Many operated subsidiary assignation houses, where discreet men connected with women and men away from downtown bordellos. Around 1890 freedom from police interruption caused wealthy procuresses to reinvest capital in male-only assignation houses. As word spread of the service, homosexual men began migrating to New Orleans, some to work in the houses and others to pay for their favors. Other madams specialized in obtaining very young girls they made available as high-fee prostitutes or else sold into permanent sexual bondage. The red-light district became a destination for many voyeurs—especially traveling men determined to return home having at least seen legal harlots—and for many sexual adventurers. It became, too, the national capital of racial and cultural collision.

In antebellum days, reputable New Orleans families took visiting reputable families to see the slaves dance in Place Congo; reputable men took visiting reputable men to see the quadroon women dance at the Orleans Ballroom. By 1900 reputable men conducted reputable male guests on tours of the red-light district, in part to drink in spectacular bars, and as Herbert Asbury wrote in his 1936 exposé *The French Quarter: An Informal History of the New Orleans Underworld,* "to see the plush and velvet parlors of the palatial mansions of sin, to shiver at the bawdy shows and dancing in the cabarets, and to peek through the shutters of the lowly cribs at the naked girls who sat patiently waiting for customers." While some of the fanciest bordellos had four-piece orchestras, others hired itinerant musicians who roamed the district. Around 1895 a group of twelve- to fifteen-year-old boys began working the district under the name Razzy Dazzy Spasm Band. Five years later their music had been taken over by an adult band calling itself the Razzy Dazzy Jazzy Band, and soon the music became known simply as jazz. The district struck many male visitors as licentious and exotic beyond words, but within the district some brothels explicitly advertised dancers and other performers as exotic. One establishment featured a well-known "oriental danseuse," supposedly the first woman in modern America to dance barefooted. By 1900 reputable women and children avoided the entire district even as men nationwide savored guidebooks offering insights into New Orleans pleasures illegal and unknown elsewhere in the country.

Across the United States after 1902, saloons, seedy hotels, and even some railroad and newsstand agents sold *The Blue Book,* a forty- to fifty-page guide to the New Orleans red-light district. Its publication followed the wild success of earlier guides, especially *The Green Book, or, Gentleman's Guide to New Orleans,* retailed mostly aboard Mississippi steamboats. Its introductory pages carried advertisements for restaurants, cabarets, liquor dealers, attorneys, and saloons. The remainder of the book listed the better-known brothels, described them and their specialties, and featured advertisements—many with illustrations—for the larger establishments, then concluded with a list of showgirls working at various clubs. "This directory and guide of the Sporting District has been before the people on many occasions, and has proven its authority as to what is doing in the 'Queer Zone,'" announced the publisher of *The Blue Book,* immediately after warning that the book could not to be entered into the Post Office as mail. Any stranger visiting "the only district of its kind in the States set aside for the fast women by law" might endanger himself without a savvy guidebook.[10]

The New Orleans guidebooks, many published under similar or identical titles, occupy a rarely remarked genre of American literature: only a handful of bibliographers know much about them, and none seem to have been reprinted. One idiosyncratic book, privately printed and now rare, stands out: the anonymous 1936 *The Blue Book: A Bibliographical Attempt to Describe the Guide Books to the Houses of Ill Fame in New Orleans as They Were Published There. Together with Some Pertinent and Illuminating Remarks Pertaining to the Establishments and Courtesans as Well as to Harlotry in General in New Orleans.* Its author argues that any supposed post-1920s modernization in sexual tolerance remains essentially urban and shallow. "Only the big cities have been affected by this gradual change, as a result of the more understandable information that is available," asserts the pseudonym-masked author, Semper Idem, of tolerance advanced by literature (especially pornographic French postcards) imported from Europe. "In the small towns and the backward counties, the old deplorable condition of ignorance still prevails."[11] Nationally distributed New Orleans guidebooks preceded the import of European books on sexual activities, including those many Americans considered dangerously deviant. Idem averred that the guidebooks not only educated many Americans boys and men but focused their attention on New Orleans as a fantastical place in which all sort of sexual activity proscribed elsewhere flourished legally.[12] Until American servicemen discovered Paris in World War I and returned with sex manuals, postcards, and other documentation of practices hitherto widely condemned at home, especially interracial sex and magic, the New Orleans guidebooks played a major if shadowy educational role.[13]

Slavery had been the peculiar institution of the Old South, but vice had been the post–Civil War industry of New Orleans. The *Double Dealer* debuted only four years following the end of legalized prostitution. However the Roaring Twenties might roar in New York, Detroit, and elsewhere, many thoughtful southerners, especially those resident in New Orleans, wondered at the supposed license sweeping the nation. Prohibition had produced liquor smuggling, speakeasies, and gangsters, and subsequent economic depression seemingly produced a spate of bank robberies, kidnappings, and murders, but all such paled before a deeper, more flamboyant, and perhaps more eerie vice still infusing New Orleans. In the 1920s and 1930s New Orleans became even more mysterious and exotic than it had been twenty years earlier: it slipped backward into the 1880s. As much of it slid too into poverty and decrepitude, its physical fabric and local culture mocked the supposed modernity of Western urban culture. In the 1920s New Orleans moved backward and downward in ways that echoed its post–Civil War slide into vice. What Hearn had remarked fifty years earlier suddenly seemed apt.[14]

Lafcadio Hearn did not invent New Orleans for readers of national magazines. But like many seasoned travelers arriving at a place outside their experience, he observed closely and created a personal view of what he saw. He realized disjunctions inhabitants accepted as ordinary, and wrote about them in newspaper columns, many of which circulated nationwide and beyond. In the aftermath of Reconstruction, Hearn found places already as mysterious as the old ways that fixed much British attention thirty years later. He found paths winding through or past the bulwarks of reconstruction, slavery, defeat, and crushing poverty. He stumbled into alignments of glamour.

Creole life and landscape fixed his attention. In time he saw the fading Creole culture best symbolized in New Orleans Creole houses, most of which focused on courtyards walled off from streets. Usually the dwellings existed in varying states of decrepitude, almost always behind "commonplace and unattractive" facades punctuated by green-painted doors and gates at ground level, and green-shuttered windows on the balconied upper stories. "But beyond the gates lay a little Paradise," he wrote in one *Item* column. "The great court, deep and broad, was framed in tropical green; vines embraced the white pillars of the piazza, and creeping plants climbed up the tinted walls to peer into the upper windows with their flower-eyes of flaming scarlet." As a botanical garden verging on tropical jungle, its banana trees, aged fig tree, and other plants, especially "gorgeous broad-leaved things, with leaves fantastic and barbed and flowers brilliant as hummingbirds," rioting about an antique fountain, the courtyard introduces its keepers. "Without, roared the Iron Age, the angry waves of American traffic; within, one heard only the murmur of the languid fountain, the sound of deeply musical voices conversing in the languages of Paris and Madrid," the sound of children talking in "many-voweled Creole." In column after column, Hearn emphasized that outside such homes "it was the year 1879; within, it was the epoch of the Spanish Domination." The inhabitants enjoyed European magazines, fine music, good Bordeaux wine, and "rich West India tobacco" despite their post–Civil War poverty. They ignored the newcomers Hearn called "Americans."[15]

"Yet some people wonder that some other people never care to cross Canal Street," he mused of a city divided along both racial and ethnic lines. Northern newcomers (his informants still called them "radical carpet-baggers") defined themselves as white and pure and dismissed everyone they defined as "colored." But racial and ethnic complexity over-whelmed their white-or-black framework. Before the Civil War, many blacks had been "free people of color," and some had owned slaves them-selves; not all postwar black people were freedmen, something that vexed Reconstruction classification efforts. The offspring of interracial affairs might be slaves or free under the law. Free or slave, however, the children of a white and mulatto were quadroons, people with one-quarter African blood; octoroons had one-eighth African ancestry. Such ethnic identity existed outside most legal frameworks but scarcely involved Creoles. The word itself derived from very old French and Spanish terms designating local, not mixed. In 1877 Hearn produced a long article about the word and its connotations, tracing usage and meaning back to 1520.

In colonial times, Louisianans talked easily of creole livestock, cre-ole boats, creole houses, using the adjective to distinguish local or native from anything—or anyone—arrived directly from France or Spain. Post–Civil War federal occupation forced Creoles to list themselves as white or black for the first time, and to distinguish themselves from the Arcadians or "Cajuns" descended from French colonists exiled in the 1760s from Nova Scotia and other Canadian colonies captured by the British. "In the North the error is usually confined to the belief that the almost-white colored residents of New Orleans are Creoles, and that Creoles are indig-enous and peculiar to the city," Hearn explained before explicating usage elsewhere in the United States and in Britain. "Probably the misapplica-tion of the term will continue indefinitely, despite all definitions of pop-ular dictionaries and all explanatory essays in popular encyclopedias, in-asmuch as it has been sanctioned by the custom of more than a hundred years." Erroneous usage "always differs more or less, however, according to locality," making philological analysis difficult, let alone correction.[16] Across much of the upland South, he argued, rural whites believed Cre-oles to be blacks who spoke French.

Hearn arrived just after the end of Reconstruction. He found late 1870s New Orleans mystifyingly rich in ethnic diversity: he cataloged Chinese, Japanese, "natives of India," Filipinos, "children of the Antil-les and of South America; subjects of the Sultan and sailors of the Io-nian Sea."[17] As an immigrant to the United States himself, the child of a Briton and a Cypriot, Hearn felt at home in some parts of the city and alien in others.

At first he dispatched articles to his former employer, the *Cincinnati Commercial.* He then resumed his fulltime newspaper career by writing for the *New Orleans Item,* a paper read chiefly by northern white new-comers. He focused on crime, social-reform issues, and the exotic world south of Canal Street—a world that newcomer readers rarely entered. "The first delicious impression of the most beautiful and picturesque old city in North America," he wrote in an 1878 column, strengthens as winter creeps into northern cities, "for in this season is the glamour of New Orleans strongest upon those whom she attracts from less hospitable climates." Glamour—visual magic—ordered much of his work. For him, New Orleans lay washed in "perennial sunshine" or slept "in magical moonlight" which produced all manner of visions. Always the city murmurs, "I am old; but thou hast never met with a younger more beautiful than I." But whatever words it murmurs, its magic is far more potent than enchantment. It is viscerally visual. New Orleans is always *she*, glamorous, sensual, and retreating from explorers who cross Canal Street.[18] Creoles proved the most glamorous of all subjects.

Paradoxically, Mardi Gras masked the glamour Hearn examined. "The romantic charm of the old city is not readily obtained at such a time; the curious cosmopolitan characteristics that offer themselves to artistic eyes in other seasons are lost in the afflux of American visitors, and true local color is fairly drowned out by the colors of Rex," he explained in 1883 to readers of *Harper's Weekly*. The grand nighttime parade fills Canal Street, and its pageantry spills into hundreds of balls and other events, easily satisfying the exoticism-seeking "American" throngs. "The strictly *local* picturesqueness of the exhibition may be studied to advantage in the antiquated French by-ways," he asserted, not only where the great carnival procession marshals itself but where smaller, less easily interpreted events materialize.[19] Americans arrive for the advertised, merchant-choreographed spectacle, which they enjoy and accept in ways some locals scorn as shallow and safe.[20]

Hearn himself often avoided the depths. He preferred that mystery but not evil accentuate the New Orleans glamour he cherished, and while he wrote regularly about everyday crime, he avoided old tales of heinous wickedness or contemporary rumors of extraordinary nastiness. In an 1880 *Item* review of George Washington Cable's Creole-focused novel *The Grandissimes,* Hearn exclaimed that "this strange, weird, powerful, and pathetic story" is "certainly the most remarkable work of fiction ever created in the South." He found the book filled with "inexpressible glamour," but "there are chapters which affect the imagination like those evil dreams in which dead faces reappear with traits more accentuated than the living originals ever possessed."[21] Eight years later, aged thirty-eight, Hearn left New Orleans after familiarizing himself with Bayou Teche, the Atchafalaya region, Grand Isle, and the Florida coast in the previous five years and writing for *Scribner's,* the *Century, Harper's Weekly,* and *Harper's Bazaar* about his exotic finds.[22] He had become a national writer overwhelmed by southern Louisiana glamour no longer pleasant and safe.

George Washington Cable surpassed him in toughness. In the late 1880s Cable moved squarely into the post-Reconstruction fight for racial justice, especially for freed slaves and their children. He tackled endemic racism both indirectly and head-on, emphasizing its propensity for fueling intermittent horrors. In an 1889 *Century* article, he swept readers into a walk through the old part of New Orleans, to a disused large house on Royal Street. He speculated that the house might be haunted. At any rate, tenants abandoned it frequently, and the owner had stopped allowing visitors to examine it between rentals. One informant told Cable that "the landlord's orders are positive that no photographer of any kind shall come into his house." Knowing visitors had numbered about three hundred in the year before he published "The 'Haunted House' in Royal Street," Cable thought that after the article appeared the number might jump tenfold.

On April 10, 1834, the slave cook shackled to one end of a twenty-four-foot-long chain had set the Royal Street house afire in order to bring help to other slaves, including children, imprisoned in the attic. Citizens responding to the blaze discovered emaciated, whipped slaves locked down with iron collars. Later in the day, the slave owner Madame Lalaurie and her two grown daughters escaped by coach to a schooner waiting off the Bayou Road south of the city. The vengeful crowd killed the coach horses and probably the slave coachman, then ransacked the house. For decades it stood abandoned and derelict, producing what Cable called "idle talk of strange sights and sounds" that deflected people from examining the true horror of a madwoman owning slaves. In the 1870s reformers devoted to racially integrated education for girls opened it as a school, and in 1874 the White League, opposed to the federal occupation government and to racial equality, stormed the building and forcibly removed the black students. Reconstruction authorities reopened the school, but in 1877, following the end of federal authority, state and city officials closed it again, and opened racially segregated high schools.[23] Cable emphasized that New Orleans had made very little progress since 1834, and that beneath the veneer of decrepitude, the old part of the city sheltered evil more profound than prostitution. He found the evil most palpable in voodoo.

His novel *The Grandissimes* holds miscegenation squirming against a mirror, then delineates the deepening power of glamour and sexuality within the context of voodoo. "The united grace and pride of her movement was inspiring but—what shall we say?—feline?" Cable says of the voodoo queen of New Orleans. "It was a femininity without humanity,—something that made her with all her superbness, a creature that one would want to find chained." The "upward-writhing images of three scaly serpents" distinguishes her drawing room from any other, and through her home moves a "dwarf Congo woman, as black as soot," enslaved outside the slavery terminated by the Emancipation Proclamation. Thirst for power draws the queen to a voodoo sorcerer, a captured African warrior forced to labor in the sugarcane fields. Finally, summoned by his curious plantation mistress, the nearly nude, still-arrogant new-made slave first sees his owner as a spirit, then retaliates with a voodoo spell cast upon her husband and her lands. The voodoo queen, intensely jealous of her counterpart's love of a white woman, entangles Creole families and Anglos in the dark magic that accompanies the working of the simplest voodoo love charms, then in a devastating collapse of morality. *The Grandissimes* makes a sharp distinction between ordinary black people and the few who practice voodoo, who deal in real raw power for good and evil until it corrupts them utterly, who know glamour beyond words.[24]

After the triumph of *The Grandissimes,* Cable wrote regularly for national magazines. In the *Century* he published a series of essays about the origins of African American dance and music in Louisiana, including sketches of dancers and pages of music and lyrics. But he probed beyond ordinary black culture into something defying Christianity and law. "The dance and song entered into the Negro worship. That worship was as dark and horrid as bestialized savagery could make the adoration of serpents," he wrote in an 1886 essay of "the orgies of the Voodoos." He benefited from ethnology; he understood that the voodoo worshippers knew "the vast supernatural powers" of a deity totally opposed to "Obi, the great African manitou or deity" and either resident in or taking the form of any snake. In Louisiana, voodoo worshippers "are not merely a sect, but in some rude, savage way, also an order." What fascinated Cable fascinated *Century* readers: the order held sway over black and white people alike, and at least some white people, not all Creoles, practiced voodoo in order to control other believers and to affect nonbelievers.[25]

Cable asserted that Hearn's transcriptions of the words of voodoo songs were in a phonetic rendering that seemed merely nonsense French: he intimated that he longed for the opportunities Hearn enjoyed. By the late 1880s voodoo had become more powerful but far less easily penetrated by inquirers than it had been even ten years earlier: a force far more powerful than gambling and prostitution that used legalized vice as camouflage. Cable claimed that voodoo "charms are resorted to by the malicious, the jealous, the revengeful, or the avaricious, or held in terror, not by the timorous only, but by the strong, the courageous, the desperate." Hoodoo, he observed, derived directly from voodoo, not from some upland southern African American tradition, and sometimes masked far more dangerous belief and activity.[26] To those who knew how to listen and look, seemingly harmless black music and dance hinted at fear of and respect for something appalling. Cable assured readers that voodoo might overwhelm the Christian faith of most African Americans and embroil the South in racial, sexual, and magical conflict.

The context of Cable's magazine articles strengthened his message that voodoo demanded rigorous attention and eradication. Between November 1888 and April 1889, he published a series of *Century* tales entitled "Strange True Stories of Louisiana."[27] Interspersed among his stories appeared two lengthy articles by Charles de Kay, "Pagan Ireland" and "Fairies and Druids of Ireland"; a sustained analysis of the remote Guanajuato district of Mexico by F. Hopkinson Smith; a highly technical essay, "Something Electricity Is Doing," by Charles Barnard; and a number of detailed articles concerning the inauguration of Washington, the issuing of the Emancipation Proclamation, and Samoa, as well as a series of articles on Siberia. Smith makes clear the revolutionary change coming to many parts of Mexico with the building of railroads into regions hitherto connected by bridle paths "and the desert trail." He asserts that "in remote regions" a distinctive Mexican culture evolved from the collision of Indian and Spanish ones, and that over 350 years it has become well-nigh indecipherable even to Mexicans steeped in Spanish colonial history.[28] Cable understood voodoo transcending time and modernity, and he described it within a framework *Century* readers understood: the collision of ancient, "primitive" power with technological, chiefly urban modernism.

Around his series the other articles seem to orbit. Many emphasize mainstream United States history, the sort by then shaping public-school textbooks aimed at Americanizing immigrant children, or else focus on remote but potentially important places, especially Samoa and Siberia, inhabited by people scarcely known to ethnologists. Several imply that technology has become powerful enough to shape culture independently of political ideology: electricity is doing something passing even beyond cultural control, exactly as Cox suggested in his Brownie cartoons.[29] The articles by de Kay suggest that scholars and other determined inquirers know almost nothing of ancient Irish culture, let alone how that culture suffuses modern Ireland, especially in out-of-the-way rural places.[30] They presage Yeats's 1893 *The Celtic Twilight*, Evans-Wentz's 1911 *The Fairy*

Faith in Celtic Countries, and even Maurice O'Sullivan's 1933 *Twenty Years A-Growing,* and they emphasize that Irish culture is *old* in ways becoming as unfathomable as high-country Aztec-Mexican culture.[31] In his introduction to the 1933 English-language translation from the Gaelic, E. M. Forster called O'Sullivan's book "an account of Neolithic civilization from the inside," a sort of old way running from the twentieth century backward into prehistory.[32] De Kay understood the depth of the Irish past and the way parts of it energized the Ireland of the 1880s, and he wondered if it could ever be analyzed or delineated. Writing about Mexico, Smith asserted, "To study and enjoy a people thoroughly one must live in the streets." He found that talking with ordinary, often very poor people gave "a closer insight into the inner life of a people than days spent either at the governor's palace or at the museum."[33] But in the late 1880s *Century* authors began focusing on the palace and the museum. Voodoo fit neither place, and its power helped force Cable from Louisiana.[34]

Cable moved from New Orleans to Massachusetts in 1885, three years before Hearn left for Martinique. While he continued publishing novels and short stories about Louisiana, often focused on Creole life in the antebellum era, Cable produced a spate of books and articles arguing for racial equality and denouncing government corruption across the South. Almost never did he make public his deepening unease with a voodoo glamour flourishing secretly in a modernizing New Orleans.[35] Hearn rarely grappled with the underlying and seemingly worsening racial divide that prompted Ku Klux Klan activity in the 1870s and almost never wrote about the sexual energy Cable introduced in *The Grandissimes* and alluded to for the next decade in magazine articles. Hearn moved to Martinique still inquiring into Creole culture, then suddenly to Japan, where he became the chief English-language explicator of a culture Westerners deemed safely exotic. He died in 1904, his Louisiana writings, especially the two thousand columns published in the *Item* and other newspapers, mostly forgotten. Cable died in 1925, his fiction, especially most of his Creole-focused stories, dismissed as genteel-tradition, local-color writing, and his political work totally ignored.[36] But magazine editors knew Hearn as far safer than Cable, reprinted his columns from fifty years before, and looked sideways at the voodoo and sexuality Cable had noticed and feared.

Modern crime, organized and otherwise, deflected Hearn and Cable from many aspects of New Orleans history. Both men left New Orleans as its demoralized, corrupt city government profited from an increase in the prostitution, gambling, and related vice it scarcely controlled and as its citizens suffered a spate of murders and other violence.[37] Beneath the veneer of an Iron Age city boasting streetcars, office buildings, booming wharves, and bustling railroad yards pulsed a sordid, violent energy barely policed and fiercely racist. Both Hearn and Cable understood New Orleans as more wicked in relative terms: as reform movements improved government in many United States cities, the New Orleans cesspool drained criminals and would-be criminals from other cities and from across the Caribbean region. New York routinely called itself a melting pot, but New Orleans presented a stove fire.[38]

Hearn hoped for the best, but his newcomer's love of the old city blinded him to the power and longevity of secret forces beyond his exploration. Voodoo had mostly vanished, he assured readers of an 1885 *Harper's Weekly* issue, with the death of the "last really important figure of a long line of wizards or witches whose African titles were recognized, and who exercised an influence over the colored population." Hearn insisted that "the influence of the public school is gradually dissipating all faith in witchcraft," and while the remaining voodoo believers will undoubtedly elect another queen, the death of the Senegal-born wizard Jean Montanet at almost a hundred years of age signaled the end of an era.[39]

Montanet, known as "Bayou John" or "Voodoo John," may have been the son of a Bambara prince; he claimed so, and his facial scars supported his contention. Hearn argued that his facial features, skin tone, and other distinguishing indicators conformed perfectly to the characteristics "by which the French ethnologists in Senegal distinguish the Bambaras." Montanet claimed to have been captured by Spanish slavers, sold in Cuba, freed there by a grateful owner, and then become a seaman, leaving his ship in New Orleans, where his wharf-side employers made him an overseer almost immediately. He had what New Orleans people called *obi,* the secret powers of foretelling the future, of making potions, healing and malefic, and casting spells, all valuable traits in an overseer of roustabout slaves. As a free man of color in antebellum New Orleans, he enjoyed many legal rights, among them the right to buy and own slaves. Soon he owned fifteen women, all of whom he married according to an African rite of his own. As his fame as a seer and healer spread along the Gulf Coast, he grew rich from fees paid by both black and white clients. Eventually he owned land and a modest but pleasant house, a fine carriage, and a superb horse, which he rode wearing Spanish costume. He distributed gumbo and jambalaya to the poor, especially during epidemics, when his healing services came into great demand. When he crossed north of Canal Street to treat a white patient, passersby fell silent. Everyone knew something of his reputed powers, and many believed in them, including the closely veiled white women who went into the old city and knocked at his door. If nothing else, he had become a very wealthy black man who eventually courted and married a white woman.

Hearn dismissed Montanet's voodoo powers and voodoo itself. Always he saw voodoo as "rapidly dying out," and at most a mere knowledge of poison. He attended some voodoo ceremonies, including one annual nighttime gathering on St. John's Eve in the swamps at the edge of Lake Pontchartrain, where he found "a scene Doré would have delighted to paint." Hearn accompanied men who knew the voodoo inner circle, and his friends interceded with the male "chief," who allowed them to watch the ceremonies at a slight distance, so long as they removed their coats and followed orders. He described the food and the "regular Voudou dance with all its twistings and contortions," but he focused on "the only person enjoying the aristocratic privilege of a chair," a "bright *café au lait* woman of about forty-eight, who sat in one corner of the room looking on the scene before her with an air of dignity." Hearn learned that she was queen of the voodoo practitioners and ruler of the annual ceremony, the precise nature of which he failed to comprehend.[40]

He underestimated the complexity and power of voodoo, asserting that "impious ceremonies" originate in voodoo believers "worshipping the prince of evil, for, in their theology, the devil is God, and it is to him they pray." Voodoo undermined Hearn's love of Creole culture and warped his personal delight in the uncanny. For Hearn had visions. Intermittently he glimpsed the everyday modern city as pure symbol only: now and then he enabled such visions by focusing intently on what he saw as exotic, chiefly Creole culture, especially its art, gardens, and dialects.

Much of his writing is now lost. Bibliographers know the mauling of his notebooks and his cryptic references to short pieces published but now vanished. Only luck and the assiduous effort of contemporaneous admirers saved much of his work from oblivion.

The collection *Fantastics and Other Fancies* appeared in 1914, carefully assembled by Charles Woodward Hutson, who despaired at collecting all of the essays Hearn had intended to publish under the title of "Ephemerae, or Leaves from the Diary of an Impressionist." Unlike many subsequent critics, Hutson concluded that Hearn had discovered profound sadness in New Orleans from the beginning, citing a letter he wrote to a friend just after his arrival, when he saw his first sunrise over Louisiana as "a dead bride crowned with orange flowers—a dead face that asked for a kiss." Hutson traced a macabre theme fitfully present in Hearn's journalism. "I cannot say how fair and rich and beautiful this dead South is," Hearn wrote to the same friend. "It has fascinated me.

I have resolved to live in it; I could not leave it for that chill and damp Northern life again." A theme of necrophilia runs through many of the imaginative sketches Hutson rescued from the incomplete files of the *Item* and from the more complete ones of other newspapers, but it remains only one theme. *Fantastics* reveals a unique awareness melding vision, time, and intense longing with intermittent melancholy: it catalogs glamour in the contexts of shadow.[41]

Much of the book concerns momentary visions accessible only in brief states of sunlight or shadow, especially at dusk. Shadows, including those formed on walls by hands held in positions producing silhouettes of geese, pigs, trees, and other forms, preoccupied many thoughtful adults from the 1840s onward.[42] Hearn wrote in the tradition of Poe, whose 1845 story "Shadow—a Parable" dealt with issues Von Reichenbach and Eastman later explored, especially luminosity and shadow as portals on another realm. Spiritualism and related occultism drove a fierce American interest in shadows and in the telluric conditions shaping atmospheric phenomena: aura and shadow sometimes fused.[43] A single shadow or "shade" might momentarily penetrate this world from another, and indeed might inveigle the unwary mind to follow it home, to shadowland.[44] But by 1865 photography blunted spiritualist argument. The devil "doesn't drive any more bargains for human shadows nowadays," averred Charles D. Gardette in "The Two Shadows: An Outline Sketch," a *Godey's Lady's Book* article. "The photographers have stopped his market."[45] Making photographs and looking at photographs ought to be safe, most of the time.[46] But throughout the nineteenth century, seeing shadows and silhouettes evolve from straightforward photography of colored objects provoked consideration of what other realms might be momentarily glimpsed at dusk, and how human will could shape both the seeing of shadows and the making of them, especially with a camera.[47] In the humid atmosphere of southern Louisiana, Hearn discovered optical effects unlike those he had known further north; they struck him as indeed fantastic and opening on faerie, the realm of genuine glamour.[48]

In 1880 Hearn told *Item* readers that just after sunset he had seen from an upper-story balcony "innumerable wrecks of kites fluttering" on the overhead lines of "the vast web which the Electric Spider has spun about the world," like "the bodies of gaudy flies." After sunset, in "the clear blue night," the kites lose all color and become the silhouettes of "malefactors mummified by sunheat upon their gibbets" or creatures "dancing grotesquely upon their perches like flying goblins" or "impaled birds, with death-stiffened wings, motionlessly attached to their wire snares." Hearn envisioned the kites as exemplars of childhood effort and fun snagged by something new that might snag other "toys of love and faith," gaudy and otherwise. Color, shape, and accident spark most of the visions.[49]

Hearn picked up a Japanese fan forgotten in a streetcar, marveled at "the grotesque foliage sharply cut against a horizon of white paper; and wonderful clouds as pink as Love," then asked, "Where did those Japanese get their exquisite taste for color and tint-contrasts?" Phrases like "sunsets so virginally carnation" emphasize the penetrating interest in light and color suffusing all his writing, but in the essay they preface an inquiry into scent. "The fairy colors were less strongly suggestive than something impalpable, invisible, indescribable, yet voluptuously enchanting which clung to the fan spirit-wise,—a tender little scent,—a mischievous perfume,—a titillating, tantalizing aroma" that leads Hearn to think of "a pillow covered with living supple silk of a woman's hair." The scent causes him to divide female odors into blonde and brunette ones, to distinguish the aroma of white roses from red, to calculate the faintness of odor emanating from a Chinese yellow rose and compare it against one as "fiercely ravishing as that of the white Jessamine," in which few can sleep without becoming faint. "Now the odor of the fan was not a blonde odor," Hearn concluded after imagining how personality and bodily shape parallel scent. "Young, slenderly graceful, with dark eyes and hair, skin probably a Spanish olive"—such a woman must have lost the fan in the trolley car.[50]

Fantastics emphasizes that the sensitive mind may hold more than consciousness admits. Some essays, especially "Hereditary Memories," explore the concept directly as an ethnological or medical issue opened by Darwin. Others approach it sideways. "Spring Phantoms," first an 1881 *Item* article, argues that for some dreamers blessed or cursed at birth, springtime brings dreams "of nostalgia, vague as the world-sickness, for the places where we shall never be; and fancies as delicate as arabesques of smoke." In quiet, such dreamers feel a languor, smell the incense of flowers, hear sound distort, then know "the sense of time and space" change as if "affected by hashish," then see sunlight shift. Male dreamers then dream or envision—they do not imagine—the ideal woman: "each year there will be a weirder sweetness and a more fantastic glory about the vision," often wrapped "in strange luminosity" like the "orange radiance of a Pacific sunset." Whatever the forces operating on sensitives, Hearn argued, they operate most effectively, most ruthlessly in secluded, quiet, abandoned places.[51]

Some of the later sketches, especially an 1884 one Hearn published in the *New Orleans Times-Democrat,* focus on travel from modern places to destinations so far in the bayous they are literally backwaters. Deep in the swamps the mind flexes: "through luminous distances the eye can just distinguish masses of foliage, madder-colored by remoteness, that seem to float in suspension between the brightness of the horizon and the brightness of water, like shapes of the Fata Morgana," he wrote of one exploration.[52] Beyond lie Louisiana islands whose inhabitants have lived almost wholly disconnected from the mainland since the postwar collapse of the sugarcane plantation economy. Hearn argued that anyone sensitive to energies and impressions need only open himself and explore Creole New Orleans and then the bayou country beyond. He understood old ways penetrating dense swamps to plantation houses destroyed in the Civil War, but he realized the necessity for traveling by boat far into the bayous.

Reality sometimes trumped fantasy and nudged Hearn into zones he found unnerving. As a *Times-Democrat* reporter, he mounted an 1883 expedition to Saint Malo, a "Manila village" a hundred miles from New Orleans. He wrote the first account of a hamlet populated wholly by Filipino men, some the descendants of Filipinos who had jumped ship in New Orleans in 1763, others deserters from the galleons sailing between Manila and Acapulco and between Vera Cruz and Cadiz. "We reached Saint Malo upon a leaden-colored day, and the scenery in its gray ghastliness recalled to us the weird landscape painted with words by Edgar Poe—'Silence: A Fragment,'" he wrote of a stilt village next to a wharf he saw resembling the spectral ship of Coleridge's "Rime of the Ancient Mariner."[53] Hearn had blundered through time and space to something timeless and unsettling. Rumor had proven true. Hearn fell back upon romantic literature typology: his pre-expedition ethnology reading seemed less than useful in a place suspended from time and reality.

After describing the brackish lake landscape for the "American" readers newly arrived in New Orleans and unlikely to ever venture south of Canal Street, let alone the bayous, he reported that the "human inhabitants are not less strange, wild, picturesque." Most "are cinnamon-colored men; a few are glossily yellow, like that bronze into which a small portion of gold is worked by the moulder." Hearn had read some ethnology in preparation for the expedition, and he knew that the Philippine archipelago included many different sorts of people; the Louisiana settlers represented more than one, but all markedly different from blacks. The men keep to themselves, except for one non-Filipino, a Portuguese, "perhaps a Brazilian maroon." Men who marry must marry non-Filipinos simply because no Filipino women live in the hemisphere. Those men quickly blend into New Orleans society after marriage, in large part because they speak Spanish. Living simply, without liquor or calendar but with modern firearms and one old clock, the single men inhabit the muddy foreshore of the Bronze Age.

Sunset seems glamorous in the isolated place. "The steel blue of the western horizon heated into furnace yellow, then cooled off into red splendors of astounding warmth and transparency. The bayou blushed crimson, the green of the marsh pools, of the shivering reeds, of the decaying timber-work, took fairy bronze tints, and then, immense with marsh mist, the orange-vermillion face of the sun peered luridly for the last time through the tall grasses upon the bank," Hearn concluded of a sunset as exotic as the inhabitants.[54] Saint Maló might be a figment of imagination, something from faerie, something from *Fantastics*. After visiting it, Hearn began to travel farther afield, caught up in exploring a Gulf Coast as culturally distant from New Orleans as New Orleans, or at least Creole New Orleans, seemed from "America."

He became a sort of ethnographer himself. He studied Creole speech in ways that still shape academic inquiry. His *Gombo Zhèbes: Little Dictionary of Creole Proverbs Selected from Six Creole Dialects* appeared in 1885. Its brief essay on Creole idioms in Louisiana derives from Hearn's sustained analysis of ethnographers studying Creole culture as far as Mauritius. He produced the first analysis of Creole cuisine, *La Cuisine Créole,* in the same year.[55] The books, both published in New York, reveal his voracious reading of British and French philology and ethnography, his correspondence with expert fieldworkers and academics, and his systematic interviewing of Creole speakers, especially housewives and chefs.[56] But Hearn never addressed voodoo in any significant way, perhaps because he misjudged the impact of the Santo Domingo exiles about which Cable proved expert, indeed perhaps expert enough to leave New Orleans.

What became the Haitian revolution began with a voodoo ceremony conducted at Bois Caïman by a legendary sorcerer, Dutty Boukman.[57] The slave uprising that rent the French colony terrified Spanish planters on the other half of Hispaniola, many of whom fled with their slaves and a number of free blacks to New Orleans between 1806 and 1810. Only a few years earlier, the French colonial government of Louisiana had prohibited the import of Santo Domingo slaves into the territory, believing that their allegiance to voodoo would foment slave rebellion.[58] Under United States rule the region welcomed the Santo Domingo expatriates, whose Spanish-speaking slaves diversified and deepened the existing voodoo belief already enlivened by the recent arrival of slaves from Martinique and Guadeloupe.[59] Voodoo probably arrived in Louisiana with the first African slaves from the Guinea coast, but as the dispirited Santo Domingo planters sipped coffee in the New Orleans Café des Exilés, their slaves and the many free blacks who accompanied them transformed Louisiana voodoo.

Before the Civil War, free people of color, especially mulattoes and quadroons, made up the voodoo leadership, and slaves most of the believers, but Santo Domingo voodoo shaped rites and beliefs from the 1820s onward. After the war, the leadership changed very little, although Spanish-language voodoo became far less noticeable: almost invariably, the ruling queen spoke French Creole. Between 1855 and the 1890s, when newspapers stopped reporting on its rites, voodoo enticed many poor whites, and many distraught middle- and upper-class white women. Cable suspected that Hearn misinterpreted voodoo in part because he did not know enough Spanish Creole to recognize the nuances of the rites he witnessed or to befriend people on the margins of Santo Domingo–based voodoo.

Hearn missed—or at least never mentioned in print—the sexual energy implicit in voodoo. In 1825 a fifteen-year-old white boy accompanied a slave woman owned by his parents to a voodoo initiation ceremony. Decades later he recalled a nighttime rite involving stuffed cats, a "black doll with a dress variegated by cabalistic signs and emblems" wearing "a necklace of the vertebrae of snakes," drumming and other music he had never heard elsewhere, and a voodoo queen waving a huge live snake over her head. The ceremony involved a dance begun by "a perfect Semiramis from the jungles of Africa" and joined by everyone except him. "Under the passion of the hour, the women tore off their garments, and entirely nude, went on dancing—no, not dancing, but wriggling like snakes," and at that the boy ran for home, terrified. "If I ever have realized a sense of the real visible presence of his majesty, the devil, it was that night among his Voudou worshippers," he recalled nearly six decades later, a few years before the New Orleans police department burst in upon a voodoo ceremony in which ten black men, nearly naked, lay on the floor surrounded by fifteen white women, all watching a nearly naked sorcerer dance among them.[60] The *Times-Democrat* reported that the officers "for a few minutes could only look on in listless apathy," then recovered their self-possession and arrested everyone, including a white seventeen-year-old girl present with her mother.[61] Hearn and Cable having departed New Orleans, no journalists scrutinized the sexuality implicit in voodoo, and the city of legalized vice turned its attention away from something it feared. Attention to voodoo might spell the end of organized vice, especially prostitution It might bring worse.

By 1920 voodoo had slithered out of modernist white southerner vision and publications, supplanted by the native African folk magic called hoodoo.[62] Educated, forward-looking white southerners studiously ignored voodoo. Just as it had long before seemed the essential energy that might spark a slave rebellion in Louisiana—and perhaps elsewhere along the Gulf Coast and northward along the Mississippi—so it became the mocking shadow of the modernist "new South" championed, advertised, and examined by so many boosters, academics, and investors.[63] Hoodoo might involve evil: practitioners knew how to hex enemies, even kill them, and sometimes worked their dark magic on behalf of paying clients.[64] A 1928 popular Paramount recording by Gertrude "Ma" Rainey, "Black Dust Blues," insinuated that goofer dust—the generations-old slave concoction made of graveyard dirt, powdered sulfur, salt, ground snake heads or skins, and anvil dust (the black metallic powder found around blacksmith equipment)—killed enemies. A year later Romeo Nelson intimated its power in "Gettin' Dirty Just Shakin' That Thing." In blues—and jazz—float hundreds of hoodoo hints, often words like *mojo,* designating the flannel bag in which Memphis male believers carried talismans against evil (bags worn by women in and around that city are still called *nation sacks*), known as a *juju* in New Orleans, where the charm is called a *gris-gris,* a corruption of a Caribbean term, *gree-gree.*[65] In a 1939 recording "I Don't Know," Cripple Clarence Lofton emphasized that goofering killed. By 1930 most United States young people knew something about hoodoo, especially goofering and the possibilities of sexual mind control, but vastly less about its far more powerful and secretive Gulf Coast relation.[66] In 1935, when Lofton sang the blues in "Strut That Thing," the sexual innuendo had become clear; black music had begun replacing European music as the armature around which spun American entertainment culture and especially a sexualized energy Hollywood eschewed.[67]

While city people marveled at what electricity did, while New Yorkers coveted the Rolleiflex and Leica cameras German tourists carried about Manhattan, while radio broadcast black music to those fortunate enough to have access to its programs, folklorists discovered terra incognita in the rural South. In the late 1890s, their work sparked by that of Hearn and other postbellum observers, antiquarians and others had begun publishing fragments about voodoo practices surviving in New Orleans and the bayou country, and related beliefs and practices in the upland, backcountry rural South.[68] By 1920 academics had begun publishing monographs built on earlier collecting infrequently reported in the *Journal of American Folklore.* In the middle 1920s appeared a spate of scholarly books focused on the potential overthrow of the white race Lothrop Stoddard articulated in his 1922 *Rising Tide of Color*. Newbell Niles Puckett's massive *Folk Beliefs of the Southern Negro* and Edward C. L. Adams's *Congaree Sketches: Scenes from Negro Life in the Swamps of the Congaree* proved especially influential after being adopted as required texts in university anthropology courses.[69]

Puckett combined intensive archival research and anthropological theory with wide-ranging field work: he examined voodoo and related practices from southern Louisiana to Missouri, linked them to similar customs along the Georgia coast, and noted the growing importance of voodoo in Pittsburgh, Philadelphia, and New York, where West Indian immigrants connected with blacks relocating from the South. He examined narratives of the circa-1900 New Orleans mixed-race orgies, and while his fieldwork led him to believe that organized voodoo might be dying out in New Orleans (he did not study the still nearly impenetrable bayou country), he befriended "goofer doctors" across the South, and learned a bit about making charms nowadays referenced in popular-song lyrics.[70] Puckett conceived of voodoo, and hoodoo and its more Americanized variants practiced by "conjure doctors," in layered ways; his many informants ranged from a small-town Mississippi police chief to black blacksmiths. While *Folk Beliefs of the Southern Negro* argues forcefully for the transfer of African culture across the Atlantic and its modification by Haitian and other immigrants, it penetrates deeply into the endurance of belief in the isolated rural areas in which fantasy writers centered their fiction.

Most importantly for contemporaneous fantasy writers who sometimes personally witnessed voodoo practices, read of them in specialist journals, or heard references to them in songs on the radio, Puckett emphasized that the beliefs and practices flowed within and outside modern media, including cinema, recorded music, radio, and even photography.[71] In his 1923 *On the Margin*, Aldous Huxley averred that cinema "audiences soak passively in the tepid bath of nonsense" when not half-consciously listening to the gramophone or radio.[72] Puckett probed further, scrutinizing how people whose intellects were dulled by modern media more easily accepted folk beliefs that were not only shaping Hollywood-centric media but also being reshaped by con artists wise to a bit of goofer-dust shop theory, if so wary of voodoo itself that they left it alone.

By 1926 voodoo practitioners and goofer doctors had integrated photography into older practices. Jilted southern blacks placed photographs of inconstant lovers upside down for nine days to lure them back. Such gentle practices coexisted with malign ones, especially hanging photographs upside down to cause headaches, insanity, or death. Putting a photograph under a dripping leak in a roof produced madness in its subject, and a conjurer might kill someone by nailing his photograph to a green tree and shooting it on nine consecutive mornings. In many instances, conjurers simply buried portrait snapshots in graveyards and sat back to await the death of the subjects.[73] In so doing they fused photography, not only with the evil or Judas eye belief Puckett found deeply embedded in both southern black and poor-white culture, but also with the zebraws, the grave-robbing hags from which conjure doctors might save both the living and the dead.[74] Photography, wind-up record players, and radio-broadcast songs by black singers did nothing to terminate voodoo beliefs and practices: instead they spread them across wider territories.[75] Technological advances, especially radio, profoundly unsettled many East and West Coast intellectuals: radio waves transmitted the blues and jazz far from the Gulf Coast and synchronized voodoo with sexuality and sinister, inchoate cultural undercurrents, most racialized.[76]

Blues was seen as destabilizing and jazz as destroying middle-class, white-based media protocols.[77] In the contemporaneous opinion of the national music chairman of the General Federation of Women's Clubs, Katherine Holton, jazz is "originally the accompaniment of the voodoo dancer," a music that can only "stimulate barbarity and sensuality."[78] As the blues morphed into a jazz only remotely related to the brothel music of the Razzy Dazzy Spasm Band, the editors of the *Double Dealer* confronted a political and intellectual trap they tried to escape by reprinting Hearn rather than Cable. The former either knew little of voodoo or wrote little about what he knew, but the latter knew a great deal and recognized its long-term political significance. Hearn thought the southern public school would eliminate voodoo. Cable had no such illusions, and realized that while belief in hoodoo made many black Americans appear simplistic or silly in the eyes of most urban whites, and consequently unworthy of political equality, belief in voodoo simultaneously made them evil and powerful.[79] In 1927 Leora Meoux Henderson toured the United States with an all-woman band called The Twelve Vampires. In a roaring era already singing about "Hard-hearted Hannah, the vamp of Savannah, the vamp of Savannah, G-A," "vampire" evoked mostly laughs.[80] Voodoo did not, especially in Louisiana and along the Mississippi River, far from muddy roads, deep in the bayou country.

Voodoo produced a 1920s resurgence of attention to sexual energy, miscegenation, and Afro-Carib music unnoticed since polite literature began ignoring the quadroons of New Orleans in the 1880s. Before the Civil War, Creole and some Anglo upper-class men attended the quadroon balls and negotiated for the favors of women they desired in ceremonies newspapers never mentioned. The women became mistresses installed in pretty houses on Rampart Street, and many retained their lovers' fealty long after the men married. Anglo women hated the gorgeous denizens of the western edge of the city. Decades after the end of the Civil War and the subsequent migration of quadroon women northward, where many were able to "pass" into white society, Anglo women loathed their memory and feared their return. "Unscrupulous and pitiless, by nature or circumstance, as one chooses to view it, and secretly still claiming the racial license of Africa," wrote Grace King in *New Orleans: The Place and the People* in 1895, "they were, in regard to family purity, domestic peace, and household dignity, the most insidious and the deadliest foes a community ever possessed."[81]

Blues originating in Memphis and jazz in New Orleans moved north along the Illinois Central Railroad to Chicago, where the music blossomed into a force that shook white culture to the east and frightened Hollywood filmmakers to the west.[82] As New York struggled to maintain its preeminence in shaping national literature, music, and visual art, as Tin Pan Alley and the producers of Broadway musicals realized their slipping grasp on the creation of popular music, the sexual energy and voodoo force of New Orleans remained a shadowy presence in national media, one rarely surfacing in Hollywood cinema.[83] However New York and Hollywood depicted "the South" before World War II, New Orleans, the Creole Gulf Coast, and voodoo played at best only cameo roles. They became far more important in broadcast and recorded music.[84]

The 1920s rediscovered Hearn but could not recover his lost New Orleans writings. The *Double Dealer* and other periodicals had made Hearn the favored explicator of something special in Louisiana and along the Creole coast. His mix of at-home anthropology, light-hearted delight in non-Anglo culture, and visual fantasy struck 1920s and 1930s readers as deliciously edgy but in the end safe. Readers admired his prose as they missed subtle references to voodoo and quadroon women. "When I awoke a woman was bending over me," relates the old Spanish priest in one of Hearn's 1880 "Fantastics." "She was wholly unclad, and with her perfect beauty, and the tropical tint of her skin, she looked like a statue of amber."[85] Quadroons, voodoo, and other subjects Hearn skirted deftly in the 1880s remained troubling a half century later. In *Gombo Zhèbes* he placed voodoo and quadroons in lengthy footnotes implying that he considered all Creoles to be believers in voodoo, and that they would use it under duress. "Thus, in a Louisiana Creole song, we find a quadroon mother promising her daughter a charm to prevent the white lover from forsaking her," he wrote in one note, before concluding airily in another, "The character of Creole folklore is very different from European folklore in the matter of superstition."[86]

Hearn may have known more than he noted in print. "There are tropical lilies which are venomous, but they are more beautiful than the frail and icy-white lilies of the North," he wrote in an 1880 letter to a friend. Charles Woodward Hutson used the sentence in 1914 as the epigraph to the first edition of *Fantastics*.[87] Hearn became the darling of the fast crowd struggling to stay ahead of voodoo, jazz, and the undead history of the older streets of New Orleans, the bayou backwaters, and the Creole and American plantation houses Laughlin photographed.

Something behind history reached into the present and teased and tormented the editors of the *Double Dealer*. The magazine published a number of poems involving the seeing of what Laughlin knew as apparitions. "The Swamp Spirit," a 1924 poem by Basil Thompson, one of the magazine's founders, revolves about something that "is no common wraith," "no meager wraith" inhabiting the emptiness beyond bayou wastes and will-o'-the-wisp flickerings. In another poem of the same year, "Timothy Spied a Goblin," a modern mother sees what her young son first reported "peeping over the fence," but she sees it just indoors, between an open window and swaying curtains. The editors accepted that something—at least in the Crescent City, elsewhere in southern Louisiana, and upstream along the Mississippi—sometimes peered just over fences or into windows.

Consequently they published a number of critical essays on modern fantasy writers. Most explicate "other ways of seeing" as reflected in the works of British writers from Alfred Watkins to M. R. James. Cuthbert Wright introduced the work of Arthur Machen to *Double Dealer* readers in 1923. In "The Mystery of Arthur Machen" he dismissed turn-of-the-century spiritualism nonsense and the frenzied zaniness of 1914, in which many British soldiers saw some sort of angel or spirit of British triumph floating above the battle of Mons.[88] Here was a writer initially condemned by British critics and at first avoided by most British readers as grotesquely immoral, especially in his linking of sexuality, decadent violence, and the power of glamour. Wright argued that a "scientifically relative" concept underlay most of Machen's fiction: "simply that matter is as awful and unknowable as spirit." In everyone's brain, although a bit more active in the brains of sensitives, is a region with the potential to sense hyperreality. Machen spoke of "seeing the god Pan," and Wright accepted that much of the novelist's success derived from linking sensitives, tradition, and modern science, especially physics and psychology.[89]

Illicit drug use in Machen's work might be, Wright told readers, "nothing less than the Wine of the witches' Sabbath—that phenomenon of satanic mania which so frightened the imaginations of our forefathers." Machen offered a unique view of something beyond the traditional Christianity seemingly shattered by modern science. "Suppose that the Fairies, the famous 'little people,' who have always been saluted in certain parts of England with signs of the Cross rather than smiles, still exist, a secondary race, fallen out of the march of evolution, but still lurking in remote and savage places," Wright postulated. The concept perforce transforms any rural-based tale in which such a creature intrudes.[90] New Orleans had a long-standing interest in energies usually outside the ken of white Anglos, especially the sexual ones implicit in voodoo. It knew brownies of its own.

Double Dealer covers typically involved woodcuts depicting nude white men and women together, often touching one another, genitals discretely masked by luxuriant vegetation. The Art Deco covers imply an awareness of sexual energy revealed annually at the Mardi Gras balls, parades, and parties, and imply some contest between whites and nonwhites, perhaps especially the descendants of slaves brought from Hispaniola, Martinique, and elsewhere in the Caribbean, rather than directly from Africa.[91] They suggest a reason why the editors published Lord Dunsany and other British fantasy authors, and American fantasy writers who otherwise found an outlet in the Chicago pulp magazine *Weird Tales*.[92] Wright understood the power of Machen's work, and its pigeonholing by both mainstream and conservative religious British critics. Machen had propelled fantasy writing toward an explication of the apparition Laughlin discovered accidentally at Belle Grove.

At the beginning of World War II voodoo had gathered strength in New Orleans. A small number of longtime white writers glimpsed its manifestations, and in 1939 Lyle Saxon published a lengthy account of a ceremony convened on his behalf. Saxon convinced a voodoo sorcerer to work a spell that might recover a lost love, and his plan worked perfectly. For ten dollars plus expenses (mostly for liquor), and his promise to report nothing to the police no matter how badly things turned out, Saxon glimpsed a midnight ritual in a storeroom beyond a French Quarter Creole courtyard. But the sorcerer, known to upset ordinary African Americans with his charms and occult knowledge, proves only a servant to an aged woman, a queen of voodoo, perhaps the queen of all Louisiana. A few participants in the ceremonies, most scantily clad, make Saxon remove almost all his clothes, and in time cut him to draw blood. Saxon catalogs the acolytes, distinguishing between "one emaciated *griffe*—a light yellow girl" and a mulatto girl, and focusing on the role of Robert, the "full-blooded Congo black man" duped into providing the ceremony on his behalf. After chants that evoke spells, the queen falls into a trance, then writhes as spirits possess her, then swallows a restorative bowl of gumbo. Then almost simultaneously with the start of the intoxicating thrumming music, the acolytes break into a dance alien to anything Saxon knows, one man imitating a rabbit munching grass, a woman licking herself as a cat licks its fur. The dance morphs into orgy.[93]

Saxon described a scene little different from what the teenage boy remembered from the 1820s. The women tear off the last of their clothes, and the men follow; a man bites a woman's breast, drawing blood. "The big Negro, quite naked now, catches a thin mulatto girl around the waist, and bears her down across the table-cloth, upsetting the candles"; other dancers smash bottles of wine. Saxon retreats from the scene, crawls around scattered furniture, drags on his clothes in an alcove, and stumbles into the New Orleans night beyond the courtyard.[94]

In 1895 Grace King traced the arrival of voodoo from Hispaniola. In *New Orleans: The Place and the People* she notes "contortions of the body, convulsions, frenzy, ecstasies, the queen ever leading" ceremonies morphing into orgies, but implies that such activities are long vanished.[95] Saxon made clear that they had become stronger, more frequent, and both more hidden from and more intrusive into white culture. Fantasy writers had already embraced them.

In 1936 the creator of Conan the Barbarian, Robert E. Howard, published "Black Canaan" in *Weird Tales*. Howard wrote many short stories about antebellum slave uprisings in Louisiana and Mississippi, most revolving around voodoo, hoodoo, and sex, especially the role of black or mulatto women in seducing white planters. Nowadays his work appears racist, but it rewards sustained attention. It is complex in obscure ways.[96] It insists especially that slavery failed to destroy much African and Caribbean culture and that upper-class white southern women feared their own sexuality might not compete with that of dark-skinned women.

"I had never before paid any attention to a black or brown woman. But this quadroon girl was different from any I had ever seen," recalls the planter narrator. The woman is graceful, exquisitely dressed, well spoken, with "features regular as a white woman's," but the planter nonetheless sees her as "barbaric, in the open lure of her smile, in the gleam of her eyes, in the shameless posturing of her voluptuous body." Her beauty makes him "blind and dizzy." As the entire remote region rises in incipient revolt, the planter understands that the "ghostly light that hovered among the trees was only part" of the released power suffusing the otherwise orderly plantation landscape. In the next few days he learns fear as he realizes that "some obscure, deep-hidden instinct sensed peril," as he remembers what he knows of "voodoo men," and as he accepts that the sorcerer leading the revolt has produced force beyond the ken of white men and domestic animals. "There are invisible *Things*—black spirits of the deep swamps and the slimes of river beds—the Negroes know of them," he admits, as his horse shies from what its rider cannot see. When he encounters the woman again, this time nude except for a sash around her hips, he understands that some fierce voodoo force empowers her. "She was alien, even in this primitive setting," and "the tattooing on her brown skin" alerts him to her role in the voodoo ceremonies into which he has stumbled. "She posed derisively before me, not in allure, but in mockery," the planter recalls. Her power is immensely old, from "the Kongo," "the Ancient Land," and his consciousness drifts into her control.[97] His power is modern, chiefly in his revolver, and it quakes before something greater, not regular, older than white settlement.

"Anyone could look at those Negroes of his and tell that they may have come (and probably did) from a much older country than Virginia or Carolina but it wasn't a quiet one," William Faulkner remarks in the first pages of his 1936 novel *Absalom, Absalom!*[98] In the end, his novel deals with the willingness of whites, and maybe Creoles, to accept incest, but to draw the line at miscegenation. Howard tapped into the same occult oldness Faulkner knew and Saxon experienced, the oldness Zora Neale Hurston depicted in her 1935 *Mules and Men* in a lengthy, detailed description of the training of a conjure doctor.[99] But Howard was not the first fantasy writer who glimpsed something rooted in New Orleans and the bayou country and spreading north to Chicago and New York.

The author of *Peter Pan* provided an introduction to the British edition of Cable's *Grandissimes* in 1898. J. M. Barrie thought New Orleans was "perhaps the most picturesque city in America," and he mused at length about the historical depth of its diverse population. Not everyone Barrie met in New Orleans struck him as even real. Creole women who complained that Cable had misunderstood their past and their present condition made him think they masked something; they convinced him that "the sweet Creoles who haunt" Cable's "beautiful pages were not always ghosts but ghost-like."[100] His is a very compelling introduction to a novel nowadays read mostly as a work of local color. It suggests that Barrie recognized how much the far distant past Cable presented not only suffused the era that produced Buchan's odd tale of women-stealing brownies but also presaged terrific racial and sexual contests in the decades ahead. Barrie realized that white men might be attracted far more strongly to dark-skinned glamorous women than to the "purest" and smartest white women they encountered. Whatever power the dark-skinned women wielded, voodoo or otherwise, it seemed fundamentally sexual, and grounded in obscure, secluded, often abandoned places.

Milo Rigaud published his *Secrets of Voodoo* in France in 1953. It appeared in translation in the United States only in 1969, perhaps too late to figure in contemporaneous criticism of the developing sexual revolution. Rigaud averred that voodoo rites take power from both "a supernatural origin" he traced to the west coast of Africa and "a geographical origin" not confined to Haiti. Western hemisphere rites "proceed from the influence of the sun in the atmosphere," something he admitted is awkward to explain, "since not everyone is endowed with the ability to comprehend the esoterics of magic." The rites emphasize a fundamental phallic power represented in the *poteaumitan* or post that supports the roof of the *oum'phor* or temple open to the sun, and an equally fundamental feminine power ordinarily embodied in both the snake and its adept servants, the latter sometimes taking on a maleness as one of the mystères or gods. Rigaud described in detail, including drawings and photographs, a religion grounded in light, vision, and the equality of the sexes and focused on the nude body as a conductor of occult force. He shaped his exegesis around the role of voodoo in the early nineteenth-century Haitian independence movement which frightened Santo Domingo planters to New Orleans.[101]

He blunted his description of its fierce sexual and sexualized energy.

By the middle 1960s that energy struck some observers as fading in white women, especially those intent on office-work careers. In *The Flight from Woman,* the psychologist Karl Stern argued that Margaret Mead, Simone de Beavoir, and other 1950s heralds of a new feminist era might inadvertently mislead young women.[102] He admitted that "for millennia women have suffered atrocious forms of social and legal injustice" and that "it is no exaggeration to say that they have been, and often still are, the victims of a kind of interior colonialism." But white women, he believed, had begun to abandon the energies Rigaud thought empowered colonized slaves to throw off their masters. "Since the French Revolution and the rise of the feminist movement, the cry for *equality* has changed into an assertion of *sameness*," he proclaimed. Sameness struck him as dubious and likely sinister. "The alleged mysteriousness of the feminine is treated with benevolent jocularity in feminist literature," when authors do not simply condemn it as one more way men keep women from careers. But in words echoing those of Rigaud, Stern insisted that "though the definition of the mysterious is that we cannot explain it, we can elucidate the psychology of it."[103] Stern thought such elucidation prudent. At a critical moment in race and gender relations, workplace change, and the tightening grip of electronic mass media, he intimated, most women might be exchanging extraordinary power for something paltry.

Anne Rice published her first novel, *Interview with the Vampire,* in 1976. Set in New Orleans and elsewhere in southern Louisiana, it introduces themes that have shaped her fiction over three decades. Vampirism, occultism, and powerful but invisible forces twine themselves in race, decay, deviancy, wealth, grandeur, and sexuality. Voodoo floats free as context, and seeing becomes dangerous. While frequently denigrated as a "women's" author, Rice depicts the deeper undercurrents of New Orleans as slowly shaping the modern American mainstream. Only New Orleans suits her purpose. Readers cannot imagine her novels set in Pittsburgh, Duluth, Spokane, let alone San Francisco or New York.[104] But they can imagine power beyond the humdrum despair of corporate-cubicle careers, power wielded by voodoo practitioners.

Apparitions haunt Rice's novels, and some characters see them. In *Blackwood Farm,* Aunt Queen sees at least a shimmer of Goblin, the eldritch double of a boy snared in the frontiers of vampirism, when she narrows her eyes. But place becomes apparition too, when the light falls just so. "I saw the branches of the trees moving, and then very slowly there came into view the ghosts again, the very same collection, as pale and wretched as before," the boy recounts of seeing something among the oaks and cypresses crowding an old graveyard. "I had a peculiar and distinct feeling about the oaks—that they were watching me and had seen me see the spirits, and that they were sentient and vigilant and had a personality of their own."[105] The protagonist descries near-parallel universes and intractable force fields akin to those Rice details in *Interview with the Vampire.* He accepts the glamour fusing plantation houses, New Orleans alleys, bayou hunting shacks, and Sugar Devil Swamp with women who denigrate high-salaried banality. His is the world Laughlin photographed, the world of ghosts along the Mississippi.

Laughlin recognized that he photographed apparitions by accident. He asserted his right to the images and to conjuring apparitions through photographic composition. The arduous effort to drive and walk far into the ecosystem of apparitions earned him the right to glimpse and shape the glamour embedded in abandoned, unsettled landscapes mocking modernity, mass-media views, and middle-brow notions of progress. "The mystery of time, the magic of light, the enigma of reality—and their interrelationships—are my constant themes and preoccupations," Laughlin proclaimed to *Modern Photography* readers in 1961. "My central position is one of extreme romanticism: the concept of reality as being mystery and magic: of the power of the 'unknown' which human beings do not want to realize, and which none of their religious and intellectual systems can really take into account."[106]

9 Old Fields

Afforested land, often ragged and interrupted by gores of wild meadow, covered most of rural New England after about 1880, always suggesting something vanished or vanquished but to some people, perhaps especially women, offering possibilities for creative experiment.

As LAUGHLIN PHOTOGRAPHED THE MOST DISQUIET-
ing scenes deep in the Louisiana back country, what he called the power
of the unknown stressed the brittle intellectual system of rural New England. Traditional understanding of local history clashed with novel ecological awareness: from the Depression onward, abandoned landscape
became fantasy theater. Early in boyhood I learned firsthand about fragments of this.

"Going cross-lots" meant penetrating decrepitude. The overgrown cart
paths, fields springing up in sweet fern as the white pine woodlots in-
vaded their perimeters, tottering wharves and other estuary marsh wreckage, crumbling dams and spillways, and cellar holes guarded by lilacs
composed my boyhood landscape. Agriculture endured but scarcely prospered. My school bus rumbled past the big farm that produced the milk
that students drank at lunch, cows ambled about the fields outside my
junior-high-school windows, and all through high school in October I
smiled at the stony fields of pumpkins heralding Halloween. But everywhere woods impinged on what adults designated *old fields,* the plowed
fields, pastures, and meadows surrendered to midwestern competition,
goldenrod, and brush. The school bus windows opened on young trees
sprouting in home acreage, on tall pines long established on back lots,
and on barnyards punctuated with clumps of juniper. Away from the school
bus routes, long-established decrepitude made children cautious and teenagers wary: so much appeared not merely abandoned but eerily derelict.
Even on sunny days, old fields sundered from schoolroom history and
aesthetics disconcerted the young. In them the past loomed, as I realized
later it did to Laughlin, as times before, not a continuum but a sometimes gentle and sometimes angry swirl. In the grown-over woods anyone
might drop into a forgotten well.

Light illuminated old fields in ways I later recognized as peculiar.
Ocean-air moisture sometimes intensified an effect produced in part by
the youth of so many trees interrupted haphazardly by tall, much older
ones. Typically beeches, the mature trees survived from the era when they
shaded livestock on summer days. They towered above seas of white pine,
the pines often only two or three feet tall at the middle of abandoned
fields and perhaps twenty feet along perimeters. Older stands of pine
flowed downhill into extensive swamps, a few covered in white cedar but
most long logged over and abandoned to hemlock, some of which dated
to colonial times. Light melted not upon pasture grass but upon whole
fields of low- or high-bush blueberry, sumac, and other primary succes-

sion plants, or of white pine. Walking or bicycling along the faint paths meant moving intermittently into bowls of light reflecting from just below or above eye level. A field of three-foot-tall white pines is scarcely a pine grove, but I had no vocabulary that correctly designated it or named the sort of light that bounced from the pines when the moist ocean wind swept over them on sunny days. Tall timothy and other hay grasses reflect sunlight in waves during wind, but young pines reflect it in ways that characterize the old-fields experience of landscape peculiar to my first photographic efforts. They bristle and vibrate and then catch the fog moving in from the beach.

In the late 1940s the telephone company abbreviated its Oldfield 9 exchange to OL 9, but part of the township beyond Valley Swamp used a different one, Triangle 8. That region centered on a crossroads graced by a post office, gas station, and chicken farms. In the middle 1950s the exchanges shifted from operator-assisted calling to direct dial, but we kept our party line and rural connectivity. We needed to dial only the last five digits of any number. While we no longer spoke them aloud to operators, the exchange names reminded us of old fields and a triangle cut off by a huge, nearly impenetrable swamp.[1]

Away from its main-traveled, paved roads, my coastal New England town offered thousands of acres of tiered abandonment. Until the end of high school, I accepted the landscape as ordinarily mine, the way local space happened to be and happened to me, and I accepted its light as ordinary too.[2] A quarter mile from our two state-numbered highways, both narrow, numbered roads maintained in part with state funds, few vehicles traveled the town ways. The roads along which I bicycled were sometimes devoid of moving vehicles for more than an hour at a time, and typically connected only with equally quiescent roads. Little traffic flowed north to south, and then only that which passed across the immovable drawbridge; even less moved east to west, for eastward lay the Atlantic. My parents worried about my being struck by a car while bicycling, but my mom worried more about my hitting a stone or stick, falling hard, striking my head, and lying in the road for a long time until someone came along to help. She had reason to worry. I had wrecked badly when I was eight, on a dirt road going cross-lots, and seemed likely to wreck again: cracks, grass, and rocks interrupted the paved edges of too many blacktop roads, but often I veered from paved roads. I preferred the derelict ways slicing abandonment, the paths that disappeared now and again into the mysterious light of decrepitude.

Long-disused cart paths made splendid shortcuts. Going cross-lots involved following scarcely discernible routes through mature woodlots, fields ten or twenty years or more abandoned after plowing or harvest, and unmowed meadows growing up in steeple bush, sweet fern, and pine. Sometimes the paths dove into brooks by then unbridged or skirted swamps that advanced in spring rains, but I never detoured. Falling trees meant lugging the Raleigh over a trunk and then pedaling, not finding another way: the paths proved to be as efficient shortcuts for a bicycle as they had for farm wagons.

I cherished the one-speed, thin-tired Raleigh my parents gave me when I turned twelve. Unlike three-speed bicycles equipped with hand-brakes and shifter, it had no cables to snag on branches and no intricate gear-changing hub to bind up when fording brooks and deep puddles. It encouraged exploration along old paths we called "brush ways" or "green ways" when we called them anything at all.[3]

Angling from shortcuts stretched the remnants of ways frequently discernible only in late autumn, after leaves fell. The remnants tantalized. Sometimes on my bicycle, but more often on foot, I followed them into imaginative exercise.[4] Decades later I read Hilaire Belloc's extended rumination on the eeriness of abandoned rural Britain and realized that I too had known faint tracks unfamiliar to many who lived and traveled along the thin-paved roads short distances from them.[5]

Now and then landscape interpretation seemed possible. A massive pasture beech had toppled, crushing a simple wood bridge across a brook, ending farm tractor access to the field just beyond and isolating the obsolete manure spreader.[6] At other times, discerning what happened took repeated visits. A chunk of estuary salt marsh had caved in, blocking the salt creek leading inland to a tiny ruined wharf. No longer useful in shallow-water navigation and thus no longer a destination for people who once visited it along a now almost untraceable path, the wharf itself collapsed into a sea of spartina grass, then floated a few hundred yards north in a gale-driven tide.[7] I could never learn why the 1930s Ford sat abandoned, a sieve of bullet holes, among white pines planted fifty years before my discovery, but it had driven over young trees to reach its permanent position.[8] And sometimes I found something that led me to trace a path.

The summer I turned ten I crested a tiny hill far beyond the active and abandoned sand pits and stopped to look ahead at the swamp beyond. I stepped forward and dropped two feet into a shallow grave: I brought home a human skull, which for convenience I mounted on a nearby femur. After my father arrived home from work and summoned the chief of police, after the crowd assembled and hiked out to the site, after county health officials removed the bones and four other skeletons, I returned again and again to the site, looking for the path that must have led to a private graveyard. I found its traces, but never a hint of the cellar hole I associated with obscured family plots.[9]

Consolidation at the start of sixth grade connected me with two other boys dedicated to cross-lots shortcuts and the exploration of abandonment. Through high school we shared our information and hunches and spent days on bicycles and afoot. We learned to shave miles from paved-road routes, and on and beyond the faint paths we blundered into all sorts of discoveries, the most important of which involved links to what we speculated were times before, something distinct from the schoolbook past. Just as we learned to make the woods tell us recent information by watching for footprints and other marks in the soil, disturbed leaves and snapped branches, and even petiole-snapped green leaves lying on the ground, so we probed older history on the ground.[10] Lying on our stomachs, we saw the long-crushed pines under the bullet-riddled Ford, looked at the tall trees around us, and estimated how long the car had been there, far from any cart path. We probed much older mysteries too.

Many of the cart paths and footpaths connected to each other in meandering ways that in time made antiquarian or agricultural sense, but others ran straight enough to be different. We found miles of what we first called "the Indian trail" because it missed most extant old houses and most cellar holes and seemed unlikely to have ever carried wheeled vehicles. Old men in time explained that it was a section of the original Bay Path between Plymouth and Boston, segments of which lay along ageless Wampanoag alignments. At one point, it crossed a seventeenth-century cart path elderly farmers called "the old river road" paralleling the north bank of the estuary. Abandoned since late in the seventeenth century and pretty much plowed over, then given over to forest, the low-lying route flooded one too many times for colonist patience. We discovered the cut-granite abutments of one of its vanished bridges, themselves flooded by an early nineteenth-century mill dam. We saw them through particularly clear ice one day when skating, and returned the following summer to dive at the site. Old-timers told us that nineteenth-century bankers had intended a railroad route along the old river road, but had given up owing to tidal-flooding worries. The old men encouraged our rummaging, muttering that at least we showed an interest in what hard work had accomplished long ago.

Mill ponds confounded our understanding of old paths, Wampanoag and colonist both, because they obscured intersections and the lazy curves that followed gravel rather than mud. By 1967 accidental interest, an inclination to be outdoors, and a sense of superiority had combined to make us value our interest. Our friends thought our rambling harmless or ridiculous if they noted it at all, but they grudgingly admitted we knew how to get around.[11]

We knew that period books aimed at tourists anxious to avoid highway travel defined our town and adjacent territory as quaint and quiet. Authors who published *The Old Coast Road* and similar guides emphasized the tertiary paved roads twisting among the marshes, swamps, and hills, now and then passing a summer-only antique shop or other tourist attraction, and intersecting at silent junctions graced with cast-iron, not steel, directional signs.[12] In 1968 the authors of *A Cruising Guide to the New England Coast* reported that the drawbridge over the estuary had been inoperable for so many decades that the upper reaches of the North River remained "quite wild country" accessible only by very small craft.[13] Like much else in the old-field landscape, the derelict drawbridge signaled enterprise long gone from an estuary whose shipbuilding industry collapsed around 1870: we launched our rowboats from overgrown gashes in salt marsh that had been shipyards a century earlier.[14] We expected an occasional summer tourist on the back roads, and the rare adventurer exploring the estuary above the old bridge, but we understood and valued far older routes, almost none open to motor vehicles. We did not understand why people from away prized quiet quaintness but feared turning onto dirt roads, or why they seemed so jittery when lost at sunset or out of gas in the meandering marshes far above the drawbridge.

We failed also to understand the abandonment still happening around us, and books taught us little, except that some photographers had begun to find it picturesque or photogenic or possessing some as-yet-undesignated quality causing it to appear in *Look at America: The Country You Know, and Don't Know* and similar folios shelved under an east window in the tiny library facing the town common.[15] We received little in the way of encouragement when we asked, especially from schoolteachers and the old: our teachers thought themselves charged with educating us away from failed farming, and the old perhaps thought us too young to know the alcoholism and other secrets of ongoing decrepitude. Ongoing abandonment struck us as something insidious, obvious yet obscure, charged with adult meaning and power and seamlessly welded to abandonment of earlier times.[16]

Adults rarely followed the paths. A handful of men went hunting along them in the autumn despite the near total lack of deer, and spring enticed a few fishermen to seek out locations they had known since boyhood, but business lured almost no one.[17] Once while breathing hard after outrunning a bull we'd surprised grazing in an old field, we encountered its owner, searching for it in an adjacent woodlot. Sometimes we encountered the local surveyor, who talked precisely and patiently with us if he were not perplexed by some colonial description of metes and bounds snarling an inheritance. But year after year, we met no men, and only a few women and girls, some getting a tan while berrying in the old fields smothered with low-bush blueberries or watching birds or collecting mushrooms or wildflowers, once the high-school beauty walking with a baby raccoon on her shoulder, but most simply rambling, usually alone, often down to the estuary to swim. The women seemed to have noticed so much more in the woods than the few men we met, and invariably seemed pleasantly surprised to find us. Unlike the old men to whom we spoke, usually when we found them sunning themselves on chairs leaned against derelict barns or kitchen ells, the women saw nothing negative in the woods and swamps and marshes. The old men saw failure and looked away.[18]

They looked away as the protagonist looks away from his abandoned sawmill in Edith Wharton's 1911 novel *Ethan Frome*. That novel came to hand upstairs in the wood-frame James Library facing the town common and Civil War monument. My town had a tiny public library, but it had the James too, a small private athenaeum erected in the 1870s from the largesse of a former townsman grown rich in Chicago. In the early 1960s it stood open only a few hours each week, staffed by volunteers who distributed the mysteries and other modern fiction shelved downstairs. Often only the ticking of the grandfather's clock disturbed its silence. Nothing vibrated the dust settled over all but the newest books. Upstairs time had stopped circa 1930 and dust lay thick. Warped shelves held first editions of all the New England authors and sometimes complete sets too, spines faded by decades of sunlight. I began reading the books in junior high school, no more surprised by my ability to check out a first edition by Hawthorne or Jewett than by the abandoned agricultural landscape nuzzling the rear of the library. I shoved *The House of the Seven Gables* or *The Country of the Pointed Firs* into the Raleigh saddlebag, and pedaled home, sometimes glad for the leather flap that kept out the rain.

While not poor, the town remained spatially isolated and peculiarly bereft of books published after 1940. Nowhere could I find one that explained why old men saw failure in the overgrown landscape most everyone took for granted and in which a number of younger women delighted. But the James held books that explained how to photograph the old fields, albeit with cameras dating to 1910: old fields offered many advantages to a photographer, including the near certainty that he would not be disturbed while making images.[19] I read Wallace Nutting's 1923

Massachusetts Beautiful with care; its photographs of old-field landscape piqued my nascent interest in landscape photography.[20] His 1927 how-to-do-it manual *Photographic Art Secrets* explained how old-fields landscape offered not only subjects worthy of intense photographic effort but sites for undisturbed photographic experimentation.[21] In high school I began carrying a camera into the woods.

College summers piqued an interest in cognitive disjunction. By then I had found books documenting the failure of agriculture in New England, the collapse of deep-sea and coastal shipping Samuel Eliot Morison elucidated in 1921 in *The Maritime History of Massachusetts, 1783 to 1860,* then the shoe-industry disarray, and even the postwar move of textile and other mills to the nonunion South. I wished for a salt marsh, south-of-Boston book similar to Harold Fisher Wilson's 1936 *Hill Country of Northern New England: Its Social and Economic History, 1790 to 1930,* but I knew just enough to learn more on my own.[22] My curiosity became the platform of my graduate-school studies and now more than thirty-five years of teaching at Harvard University. I got started by looking around at abandoned environments, wondering how they came to be and what they meant and mean to their inhabitants (especially to children), and then photographing them.[23] But the poetry of Robert Frost and Edwin Arlington Robinson, the novels and short stories of Sarah Orne Jewett, Edith Wharton, Ruth Moore, and Mary E. Wilkins Freeman, and the paintings of Edward Hopper and Andrew Wyeth intermittently redirected my attention at something suffusing the old-fields landscape.

In summertime my parents' home offered a portal on an understanding I missed in college and graduate school. By my midtwenties, I found myself ensnared in a cognitive disjunction involving failure and masked success, cruelty and power sometimes forgotten and sometimes deliberately obscured, and a fierce sexuality, one represented sometimes by exposed belly buttons. I began to encounter the tracings of glamour, usually along the overgrown paths grown suddenly even more abandoned and often shimmering like a force field in a haze I came to treasure.

Ten-speed bicycles arrived around 1970, and within three years children and teenagers no longer rode the old paths. Wheel rims built for speed twisted when bicycles struck rocks and roots. Delicate cables and derailleurs failed after striking branches or sticks, or after a splash in muddy or sandy water: salt water corroded them immediately. Corrugated metal pedals ended barefoot bicycling, and shod bicyclists stuck to paved roads, where they rode fast, often to the estuary swimming areas and sometimes to new backyard pools. Between the era of ordinary bicycles and the advent of mountain and trail bikes, I rode my thin-tired, one-speed English Raleigh along unpeopled paths. In the early 1970s the lack of children struck me as heralding a new era, one focused on main roads and television.[24] Between 1970 and 1975 even the narrow centerline of the most-used shortcuts grew up in weeds and scrub, and my rambles on my bike and afoot led me into conversation with the people whose backyards and back lots by then abutted woods wholly bereft of children. I began to listen to women, learning that their interpretations of the changing old-fields landscape elucidated gender- and class-differentiated distinctions absent from university classrooms.[25]

In my 1970s graduate-school summers I realized that the warnings about cinema, advertising, and television came chiefly from middle-aged women who still rambled in the abandoned woods, fields, and marshes, and who swam in the estuary.[26] They came too from a few men who knew the abandoned landscape well, although I almost never encountered them in it: the elderly surveyor first alerted me to ways real estate developers reimagined old ways. The warnings differed from the remarks of very elderly local women so markedly that I began paying close attention.

Old women began giving me books, typically telling me that I might not need them immediately and perhaps ever, but that the books needed a good keeper. I found it difficult to accept a 1702 edition of Cotton Mather's *Magnalia Christi Americana: or Christ's Mighty Deeds in America,* let alone volumes by subsequent New England authors. I explained their value as collector items, but the women dismissed my opposition, often brusquely. They retorted that I valued things from the past, and that as a future academic I might find them handy.[27] I could not get clear what they meant, or even what past they thought I valued. The abandoned acres reflected multiple pasts, including the three years when children and bicycles disappeared from the old paths left to a handful of college-educated women and me.

The elderly local women dismissed ordinary schoolbook history and told me to attend to everything predating cinema, television, and advertising. Their value system had gone to ground, grown up in sweet fern, summersweet, juniper, and white pine, and become invisible except when the light fell just right. Younger people mocked it. But it lingered, glimpsed now and then from the corner of the eye. They asked that I look through the abandonment toward what had been abandoned and ignore for a while the causes of abandonment.

They wondered not so much at failure but at darker forces latent in the abandoned landscape. "Later, Frost affirmed and proved, as no one else for many years, the depth and the vigor of life that subsisted in New England," asserted Van Wyck Brooks in his 1940 critical study *New*

England: Indian Summer, 1865–1915, a book I first found in the James. "But he knew how much was morbid in it, and his early poems reflected a world of dearth, decay, and desiccation." Brooks cataloged authors permanently and deeply affected by "the black old tenantless houses, where the windows lay in the grass and the roof had tumbled in, the houses, damp and cold, with people in them, where the rain had rotted the shingles, the barns with wooden cages in dark corners, the double houses of brothers who never spoke, the thresholds that had never been crossed since someone's death." He directed readers to authors who wondered "about the Yankees who had shut out humanity, like all those sinister characters in Hawthorne's tales, in whom the force of the past, repressed and turned inward, reeked with suspicion, hypocrisy, hatred and poison." By 1890, he insisted, New England authors believed that the Yankee sun had set and that "it was time for the moon to have its say." He wrote explicitly of writers who believed that in remote places "there were colonies of savages," most "queer, degenerate clans that lived 'on the mountain,' the descendants of prosperous farmers." He claimed that post-1880s New England writers, along with Edith Wharton and other summer visitors to the New England backcountry, heard stories of "old women poisoners in lonely houses," "heroines in reverse who served the devil," "Draculas in the northern hills and witch-women who lived in sheds," and lunatics in attics. In the end, Brooks said bluntly, Yankee power "at last inverted, devoured itself. There were Yankees like Heine's gods in exile, the gods who became diabolic when they could no longer be divine."[28] He knew stories like those the oldest women told me.

Brooks knew too the withering rural and small-town landscape. "How many thousand villages, frost-bitten, palsied, full of a morbid, bloodless death-in-life, villages that have lost, if they ever possessed, the secret of self-propagation, lie scattered across the continent," he wondered in a 1918 essay focused on rural decrepitude.[29] He scrutinized the plight of women in such places by reading widely in a literature nowadays largely ignored, even by women's studies professors indefatigably recovering the work of long-forgotten women authors. "Such was the setting, and the people were in harmony with it. They were mostly old, and mostly women," and they were "village-bound and house-bound," he wrote of frost-nipped New England villages. Visitors, except for Wharton, Jewett, and a very few other perceptive ones, rarely inquired deeply about the worldviews of lonely women whose children had moved west or to cities. "Beyond the horizon of the village, they had no thoughts; and whether they had thoughts below the village was a question that strangers asked as seldom as whether or not they possibly had thoughts above it."[30] Brooks fixated on the downward thinking, arguing that the women usually knew the blackest secrets of the poverty-stricken, decayed society reflected in a half-abandoned landscape that repelled even train travelers gazing from Pullman car windows.[31]

In *A Humble Romance, A New England Nun,* and perhaps especially *People of Our Neighborhood,* Mary E. Wilkins wrote icily about the people of a town, even then not a suburb, in which she had grown to adulthood and to which she returned in 1883 to write. "It was a fading Yankee village, and this was the moribund village—and the symbol of hundreds of others—that appeared in her stories," Brooks noted. In high school I read *A New England Nun* because it stood on the dusty second-floor shelves of the James Library. Although I thought the town fictitious, I recognized the abandonment Wilkins depicted as generic late nineteenth-century decrepitude. In the summer of 1974, home from graduate school and by then acquainted with Brooks's study of cultural Indian summer and reading New England writers to further my understanding of landscape, I brought home *People of Our Neighborhood* from the dusty second floor and learned when my mom recognized its title that part of our family had lived in Wilkins's neighborhood for generations. As I thought for a moment about my great-grandparents' generation being the prototype of characters in the novel, my mom mused aloud about women ancestors who had lost husbands in the Civil War.

Her aunt had known such things more precisely, but she died in my boyhood, the last of the family in that town. Aunt Lily had told me of one of my forebears, a prosperous farmer who disciplined his horses so well that the day he rolled, drunk from celebrating a financial victory, from the rear of his hay wagon and yelled "My back, my back" in pain, the matched Belgians immediately backed the wagon over him, snapping his neck. Mary E. Wilkins's neighborhood suddenly seemed a bit too close to home. I remembered that Aunt Lily believed in communicating with the dead, had assembled a sophisticated collection of books on it and related subjects she bequeathed to a specialized library, and that the finest of the books had stood in a glass-door case that dropped a revolver into one's hands from a secret compartment below its top shelf. I asked my mom what else she remembered of the background of Wilkins's novels, but she knew only fragments from her visits to very old people circa 1940: the family had run out of children and some of the women had turned to the occult.

In the early 1980s I wrote about the abandoned landscape of New England. I concluded my *Metropolitan Corridor: Railroads and the American Scene* with a chapter about the wildering of agricultural countryside from which railroad companies withdrew their tracks. The German word *ortsbewüstung* properly captures something that disturbs Americans accustomed to thinking of their landscape as hacked from virgin wilderness. Wilderness returns when enterprise fails.[32] For thirty-five years I have elucidated the concept, typically using a courageous, incisive book by Hal Barron, *Those Who Stayed Behind: Rural Society in Nineteenth-Century New England*, which appeared a year after my *Metropolitan Corridor*. Barron demonstrates that the poor first emigrated from rural New England, especially from Vermont, New Hampshire, and Maine, and that their departure enriched those who remained. At the time, canny Yankees observed that they might prosper by shooing away people dissatisfied with lack of jobs and few chances to buy farms. The poor tended to clog schools and poorhouses, and often became criminals.[33] While almost never mentioned in newspapers and other journals, which typically editorialized about the sad loss of young people to western states and to urban factory jobs, the emigration for a time enriched people remaining in places census data defined as depopulated.[34] Brooks comprehended a subsequent rural abandonment spreading north from Massachusetts and Connecticut around 1875 but leaving few prosperous families in its wake.[35] While mitigated by the nascent suburbanization and by the buying of abandoned farms in scenic areas by city people anxious for summer retreats, which I describe in *Borderland: Origins of the American Suburb, 1820 to 1939,* the second phase of abandonment produced decrepit landscapes scarcely rehabilitated by 1960 and nowadays still found across much of northwestern New England and upstate New York.[36]

This second phase of abandonment produced deep-seated unease, especially among women authors writing after Jewett, Wharton, and Wilkins, although Wharton glimpsed enough of it to realize its power in her 1915 novel of seduction, *Summer.* It shaped the writing of Lovecraft and his fantasy-focused contemporaries who saw what Brooks discerned—a gloomy landscape become the theater of the bizarre and the grotesque, laced by poor roads and lanes dead-ended in superstition, atrocity, and perhaps the triumphant return of the Indians.[37] If anything, the post-1920s abandoned landscape mocked modernist, progressive ideology while indicating something gone wrong in the blood of its makers and deserters—perhaps a failure of nerve or a failure of sexual energy.

In 1926 Amy Lowell published a volume of narrative poems, *East Wind,* which underscored the thinking Brooks subsequently framed, and provided him with examples of weirdness become the raw material of art. "A Dracula of the Hills" traces the transformation of a dying woman into a vampire. The selectmen of her rural New England town finally exhume her body and find what they expect, a live heart amid the decay. "Oh, they burnt it; they al'ays do in such cases,/Nobody's safe till it's burnt," concludes the teller of the tale, remembering "some queer goin's on" a few decades before the telephone and automobile brought summer people from cities. In "The Real Estate Agent's Tale" a different narrator warns a newcomer that a house rented furnished shelters a clock which unnerves the town: he explains that he once saw its owner hold legal papers to its face: "I might be seeing a heathen devotee/Making oblation to a heathen god,/A wood and metal thing without a soul/But furious with abominable intention." Many of the narratives trace the collapse of human spirit, especially will, in the face of inexplicable oddness: clinical depression might explain the symptoms manifested by the woman in "The Day That Was That Day," but in the end the narrator says she wants a change from the hills, and hopes to see the ocean "or a real big city." Certainly she wants out of the house in which she lives a threadbare life as humdrum as the ticking of any clock, even one brought from England decades earlier by a half-crazed mariner.[38]

Lowell perfected the motif of the modern vacationer as discoverer, learning from Sarah Orne Jewett that with luck the outsider relaxing on a half-abandoned farm for an entire summer might glimpse things ignored in 1930s cities. "A gate-legged table/Of old mahogany, as soft as skin" opens one of Lowell's most evocative narrative poems. The psychologist who pulls a notebook from its tiny drawer recounts his chance discovery during "a little trip into the Berkshires/Last autumn in my car." On a whim he stops at a farm auction—"The old stock ended—it was the usual story—/Gone West, or dead, no one to keep the farm"—and buys the table, has Railway Express ship it back to the city, and discovers the journal scribbled by someone confronting power as great as voodoo. The hard-worked, exhausted alienist finds the journal fascinating but dispiriting, exemplifying an array of madness. It pulls him back into the hill country to a tiny village near the farm, and to a man who knew the place in the late nineteenth century. The psychologist learns only that the notebook author hanged himself from a harness strap in the barn. The suicide makes him muse on late nineteenth-century physicians who prescribed rest in the country for nervous-wreck businessmen and other sufferers. The old-fields countryside harbored too many psychological dangers for the healthy, let alone the mentally exhausted. Even in the 1930s, anyone who walked away from his parked car might encounter the abandoned house surrounded by catbrier, its interior walls covered with wallpaper pasted up by selectmen anxious to mask drawings no one should see.[39]

Other authors followed Lowell's precise, indefatigable rummaging. In 1930 Rachel Field published *Points East: Narratives of New England,* a collection of chilling poems emphasizing how much oddness had taken root in what she called "the old pasture" long bereft of livestock. But unlike Lowell and her predecessors, Field often located the origin of oddness far beyond the New England coast, insisting that seamen, ship-masters, and even the ships themselves brought home more than clocks, curios, and gimcracks.[40] Modernity did nothing to stop the spread and power of exotic weirdness or end the transmission of tales from one woman to another.

Field details the uncanny experience of a midwife called out one foggy night by a strange man, brought to an island she cannot identify, and given a salve different from her own herbal mix to wipe on the eyes of the newborn child. The man returns the midwife home, but years later she sees him at the county fair, and he realizes that she touched one of her eyes with the salve. He blinds that eye instantly and returns to his ordinary in-visibility.[41] In another narrative, "The Shell, the Comb, and the Bird," a widowed seaman given up for drowned returns from a long-distance pas-sage with an exotic wife his mother instantly hates. The beautiful woman gives no offense, but her gorgeous comb and brilliant caged bird, and perhaps especially the tropical shell in which she listens, produce only bitter, jealous sullenness. When she dies, her husband buries nothing in a stony grave: her body has vanished into thin air, more rapidly than the caged bird released into the New England winter night. Outside any window in any old house in Depression-era coastal New England, Field suggested, lay a view that once included sailing ships returning from the Far East and an alien ancientness that took root, grew, and sometimes blossomed when it did not choke.[42]

Lowell and Field represent awareness still outside the parameters of most scholarship.[43] Urbanization and mass media directed attention away from rural places after 1930. By the end of World War II the farmer had become a hick in most urban-produced imagery.[44] After earlier ex-periments ridiculing rural families, the success of *Ma and Pa Kettle* in 1949 prompted Hollywood to produce a plethora of films about yokels; television simply followed its lead, and that of radio. The prime-time tele-vision show *Green Acres,* which aired from 1965 to 1971, originated in a thirteen-part CBS radio series aired in 1950 that was revised by its origi-nal scriptwriter for television. Both shows present a simple premise: well-to-do, educated city people move to the country and encounter laughable bumpkins.[45] By 1960 television made national viewers armchair anthro-pologists. Beginning with *The Andy Griffiths Show* (1960–68), and its spin-off, *Mayberry R.F.D.* (1968–71), and *Petticoat Junction* (1963–70), it showcased hicks at home. In *The Beverly Hillbillies* (1962–71) it depicted hicks who had moved to the city. While these rustics sometimes knew more than the newcomers, they remained simple—and invariably simpler than the audience.

Postwar rural depopulation explains only in part advertiser willingness to sponsor shows spoofing rural families. Rural viewers who watched might purchase all sorts of goods in a determined if unconscious effort to prove themselves not hicks: insulting people stimulates buying, although advertising experts rarely mention it.[46] Mass media—and especially television—ignored the creeping rural desolation airline travel both created and obscured.[47] "But the new West/Cut farming into bits all through this country," snaps the narrator of Lowell's "Real Estate Agent's Tale."[48] Those who stayed behind often suffered pain and emptiness even if they acquired more wealth, especially in the 1920s and 1930s. But they had no way of knowing how many people would abandon rural places, even in the West, immediately following World War II, producing the decrepitude and aching loneliness. Rural America became fly-over land. Urban motorists on long-distance trips find it dark at night, and away from interstate highways, poorly signed, seemingly free of gas stations, and fraught with unfortunate possibilities.[49]

In my college summers I began to discern that two cohorts of women understood abandonment differently. Elderly local-born women insisted fiercely that the abandoned landscape represented moral failure and much worse. They argued that people who prospered in a harsh climate on rocky soil produced around 1920 a generation that could not even maintain what it inherited: by 1940 a half century of continual failure had become something grotesque. They thought its outlines worth retelling to a young man in his early twenties willing to listen as he helped weed a flower bed or patch a henhouse roof. But younger, middle-aged women, most "from away" and recently arrived, saw the 1960s landscape as representing an ecological transformation outside history and morality that provided opportunities for them to prosper in ways impossible in cities and suburbs warped by mass media. They found the views of the elderly women outdated, and instead juxtaposed the power of landscape against that of contemporary media. Morality governed the viewpoints of both groups, but the viewpoints lay almost two generations apart.

Moral decay orders John Ellis's 1884 pamphlet *The Deterioration of the Puritan Stock*. Ellis had visited his boyhood home, Franklin, Massachusetts, for a school reunion, and marveled at the landscape decrepitude and the large proportion of immigrant farm families working acreage Yankees had abandoned. After a year of research, including analysis of population statistics, he concluded that moral rather than economic forces drove the changes he found. An "inability to bear, care for, and rear children, which is largely the fault, either physically or mentally, of the native women" lay at the core of his argument. Something had gone wrong with Yankee women, and he traced the problem to Yankee girls caught up in stylish dressing and other new trends. "Women presenting the greatest deformity from tight dressing" on stage had warped national costume, and corsets worn by very young girls destroyed their childbearing ability. Overindulgence in tobacco weakened the men, he admitted, but a bizarre following of fashion other than clothing caused young adults to postpone marriage. Many men believed they could not support girlfriends in the manner in which they lived in their parents' homes, and often left small towns to earn more money in cities, where they married newly met girlfriends, leaving rural women to marry badly or to live as spinsters. Ellis believed that advertising and fashion proved most culpable in altering rural New England thinking and behavior. While he touched on other issues, arguing that children did not get enough physical activity to grow into robust adults, for example, he shaped his argument as a cultural collision symbolized by fancy female attire and decayed rural landscape within a larger context of failed sexuality.

Unlike many of his contemporaries, Ellis took on the shadowy issue of abortion. "Unprincipled physicians" performed many rural abortions a year, he determined, and not just for unmarried young woman: married women routinely sought abortions too.[50] Smaller families meant fewer children to work farms, and increased the chances that disease, accident, and migration might tip a town into depopulation, but abortion meant too that especially robust, industrious, or bright children might never exist. His argument echoed the mid-nineteenth-century rural Yankeeism that all the folks with get up and go had gotten up and gone, leaving behind the weak, including women too frail to bear many children, let alone raise them. At its base lay the contemporaneous fear of witch women, herbalists, and midwives who know how to forestall conception and initiate abortion, and who compete with male physicians. "She didn't hanker for a snarl of children/To fill her house and trample down her plants," wrote Field of a midwife whose plant knowledge is slightly suspect even among her friends.[51] Ellis stated the modern difficulty bluntly: many rural women wanted to see the ocean or a real big city now and then, and having snarls of children prevented their having recreational time and the store-bought items they coveted. Ellis missed what Field knew a half century later: abortion nested in female-only plant lore. Indeed, he missed the whole woman-only understanding of collapsing rural economy, urban media, and controlled sexuality.

Rural abortion typically began—and begins—with pennyroyal tea. In the first weeks of pregnancy, tea brewed from fresh or preserved pennyroyal leaves works as an emmenagogue, a substance that stimulates menstrual bleeding. Only when I reached college did I first hear of rusty coat hangers, something as alien to my boyhood landscape as dark alleys. Many years later, when tracing how rural women shielded plant lore from a male-dominated medical profession, I noticed that even Alice Henkel's 1912 *Weeds Used in Medicine* omits all mention of emmenagogues.[52] Conception, abortion, childbirth, and related topics intrigued me a bit in college, since what I knew of them differed greatly from what my city-reared friends considered normal. I watched one birth-control advocate arrested for publicly displaying a birth-control device and I knew that contraception issues sparked the first tentative feminist demonstrations. But what I knew of such subjects made me feel like a hayseed, and I kept quiet. "Anybody knows/Who knows the smallest thing about such doings,/That children always come with a flood tide," writes Field in her long narrative poem about a midwife who wanted no children herself.[53] In my early twenties I knew that the menstrual cycle mimics the lunar calendar ordering the tides in the estuary downhill from where pennyroyal grew. My knowledge about the relation of tides, childbirth, and pennyroyal tea struck me then as part superstition, and certain to provoke laughter in urban conversation.

But I knew elderly women who might have told me more, had I asked. Now and then they intimated that they understood natural means of contraception and other uses for plants about which no one cared any longer. Henry N. Snelling's 1849 treatise *The History and Practice of Photography,* which explains how to sensitize paper using juice squeezed from the petals of red poppies, wallflowers, marigolds, and other flowers, later struck me as one more component in a forgotten shop theory of plants known mostly to elderly women who still walked along old paths to collect herbs.[54] The women knew a lot about concerns which ordered the work of Lowell and a few other writers, and they knew much about the travails of women buried in local graveyards.

One woman showed me hundreds of identical glass bottles, all square and each about three inches tall, buried like a subterranean carpet in the pathways of the dooryard garden of her old house. She had researched the patent medicine and learned it consisted largely of alcohol and morphine. Its maker retailed it to women who had "womb complaints," and my elderly friend thought it addictive. The massive carpet of bottles fascinated her, and it made me sad, for I concluded that she guessed right: a woman buried the bottles secretly, almost certainly out of sight of her husband. In the years when the Pilgrim Society, the descendants of the *Mayflower* colonists, planned and erected the colossal Forefathers Monument just down the coast in Plymouth, the drug addict had failed her bloodline and abandoned female-kept herbalism too.

One of the strangest and least-known historical monuments in the United States, the Forefathers Monument memorializes not the Pilgrims but what they brought to the New World. A gigantic figure of Faith tops the monument; around her sit Morality, Education, Liberty, and Law. Dedicated in 1889 with much fanfare, the monument reflects an assertion of ancestral accomplishment that had become a joke by the late 1960s. In my college years the monument had begun to decay, and few tourists found its location: they preferred Plymouth Rock and the *Mayflower* replica. As a son of Plymouth County, I considered that everything important and transcendent in North America had arrived with the Pilgrims: Plymouth Colony had been a going concern for a decade before the new arrivals settled at what they called Boston. On one level, no one took Jamestown seriously, and by the time I turned fifteen I knew the stock jibes about it and the Lost Colony of Roanoke being figments of southern imagination. But one summer day, showing a college friend around Plymouth, *Mayflower* replica and all, I drove up the hill to the monument and thought for a moment about the woman burying the glass bottles and about the statue of Leif Eriksson on Commonwealth Avenue in Boston. Erected in 1887 by the Scandinavians of Boston with the guidance of scholars fascinated by the Norse discovery of North America, it balanced my Plymouth Colony bias. In the late 1880s many immigrant groups strived to demonstrate that they had contributed something special to the melting pot. For the first time in my life, gazing at the Forefathers Monument, I knew myself as part of a defined cohort and suspected that the monument exaggerated what the *Mayflower* freighted. I understood its site as an old-fields landscape, the grass mowed erratically.

The elderly local-born women who valued the spirit and industry that preceded the 1880–1920 "moral collapse" knew the monument and venerated it, seemingly accepting it at face value.[55] The old-field neighborhood in 1968 framed something distasteful to the elderly women, who thought that younger men and women no longer cared about what the failed agricultural environment revealed. In roundabout ways, they understood abandonment as the emblem of diminished character, spirituality, and virility and fertility too, the decline I knew from reading eighteenth-century theology, which characterized Puritanism and religious declension as the armature of New England culture.[56] Almost no one, often not even their daughters, was interested in the point of view of the elderly women. Sometimes in their voices I heard a dislike of African Americans, southern European immigrants, and Asian Americans that was grounded in envy of energy, especially sexual energy the women condemned as immoral even as they stood jealous of it.[57] They distrusted the younger newcomer women whose brief attire, sunbathing, and tans linked them with darker-skinned racial vitality, not with the tradition of imperiled whiteness and decrepit landscape.

The newcomer women to whose conversation I paid careful attention in the 1970s and later viewed the old-fields landscape as a theater of operations, the ground of personal exploration and development. All had chosen years earlier to move to a quiet old-fields place; they loved the outdoors, disliked cities, and cared little for local history of any sort. None lived as though well off, even if they traveled sometimes in Europe, the Caribbean, or the Pacific islands.[58] Their modest houses and home-centered lives struck their less observant neighbors as oddly parsimonious. Many locals their age and older did not understand why they painted their own houses, built lawn furniture, gardened, and chopped down trees, often without the help of husbands or hired men. The women read a lot, typically outside in the sun in summer: they tanned while they read French, German, and Swiss books they ordered from afar or magazines to which they subscribed. They talked easily with me about what I read in my college literature and history courses. I ran into them at the James Library, sometimes upstairs. More frequently I ran into them outdoors, where the old paths edged into their fields and gardens and the breeze rattled the pages of their books and magazines.

In the summers when home from college and graduate school, I learned something of the range of their capabilities. Several gathered together monthly to lunch at each other's homes, speaking in French about novels they read in French. All quietly supported a wide variety of environmental organizations and efforts, and some did well financially but worked as consultants. The latter profited from stock-market investments based on anticipating long-term trends, or had real estate licenses and now and then sold a house before most townspeople knew it to be for sale. Three operated wholesale antique and imported craft businesses from their homes. A handful did freelance illustration work or other graphic design. All enjoyed robust health. I knew them as inveterate walkers long before jogging, running, and other aerobic exercise became fashionable. They swam in the estuary, skated on the millponds in winter, and walked constantly in the old-field landscape of abandonment, never on the side of paved roads.

These women valued houses secluded by woods and marsh: delight in living in spots others dismissed as lonely or isolated accompanied a fierce desire for spatial privacy. I knew little about their social lives, but by 1975 I understood that they prized spatial solitude and found it anything but lonely or lonesome or isolated. Unlike the elderly women who saw old fields as the manifestation of failure and who lived in the village or in crossroads clusters, the younger women reveled in seclusion. Now and then they spoke explicitly of their happiness in living out of sight of roads, passersby, and nosy neighbors, and being free to wear whatever they chose.[59]

Always toughness spiced their comments. Their kindness to children, old people, and injured wild animals coexisted with a ruthless vitality that sometimes shocked acquaintances.[60] I learned to think of them as a cohort adapted to a harsh climate and half-wild environment, but also to ballroom floors and ocean liners. They walked in the rain, split wood in the snow, and swam early in the spring and late in the fall. In private they spoke their minds and behaved differently from most other women I knew or have known since. They were the first people I encountered who pondered the meaning of a liberal arts education in times of great change and who consciously forged lives rather than careers.[61] Their curiosity, range of interests, and ability to teach themselves anything they chose made me respect them and classify them as a group different from any other in town. In the middle 1970s I decided they were Protestants nearly sundered from the Puritan tradition fixating the elderly women and well-nigh gone to ground, merging with the trees at dusk, using the abandoned landscape as camouflage and drawing its cloak around them for private purpose.[62]

The women scorned much contemporaneous thinking and many people in turn scorned them. Certainly many other women distrusted them, sometimes only for their appearance, sometimes because they could not classify their ideas and ways of analysis.[63] The women dismissed the feminism that newly inflected news media and transformed the thinking of most women my age after 1970. At one time or another, several insisted that "using" a liberal arts education meant more than finding an office job, and explained to me the distinctions between jobs and careers, careers and lives, and between earning a salary and making money, especially as such issues involved women. They viewed the feminist movement as contorted, Marxist, and essentially bloodless.[64] Liberal arts education had failed college-educated feminists who condemned the "patriarchal society" in which they feared to compete as intellectual, physical, sexual, and visual equals. In the early 1970s such sharp criticism of the feminist movement antagonized many women, particularly when it originated among educated women. I found it compelling, though especially the components concerning observing, sexuality, and appearance within a context of something older, harsher, and perhaps as peculiarly New England as the light washing the old-fields landscape.[65]

In the aggregate, the younger women I listened to lacked faith in government, religions organized beyond the parish level, public school systems, and people who talked about doing things rather than accomplishing them. They disliked self-appointed advisers on child rearing, prevention of illicit drug use, sex education, physical safety, and proper adult behavior: they thought such self-appointed advisers and advocates fundamentally insecure, perhaps intellectually, certainly socially. They disdained keepers of public morality and condemned them as desperate to maintain or advance their social position and anxious for publicity.[66] They equated cinema and television with the ruination of the free-thinking, educated American: media crippled the imagination of the poorly educated and eroded the independence of middle-income families while deflecting attention from rich, unprogrammed visual realms. In sum, these women seemed competent, satisfied, successful, and happy with lives my women contemporaries either dismissed out of hand or, I first suspected by about 1975, did not know existed.

In college I wondered if the middle-aged old-fields women who scorned cinema and television spoke from some upper-class-based platform I might discern with effort.[67] In my graduate-school summers I determined that whatever their childhood privilege and solid liberal arts educations, they spoke from positions not necessarily based on wealth and not easily analyzed in class terms.[68] They seemed financially and socially secure, but out of step with Hollywood and prime-time broadcasting. Often they wore threadbare, faded clothes, and only one among them bought new automobiles. None had large houses like those built by the executive-headed families moving into the town. All routinely "made do" by repairing and rebuilding things; they intuited a sort of shop theory of old-fields living. I wanted to know what they were in step with, and how the abandoned landscape, by then changing with suburbanization, fitted so precisely into their scheme of endeavor. Women who visited Europe, read in languages other than English, bought gardening books in London and bikinis in St. Tropez, and queried me knowledgeably about my latest courses, independent reading, girlfriends, and cameras found something as valuable in the old fields as I did. What they found involved more than the landscape itself and more than its ordinary local history and the deeper, usually darker history explicated by the elderly local women.

The summer day in 1968 when one of the coterie told me that the Hollywood Production Code had produced a generation of unthinking viewers afraid of the human body I remember not only because her comments ordered cinema details I had noticed. The woman wore a bikini far briefer than any worn by women my age, or in the few films I saw. The bandeau suit stayed in place with minimal adjustment, but when it slipped a bit it revealed only more tanned skin. I had seen one like it advertised in the back pages of a glamour photography magazine. On her own land, out of public view, this woman wore what she chose, as did so many other women, but what she chose differed markedly from what women wore on public beaches and aboard pleasure boats—and around college guys who stopped to help repair a rickety shed. As she reinforced this structure with third-hand boards, I wondered at both her poise and her ease, and I felt complimented that she had not pulled on a shirt when I arrived. Then I noticed that the exiguous suit was all her attire: she had no cover-up with her, no shirt or towel nearby. She worked well away from her house wearing almost nothing. As she drove in one nail after another, swinging a correctly weighted hammer accurately again and again, now and then shoving back her graying blond hair, I thought she might make a perfect photograph. She seemed the spirit of her place. I imagined photographing her, noting her ease in nothing other than her skin and two wisps of nylon. I recognized her as an intellectual being, but as a physical being too, happy in the sun and happy repairing a shed so decrepit every gale threatened to collapse it.

She might have been the genius loci of that notch of sunlight adjacent to the abandoned old fields and tangled woodlots. Thoreau spoke of farmers who owned the land and the rare cognoscenti who own the landscape: that day she owned the landscape.

In 1968 I could distinguish between *nymph* and *nymphet*. The former term designated one of the minor divinities dwelling in the fields, woods, mountains, and seacoasts of classical mythology. *Nymphet*, ten years after the publication of Vladimir Nabokov's *Lolita*, connoted not merely a young nymph but a very young girl prone to running about nude and sometimes seducing older men.[69] I wondered if a middle-age woman, no matter how fit, might be a nymph. I knew enough of mythology to realize that maidens represented nymphs in the classic tales, and enough of Theocritus to know that he called nymphs "terrible divinities."[70] Nereids lived in salt water, and about their age and other attributes I knew little.[71] When this woman dove into the estuary another day I thought she might be a nereid: she swam far better than I, with abandon. I wondered at what distinguished her and her friends from the older women and from women of their age born in the town but not well educated, and from the feminists I encountered in the university. One thing struck me as obvious: their ease and confidence made them at home in the old-fields landscape.

Classical nymphs exist outside history. They disport themselves in discrete space, and tend to stay in what might be called ecological niches. They neither know nor own history, they model space around themselves, and they sometimes draw humans into it.[72] *Nympholeptic* designates the state of being *taken with* the nymphs, not by them, as one is taken with a spectacle or image or ideas. The human taken with the nymphs is not in contact with them directly or consciously, but always slightly separated from them.[73] What I encountered on summer days seemed outside the sexual revolution and anything reported in contemporary media: it resided in classical mythology.[74]

In his 1937 book *Pipe All Hands,* H. M. Tomlinson caught something that stopped me thirty years after that day by the shed. "Look at that girl now, beneath his window, leaning over the sea-wall! She was harmonious, even in that outlandish splendour. Wasn't her shape just right for the day of a legend? No wonder we had to go wary, once on a time, for occasionally the gods were about," he wrote. "And that woman was a visitor, by the way she was dressed. No local woman would dare to go out in stuff so rare and scanty. Such a girl could afford the innocency of the immortals, and perhaps she knew it."[75] The young woman Tomlinson describes is perhaps twice a visitor, certainly once to the sleepy coastal town in which she arrives at night, and perhaps from some lower height of Olympus too, momentarily intruding into ordinary landscape and society. Tomlinson viewed film, especially Hollywood film, with deepening suspicion. "We gape, and hardly know why, at a distant and bloodless wonder," he wrote in *Out of Soundings* in 1931 of people fixated on cinema screens.[76] Few people encountered the lesser divinities in the flesh. Instead they paid money to see simulacra of substitute divinities flickering on screens. Meanwhile they avoided the locales where the lesser divinities disported themselves.

Among a handful of especially perceptive writers, the year 1937 marks a pivotal point in the perception of the film industry and its products. J. B. Priestley wondered at the "flavorless and phantasmal" boulevards of Hollywood, finding them in the end simply unreal. "Reality there was to be found in the millions of sharply-lit little photographs that were always being projected and examined by the producers and directors and cut-ters," he observed, adding that he "felt the same about most of the stars themselves," who "were people born to achieve reality in a photograph." Invariably, "a film star dwindles and fades in the flesh," and the public-relations fuss made over them when "they emerge as persons, descending upon the outer world," is simply absurd. "It is the photograph that should be waited for and cheered, not the actual person," he concludes. "This is particularly true of the young women, who may in reality be pleasant, handsome, intelligent actresses, but who can never in person be anything but ghosts of their screen appearances, though these in turn are only shadows." On banal Hollywood streets Priestley found a high number of "attractive-looking people" but knew them as the "raw material" of studio shop theory. "The film producers would like us to believe—and easily succeed in persuading most of us—that they are using the screen to convey to us a little of the essential glamour of these delicious beings, but the truth is, and nobody knows it better than the producers, that it is only on the screen that these stars really achieve glamour." In the end, he found the studio-produced glamour "cheap," and damaging to the stars, for "with them, the substance must always be less than the shadow."[77] The very technology of cinema in the hands of the cinema industry de-stroyed the raw material talent scouts collected on sun-washed, surreal boulevards to be projected later in darkness.

Not long after Priestley published *Midnight on the Desert, Film Fun* and other Hollywood fan magazines began to emphasize candid pho-tographs of cinema stars, minor actors and actresses, and even people with chorus-line or crowd-scene roles. Newsreel footage almost certainly drove fan magazine paranoia and effort. Hitler had become larger than life, exactly as Tomlinson and Priestley might have predicted, and by the late 1930s wary Americans, especially those who had traveled in Europe since 1936, knew the evocative and controlling power of film as propa-ganda. Fewer and fewer people encountered genuine glamour. Instead they encountered films, what Tomlinson, Priestley, and others dismissed as machine-made, simulated glamour. Nazism triumphed in film.

In 1968, helping her repair her shed and listening to her comments on Hitler and Hollywood, I knew in the back of my mind that the "nereid" wore a bikini intended for photography and that she lived in that bikini all summer, but consciously I realized only that she wore the suit well, in-deed effortlessly, in total confidence. Years later I identified her not as the owner of a swath of old fields and forest, but its newcomer spirit, glam-orous in a way different from Hollywood glitz. Unlike the flickering-light stars and starlets of Hollywood cinema, her glamour existed in reality, outdoors in the sun, naturally. Another day, when I asked if she had found the bikini advertised in a photography magazine, she grinned, nodded, then said, "Briefer and cheaper than anything European."

She and her friends lived, sometimes, with abandon, a concept over which I stumbled repeatedly in junior-high-school English class, then again in high school.[78] A good deal of abandonment lay outside the classroom window, but we never connected it with a lack of responsibility, or violation of rules, or fierce positive energy. Old fields represented *lack* of energy. I saw few things done with abandon until I met the newcomer women. By then *abandon* drifted between two generations of dictionaries. The 1934 unabridged Webster's defined the term simply enough: "a yielding to natural impulses, freedom from artificial constraint, careless freedom or ease." But from my teachers I absorbed the notion that abandon connoted something incorrect: I wondered about abandoning ship.[79] In 1967, the year I graduated from high school, Random House defined it as "a complete surrender to natural impulses without restraint or moderation: freedom from constraint or conventionality: *to dance with reckless abandon*." Thereafter *reckless* seemed welded to *abandon*. In November of that year Jane Fonda appeared nude on the cover of *Time* as the fantasy adventurer Barbarella, illustrating a feature story on the permissive generation. Abandon made less and less sense to me, especially when I walked through the woods past women a generation older than I living with abandon, or at least gardening sans bikini tops. "I love 'abandon' only when natures are capable of the extreme reverse," the nineteenth-century intellectual Margaret Fuller asserted.[80]

In the James Library I found the 1869 edition of her book *Woman in the Nineteenth Century.* Fuller meant human natures, not the nature that overwhelmed pastures and meadows. She drowned in an alongshore shipwreck, and I wondered whether she had not known how to swim, how to abandon ship with abandon.[81] All the newcomer women who did things with abandon, at least now and then, reverted quickly into logical, number-crunching, hard-questioning, methodical inquirers and makers when necessary, and Fuller's remark about extreme reverse made instant sense. All could swim well too, and they dove into the estuary or ponds with abandon: none waded into the cold water, or even into the warm water of ponds and swimming pools. They dove, and when they dove, they made the water rise to meet them. When they swam, they made the water surround them. They made woods and fields and vegetable gardens surround them too, in ways that only classical mythology ordered.

In them the New England conscience had morphed into a consciousness that embraced abandon, not abandonment.[82] The old fields, third-growth pine woods, and wild estuary marshes surrounding their isolated homes made a sort of theater in which they experimented in ways older women dismissed as frivolous or wicked, and other women their own age feared or envied. Instead of bemoaning bewilderment, the women accepted natural forces as energizers of something new. Their view of the decrepitude surrounding them was unstained by pessimism; instead they took a positive if realistic view of happiness in a decaying, bewildered landscape they used to their own advantage. They discovered that landscape as supportive, even luxurious: they discovered with abandon. They became part of that place, its genii loci, and invented a new ecology.

In 1978 I bought a house in the town and continued exploring the old-fields landscape, marveling at the quickness of ecological succession and suburbanization and the willingness of so many newcomers to live unlearned in any local history at all. Acclaimed one of the most beautiful, quaint, and rural towns within fifty miles of Boston, it attracted people who liked to see its natural beauty from the comfort of their new houses and automobiles.[83] Its backlands grew less and less visited, and many of the old greenways closed in entirely. Few blamed television, video games, and a generalized fear of wandering for the paucity of children along the old ways. The absence of adults concerned no one: the elderly women I had known in my boyhood and college years died, and then most of the newcomer women. In 1984 I bought the remains of a farm down the road, and a 1953 John Deere tractor, and began a continuing struggle against the forces of bewilderment. When I plowed the west field, already grown up in juniper and steeple bush, an abutter complained that she had not moved to the country to look at farm land: she prized what she called "the Currier-and-Ives wildflower" look of my place. I reminded her that her land abutted Brookside Farm and went back to plowing, watching the great notched coulter wheels cut into the sod and saplings.

In the mid-90s, to all but a few children (my twin sons among them) the vast expanse of back land grew alien. Preserved from development by wetness and fierce conservation efforts, it became a dark green blur to new arrivals attracted by scenic beauty and a superb school system. It is the undiscovered country of childhood, since only a few children probe far into it. Parental caution keeps children close to home, of course; but so do team sports and other organized activities, and especially electronic media. The one electronic gadget that does not seem to interest them is a GPS unit: they feel no need for the spatial-locating technology, in part because they do not enter the woods and marshes. They fear getting wet feet and getting lost, and they fear too an amorphous unknown vaguely conveyed to them by their parents.

Anything might be in the woods behind so many backyards, just beyond the piles of leaves and lawn clippings dumped over the edge of ordered landscape. "Anything" typically connotes bad. Coyotes howl at night, but perhaps homeless men live far out in the swamps. Mothers speak of quicksand; fathers wonder about out-of-season hunters, mentioning gunshots far off. But mostly, all but the enduring local families worry about getting lost, becoming bewildered, hearing the rushing voice of Pan fill their heads, finding themselves panicked and unable to return to quiet cul-de-sacs, mowed lawns, and clean floors.

Fantasy fiction thrives on such fears, especially the delicious fears of children and teenagers. Much of it is trash, but the best builds on themes reaching to M. R. James, Machen, Tolkien, and others who knew untraveled paths and lanes. R. A. Salavatore's *Woods Out Back* exemplifies two themes Susan Cooper and Ursula Le Guin discerned in the 1970s and that reward scrutiny now: the way suburban woods in time evolve from abandoned to wild as memory fades and built objects decay, and the way such unpeopled neo-wilderness fosters a new ecology of the imagination. Both themes invite consideration now because the best contemporary fantasy fiction has begun to abandon them.

Such works emphasize urban space and structure as entire setting. Exemplified by Neil Gaiman's *Neverwhere* and China Miéville's *Un Lun Dun,* the books embrace the hidden places of great cities. Such fiction almost certainly represents a reaction against modern architecture and urban design. Young faculty in architecture schools may worry about its long-term impact, knowing its Dickensian nooks and crannies make modern structures seem pallid. The books also represent a concerted effort to wrench fantasy fiction from the orcs-and-armor motifs central since *The Hobbit*. Much of it involves technology—"steam punk." Chiefly, though, it represents a continuation of Philip Pullman's attack on the formal educational system and an extension of the science-fiction notion of parallel universes. "His life so far, he decided, had prepared him perfectly for a job in Securities, for shopping at the supermarket, for watching soccer on the television on the weekends, for turning up the thermostat if he got cold," thinks one character in *Neverwhere*. "It had magnificently failed to prepare him for a life as an un-person on the roofs and in the sewers of London, for a life in the cold and the wet and the dark." In the steam-punk-technic uncities beneath London, Bangkok, and elsewhere, education falters: in most very recent urban fantasy, visual education fails completely. "It is dark, broken by phosphorescent patches on the wall, greenish grey fungi that give light enough to fool the eye, light enough to walk by."[84] The explorer does poorly, even the experienced one. He or she seldom sees what J. K. Rowling introduces so cleverly in the Harry Potter novels, Diagon Alley, camouflaged beneath modern architecture.[85]

Woods-based exploration fails to interest fantasy writers today in large part because the woods are officially accessible, unlike urban sewer systems, subway tunnels, and electrical conduits. Moreover, woods, fields, swamps, marshes, and other more or less natural places tend to be quiet and sparsely populated, and so simultaneously conducive to both looking around and thinking. Contemporary urban fantasy thrives on fast-paced adventure, which inhibits sustained reflection or even thought itself. The novels read almost like computer-game scenarios. Natural places threaten the primacy of fast pace. But more importantly, natural places encourage sustained thinking about ecosystem over time and over landscape once far more ordered than it is now.

People with time to think are likely not to think about the remote local past. They are likely to associate such places with the background settings of advertisements and articles in *Vanity Fair, Vogue,* and other fashion magazines aimed at women. Since the 1970s the images have attracted intermittent condemnation, typically ideologically based, but less sustained critical scrutiny. All too often critics focus on the model and her attire (or lack thereof), and wholly ignore settings beyond remarking their silliness or inappropriateness.

A number of my women students have noted that much contemporary fashion photography emphasizes ruined, often overgrown landscape, not austere urban space. They accept the setting as given: indeed they cannot imagine well any other setting, especially for formal attire clearly intended to be worn in urban venues. When I catalog setting elements, noting the stone bench, the stone steps, the stone balusters, and so on, the students frequently remark that they had never noticed the elements. When I note what rarely appears in the images—say wood decks or stairs or benches—they admit that they had never studied the settings or thought of them as worth studying. They agree that the models often appear disoriented or frightened or otherwise disconcerted, and while male students interject that anyone dressed in a long gown and spike heels might indeed feel such emotion when struggling among vines and collapsed walls, all of my students grow quiet when asked to explain the meanings implicit in long-running visual motifs. Then they begin talking about women wielding visual power, or overcome by such power or by their failure to use it deftly, and they begin to accept glamour as a power equal to any other.

When I suggest that the images imply that women are either about to find themselves in a novel and perhaps challenging ecosystem, or perhaps that some women have become the genii loci of places still alien to most others, my classroom explodes in energetic conversation. Advanced students who have studied old-field landscapes in my previous courses suddenly make connections between twentieth-century abandoned landscapes and the settings of the fashion magazine images. Invariably some students designate the images "fantasy-like": might their makers work in a tradition paralleling that of modern fantasy writing? As the discussion swirls about me I remember the newcomer women to whom I listened so attentively in the 1970s, the women who made abandoned landscape into their private theater, who made that landscape surround them.

10 Imagers

Abandoned houses, in the South after the Civil War, across much of New England after about 1880, in much of the Midwest after about 1920, often stirred gothic imaginings that frequently shaped fantasy literature.

QUIETUDE ENCOURAGES PHOTOGRAPHIC EXPERI-
mentation, especially among skilled enthusiasts free of the time constraints professionals loathe. Beginning in the Depression, photographers
working in abandoned landscape with equipment they had modified themselves valued uninterrupted time, and their models enjoyed the lack of
any observers, especially censorious ones. Clarence John Laughlin spoke
for many photographers when he explained that the figures in his images
served not as actors on stage but as manifestations of fears, dreams, and
other emotions evoked by forces suffusing specific abandoned places.[1]
His images and those made by many other old-fields photographers originated in extreme sensitivity to place-evoked intellectual and emotional response and in fierce devotion to shop-theory photographic effort evolved
since the early 1900s. The effort endured always just adjacent to trick
photography.

Lafcadio Hearn excoriated trick photography in a newspaper article
in 1875. Images purporting to show the presence of ghosts, especially the
ghosts of dead children and other deceased loved ones, preyed upon the
credulous living. Hearn lambasted "spirit photography" as "total bunk,"
but he knew that condemnation alone would convince few *Cincinnati
Commercial* readers. The images seemed genuine, veracious records of a
most convincing glamour.

"A very weird effect was produced in some of the photographs by the
presence of a ghost—generally that of a woman or child—embracing the
living sitter," he explained of the first such images produced in Cincinnati. "A number of queer monstrosities and nondescripts were also exhibited to us as the work of spirits."[2] Such images struck most observers as
so convincing that Hearn embarked on a step-by-step description of the
photographic process that produced them. He led his readers away from
studios and other photography locations into darkrooms.

"The ordering process of photography" contains many steps, but the
"most important preparation of the glass plate for the negative is termed
'sensitizing,'" he wrote, and sensitizing and negative development order
his attention. His lengthy newspaper article, published posthumously as
a book in 1933 by a bibliophile, contains one of the most detailed and
evocative descriptions of early darkroom work, involving both the coating of the glass plate and its postexposure processing. "Here and there
the creamy white of the film fades away, black shadows come out here
and there, and the picture grows out from the pallid surface, first in pale
shadows, which ultimately develop to strong reliefs of white and black,

like the shadows on a wizard's mirror." Modifying the sensitization process and double-printing negatives, and retouching, produce at the printing stage "extraordinary spectral effects, such as that of a man shaking hands with his own ghost, cutting off his own hand, or followed by his own *doppel ganger*."³ Hearn called the printing process "making" and insisted that its nuances would overwhelm his already long article. But he warned that a photographer wise in the ways of making might utterly subvert the photographic process most people thought straightforward and truthful: the photographer sensitive to chemical manipulation and to human emotion might produce an uncanny image by design. That photographer might create not glamour but a deceitful record of false glamour, and in so doing evoke the most wrenching emotions imaginable.

Hearn insisted that anyone intending to be photographed in séances or while visiting self-styled spirit photographers had only two defenses. In a séance, the visitor must suspect a medium who did not keep his or her hands open with fingers spread upon a table. Too many charlatans used simple sleight of hand to produce illusions that cameras faithfully recorded—and that subsequent viewers of photographs took as documentation of spectral events they accepted, and continued to accept, as truthful records of apparition. Hearn warned visitors to spirit photographers to bring not only photographs made of themselves by other photographers but the photographers themselves; they should "induce a first-class photographic artist to accompany them through the order." The photographs provide a standard by which to judge the images made by the spirit photographer, and while the experienced photographer will be unable to learn much about plates already sensitized and waiting to be exposed, he can scrutinize double printing and other darkroom techniques. "The spirits will probably feel indisposed or indignant, and victory will smile benevolently upon" the sitter, whose actions will help terminate trickery preying especially upon the bereaved, particularly heartbroken parents, and will bolster understanding of photography as a malleable technique, not a fundamentally representational process.⁴ Hearn understood spirit images as contrived photographs of something essentially emotional. Intended and designed to play upon emotions, they nonetheless originated in the purest form of technical manipulation.

More than intense emotion and the post–Civil War fascination with spiritualism prompted many Cincinnati residents to accept so-called spirit images as honest. Hearn wrote at the close of what historians now consider the pioneer period of photography—roughly a forty-year time following the discovery of the medium in 1839—and the beginning of the spiritualism fad Von Reichenbach, William James, and others addressed at length. By 1875 portrait photography had become formulaic.[5] What Hearn condemned marked only one shift of many that reshaped the circa-1880 reinvention of photography as both cultural phenomenon and mental reflex.

Spirit photography had prospered in part because most photography, especially most portrait photography, struck most American subjects as simultaneously highly technical and humdrum.[6] The 1880s change to dry-plate negatives caused many professional and advanced amateur photographers to look away from innovations in wet-plate photography, the entire technology of which they quickly derided as old-fashioned, but it did not stop many highly skilled wet-plate photographers from using techniques perfectly suited to spirit photography.[7] Hearn denounced innovations that preyed on nonphotographers predisposed to believe the trick images, and he did so at a critical juncture in the history of photographic technology. Within a few years, innovation of photographic technique had transformed the popular understanding of photography: photography had become vastly more accessible to the public and more interesting.

"The discovery of 1839 was suspect from the beginning: this mystery smelled strongly of witchcraft and was tainted with heresy," Nadar (pseudonym of Gaspard-Félix Tournachon) contended in 1899. "Nothing was lacking for a good witch hunt: sympathetic magic, the conjuring up of spirits, ghosts, Awesome Night—dear to all sorcerers and wizards—, a made-to-order temple for the Prince of Darkness." Nadar dismissively singled out the novelist Honoré de Balzac for believing that "every time someone had his photograph taken, one of the spectral layers was removed from the body and transferred to the photograph." Balzac thought that man could not make something material from an apparition, and that consequently the camera stripped away, layer by filmy layer, some kind of energy from his body. While that energy might produce the ghosts and other apparitions of traditional folk belief, its removal by photography must necessarily produce death. Nadar admitted that he could not judge the genuineness of Balzac's feeling, but in the end he thought it honest and real. The novelist knew much about the beginnings of daguerreotypy and photography, and he died in 1850, just as portrait photography became ordinary, formulaic, and seemingly safe.[8] It became common, too, in a way Nadar had difficulty explaining to his readers fifty years later.

Nine years after Balzac died, Baudelaire blasted photography in "The Salon of 1859," a criticism of the first Paris exhibition to include both paintings and photographs. A friend of Nadar and devotee of Poe, who championed daguerreotypy in the United States, Baudelaire attacked photography as a threat to the traditional fine arts. "Photographic operatives," as he termed them, came from the ranks of failed or lazy painters, but their products produced a frenzy. "A madness, an extraordinary fanaticism took possession of all these new sun-worshippers," he wrote of those who flocked to photographic studios. "Strange abominations took form," perhaps the worst being people costuming themselves as characters from mythology or ancient history. Each technological advance produced further frenzy: the stereoscope soon had thousands of well-to-do individuals staring through its peepholes "as though they were the attic-windows of the infinite," and pornography evolved from print to photographic imagery.[9] Two years after he wrote *Les fleurs du mal,* Baudelaire attacked a medium he condemned as threatening the powers of the imagination, and perhaps especially those powers that enabled the painter or poet to imagine things salacious or deviant.

The invention of the gelatin dry plate (and, soon afterward, roll film) and the popularization of amateur photography of the sort Ralphson describes in *The Boy Scout Camera Club,* refuted the thinking of Balzac, Baudelaire, and even the retrospection of Nadar. Over four decades, Alfred Watkins and other dedicated amateur photographers revolutionized the medium, sometimes by becoming professionals and sometimes by manufacturing new products. The Eastman Kodak Company nudged, prodded, and lured them along.[10] A coterie of the amateur photographers became critics of a new sort: active photographers who critiqued the work of others not on aesthetic grounds but on technical ones.

The British dramatist and socialist George Bernard Shaw wrote extensively about photography, but always from the viewpoint of an amateur enthusiast who moved from older cameras to an early Kodak box camera to a series of sophisticated cameras he modified himself, and finally to early 35 mm cameras. In the 1880s he published columns on two subjects especially, lens choice and darkroom procedure. In his Kodak years he printed mostly on POP, inexpensive printing-out paper intended for snapshot enthusiasts contact printing their own large negatives, but he moved on to platinum, bromide, and other papers and processes, experimenting especially with pyrocatechin and metol, eventually condemning the latter as unreliable and "a leprous poison."[11] After 1907 he dabbled with the Autochrome color process, making one image jurors selected for publication in a special 1908 edition of *The Studio* entitled *Color Photography and Other Recent Developments of the Camera.*[12]

Throughout his life, Shaw delighted in photographic gadgets and innovations. He knew he might never be a great photographer, and told one professional photographer attempting to write plays that "playwriting is like photography: you have to spoil a prodigious number of plates, and wear out the interest of quite commonplace snapshots and portraits and views for some years before you cease to care for your pictures merely because you made them."[13] Shaw made thousands of photographs, most still not cataloged and only cursorily examined, but the images offer some insight into his essays and addresses on photography and on a new if still obscure sort of criticism. Baudelaire wrote as an observer of photographs—Shaw wrote as a photographer.

In a 1906 catalog essay for a show of Alvin Langdon Coburn's photographs, Shaw defined the twenty-three-year-old photographer as experienced, noting that Coburn began photographing at age eight. "He has fifteen years technical experience behind him," Shaw noted, which produced "his command of the one really difficult technical process in photography—I mean printing." Then Shaw made a statement others quoted frequently: "Technically good negatives are more often the result of the survival of the fittest than of special creation: the photographer is like the cod, which produces a million eggs in order that one may reach maturity."[14]

In the 1930s denigrators of recently invented 35 mm cameras filled with thirty-six-exposure roll film and their machine gun–like users insisted Shaw spoke correctly. But in 1906 Shaw referred to amateur photographers unwilling to learn how to use one sort of film and one set of technical processes well before moving on to others. Coburn avoided "dark dexterities" of trick photography, especially the superimposed negative printing that so angered Hearn a generation earlier, and he experimented constantly. Shaw noted that even expert photographers "prefer to ascertain how his [Coburn's] prints are made by the humble and obvious method of asking him." He saw Coburn as having the "faculty of seeing certain things and being tempted by them," and as having the technical expertise and disciplined darkroom inventiveness to produce different sorts of prints, including "the device of imposing a gum print on a platinotype as a means of getting a golden brown tone quite foreign to pure or chemically toned platinotype."[15]

Unlike Shaw, Coburn traveled with simple equipment and a limited range of film types: part of what advanced his faculty—and efforts—involved technical mastery in the field, especially getting the exposure "precisely right," and in the darkroom, which Coburn kept "really dark."[16] Along with Watkins, Coburn wanted more than most professional photographers, and he achieved what he wanted. In 1917 he produced the first abstract photographs ever made, so-called vortographs created by focusing a camera lens at bits of glass at the ends of tubes of mirrors. The Vorticists, among them Wyndham Lewis and Ezra Pound, had probed new territory. Shaw found the images difficult to analyze, although he admitted instantly that only a master of camera and darkroom could have produced them. But Shaw understood Coburn's intense willingness to "not make difficulties until he meets them, being, like most joyous souls, in no hurry to bid the devil good-morning." In 1906 Shaw commented that Coburn's landscape photographs represented a genuine happiness rather than some morbid mood accentuated by "impoverishment or ar-tification," and implied that the happiness that led Coburn into particu-larly fruitful temptations originated at least in part in total confidence in very dark darkrooms indeed.[17] The twisting, unvisited lanes of England tempted and energized Coburn, who found light enough among the shad-ows to facilitate his photography of places whose forces affected his al-ready happy psyche.

In the early 1930s a consortium of photographers active in the San Francisco area formed Group f/64. Although women joined it and simi-lar groups, they were treated with a lack of respect bordering on hostil-ity. Edward Weston and Ansel Adams prided themselves on their tech-nical ability and found women "impure" and too emotional. Dorothea Lange, dismissed as "messy in the darkroom," retorted to a male pho-tographer that "the print is not the object; the object is the emotion the print gives you. You look past the print to the inner meaning."[18] In re-turn, men waved away such comments as masking incompetence and as generally silly.

For Weston, Adams, Van Dyke, and other California greats, techni-cal excellence mattered as much as choice of subject and composition. How a photographer behaved in the darkroom and how his negatives and prints manifested that behavior governed both reputation and opportuni-ties. Darkroom technique separated men from boys, and almost all males from women, no matter how otherwise accomplished.

Dorothea Lange offers an excruciatingly painful example. An elderly itinerant photographer rented a chicken coop behind the Lange family home and converted it into a darkroom, but he taught Lange mostly ob-solescent processing techniques. Another professional told her she knew nothing about making quality negatives, a charge that sent her to night classes at Columbia. As a quasi student, probably never officially enrolled, she studied developing, printing, and mounting, but she may not have encountered enlarging, the coating of paper, or advanced manipulation of negatives. After she moved to California, she joined the San Francisco Camera Club in order to have access to a darkroom, and only when she opened her first portrait studio in 1919 did she build her own darkroom in the building basement. For years she did only portraits on commission, and she placed a special emphasis on producing fine prints. "I knew something about what a good resonant print is," she recalled years later. "You must start with a good negative, of course, but the print in its range, its vibration, is impregnated with a life of its own," something like "a full fine chord of music in its richness and depth." But many of her peers judged that she rarely started with a good negative, and often struggled long into the night to make a superb print from a defective negative.

Once she abandoned formal studio portraiture, Lange's lack of technical training precipitated continual crises in developing film. She acquired better cameras, spurred on by the work of friends and mentors who used Rolleiflex medium-format ones, but instead of making her darkroom work easier, new film, chemicals, and paper challenged her. The lack of her own darkroom soon proved so irksome that she built one in her home basement, buying new equipment—including an enlarger—with her first paychecks from the Farm Security Administration. But from then on, she worried the FSA with letters about her poor-quality negatives and assurances that she could make fine prints from them. In one exchange, Roy Stryker, the head of the FSA photographic division, insisted that heat could not have adversely affected her film, before or after development: two other photographers, Arthur Rothstein and Walker Evans, had worked in the South in the height of summer too, and produced exquisite negatives "that show not the least sign of deterioration." Stryker pushed Lange hard. "Are you sure it isn't the developing rather than the heat?" he asked of negatives exhibiting poor developing and fixing.

Lange rarely made test exposures, used light meters casually, and gave processing too little attention. She relied on traditional chemicals and papers, and when manufacturers discontinued them she became uneasy. New developers replacing old especially upset her, and some assistants knew she bought paper unsuited to the printing tasks at hand.[19] As she became famous, her contemporaries accepted her lack of darkroom expertise, putting it down to simple lack of interest. Younger photographers, including Mary Jeanette Edwards, tempered their criticism, although as her assistants they knew the darkroom problems firsthand. Lange often spent a full day printing from a single poor-quality negative. She may never have become comfortable with the cropping capacities of enlargers, something that still dogs critics evaluating her work. Toward the end of her career she constructed a small outbuilding for a studio and darkroom, but she emphasized the studio. Even her friends wrote almost slightingly about her technical skills. Willard Van Dyke noted in a 1934 *Camera Craft* essay that Lange used a Weston exposure meter rather simply and infrequently, and that no "preconceived photographic aesthetic" drove her efforts. "For her, making a shot is an adventure that begins with no preconceived idea for success," he asserted, implying that her technical skills produced fewer great images than did luck.[20]

Lange was not the only woman photographer belittled by male colleagues. In his posthumous tribute, Ansel Adams said that Imogen Cunningham "wasn't very exacting about the way she made photographs. She was inclined to be a little sloppy." Adams sniffed that her final prints "never quite achieved what she had intended" in part because "her printing was extremely uneven." When he visited her darkroom he found drying racks made of long-browned cheesecloth, rather than up-to-date plastic screening. On one occasion, Adams recalled, Cunningham asked, "What bromide did in the developer—she knew it did *something*. She'd ask simple questions and expect simple answers."[21] Van Dyke shrugged that her "images often weren't all that sharp."[22] Women photographers tend to praise Cunningham, while men continue to damn her with faint praise. Van Dyke remarked patronizingly that "it was her unique way of seeing things that was important, and we all respected her for that," but critics condemned some of Cunningham's earliest images of male nudes as pornographic, and no one appeared to defend them or their maker, or to defend her subsequent experiments with double exposure and other techniques.[23] Her way of seeing proved less important to many of her contemporaries than her "inferior" darkroom technique.

In 1901 Cunningham made a self-portrait at Coburn's request, but what the master of innovative darkroom technique knew of her skills no one knows. In many ways, the pre–World War II darkroom might as well have been the men's room. Yet Cunningham had studied chemistry and photography in Germany, and in 1910 published a research paper, "About Self-Production of Platinum Prints for Brown Tones," detailing how lead and mercury might be added to the coating of sepia platinum paper.[24] The paper is well worth reading, because the photographers who coated paper with light-sensitive salts of platinum rather than contemporary modern silver salts intended to contact print negatives. Even the platinum papers produced commercially, all providing slow emulsions and a very wide range of middle tones and all extremely expensive, existed for contact printing. When Cunningham went to Europe she had the 4×5 camera she bought in college and a small folding Kodak snapshot camera given to her by fellow employees when she left her full-time job in an establishment that printed negatives. She could scarcely afford film for her 5×7 camera while in Europe, came home and opened a portrait studio, and thereafter moved gradually from one artistic concern to another, and from one format to another. The juxtaposition of concern and format nudged her away from the f/64 group, which emphasized the use of the camera as "a direct window to the real world." But as Weston and others strove for directness and superb if stark technical excellence, Cunningham moved toward double exposures and other concerns, and in time her darkroom technique puzzled her male counterparts.[25] Questions about bromide puzzled them even more. They knew she had shifted from large-format cameras to a Rolleiflex, but they did not comprehend her abandonment of previsualization.[26] Perhaps they never bothered to understand that she—and Lange—had a different notion about both the act of photographing and subsequent darkroom effort.

The charges of shop-theory carelessness or ignorance which still dog Cunningham, Lange, and other women photographers originate in a championing of one shop-theory framework over another. Always some men leveled the charges, repeating them often enough that they stuck despite very scanty evidence. Their championing of one framework over another segregated many male photographers too. Self-appointed male experts in darkroom technique tended to dismiss women as either congenitally messy or simply uninterested in bromides and much else, but by the early 1930s they were deriding male photographers whose darkroom innovations threatened the hegemony of self-styled straight or pure photographers, such as Group f/64 and its admirers. In short, the purists denigrated all photographers who did anything other than contact print large-format negatives. In their first exhibition, Weston, Adams, and Van Dyke acted as the "jury of selection" and emphasized that photography "has a definite and distinctive work field of its own, without intruding into the fields better handled by other media."[27] Beaumont Newhall routinely repeated their ideological message and devalued photographers who thought and worked differently. "Also it's hardly possible to understand f/64 without knowing the low level of west coast photography in the 1930s," he asserted in a Cunningham memoir. "It was all Photo-Secession derivative, and there was William Mortensen, a very colorful Hollywood makeup artist, who shocked people with his subjects and who manipulated his photographs in a way that was considered an absolute no-no."[28]

Some early twentieth-century photographers saw through prisms of glamour. When Lange asserted that the printing process must be secondary to the making of the negative and to the emotion produced by the print, perhaps especially the emotion the print creates in the photographer as she makes it in the darkroom, she explicated something that shaped Cunningham's entire career too. Cunningham had an early interest in theosophy, and especially in the concept of the astral body, a belief that shaped her life work.[29] "Those who are clairvoyant (clear-sighted), which means that they have developed the power of seeing this finer than physical matter," stated Ethel M. Mallet in *First Steps in Theosophy* in 1905, "tell us that when they look at any one of us they see the physical body, the ordinary form, which is all that most of us can see, and that within this they see a form of finer matter which interpenetrates the denser physical matter, and also stretches beyond the physical form, appearing as a kind of cloudy shell or halo surrounding the physical body."[30] The clear-sighted see the astral body around some people, and glimpse what AE sees as he walks about the country roads in Ireland, the "luminous quality" that manifests itself as an almost intolerable luster of light, pure and shining faces, dazzling processions of figures, somehow prolonged "into spheres which were radiant with actuality" and opening on entire cities in the sky. Meditation produces a readjustment of human faculties. "We are creating our own light," AE continues of those who practice, and that light enables the clear-sighted to see not only far into other dimensions but through the "cloudy gloom through which vague forms struggle sometimes into definiteness."[31]

This is the visionary glamour Pullman describes repeatedly in His Dark Materials novels. The aurora enables Lyra the clear-sighted to see something beyond it: "And behind the ever-changing gauze of light, that other world, that sunlit city, was clear and solid."[32] Lyra sees what Lord Asriel photographs using his special emulsion, the radiation Von Reichenbach descried. Lyra sees Od, known to Cunningham as the astral body of some people and the luminous glow of other-worldly creatures that AE says produced ancient "legends of nymph and dryad."[33] Lange and Cunningham and many male photographers never abandoned what they and others glimpsed in the first decade of the twentieth century. They continued to focus on what most photographers never noticed, especially after the California-based purists marginalized aesthetics and techniques other than their own.

Prisms of glamour often arrived by Railway Express. When she was in high school in 1901, Cunningham sent fifteen dollars to the International Correspondence School in Scranton, Pennsylvania. It shipped a 4×5 camera, a course of instructions, and a box in which developed glass negatives might be returned for analysis and comment. Her father built her a darkroom in the family woodshed, and she developed her first negatives by candlelight.[34] She had no personal instruction in the beginning, and simply worked her way into photography, following directions. Soon she was photographing herself nude in a quiet meadow. After a public outcry following a newspaper story reporting that she had photographed her new husband nude in mountain meadows, Cunningham put away many negatives for more than half a century, not returning to them until just before her death at the age of ninety-three in 1976. She began photographing when George Eastman still thought of photography chiefly as fun; many second-generation photographers discovered new possibilities latent in Kodak cameras, films, and darkroom processes; and many beginning photographers learned not from instructors but from books, manufacturer directions, magazine articles, and above all by doing. The range of her work reflects more than genius and sustained dedication: it reflects something of how photography engendered glamour—and fun—in the years immediately after 1890, perhaps especially for bold, free-thinking women.[35]

"When I started out in 1935 I was a kind of purist because I had just discovered Paul Strand and Edward Weston and Ansel Adams in magazines," recalled Clarence John Laughlin in a 1988 interview. "But by the end of the 1930s I had started to do these photographs where I use human figures with certain backgrounds picked out just for these figures, and with objects brought there; I started to do pictures suggested by what these things did to my subconscious mind." A half century after he began making photographs, Laughlin understood that he had drifted quickly from purism to something he sometimes called "surrealism," in part because he lived in New Orleans and wandered the outlying bayou country. "I became very interested in old houses and cemeteries, and everything that seemed strange or out of the way." He grew fascinated with creating a "system of symbols," and by 1940 knew that "everything, everything, no matter how commonplace and how ugly, has secret meanings," perhaps especially the abandoned plantations along Louisiana back roads. By then he had begun to distrust the darkroom technique purists advocated. "I never pay attention to technicians anymore, including Ansel Adams," he explained.[36]

Shop theory influenced Laughlin's first darkroom and all its subsequent improvements, and the darkroom equipment shaped his photography. He made his first developing tank from a glass battery jar, and his first enlarger from a wooden box. In 1988 he told an interviewer that he built his first sophisticated enlarger from directions in *Popular Science*, noting only that it used tinfoil, a headlight reflector, the camera lens, and worked horizontally. "I had really to conserve on money because I didn't have much: I had a very low-paying job."[37] In the Depression many other photographers found themselves in similar circumstances, but they had discovered a wealth of older, pre-Kodak cameras for sale in junk stores, cameras made obsolete by roll-film technology.[38] They followed detailed instructions and built photographic equipment from cannibalized junk cameras and ordinary materials.[39] Their idiosyncratic, homemade darkroom equipment reflected and then shaped their personal visions, but technical excellence characterized their work always.[40]

Laughlin built an enlarger using an automobile headlight reflector, and in 1988 he was still using it. "You go in this darkroom I have now, there's not a single piece of expensive or complicated equipment in there. My enlarger is completely primitive, everything has to be done by hand, it doesn't even have condensers. When I tell some photographers this they don't believe me. They're so used to all these expensive enlargers, all kinds of gadgets—everything can be done automatically or semi-automatically—that if they saw this darkroom they would hardly believe it's a darkroom."[41] When he dismissed the purism of the f/64 group, Laughlin owned only one camera, the lens of which he used on his homemade, condenser-less enlarger.

Condensing lenses spread out light through the negative. Found only in high-quality electric-light enlargers—in the 1930s called "projection printers"—they work in pairs, their convex sides toward each other between the light source and the negative slid just below them.[42] Before World War II, photographers knew the arrangement as that inside magic lantern projectors throwing enlargements of glass slides upon walls and theater screens.[43] Cinema made magic lantern technology obsolete except in university classrooms, where art history professors valued the detail capacity of large glass slides, and many photographers rebuilt magic lanterns into enlargers. Rebuilding demanded some knowledge of optics: a 4-inch magic lantern lens could enlarge negatives up to $2\frac{1}{4} \times 3\frac{1}{4}$ inches, while a $5\frac{1}{4}$-inch lens managed negatives $3\frac{1}{4} \times 4\frac{1}{4}$, so photographers scrounged for projectors that supported negative formats. Most rebuilt magic lanterns worked only horizontally, and often awkwardly when compared with novel concave reflector enlargers. The reflector placed behind the light source spread out light over the negative in ways that satisfied most amateurs, especially since it used smaller bulbs that proved less likely to melt negatives. Soon manufacturers produced belt-and-gear reflector enlargers that kept images focused as users changed image size.[44] Technically minded photographers, including f/64 group members, trusted only condenser enlargers when they condescended to enlarge rather than contact print negatives.[45] But shop-built enlargers offered a wealth of opportunities to photographers anxious to achieve something other than the standardized technical perfection purists and manufacturers of close-tolerance equipment defined and championed. When photographers used such enlargers with other homemade equipment, they often found themselves working in ways that encouraged experimentation.[46] Shop-built cameras and darkroom equipment, even those built from plans, often proved ideally suited to idiosyncratic intentions and aesthetics.[47]

Laughlin found his enlarging camera perfect in his quest for "placing figures in settings, not as actors on a stage, but as symbolic manifestations pointing to unconscious fears or dreams." In many cases, the enlarger made superb prints of ruined plantation houses and other decayed period structures, each in his words "evoking qualities of its spiritual past far more complex and critical than the recent nostalgia for ante-bellum life." For decades he photographed the detritus of the slavery landscape in a way that jarred both sentimentalists and the nascent Civil Rights movement.[48] Often he peopled the ruins with figures according to what he called a "preconceived, pre-sensitized concept" he found hidden in his imagination or subconscious.[49] But often he superimposed negatives in the darkroom, creating images that many viewers found off-putting or contrived or surreal or suffused with unnerving light.[50]

Laughlin meditated deeply on meanings of rationality, inserting in some photos (by multiple exposure) images of human forms returned "from the great gulf of the past; that past, which mathematicians now assure us, is co-existent with the present."[51] He produced image after image demonstrating a mastery of on-site and in-darkroom recombinant imagery making, forcing the viewer to acknowledge if not accept his peculiar understanding of "looking with the eye of the mind, which, driven by memory and desire, recombines the elements of the natural world."[52]

After the widespread sales success of *Ghosts along the Mississippi,* Laughlin's photographs of plantation houses and late nineteenth-century San Francisco mansions now and then appeared in American and European photography and design journals and decorated the pages of mass-circulation magazines.[53] In 1950 *Flair* reproduced *Greenwood Plantation: The New and the Old* full size, perhaps to demonstrate how a medium-format view camera records a reflection in an automobile hubcap.[54] Five years later, the British annual *Saturday Book* reproduced a series of Laughlin's work involving trees, introducing the images with a comparison involving the paintings of Bosch and Paul Klee.[55] Magazine editors generally chose the seemingly simpler images: they eschewed any involving Laughlin's arrangement of found objects or darkroom exposures resulting from overlaid negatives. In 1955 *Coronet* published a selection of eight images from the book, but with altered captions. Laughlin had set out to become the first photographer to fuse words and images, but despite the care with which he wrote captions, *Coronet* shortened them by eliminating all mention of out-of-the-ordinary perceptions.[56]

In 1960 *Life* reproduced ten Laughlin images. I found them in my junior-high-school library about a year later. Most of the images struck me as documentary. But several seemed elegiac in ways about which I had learned from reading railroad magazines. A disused, weed-grown track, a derelict station or water tower, perhaps a semaphore signal rusted into the "stop" position, by then illuminated many issues of *Trains* and *Railroad:* as the railroad industry contracted, many photographers sought out lightly trafficked and abandoned routes. Many of their images originated in formulas I had begun to understand, especially the passion for late-afternoon sunlight indicating end-of-an-era concepts. But several Laughlin images transcended the railroad photographs.

By 1975 I knew a bit more about Laughlin, but not a lot. I had not known of his 1973 show at the Philadelphia Museum of Art, but when I found a review of it in *Photography Year 1975,* an annual published by Time-Life books as part of its photography technique series, I knew I had missed something that mattered to me. While noting that Laughlin had had more than two hundred shows and had images published in *Vogue, Life, Mademoiselle,* and other periodicals, the editors understood that most people who knew his work saw it through *Ghosts along the Mississippi,* a folio that delighted and disturbed. "This is hardly the career of an obscure photographer, and yet there is a sense in which Laughlin is unknown," they concluded.[57] But Laughlin worked in a realm far beyond the one Newhall and others defined as central. The few images Time-Life selected suggested that Laughlin received no attention from mainstream photographic historians because his work fit no established genre.[58] It had fit no genre for decades.

"I have been fascinated by the mystery of light . . . by the amazing and inexhaustible magic of light itself—which is related, on the one hand, to the basic vital processes of all living things; on the other, to the inner nature of time," Laughlin wrote in *The Personal Eye,* one of the two volumes that accompanied his 1973 Philadelphia show.[59] Laughlin understood two sensitive surfaces, film and the mind's eye, but he believed that a sensitive mind's eye saw far more than the fall of light on a place. Insisting that "technique and technical proficiency mean nothing in themselves," Laughlin introduced a range of superb photographs. "Much of the pathetic and moving emotionalism which the old Creole families of New Orleans centered around their devotion to the dead . . . ," begins one caption. "There is about this oak a sort of visual magic . . . ," begins another. "In 1955 New Orleans still had a few streets—unpaved, where one had the feeling not only of going back in space, but also back into time—streets whose ancient, shabby, and secluded quietness, free from cars, breathed the feeling of an older day . . . ," begins a third. In these captions readers of Hearn and the *Double-Dealer* find glimpses of what Hearn designated fantastic. But Laughlin's captions deal too with the making of the photographs, one concluding that "because of the great range of light values here (and careful control work on the print)—the white vase at center starts to become unreal—and to lose its position in space." Laughlin implicitly accepted what he called "the special and indigenous fantasy" of New Orleans, and linked much of it to the powerful force of legalized prostitution within a larger matrix of multiracial and multiethnic forces underlying the civil rights movement.[60] Fierce abandon produced much of what captured Laughlin's attention in and beyond New Orleans. An understanding that cameras (and enlargers) often act on their own fixed much of his willingness to invent and explore.[61] He strove to bring his camera into places so charged with multiple forces that the camera might respond willfully.

Stories by Lafcadio Hearn structured the catalog of the 1973 Philadelphia Museum of Art show. Interspersed among groups of selected images and preceding Laughlin's lengthy captions appear "The Night of All Saints," "Spring Phantoms," and other tales from *Fantastics*. "One of my basic feelings is that the mind, and the heart alike, of the photographer must be dedicated to the glory, the magic, and the mystery of light. The mystery of time, the magic of light, enigma of reality—and their interrelationships—are my constant themes and preoccupations," Laughlin noted at the beginning of his introduction, "A Statement by the Photographer." He understood that depicting "the unreality of the 'real' and the reality of the 'unreal'" would disturb many viewers, especially those unused to "*extreme romanticism*—the concept of 'reality' as being, innately, mystery and magic; the intuitive awareness of the power of the 'unknown'—which human beings are afraid to realize, and which none of their religious and intellectual systems can really take into account."[62] Many of the photographs exist not only by virtue of sensitive film and a sensitive mind's eye, then, but because of extremely nuanced darkroom manipulation. A store-window mannequin exhibits a human leg, a mirror reflects the core of a painting, a fragmented icon floats in the clouded sky above a ruin plantation house—those and many other images exist because Laughlin used not only fragments of the darkroom trickery Hearn condemned but countless other shop-theory methods and a one-off enlarger combined to produce one-of-a-kind images.

"He is the Master of Ignored Ghastliness, the Eldritch, the Psycho-pompous, the Metamorphic, the Mephitic, the Fearsome, and now and then of Trumpery and the Fulsome," wrote Jonathan Williams of Laughlin in the catalog introduction. "Purists and the mean in spirit have regarded him with distain for almost 40 years and have ignored him."[63] But Williams saw the Philadelphia show as a sort of reckoning. He thought the academy and the critics would finally realize Laughlin's genius. Laughlin thought otherwise, and proved right.

Too many of the Laughlin images displayed in 1973 hinted at what Depression-era fantasy writers had drawn from Hearn, Cable, and other turn-of-the-century writers, and at what postwar folklorists delineated in ways that shaped pulp magazine fiction. Between 1946 and the early 1960s, articles on voodoo appeared in the *Journal of American Folklore* that made rural North Carolina African Americans seem as immersed in voodoo as locals in the northern part of Haiti. What one folklorist called "patterns of malign occultism" and "maleficia" (misfortunes attributed to evil) stretched deep into the colonial and preslavery pasts and into on-going Haitian contact with the American South, and seemed likely to inform the future of African American culture, perhaps especially music.[64] By the mid-1950s, men's pulp magazines regularly published nonfiction articles based on recent folklore scholarship and supposedly firsthand exploration of voodoo and other occult beliefs among African Americans.[65] Brian O'Brien's "Voodoo Queen of New Orleans," a 1956 *For Men Only* article, recycled tales related by Hearn, Cable, and others, albeit in modernized form.[66]

In 1973 Laughlin's images seemed part of an older cultural framework suddenly politically unpalatable. The neat boxes post-1960s academics crafted to contain revisionist understandings of slavery, aesthetics, ideologies, eroticism, and film could not contain his photographs, any more than they could contain the work of specialist folklorists working in the rural South until the late 1960s. Laughlin photographed in places vanquished by slum-clearance programs, bayou floods, great mansion house fires, and even simple rot, and in cultural contexts folklorists delineated until their scholarship collided with politics. The decrepitude Laughlin found along Bayou Lafourche and other places had disintegrated into memory and then disintegrated memory itself: the sensitivities Von Reichenbach analyzed might have explained complexities northern critics chose to ignore.[67] When Laughlin worked in California, the locus of Ansel Adams and other purists, he accepted the local dominance of Group f/64 and its devotees and "tried to do something more subtle: to incorporate 'Purism' *merely as a basis*" upon which to build a personal vision.[68] But after 1951, when he began photographing Louisiana women within contexts he conceptualized as unreal or fantastic, he realized that his "hyper-real" visions would create trouble as "the erotic element becomes all the more intense." Laughlin had been careful for two decades. "Due to the puritanical code dominating this country till recently, none of these pictures have ever been published or exhibited before," he noted of images juxtaposing vaginas, penises, flowers, breasts, and the heads of lions against fragments of decrepit antebellum houses or gardens.[69] The images transcend abstraction, but in ways the followers of the f/64 group understood to be almost hokey.

After the Philadelphia show a handful of critics discovered or reassessed Laughlin's photography, most unknowingly following the lead of a 1966 *Saturday Book* selection of his work entitled "American Fantastica." Laughlin insisted simply that buildings often "tell us something of what was happening *inside* human beings. Some of these buildings speak to us of the secret desires and compulsions of particular men." Laughlin attacked architects of the "less is more" school: "Eventually we are going to have to do something about giving our buildings more character. In our search for 'purity of form' we have ended up, mostly, with nothing but a cold and inhuman blankness."[70] Despite the seeming illogic of his view (why blankness does not indicate something of desires and compulsions escaped him), Laughlin rammed his images straight into the urban-renewal engine and against the power of Group f/64, its followers, and especially Newhall. His arguments angered many of his contemporaries, and despite his 1973 show, when the Center for Creative Photography at the University of Arizona produced a slim volume devoted to his work, Henry Holmes Smith maintained that the avoidance or scorn of his work by critics correctly indicated either unevenness of production or second-rate achievement.[71] Despite Susan Sontag's passing notice in her 1977 *On Photography* that Laughlin's extreme romanticism enlarged "the familiar iconography of mystery, mortality, transience," others of the Walter Benjamin school of critics avoided her hunch that Laughlin represented something original and well ahead of critics.[72] Laughlin died in 1985, still an enigma and still—perhaps—a threat.

In 1990 appeared *Clarence John Laughlin: Visionary Photographer,* a volume containing essays by three scholars, among them Keith F. Davis, the chief curator of the Hallmark Cards, Inc., collection of photographs.[73] The Historic New Orleans Collection produced another in 1997, featuring essays by senior photographic historians and critics, among them Jonathan Williams and John Wood. Like the Hallmark volume, *Haunter of Ruins* introduces Laughlin's photographs as well as interprets them;

both books emphasize the fact that Laughlin remains an obscure photographer despite the success of *Ghosts along the Mississippi* and deepening respect for his first book, *New Orleans and Its Living Past,* which appeared in a limited edition in 1941.[74] Several of the essays in *Haunter of Ruins* make uneasy reading: they avoid Laughlin and focus on Louisiana circa 1940, detailing a time-place continuum still unknown to most American intellectuals. The prose seems circumspect, and almost timid, as if the authors sense that the photographer's career might contain difficult-to-analyze forays into genres critics still dismiss. Such suspicion is well founded. The Center for Creative Photography bibliography fails to include much of his work.

Art Photography: Sophistication in Pictures nowadays might strike a discoverer as a girlie or "men's photography" magazine masquerading as a photography journal, but only contemporary prudishness and ignorance produce the incorrect designation. Cheesecake magazines, especially the pulps so common before *Playboy* changed publishing standards after 1954, rarely appeared on glossy paper, let alone featured full-page advertisements for Nikon, Minolta, and other expensive cameras, cover photographs of Sophia Loren, or articles detailing the abstract photographic experiments of Weegee, the New York street photographer famous for his images of homicides, car wrecks, and other urban trauma.[75] The photographs of nudes might be cheesecake, pornography, or something else altogether that shatters simplistic contemporary views of the 1950s, and few contemporary observers find words to fit them.[76] They might be the glamour images against which contemporary critics and photography faculty warn young professional photographers and advanced students. "Avoid so-called glamour poses—they usually look ridiculous in pictures," cautions Ralph Hattersley in *Photographic Lighting: Learning to See.* "They also tend to look pornographic because glamour is a deliberate projection of sex. It is all right to have a picture project sexuality, so long as you do a good and honest job of it, but a failure in this respect nearly always comes out as pornography."[77]

But Laughlin's images are not pornography, and not in the tradition of *Vanity Fair* glamour imagery, either. *Art Photography* jars contemporary viewers, forcing them to realize that Hattersley and others fail to define "usually," and that Laughlin and a handful of other photographers long ago pushed far past the limits of cinema- and fashion-magazine glamour imagery. Laughlin knew in the 1930s that visual magic involved far more than deliberate projection of sex and poses already hackneyed in film-fan magazines. He knew that a photographer might make something vastly different from pornography and that it might be equally disturbing to many viewers.

In "Backgrounds and Models" Laughlin argued that formulaic how-to-do-it photographic instruction produced "a stereotyped style of 'cheesecake' picture" instead of ones demonstrating individual imagination. He condemned collections of expensive equipment, professional models, and even sophisticated cosmetics, unconvincing "stagy" special effects, and figures who seem aware of the camera. At the heart of this lengthy article pulses the signature Laughlin energy. He observed that the photographer should have something to express about a setting and a figure, and now and then be fortunate enough to find the two fitting perfectly. Laughlin thought purism attracted poorly educated, fundamentally unsophisticated photographers fixated on surface aesthetics. He suggested that photographers should read poetry, and understand that great poetry evolves from the "inner world" of the poet in place. In one photograph, a young woman in a strapless sundress stands on the porch of a decrepit cabin; above her dangles Spanish moss, and a great spiderweb veils her face. Laughlin says little about the image, only mentioning the folktale of the spider and fly, but stabs at something else. The woman is not trapped: her beauty traps her, and makes her a spider. In many of the other images the female figure, often robed in black or nearly lost in jet-black shadow, is the genius loci of derelict plantation houses, "of ruin-haunted grandeur."[78] Often, she is masked.

Laughlin worked with masks all his life. Certainly Mardi Gras festivities intrigued him, but in the 1950s he decided that most people wear masks concealing their true selves, and that in time the masks become ersatz selves. With a shattered store mannequin head, he created an image via double exposure, having discovered a woman whose face resembled the half face of the mannequin. Using an f-stop of 16 to produce great depth of field, Laughlin made one exposure with the woman covering half her face with the half mask, at 1/5 of a second; he made the second, without the mask, at 1/10 of a second. What he implies, but fails to say, is that the model must remain as still as the tripod-mounted camera.[79] "Backgrounds and Models" explains how and why he made several of the images critics discovered in the 1970s and have begun to value today, but it reveals far more about his understanding of glamour. For Laughlin, glamour involves something utterly different from the outpouring of images in cinema, girlie, and other magazines before television transformed the serial publishing industry in the late 1950s. It involves something the editors of *Art Photography* struggled with from 1949 onward: the use of the female figure in images that defied ordinary understanding of film star, cheesecake, and pornographic poses while emphasizing what Laughlin called extreme romanticism, typically in places peculiar to it.

In "Background and Models" Laughlin implied not only that the work of William Mortensen had influenced him but that he had deliberately moved beyond the frameworks of the photographer so many Group f/64 devotees excoriated. When Laughlin built his own enlarger, Mortensen already exerted a strong influence not only among so-called pictorialist photographers but among photographers deeply intrigued by glamour, mixed-media image making, and home- or custom-made, simple and sophisticated, photographic equipment, and with a determined refusal to follow cinema studio aesthetics grounded in Production Code prudishness.

Mortensen left Hollywood in 1931, disgusted at the formulaic studio culture evolving from the making of sound films, and already famous as the photographer of Jean Harlow, Marlene Dietrich, and other stars. His film stills for the Cecil B. DeMille film *King of Kings* proved innovative and wildly successful. Mortensen took a small camera directly into studio cine-film shooting activity, producing publicity images that crackled with energy and became part of a hundred-volume limited-edition portfolio sent to heads of state, the Vatican, and other powers uneasy about the New Testament theme. But Mortensen wanted more than innovative film studio work. In Laguna Beach he became a specialist portrait photographer to the stars and established a small photography school in which he eventually taught some four thousand advanced students. For thirty years he resolutely withstood attacks by purists. Mortensen published more than two hundred technical and critical articles in *Camera Craft* and other photography magazines, and a number of books. He wrote well, and his cogent arguments proved valuable to Laughlin, who prized the writing of succinct, straightforward essays and captions and valued anyone who urged individual photographers to follow their own dreams. Now and then Mortensen responded to critics: he repeatedly asked purists why news and other photographers, especially ones employed in topographical survey work who contact printed large-format negatives, did not deserve the purist designation.[80] By the middle 1940s he essentially ignored the f/64 group–based "purism" Newhall and other critics had fashioned into what most intellectuals considered the mainstream of United States photography.

Mortensen continued to publish, often updating his books as new technology appeared, and he continued to teach. In the 1950s he manufactured and sold darkroom accessories, including texture screens for use in darkroom projection.[81] "In exploiting the camera's capacity for dealing with the humorous and fantastic, students have discovered a field of photographic expression that far transcends the merely 'candid' or 'pure,'" he wrote in 1940 of one component of his curriculum. As mainstream critics and historians determinedly marginalized his thinking, Mortensen produced juxtaposition of settings and models in compositions that extended meanings of glamour far beyond anything Hollywood contrived.[82] In the middle 1930s his photographs and writing appear to have encouraged Laughlin to abandon the path blazed by Adams, Weston, and other Group f/64 members and to follow bayou back roads. Today Laughlin's advocates make clear that the photographers and critics who marginalized Lange, Cunningham, and other women photographers strove even harder to marginalize a man who proclaimed—along with Lange and Cunningham—that "the whole program of the purists inclines to overlook the basic truth that the final concern of art is not with facts, but with ideas and emotions." Mortensen respected the purists and easily admitted that he did not understand their condemnation of so much photographic enterprise. Only occasionally did he write bluntly: "A chemical fact can never become a picture unless an idea and an emotion are also present, and these are qualities that cannot be added to the developer."[83] He distrusted any theoretical framework that tacitly accepted the camera as an instrument functioning solely as a machine.[84] His questions about the "purism" of topographical and other photographers working in the sciences effectively silenced Group f/64 members and allied critics.

For twenty years following the mid-1930s ascendancy of the f/64 group in art and photography magazines, Mortensen and others argued that technical proficiency merely enabled individual photographers to work out personal agendas evolved from experience outside photography.[85] In 1936, for example, George Allen Young told *Camera Craft* readers that most photographers who move on from the snap-shooter stage bog down in the technical stage. They experiment with too many manufactured items, especially darkroom chemicals, and they never learn how to make technically perfect images of anything. Advertising traps most in a decades-long gadget-acquisition fixation that deflects them from learning to use well the most basic, often homemade equipment in pursuit of individual enterprise. Young suggested that such overequipped but often demoralized photographers might begin photographing a fragment of ordinary landscape already intimately familiar. Such photography develops "the power of observation" by deepening familiarity with something already well known: the ostensible subject becomes less important than the variety of lighting and atmospheric conditions which must in the end center the attention of the photographer.[86] With much effort, the determined photographer becomes proficient in the technical expertise enabling him to work out his individual agenda. In his numerous monographs, Mortensen explained technical details Young and others only mentioned, always insisting that photographers could make much of their own equipment.[87] It is difficult to overestimate his impact on United States photographers between 1930 and 1960.[88] It is equally difficult to find any mention of that impact in standard histories of photography.[89]

In 1940 Mortensen published *Outdoor Portraiture,* another in a series of sophisticated books dissecting challenges most amateur and professional photographers confronted. As he had in *The New Projection Control* (1934), *Pictorial Lighting* (1937), *Print Finishing* (1938), *The Negative* (1940), and other monographs, Mortensen emphasized "the negative approach," stressing what photographers should not do rather than what they must do. He argued that outdoor portraiture typically preoccupied most neophyte photographers, usually disappointed them immediately, and very frequently ended their love affair with both simple and expensive cameras. "A good outdoor portrait has a directness and sincerity that is rarely achieved in the studio product," Mortensen remarked. Learning to make superb outdoor portraits teaches much about other photographic situations, especially studio work in which the photographer controls the lighting. *Outdoor Portraiture* deals at length with problems posed by incorrect backgrounds, especially those never seen—"realized" is perhaps a better term, although Mortensen uses "seen"—by the photographer. "The literal minded camera" records in a very purist way, and "turns up all sorts of strange things in the background that the photographer has overlooked completely."[90] By "background" Mortensen meant everything surrounding the subject, including foreground details. All too often photographers noticed cluttered backgrounds, litter, and shadow only when they developed negatives or, sometimes, when they printed them. Most of the time, the literal-minded camera recorded the total absence of photographer control.

Control figures prominently in all of Mortensen's books and articles, but always in two ways. He argued that too few photographers practiced enough with newly acquired cameras and accessories, and with enlargers, darkroom chemicals, and photographic papers, to control them well enough to accomplish personal agendas. In *Flash in Modern Photography* (1947), he detailed how flashbulbs had made exposure "a very touchy and treacherous problem," and how magazine advertisements by flashbulb manufacturers demonstrated the use of the bulb but rarely illustrated "good photographic technique." In his view, flashbulbs and synchronizers were two more gadgets that fascinated photographers too enthusiastic or overwhelmed to integrate them properly into established techniques.[91] By 1940 he longed for Depression-era forced simplicity. In *The Negative* he detailed the damage wrought by the gadget craze and condemned many photographers, especially well-to-do ones, as immature. "You must learn," he urged, "not only the mechanical finger movements and the various other matters of rote and ritual that any bright ten-year-old could master, you must also *grow up* in your approach to photographic problems and learn to understand the basic principles that will give the solution to your problems." He argued against experimentation before learning standardized control techniques worked out by highly skilled technicians employed by film and other manufacturers.[92] He chastised photographers for controlling lighting and composition, especially outdoors, all too rarely. He blamed their lack of control on immature enthusiasm and an arrogance born in the purchase of expensive cameras, and he asserted repeatedly that making high-quality photographs required intelligent and disciplined practice in controlling the camera and in understanding the environments in which photographers intended to use it. What photographers did with accomplished technical skills, Mortensen noted, did not concern him. He knew what he did with such skills, and he valued control in part because letting it slip slightly now and then produced valuable surprises.

He counseled photographers experimenting with the new 35 mm cameras to try outdoor portraiture in tightly controlled ways and then to relax some one or two components of control. "Were photographers more honest than they are vain, they would freely admit that the *factor of the accidental* plays a large part in their best work," he commented. Mortensen understood both the inability to realize background when aiming a camera and the accidental images the camera records—the armature around which Ralphson's Boy Scout thriller turns and on which so much of Watkins's counsel depends—and the potential successes resulting from deliberate seeking after accident. "When the hampering restrictions of logic, common sense, and conscious technique are gaily chucked overboard, one is most apt to accomplish things that are fresh, spontaneous, and vital."[93] But until a photographer had learned to see everything revealed in the camera viewfinder and a range of nuanced skills, he could not know how to invite serendipitous accident. "If the idea is fantastic, be fantastic," Mortensen advised, having warned his reader that fantasy imagery originates in technical discipline too. "The *meanings of things,* not things themselves, are the ultimate material of art," he concluded, seconding the thinking of contemporaneous women photographers.[94] Meaning might be real, surreal, or something else entirely, including what Hearn described in *Fantastics*.

The darkroom trickery Hearn condemned in 1875 originated in deft projection control. Mortensen's *The New Projection Control* explains not only how to print a negative but also how to alter both the projected image and the image that emerges on the developed sensitized paper. *The New Projection Control* details what Baudelaire and Coburn knew and what Shaw at least glimpsed, that the photographer might control far more than the camera itself. He might control the making of the latent image and control too its projection, altering that projection to suit ends other than the ostensibly objective ones most people equated with photography. But what Hearn descried in 1875 proved instructive years later: the photographer in control might see in ways as peculiar to any place as Hearn discovered in New Orleans and the bayou country.

"To render flesh, for example, in terms of pores, hairs, and wrinkles, no matter how accurately it is done, fails utterly to give an *experience* of flesh," Mortensen told *Camera Craft* readers in 1934, going on to warn them that "our perception of flesh is to only a limited extent made up of visual facts: impressions gained from other senses, such as warmth, smoothness, and firmness, are just as important as surface topography."[95] Mortensen clearly valued images that do more than convey visual facts. Like so many women photographers of his era, and like Laughlin, he struggled to produce images of emotion originating in light and time.

Nowadays few viewers of photographs by Laughlin and Mortensen can say much about how the photographers made the images. Photographers who worked with homemade or customized cameras, enlargers built from automobile headlights or aluminum cocktail shakers, and overlay negatives often produced one-of-a-kind images that reject machine replication.[96] Photogravure and other mass-production technologies reproduce only *facsimiles* of photographs, legible, on some levels at least, only to other photographers familiar with photographic shop theory.[97] Hearn felt that darkroom controllers violated public trust. But control involves far more than deliberate multiple exposure. It means—among many other things—understanding lighting and composition as frames to which (and from which) what almost everyone accepts as natural can be added and subtracted. Mortensen examined only the borderlands of such control in *The New Projection Control* and *The Negative,* and those and his other books remain almost the only larger portal through which contemporary photographers pass into something utterly different from Group f/64–based photographic technique and tradition.

A clock smothered in cobwebs may reveal much about how Laughlin found the abandoned countryside along Bayou Lafourche. But perhaps it means only that Laughlin knew William A. Palmer's 1935 *Camera Craft* article explaining how to produce fake spiderwebs that seemed natural.[98] A tin cup with tiny holes drilled about its lip, mounted on the armature of an electric motor (nowadays an electric drill does superbly), and filled with carpenter cold glue spins out perfect webs by centrifugal force.[99] Cobwebs are where a photographer finds them, but also where he or she needs them to be.

Cobwebs covering anything in photographs made after the early 1930s prove as suspect now as any spirits Hearn condemned. The shop-theory methods of cobweb making escape many experienced critics of photographs. A universe of shop theory shaped photography between 1910 and the beginning of World War II; fragments of it endured into the early 1960s. But such shop theory challenged and then repulsed many photographers who embraced 35 mm photography in the 1930s and found themselves suddenly imprisoned in small-format image making and the collecting of standardized accessory lenses, filters, enlargers, and other equipment. Not only did they make little of their own equipment, they prized regular image making, expecting their new-format cameras to work repeatedly in regular, predictable ways and to display none of the willful, idiosyncratic behavior Mortensen and Laughlin thought perfectly suited to abandoned rural landscape and to photographing what both photographers considered its genii loci.

11 Rolleiflex

Not only did fashion photographers typically use Rolleiflex cameras; fashion models frequently held them while being photographed. The square-format cameras exuded classiness and class distinctions.

ONLY ACCIDENT LINKED MY BOYHOOD OLD-FIELDS landscape and my early interest in Depression-era photographic technique. Medium-format photography, what I unhesitatingly and thoughtlessly considered "photography," began to fascinate me around the age of eight, and within three years I had begun dismantling and altering hand-me-down medium-format cameras, then taking them into the old fields and the marshes, and into rowboats. I never worried about damaging any of them, or even losing them overboard, and by my early teens I had learned enough of the Depression-era and older shop theory of image making to connect medium-format photography with a particular response to abandoned rural landscape.

My parents, grandparents, and great-uncles and -aunts used only medium-format cameras. Only the oldest, never-used cameras, mostly monster collapsible Kodaks and a shelf full of box camera Brownies, made rectangular images: the others made square negatives. Although adults in my family made snapshots, no one devoted much attention to photography; but everyone older than I said that good-quality cameras made picture taking easier. In the late 1950s I began using third- and fourth-hand cameras, all square-format, waist-level viewfinder models. I preferred the cart paths and footpaths winding through the old fields and woods of the town to the paved roads, and the vintage cameras seemed specially suited to such quietude. They were tricky to work, liable to accidental image making, and thought provoking in their operational limitations and difficulty: they forced me to work slowly and deliberately.[1] In the brilliant beveled-glass viewfinder of an old Kodak Duaflex II I first puzzled over the optics that causes mirrors to produce reversed but not inverted images. I decided that the reversed image caused me to consider composition more closely, since the image in the viewfinder moved opposite to the lateral direction in which I moved the camera, but I found little in the school library or at the dusty James which illuminated the vagaries of medium-format camera optics.[2] The chunky curved-glass viewfinder seemed a direct descendant of, if not a close cousin to, the shewstones of sorcerers. In it I saw startling reflections, even when the camera lay beside me as I munched a sandwich: inside the camera, even midway in the thick, beveled viewfinder, now and then a world of glass.

Euclidean geometry failed to explain my seeing in squares or my love of square-format photography, and it failed to explain some optical issues too. As an undergraduate, I decided that I had missed something in my sophomore and senior years of high school. My fascination with small-boat navigation had skewed my teenage understanding of geometry, and senior year physics classes emphasizing reflection and incidence avoided curved surfaces, something that made me ponder diffusion versus condenser enlargers. In university art history classes I wondered about the mathematics of the golden triangle, curved-surface prisms, and matters of proportion. In my cameras, round lenses threw images onto square negatives.[3] Occasional questioning taught me only that art history professors knew very little math and optics, and even while photographing my women friends I thought about the ways people chose cameras. The Duaflex II and its many successors, even the Tower Twin-Lens rangefinder, produced a top-down, square-format viewfinder complexity I missed when I began carrying the eye-level, square-format Kodak S-10 so useful for candid shots. The enantiomorphic (opposite handedness) nature of my obsolescent cameras made me wonder if American visual perception changed as camera styles changed or if changes driven by cinema and television forced manufacturers to create new models easier to work.[4]

Squaring the circle vexed me. As nearly as I could learn as an undergraduate, Euclidean geometry offered no means of squaring a circle. Alchemists cherished the squared circle because only divinity accomplished it. Where boat-building jigs fit into such august conceptual frameworks I could not imagine, although shop visitors who watched perfect circles emerge from square or even irregularly shaped pieces of plywood marveled at what they called magic.

"Make a circle around man and woman, then a square, now a triangle; make a circle, and you will have the Philosopher's Stone," explained Michael Maier in 1617. Maier provided an illustration whose details mislead: how the t-square figures in his shop theory remains as obscure as the fractured protractor. "If this is not clear, then learn Geometry, and know it all," he counsels. His epigram mocks geometers: "Around the man and woman draw a ring, from which an equal-side square springs forth." Maier—and Robert Fludd—seem to have visualized squared circles materializing from nothing, but geometers still cannot accomplish what Maier claims originated in the essence of man and woman.[5] Maier suggests that the philosopher's stone originates in a making that is essentially visual: the stone itself is a visualization or a visualizing capacity, something that springs forth in a way that even then reminded me of the ah-ha moment when an adjustable-lens medium-format camera suddenly snaps an image into focus.[6] Some people may be born with the capacity to bring forth a visual image, as Von Reichenbach seems to have believed, while others may achieve it. The so-called stone may well emblemize a rare way of seeing that enables subsequent making, especially of visual-izations and apparitions.[7]

In graduate school I gave up trying to explain why a Kodak Duaflex II viewfinder image differed from that in an ordinary 35 mm camera view-finder.[8] Few friends knew anything of optics or had ever pondered their own images reflected in mirrors.[9] Flat mirrors produce a genuine virtual image, one seemingly as far behind the mirror as the reflected object stands in front of the glass.[10] An object three feet before a mirror ap-pears in the mirror three feet behind it, with the same size, shape, and orientation, but with handedness reversed. Holding an analog clock face perpendicular to an ordinary mirror produces a forward-backward trans-position of numerals so that the mirror seems to invert up and down, which makes thoughtful nonphotographers pause when they see a Rollei-flex Twin-Lens Reflex camera fitted with a right-angle accessory.[11] The right-angle accessory, offered only in the 1930s, enabled photographers to orient themselves and their cameras ninety degrees away from their subjects.[12] It evolved from the 1920s fascination with surreptitious or candid photography done with cameras smaller than the medium-format Rolleiflex, but in my mind it raised even more optical issues about hand-edness, inversion, and acute-angle reflection.[13] In the early 1970s I met no one who cared about such issues.

I gave up too explaining how a circular lens produced a square image on the viewfinder ground glass or beveled glass, let alone on the nega-tive. Giving up proved less than onerous: almost no one bothered to ask.[14] Usually a woman, perhaps smiling too long into the lens, began to won-der. I explained the "circle of confusion" based on the fact that the typi-cal human eye cannot distinguish between a true point and a disc smaller than 0.01 inches (0.25 mm) from a distance beyond ten inches.[15] A pho-tographic print intended to be viewed from a distance of ten inches by a typical human untrained eye must therefore be produced from a negative reaching a specific standard of sharpness. Photographers tended to agree that ideally people would view a photograph from the same distance as the focal lens on the camera that made it. People would stand four inches from a photograph made with a lens having a focal length of four inches and eight inches from one made with a lens twice as long. Enlarging a negative to produce a large print caused difficulties: people looked at enlargements so closely that they discerned lack of sharpness. Many pho-tographers, especially commercial ones, gloried in massive enlargements, and found themselves refining the circle of confusion. They realized in the 1920s that a circle of confusion having a diameter of 1/1000 of the lens focal length fails to satisfy, and lens makers began aiming for diameters of 1/1500 or 1/2000 the focal length of the lens.[16] The diminishing size of negatives, and especially the novelty and then proliferation of the 35 mm camera, produced intense concern about graininess of film that submerged the more nuanced issues implicit in circle-of-confusion arguments. Enlarging tiny negatives so frustrated photographers delighted with the new miniature cameras that most simply ignored the optical questions implicit in using circular lenses to produce images on rectangular negative film.[17] In my undergraduate years I found my boxy square-format, clunky cameras disarmed. Wealthy student photographers carried Leicas and other 35 mm cameras like chivalry standards, but my cameras seemed old-fashioned and decidedly unthreatening to sunbathing girlfriends.

At the beginning of the 35 mm era a few photographers analyzed optical issues linking specific lenses and camera formats with specific subjects, particularly figures in rural landscape. Vaughan Cornish, a British geographer-photographer concerned with many of the nuances of light that fascinated Alfred Watkins, especially the fall of light on uneven topography, and the ways light accentuated or cloaked landscape antiquities and perhaps revealed patterns discernible to those sensitive to light, performed many experiments tracing the ways medium-format handheld cameras shaped scenery values.[18] In many parts of England, old paths often curved just below the tops of low hills, producing a skyline not more than two hundred yards away. Serious photographers walking old paths consequently found that "the figures of the horse and his rider, or of the ploughman and his team, are outlined against the sky at an effective distance." The location of old ways, therefore, subtly produced a type of landscape image that struck most Britons as ordinary. Cornish understood the optical relation of the lens and the quarter-plate-size film in an unusual but not rare way: his camera made each exposure on a rectangle 4¼ × 3¼ inches, roughly in the same proportion that his lens captured degrees of horizontal and vertical arcs. Only when he aimed his camera at more distant views, especially the cross-valley hillside views in which Watkins discerned alignments, did he discover its limitations. "The ordinary camera lens ceases to be satisfactory, for it not only embraces more of the horizon than the eye compasses in such a landscape but a large angle of foreground unnoticed by the observer obtrudes in the photographic picture."[19] In his argument, the camera becomes an important if usually unnoticed portal linking the eye of the photographer and the scenic subject in ways that drawing textbooks and painting shop theory fail to adequately explain. Whatever the origins of lens types and negative sizes, most mass-produced cameras combined them in ways that made some rural landscapes far more effective in photographs than others.

Just as the observer unconsciously ignores much of the immediate foreground when looking across wide distances, so sketchers and painters of landscape ignore it as a matter of rule, aiming for a ground line roughly thirty feet away and about ten degrees below the horizon that bounds the view. "With an eye-height of 5 feet 3 inches the 30-foot ground line is 10 below the horizon," Cornish noted. "A hand camera with the moderate angle of 33 vertically (for the long picture) if held level brings the ground line 16½ below the horizon, which, for the same height, would be a distance of only 18 feet." Anything below the thirty-foot ground line lies "outside the ordinary landscape view" and poses a serious optical problem. Few cameras in any light can produce a negative in which a "spray of leaves on a hanging bough" or any other foreground feature is in focus as sharply as distant objects.[20] When they notice it at all in viewfinders, the foreground distracts many photographers unfamiliar with camera optics. Often it vanishes in the darkroom, when photographers crop it out during the printing process, and nowadays it disappears when photographers bring favorite factory-processed prints to a framing store.[21] Cornish's concern with degrees of arc in hilly landscapes where old ways ran just below ridges, and especially with the relationship of eye height and ground line, originated in sustained analysis of how twentieth-century Britons saw landscape in culturally determined ways, and in late 1920s camera format changes that reinforced or clashed with tradition.[22]

In *The Beauties of Scenery: A Geographical Survey* Cornish first analyzed his own ways of looking within landscapes he and his countrymen tended to find most beautiful. Woods rather than forests or jungles intrigued him especially, since they block long-distance views but are often components within much larger British landscapes seen from the ridges Watkins and other photographers walked. By experiment Cornish determined that someone standing or sitting in ordinary English woods enjoyed a range of vision extending about 150 feet in any direction. Beyond that limit, the trees formed a visual barrier in which clarity disappeared along with light. Cornish likened the once-recognized effect to sitting in the center of a deep quarry 300 feet in diameter, asking his readers to imagine the forest minus the trees within the 150 limit but with a ring of tall trees blocking longer views as the rising walls of the quarry would, and thus producing all manner of shadow normally masked by trees closer to the viewer.[23] The elm and beech woods through which

Will trudges in Cooper's *The Dark Is Rising* fit precisely into a framework Cornish articulated. "Looking upwards where the golden crown of beech or elm or birch stands out against the blue sky, it will at once be recognized that the blue is much deeper in the immediate neighbourhood of the foliage than in more distant parts of the background," Cornish explained before noting that "it may however be inferred from the circumstances that the violet sky of late twilight imparts a recognizable tint of pale gold to the moon." The type of woods fascinated him, especially the density, extent, and species of trees producing specific visual effects and seeming effects, gold, bronze, and silver appearing against other colors, especially the pinks and violets of high-latitude evening.[24] Over decades Cornish pieced together an aesthetic that readers of books by Belloc, M. R. James, Watkins, and other old-ways explorers, and by Tolkien and subsequent first-rate fantasy writers, instantly recognize. Its core involves the "outdoor habit" that acclimatizes the body in ways that sharpen the senses.[25] Cornish considered woodland beauty to be something predicated on physical limitations and variations of longer-distance views that for some people, walkers especially, proved stronger the more they consciously noticed them. Awareness often originated in simple sensitivity, but it might be acquired or heightened through self-disciplined practice.[26]

Wallace Nutting addressed changes in viewing habits in his 1927 *Photographic Art Secrets,* a shop manual emphasizing the worth of medium-format and large-format cameras. Nutting had made hundreds of thousands of photographs in the United States and Europe, emphasizing the rural scenery he made famous in his States Beautiful volumes. *Pennsylvania Beautiful, Massachusetts Beautiful,* and other volumes emphasized abandoned or disused countryside as worth repeated, receptive visits. In *Photographic Art Secrets,* a shop manual hovering on the very edge of the 35 mm era, he noted that "one of the best features of tripod work is that it enables us to cut out objectionable foreground." Nutting loathed lawns and light-colored paved roads, contended that the two-rut roads of horse-and-buggy days made far more intriguing images than the roads Thomas Murphy favored, argued that photographers should seek out trees and woods in which light reflected upward against the lowest limbs, and crafted an aesthetic of forest and old-fields paths, open spaces, lone trees, derelict houses, and brooks. While not nearly as sophisticated as Cornish, Nutting warned readers that woods and old-field foregrounds might defeat photographers, and noted acerbically that he carried an ax with him to excise objectionable saplings and other brush.[27] Byways and footpaths, he believed, typically led into lonesome, period-piece places in which the photographer might work slowly and carefully. He scorned snapshots and small cameras equally.

Some large-format photographers explored the capacities of early 35 mm cameras and enlargers. Ansel Adams told *Camera Craft* readers in 1936 that in order to make superb enlargements from such tiny negatives, darkroom shop theory mandated condenser-equipped enlargers unlike those Laughlin and other tinkerers built for themselves. Resulting prints would have slightly higher contrast. "The problem of negative grain seems to be a real bogy to most miniature camera workers," Adams noted before explaining that he preferred rich tonal values and "a *little* grain than *no* grain and an unsatisfactory tonal quality." He understood camera optics as well as Cornish, but in wholly different terms, explaining that if "film granularity is finer than the lens definition, the resultant effect is one of *apparent* increased definition: the large disc of confusion of the lens image is broken up into sharp points of tone." He expected that photographers using novel miniature cameras would despair when they found contact prints grainy, and would not be satisfied with enlargements fifteen to twenty times the size of the negative. Adams had no illusions concerning the ability of miniature cameras to duplicate the work of 8 × 10–inch and larger tripod-mounted view cameras, and he asserted in "My First Ten Weeks with a Contax" that his "main aesthetic objective has been to find the 'rightness' of subject in relation to the apparatus" rather than attempt to imitate work done with large-format cameras. He discovered that the Contax and its chief competitor, the Leica, might produce superb work far beyond "the 'hobby' quality dominating to an alarming degree" prints made by devotees of 35 mm cameras.[28] But such work would evolve from wholly different subject matter.

Underlying Adams's evaluation were disputes about taste and optical effectiveness, and beneath them, intractable issues of technology, wealth, and class.[29] In the Depression many photographers prized the first 35 mm cameras for their portability, usefulness in candid photography, interchangeable lenses, and large magazines: having thirty-six exposures on a roll of film encouraged many photographers to bracket exposures and experiment with different camera positions, and reduced the aggravation of frequent reloading, something Leitz Inc., the manufacturer of "the original cat's eye Leica," emphasized in advertising.[30] But photographers discovered that only the premiere Contax and Leica provided reliability (even first-generation Contax models were recalled for shutter-failure problems), interchangeable lenses, and above all, the high-quality lens permitting enlargements of high-speed emulsions producing relatively little grain.[31] Lenses nearly free of aberration produced circles of confusion between 1/500th and 1/750th of an inch that enabled owners of Contax and Leica cameras to enlarge negatives forty to sixty diameters, using new darkroom chemistry and high-quality, condenser enlargers.[32] "Such lenses cannot be manufactured and sold on the same basis as the ordinary lens," opined one *Camera Craft* author of a series entitled "Practical Miniature Camera Photography." "Precision cannot be built into a camera except at additional cost."[33] The finest 35 mm cameras debuted as expensive apparatus requiring expensive enlargers, usually novel developing chemicals, and much difficult decision making.

American camera manufacturers proved unable to design and build high-quality 35 mm cameras: Eastman Kodak subcontracted such work to German firms. Historians of photography typically ignore the convoluted and emotionally charged history of 35 mm cameras, and most camera historians emphasize only technicalities.[34] Not until well after World War II, when Japanese manufacturers offered high-quality 35 mm cameras at prices below those imported from Germany, did 35 mm cameras become popular in the United States. Japanese imports, especially the Nikon line, put late 1940s domestic manufacturers out of business. Nowadays almost no one remembers the Argus (so heavy photographers nicknamed it "the brick") and other cumbersome United States–made 35 mm cameras.[35] Until the 1950s the price of 35 mm cameras deflected many would-be photographers, just as their format deflected many others; as late as 1949, when Bell & Howell produced its Foton, its $700 price tag put off many shoppers.[36] Inexpensive imported cameras eventually caused the camera format invented to test exposures of 35 mm cinema film to overwhelm all others, by 1975 making medium-format photography almost as rare as the large-format photography Laughlin, Mortensen, Adams, and others practiced.[37] But even as well-to-do Depression-era photographers shifted to Leicas and other 35 mm cameras, Lange, Cunningham, and many other impoverished professionals moved to equally expensive medium-format cameras, especially to the Rolleiflex.

Viewpoint difference attracted many photographers to the Rolleiflex. The medium-format camera opened at the top, with four metal sides springing automatically into a square-shaped shade surrounding the square ground-glass viewing screen. Its inventors intended photographers to hold the camera at waist level, supported by a strap for stability, not against the face, although the shade came with eyeholes and frames for eye-level use, especially at sporting events.[38] The Rolleiflex caused users to bow toward subjects: most photographers not only bowed their heads over the shaded ground glass at the top of the camera but also slightly hunched their shoulders and pulled in their stomachs, bending their bodies at the waist. While the posture often relaxed subjects, who saw it as respectful and studious, it also eliminated the broad foreground Cornish condemned: it replicated the traditional point of view of post-1880 hand-held cameras used at waist level. Waist-level position and top-of-camera viewfinder link the Rolleiflex with the Kodak Brownie and contemporaneous sophisticated Eastman Kodak Company cameras, and even with the pre-1880 large-format, tripod-mounted view cameras Adams and other Group f/64 photographers cherished in the 1930s and 1940s. View-camera photographers typically set cameras roughly at chest level, to make easier the ground-glass focusing done beneath a black cloth. Francke and Heidecke provided a ground-glass accessory back for the Rolleiflex, which enabled photographers to use the camera at the same height they positioned large-format ones. The Rolleiflex debuted roughly simultaneously with the 35 mm cameras, but its design encouraged photographers to hold it at waist level and so produce images from a fundamentally different angle of vision.[39]

The top ground-glass viewfinder serves also as a focusing screen and produces the lateral-reverse effect common to all twin-lens reflex cameras.[40] From the mirror set at a forty-five-degree angle behind the viewing lens, the viewfinder image appears right side up but reversed. Objects to the right of the camera appear on the left of the ground glass, although correctly on the film exposed through the taking lens below. "Rollei photographers say with fair unanimity that they soon become used to this feature, and have learned to cope with it instinctively, even in the case of reverse lettering," wrote Jacob Deschin in *Rollei Photography,* but the firm provided the viewer-finder focusing eyehole and frame because the mirror imaging frustrated photographers at sporting events until they learned to move the camera opposite to the direction of action.[41] Its manufacturer assumed that most Rolleiflex users would either compose and focus scenes deliberately or use the camera so frequently that shifting it opposite to moving subjects became second nature.

In low-light conditions the ground-glass screen, typically 95 percent efficient at transferring light from the mirror behind the viewing lens, vignetted, its center remaining bright but its edges darkening dramatically. As the screen darkened, the lack of uniform lighting irritated users. In the late 1940s Eastman Kodak produced a wafer-thin Fresnel lens that Rolleiflex users installed beneath the ground-glass screen. The Ektalite Field Lens not only made the lens brighter in bright sunlight but reduced vignetting significantly in subdued-light conditions.[42] In time Francke and Heidecke introduced its own Fresnel-lens brightening accessory, the Rolleigrid Field Lens, which dropped onto the top of the ground-glass screen and so did not interfere with ultra-accurate focusing. Vignetting characterizes all twin-lens reflex cameras, and most manufacturers accept it as secondary in importance to close focusing: curving the glass eliminates vignetting at the cost of edge-screen focusing distortion. The inexpensive Eastman Kodak Duaflex box cameras have a startlingly bright viewfinder lens made of heavy curved glass, since the cameras focus by range-finding scales, and neophyte Rolleiflex users wonder why screens are not as bright as their childhood box camera lens. Flat Fresnel lens accessories annoyed Rolleiflex users peering downward through the magnifier eyepiece attached to the viewfinder hood for extreme focusing accuracy (the eyepiece revealed the concentric rings of the Fresnel form), but not until the twentieth-first century did aftermarket screens appear that solved the vignetting problem without altering focusing accuracy.[43]

The Rolleigrid Field Lens accomplished something more than brightening screens. Its grid of very thin black lines making up twenty-five squares enabled photographers to level and plumb the camera when photographing any subject having horizontal and vertical straight lines. While the feature pleased photographers of architecture, it delighted photographers whose subjects stood before buildings, or those who made images of decrepit buildings in more or less natural landscape. No longer did buildings appear to lean slightly, or straight-back chairs seem slightly askew.[44] More importantly, serious photographers discovered the Rolleigrid Field Lens as a useful but not necessary accessory advancing the seeing in squares within the larger square of the viewfinder glass.

In his 1933 *The Rolleiflex Book,* and for decades afterward in subsequent expanded editions, Walther Heering addressed the difference between rectangular and square negative formats, arguing that the Rolleiflex square shape originated in technical necessity—the square being the better shape to exploit the "precisely defined circle" produced by the circular lens. "Expressed the other way round," he continued, "good taste likes the genuine thing which has developed organically out of the technical necessity."[45] Heering took his analysis directly into the path of cinema. In 1934 he stated that "the format of a picture should have incisiveness, power, and character," something he altered in 1954 to "the size of a picture should have style, verve and character in its representation." In 1934 he argued that rectangles, particularly those in the ratio of 2:3 or 3:4, are "too ordinary, too easily mediocre"; twenty years later he dismissed them as "too cozy, too much golden mediocrity." Against such oblong images "the weighty mass of the square is modern, all concentrated realism, calm and serene," a phrase that became by 1954 "the powerful block of the square is highly fashionable, full of concentrated reality, quiet and clear."[46] Over three decades, Heering explicated something many other Rolleiflex experts championed: anyone using a Rolleiflex freed himself from the tyranny of cinema-made rectangles.[47]

In 1953 Jacob Deschin pointed out that for Henri Cartier-Bresson and a few other brilliant photographers, the 35 mm rectangular format worked a similar magic, freeing them from older rectangular-ratio formats. But by the 1950s miniature camera users had begun jamming every subject into a fixed rectangular format, rotating the camera ninety degrees from landscape to human subject and back. "Once released from the behest implied in the 2¼ × 3¼ frame, the Rollei photographer's thinking began to move gradually in the direction of choosing a format to fit the subject instead," Deschin wrote, although he acknowledged that experienced Rollei photographers generally printed only about one negative in a hundred as a square.[48] The square format dictated their way of seeing. In the darkroom square-format photographers enjoyed the luxury of negatives large enough to crop before enlarging with home-made enlargers—large enough to contact print and give away as finished photographs. But so many photographers scorned the square format that Deschin suggested a shop-theory experiment.

He told skeptics to cut a piece of metal or cardboard into a rectangle ½ inch wide and about 2¼ inches long, and drop it onto the Rolleiflex ground-glass viewing screen. Covering the glass on the right produced a vertical image; covering the top edge of the glass produced a horizontal one. Deschin suggested attaching a tiny handle to the rectangle so it might be removed without upending and shaking the camera, and explained that after some experimentation the skeptics would understand the power of the square.[49] It remains a valuable shop-theory technique to elucidate the culturally coercive power of rectangular imagery and the shocking power of the square-format ground-glass image.

By the late 1930s the Rolleiflex square negative had proven itself in another arena altogether. Not only did medium-format color transparencies make 35 mm slides seem puny when projected in comparison tests, the square images thrown by powerful projectors, including those manufactured by Francke and Heidecke, radically reconfigured audience understanding of cinema views.[50] Cropping square negatives in the darkroom became the norm almost immediately after the firm introduced the Rolleiflex. Only in the 1930s did explorers, professional lecturers, and university professors begin to savor the wallop of gigantic square slides projected in ways so bold that rectangular cinema imagery seemed mediocre.

In 1937 Deschin published *Making Pictures with the Miniature Cam-*

era, one of many books that appeared as the miniaturization fad became a permanent photographic phenomenon.[51] *Minicam: The Miniature Camera Monthly* debuted in the fall of that year, its first issue filled with full-page ads for Leica, Zeiss Ikon, Contax, and other 35 mm cameras, sophisticated exposure meters, and Omega and other enlargers suited to tiny negatives, and with a painstakingly chosen set of articles. Several feature articles emphasized candid and sports-action photography, which manufacturers thought most fitted to small cameras. Others detailed how to build an entire darkroom inside a large cabinet and how to process tiny negatives for excellent contrast and slight graininess. "High Quality Negative Development" chiefly compares the plethora of new developer chemicals manufactured especially for 35 mm photographers, but it dovetails with other articles comparing miniature cameras according to features and costs. *Minicam* rode the crest of the manufacturing wave, but its editors balanced the miniature camera fad against innovations that might pass by 35 mm photography. Their conviction was that miniature cameras might make paper negatives and superb color photographs as well as larger cameras, but the editors realized that manufacturers had to broaden their lines of film and chemicals. In the end, however, the full-page, full-color reproductions, especially a stunning image of a nude woman atop a sand dune made by Remie Lohse, a Danish Puerto Rican immigrant photographer who had burst from a New York factory job into the national limelight barely four years earlier, proved the point on which *Minicam* based its long-term efforts. Determination, practice, and flair enabled anyone to make superb photographs with a miniature camera. Deschin and others argued that medium-format cameras produced far higher quality negatives capable of great enlargement—along with other bonuses such as medium-format slides—and responded to the visceral needs so many photographers felt in a world shaped by cinema film.

In *Making Pictures with the Miniature Camera,* Deschin asserted that 35 mm photographers must pay particular attention to the "so-called aerial perspective, that stereoscopic quality in a photograph that makes us feel the separation of foreground, middle distance, and distant planes that constitute the original view as seen by the human eye." He understood the composition concepts—especially the flood tide of foreground in so many landscape images—that concerned Cornish, and clarified them by depicting two 35 mm vertical images joined to make a near square, but implicit in his larger argument was a worry that too many purchasers of 35 mm cameras simply did not understand that in choosing a rectangular-format camera they necessarily involved themselves in awkward optical limitations that might shape choice of subject matter.[52] Richard L.

Simon published *Miniature Photography from One Amateur to Another* in 1937, too, and wholly avoided the composition issues that concerned Deschin. Simon argued that half of the buyers of 35 mm cameras "expect to do night and indoor 'candid' photography" and usually found themselves disappointed. While he blamed poor-quality developing chemicals for the graininess that destroyed neophyte hopes, he offered advice only on making close-up shots outdoors in bright and hazy sunlight. He insisted that lack of attention to lighting created exposure-setting problems that camera-store developing and printing merely exacerbated. "No camera made (even the ones that sell for a dollar) can be as bad as much (I might almost say most) of the developing and enlarging that is being done by commercial processors." *Miniature Photography* recommends that photographers build a well-equipped home darkroom and develop and print negatives in ways that correct errors peculiar to miniature cameras. This was nothing new: the first issue of *Minicam,* in an article entitled "Build It Yourself," devoted itself to the proposition that every 35 mm camera owner, even apartment dwellers, should build a darkroom to control the developing and printing process.[53] While Deschin championed the Rolleiflex as a camera that simplified the making of superb images, Simon and many miniature camera magazines hammered away at darkroom improvement of poor-quality 35 mm negatives. Together Deschin and Simon framed issues now obscured by the multiplicity of miniature-photography magazines hatched in the Depression as photography split repeatedly into special-interest groups that tended to ignore the successes and advice of Adams, Mortensen, Cornish, and Lohse.

In a chapter entitled "Is It a Vogue, a Trend, or What?" Simon acknowledged that Eastman Kodak had produced "vest-pocket" collapsible cameras by 1912, and that the Depression-era miniature camera fad began in 1929 as German and Austrian tourists brought Leicas with them to record their American visits. Just as Depression-era poverty produced a massive fascination with building radios—and sometimes grounding them to bedsprings—so it strengthened the 35 mm fad. In 1937 bulk loading 35 mm film let photographers buy it for a penny a frame, and even in Kodak reversal canisters a frame cost only slightly less than two cents in a thirty-six-exposure roll. Commercial developing and printing cost about three dollars per roll.[54] While the 35 mm fad may have blossomed in very late 1920s prosperity and experimentation, its roots reached deeper. Simon barely acknowledged the Eastman Kodak experiments or the continuing availability of 127-size film. In the Depression, carrying an expensive Leica, Contax, or other German-built miniature camera indicated a degree of prosperity in a time when many photographers could not afford automobiles or houses. But as a handful of thoughtful experts insisted, it indicated something dating back to 1912 at least—something that had not worked out especially well.

In 1935 the editors of the *New Photo-Miniature* dismissed the claim that the Germans had invented the miniature camera in 1925 as "too absurd to deserve more than mention and dismissal as a bit of Teutonic nonsense." In a lengthy, detailed, footnoted article entitled "Miniature Camera Work," the editors traced the history of small-format photography, noting that as early as 1861 a French maker of optical instruments demonstrated a small fixed-focus camera that made negatives 2¼ inches square that he claimed to enlarge to three feet square with perfect sharpness. Not until about 1910 did many well-off amateur photographers begin to complain about the bulk and weight of the so-called hand cameras like those Ralphson's Boy Scouts used. By 1912 European manufacturers and Eastman Kodak had produced small cameras especially suitable for travel photography—at that time understood as the making of casual snapshots of landscapes, buildings, and people during business and vacation trips. Professionals and advanced amateurs continued to use larger-format cameras, and most other adults and almost all children continued to use Brownie and other box cameras or the larger-size folding cameras. Nonetheless, many travel-camera photographers were using small but still "chunky in the pocket" travel cameras and their descendants in 1935. The editors of the *New Photo Miniature* blamed Leica advertising both for the 35 mm craze and for slicing smaller-format photography from its historical and technological roots: the Leica and its four hundred accessories had not "created an entirely new photographic method."[55] But the Leica and Contax, Pupille, Beira, and Argus advertising had sparked an unthinking acceptance of rectangular-format 35 mm roll-film technology as ultramodern even as it shaped photographer expectations that often ended in frustration, camera trade-in, the conversion of older small cameras to 35 mm film, and the purchase of expensive accessories and aftermarket gadgets.[56] In the end, Simon admitted, two years after the *New Photo-Miniature* struggled to explain and analyze a miniature camera technology and practice in the face of a splintering photography magazine situation, "way back in the eighties and nineties Alfred Stieglitz with an old-fashioned box camera made photographs as good as any of today" not only because he had extraordinary talent but "because his big box camera made big negatives."[57]

In 1938 Willard D. Morgan and Henry M. Lester published a folio, *Miniature Camera Work: Emphasizing the Entire Field of Photography with Modern Miniature Cameras,* in which they and many contributing photographers and manufacturers' representatives extolled the virtues of post-1925 miniature photography. Funded largely by Eastman Kodak and other companies, the lavishly illustrated book ranges far beyond Leica-based issues and deals especially closely with Kodachrome and other new Eastman Kodak color products. About a quarter of the way into the book, Ansel Adams urged readers to familiarize themselves with the geometry of enlarging small negatives. He informed them that the "ideal size of print from a 1 × 1½–inch negative lies between 5 × 7 and 6 × 9 inches," and that a 6 × 9–inch print from a 35 mm negative is "proportionately equal to an enlargement *five feet long* from an 8 × 10 negative." He emphasized that hanging prints made from enlarged negatives of different formats often made miniature photographs appear insignificant.[58] Five years earlier, in reporting the rocket-like rise of Remie Lohse—"last January he was nobody. Last week his photographs were featured in six magazines (*The Stage, Vogue, Vanity Fair, American Magazine, Cottier's, Town & Country*) and he held a one-man show"—*Time* revealed that he worked with "a tiny Contax camera looking like a child's harmonica" and made images of strippers and chorus girls, singers, newsboys, and other people, none posed. Lohse had enlarged each negative only six times, and when seen at his one-man show, the small prints succeeded superbly.[59]

Wealthy professionals and amateurs bought Leicas and Contaxes, often on time-payment plans. *Time* reported that Lohse's "little Contax special cost him $225" and that he often used an $80 telephoto lens, along with a right-angle device that tricked people standing beside him.[60] In the same year, the editors of the *New Photo-Miniature* urged readers to buy the American-made Argus, a multifaceted 35 mm camera "at the incredible price of $12.50."[61] But the Argus lens compared poorly with the Leica one. The American camera had a f/4.5 aperture, while Lohse enjoyed an f/1.3 one, and as color photography became increasingly important, especially to academics and other lecturers using color transparencies, the Argus and other slow-lens cameras seemed more and more inefficient in low-light situations.[62] Even the Eastman Kodak Retina, introduced in 1935 as an American-built "continental kind" of 35 mm camera retailing for $57.50, failed to approximate the Leica and only exacerbated the confusion among pro–miniature camera photographers.[63] "Individual taste, requirements, and the amount of money available are perhaps more deciding factors in choosing a camera than they are in the selection of a motor car," opined one *American Photography* author in 1935.[64] Money bought a dramatically better 35 mm photographic experience from 1925 until about 1960, when Japanese-made cameras began to narrow the price differential, in the process putting almost all United States manufacturers out of business.

Color photography added to the frustrations of many 35 mm photographers equipped with the finest cameras and already irritated that new film, filters, and electric light had complicated monochrome photography after 1930. "A portrait of a blonde-haired person with blue eyes and red lips, taken without a filter in tungsten light looks queer. The eyes are rendered quite dark, the lips much too light, and the facial color rather pale and without life," remarked one Depression-era columnist reporting on unforeseen shortcomings of panchromatic black-and-white film. New blue filters corrected the tonal values of blond, blue-eyed people photographed under ordinary light, but required exposure increases of up to 50 percent.[65] In *Miniature Camera Work*, Harris B. Tuttle, an Eastman Kodak expert loaned to the book-project team, emphasized two problems confronting miniature photography. He thought it would be years before many people developed an understanding of color prints and transparencies. "As a rule the untrained eye is very critical of color pictures, the trained eye very tolerant," he wrote in a phrase he considered so important he italicized it. More immediately, he argued that most 35 mm photographers began with color film, which he thought far more prone to unfortunate accident than black-and-white film.[66]

Side- and backlighting increased monochrome contrast; in color photography contrast originates in differences among colors. Not surprisingly, most of the full-color images illustrating his chapter capture beach, snow, and other full-sunlight scenes that fall well within the limits of the Argus and other low-priced cameras. Eastman Kodak color film is balanced for noontime sunlight, and most of the images appear to have been shot at midday as well: all seem carefully chosen to make the most of color juxtaposition. Unfortunately, as so many experienced photographers by then knew well, noonday sun often creates the worst of glare and shadow problems, causing the cognoscenti to take long lunches and perhaps snoozes.[67] Photographers attempting to shoot color transparency film with 35 mm cameras quickly discovered that the new type of film had very narrow latitudes of exposure and did not render all colors equally well.[68]

By the middle 1930s camera manufacturers, wholesalers, and retailers struggled to portray larger-format cameras as modern, noting that film manufacturers supplied color and other new film in formats other than 35 mm. In a 1935 issue of *American Photography*, Willoughby's, a New York photographic store, advertised the collapsible Ebner, which made sixteen 4½ × 6 cm exposures on an eight-exposure roll of 620 film, as "armour-plated," "as modern and dynamic in style and construction as the new Union Pacific train," and designed without "a protruding gadget on its entire surface" to slip into "side pocket or purse."[69] Four years later, it announced in *Popular Photography* the new Voigtländer Focusing Brilliant, a medium-format, square-format twin-lens reflex camera, as "an entirely new type of camera" having a "special optical focusing system [that] 'tunes' in the image like a radio tunes in sound."[70] Such advertising did little to counter a fad that Mortensen lamented had evolved "into a sort of scientific black magic" in which 35 mm photographers, assuming "the manner of initiates performing mysterious rites at the dark of the moon," made a ceremony of every exposure. In 1934 Mortensen laughed at the 35 mm photographers, concluding that for all their expensive cameras and arcane language about film types they usually found themselves satisfied with drugstore quality prints.[71]

In one 1934 *Camera Craft* article, "Notes on the Miniature Camera," he insisted that "the use of new things is prone to run ahead of the proper understanding of them," and concluded that "in equipment of the extremest simplicity" lay all hope for 35 mm camera success. Along with many other larger-format photographers, Mortensen lit into the miniaturists with sarcasm, claiming that their love of gadgets resembled "the well-known feminine habit of buying a new hat to rouse the drooping spirit," and that buying complicated equipment to make excellent photographs is "like differential calculus in order to learn to add two plus two." He understood miniature photography, especially 35 mm photography, as likely to sour many educated, well-off adults and teenagers on photography forever. Fads within the miniature fad, especially the one involving monochrome color correction with filters despite the availability of new films far more sensitive to color variation than older ones, only further annoyed photographers increasingly frustrated with overcomplicated, gadget-encrusted, expensive 35 mm cameras.[72] In the end, Mortensen and many other experienced photographers who tried 35 mm cameras extensively, argued—usually in long-established photography magazines aimed at professionals and advanced amateurs, not in the ones founded in mid-Depression and aimed chiefly at 35 mm enthusiasts—that less expensive, medium-format cameras (and sub-medium-format ones like that Willoughby's advertised) might serve most photographers better than any but good box cameras.

Even the new *Popular Photography* embraced a bit of the larger-camera attitude by early 1939. In "A Beginning and a Box Camera" John B. Dilworth told an anonymous young woman at length why her photographer boyfriend's gift of a five-dollar box camera might mean more than a present of a 35 mm jewel. The camera would make excellent snapshots under the right conditions, and its yellow filter would prove handy on sunny days when subjects stood in front of green foliage. While it cost only five dollars, the box camera and its film amounted to something far better than anything most professional photographers used only a few decades earlier. Practice would quickly produce excellent snapshots if discipline and attention guided her efforts. While acknowledging the arguments of Mortensen—who had published an extensive article, "Glorifying the American Snapshot," four years earlier arguing that box cameras made exquisite images when photographers accounted for available light (especially around noonday), reduced foreground material, and emphasized lone main subjects in compositions—the editors of *Popular Photography* perhaps understood a need to broaden readership and advertising in the demoralizing 1938 downturn.[73] In May the magazine published a feature article detailing the experiments of four well-known professional photographers handed identical three-dollar Eastman Kodak Brownie or Agfa B.2 Shur Shot box cameras and Kodak Super-XX panchromatic film. One of the photographers started his experiment late and made several box camera images during a lull in a fashion shoot: one appeared in *Harper's Bazaar,* something *Popular Photography* noted as proof that in the right hands a three-dollar box camera might do wonders.[74] Part of the awakening interest in box cameras derived from the frustrations of 35 mm photographers finding "amateurish" friends and even children making excellent images with chunky cameras, but much of it originated in the quiet success of the boxy Rolleiflex camera.[75]

Priced at about $130 in 1939, the Rolleiflex fit nowhere in ordinary magazine articles addressing cost-value ratios, in large part because it struck many editors and readers as an ultrasophisticated box camera and many columnists as a camera marketed chiefly to well-to-do, well-educated, tradition-minded professionals. Wealthy advanced amateurs definitely preferred it (railroad photography hobbyists, which for some reason included many well-to-do physicians, delighted in the Rolleiflex throughout the Depression and well into the 1960s), usually citing its square format and large negative size, but sometimes championing its medium-format transparencies.[76] The Rolleiflex raised nuanced issues of format (square and medium both), technology (especially the importance of ground-glass viewfinders and vibration-free shutter-release movement), and shop-theory taste (its large negatives proved easily contact printed and enlarged with simple equipment, something that mattered to railroad hobbyists and others anxious for the renown and payments provided by magazines reproducing their images). But in the end its size mattered. No one slipped a Rolleiflex in a side pocket or purse. Carrying a Rolleiflex announced incipient photograph making of a peculiarly intentional kind.

In 1935 Antoinette Perrett explained the growing oddness of Rolleiflex photography. She did mostly interior and still-life photography, the former often in cramped conditions, and chose the Rolleiflex first because its slightly wide-angle lens nudged her from the interior distortions produced by wider ones. "I love to look down onto the ground-glass screen with its brilliant upright picture, because it gives me an opportunity of quietly and carefully studying my compositions," she admitted. The large, bright viewing screen had prompted her to begin portrait photography, because the lens that photographed closets worked splendidly in close-ups of faces. Perrett deemed the Rolleiflex "modest and self-effacing" and commented that it makes sitters relax. "It looks so very amateurish that they never suspect how penetratingly professional it can be," she confided.[77] To most people the Rolleiflex looked like an obsolescent box camera. It made its user appear innocent or playful or studious, not threatening.

While in experienced hands the Rolleiflex easily managed sport and other action photography (its manufacturers struggled against the late Depression popularity of 35 mm cameras by advertising the usefulness of the Rolleiflex in photographing birds on the wing), the camera quickly became the favorite of photographers anxious to photograph still subjects as well.[78] The Rolleiflex collapsible hood shielded the ground-glass screen, making its bright image even brighter, but parts of the hood instantly converted to a simple viewfinder device that enabled users to hold the camera against their face. Many undoubtedly made use of the feature, but most appeared willing to compose and focus while bending over the screen. Holding the Rolleiflex just above waist level—Francke and Heidecke insisted that users loop the long leather strap about their necks to suspend the camera in a way that nearly eliminated handheld motion—produced a different angle of vision immediately apparent on the viewing screen. Some photographers found it the view of a child—if not innocent, at least not an ordinary full-height adult perspective that produced ordinary angle-of-vision images.

Many women thought of the bulky Rolleiflex as a sort of purse, swinging on its shoulder strap, exactly as Mildred S. Sullivan, a freelance professional, outlined in a 1932 *Photo-Era* article. With the camera slung around her neck at waist level, Sullivan found her hands free to write in her notebook as she walked from one subject to another; the flip-up magnifier inside the viewing-screen shroud made possible superb focusing under low-light conditions as the strap helped steady the camera for long exposures. "The entire outfit weighs slightly less than two pounds," she wrote, "and I can swing along with it as comfortably as a lady who carries but a lightweight handbag."[79] Men accepted its bulk as too chunky for pockets, and learned to manage it exactly as women did, as an accessory handing from a long strap.[80] The bulk and weight of the Rolleiflex signaled serious photographic intention that shaped other effort from casual walking to hiking to striding down a city street. A photographer might carry a Leica in her pocketbook or his jacket pocket, and pull it out when needed, but the Rolleiflex swaying on its strap announced the primacy or near primacy of photography among the activities of the person carrying it. To thousands of Americans suddenly irritated by candid-camera fanatics, the obvious Rolleiflex announced not only an old-fashioned or innocent or light-hearted photographer but one who intended to make a photograph, not snatch a picture.[81]

Just as the Eastman Kodak box camera had angered beachgoers, especially bathing-suited women, in the first years of the twentieth century, so the 35 mm camera and its users' passion for rapid-fire candid imagery angered Americans, again especially on beaches, in the last summers before World War II. The 35 mm camera smacked of Hollywood glitz and voyeurism.

"The movies have exerted a harmful effect on photography, with their jazz replacing aesthetic beauty, their harshness replacing gradation, their excitement replacing calm contemplation," complained Paul L. Anderson in *American Photography* in 1935. A professional photographer committed to technical excellence, he asserted that only one Hollywood cinematographer, Karl Struss, who filmed *Ben Hur* in 1925 and won an Academy Award in 1927 for his filming of F. W. Murnau's *Sunrise,* consistently produced a first-rate image, and he particularly praised Struss's night scenes in *Sunrise.* He claimed that Struss struggled against the same glitziness that forced Mortensen away from Hollywood, and that mirrored the growing use of harsh, contrasty photography in advertising. But Anderson reserved his real fury for the Eastman Kodak Company and German 35 mm camera manufacturers.

The American firm produced such a surfeit of films and papers that even professional photographers found themselves unsure which to use in a given assignment, let alone for their own independent artistic purposes.[82] "Artistically, the effect of the panchromatic emulsion is to minimize study: when one is using a color-blind emulsion it becomes necessary for him to see light and to study it, that he may adjust the lighting of his subject so that the scientifically untrue values will say what he wishes them to say," Anderson concluded following a lengthy diatribe against infrared film used with K- and X-class filters and other emulsions rendering only violet and ultraviolet light.[83] German manufacturers produced the 35mm camera that gobbled the new films.

Advertisements disparaging camera bulk and weight especially angered Anderson and other late 1930s commentators, who believed simple physical laziness drove photographer love of small, lightweight 35mm cameras.[84] Earlier generations of photographers had slogged for miles carrying heavy equipment; surely the Rolleiflex did not weigh so much that it exhausted modern walkers. In sophisticated magazines and a few books, experts pointed out that few late 1930s photographers lugged cameras far. Most walked relatively short distances in cities or drove in automobiles almost to the sites where they made photographs. Many made images while standing next to stopped cars.[85] The new desire to own 35mm cameras originated in advertising trumpeting convenience and seeming modernism over quality image making. That advertising prompted many minicam faddists to abandon tripods: such photographers often produced badly focused, underexposed negatives, in large part because they believed advertising extolling superb pictures made by handheld cameras with shutters set to a tenth of a second, often in low-light conditions.[86] Anderson and others condemned such image making, scorning the advertising-based, walk-light fad indirectly creating it and noting that more and more 35mm photographers seemed satisfied to make snapshot-like photographs, perhaps to avoid issues of graininess during enlargement and printing.[87] The proliferation of 35mm images, most made by handheld cameras and often when a subject suddenly presented itself to a camera-carrying photographer involved in other activity, shaped mass-circulation magazine editorial expectation by 1940. Illustration editors frequently preferred snapshot-like photographs, especially ones they designated "action," to the better composed and illuminated ones made by professional and amateur photographers using Rolleiflex and other medium-format cameras.[88]

One *American Photography* author glimpsed distinctions beyond the willingness of 35mm photographers to accept lower payment for their images. Don Wallace told readers to study magazines in the "class publications group," especially *Vogue, Vanity Fair,* and *Harper's Bazaar.* In such magazines appeared images different in composition and light from the cinema-like images made by most 35mm photographers and shaping the miniature camera, rectangular-format aesthetic dominating magazines aimed at the same population that devoured Hollywood films.[89]

With devastating accuracy, Wallace pinpointed the deepening class divide separating medium-format photographers from 35 mm photographers. As World War II loomed, mass-market photography magazines, especially *Popular Photography,* veered closer toward embracing not only amateur cinematography but the still photography, including trick photography, used in Hollywood and especially in film fan magazines.[90]

Controversy arose over issues of format, film type, photograph aesthetics, and camera handling itself well into the 1960s.[91] World War II not only stopped much camera manufacture but also halted imports of Rolleiflexes and other German-built cameras. In 1945 the Soviet Union confiscated the world-renowned equipment in the bomb-damaged Carl Zeiss lens factory in Jena, but before its troops occupied the town, American soldiers, at the behest of Zeiss executives, transported its top scientists and technicians two hundred miles west to Heidenheim, thus assuring the western-zone camera manufacturers of superlative lenses.[92] By the early 1950s German firms had introduced improved models of the Rolleiflex and 35 mm cameras, destroyed the nascent American fine-camera industry, and found themselves competing on United States soil against Japanese-made imitations of 2¼ and 35 mm cameras.[93] In a 1958 issue dedicated to 35 mm photography, *Modern Photography* published a special report, "Made in West Germany," emphasizing the research-and-development effort indirectly showcased annually at the Photokina trade show in Cologne. But no longer did Leica products seem expensive: that year its M-2 retailed for $276 while the Nikon SP sold for $369. Japanese competition had driven down the prices of most 35 mm cameras (a versatile Fujica sold for $70) but not the price of the Rolleiflex, which retailed for $260, more than twice the price of a Japanese-made Minolta square-format camera.[94] Not until the early 1960s did a handful of thoughtful experts take stock of a marketing situation shaped by late 1930s advertising and technological development.

In 1962 *Popular Photography* published "After 35 mm. What?," a lengthy lead article by David B. Eisendrath that committed the "sacrilege" of predicting developments beyond 35 mm cameras. Eisendrath prophesied that electronic cameras would appear in the near future, developed from television electronic imagery technology supported by lavish research-and-development funding devoted to making commercial television cameras more portable. He averred that 35 mm camera design had been restricted for decades by the desire to keep cameras small: major innovation might require enlarged bodies, and even minor improvement might force manufacturers to increase the number of projecting buttons and dials controlling innovative features.[95] In the end, however, the editors of *Popular Photography* commented indirectly too. Facing the first page of his article stood a full-page advertisement for the Rolleicord, the cheaper version of the Rolleiflex introduced to make the medium-format camera more affordable to lower-income photographers determined to move from 35 mm photography. So long as cameras used film, and perhaps into some postfilm electronic era, a larger camera would almost certainly make better images than a small one. Size necessarily involved photographers in issues of bulk and weight, as well as in issues of image quality. It thrust manufacturers into intractable issues of economic class too.

Since Eastman Kodak and its competitors sold the same film types in different formats, medium-format photographers tended to fare better than 35 mm ones, something the editors of *Photo-Era* realized as early as June 1931. "Owners of roll-film cameras should have a remarkably successful summer photographically," they opined in a column. "Our reason for this optimistic outlook is the arrival on the photographic market of the new Kodak Verichrome Film and the Agfa Plenachrome Film, both of which embody radical improvements in roll-film manufacture."[96] Three years after the first explosion of interest in 35 mm photography and the importing of the Rolleiflex, *Photo-Era* predicted the symbiosis that revolutionized not only miniature photography but medium-format photography as well. Developers and other chemicals intended to reduce grain in 35 mm negatives reduced grain in medium-format negatives too. Larger-format negatives continued to produce finer-grain negatives (with better contrast) and prints than 35 mm ones, no matter how industriously 35 mm photographers worked in their darkrooms with new products from film and film-chemistry manufacturers. Technological innovation scarcely narrowed the gap between 35 mm photographers, even those equipped with the latest and most expensive imported cameras, and the users of Rolleiflexes and the handful of similar medium-format cameras.

In 1960s issues of *Popular Photography* and other low-end, mass-circulation photography magazines, I learned from rare, subtle remarks that under certain conditions the Kodak Duaflex II medium-format camera I carried might make a better negative than a sophisticated 35 mm camera, especially if I estimated distance correctly and noticed ambient lighting accurately. Its top-mounted, bright, beveled-glass viewer enabled me to compose carefully, and its serviceable lens worked reasonably well in the hands of a thirteen-year-old boy alone, uninterrupted, and taking his time in the quiet old-fields sunlight to photograph things essentially motionless. The Duaflex II made a large negative on the same excellent

Eastman Kodak film used by professional photographers holding Rol-leiflexes.[97] Not only did its square negatives enlarge well, but parts of them—carefully circled in red pencil on glassine sleeves at the rural drug-store before dispatch to some far-off processing facility—enlarged well too. The camera banged and bounced a bit as it hung from the plastic strap tossed over my shoulder, but its product made me happy to receive as a gift a used and battered Tower 2¼ camera with a faster lens that led to more experiments along the overgrown paths.[98]

In 1926 Walter Prichard Eaton published *In Berkshire Fields,* one of a series of books tracing his quiet adventures in the hill country of western Massachusetts. In "Forgotten Roads" he explicated the mean-ings through which wound almost untraveled roads growing up in grass or brush. Eaton had been tramping since his college days, and made a living from his magazine columns and books centered on an abandoned landscape he interpreted by consulting ancient gazetteers, elderly gos-sips, and the landscape itself.[99] His work echoes not only that of Amy Lowell and others who scrutinized the rural New England landscape in the late nineteenth century but also that of Lovecraft and other fantasy writers who failed to make that landscape as mysteriously evocative as the rural British ones M. R. James and others depicted. But in *Green Trails and Upland Pastures* and *Barn Doors and Byways,* and perhaps most forcefully in his *In Berkshire Fields,* Eaton pondered the role of the meditative walker who blunders into "a half dozen other abandoned farmhouses or barns, like elephants browsing over the hills," glimpses the pudgy motorists bewildered on a rural detour and gunning their en-gines while studying maps at a crossroads, and who finds only four miles from a "busy modern town, on the main line of a railroad" a place that seems lifted from ordinary history and even from ordinary time. "In this beautiful, breezy, forgotten place no people pass, no sound breaks the stillness," he wrote of an abandoned farmstead reached along a twisting, half-distinct cart path. "Only the memory walks of a vanished commu-nity; almost, it seems, of a vanished race."[100] In such places Eaton found the square image, decades before I discovered it for myself. He found the barn-doorway frame.[101]

As a boy I found what Eaton found, and savored it, but until I discov-ered Eaton in middle age I thought I alone knew the intensity with which a square barn doorway frames the landscape beyond for anyone willing to stand deep within the dusk of the barn itself. "Moosilauke is a noble mountain, even if it is absurdly easy of ascent. Its blue bulk walls in the southern end of the Ham Branch intervale with an almost grandiloquent self-sufficiency," Eaton noted in 1913. "Yet without trouble it fits into a barn-door vista, a topaz in a setting of golden hay."[102] Hay transport dictates the square shape of barn doorways. In summer and early autumn farmers backed loaded hay wagons into the main bay of their barns, then forked the hay upward into lofts. Unlike pedestrian doorways, vertical and narrow rectangles too narrow to pass a mule, barn doorways make immense squares. To the observer inside looking outward, even a boy growing intrigued by optical illusions in the old-field landscape of half-abandoned barns and fields, the dark of the barn sharpens the light framed in the square-shaped doorway.

As a young teenager I realized a similarity between the brilliant, shroud-surrounded waist-level viewfinder image and the brilliant intensity of sunlit landscape framed beyond the barn-doorway square. I looked out from deep within Loring Jacobs's barn, across his sunlit fields to the abandoned woodlot, and felt the square-framed light almost sear my eyes. At age fifteen I understood that framed view to be something akin to the illuminated rectangular screen in a darkened cinema, but something far different too, in ways beyond simple squareness. In the next few years I slowly realized not only that the barn offered quiet to view the spectacle of light framed in its doorway, but that the spectacle itself differed markedly from the ever-shifting cinema image. Through the doorway, light fell quietly on open land, free from busyness. The barn seemed a dark chamber resembling the interior of my clunky square-format cameras, and the doorway a ground glass on which hovered square-framed images, some bright, some dim, all squaring the circle of my eyes I watched. The abandoned, rarely visited landscape seemed the perfect theater of operations for my derelict square-format cameras, cameras everyone in the early 1970s derided as old-fashioned, too slow to make quickly images valued by a fast-moving world.

Nowadays I stand deep inside my own barn, its great rolling doors slid wide open, and look east into the sunlit woods, still wondering at the wrenching of light and shade and format so akin to the view down through the Rolleiflex ground glass.

12 Tutorial

Just before World War II, European manufacturers produced small square-format cameras intended to capitalize on the Rolleiflex success and stem the popularity of 35 mm models; relatively few of the cameras ever reached the United States.

I N 1935 ALBERT JOURDAN DISCOVERED HIS WIFE
framed in a doorway, eating a cluster of grapes she had just picked. "I
sneaked up and took five minishots of her just like firing with a six-
shooter," he reported in *American Photography.* "While aiming the sixth
to-be-mortal shot she saw me and dared me to shoot again, and I took
the dare and bagged a grin." Jourdan concluded that the 35 mm camera
resembled a tiny pistol, "because like any other concealed weapon a minicam can be used surreptitiously and nefariously and so provide a lot of
fun, very cheaply too, in my case 16 deadly shots for only 25 cents." While
Jourdan wrote regularly for the magazine, the colloquial tone of his article on 35 mm photography distinguishes it from his other feature-length
pieces and from almost all other articles appearing in the journal over
decades. "I can stuff about three hundred rounds of ammunition in my
pockets and do slaughter right and left most any old time, rain or shine,
winter as well as summer apparently," he concluded of an experiment
that he admitted reflected foolish and immature behavior.[1] *American
Photography* published none of his six-shooter images. The magazine had
long aimed at serious photographers who prided themselves on making
superb images under all sorts conditions, not on rapid-sequence ocular
flaying that called to mind turn-of-the-century complaints about Kodak
camera fiends roaming beaches. What Jourdan described seemed worse
than colloquial. It seemed like slumming.

American Photography had absorbed thirteen other photography magazines over the years, including *Anthony's Photographic Bulletin,* founded
in 1870, *Photo Era* and *Camera and Dark Room,* both established in
1898, and the first *Popular Photography,* founded in 1912. It had agents
in London, Berlin, and three cities in New Zealand, a history of publishing innovative articles by professional and amateur photographers, and
monthly columns both on nature photography and other traditional topics, and on aerial and minicam photography and other novelties. Unlike
the competitors that blossomed in the depths of the Depression, *American Photography* reproduced, usually one per page, superlative images
from international competitions and from readers' submissions. It featured a monthly schedule of forthcoming exhibitions and competitions
across the United States and Europe not only for potential entrants but
for travelers, and it routinely reviewed photography books published in
French and German. It presumed at least some college-educated readers
capable of understanding Alex Strasser's *Mit der Kamera im Schnee,* and
expected that several might submit articles detailing their success or fail-

ure in following its advice on photography in snow.[2] Today the magazine resembles a contemporary academic journal: it nudges any thoughtful reader into wondering at the class divide separating it from the new *Popular Photography*, founded in May 1937.[3]

American Photography understood how miniature cameras might make nighttime slum photography feasible. In 1935 it published "Night London with a Minicam," a brief article by Francis Sandwith describing doss house photography via oil lamp, recording the condition of a corpse washed ashore in the Thames, and pacifying and photographing the owner of a Chinese restaurant who mistook the tiny camera for a bomb.[4] But the magazine stepped back from the sort of rapid-fire candid photography about which Jourdan wrote, and from the sort of feature articles and image making *Popular Photography* championed from its inception.

"Shooting the Burlesque from the Center of Baldheaded Row" explains how its author used a "a Contax Camera, list price $399," with a f/1.5 lens to shoot striptease dancers at Minksy's Burlesque Show. Pat Terry explained that other cameras might work in such dimly lit spaces, especially if photographers anticipated dance movement, but emphasized that a small, fast-lens camera provided the best photographs of women revealing belly buttons and breasts while dancing in one-piece cutaway outfits.[5] The article reinforced the cover photograph of a towel-clad woman in a shower, and the accompanying feature article, "Shooting Our Cover in Color." Along with its competitors, especially *US Camera* and *Modern Photography*, *Popular Photography* showed lots of female skin, usually in candid photographs or ones masquerading as candid. *American Photography* published far more technical if by comparison sedate articles like F. Allan Morgan's "Panorama Pictures with the Rolleiflex," and always in monochrome, but it routinely reproduced images of nude women enjoying themselves outdoors, sometimes posed but usually not.[6] The magazine subtly acknowledged more than a deepening class divide in the United States; it embraced the easiness with which Europeans accepted the nude, and the casualness with which many Americans had begun sunbathing and swimming in the buff. As Nora E. Reisman explained in "The Photographic Nude," a mid-Depression article, appropriate backgrounds idealized the nude body: beads, masks, or contortions shielding certain body parts seemed cheap, Hollywood-based contrivance.[7] *American Photography* asserted that nude Americans, and ones wearing very little, might be photographed superbly while at ease around photographers. In its pages women who doubled as both models and photographers argued that many accomplished photographers understood the difficulties involved in photographing the human figure and so did not attempt what some successfully managed by avoiding the poses snatched from burlesque houses by candid minicams.[8] Its editors knew too that nude and scantily clad Americans had become the target of "candid cameramen" incapable of posing nude people in sensible, relaxed ways and undoubtedly voyeuristic in their attitudes toward casually exposed flesh. They saw nudity and near nudity as upper-class phenomena attracting lower-class photographers.

Until the start of World War II, *American Photography* featured foreign scenes on about half of its covers each year. Dutch polder landscapes, British rail yards under low clouds, and Berlin streetcars operating in snow merely introduced the cosmopolitan mix of "principal images" reproduced in the pages that followed. While Americans made some of the photographs when abroad in Europe or the Near East, many were the work of Europeans publishing in *Das Deutsche Lichtbild* and other annuals.[9] Just as the magazine routinely reviewed books published in French and German, so it attempted to publish the very best images made overseas. Rather than choose only from images submitted by subscribers, *American Photography* frequently reproduced prizewinning photographs from United States and foreign competitions, many of them outdoor nudes. Its editors assumed that readers viewing excellent images might learn as much from them as from those illustrating technical articles, and from translated technical articles, usually from *Die Photographische Industrie* and other German journals.[10] *American Photography* connected directly and explicitly with readers who understood photography in a global context, and who saw 35 mm candid-camera photography as anything but German.

Camera Craft, The Camera: The Photographic Journal of America, and other magazines corroborated the stance of *American Photography* that the candid-camera craze revealed a deepening split in the ranks of American photographers. Despite the steep price of Leica, Contax, and other 35 mm cameras, let alone the exorbitantly priced but even smaller Compass introduced just before World War II, the craze splintered photographers. Traditional magazines saw the minicam and candid-camera craze as beneath contempt, and far down the scale of common sense, propriety, and even good fun, not only driving ferocious effort in film-chemistry modification to make quality small negatives produce quality large prints, but firing an equally ferocious and increasingly rude fad of photographing people unaware, often in the low-light conditions inspiring film manufacturers to invent ever faster film. Their editors wondered routinely at the American nature of the craze and mused about its impact on children and teenagers still satisfied with large-format box cameras.[11] As

Europe collapsed into war in late 1939, the traditional American magazines acknowledged the temporary cessation of European tutelage; their
editors promised readers continued commitment to high aesthetic and
technical standards. Mass-circulation magazines instead savored freedom from European (and especially German) constraint. They extolled
35 mm candid photography as patriotic and distinctly American.[12]

In the years 1938, 1939, and 1940 photographers uninterested in rapid-
exposure 35 mm shooting enjoyed a sudden outpouring of books on light
and color in medium-format terms. The year 1938 witnessed the publication of *The New Photo-School,* an idiosyncratic but sophisticated book by
Hans Windisch published simultaneously in English and sold at Rolleiflex dealers. The book is part of a larger, late 1930s European attention
to natural phenomenon nowadays best examined in M. G. J. Minnaert's
1937 *Light and Color in the Outdoors.* Minnaert and other experts explained that quality cameras and new color film in educated hands offered insights into natural phenomena: backyard photography of the Big
Dipper revealed that of the two right-hand stars, the upper one is far
more yellow than the lower.[13] *The New Photo School* addresses some technical issues that Watkins confronted decades earlier and others as new as
the beach images of women in two-piece swimsuits posing in four photographs reproduced on its first page.[14] Windisch argued for photography
by premeditation, not by candid accident. The scantily clad women represent novelty and challenge as did any new color film, and together they
posed problems of photographing figures in jarringly colored suits in
bright sun and glaring reflection.[15] *The New Photo School* exemplifies
the aesthetic stresses produced by European photography manuals, annuals showcasing prizewinning photographs, and magazines produced by
individual camera manufacturers. The women posing naturally on a beach
did not merely illustrate problems bright light posed for late 1930s photographers bereft of Rolleiflex camera exposure tables. They pushed *The
New Photo School* just a bit beyond the Remie Lohse photographs featured in a two-page center spread six months later in the August 1939
issue of *Popular Photography.* Purchasers of Rolleiflex and other excellent German-built medium-format cameras acquired manuals, compli-
mentary magazine subscriptions, and access to books emphasizing a photographic aesthetic markedly different from that espoused by Hollywood
and mass-circulation American photography magazines.

In the month before World War II debuted the Pilot Super, a chunky,
near-cube-shaped square-format camera produced by Kamera Werkstatten
in Dresden and imported and distributed by Burleigh Brooks. A single-
lens reflex camera making medium-format images on 120 film, the Pilot

Super appeared suddenly from a Chicago-owned German camera firm known for producing extremely thin, folding, medium-format plate-film cameras. The Etui line of Kamera Werkstatten cameras remains a delicious prewar obscurity. The expensive and rare cameras typically appeared in bright red or dark blue leatherette, usually with red or blue (and more rarely, purple) bellows and extremely fine lenses. Each carried a single piece of rectangular-shaped film: without a roll of film to accommodate, the cameras collapsed into an oblong advertised as "wafer thin." While the Eastman Kodak Company produced much larger folding cameras in several colors of leatherette decades earlier, the KW Etui cameras mystify collectors willing to pay exorbitant prices for cameras made in lots of perhaps only 750. Nowadays considered to have been an expert woman's camera, colored to match clothing ensembles, the various Etui models imply that some photographers, perhaps chiefly women, preferred a one-shot, medium-format camera that slid easily into a pocket or handbag rather than an expensive but far thicker 35 mm Leica or Contax.[16] The Pilot Super arrived in the United States late in the summer of 1939 as an instant puzzle, a relative of some of the rarest German cameras ever imported and a challenge to the 35 mm craze.

Burleigh Brooks advertised the camera as innovative and low-priced. It made twelve standard images 2¼ inches square or sixteen smaller, rectangular ones using 120-size film, had both eye- and waist-level viewfinders, a guillotine shutter featuring speeds from B and 1/20 to 1/200 of a second, a double-exposure prevention lock, and a unique light meter. It cost $45 when equipped with its fastest (f/2.9) lens, and only $28.50 when equipped with its slowest (f/4.5). For an additional $20, the camera came with a second, four-inch lens that interchanged with the standard focal-length one, offering some telephoto capability.[17] It appealed to photographers wanting a quality fast-to-use camera producing much larger negatives than its 35 mm competition.

The Pilot Super appeared exactly as Franke and Heidecke, Burleigh Brooks, and other medium-format manufacturers and distributors seemed poised to effectively counter the 35 mm candid-camera fad. Nothing about the new camera made it pocket friendly. Its shape resembled the bottom half of a Rolleiflex. But its features suggested an incipient change among photographers abandoning the candid-camera fad, ready to move up from Eastman Kodak and similar basic box and folding cameras to something less expensive than a Rolleiflex but able to make large, high-quality negatives.

Its user lost the viewfinder image as the shutter fired. In this the Pilot Super worked in a way similar to many single-lens reflex 35 mm cameras. Its user could experiment with interchangeable lenses, something the manufacturer of the Leica and other expensive 35 mm cameras—and minicam users like Lohse—championed as driving the candid-camera enterprise. It carried a simple but effective extinction-type light meter requiring neither selenium cells nor batteries; the meter worked rapidly with a minimum of scrutiny.[18] Above all, it allowed its user to focus precisely, using both the scale marked on the lens barrel and the image displayed right side up on the ground-glass focusing screen. Apparently intended as a full-figure, natural-portrait camera, the Pilot Super provided a low-cost alternative to small-format minicams. But it competed too with far less expensive Rolleiflex knock-offs.[19]

The Pilot Super might have nudged many photographers toward high-quality medium-format photography, and especially toward buying Rolleiflexes, had war not eliminated the supply. Even before World War II began in Europe, American importers and publishers anticipated the fracturing of the global camera industry: in 1939 Central Camera refused to accept any Altiflex orders beyond its present stock, and *Popular Photography* began suggesting that readers vacation in the Caribbean and in Central America.[20] In the close-to-home tropics they might find bold natural color, near-empty beaches, and American women wearing swimsuits they chose not to wear at home, if they wore suits at all.

As early as 1938 Fawcett Publications introduced an important annual, *Good Photography,* to supplement its already successful new annual, *Photography Handbook.* The bulk of each book showcased successful photographs and shop-theory projects, often extremely nuanced ones that nonetheless required little in the way of high-priced material. In 1939 Everett Rudloff told readers how to construct "an air-conditioned, vibration-less enlarger designed along simple lines, that anyone who is handy with a saw, bit brace, and screwdriver can build" from scrap wood.[21] *Good Photography* published photographs by professionals, but operated an annual competition open only to amateurs: often amateurs won by imitating the work of Lohse and other professionals using 35 mm cameras to photograph swimsuited women playing on beaches, or by following the technical precepts and aesthetic notions of Max Thorek and other amateurs intrigued by nudes. Thorek, a famed surgeon and first president of the Photographic Society of America, told readers how to use his paper-negative process, and illustrated his instructions with images of women posed in Mortensen-like ways, one as an odalisque.[22] The editors of both annuals emphasized 35 mm photography and by 1940 knew they had well-nigh cornered the market on up-to-date photography information and shaped advertising by American manufacturers. The publisher of *How to Built It* and other do-it-yourself annuals, and magazines ranging from *Mechanix Illustrated* (a monthly that competed aggressively with *Popular Mechanics*), *Motion Picture,* and *Movie Story* to *Startling Detective Adventures* and *For Men,* had discovered the opportunity world war offered. It spent the wartime years fine-tuning its understanding of the class hierarchy of American photography, dismissing entry-level photographers except as potential purchasers of expensive cameras and darkroom equipment, and integrating its understanding of shop theory, Hollywood cinema, and men's magazine approaches to photographing women. At the end of the war, Fawcett Publications owned a foundation on which it then built a photography book empire, much of it centered on what the firm announced as fundamental American aesthetic principles grounded in 35 mm format and wartime glamour photography.

Between the summer of 1938 and early 1940, 35 mm photography, especially candid photography, triumphed in almost all United States publications outside traditional, upscale photography magazines and those aimed at box camera snapshooters. Instructional authority shifted from professional photographers to Windisch, Thorek, and other knowledgeable amateurs, but by 1940 most British and European authorities, amateur and otherwise, had grown distant from American publications. The incipient shift away from 35 mm photography, evidenced by Kamera Werkstatten designing and producing the Pilot Super, imported, distributed, and advertised by Burleigh Brooks as a threshold to Rolleiflex photography, ended by the summer of 1940 as publishers of annuals and monthly magazines cast off what they classified as the cameras, instruction, and aesthetic of Europe. Popular magazines made medium-format photography suddenly old-fashioned again. All German-built cameras, Rolleiflexes especially, suddenly seemed unpatriotic, their superb quality threatening a United States camera industry capable only of buying German firms or contracting out camera development and production. The Pilot Super vanished overnight.

World War II brought about a hiatus in which *Popular Photography, Minicam, Modern Photography,* and similar magazines grabbed the great bulk of American photographic readership, including servicemen stuffing tiny cameras in duffel bags. While they made efforts to include the Rolleiflex and other square-format cameras in the classification they celebrated as miniature, they failed, in part because after the end of 1939 no one could purchase a new first-quality twin-lens reflex camera.[23] By 1950 Americans intrigued by medium-format photography could only build on their late 1930s European tutors and move forward as a self-defined cadre dedicated to anything but candid picture making.

In 1961 I found tattered photography magazines in my junior-high-school library, but over two years I realized that my seeing in squares apparently appealed to very few editors and writers. I did learn that a Rolleiflex remained a very expensive camera indeed, however, and that knowing a bit of German might not only prepare me for owning one someday but also advance my haphazard, old-fields square-format image making with cameras that at least made square negatives.[24] By the time I entered college in 1967, the Rolleiflex seemed even more mysterious in mass-circulation photography magazines. By then I could read the literature its manufacturer published for German readers, and sometimes translated for British, Australian, and American ones. I knew too that fashion photographers preferred the Rolleiflex, and that they often spoke of doing glamour photography, something they distinguished from candid photography.

Distinguishing the divergence of square-format, Rolleiflex-based glamour photography from candid and other sorts of 35 mm photography is important.

It demands attention to Walther Heering's *Das Rolleiflex Buch*. After its publication in 1933, Rolleiflex users understood what Francke and Heidecke appear to have decided a year or two earlier. While the Rolleiflex must compete with the Leica, Contax, and other 35 mm cameras, its bulk handicapped photographers of action sports and other activities requiring instantaneous, eye-level decision making and made much candid photography impossible. At the same time as the manufacturer determined to find a niche in which the Rolleiflex might triumph, Heering realized what its users already knew. The Rolleiflex proved superb at full-figure portraits, especially so-called natural ones, and at landscapes in which figures dominated foregrounds.[25]

Between 1933 and 1940, but especially between 1938 and 1940, the Rolleiflex and glamour fused into a whole. Driven not only by photographer discovery and interest but by the determined advertising and technical information of Francke and Heidecke, the camera itself became a portal on faerie.

Illustrated with images that varied between the German and subsequent English-language editions, *The Rolleiflex Book* profoundly shaped other manuals. Heering proclaimed that the Rolleiflex enabled a skilled photographer to make unposed group portraits, especially since the downward gaze of the photographer "has a very steadying effect" on the most self-conscious of subjects. "The technical details—stop, exposure, etc.—will of course have been thought out beforehand," he acknowledged. "The chief thing is the psychological achievement, the correct moment, the characteristic expression of the sitter, which must be brought out of him by personal contact."[26]

For Heering, the key to photographing people with the Rolleiflex was to aim the camera at people who knew they were being photographed but who sooner or later began to ignore the camera and its downward-gazing holder. "Head pictures are the easiest, full figures the most difficult, whilst hands are very important," he observed. "Two-point focusing and presence of mind are the necessary requisites," and "the manner in which the photographer approaches his subject decides the extent of his success or failure."[27] Through numerous editions Heering continued to maintain that a Rolleiflex made superb portraits both indoors and out, in artificial and natural lighting, and that it did best when aimed at people wholly one with their surroundings.

In the 1954 edition (the sixth), entitled *The Rollei Book*, Heering tacitly accepted the primacy of the Rolleiflex in fashion and glamour photography, and devoted many pages to explaining how to achieve results resembling those in *Vogue, Vanity Fair*, and other high-end magazines. Much of his advice derived from trends established in World War II and emphasized in the immediate postwar years, especially in United States fashion magazines. "Make them do something, give them a book, a fruit or a flower, but don't give the flower to an old man with gnarled fingers or a scientific book to the blond teenager," he recommended, and schooled readers on ways to bring out highlights in women's hair, achieve soft-toned, blemish-free skin. "Good modeling on the features and clothes and naturalness of expression," he reminded readers, "all that has to be done with the light!" Heering knew that fashion magazines had begun to reshape sitter expectation of slightly out-of-focus backgrounds and that the photographer might accomplish only so much: "You can't make a Jane Russell of a plain peasant girl, so don't try it," he warned. But many sitters would find themselves pleased with portraits, so long as the photographer kept peering down, "talking freely and quietly, asking and replying to questions," and watching "unobtrusively" a subject no longer called "the sitter" but "the model."[28]

In the 1954 edition, Heering tacitly traced the transformation from fashion to glamour photography wrought by the Rolleiflex since 1933 and noted in earlier editions. "Only one who has some knowledge of psychology can be a master," he concluded.[29]

Unlike many writers, Heering understood the power of shop theory and experience in terms of Rolleiflex users. He adopted terminology Mortensen invented, especially that of plastic light produced by two or more photofloods used indoors or by employing ambient light outside. A

Rolleiflex photographer acutely aware of lighting and color created the continuum conducive to making excellent images of people and setting as a whole. He understood such image making as deliberate.

Remie Lohse epitomized the so-called candid portraiture of very late 1930s 35 mm photographers. His books advanced his straightforward argument that 35 mm cameras performed well, especially on beaches: their long film rolls enabled users to photograph cavorting nude women in ways that captured what he called "natural character." His *Rhythm and Repose,* a 1937 folio almost entirely devoted to nude women at the seashore, nonetheless included several square-format shots made with a Rolleiflex.[30] Two years later, his *Miniature Camera in Professional Hands* almost wholly dispensed with Rolleiflex images, and emphasized his work for magazines and advertising agencies. Lohse republished many images readers had seen in advertisements for Socony Gas and Oil, Old Gold Cigarettes, Paramount Pictures, and Gantner's Bathing Suits, as well as several he did for Agfa Ansco, a manufacturer of photographic film and other materials. He explained how he made each, including how he manipulated film development and printing, and offered a set of rules for remaining inconspicuous at events and deflecting curious bystanders.[31]

In the end, Lohse's books emphasize his proposition that "action adds greatly to the life in a photograph, and a little 'arrested motion' generally improves the picture, provided it harmonizes with the scene."[32] What he taught himself while making images of nightclub performers in very poor lighting blossomed on the beach. He admitted bringing carloads of models to beaches, and photographing each woman until she became exhausted. Given his predilection for movement, especially gamboling in waves and running down sand dunes, his daylong shoots undoubtedly tired models as his five or more miniature cameras consumed hundreds of rolls of film. Often his images jar because the arrested motion seems too obvious. But his books accomplished more than simply confirming the growing popularity of seaside nudity among upscale Americans. They welded glamour magazine photography, general advertising imagery, and advertising for new photographic materials (especially very fast, fine-grain film and high-contrast paper) into a new way of making "candids" that overwhelmed others.

The bulk of postwar portraits divided into three classes: snapshots, formal posed portraits, and informal action shots à la Lohse. By the late 1950s, as Otto Croy's 1940 *The Photographic Portrait* (translated from the German after the war) influenced medium-format photographers, the relaxed personalized portrait that "happened" during the longer photographic effort influenced fashion and glamour photographers. *The Photo-*

graphic Portrait nowadays makes difficult reading, in large part because even in translation it remains a very Austrian book: like Windisch's *New Photo School,* it aims at a reader educated in matters beyond photography. It distinguishes between shots of profiles that show "most clearly the person's racial characteristics" owing to the emphasis on bone structure and full-face views that reveal "personal qualities, irrespective of the person's origin." It explains the importance of foreheads in shots of men versus the importance of hairstyle (and the relative unimportance of foreheads) in images of women; distortions caused by projected hands and feet; and a wealth of other precise technical information. Its images of Marilyn Monroe made in 1945 and 1950 illustrating slight facial change over time seem more oriented toward physical anthropology than photography, let alone art, and its lengthy analyses of the impact of top lighting on spare and blond hair and similar details sandwich technical information among brief essays by postwar photographers working in ways alien to Lohse.

"I have always succeeded especially well with pictures of young women, so these are the only pictures I shall show here," remarked Andre De Dienes, who in his essay in Croy's book confessed himself unwilling to write much about his portraits. He thought that American young women "are the most beautiful in the world" largely because most are of mixed ethnicity and eat right: they are healthy and fit. They represent "everything young, happy, amusing, bright, and lovely," but each is an individual, something critically important. "I always aim at capturing the girl's charm as I see it in reality. At the same time, I allow myself to be influenced by poetic feeling."[33] De Dienes obliquely confirmed Croy's insistence that profile shots reveal ethnic characteristics, among other minor details, and he corroborated Croy's assertion that the prudent photographer carried one camera, a small stand, and one compact lighting unit to set atop the stand. While Lohse photographed groups of women on the beach or showgirls in strip clubs, De Dienes did as Croy insisted, and photographed young women one at a time, avoiding both the Group f/64 aesthetic and honoring the poetic feeling—or license— Lange, Mortensen, and others championed.

Croy wrote for the accomplished amateur and the aspiring professional willing to pore over charts entitled "Treatment of the Face," "Treatment of the Nose," or "Treatment of the Chin" to learn how to "characterize or emphasize" or "idealize" certain features the photographer had already identified and classified. "As every schoolboy knows, it protects the lens against the strong oblique light rays in outdoor photography," he said of the Rolleiflex lens hood, before going on to explain how it alters lighting that otherwise separates the model too much from background.[34] *The Photographic Portrait* addresses neither the faint of heart nor schoolboys, and it emphasizes the advantages of the medium-format camera over the miniature cameras become so popular.

Heering's 1954 *Rollei Book* moved well beyond earlier editions to emphasize the creation of portrait glamour. It explains that sensible portraitists realize that one main lamp must illuminate the sitter, lest eyes reflect multiple highlights that give "an uneasy look." Sophisticated studio effort, however, must involve three lamps properly placed. Heering understood the plastic light Mortensen identified and refined, and provided detailed information on placing up to three lights around a sitter. "Don't mind all the beautiful 'rules,' and try it this way," he advised. "Give the model a stool to sit on, not a chair (this means 'not too comfortable') and 'stalk' the sitter with your two lamps, try this and vary that, you know, and finally add a third lamp from above to give the hair that glamorous sheen, which is often the solution of the whole problem."[35] Using a camera identical to those high-fashion photographers used, an advanced amateur or aspiring professional might produce a glamorous full-figure portrait, often with simple lighting equipment he made himself.

Rolleiflex users devoured books, keeping many in print through multiple editions as Franke and Heidecke produced improved cameras and added to the tiny range of Rolleiflex accessories. Typically erudite, technically detailed (often to extremes unknown outside a handful of technically oriented photography magazines), and handsomely printed, the books not only suggest the wealth of Rolleiflex photographers but imply that few Rolleiflex photographers began photography with a Rolleiflex. Often the manuals assume a reader moving directly from box camera image making to owning a Rolleiflex; sometimes they address a reader determined to forget candid-photography tricks. Most assume readers familiar with European trends in photographic aesthetics as well as with European-built cameras, often through the Franke and Heidecke magazine, *Photography with the Rolleiflex and Rolleicord.*[36] Despite the continuing popularity of Heering's *Rollei Book,* Americans and Britons wrote most of the competing volumes, making certain to illustrate them with a mix of American and European (and sometimes South American, Asian, and African) images.

A handful of writers produced inexpensive books intended to introduce the Rolleiflex to potential purchasers. In 1945 F. W. Frerk extolled the Rolleiflex as the camera prizewinning photographers preferred across a broad range of contests: he called it the best serious camera to buy. "The chief merit of the Rolleiflex—and of the whole Rolleiflex family, including a large number of illegitimate children of very similar appearance but different industrial parentage—is just that it makes a sensible and modern 'general' camera," he wrote in the beginning of his *Rolleiflex and Rolleicord Guide*. Frerk enumerated the defining features of the Rolleiflex, emphasizing especially its ground-glass focusing, its medium-size negatives, its square format, and its waist-level user position, concluding that it is not the fastest camera in shutter speed or ease of use and so not well adapted to potential purchasers already "all for excitement, fast tempo, or big sports," in other words, for the candid-camera aficionado. But the Rolleiflex is not fussy, operates in straightforward ways, and *"is one of the best 'picture' finding and 'picture making' instruments"* available.[37]

In 1951 appeared L. A. Mannheim's *The Rollei Way,* a sort of technical manual and anthology of expert essays. It aims at explaining why many photographers see a few carrying what is "in a sense a very superior sort of box camera" in an age when most amateurs use either a simple box camera or an often-pricey 35 mm camera. It includes essays by European portraitists insisting that natural portraits evolve from photographers willing to leave subjects alone—Hugo van Wadenoyen's perceptive essay, "People Out of Doors," emphasizes that "no coaxing or ordering, no posing or arranging, no matter how cleverly and cunningly done, can ever give that air of authenticity and complete naturalness possessed by a good expressive shot of a real happening" and emphasizes that the "easiest light is sunlight diffused through light clouds," since it "will bring out the 'modeling' of the subjects"—but its tone is both introductory and exploratory.[38] It introduces a different and expensive sort of camera definitely related to Brownie box cameras while exploring how the Rolleiflex user embraces a picture-making effort different from that casually accepted by 35 mm photographers. *The Rollei Way* insists that looking down through the ground-glass square viewfinder subtly alters the way the Rolleiflex photographer sees potential images around him all the time. It reminds readers that 1900-era box cameras perhaps worked their own visual magic on subjects in part because they shaped photographer stance.

Many photographers sacrificed to buy Rolleiflexes. Writers considered the expensive cameras not only worth their retail price but worth spending money to learn about from high-priced books. Major improvement substantially increased Rolleiflex list prices within four years. In 1957 the Rolleiflex 2.8E, which came equipped with an integral light meter and automatic Exposure (or Light) Value System (which kept shutter-speed and f-stop ratios constant during alteration of either setting), retailed for $350, worth about $2,428 (based on the CPI) or $3,153 (based on the unskilled wage rate) in contemporary dollars. In that year mail-order retailer Montgomery Ward sold the new Rolleiflex and its much less expensive sibling, the Rolleicord, but also retailed several imitations. The meter-equipped Minolta Autocord L sold for $135 and the Ikoflex Automatic Favorite with meter sold for $209; but the Yashica twin-lens reflex, with meter, sold for only $69.50, only about a third more than the similar but unmetered company brand Wardflex II, which retailed for only $47.50.[39] Fair-trade laws and federal import tariffs alone did not explain the rapidly rising retail price of the top-level Rolleiflex model: Franke and Heidecke improvements had nudged the Rolleiflex price beyond that of any similar camera, and catapulted it far beyond expensive 35 mm cameras and new Polaroid instant cameras too.

In the 1960s American distributors distinguished the Rolleiflex by extolling its use in glamour photography. They ran full-page ads in *US Camera* and other mainstream photography magazines emphasizing the size of the viewfinder image, negative, and color transparency as perfect for full-figure portraiture, citing the well-known fact that almost every fashion magazine photographer used Rolleiflexes. They secured the place of the Rolleiflex as an upscale camera for advanced photographers, and particularly for men, defining it against 35 mm candid photography and building on twenty years of technical publication.

While television censored belly buttons, Rolleiflex advertising emphasized them and bikinis, often bikinis briefer than those appearing in United States advertisements for swimwear. Between 1953 and 1961 Franke and Heidecke and its American distributors orchestrated an advertising effort that made the Rolleiflex the camera for a new elite, one comfortable with scanty attire, sexuality, and photography requiring and rewarding practice. The advertising campaign piggybacked atop a serious educational effort made by two well-respected photography experts, Jacob Deschin and Alec Pearlman. Deschin's *Rollei Photography: Handbook of the Rolleiflex and Rolleicord Cameras* appeared from Camera Craft Publishing in December 1952. Eleven months later, Pearlman's exhaustive *Rollei Manual: The Complete Book of Twin-Lens Photography* launched simultaneously in London and New York. Deschin published a revised version of his book in June 1953; the second edition of Pearlman's volume appeared in April 1955, and thereafter Pearlman updated *The Rollei Manual* as Franke and Heidecke produced new versions of its Rolleiflex. Burleigh Brooks listed Deschin's *Rollei Photography* in its wholesale price lists immediately following its publication, classifying it more like an accessory than a book. Montgomery Ward advertised Pearlman's *Rollei Manual* in its retail catalogs, pricing it at $7.50 (in contemporary dollars, $52 [CPI] or $68 [unskilled wage]). By the middle 1950s even books about the Rolleiflex debuted as expensive volumes no longer aimed at the bulk of photographers—amateurs and professionals—but at an elite.

By 1957 Rolleiflex-centric advertising was triumphing over lingering postwar anti-Germany attitudes and over Japanese twin-lens camera competition. It triumphed too over bitterness involving the collapse of United States twin-lens camera manufacturers unable to compete against either Franke and Heidecke innovation or Japanese low price. In the decade following V-J day, a number of domestic manufacturers produced reliable, mid-range-quality twin-lens cameras, the best known at the time probably being the Ciro-flex.

Bruce Downes published his *Photography with the Ciro-flex: A Basic Book on Twin-Lens Reflex Camera Technique* in 1950, assuming that the Ciro-flex would become the standard TLR camera in the United States and perhaps the world. Down aimed his book at an arty sort of younger reader, upwardly mobile, perhaps the GI home, employed, and settled down with a wife but just a bit different from others buying new houses and starting families. He aimed it at men who enjoyed photographing women in pants, who embraced and even relished wartime changes in women's roles and outlooks.[40] Yet within seven years Montgomery Ward no longer listed the Ciro-flex. Cameras built in war-ruined countries had supplanted it, and the Rolleiflex nestled in the hands of the young cohort Downes so precisely identified even as the cohort merged seamlessly with the established Rolleiflex-owning elite.

In 1952 Jacob Deschin saw the Rolleiflex elite snatching the heart from 35 mm photography. As a *Popular Photography* author since the first issue of the magazine in 1937, and as camera editor of the *New York Times* from 1941 on, Deschin shaped American photographic thinking as Europe devolved into the war that stopped the flow of imported cameras and thinking alike. His *Rollei Photography* includes essays by five Rolleiflex users, among them Andreas Feininger, who authored "On City Life," and Fritz Henle, who wrote "On Travel," but it presents Philippe Halsmann's essay on portraiture first. The essays follow Deschin's chapters on using the Rolleiflex, but the chapters revolve around chapter 9, "Rollei 35 mm Photography," which describes the Rolleikin.

The compact Rolleikin accessory kit, chiefly two special spools that accommodated ordinary 35 mm film and a mask that dropped over the viewing glass so photographers could easily see the rectangular-shaped image full size, came in a small leather case. Deschin admitted that photographers devoted to 35 mm photography would undoubtedly purchase a 35 mm camera, but that medium-format devotees would find the accessory package "useful in extended series pictures, as in picture 'note-taking' of action subjects by artists for use in drawing or painting" and "for portraiture."[41] While the telephoto effect nudged Rolleiflex owners into realizing they had—in a way—a second lens, it made the Rolleiflex accomplish what 35 mm cameras did only with a second lens. *Rollei Photography* did far more than explain why so many illustrious photographers used Rolleiflex cameras and why an advanced amateur might find the Rolleiflex superbly useful. It explained that the Rolleiflex alone could shoot 35 mm film too, something its illegitimate cousins could not do, and in so explaining wrenched the medium-format versus 35 mm argument sideways. No 35 mm camera accommodated medium-format film. Rolleiflex users could shoot 35 mm film—if they chose to do so. But most probably would not, except under rare circumstances.

The chapter entitled "The Rollei in Fashion Photography" in Alec Pearlman's *Rollei Manual* emphasizes that fashion photography had morphed into glamour photography in the early 1950s, and that fashion and glamour photography drove the shift to naturalistic, often outdoor full-figure portraiture using existing lighting in specific sorts of settings.

"It is the one serious camera which can be taken on location with the greatest of ease, and the least discomfort—to fishing villages in remote places, to sun-drenched beaches, to city pillars and country hedgerows," Pearlman asserted. "It can even be draped round the neck of the model herself to give the impression of carefree holiday snapshooting at home or abroad." The Rolleiflex had earned its position as the most versatile fashion photography instrument, but luck seemed to have played an initial role. The 75 mm (and later, on the 2.8C and other 2.8 models, 80 mm) lens *happened* to be the perfect lens for the 2¼ square format: the same-size ground-glass viewing screen made the composing process straightforward if rarely simple. The same lens offered about ten degrees more horizontal arc than that used by Cornish, and so tended to mitigate many problems posed by rectangle-format 35 mm cameras when used in landscape photography; it proved perfect for the burgeoning fashion photography industry situating models in landscape.

But Pearlman insisted that facility with the Rolleiflex did little to make a fashion photographer. Instead, the would-be photographer needed years of experience in "visual presentation in a variety of fields," a background in art, and perhaps some kind of "basic training" in painting or sculpture. Without such grounding, "he will be unable to live and work on the same plane as his educated and worldly clientele—unable to appreciate the finesse of the subtle drape, or the special significance of the latest hemline or neckline." Pearlman assumed a male aspirant, and warned him that he must "understand how cut and style affect the woman at whom all his work is eventually aimed," as well as how to get the "best possible cooperation" from his models while "imprinting his own personality on the finished product which is composed of gown, model, and setting." Unlike his competitors, whom he eventually vanquished, Pearlman dealt at length with each of the mainstream uses of the Rolleiflex, and he saw fashion photography as the epitome of photographer skill. It achieved genuine glamour.[42]

He advised aspirants to employ professional models accustomed to posing before cameras and possessing "that nonchalant air of insouciance which is the envy of most women, and which does away with the 'feel' of the camera's presence." Given the Rolleiflex lens, the woman should be above average in height, since the 75 mm lens tends to add slightly to the weight of anyone. Pearlman suggested the ideal model as 5 feet 7½ inches barefoot, with a bust of 34 inches, waist 22½ inches, and hips 35 inches: shorter models worked well in half and three-quarter shots, but not in full-figure ones. In the end, the ideal model is the woman with "that special flair for wearing clothes—that something which cannot be taught but which comes naturally to some girls, even at an early age."[43] With a bit of makeup, especially at the corners of the eyes, such a model satisfies industry requirements and the technical characteristics of the Rolleiflex—and satisfies the woman at whom the images are aimed by the photographer, the advertiser, and the manufacturer, the ultimate end user, the potential purchaser. Everything else, studio and outdoor lighting especially, the successful photographer manages in relation to his Rolleiflex, which he usually holds in his hand, waiting for the perfect composition and perfect facial expression. "The shutter is then released when the pose, the expression, the juxtaposition of background and model, the swing and drape of the material are all quite perfect." What Franke and Heidecke advertised in the late 1939 as the total control peculiar to the Rolleiflex had, by 1955, made the Rolleiflex the premiere camera of the fashion industry, especially among photographers working outdoors in new, naturalistic ways.

Successive editions of *The Rollei Manual* adapted to new cameras and new accessories, and to new aesthetic standards. Pearlman scarcely altered his text, but he did change illustrations. In 1955 many of the images came from the fashion industry, and several from stark-background studio series.[44] By 1960 far more casual images of women had replaced the earlier ones: the new images depicted women at work, usually in urban settings.[45] Six years later the portrait chapter images had shifted again, toward far more naturalistic, spontaneous-seeming poses, including bikinied women on beaches and nude women just in from swimming. Those images parallel a similar change in the fashion photography chapter, where bikinied women on beaches, windblown women in shallows, and well-dressed women casually posed in doorways supplant most formally gowned models.[46] In the fifth edition, published in 1971, Pearlman replaced nearly all the illustrations in the fashion photography chapter, choosing outlandishly clad models in outlandish settings—and one woman seated on the floor, a nude five-year-old girl between her spread legs. He replaced most of the female-centered images in the portraiture chapter with even more daring images, including one of a woman clad only in metal jewelry and another informally posing in a transparent blouse.[47] Each edition addressed new-model Rolleiflex cameras and accessories, something that necessitated new editions, and sometimes partial revisions. After 1966 Pearlman deleted much information about prewar cameras and emphasized recent innovations, but his evolving text and strikingly changing images illustrated the fact that the Rolleiflex adapted well to new subjects, new notions of lighting, and above all to the increased impact of fashion and glamour photography on full-figure portraiture and even on landscape imagery. Pearlman argued that the camera drove such change.

The Rollei Manual unwittingly traces the impact of postwar fashion photography on full-figure and even half-figure portrait photography. Reverse-reading Pearlman's many editions only makes the road that much more apparent, in a way that recalls Watkins's discovery of the alignments. "Fashion usually demands a tall model and often a long-length leg, and for such effects, the low camera angle is usually called into use— with the Rollei the floor is the limit," Pearlman opined in 1953.[48] The Rolleiflex photographer might set his camera on the floor, look down as usual from above, and create the low-angle shot that shaped fashion photography from the late 1950s onward until it dominated fashion imagery after 1975. But as early as 1953 Pearlman glimpsed the potential long-term impact of Rolleiflex-driven fashion photography on full-figure portraiture. Given the very short exposures necessitated by high-speed emulsions, the "net outcome of all this is that split-second timing of the pose becomes possible and the swing of a skirt, the point of a toe, or the characteristic gesture can be captured without tiring the subject or model and avoiding the strained and unnatural look."[49] No longer did the photographer need to exhaust groups of models on the beach or even tire his favorite subject. Full-figure portraiture segued further into fashion photography format and far from 35 mm candid photography, becoming a new genre: glamour photography, driving an upscale marketing of film, subject, and aesthetic targeted at both men and women.

Heering too distinguished what Pearlman noted. In 1963 he produced a revised version of his book, never translated into English. In *Das Rollei-Buch,* Heering emphasized a new genre of portraiture characterized by acute angles of view, composition juxtaposing figure or face with slightly out-of-focus backgrounds, and color. He distinguished sharply among images made as documents, art, and advertising and those made as glamour.[50] Although the last edition of *Das Rollei-Buch* never appeared in English, it had an impact on at least some American photographers, especially United States servicemen stationed in West Germany who returned home with a Rolleiflex purchased duty-free at the post exchange.[51] In it Heering argued for a new genre of portrait photography welding people and animals to place in magical ways. Pearlman accomplished Heering's vision, detailing how photographers long dissatisfied with candid imagery might create images fusing specific place and specific models.

After the late 1930s, medium-format photographers worked outside the aesthetic parameters espoused in *Popular Photography* and similar magazines and outside the 35 mm–format aesthetic Fawcett Publications extolled. By the late 1950s, Rolleiflex users constituted a small but well-to-do cadre confident its decision to avoid 35 mm photography and centered on a new genre evolving from fashion photography.

Glamour photography emerged from novel approaches to photographing women in landscape, but the medium-format photographer's embrace of a new kind of woman thrust both glamour photography and the Rolleiflex into an upscale modernity that discomforted 35 mm photographers accustomed to mass-circulation magazine aesthetics. While late 1930s inventions in color negative and transparency film caused experienced photographers to rediscover light in ways Windisch and others detailed, an energizing symbiosis of medium-format image making and female sexuality caused many American photographers to rediscover the Rolleiflex as the conjurer of visual fantasy.

13 Chrome

In the mid-1960s, Eastman Kodak advertised its aluminum, collapsible S-10 as a psychedelic camera intended for young women. I carried one everywhere in college and aimed it only at women.

IN THE LATE SPRING OF 1972, IN THE EARLY AFTER-
noon when the moist air caused the slanting sunlight to turn golden,
I found the near-perfect nereid wading a few yards ahead of my boat.
Relaxed among chartreuse marsh grass and wearing a chartreuse bikini,
she smiled at me and suggested the time had come for me to point the
Rolleiflex toward her. At age twenty-three I recognized the opportunity:
a woman my age, confident and happy in the marshes we both loved,
drenched in yellow light and wearing a bikini matching the color of the
grass. She made the marsh surround her, and seemed to radiate light and
some indescribable force too. The light bouncing up from the shallow
water below her knees made her seem to float among the marsh grass
hiding her feet submerged in black mud. She posed confidently, with
abandon.

And the Eastman Kodak color transparency and negative film registered the chartreuse as a sickly, chemical-spill yellow or olive drab: the
marsh materialized on film as a hazardous waste site and the bikini as
faded and splotched. The photography store proprietor telephoned his
specialist processor at once, then handed me the phone. A bored, technical voice informed me that Kodak color film registered chartreuse
poorly. The processing plant could do nothing about the transparencies,
but offered to correct prints made from the negatives so long as I submitted a swatch of material. I replied that the bikini existed as little more
than a swatch, and vowed to never again photograph a model wearing
chartreuse.[1] The bikinied woman belonged in the salt-marsh creek at the
head of the bay, and so did I, my boat, and my medium-format camera.
But perhaps color film did not. Later the nereid scowled at the images,
heard my film chemistry explanation derived from Eastman Kodak Company technical leaflet E-73, then smiled and suggested we try underwater
photography. She would wear a black bikini, and surely I could photograph that in a way transcending fashion-magazine imagery.

I did not own (and still do not own) a Franke and Heidecke Rolleimarin unit, the sealed housing that enables a diver to take a Rolleiflex
under water. But I knew that such imagery fixed the attention of many
young women, especially those casually confident in very brief suits, not
only on beaches and in boats but in the water. Hans Hass invented the
Rolleimarin around 1946 to facilitate his marine biology work. By the
early 1950s professional fashion photographers knew it as a reliable if
astronomically expensive Franke and Heidecke accessory enabling image
making beyond the reach of all but the most determined well-off enthusi-

ast photographers.[2] Hass's books demonstrated that color film registered differently below the surface, especially in sunny shallows, that water foreshortened distance, and other technical issues new to most photographers.[3] The postwar woman confident in scanty attire and swimming with abandon morphed into a nereid in the habitat Hass and other marine biologists explored: she became a new creature, or at least one newly discovered, one somehow superior to the dune-jumping girls Lohse photographed.[4] Owners of 35 mm cameras disliked the Rolleimarin. It reinforced the role of the Rolleiflex as the facilitator of glamour and catapulted the bulky, square-format camera into a new era charged with physicality and sexuality, both emblemized by bikinied woman, especially those at home in the sea.

Rolleiflex owners knew Hass and his experiments early. Only a year after his first book on photographing Caribbean coral and sharks appeared in 1941, Walter Heering published his underwater-photography technical manual.[5] By then Hass had joined an elite German army underwater unit, where he began developing what became the Rolleimarin immediately following the war. Franke and Heidecke emphasized the accessory as soon as the firm began manufacturing cameras again; it became an icon demonstrating technical mastery, wealth, and welcome for a new woman. After the wartime hiatus, company advertising (especially flyers distributed in photography stores), the magazine *Rolleigrafie,* and technical manuals acquainted American Rolleiflex photographers not only with the Rolleikin but with the radiance characterizing bikinied women.

In 2001 Humberto Fontova recalled his experimental attempts at diving with aqualung equipment under the offshore oil rigs in the Gulf of Mexico. Among the first divers in the United States to test the self-contained underwater breathing apparatus (SCUBA) invented by Jacques Cousteau for the German navy in World War II, Fontova embraced half-known risks in June 1952.[6] Just using the breathing gear taxed his skill. Spear fishing proved dangerous, and he and his friends began diving in football helmets and shoulder pads to reduce injuries from collisions with barnacle-encrusted oil rig pilings. Fontova recalled the day they speared their first fish because they surfaced to see "women in a new bathing suit called a 'bikini'" watching them from the deck of a large pleasure boat. "We liked to go nuts," remembered one of Fontova's dive buddies. "They were wearing these two-piece bathing suits! And it was unbelievable— their navels were showing. To us it almost seemed like they were naked. Remember this was 1952. No *Playboy* or anything."

The opening pages of Fontova's *Helldivers' Rodeo* juxtapose men wearing extremely brief, navel-displaying bikini-like suits and novel technological equipment (including football gear), and women wearing even more exiguous swimsuits. The women seem new creatures, totally relaxed aboard a boat carrying no men and utterly confident in both their tiny suits and in their abilities: when one diver cut himself, the women smoothly ran their boat alongside and provided expert first aid. *Helldivers' Rodeo* epitomizes a new genre of books written by men and women who pioneered underwater exploration fifty years ago employing shop-theory innovations like wearing football helmets underwater and building underwater camera housings.[7] The genre proves a treasure trove of facts and photographs still drifting beyond mainstream critical analysis, but offers one portal on the role of underwater photography in shaping the glamour photography emerging from fashion imagery.[8]

Fontova's book describes Jacques Cousteau visiting New Orleans in 1957 to support one of his most successful equipment retailers, a sporting-goods store on Canal Street. There Cousteau ran a workshop devoted to spearing fish efficiently.[9] Beyond its straightforward retrospective look at early scuba diving and the efforts of Cousteau and Hass to encourage spear fishing and undersea photography in America, *Helldivers' Rodeo* records the collision of upper-middle-class, envelope-pushing bikinied women and working-class men pushing a technological envelope.[10]

Bikinis represented a new demarcation grounded in class and modernity, but only rarely did postwar writers confront the class implications. In *The Wind Off the Island*, a 1960 yachting narrative, Ernle Bradford recorded the impact of British bikinis on Sardinian fishermen. A group of vacationing London ballerinas ran happily into the sea, returned to sunbathe, and scandalized and stupefied men who refused to speak with the women trying to make conversation. "None of the fishermen had ever seen women displaying themselves like that before. Even the married ones, most likely, had never seen their wives naked," Bradford concluded. "It was probably the first occasion that any of them had ever seen a bare female belly and navel in their lives."[11] Bradford meditated a bit on the incident. He and his wife realized that men who still feared the possibility that blue-eyed people might put the evil eye on their children distrusted the bikini as a constituent of glammyre. Bradford admitted that offshore they sailed their ten-ton sloop nude, and that the British yachting fraternity accepted nudity and scanty attire in ways alien to Italian fishermen and other uneducated and poor people and scarcely known to middle-class readers. The bikinis worn by the ballerinas involved Bradford in meditations about spectacle, performance, and above all, power: he understood them as more modern in some ways than the easygoing British nudity afloat. He knew the bikini symbolized the French Riviera reborn after war, and the bikinied woman represented an evolution of glamour.

Late 1940s Mediterranean yachting narratives confirm Bradford's hypothesis. In his 1948 *Isabel and the Sea,* George Millar noted that he and his wife sailed their ketch and swam nude in 1946 and worried only that new bikinis might fall off in the water. He thought the scanty, strapless suits originated in Bandol.[12] The so-called bandeau bikini may take its name from that resort town, but is still spelled phonetically in English. It did not alarm yachtsmen cruising fifteen years before the Bradfords.

The two-piece suits extolled after 1946 by Riviera publicists quickly erased the postwar malaise of the resort. "Instead of dying, the bikini merely shrank," remarked French American journalist Geoffrey Bocca in 1960 in *Bikini Beach; the Wicked Riviera—as It Was and Is.* "On the mine-swept and tank-trapped Riviera, the brown and almost-naked girls accumulated, and the Riviera, stimulated, seemed somehow to stir and revive." At Saint-Tropez appeared bikini tops "wired below rather than over the breast and held up by two loose shoulder straps, permitting the nipple to peep over the top." Throughout the late 1940s and well into the 1950s, such suits horrified low- and middle-class American women and the magazines that catered to them, Bocca snickered. Even in 1960 such women recoiled when confronted by images of bikini-wearing women.[13] The bikini was actually a prewar invention that first reappeared along the southern New England, Louisiana, and Texas coasts well before it triumphed in California and elsewhere.[14] To many 1960s readers of Franke and Heidecke literature and other Rolleiflex-oriented material, the bikini presaged a new era of nudity.

"The nude figure is no longer a matter of speculation, but one of the facts of life," remarked Ica Vilander in a 1969 feature *Rolleigrafie* article. "It is a new situation in our present age." Vilander had already published one book, *Akt Apart,* when the magazine profiled her work. Sometimes concentrating on figure studies and sometimes working in advertising, she emphasized nudes. Much of her work originated in advertising contracts, especially for jewelry. "A picture is an impression of one's own thinking," she explained, and she centered her efforts on "attractive eroticism as an eye-catcher to turn attention to the product." Already featured in a collection entitled *Nudes 69,* her work emphasizing nude men playing on beaches appeared a year later as a book entitled *Akt Adonis.* The editors of *Rolleigrafie* emphasized that her advertising work was almost entirely for women readers and formed only a part of her larger effort to "overcome the equivocalness of a naked body" in sexually liberating ways.[15] *Rolleigrafie* was a part of that effort.

In "White Slavery: Sex times Sex," the magazine profiled Eric Bach, a young, successful advertising photographer who insisted that "pure art in photography does not sell well." In 1969 the twenty-seven-year-old photographer had been freelancing for three years. He owned two studios (one set up only for portraits) and a darkroom fitted for both color and monochrome processing, and he employed three assistants. *Rolleigrafie* followed him through a day of shooting, noting that Bach had begun using his own sailboat as a prop for advertising commissions. "In the meantime, the model has got 'dressed'—micro-bikini, loose mane of red hair," the editors note. "Work can begin. First, bikini shots—the girl in the cabin, at the wheel, in the bows—the goods for countries that prefer veiled sex." Then the model removes the bikini top, and Bach repeats most of the poses; by late in the morning she is nude, posing on a beach thronged with slightly curious nude sunbathers. Bach uses Rolleiflex cameras in a wholly modern, global enterprise: "He produces series of pictures in numerous variations, consistently adapted to the market in question. For Japan very nude, for Brazil very buttoned up."

Rolleigrafie takes neither an aesthetic nor a moral stance, but traces the technical permutations of a photographer alert to global cultural preferences dictating how popular media depict the scantily clad or nude female form. The editors make clear that the nude model poses on a beach where ordinary Germans enjoy themselves sans clothes: clothing, not total lack of it, accentuates Bach's imagery. They assume *Rolleigrafie* readers around the world understand that clothing often makes for a more sexually charged image than skin alone. Like so many other articles in *Rolleigrafie,* the profile of Eric Bach emphasizes how a Rolleiflex-using photographer succeeds: it makes no value judgments other than photographic ones. But it and the Vilander profile advance a subtle agenda evident since the 1950s. They emphasize that the Rolleiflex owner, like the profiled professional photographers, thinks more independently and less parochially than other photographers. *Rolleigrafie* advances an upper-class vision of power, especially of glamour, rather than the vision of Hollywood, television, and 35 mm camera manufacturers.

Dedicated advertising proved successful for Franke and Heidecke after 1935. Walther Heering did wonders with his *Rollei Photography,* but succeeded beyond words with his 1936 *Golden Book of the Rolleiflex,* a square-format folio of superb images, all made with Rolleiflexes. A year earlier, the firm had sponsored a Europe-wide photography competition, and the folio showcased the winning entries. It showcased too the Franke and Heidecke factory, in multiple images emphasizing the technical wonders-to-come depicted on corporate drawing boards. The many competition images, most made by amateurs, demonstrate above all the capacity of the Rolleiflex to make exquisite images, often under poor conditions, especially in low light and in rain or mountain mist. "While the handling and technique of the camera may be learnt from instructions and descriptions, the laws of designing, the choice of motif and the mastering of the line can only be gleaned by the eye from a comprehensive series of model snaps," Heering argued. "That was the basic idea, and from it arose this publication as a textbook of the motif, as an Advanced Schooling of the Eye." Heering sifted through tens of thousands of anonymous entries to create what he called an "imposing review." If nothing else, the folio demonstrated that amateurs could make very arresting images indeed. "It cannot be said to advertise a camera—it is rather the other way about, as it was indeed the Rolleiflex which made this magnificent collection possible," he concluded disingenuously. *The Golden Book of the Rolleiflex* of course advertised the camera, and especially the relative ease with which it enabled users to compose images, to have the opportunity of visual construction.[16] The range of subjects, from dancers to sailing vessels to speeding cars to peasant faces to stainless-steel boilers, in the end scarcely interested Heering. Composition mattered—and technical accomplishment. *The Golden Book of the Rolleiflex* is not shop theory made manifest, but something akin to shop theory–technical accomplishment and compositional design involving one type of camera that did especially well with full-figure portraits.[17]

International acclaim prompted the firm to inaugurate *Photography with Rolleiflex and Rolleicord,* a quarterly magazine mixing technical explanation with superb images, albeit ones typically made by professionals. The magazine provided up-to-date information in ways book authors could not. It emphasized using new film, especially color film, in both traditional and novel approaches—in "Colour Photography with the Rollei Camera" Hans Windisch stated bluntly that "colour photography is a half-way house and tends at the moment to lack style: it is neither one thing nor the other, a new land without landmarks"—and it explained even the most modest of Rolleiflex camera innovations.[18] While much of the information is technical—articles elucidated how to conserve pricey color film by knowing the perfect portrait moment when it appeared on the ground-glass screen and how to combine flood lights with expensive flash bulbs when photographing dancers—its main thrust involved publishing superb images as models.[19] Landscapes, dogs, and even cacti figured in many images, in part to make the magazine appeal to Franke and Heidecke customers around the world, but most full-page reproductions featured portraits, often full-figure ones or one in which people form the foreground of landscapes. In the summer of 1939 the magazine announced another competition, this time global in scale, and in "How to Win Prizes" bluntly told amateurs to learn from prizewinning photographs published in the magazine and elsewhere. "It is not only originality of subject that counts, but also perfection of technique," one editor insisted. In the back pages, readers learned that perfection of technique might be helped along by products advertised by firms other than Franke and Heidecke. For example, the June issue carried an announcement of Windisch's *New Photo-School* and a half-page advertisement, emphasizing a miniskirted woman slouched in a tiny sports car, for Agfa film.

The editors also thought that entrants ought to know the qualifications of the judges, and *Photography with the Rolleiflex and Rolleicord* profiled the seven judges, each of whom had a reputation for "definite views on photography," and each of whom had won awards, always for images made with Rolleiflexes. The contest would produce a folio, tentatively entitled *The Magic of Light,* which would reinforce the power of *The Golden Book of the Rolleiflex.* The editors expected tens of thousands of entries, including thousands of color transparencies, each of which they dictated should be mounted in glass and packed to arrive undamaged.

In 1951 Franke and Heidecke published the first *Rollei Annual,* reproducing Rolleiflex-made images chosen in a global competition organized the previous year and accompanied by sophisticated, up-to-date, and lengthy back-matter articles on Rolleiflex technical innovations and issues, especially film chemistry.[20] The photographs reproduced in the first annual owe much more to the prewar quarterly than they do to *The Golden Book of the Rolleiflex.* Only a handful, especially Fritz Henle's untitled shot of two women in abbreviated swimsuits on a tropical beach, demonstrate a marked postwar modernity.[21] Introductory front matter deals with matters of composition, especially issues of foreground in landscape shots, in ways that generally follow the outlines Cornish established: it makes definite that the Rolleiflex is no minicam, but instead a "medikam."[22] It emphasizes the view through the Rolleiflex camera, and especially the role of the ground-glass screen gridded in a way directly evolved from the Renaissance "rule of thirds" composition system favored by Old Master painters.

The editors of the 1952 *Rollei Annual* stress that in most of the reproduced photographs "the main point of interest in each photo (lines and planes of the main motif) has been pushed aside from the middle of the format, near to the second line of the grid." Only the Rolleiflex owner, or someone lucky enough to borrow a Rolleiflex and experiment with seeing through the gridded glass, might understand the composition of the reproduced images. "The engraving on the screen has not been done by chance, but with reason," the editors insist. "We ought to always train ourselves to 'read' illustrated volumes in this way."[23] Sustained effort to read any volume of prizewinning photographs would produce some awareness of the painting-derived composition rules that govern most prizewinning photographs made with any camera, and would reinforce Rolleiflex owners in their decision to use a square-format camera featuring a viewing glass that made the rules obvious and somewhat easy to follow.

Sustained scrutiny also produced an understanding that even in the tense Cold War years photography often produces images of serenity. "Surely and certainly the old world begins to loose its nerves," one editor concludes, "but the unrest of the times has not yet been felt in photography." Indirectly, the *Rollei Annual* editors recognize that in 1950 and 1951 the bulk of entrants were older, if not middle-aged at least not extremely young, and if in their late twenties, often seeking postdischarge serenity; they may well have been guided by the images that won prewar contests. The bulk of winning entries published in the first two annuals resemble those published in *The Golden Book of the Rolleiflex* and in the subsequent quarterly magazine issues. "The traditional characteristics of Rollei-photography have been preserved—that vivid plasticity and the technical quality of the photo, in which the twin-lens Rollei has gained a key position," Carlheinz Albrand concluded. He and other editors worried that "it is a pity that experimenters with the Rollei modestly kept aside" and mused that too few photographers submitted images graced by "a cool objectivity" that had begun to transform advertising imagery. "This illustrated work is to stimulate Rollei activity: this being its most urgent task and aim," Albrand asserted simply.[24] He and his colleagues wanted what the firm knew it must have: images made by younger Rollei users that would make the camera the favorite of a rising generation of professionals and expert amateurs. Franke and Heidecke appear to have glimpsed, then fastened on the glamour of the bikinied or nude woman as the perfect way to connect very young photographers with the Rolleiflex.

The 1953 *Rollei Annual* was transformed from its predecessors. It offered many images in color, including a cover photograph of a woman posed on a ski slope in a fashion magazine, casual stance. The winner of the third prize "is an example of the recently discovered photographic style often described as 'the camera released from chains,'" wrote Albrand, and many of the images depict the coolness lacking a year earlier.[25] One image of the eighty reproduced depicts two bikinied women sunbathing, most definitely displaying navels, and another is a full-figure portrait of a formally gowned young woman posed against a floor-length mirror. Several others depict formally attired young people in sophisticated poses, all decidedly cool.[26] A quiet revolution had stirred the editors of the annuals and apparently the entrants too: suddenly many of the featured images by young photographers depicted young women utterly modern and well-to-do.[27] The next year the annuals began to specialize, the 1954 focusing on outdoor portraits, the next on artificial light, and so on. Having accomplished its first postwar aim, that of rebuilding the place of the Rolleiflex in world markets, the firm moved toward advertising the Rolleiflex as the camera for an elite devoted to something other than mass-media, 35 mm camera imagery and middle-brow aesthetics, including morality-based aesthetics, and thus devoted to something other than cinema and television too. In 1953 Franke and Heidecke no longer needed the expense of operating worldwide photography contests. The firm merely piggybacked on the work of others showcasing contemporary postwar photography, especially that sort *Rollei Annual* editors identified as cool.

It and its United States distributors instantly recognized the power of *Photography Annual,* the flagship publication of *Popular Photography* that debuted in 1951.[28] The annual featured short technical articles aimed at neophyte and moderately advanced amateur photographers, especially those struggling to make better than snapshot-quality images, but showcased prizewinning images selected by the editors of *Popular Photography* from competitions around the world and those submitted for publication in the magazine. Chapters entitled "The Versatile Lens," "Pictures after Dark," and "The Camera Indoors" opened with brief essays followed by many images, most reproduced full size on 8×11–inch pages. "The pictures in this section provide interesting examples of the use of special purpose lenses which add still another dimension to photographic control," concludes "The Versatile Lens" before a run of seven images ranging from a close-up of Gutenberg Bible text to an aerial view of a boat under full sail. The annuals existed to sell advertising: from the first they ran many pages touting all sorts of film, and almost as many advertising cameras, and the last pages featured a host of tiny advertisements ranging from darkroom equipment to light meters. In 1952 Burleigh Brooks bought page 9 for a full-page Rolleiflex ad directing readers to note that "in the photo publication, the annuals, the news magazines or wherever else the outstanding work of the leaders is shown, credit-line after credit-line reads *picture by Rollei.*[29] The distributor of Rolleiflex cameras exploited a *Photography Annual* editorial quirk that dramatically advanced sales of its cameras. From the early 1950s onward,

Rolleiflex owners won a disproportionate share of prizes in *Photography Annual* and its competitors, in part because Franke and Heidecke alerted Rolleiflex photographers to emerging, very powerful subjects and composition aesthetics. The Rolleiflex viewfinder grid not only facilitated a very steep learning curve but enabled thoughtful Rolleiflex photographers to create images ahead of the mainstream curve.

The Ziff-Davis Publishing Company intended its annuals as educational. The back pages of every issue carried a brief technical description of each reproduced photograph. Thus Peter Gowland's *Modern Mermaid,* an image of a brief-suited woman tugging on seaweed in the shallows of a Pacific Ocean beach, appeared as a complete work on one page of the chapter entitled "Putting the Sun to Work" in the 1952 annual. Two hundred pages later, the thoughtful photographer learned not only where Gowland lived and the name of the beach, but that he used a Rolleiflex "with a 75mm. lens and Kodak Super-XX film," that "the sun was bright, and the sea acted as a reflector, illuminating the shadows," and that exposure was 1/250 second at f/8. The brief technical synopsis concluded with a caution: "A natural or artificial reflector, if not a supplementary light source, is often necessary to avoid excessive contrast when shooting under a very bright sun."[30] In "Focusing," the 1952 annual reproduced another Gowland Rolleiflex-made image, *Nude at Noon,* of a woman sitting on a California beach, and again cautioned the reader to understand that Gowland placed his model so that the sunlight reflected upward from the sand. Moreover, "by keeping his depth of field shallow, he played down the background, particularly the horizon line, which, if sharp, might easily have arrested the viewer's eye from the center of interest in the scene."[31] Burleigh Brooks merely noted what becomes evident from reading the technical notes: a great many photographers used Rolleiflexes, and almost all photographers making full-figure portraits.

From its inception, *Photography Annual* featured decorous nude or nearly nude women on its color covers, and at least a handful of full-color reproductions inside, some depicting nude women. In its first years, the images were pictorialist, almost staid, what most photographers knew as "arty" in art school ways. By 1953 the editors recognized that Europeans had begun swimming and sunbathing nude, and that a cohort of educated, rural, often wealthy American families had been experimenting with private nudity since before the war. While they sometimes reproduced images of nude American women enjoying beaches, they tended to avoid the subject, apparently because the images seemed too akin to the voyeuristic ones appearing in downscale girlie magazines.[32] But they easily accepted close-up, low-level shots of men wearing very brief suits that outlined their genitals.[33] Anthony Lick's crotch-level shot of a waterskiing champion, made with a Rolleiflex, represents a broad acceptance of the human form: frontal nudity still could not move through the United States Post Office, but it had appeared at the edges of American-made, Rolleiflex-based photography.[34]

Nudity, especially female nudity on isolated beaches, grew increasingly important in the mid-1950s annuals, but always associated with wealth, education, and privacy, and with glamour. The 1954 annual featured a nude woman (wearing a broad-brimmed straw hat) sunbathing at the edge of sand dunes. Such images differed from those depicting brief-suited women gamboling in surf, and from very cool studio images, usually European, of nude women juxtaposed against mirrors or reclining on newspapers. They differed too from candid images, usually made with 35 mm cameras, of showgirls and other stage performers.[35]

By 1955 studio nudes had begun to supplant beach nudes, although Rolleiflex-made images of brief-suited women playing on beaches continued to illustrate "Shutter Speed" and other chapters directing attention at stop-motion imagery. Andre De Dienes's *Exuberance* demonstrated not only a Rolleiflex operating at 1/500 second and f/8, but how lighting on a Cape Cod beach differed from that on California beaches.[36] Lighting the nude preoccupied annual editors from 1956 on. While a handful of the images depict women nude on beaches, and young and adolescent children nude on beaches and elsewhere outdoors, the editors emphasized nudes photographed indoors, usually in the most modern of spaces. Full-figure studio portraits produced multiple lighting problems, but since the editors saw them shaping the core of indoor glamour photography, the annuals devoted more and more attention to them. "Glamour: Figures . . . Faces . . . Fashions," a chapter in the 1956 annual, distinguished between fashion advertising—in which the woman wore something, presumably created by a manufacturer and offered for sale—and glamour photography, in which the nude or nearly nude woman worked a power of her own, one the editors distinguished from cheesecake, which they depicted too.[37] Throughout the late 1950s, the editors of *Photography Annual* sharpened the distinctions they developed around 1955, understanding that some women behaved nude naturally on beaches and deserved accurate rendering in photographs, that the nude formed a major component of studio full-figure portraiture, and that scantily clad women had emerged as a driving force both in cutting-edge fashion photography and in a range of genres shoving hard at code-restricted Hollywood cinema and television.

Studio nudes and nude or bikinied women on beaches were subjects totally different from strippers ordinarily photographed through tobacco smoke.[38] As subjects, they represented a new appreciation of the healthy female body paralleling a less developed but intensifying appreciation of the male body. The 1958 *Photography Annual* demonstrated that female and male bodies of all ages demanded attention and respect, and that such attention and respect evolved from very recent cultural changes.[39] Editors struggled to delineate vexing issues of class, education, and power: people casually nude outdoors, especially in largely private places, challenged mores and aesthetics grounded in strip-club behavior. And no longer could American photography magazines and annuals ignore the force of European thinking, especially as Franke and Heidecke reflected it in advertising aimed at advanced, determined, well-to-do photographers who could afford both Rolleiflexes and color photography.

Color film challenged *Photography Annual* editors in the middle 1950s, awakening concerns dating to the late 1920s. "One of the few drawbacks of air-photography is its failure to register colors," Osbert Crawford and Alexander Keiller cautioned readers of *Wessex from the Air.* "As seen from the air the ground in summer appears clothed in many beautiful colors, olive green and yellowish, brown, both tinged with a suspicion of blue, prevailing." Readers of their monochrome folio missed something that struck photographers aloft. "The faint dark ring was caused by poppies and actually appeared as a semicircle of brilliant scarlet, sharply outlined against the bright yellow of a field of oats," they continued. "That is the essential archaeological fact of the photograph, and of the preceding observation which it records. The inference is that the scarlet circle depicts the outline of a vanished hill-fort."[40] Watkins never worried in print about the lack of color in his photographs, but by 1928 Crawford and Keiller recognized that while monochrome imagery conveyed the shadows of the past, the public longed for color photographs. At least sometimes, it wanted to see the red of the poppies. It waited decades.

In the 1950s black-and-white photographs still distanced viewers from subjects, and at least some subjects from awkward aesthetic and social issues. Reproducing black-and-white images of nudes, or even women wearing exiguous suits, struck the editors as far less challenging than reproducing full-color images. Money could solve the technical problems inherent in reproducing full-color images, but not the sensitive issues centered on too-lifelike photographs. In 1957 Ziff-Davis introduced its *Popular Photography Color Annual,* again partly as an advertising vehicle intended to entice manufacturers of cameras and color film but largely as a way of avoiding growing friction between photographers devoted to monochrome as the best medium for creating superb images of fraught subjects and younger innovators fascinated with color and impatient with constraints they dismissed as prudish, downscale, and old-fashioned.

Burleigh Brooks purchased a full-page ad in the first pages of the new annual, emphasizing that the Rolleiflex produced three sizes of color transparencies, massive 2¼ by 2¼ ones, and both its proprietary "Super Size" square-format slides projected by ordinary 35 mm slide projectors and ordinary 35 mm slides made in Rolleiflex cameras momentarily fitted with Rolleikin attachments carrying 35 mm slide film over different-shaped masks. The advertisement reproduced the slides full size, hinting at the slamming power of the medium-format images projected by Franke and Heidecke projectors.[41] No professional photographer doubted the ability of the Rolleiflex to make superb color images: fashion and glamour photographers preferred it above all others. But the greater expenses involved in color photography produced marketing headaches; many photographers chose to spend much more money on film and professional processing rather than buy new cameras. What masqueraded as debate concerning aesthetics really pulsed as marketing and economic issues shoving editors into class division nastiness involving Technicolor motion pictures, full-color magazine advertising, and the specter of color television.[42]

Much of the problem involved full-figure photography, especially that involving fashion, glamour, and nudity, especially when photographers made medium-format transparencies and projected them at gigantic scale. A black-and-white print of a nude woman struck many viewers as wholly manageable, and an otherwise identical color print as a bit too flagrantly literal, but a wall-size color transparency unnerved too many observers accustomed to Hollywood prudishness.[43]

"To the conditioned consciousness the camera's nudes come often as a shock. The model too often appears as no more than a naked woman standing self-consciously before the merciless lens," conceded Bruce Downes, one of the editors of *Popular Photography Color Annual,* in a long article juxtaposing photographic nudes against ones in period painting. "Unlike the painter who can work and rework the image, the photographer must perforce produce *his* image instantaneously. For a successful picture everything must be 'right' at the moment of exposure. There must be uninhibited rapport between the photographer and model; pose, lighting, attitude, and expression must be 'right.'"[44] By 1957 too many viewers of photographs had become conditioned to black-and-white images as standard representations of the reality in front of the camera lens.[45] They often unthinkingly accepted that "there should be an ideal placement of in-focus and out-of-focus planes," but they understood almost nothing about color processing chemistry. "If color is involved, the exposure should be controlled to achieve the degree of brilliance and saturation that will best suit the mood of the picture."[46]

Photography magazine editors understood the frustrations color film produced among beginners, advanced enthusiasts, and many successful professionals confronting demanding clients: they reoriented *Popular Photography* and other mass-market magazines to address them. But they feared the confusion color photography produced among different segments of the American population, and especially the chaotic mixing of painting, World War II and pinup cheesecake drawings, and racy, raunchy, and even pornographic imagery reshaping male-oriented pulp magazines stunned by the appearance of *Playboy* in 1953 and especially its full-color centerfolds. They worried that color photography might quickly plunge downscale, especially if conservative, well-to-do people realized its chemistry might prove far less stable over decades than black-and-white.[47] They were concerned too that many Americans would connect bikinis, nudity, and color film with racial and sexual-orientation issues beginning to freeze public discussion. Always at their back the editors felt the financial muscle of film manufacturers anxious to sell cinema film to Hollywood and similar film to photographers.[48]

Advertising revenue and technical innovation let Eastman Kodak, Dupont, Agfa, and other manufacturers of photographic materials govern the content of all American photographic periodicals after the early 1920s. In the long run, technical innovation proved more coercive than money spent on advertising, since readers demanded articles about new film and other novelties manufacturers advertised. While Eastman Kodak published its own in-house magazine, *Kodakery*, for decades after 1905, it and most other firms relied on magazine advertising and in-house brochures and brooklets distributed gratis or at low cost, usually in camera stores but always available by mail order, to advertise individual products and groups of related products. An educational force all too often ignored in histories of twentieth-century American life and nonschool technological and aesthetic learning, and even in histories of photography as art, the magazine advertisements, brochures, and booklets grew critically important in the last years of the 1930s, and again in the middle 1950s, as film manufacturers asserted and reasserted the primacy of color film and attendant chemistries as fundamentally modern.[49]

In 1935 Eastman Kodak introduced Kodachrome, the first color transparency film. Overnight it shifted color photography from the experimental to the commercial stage. In fits and starts thereafter, the company introduced other color film products. In 1941 it began selling Kodacolor, a color-print negative film, and in 1946 Ektachrome, the first color transparency film expert amateurs could process at home. Kodachrome II, a transparency film with greater exposure latitude and a speed raised from ISO 10 to ISO 25, debuted only in 1961. At the beginning of the 1960s Eastman Kodak struggled to market color film to snapshot photographers and many amateurs not only pleased with its black-and-white films but confident in their use. Many professional photographers remained committed to black-and-white film, especially if their clients preferred monochrome images, but particularly to keep down reproduction costs. From the late 1930s through the middle 1960s, film manufacturers consequently produced two overlapping sets of literature, unless they went out of business in the face of Eastman Kodak competition.

Better Photography Made Easy, a 1938 Agfa Ansco Corporation booklet, represents the older set: it emphasizes "taking *better* pictures" largely by understanding light, filters, and film. It supposes readers using box cameras or folding cameras, but not 35mm or sophisticated medium-format ones. It advertises Agfa film subtly, identifying each image by exposure, shutter speed, filter (if any), and film type. Readers discover differences between Agfa Superpan (especially useful for landscapes and beach subjects) and Agfa Infrared (useful for harbor shots of steamships and other vacation subjects), among other types. While Eastman Kodak produced a plethora of such books after 1900—one series alone, entitled *How to Make Good Pictures,* passed through perhaps thirty versions by 1960—it also produced a series entitled *Kodak Films,* which after 1935 carried different titles; by 1943 it appeared as *Data Book on Black-and-White Kodak Films.*[50]

Kodak Films existed for the expert photographer, "the photographic craftsman who desires more than a superficial knowledge of negative materials," not beginners or even devoted box camera amateurs. It cataloged the entire Eastman Kodak line of films and described each in painstaking detail, from the ISO 50 Verichrome to the new Super Panchro-Press, Sports Type with an ISO of 250, according to prospective uses. Each description carried charts illustrating the color sensitivity of each black-and-white film. In 1943 readers learned that Verichrome had a high sensitivity to blues and greens but essentially none to red, which it rendered as black, and that it had been developed especially for "beach, marine, and snow scenes," and especially for people in such settings.[51] In subsequent editions, in 1945, 1947, 1951, and 1952, readers learned of innovations, and the changing relations of one film type to another: by 1952 the firm recommended Super XX-Panchromatic film too for people in marine and beach scenes, noting that it had much greater sensitivity to reds.[52]

In that year Dupont produced a new edition of its *Photographic Films,* with charts similar to those Eastman Kodak used, but with more attention to rendering skin. It emphasized that its X-F Ortho film "is particularly suited for portraiture of men where the orthochromatic rendition emphasizes skin texture." It suggested that the photographers choose its X-F Pan or Arrow Pan films when photographing women, since both films minimized the lines X-F Ortho brought out to give "character."[53] Film varied from manufacturer to manufacturer, and competent photographers experimented with different types, especially when photographing men, women, and children outdoors.

Expert, determined photographers followed the arguments Eastman Kodak made over decades in *The Photography of Colored Objects.*[54] A clothbound book emphasizing the differences between sunlight and several types of artificial light, it had passed through fourteen editions by 1938, the year Windisch published *The New Photo-School.* It includes full-color plates illustrating the interaction of colors as they structure photographic chemistry, the impact of filters, and so on, but its chief subject is the photographing of white, black, or gray objects (it illustrates the usefulness of red "A" filters with images of typewritten words on white paper), since they illustrate ways of understanding the photographing of multicolored objects. While the 1938 volume analyzes some issues historically, especially the ways panchromatic cinema film caused Hollywood studios to scrap mercury vapor and arc lights for incandescent bulbs, most of it minutely examines differences between the sensitivity of the human eye and Eastman Kodak films toward light reflected from colored objects. It stresses the changing understanding of photographers toward subjects photographed with new films. But it hammers away at the unwittingly trained consciousness of photograph viewers who no longer recognize that in spring, for example, trees and hedges are often far more brilliantly reflective than grass, and so think a photograph showing hedges lighter than lawns must be "over-developed."

More acutely than most brochures and booklets displayed on camera store counters, *The Photography of Colored Objects* distinguishes the aesthetic and technical structure revolutionized by color film. It is a serious, sophisticated, and authoritative volume directly addressing problems such as those posed by scarlet poppies. "It is convenient to memorize this chart since by means of it the approximate position of the absorption band corresponding to any color can be found," the authors suggest early on. At some point, any photographer might encounter a woman in a lemon-yellow dress standing under a light-blue sky against a magenta wall, and memorizing the chart of residual colors made by the bands might cause him to suggest she move to another backdrop.[55] In terms that mimicked the framework Von Reichenbach had created, some photographers turned out to be far more sensitive than most.[56] Some people wore clothing that seemed to radiate light (or Od or some other force) that befuddled color film chemistry. Others noticed color inconsistencies and variations most viewers ignored.

Innovation in film capability necessarily forced photographers to see differently as they attempted to predict how new film types functioned in certain lighting and with certain subjects.[57] A book bound in scarlet would appear bound in black when viewed under mercury vapor light, which produces no red wavelength light for it to reflect. Eastman Kodak recommended that given the changes transforming cinema, a prudent photographer "should form the habit of considering a red object, not as one that reflects red, but as one that absorbs blue-violet and green." *The Photography of Colored Objects* consequently investigated issues of photo reproduction originating in the juxtaposition of colors in the subject composition as seen by both the photographer and the viewer of the final image. Some emulsions might cause a man in a blue jacket to merge almost seamlessly into the green hedge against which he stood for his full-figure portrait. Others might cause a pale-skinned woman wearing a light-pastel and very brief swimsuit to appear nude in the negative, and almost certainly in the print. Black-and-white films offered few such vexations.

In 1938 Eastman Kodak knew that the burgeoning fascination with antique furniture made many photographers eager to learn why using a panchromatic film with an orange or red filter produced photographs in which furniture appeared without scratches but with pronounced grain. "So startling is the difference, that probably many readers might think that the example is faked," the authors noted, "but if they try the experiment they will get similar results."[58] In the end, the technical treatise offers extremely detailed information, but suggests as well a shop-theory approach involving photographing both black and purple typewritten words on white paper. Eventually a photographer might train himself to see light so acutely that he understood that the fall of light on colored subjects demanded a particular type of film, and probably a specific filter as well. Experimentation sold film, of course, but it often produced satisfied photographers whose work, even amateur work passed around to friends or coworkers, elicited both praise and greater sales for film manufacturers. Until the late 1930s, the conscious eye of the photographer, trained by camera manufacturer manuals and general books, understood color as something on the far side of the camera lens and typically not critically important.[59]

After the 1935 mass production of color film, everything changed, but the enduring stringencies of the Depression combined with World War II shortages caused the initial change period to last into the early 1950s.[60] As early as 1937, when Clifford A. Nelson published his remarkably perceptive and prescient *Natural Color Film: What It Is and How to Use It: A Work Devoted to the Technique and Handling of "Kodachrome" in Motion Picture and Still Photography*, Eastman Kodak knew it faced marketing challenges. Nelson anticipated many of the challenges, recognizing that most people do not see color very precisely in the first place but are easily insulted when told they do not, and are often infuriated when confronted with tests demonstrating their inabilities. "The peculiar mental reactions to color which vary with individuals and the failure of color memory are far more common than failures of the film to record facts," Herbert C. McKay noted in his introduction to the book.[61] Nonetheless, Kodachrome produced a surfeit of odd effects, many technological, but many more cultural.

Eastman Kodak at first produced Kodachrome only in 35 mm format but in two types, the mainstream one and Type A, to be used only under incandescent light.[62] The film required much more light than most black-and-white films, and did its best work under "a more flat and evenly diffused light," something that perplexed even experienced photographers. Kodak told photographers to choose subjects illuminated by "light falling directly on the front," but the narrow exposure latitude of the film frustrated those who found most exposures either over- or underexposed. Since the film tricked many light meters too, it furthered sales of 35 mm cameras. Photographers loaded with Kodachrome, then, made multiple exposures, bracketing stops widely and hoping for one good image in six or eight. Franke and Heidecke had introduced the Rolleikin accessory at precisely the right moment: Nelson noted that it made the Rolleiflex an extremely useful camera for shooting Kodachrome. But Eastman Kodak could only begin to describe correct shutter speeds and exposure settings for most subjects, which it referred to as "light-colored" and "dark-colored" on the sheets packed with each roll of film.[63] Its booklets perforce avoided what thoughtful, shop-theory-inclined photographers quickly intuited about Hollywood cinematography: studios chose costumes and props, and even backdrops, suited to the new color film, and lighting experts scrapped a whole generation of studio lighting. Away from studios, photographers lacked the luxury of dictating costumes and backgrounds; they had to make do, knowing that color memory varies wildly from one individual to another and that contiguous colors sometimes cause color film to register incorrectly. In many outdoor locations, especially along paths winding through woods and scrub, they found it difficult to find the front-falling light Eastman Kodak preferred.

Color film meshed 35 mm photography and Hollywood cinema. The year 1940 witnessed the publication of a folio, Ivan Dmitri's *Kodachrome and How to Use It*, reproducing 101 images in full color. Simon and Schuster boasted that it "represents the epitome of the photo-engraver's and printer's art," and extolled the technical capacities of its partner, Conde-Nast, the publisher of *Vogue*. In the book Dmitri published both superb photographs and awkward ones, struggling to define the compositional problems produced by clashing and complementary colors. "The reader will notice that the book deals entirely with the use of the miniature camera," he noted in his introduction. "This is so because the miniature is the most flexible and popular of all modern cameras." While he admitted that experienced photographers would have to relearn many rules (overexposure produces lighter colors in Kodachrome, underexposure darker shades, for example), he insisted that the minicam "offers a chance to get pictures in situations where a more bulky camera would probably fail." Part of his partisanship for the minicam originated in a fierce attempt to convince photographers to notice the colors of backgrounds, and to shoot from lower than usual angles, often at very low angles. Much of it derived from an understanding of angles of vision remarkably like those enunciated by Cornish but a bit modernized. According to Dmitri, a person viewing a street scene sees a range of about 48 degrees, the angle of a typical 50 mm lens, and that a much longer focal length lens, about 90 mm is needed for quarter-length portraiture requiring 27-degree arcs. Shots made from airplanes, however, demand lenses between 28 and 35 mm providing about the 65–76 degrees of arc to produce the sensation of airborne spaciousness. Some of his partisanship began too in his understanding that most photographers would project Kodachrome slides in their homes or elsewhere. But the bulk of his support for the minicam originated in simple marketing reality: Eastman Kodak made the film available only in 35 mm format.

Consequently, *Kodachrome and How To Use It* emphasizes four cameras: the Leica, the Contax, and two made by Eastman Kodak—the older Bantam Special and "the new line of Kodak 35's." The book champions 35 mm photography, but also advises readers that the Kodak 35s (three cameras offering three speeds of lenses and priced from $15 to $35) "are especially designed for the convenience of amateurs who work with Kodachrome film."

The dust-jacket image of *Kodachrome and How To Use It,* reproduced toward the end of the volume, featured a blonde woman wearing a very tight-fitting, nearly translucent one-piece white suit and holding a short robe behind her, against the wind. She might be standing atop a dune, or jumping from a low but steep rock: almost the entire background is a navy-blue sky darkened by a polarizing filter. However striking, the image represents more than the Remi Lohse approach to cavorting models; it transcends the limits the Hollywood cinema industry imposed on itself, and indirectly implies a woman in flight. Even today, it perplexes students, only a few of whom quickly realize that its color density, deepened by a two-stop added exposure to compensate for the polarizing filter, means that the model must have been standing still. The photograph, which Dmitri made, complements many others showing women in abbreviated suits, always in very sunny, simple locations and photographed in flat light.

But color film forced new compositional decisions. "To complement the purple-magenta coloring of the bathing suit in this picture the photographer selected the warm brown skin of a well-tanned model," Dmitri wrote of a Tony Frissell image. "This color scheme was carried still further by the choice of the brown lava rocks for the general background and a brown-colored dachshund to add to the story-telling value of the picture. Several exposures were made from which this one was chosen." While images of sunflowers, historic houses in Williamsburg, Virginia, and flowering shrubs exemplify his argument that any sort of angle can produce a quality Kodachrome image, almost all the images of women are shot from very low angles against a background chiefly composed of light-blue sky. "Here is an excellent example of how a full-length figure posed against a simple background was given emphasis by photography from a low angle," he wrote of a yellow-gowned woman standing atop a dune, lifting her overskirt slightly to catch the wind "to give the picture a feeling of movement."[64] The reader eventually realizes the cinematic imperative ordering so many of the images. Although presented as still images, composition caused viewers to interpret them according to cinema aesthetics. Dmitri stressed, as Lohse did at the same moment, the symbiosis of Kodachrome and extremely active women, some so active they appeared to fly.

Screening Kodachrome images produced more than novelties in aesthetic appreciation of massively enlarged photographs. It produced too a sale of slide projectors. The purchaser of a Kodak 35 mm camera quickly discovered the need to acquire a projector and a specially made reflective screen. For a brief time, roughly 1938 and 1939, the Eastman Kodak Company seemed poised to control an entire Kodachrome-based market. But incipient monopoly had already shattered in Germany.

The Rolleiflex Rolleikin adapter rattled Eastman Kodak 35 mm Kodachrome hegemony. It put 35 mm Kodachrome inside a medium-format camera offering a massive ground-glass viewing screen experience. The 1938 debut in Germany of Agfa color transparency medium-format film ended whatever hopes the Rochester firm had for controlling a new film and film products market. War masked the rapid development of German color film technology. American manufacturers knew little of changed aesthetics too. In 1942 Paul Wolff published a folio, *Mein Erfahrungen Farbig,* reproducing fifty-four large-size images made with a Leica 35 mm camera. In it, he pondered many of the issues that perplexed Dmitri.[65] In particular, he worried that black-and-white photographs of nudes, often made with slightly soft-focus lenses, proved far less embarrassing to many viewers than ultrarealistic full-color images. Part of the problem lay in power of fashion magazine imagery: even aesthetes had little experience in judging color images produced outside advertising. "The large color prints of Conde-Nast are among the most beautiful ever produced," Wolff maintained. He attributed this to a distinctly American expertise involving three-lens cameras making three separate negatives simultaneously for the three-color reproduction process. But fashion magazine imagery emphasized models in clothing, and in the end involved advertising illustration, not art.

"We are not prudes and have absolutely nothing against anyone who wants to take outdoor pictures of a girl in a state of more or less undress," Wolff wrote, "but this has nothing to do with 'color art photography.'" Wolff worried about "stale realism" driving public expectation of every color image. Advertising had only begun to prepare the educated public for color photography, and few readers of *Vogue* and other such magazines knew anything of the "maximum effort of highly paid cameramen expended to create studio images giving the impression of outdoor shots, particularly in advertising pictures."[66] Wolff harbored deep reservations about the aesthetic flexibility required to make, accept, and evaluate genuine outdoor color 35 mm images, especially when women wore little or nothing. He understood the color juxtaposition issues that haunted Dmitri; indeed, he chose models with skin and hair color and swimsuits similar to those Dmitri portrayed.

Kodachrome and How to Use It provides a chart organizing Dmitri's thinking about the juxtaposition of clothing, hair color, and skin tone in 35 mm color photography. Emphasizing that light soft colors are "most effective and should be chosen to harmonize with complexion and hair color," it warns against black and very dark colors, but also against colors of such high brilliance that they divert attention from the face. It explains that children should be photographed in very light colors against "white or very light tints." Men wearing brown or tan should be photographed against buff backgrounds, those in gray against dull blue, those in blue against gray or buff, and those wearing white against "any light color harmonizing with the subject's hair." Women presented far more complex issues: the chart notes that women in pink should stand before "gray blue" or "jade green" backdrops, those in blue against yellow or dark blue grounds, and those in yellow against gray blue surfaces: women in gray should stand against dull blue backdrops, in green against lavender or gray surfaces or ones of a darker green than the clothing, and women in white against "any light color harmonizing" with their hair.[67] The chart reveals a bias against photographing almost any clothed person against a backdrop of lawn, hedges, or trees, coniferous or deciduous, and emphasizes the extreme awkwardness of photographing pairs or groups of people attired differently. And while Dmitri notes that Eastman Kodak research underlies his chart, *Photography with Kodachrome Professional Film*, a 1941 corporate guide aimed at professional photographers, insists that men wearing brown, tan, or gray suits should stand before maroon backgrounds, and that maroon made a second-best (after blue but before green) ground for women in gray.[68] Much of what Dmitri counseled had been said by experts working in monochrome: "Finally observe the *color* of the skin in both highlights and shadows," Frank R. Fraprie advised readers of his 1935 *Portrait Lighting by Daylight and Artificial Light*. "Unless you can see the local tint of the sitter's complexion in both, the lighting is too harsh."[69] But Wolff knew that his readers faced a new challenge: color film behaved almost erratically.

Dmitri's chart explains much of Wolff's thinking about differences in the ways color film rendered color. "Generally, the colors of the American films are livelier," Wolff decided of American motion-picture Kodachrome. "One could almost say, more optimistic, fresher, and warmer," something that he concluded reflects the character of the American people or at least their attitude toward life, "gay, animated, and radiant." Agfa-based motion pictures provide something much more subdued and nuanced, which Wolff identifies as distinctly European.[70] Heering seconded Wolff's thinking in a superbly illustrated anthology of essays published in 1943, *Im Zauber der Farbe,* in which Otto Croy and other expert photographers teased out the significance of color film chemistry. In a lengthy chapter entitled "Das Agfacolor-Papierbild," H. G. Wandelt detailed the rationale underlying the more subtle colors of Agfa chemistry aimed at three markets, cinema, transparency, and color photographs; and in "Farbige Bluemenaufnahmen" Wolf H. Döring probed at the oddnesses bedeviling photographers of specific flowers. Heering chose essayists who centered their work on components of the color photography issue. *Im Zauber der Farbe* emphasizes differences confronting nature photographers, especially photographers of flowers, who necessarily confront a range of colors against green backdrops, and portrait photographers, at least of few of whom had discovered that underwater photography might involve low-angle, upward shots that turned water into almost uniformly blue background.[71]

Year after year Eastman Kodak responded to professional photographer frustration by publishing highly specialized shop-theory booklets offering detail technical information and step-by-step procedural advice.[72] Its 1950 *Color Photography in the Studio* emphasized that lighting models for color transparency work demanded an understanding of how spotlights work. Color temperature tended to drop precipitously at the edge of the beam, and some brands of bulbs produced subtly colored fringe illumination: so-called feathering of light, in which the direct beam angled past the subject, thus producing erroneous color on the subject.[73] Projecting transparencies only magnified errors of composition, lighting, and color in ways that irritated even die-hard champions of 35 mm cameras. By 1950 so many photographers projected slides that none could take refuge in Lohse's presentation of negatives enlarged to roughly 8 × 10–inch format.[74] Close-up portraits emphasizing the face so perplexed even professional photographers that Eastman Kodak advised photographers to emphasize the three-quarters or full-figure pose.

The full-figure pose offered immediate advantages. The greater distance of camera from subject led to increased depth of field, which compensated for the larger lens openings most photographers found themselves using with the "chrome" films. Depth of field did not always produce greater sharpness: checkered or herringbone fabrics sometimes appeared blurred, and diffused flesh tones appeared less lifelike than undiffused ones, but the firm insisted that sharpness was generally more desirable in color work than in black-and-white fashion photography. Full-figure poses provided more reliable light-meter readings: Eastman Kodak recognized that too few photographers worried about changes as slight as a ⅓ f-stop. Finally, the full-figure pose eliminated problems caused by the merest movement of the model's head or eyes, problems caused by photographers forced to use slower shutter speeds than they did with black-and-white work. In general, the full-figure pose enabled a careful photographer to arrange artificial lighting—or pose a model perfectly outdoors—in such a way as to "obtain the maximum illusion of depth in the reproduction."[75]

Into the 1960s Eastman Kodak worked to reeducate photographers long experienced in black-and-white image making, accustomed to wide freedom in printing negatives in darkrooms, and often unable to notice the interplay of light and color, especially outdoors. Studio work at least offered the chance to control some color and some lighting, and the firm indirectly urged experienced photographers to begin their reeducation indoors. *Applied Color Photography Indoors* emphasizes, often in italics, what photographers needed to unlearn or learn anew. *"The saturation of a color increases when surface reflections are decreased or removed,"* it counsels in a section warning of the difficulties posed by shiny objects reflecting larger contiguous luminous areas.[76] For more than three decades after it introduced Kodachrome, Eastman Kodak fought a three-front battle: it struggled to educate photographers in the use of its black-and-white films, to reeducate experienced photographers to succeed in color photography (and especially color transparency photography, since the latitude of exposure error was minuscule and so many photographers projected transparencies), and to introduce color photography to young people with no experience in black-and-white photography.[77] While booklets and leaflets, often sold at slight cost in camera stores attempting to nudge snapshooters toward more sophisticated picture making, carried part of the corporate educational burden, trade publishers intermittently issued volumes by Eastman Kodak experts writing as experienced individuals.[78] Often only the most sophisticated trade publications dealt with successes involving photographing women outdoors. If background, costume, and body coloring combined perfectly in ambient light, the woman appeared to radiate the kind of energy Wolff defined as peculiarly American.

In 1959 Wiley and Sons published a massive work by Ralph M. Evans, director of the Kodak Color Technology Division, entitled *Eye, Film, and Camera in Color Photography.* It advanced a novel, even daring idea concerning photography in color. In arguing that "lovers of beautiful color want to experience increasingly beautiful examples," just as lovers of black-and-white photography sought for improved line, spatial relations, and other compositional elements, he suggested that people became addicted to superb color imagery and inadvertently to the way it rendered human beauty, perhaps peculiarly outdoors. People who sat for portraits wanted no "reproduction of themselves" but rather an idealization "of their ideals of beauty for that kind of face or toward an idealization of a kind of character they feel they possess." But by the late 1950s the personal idealization often derived from fashion photographs, which together produced a generalized idealization overarching the personal one, a definable visual concept of "a beautiful woman" projecting "an impersonal beauty not to be identified with a living person but as an example of how an impossibly beautiful person might look." Evans stopped just short of trying to "draw a parallel between this and the so-called 'glamour' photography," but admitted that he thought it no "exaggeration to say that the people do not look much like the photographic results."[79]

He argued further that photographs, and perhaps especially color photographs, had begun to unconsciously shape the visual memory of educated individuals. He asserted that "one of the best, if perhaps the most dangerous of examples is the simple fact that most men are unable to remember the exact appearance of their wives' faces" but instead remember an image in a favorite photograph.[80] Here Evans elucidated a crucial concept. People (perhaps especially husbands) do not remember faces because faces are seldom stationary except in sleep. A fine photograph consequently meant vastly more than a film, because people might stop and scrutinize a photograph repeatedly until the image shaped their conception of its subject. Given the peculiarities of color transparency film to record colors the eye typically missed or autonomically corrected, the color image became powerful in ways that made observers want ever starker, more powerful, more beautiful ones angled toward something unreachable, the image of the impossibly beautiful person.

Perhaps the desire originated in the way Americans saw objects rather than light, something that might explain the differences between Kodachrome and Agfachrome Wolff articulated. Evans insisted that most people rarely noticed changes in light, but instead saw objects as having fixed visual properties unaffected by altering illumination: he explained that a white tennis ball standing in sunlight is slightly yellowish on one side and gray or bluish on the other, but that few observers notice the variation.[81] He directed readers to the work of Cornish, making clear that the ways some people focused on mid-ground constituents in landscape illustrated other ways autonomic thinking distorted seeing. Painters and photographers trained themselves to see light, and to mark its changes, especially on objects that intrigued them, and to note how changing light separates objects from backgrounds. Color transparency film changed all equations by forcing viewers to align expectations against recorded color.

As it sharpened differences in lighting and in color (perhaps especially in contrast and saturation), it provoked inchoate feelings rather than critical thinking.

Skin caused special problems. "Its color varies both when the direction of the light is changed and when it is looked at from different angles," Evans concluded.[82] The fashion or glamour photographer, head bent over his Rolleiflex and body moving constantly to find different angles, might or might not realize how either he or Kodachrome records skin color. But unless he forced himself to learn, and to unlearn what Evans knew as the bedrock conceptualizations of black-and-white image making, his images would most often disappoint subjects, viewers, and magazine editors. Almost invariably, the fashion photographer concentrated on the clothing worn by his model in a studio. The glamour photographer more frequently worked with a nude model outdoors, making most issues of light and color more complex, but eliminating the vexations caused by clashes of clothing and skin color.

Skin tone and skin color issues underlay much postwar frustration with Kodachrome and Ektachrome, and even with the more exposure-error-tolerant Kodacolor. As Eastman Kodak changed its color films it eliminated some frustrations but created new ones. In a 1985 technical advisory, the firm explained to advanced photographers that "good reproduction of flesh tones is a primary consideration in designing a color film," along with accurate rendering of neutrals (whites, grays, and blacks) and "common 'memory' colors such as those of sky, grass, sand, etc." It designed its color films to reproduce such subjects well under a variety of conditions, and in so doing indirectly created films that sometimes failed: "Other colors—such as shades of chartreuse, lime, pink, and orange—may not reproduce so well." A chartreuse bikini against deeply tanned skin, for example, even front lit, might register as a sickly yellow.

Why a Color May Not Reproduce Correctly explains that color film is sensitive to ultraviolet radiation. A fabric that reflects ultraviolet light will appear bluer than seen by human eyes, something not necessarily frustrating if the fabric is blue anyway but confusing and irritating when a fabric apparently neutral, say a black tuxedo made of synthetic material, appears blue in a transparency. Other neutrals absorb ultraviolet light and then fluoresce it in the shortest wavelength portion of the visible spectrum, something most people cannot see happening but which materializes almost spectrally in color transparency film. Some wedding gowns made from certain materials fluoresce, and show up blue in transparencies, often ruining wedding photographs. At the other end of the visible spectrum are the flowers that agitated Wolff, Heering, and other

German experts in World War II. High reflectance at the far red and infrared end of the spectrum, "where the eye has little or no sensitivity," produces anomalies in color transparencies of blue morning glories, gentians, and ageratum flowers. Certain inexpensive dyes used by clothing manufacturers produce the same problem of high reflectance in the high red zone, sometimes so much that medium- or dark-green fabrics show up as grays or even warm pastels, since the reflectance neutralizes the green appearance obvious to the eye but not to the film.

Eastman Kodak commiserated with professional photographers and with advanced amateurs asked to make images of friends, admitting that neither it nor photographers could force fabric and clothing manufacturers to eschew dyes that photographed badly and that photographers often had no way of identifying such fabrics until viewing exposed film. "In most cases, people choose fabrics for their visual impression, not because of the way the colors may appear in photographs," the leaflet concludes. While filtering the lens with a Wratten Filter (often a #2B or a #70) or filtering the light source in a studio sometimes helps, in most cases (especially outdoors) the photographer can do little. Eastman Kodak advised professional photographers to examine fabric through a Wratten #70 filter and instantly see the difference between natural-fiber fabric and synthetic materials.[83] What they saw might work on human skin too.[84] It might work especially well if no contiguous clothing sparked autonomous color correction.

A year after the appearance of Evans's book, a color photograph of the model Venetia Stevenson graced the cover of *Photography Annual 1958*. The editors reproduced the Don Ornitz Kodachrome Daylight image inside the volume, too, referring to the model as "the most photogenic girl in the world." Ornitz used an out-of-focus screen as a background, which produced internal reflections in the camera lens, which in turn produced a soft-quality image of the blonde, fair-skinned woman.[85] At age twenty, the British-born Stevenson had completed the transition from modeling to appearing in minor roles on American television and in Hollywood films, but for several years her face appeared routinely in photography magazines.[86] Her hair, skin, and eye coloring fit perfectly the design parameters of Kodachrome. Nowadays undergraduates gasp when they see a slide of the Ornitz image. Stevenson seems the prototype of the first Mattel Barbie doll, only more austere and sophisticated.[87]

Despite its full-color glamour cover photography, by 1968 *Photography Annual* no longer showcased images made largely with Rolleiflex cameras but instead featured a mix of American 35 mm photojournalist images, candids, and photographs altered in darkrooms in which Hearn might have felt at home. Landscape images resembling Laughlin's competed with images mimicking the paintings of Edvard Munch and other artists. Many of the photographs, especially of rural landscape and related subjects, achieved a quasi-surrealist frisson.[88] Over a decade the editors had completed a subtle but successful swing away from medium-format images, especially color ones: the images that readers knew as intimately linked with fashion and glamour photography by then appeared in the color photography volumes.[89] The editors emphasized American subjects photographed by American photographers. Not only did most reproduced images differ substantially in subject from those reproduced in *Rolleigrafie* and other European corporate magazines and in *Das Deutsche Lichtbild* and other European annuals, *Photography Annual* contained relatively little material made by non-Americans, including photographers in Asia. The annual had turned inward, away from medium and larger formats, and away from color imagery too.[90]

Fashion photographers contended with the contrast problems created by scraps of bright-colored, often florescent fabric photographed under bright sunlight against highly reflective waves and sand. By the middle 1970s a modest number of American women had begun to shed their suits in private—eliminating a chief technical problem posed by color transparency photography—and become the genii loci not only of place but of a new era. Medium-format photography, especially that accomplished with Rolleiflex cameras, began moving further upscale and away from mass-market American photography magazines and annuals. Rolleiflex-owning photographers avoided contesting bourgeois social mores and quietly followed European guidance, moving along ways unseen by most 35 mm popular photographers. Rolleiflex cameras themselves began to seem risqué or subversive in the eyes of many amateur photographers using expensive and increasingly automatic 35 mm cameras.[91]

In the summer of 1972 I learned firsthand of the vagaries of Kodachrome when it confronted synthetic fabrics and dyes, ultraviolet and infrared radiation reflected from salt water through moist air, and the chance juxtaposition of a bikini and acres of chartreuse salt marsh. By then I knew that the chartreuse of late springtime salt marshes photographed haphazardly no matter how carefully I exposed film at any time of day. Even the early morning or late evening sun Windisch and others specified (and that *Rolleigrafie* championed) did little to make transparency film render spartina grass accurately, and summer diminished the color registration problems only marginally.[92] I wondered if the weaknesses of Kodachrome and Ektachrome had made some landscape constituents and even landscapes themselves less photogenic, and perhaps less common in calendar art and other publications reflecting and shaping American scenery values. I had begun experimenting with Fuji-chrome simply to see if it did a better job in salt marshes, but that day I photographed the bikinied nereid I had on board only Kodachrome and Kodacolor.[93] Still, I saw something more complex gleaming in the big viewfinder screen at the bottom of the light well. I saw a woman at home in the marsh, confident in her energy and sexuality, and determined to be photographed in a way that transcended fashion magazine imagery. I saw a new energy come to the old-field landscape at the head of the marsh.

14 Spirit

Whether fashion, glamour, or cheesecake imagery, poses such as the one shown here, however awkward they may seem today, reveal the origin of the bikini as a posing suit that still provokes questions of nudity, modesty, and sexuality in a feminist era.

S<small>UZY</small> P<small>ARKER</small> B<small>ROUGHT</small> B<small>IKINIS</small> I<small>NTO</small> M<small>AINSTREAM</small>
American media in the early 1960s. The premiere American model cham-
pioned the suits as heralding a new era of female freedom. No longer risqué Riviera beachwear, the suits emblemized a new, confident physicality
fused with natural surroundings,[1] twenty-five years after some American
women began wearing bikinis in boats and elsewhere in private, and in
photography magazines. Parker demonstrated that well-to-do adult women
had embraced the navel-revealing suits working- and lower-middle-class
women feared and Hollywood shunned.[2] Parker's adoption of the bikini
convinced most American women that bikinis, first advertised to models
and glamour photographers, heralded not the imminent triumph of mid-
1930s nudism but the freeing of women from old-fashioned prudery.

In the late 1950s Suzy Parker personified both sophistication and
down-to-earth simplicity, an amalgam of European smartness and American spontaneity. Rolleiflex-made photographs of Parker wearing formal
clothing appeared not only in *Cosmopolitan* but in *Look,* and in dozens
of other magazines.[3] In 1961 *Redbook Magazine* designated her "the
world's most beautiful woman," a year after *Newsweek* called her "the
girl next door."[4] American readers, especially women readers of women's
and fashion magazines, read that Parker had moral values as high as her
cheekbones, a determination to represent American women as educated
and competent as well as beautiful, and a belief that beauty depended on
good health, physical competence, and a radiant energy long assumed the
province of Creoles and other darker-skinned women.[5]

By the middle 1960s American advertising experts, manufacturers,
and editors realized that Suzy Parker could realign the thinking of millions of potential buyers. Images of her in a bikini might forestall the arrival of the European fashion aesthetic they envisioned following on the
heels of the Beatles and other offshore musicians. They saw cinema and
television shoving all but upper-class nonviewer women into a frumpy,
downscale prudery unlike the vivacious exuberance of the immediate
postwar years. Suzy Parker served the short-range interests of advertisers
caught up in the Cold War effort to present American womanhood as
beautiful, healthy, and virtuous—and unafraid of the bikinis freeing European women from obsolescent inhibition.[6]

Parker photographed superbly in color. Unlike World War II models,
Hollywood starlets, and other women who appeared in countless black-
and-white publicity photographs GIs pinned up in barracks, and unlike
those who appeared in immediate postwar and Korean War monochrome

images, Parker represented the triumph of fashion magazine full-color reproduction. But the first supermodel could not avoid the bikini American tourists discovered everywhere in Europe and the Caribbean, the suit photographers understood through the shop-theory prism of European photography magazines and annuals.[7]

In the 1960s *Rolleigrafie* provided a square-format window on photography unlike that appearing in United States photography annuals and almost all photography periodicals. The English-language edition debuted in 1964, edited and published by Walther Heering. More than a simple translation from the German, the first issue appeared as a compilation of earlier German issues. Intended partly to advance the agenda of Honeywell Photographic Products, the American conglomerate that had purchased Franke and Heidecke, and to showcase new Rollei products, including a square-format, single-lens camera somewhat akin to the prewar Pilot Super, *Rolleigrafie* found photographers only by subscription and at Rollei dealers, at fifty cents a copy. The first English-language issue had been assembled, Heering announced, "with our American audience in mind, the aim being to provide a good balance of technical information, pleasant reading and looking, and thought-provoking articles." For thirty years Heering had championed Rollei photography. *Rolleigrafie* gave him a platform to emphasize the elitism of Rollei photographers in part by reproducing photographs alien to mainstream American photography magazines and mass-circulation periodicals. It offered a rare opportunity to demonstrate that elitism in shop-theory terms of landscape, genii loci, and photographic technique.

The inaugural issue set the tone for those that followed. Most of *Rolleigrafie*'s articles emphasize technical subjects, including underwater exposure and darkroom trickery producing eerie final effects, but its longest pieces deal with color composition, close-up color photography, projection of color transparencies, and fashion photography in color. Its full-color, full-page images showcase success with subjects having one or two defining colors: "good looking" means rewarding looking for photographers anxious to produce better color images, especially on brightly lit summer beaches. But one of the final articles, "Rollei Photography with the Older Rolleis," raises a subject rewarding scrutiny now.

In 1964 *Rolleigrafie* observed the drift of some college students and other money-short young photographers toward second- and thirdhand Rolleiflexes as second cameras. As owners of early Rolleiflexes died and their cameras became available at low prices, young photographers aware of their use by professionals acquired them as experiments in non–35 mm image making. *Rolleigrafie* explained that older Rolleiflexes might be updated with flash contacts, new and brighter focusing screens, and "even the very latest Rolleiclear screen with a built-in split-image rangefinder wedge."[8] It showed a new generation what very young European photographers were doing with reliable cameras often nearly forty years old.[9] Indeed at times the magazine editors appear surprised at the vitality with which very young postwar photographers used old Rolleiflexes, especially in the photography of young women outdoors in largely natural landscapes. Young European photographers aimed old Rolleiflexes chiefly at young women—often bikinied, sometimes nude—enjoying the landscape in ways that shocked "the typical American." The heavy, bulky cameras captivated many young photographers: they seemed perfectly suited to exiguous-suited models and often possessed by Brownie-like independence.

By 1968 *Rolleigrafie* appeared as a folio juxtaposing advanced technical articles and superb images unlike those reproduced in any American publication.[10] Its page size and square shape emphasized the enlarging capacity of medium-format square negatives and transparencies: exquisite color reproduction reinforced the large-page message. The technical articles surpassed anything appearing in *Popular Photography, Modern Photography,* and the other periodicals that had well-nigh obliterated more sophisticated journals aimed at experienced, innovative, well-to-do American professional and amateur photographers.[11] Its images grabbed the attention of young American photographers accustomed to American-produced photographs, 35 mm–format images, and the deluge of films and shows from Hollywood and television producers shaping mass-media still photography. *Rolleigrafie* showcased nuanced images of powerful and daring yet young, seemingly unsophisticated people, almost invariably European, made by photographers working free of the Production Code context that hamstrung United States makers of cinema and television. In October 1968 it emphasized that one way of eliminating problems posed by bikinis made of synthetic fabric that tricked color transparency film might be to discard the bikini, just as technical photographers had learned to discard white laboratory coats which fluoresced so strongly that the light contaminated subjects.[12] *Rolleigrafie* subverted the entire Suzy Parker effort.

However subtly stated, such advice floated far above even the more sophisticated American photography manuals available to amateurs determined to make images that surpassed snapshots and even those photographs in *How to Make Good Pictures* and other film manufacturer books. Outdoor color photography away from lawns and hedges, and far from sylvan suburban backgrounds, by then struck some advanced amateurs as necessary for success. "Green is an awkward color. If it comes out too dark it looks like spinach," opined W. D. Emanuel in the seventieth edition of *The All-in-One Camera Book*. "Slight over-exposure immediately produces a violent hue. The eye is much more critical of distortion in green than in the other colors, red and orange, for example." In 1973 he asserted in his frequently updated book that "in the case of reflections the photographer should remember that a green shadow on a face will give an extremely strange effect when the tree which causes it is not in the picture." Deep-blue cloudless summer skies may be enchanting, but without careful handling are "apt to look a bit gaudy" on transparency film, and wintertime blue skies simply produce blue shadows on snow. In the end, Emanuel cautioned against compositions too "variegated" in color.[13] Sensible photographers determined to work in color should abandon lawns and shrubbery and find outdoor landscapes appropriate to color film chemistry, models, and attire, especially attire skimpy enough that the photographer conscious of color film vagaries might concentrate on skin rather than fabric.

The many editions of *The All-in-One Camera Book*, originally published in December 1939, now make up a finely segmented chronology of photo-technology innovation prompted by advertising, photograph annuals, illustrated news magazines, and above all changing photographer interest. They offer a window on evolving advice offered by experts to advanced amateurs able to buy whatever equipment they needed and willing to invest time and money in shop-theory effort running counter to Hollywood (and subsequently, television) enterprise. Emanuel commented in 1944 that "dressing up for portraits, whether of children or grown-ups, is a bigger mistake when taking colour photographs than in black-and-white photography." In an example image of a blonde, fair-skinned girl in a pale blue dress lying on a cream-colored rug, reproduced in full color, he explained that "the charm of this child's portrait is due to the fact that the complexion of the child presents the most vivid colors of the whole."[14] Later, in the 1958 edition, Emanuel confronted the problem that vexed him thereafter: an example black-and-white photograph of a confident woman wearing a bikini very brief by contemporaneous American standards and in a pose accentuating her stomach illustrated monochrome beach full-figure photography perfectly, but proved a less useful example to photographers working with transparency film and "the sort of light you find only at the seaside."[15] While the suit in the black-and-white reproduction pushed the limits of mainstream American tolerance, it reflected the late 1950s fashion of Germany, Spain, Italy, and other European countries in which Emanuel's guide appeared in translation.[16]

A year earlier Emanuel had published his *Rolleiflex Guide: How to Make Full Use of Your Rolleiflex,* in which this Rolleiflex-made photograph would have fit more easily. In an advanced but general American photography manual, it fit uneasily, and then only because it appeared in monochrome: color would have made it unacceptably risqué. Over decades, *The All-in-One Camera Book* illustrates not only the divisions between European and American shop-theory photographic aesthetics but also those between middle-income American photographers and those wealthy enough to afford both a Rolleiflex and the aesthetic Franke and Heidecke promulgated.

The divisions vexed Aaron Sussman when he took over authorship of *The Amateur Photographer's Handbook* in 1940. The first edition appeared in 1925 and passed through many printings without change; by 1940 technology had changed so dramatically that Sussman rewrote the entire book. He found himself caught in the trap of presenting a hitherto respected, mid-range reference work to readers expecting only minor change and not especially anxious to face European-style photographs.

The fifth edition appeared in 1952, featuring a full-color frontispiece captioned in an epigraphic way: "Color film can produce consistent and fine brilliance. This informal portrait was made on Kodak *Ektachrome* film." Only far later in the book did the reader acquire any information about a blonde, fair-skinned model wearing a blue dress, leaning on the back of a blue sofa, and placed before a light-blue backdrop. Almost exactly as Emanuel had insisted, Sussman made clear that the best color portraits evolved from models wearing clothing that accentuated their complexion and hair and posed on or before neutral grounds (not spinach). But Sussman devoted little attention to women posed on sand.[17]

The Rolleiflex had forced Eastman Kodak to produce 120-size Ektachrome film, just as it had forced a competitor, Ansco, to manufacture its transparency film in medium format. Implicit in Sussman's directions for exposure and elsewhere floats awareness of Rolleiflex idiosyncrasies, especially its 1/50 rather than 1/60 shutter speed, as well as a more subtle awareness that Rolleiflex owners would read *Rolleigrafie* and other German publications rather than his book. He knew Rolleiflex owners accepted an aesthetic many American photographers, especially 35 mm photographers, distrusted.

While he offered example beach illustrations, chiefly one of a young mother and her child, Sussman wrote remarkably little about beach color photography, and even about color photography outdoors. In the seventh revised edition in 1965, he changed only the beach illustration: in it a young girl jumps over her older brother.[18] In that edition, and the next, which appeared in 1973, he cautioned readers to make at least three exposures of every subject shot with color transparency film.[19] Between 1940 and 1973, Sussman biased *The Amateur Photographer's Handbook* toward 35 mm photography, away from German medium-format technology and example, and toward family-oriented subject matter.[20] Despite the fast-growing popularity of color photography, the multiple editions pay it remarkably little attention; instead the bulk of each edition deals with black-and-white work, and with corollary darkroom techniques.[21] While widely regarded at the time in the United States as the leading general handbook for dedicated amateurs and even for many neophyte professionals, its emphasis on black-and-white photography makes it appear elementary alongside the multiple editions (1940, 1947, 1955, and 1963) of Paul E. Boucher's university textbook *Fundamentals of Photography, with Laboratory Experiments.*

Boucher had little interest in aesthetics, and even in composition beyond those arrangements producing color-clash problems, but he analyzed the various color films minutely, and dealt especially precisely with Ansco and Printon films as fundamentally different from Eastman Kodak products.[22] He devoted less attention to beach photography than Sussman, however, despite his publisher using a beach photograph on the jacket of the 1963 edition.

Beach photography produced nearly intractable problems of composition, lighting, color, exposure, and propriety. It ranged traditional black-and-white insistence on side lighting (especially in morning and late afternoon) against the flat light color film manufacturers insisted must come from behind photographers.[23] Shadows frustrated beach photographers—even hitherto successful box camera users—as soon as they saw their first developed roll of color transparency or color negative film.[24] By the late 1960s expert photographers understood and used the strong light reflected from waves and sand in color work, but even accomplished amateurs equipped with fine 35 mm cameras struggled to achieve the success Lohse and others found in 1940. Sophisticated advice offered throughout the 1950s to photographers working in black-and-white failed to re-educate photographers working in color.[25] "How to Pose a Pretty Girl," a 1951 *Photokinks* article, offered advice on "interesting results with mirror reflections, rural backgrounds, glamorous close-ups and shooting against the sun," noting simply of the model that "as long as she's pretty it's sure to be pleasing."[26] It and another article, "Bathing Suits," suggest the arrival of a new force changing the photography of women: the women had changed in a fundamental and mysterious way.

"Pretty" suddenly designated women who photographed well in both black-and-white and in color, often wearing so little that the tone of their exposed skin dominated exposure settings and color rendition. Photographers had discovered that many experienced models looked less than pretty in outdoor color images (often because neither they nor the photographers knew how to choose attire that complemented complexion and surrounding vegetation, let alone neutral beach sand), and had begun making beach photos indoors, in studios offering filtered, arranged lighting.[27] Studio photographers controlled lighting in ways that sped black-and-white image making in unanticipated but profitable ways, but they found the biggest gains in color work.[28] They also found themselves free of onlookers critical of scanty attire, something that became increasingly important after about 1955 as urban-based photographers found suburbanites flocking to hitherto isolated beaches and rural areas.[29] *Rolleigrafie* offered technical help grounded in the waist-level, giant ground-glass viewing screen of the Rolleiflex that made composition (especially for color work) far more efficient, and examples of color images of women wearing everything from variegated-color suits to nothing but skin. *Rolleigrafie* began redefining "pretty" in a full-color-image era. It emphasized that a pretty woman made genuine outdoor settings surround her. She did not need artificial lighting and other studio crutches.

Rolleigrafie shouldered aside its competitors. Its first issue in 1968 featured a cover image of Caribbean carnival revelers wearing iridescent, variegated-color costumes thronged in a narrow sunlit street. The "blaze of glowing, joyous colour" demonstrated the poverty of the advice offered by Emanuel, Sussman, and Boucher, and rammed home the power of the Rolleiflex. Inside, the reader found collections of photographs and articles, among them one by Berndt Heydemann, "On the Importance of Sharpness in Photography," illustrated with a gigantic color image of the iridescent colors of the head of a tiger beetle; another on close-up color photography of flying birds; and a full-page image of a nude woman showing off her bikini lines.[30] The subsequent issue again provided a range of articles, among them one by Paul Swiridoff dealing at length with the photography problems posed by International Style architecture, another examining glacier and ice photography, and one by Heinrich Metrios, entitled "Outdoor Portraits," that included a full-color image of an adolescent girl posed nude on a beach to illustrate the usefulness of the Rolleiflex-Ektachrome combination. "Several test shots had to be made to get over the young model's initial camera shyness," the editors reported of Leo Alexander's photograph illustrating Metrios's article. "But the wish to see herself photographed according to her own conceptions very soon produced natural poses needing only a minimum of direction."[31] In its second issue *Rolleigrafie* hit a stride that never varied thereafter. It provided intense technical information that bluntly contradicted and transcended American magazine photographic advice. Metrios emphasized that "it is a mistake to place your model in front of a wall in an effort to get a 'restful' background"; that sentence alone contradicted much American shop theory. It reproduced images of subjects far outside mainstream American aesthetics.[32] Suzy Parker appearing in a bikini in fashion magazines might reassure many American women, but a nude fourteen-year-old girl on public beaches and in American photography magazines was a different matter. By the second issue, *Rolleigrafie* readers knew they held a magazine far more advanced than any published in the United States, one that seemed a veritable palantír. It showed another realm of photographic shop theory and an aesthetic far removed from Hollywood and its Production Code, one any intrepid, determined, Rolleiflex-owning photographer might explore.

In March 1969 the magazine began showcasing the work of very young European professionals working with Rolleiflex cameras. The photographs fit perfectly with the *Rolleigrafie* editorial mission: technical excellence informs images of fantastically attired women in fantastic outdoor environments, but also images of people without clothing nonchalantly inhabiting nature. The nudes are nude in places, especially beaches and other locations suited to sunning, where European young people had abandoned clothing. The images make up a genre distinct from fashion imagery, even that subgenre featuring people attired in ways incongruous with their settings.[33] Nudity, of course, subverts fashion photography.

The juxtaposition of attire, nudity, and setting informs the whole of the June 1969 issue, devoted to the photography of women in "hyperspatial" ways that are "far from glamorized sex, yet romantic in a very modern way."[34] In articles entitled "The Naked and the Rollei," "Oh Leg—Thou Art a Mirror," "Of Maids and Men," and others integrating technical data and cutting-edge aesthetic extrapolation, the editors and authors slice deeply into the power of images featuring both unclothed women and gorgeously attired women in swamps, forests, fields, and other outdoor settings. In subsequent issues Walther Heering and other attempted "a glance back into the future of photography," attempting to extrapolate short-term futures from experiments of earlier decades which proved too avant-garde.[35] Longtime fashion photographer Hubs Flöter teased out the loss of American preeminence in fashion photography, which he claimed had peaked with *Harper's Bazaar* in the late 1930s, as an extension of Rolleiflex-based portrait photography. The Rolleiflex "for the first time made photography from the navel to the eye" possible, especially outside studios, transformed much advertising imagery from static to natural, and produced "a flair of natural things" that emerged, not in New York or Los Angeles after the war, but in Paris and then elsewhere in Europe.[36] By the middle of 1970 *Rolleigrafie* sniped that American photographers had lost both their leadership position and their nerve. They had succumbed not only to 35 mm candid photography and to the sloppy bracketing of color transparency film but to Hollywood-based prudery and stodginess, preferring photographs of formally attired women aboard boats, on beaches, and elsewhere to nude women anywhere.

The June cover illustration, a Peter Raba photograph of a nude woman in a fern glade, illustrated a key feature, "Colour-Subjective Picture Element." The article argued for "a new colour aestheticism of subjective transformation" evolving from the work of young European photographers as free of black-and-white image-making tradition as the woman is free of her clothes.[37] By then *Rolleigrafie* had punched through many American envelopes, emphasizing the use of color film to depict African American skin and jewelry, tracing the work of expatriate American fashion photographers in Europe, and depicting in full color a nine-year-old nude girl posed on a sofa with her ten nude dolls.[38] It forced American readers to confront the deepening photographic conservatism and the tightening cultural constrictions driven by prudery: even its advertisements for women's raincoats and vodka surpassed any in American magazines.[39] While American mass-circulation magazines titillated readers with images of navel-baring bikinied women, *Rolleigrafie* suggested that nudity might prove less erotic and far less sexualized than bodies exiguously attired, and that nudity itself might be a force for good health and simple, natural living.[40] It argued that American fashion photography had to catch up to global standards, but it announced that some photography had transcended fashion photography itself.[41] It had become fantasy imagery fusing specific women with specific places.

Most of the December 1969 issue focused on the wide latitude and generous financing European advertisers offered to daring young photographers creating images for young, upwardly mobile magazine readers, as well as for record album jackets, posters, and the like. In addition to explicating Ica Vilander's photos juxtaposing jewelry and nudes, and Peter Bach's subtle but erotic black-and-white and color images, *Rolleigrafie* asserted that advertising, especially fashion magazine advertising aimed at sophisticated women, would follow a trajectory away from Hollywood cinema and mass-market commercials. Jürgen Theis, in a seminal article entitled "Advertising Photography: A Synthesis of Art and Craft," likened his Rolleiflex-based work to that of a goldsmith mingling technical excellence and artistic vision. He thought "made-in-USA" advertising detrimental to both technical innovation and to artistic experimentation, and counseled young photographers, European and American, to eschew it.[42] In "The Manipulated Consumer," Goetz Sobek argued that the more savvy, upscale European viewers of print advertising valued a sort of frisson based on "snob appeal and spiced with a soupçon of sex." Visual education in childhood produced viewers attuned to nuances of lighting and to the interaction of color: educated women especially understood the sexual power driving a new aesthetic.[43] While a few films evolved from comic books (*Barbarella* being a prime example), the evolving aesthetic originated in a collaboration between advertising agencies and photographers attuned to their era.[44] Advertising and other imagery, especially images fashion photographers made for themselves rather than clients, had moved far from cinema, and even further from television, and especially far from American film and television.[45]

Rolleigrafie insisted repeatedly that photographs might ensnare the eye and the mind alike, and lead thoughtful viewers into other realms. After the middle of 1969, it made clear that some fashion magazine advertising photography often transcended its primary purpose, offering scenes from stories viewers imagined strongly enough to remember.[46]

The June 1969 issue of *Rolleigrafie* revolved around the photography of women in landscape, and especially the making of photographs of women in ways that intrigued women viewers determined to explore change. In "Women in Front of the Camera," Karl Pawek posited that women had become increasingly photogenic as their roles in society changed. Man "still runs around exclusively in trousers," but women often presented themselves in a variety of ways and thus produced extraordinary visual diversity on any urban boulevard or village beach.[47] Hans von den Socken produced an entire article on the photography of women's legs, in pants and otherwise; Richard von Frankenberg, in "Maidens, Men, and Motors," traced a bit of the evolving aesthetic juxtaposing women against machines rather than women dressed incongruously in natural environments; and Georg Stengel dealt with female-male couples in a variety of different photographic venues. The visual approach of all these was grounded in the full-figure portrait that the long-focal-length Rolleiflex had made world famous.[48] But it was Alexander Spoerl who observed that women had begun to understand themselves as more than clothes-horses or the wearers of jewelry. The woman who "admires herself" had begun to realize that she did not need accessories to be whole—or the subject of a photograph.

In "The Naked and the Rollei," Spoerl concentrated only on the real-politik of full-figure photography in a new era. There was, he said, "just one rule: the more abundant the curves of the subject, the longer the focal length should be."[49] The Rolleiflex had reinvented fashion photography after World War II, and it reordered full-figure photography too, especially in Europe.[50] The magazine had made its case and modestly suggested that readers pay close attention over the years to its long-term projections. It not only discerned a class and aesthetic divide in America but predicted the divide would deepen: some women would value health, vitality, sexuality, and idiosyncratic radiance as components integral to an emerging understanding of nature, ecology, and aesthetics. Others would just buy more clothes.

American commercial photographers seemed especially likely to abandon outdoor location work for a new kind of indoor image making, one grounded in the optical trickery Hearn scorned.[51] Rear projection of backdrops originated in the cinema industry. Cine cameras recorded the movements of actors before a static image projected from the rear onto a screen behind the actors. In the black-and-white cinema days the illusion worked, although it required studios twice as large as regular ones (the lantern slide projector had to be placed far behind the translucent screen). Color cine film and then television produced problems with the technique and eventually expensive solutions, most involving high-output, 6,000-watt Xenon color-balanced light bulbs. But commercial photographers unable to afford the large studios and the expensive equipment turned to front projection using medium-format color transparencies made with Rolleiflex cameras: 35 mm slides produced images too poorly resolved. Lighting the subjects posed before the transparency front-projected onto the screen proved exceedingly difficult: the subjects could cast no shadows on the projected image lest they destroy the illusion. The Scotchlite high-intensity screen, which offered very high reflective power within an angle of two or three degrees and so allowed the projector location almost exactly behind the camera, solved most studio problems. While the background image appeared brilliant and its color tones approximated natural ones, it did not adversely affect the color contrast of the subjects set before it.

In 1973, looking back at a breathtakingly rapid advance in advertising—and especially fashion—photography, Ignatius Storr explained to readers of the German magazine *International Photo Technik* that the expensive, fast-evolving technique nonetheless depended on the medium-format cameras professionals traditionally used. In "The Versatility of Front Projection" he cataloged an array of shop-theory issues: lighting, color, composition, and above all depth of field challenged even the photographer ordinarily making very large transparencies for magazine, calendar, and poster reproduction. He did not use the term *virtual reality* for a technique that transformed studio advertising imagery, then much studio art, and that nowadays many readers of 1970s magazine cannot discern from straightforward images made outdoors.[52] But he correctly identified the inability of most viewers to note the trickery.

Front-projection vagaries saved photographers substantial sums. No longer did they have to travel to the tropics to photograph summer fashions, and often they escaped inclement local weather too. But the technique did nothing for the photographers of very small objects, subjects that could not be brought indoors, and models intended to look natural in movement.[53] Front-projection technology thrust some photography backward into situations reminiscent of nineteenth-century portrait-studio work: sometimes models moving only slightly destroyed the perfectly angled lighting on which the entire illusion depended. While photographers often made on-the-spot Polaroid images to verify lighting decisions, many created images that nonetheless seemed static and posed—which they were. The expensive technique split fashion photography circa 1970, driving many photographers to work in real surroundings.

International Photo Technik traced the subtle changes skewing the most sophisticated professional effort. Even "when all factors down to the most delicate mimic expressions have been determined and observed by the photographer or the director," one expert lamented, "certain dangers" stalked the photographer. "The model may blink her eyes at the critical moment, her winning smile may fade or be lost altogether, the position of the hand may imperceptibly change, etc." All such change ruined photographs by the middle 1960s, because they paradoxically eliminated "liveliness" from the images in ways the public no longer accepted.[54] But the public unthinkingly and instantly rejected many natural images too, especially ones featuring people standing in waist-deep, clear water: refraction distorted the lower halves of bodies in ways that made photographers and advertisers shy from high-viewpoint shots of people standing in shallows.[55] Some photographers tried to control setting using front-projection techniques, but many others, especially those aiming cameras at people in moving water (or even worse, hang gliders in midair), improved their natural, outdoor techniques.[56] All preferred

Rolleiflex and other medium-format cameras with large viewfinders that kept subjects in view until the literally split-second close of the shutter.[57]

After the middle 1960s *Photo Technik* became almost obsessively aware of changing perceptual frameworks. In "Photography and Visual Perception," for example, Manfred Riemel explained that "to the human eye the moon only appears natural in one quite definite size," and that on an 8 × 10–inch negative made with a normal-focus lens the moon appears a disc about 1/10 of an inch in diameter: "To the viewer of such a picture however the effect is natural only with a moon at least four times this size." Often amateurs and even young professionals did not understand why night photographs appeared vaguely "wrong." Riemel insisted that "a peculiarity of visual perception, this, for the size of the moon's image on the retina is always the same, subtending an angle of 31 minutes" of the arc of the horizon line. Just as viewers of salon photographs and magazine advertisements unconsciously corrected the oval image of the top of a tumbler and perceived it as circular, so they misjudged the scale of the moon. A modern professional photographer charged with photographing many small items from jewelry to model railroads needed to understand why viewers required "appropriate dimensional reference standards included in the picture." Without such clues modern viewers could not quite apprehend the scale of the objects pictured, and once scale (and sometimes other components of composition, especially reflective intensity) jarred them ever so slightly, they dismissed an image as instantly as they dismissed ones lacking liveliness.[58] However art critics and social historians evaluated photographs, *Rolleigrafie* and *Photo Technik* writers defined a striking new division between studio and natural photography grounded in technology achingly difficult to use perfectly. They defined too an emerging perceptual distinction between exiguously attired women and women not attired at all that paralleled the studio-nature divide.

In "Are Pin-Ups to Be Taken Seriously?" Gilbert Petit asked 1971 *Photo Technik* readers to consider the subtle, unconscious links between projection-created advertising images and traditional pinup imagery circa 1935 to 1960. "The expressions 'erotic,' 'sex,' and 'pornography' are still very confused with one another today," he commented, "and are condemned outright by a code of morals which has become somewhat dusty and is fortunately beginning to lose its validity." Few signs marked the border between good taste and vulgarity in the new pinup photography. No longer did young Europeans condemn all pinup photography as tasteless. Petit insisted that a new generation freed of "old conceptions of the smug bourgeoisie" wanted something other than "the former 'cheese-cake' girl with net stockings and frivolous undergarments or with a bi-kini in imitation panther skin plus a mischievous come-hither look." Pro-ducers of calendars and other buyers of pinup images delighted in Petit's images, most made with front-projection techniques that permitted him to pose models as diminutive creatures standing atop flowers, cupped in the hands of sorcerers, or trapped in webs of tangled videotape. Only a few of his models stood nude, or even in scanty attire. Novelty of scale alone made the images powerful. "Front-projection equipment is not only capable of apparently transferring a model into a remote landscape, but is also useful for achieving surrealistic effects by mixing up motifs of differing scale," he concluded. Petit scoured agencies for willing models, finding few who would enter into the spirit of the work without embar-rassment or without reverting to the suggestive or pornographic poses they accepted in their ordinary work. Not many models wanted anything to do with such image making. Still, Petit did more than juxtapose mod-els and front-projected images (he completed many of the images using "complicated subsequent montage," since he intended that his models stand in some virtual images and in front or among others), and he cat-apulted pinup work to the cutting edge of fashion photography and the illustration of record album covers.[59]

In the early 1970s *Photo Technik* uneasily accepted the new reality. Some photographers had begun producing images that at first glance seemed produced by front-projection techniques but varied just slightly enough to puzzle all but experienced medium- and large-format photog-raphers. "Enormous artificial flowers right in the midst of nature are bound to conjure up a fairy-tale effect," the editors explained of an ar-resting image Jean-Pierre Ronzel made on an 8 × 10–inch piece of Ek-tachrome sheet film. Ronzel "did not arrange the flowers in such a way that the Scheimpflug law could be utilized, since unsharpness was to be employed as a design element."[60] In the first years of the 1970s, both *Rol-leigrafie* and *Photo Technik* assumed photographer readers deeply versed in the compositional and color technique possible with camera formats much larger than 35 mm. They knew too that their readers had begun segueing into a still-nameless shop-theory realm in which a handful of adepts familiar with the Scheimpflug and other optical laws might ever so subtly tease less educated viewers.

Against studio-produced pinup images *Photo Technik* juxtaposed out-door casual photographs made for young, well-to-do clients, one of the few American aesthetic innovations it understood as presaging global aesthetic change outside the purview of Hollywood. In his article "Is the

Photographic Portrait Still Up-to-Date?," Heinrich Freytag asked rhetorically if the sort of portrait honored in *Das Deutsche Lichtbild, Rolleiflex Annual,* and other Europe-based photography annuals still shaped portrait imagery. The answer was no. He pointed out that much pre-1960 portrait nuance had been lost as professionals retired from a no-longer-profitable part of the photographic studio business. Machine-made passport photographs, for example, had replaced older photographs intended to "be clear, matter of fact, and give the observer as much favorable information as possible about the person portrayed." Freytag emphasized that a good passport photograph made the subject look natural in ways customs officials equated with probity.[61] He argued that department stores had captured the baby-portrait business and that young people accepted 1930s-style graduation portraits simply because they knew nothing else. Joachim Schrobsdorff, a young German professional photographer working in Massachusetts, replied to Freytag two years later. He had learned that women graduating from elite Massachusetts colleges wanted outdoor images beyond those they saw in upscale fashion magazines, and they wanted them in color. He produced them, doing all 130 members of one senior class alone, and reveling in what he called "controlled messiness." He learned a bit about each girl from her attire and posture, and used a variety of techniques from positioning to the intermittent application of Max Factor Erase Stick. "I use medium-format cameras because the negative can if necessary be retouched," and because "there are always people who, no matter how many close-ups I take, insist on having a full-length photo enlarged to a headshot."[62] But his Rolleiflex cameras mattered for a more critical reason than negative size.

Schrobsdorff posed the women outdoors, among woods, in trees, lying on the ground, leaning against barns or rocks, and often sitting by water. His Rolleiflexes worked perfectly in such environments, and he struggled to make the women appear as the genii loci of New England woods and fields or the actual campus itself. Meanwhile, *Photo Technik* was suggesting that all photographers should record natural environment degradation caused by pollution.[63] Schrobsdorff's work justified the faith *Photo Technik* editors placed in medium-format cameras usually mounted on tripods in often difficult outdoor environments, but often handheld: it blasted past rear- and front-screen projection technology.[64]

"Candid Outdoor Portraits" marks a crucial turning point in American aesthetics, one its author recognized at the time. "The easiest light to work with is overcast sky," Schrobsdorff wrote. "One can use any background, turn the model in any position, and get beautiful skin tones." Sunny days he found more tricky, "but the extra sparkle pays for the extra effort" he took to "keep the sun behind the subject and lighten the face with a silver reflector, morning and afternoon giving the best results." He detailed the lenses and color film he used, the wide apertures "that give a delicate diffusion to the fore- and background," and the way that he demonstrated useful poses and so made the women laugh. "I start a session walking around the campus with my subject and, keeping in mind the clothes she wears and the way she looks, hope that inspiration may strike me. . . . Lakes, ponds, and foliage all make excellent 'straight' backgrounds, and go with nearly any type of clothing." He also used pumpkins, horses, swings, and other props. Not all parents liked the images—some still expected the dress-with-pearls quarter-figure monochrome shot—but so many did that they hired him to photograph themselves and their other children outdoors. Schrobsdorff took this as evidence that an ecological-aesthetic revolution begun in upscale women's college graduation portraiture would eventually reach public colleges and universities.[65]

His article exemplifies the welding of technical information and practical aesthetics that made *Photo Technik* a crucially important journal to both professional and amateur medium-format photographers battling Hollywood and high-tech commercial advertising aesthetics. It also exemplifies what *Photo Technik* and *Rolleigrafie* now offer to any retrospective observer of college and high-school yearbook photographs made after 1965. Around 1969 "candid photography" suddenly designated something quite different from Albert Jourdan's surreptitious rapid-fire snapshooting of his grapes-eating wife. For most Americans, it still meant a sort of sophisticated surprise snapshot made with a 35 mm camera. For young, more sophisticated subjects, the phrase designated naturally posed color images, almost always outdoors and almost always made with medium-format cameras, especially the Rolleiflex. Equally importantly, it designated images fundamentally different from most outdoor color photographs. *Photo Technik* readers immediately understood the import of Schrobsdorff's statement that he put the light behind his subjects. Eastman Kodak experts and almost everyone else had insisted since the late 1930s that flat light worked best for color film: Schrobsdorff knew that in medium-format photography light other than flat front light accomplished much more that most photographers had recognized.

He knew what *Photo Technik* and *Rolleigrafie* had told their readers as part of a tradition originating in Windisch's *New Photo School* and similar works published in Germany in World War II but not sorted out until the middle 1950s. In color photography, color works on three levels. One is conscious, or at least seemingly so, as when the viewer holds a color photograph and remarks that one or more colors do not seem right. Most of the time the viewer says nothing, even if he has long forgotten the late afternoon light that cast a yellow tone over the subject. The other levels are subtle. "The purely sensual associations a colour summons up are only on the surface of our conscious mind, whereas the real subconscious psychological aspects remain at first concealed," argued one *Photo Technik* author in 1971. One level is traditional, and perhaps archetypal. The third and most obscure level is personal. "A colour picture must under certain circumstances be capable of appealing to both layers of the mind—the archetypal and the personal unconscious," H. Frieling argued in "Colour as a Mode of Expression." He observed that people tended to forget "to compensate for the grey veil that shrouds our mind," which often dulls or otherwise alters the colors in the image. He thought the color theory expounded by Goethe, rather than the far more popular one of Newton, perhaps explained postwar lack of attention to the relation of contiguous colors. "Although every colour has its own inherent symbol (yellow = mobile as quicksilver, red = exciting as Mars, green = cherishing, blue = separating), it is really the colour sequence which has dramatic content." Frieling insisted that alchemical frameworks might prove as useful as Jungian archetypes to professional photographers working in color and determined to triumph over 35 mm snapshooters. Color photographs might work on the individual psyche as Robert Fludd averred of his imagery.

In a civilization that reads from left to right, "one projects the future to the right at the top (here also the aim), whereas one places the origin in intellectual matters top left, corporal matters are to be found at the bottom left, and finally the realization at the bottom right-hand corner." Goethe's color theory, based on an observer looking down into a glass cylinder filled with various liquids and gums, explained what the alchemists sometimes envisioned and what seemed to work (almost too well) in both advertising and artistic color photography, including color full-figure photography. Frieling offered examples. A rocket exploding over a ground area in the upper left of an image threatens the fate of mankind. One exploding over the top right is "a pleasant firework, an effect, a wish which at the present moment is of no danger"; one bursting at the bottom right is a historical event; one exploding at the right might or might not threaten according to the composition of the image.[66] *Photo Technik* might disagree with Frieling's argument, but the magazine editors had been working out a similar hypothesis since the middle 1960s: color changed composition and its meanings. But working outdoors in color made some photographers especially aware of the power of compositions they descried by looking down into the cube-shaped Rolleiflex viewing surround darkening the ground-glass screen into austere brilliance.[67] Peering down into the surround evoked Goethe's color experiments and theorizing, and perhaps the show-stones Tolkien imagined.

"Precautions have to be taken when photographing in the woods," wrote the editors in the summer of 1973 of a most successful photograph by Monika Wegler. "The domination of green areas often results in an overall colour cast which lends the model a not very flattering deadly green complexion." Wegler had taken risks, dispensed with the ordinary filters, caught a momentary ray of direct sunlight on her model's skin, and produced an arresting image of a woman in a white shirt standing among ferns against a backdrop of trees anything but spinach green.[68] She had triumphed naturally, outdoors, in difficult light. But Wegler tended to work outdoors anyway and specialized in documenting landscapes ruined by pollution. In the spring of 1973 *Photo Technik* featured her Agfachrome work. Of one locale the editors commented, "No fish, no plants, no sign of life—nothing but a stinking bog, but it did have structure and colour. . . . The late evening sun helped to exaggerate the intense colours of the refuse. According to the chemical composition the swamp constantly changed in colour." Wegler used a light red filter to enrich the shades of brown, and other filters to accentuate the patterns constituting an extreme landscape of the sort all photographers had a duty to present to viewers as a warning.[69] The photograph the journal reproduced full-page later that year, depicting an exiguously attired woman surrounded by ferns, made explicit Wegler's juxtaposition of two types of beauty: the dead marshes might be as gorgeous as the woman among the ferns.[70] But Wegler moved a step further, making the woman the genius loci of a place that had to be saved from destruction unless it became the new norm of beautiful outdoor landscape.[71]

By the spring of 1976 the editors had coined the expression "extreme landscape" to designate landscape images having arresting juxtapositions of viewpoint, perspective, and lighting.[72] But by then they had published articles linking the shop-theory technicalities of photographing microcircuits with others centered on photographing jewelry, eye shadow, and especially human skin. In every instance, the word "arresting" proves important. *Photo Technik* stressed images that stopped and held the gaze long enough for viewers to think and feel. In an age already overwhelmed with images, it realized the necessity of producing ones that seized viewer attention. But as Schrobsdorff made clear in a long aside about the protests and other changes defining the undergraduate experience by 1969, arresting images result from photographers understanding that something new and daring is informing their subjects.[73] Schrobsdorff and Wegler abandoned many rules, first scrapping the front-light one expounded by Eastman Kodak since its invention of Kodachrome, then most of the traditional rules of portraiture and landscape.

Backlight made natural full-figure color portraits seem mysteriously different from so much contemporaneous advertising imagery and from traditional college yearbook portraits.[74] It made the women of Mount Holyoke College special.

In the early 1970s many astute would-be sitters wanted (albeit vaguely) portraits different from the traditional ones so valued between the late 1930s and about 1960 but equally different from the Hollywood and advertising images few viewers understood as front projection–based images.[75] Professional and amateur photographers created the images the sitters wanted by combining two technical innovation–based modern traditions, one originating in medium-format nude photography, the other in pinup imagery, both themselves shaping new depictions of landscape. While *Photo Technik* held sway over the innovations by 1973, *Rolleigrafie* had introduced them a few years earlier, simply by documenting the work of Fritz Henle.

In June 1970 *Rolleigrafie* readers encountered a feature article on Henle's work that began with a series of rhetorical questions about his photography of the Virgin Islands. In "Caribbean Island Paradise of Dreams" the editors mused on what might be expected from "an El Dorado for the eye, a lure, composition that is pure delight," and concluded that Henle's images defied designation and classification. They understood every image as arresting in ways beyond contemporaneous documentary work: Henle "plays mirror to an island dream world which now only exists in dreams or dream factories, and that is why his pictures exert a magic fascination," they determined of the "striking sharpness," of his images. "The philosophy of his Rollei belongs in this world of illusion," they concluded.[76] His work functioned in 1970 as an indicator of the ways upper-class, highly educated people watched middle-income, college-educated people veering toward a different aesthetic. The *Rolleigrafie* editors knew Henle as a long-accomplished, risk-taking photographer whose work whispered to the elite holding a course from which most educated Americans had begun to diverge.

As early as 1963 the editors of *Popular Photography* sensed the first tremors resulting from their devotion to 35 mm photography. They praised the work of South African glamour photographer Sam Haskins in *Photography Annual 1963,* but warned readers that the world-class fashion photographer had transcended fashion imagery. "The freshness of his approach to glamour is a welcome change in an area of photography that, at least in the United States, has produced few original or interesting pictures in recent years."[77] At age thirty-five, Haskins had just published *Five Girls;* he had owned his own studio for ten years, built a global reputation as a fashion photographer, and on his own time had struck out on a new path, photographing amateur models as genii loci.[78] The editors extolled his accomplishments. Buried in the fine-print back pages of the annual appeared something a bit out of tune with the times as *Popular Photography* reported them, however.[79] The young photographer made all of his images with a Rolleiflex or a Linhof, the large-format camera *Photo Technik* championed. Haskins's images had not appeared from thin air: any reader of *Photo Technik* understood the power of the Rolleiflex and the Linhof in shaping a new aesthetic and making possible the realization of an implicit idea. Any reader of Franke and Heidecke–supported advertising understood it too as grounded in the work of Fritz Henle, whose images proved powerful enough to divert very young photographers from the 35 mm format *Popular Photography* advocated.

A powerful if reserved elite favored Henle's images as 35 mm photographers struggled to compete with medium- and large-format photographers reinventing glamour photography. His 1970 triumph evolved from a twenty-year career in the avant-garde grounded in his devotion to Rolleiflex photography. Franke and Heidecke's support contributed to his success: in 1970 Henle's work had become synonymous with Rolleiflex photography, in part because it appeared in Rolleiflex advertisements.

As early as 1957 *Popular Photography Color Annual* recognized Henle's Caribbean figure work as transforming American notions of beauty and propriety. Laughlin had skewed such notions with his work on Louisiana plantations and New Orleans courtyards, but Henle made clear that the Virgin Islands might reshape them altogether. Bruce Downes understood Henle as one of the few photographers making a successful transition from black-and-white to color. He succeeded in part because everything was "right" at the moment of exposure, and he triumphed because he worked outdoors using natural light.[80] At first based in New York after emigrating from Germany in 1936 with three cameras (two of them Rolleiflexes) and little else and finding work as a *Life* staff photographer, Henle discovered the Caribbean while doing fashion shoots for *Harper's Bazaar*.[81] When he published *The Caribbean* in 1957 he already enjoyed a reputation for producing volumes of stunning photographs, each devoted to a specific place: Mexico, Hawaii, Paris, and elsewhere.[82] Many sophisticated readers, especially those who traveled frequently, were aware of Henle as a photographer who traveled a lot himself and made arresting photographs on many scales; his 1964 *Holiday in Europe* proved one more arresting volume.[83]

But Henle did more than produce folios of arresting images while keeping a breakneck schedule as a freelancer for New York magazines. He explained how readers might use the volumes to improve their own photography. In "A Note for Photographers" at the end of *Holiday in Europe* he suggested that amateurs make images distinct from postcard ones: they might frame shots through doorways or try for "intimate, characteristic details that contribute to the general atmosphere of each place you visit." He urged photographers to capitalize on bad weather, to note the "matchless" quality of light just before and after storms, to shoot from under awnings, and to learn from storm light why early morning and late afternoon light produces far better images than noontime sun. He advised everyone to buy a Rolleiflex because its viewfinder, lens, and massive negative made superb photography far more approachable. In fact, he suggested people buy *two,* one for black-and-white and one for color, and learn to recognize which subjects would render more beautifully on one type of film or the other.[84] Unlike so many of his contemporaries, Henle enjoyed explaining photographic shop theory to amateurs and professionals alike, and he saw no reason to tell beginners why they should not dream of owning a Rollei or two.[85]

As early as 1950 he published a folio of his own work, *Fritz Henle's Rollei,* that demonstrated the range of his capabilities. While many people knew him as a travel photographer and others "as a 'fashion expert,'" the volume emphasized his love of outdoor work in natural light. By 1940 he had convinced the editors of *Harper's Bazaar* to abandon their commitment to studio photographs made with large-format cameras. His photographs made outdoors (with his Rolleiflex held in his hands, not fixed to a tripod) presented models naturally. He requested, and in time required, models endowed with more than good looks and poise: he wanted women "endowed with imagination and intelligence," and he never gave them directions, but instead let them lead. While he used reflectors (usually a white wall or the white sand of a beach), he never brought flash or photoflood lights to outdoor locations. With camera in hand, away from light stands and other impedimenta, he worked with a new sort of model to produce naturalistic images that transformed most fashion photography in the postwar years.

By 1950 Henle had advanced his hypothesis that extremely beautiful models did little to make women viewers identify themselves with the ones in the photographs. He thought more ordinary and intelligent models might merge with the landscape into something vastly more powerful, and he emphasized foreground items that accentuated viewer realization of setting. The foreground items, often extremely minor within larger compositions, became a signature element in his work. Viewers of fashion images might consequently imagine themselves in both the attire and the landscape. Viewers of his travel books might imagine themselves in the scenes or creating them. Most importantly, photographers viewing the images might ponder how he made them. In her introduction to the folio, Vivienne Tallal Winterry contended that Henle's books "transcend mere 'travel picture books'" in large part because Henle intended them to show the advanced amateur what might be done instead of assembling the "hodge-podge of meaningless trivia too often produced by the tourist."[86]

Four years later appeared his *Figure Studies,* dedicated to his favorite model, his wife, Marguerite, who posed often on a stretch of Caribbean beach near their home. Henle insisted he had not produced a book about how to photograph nude women, but instead had made a "book of pictures, simple statements about a woman, which speak for themselves." He understood realism, and he insisted that nudity formed a large component of Virgin Island living, at least for some people wishing to merge with the environment. They lived nude casually in a place in which such behavior meant something far different from nakedness or the tawdry display of flesh sold by the pornographer. Henle explained his method in detail in "The Technical Problem." "A soft sunlight, diffused by haze or mist, is wonderful for beach shots," he wrote. "This gives a soft over-all illumination without heavy shadows to worry about under the eyes or breasts." He dissected the general fabric of the photographs, discussing his signature foreground items, and emphasizing how much of the photographs depended on Marguerite, who despite not being a professional model "approached this work without inhibition and with an amazing ability to take suggestions and directions."[87] *Figure Studies* touches upon everything from Rolleiflex close-up accessories to Henle's favorite film, Ansco Supreme, but most significantly it emphasizes the value of an amateur model, one who radiates the energy of the landscape surrounding her.

Henle had succeeded with all sorts of portraits and reproduced some of his most important ones (often done for biographical articles in *Life* and other magazines), but *Fritz Henle's Guide to Rollei Photography* emphasizes full-figure outdoor images, none perfectly posed but all "natural." It veers sharply from the work of Croy and other portraiture experts, and advances a simple hypothesis: the formal studio portrait is already a thing of the past, and "in modern photography, the truthful portrait, frequently made in the subject's natural surroundings, is becoming accepted everywhere." His manual is the first monograph to propose that "the portrait is a live and natural picture," explains the technicalities involved in making such a picture with a specific camera, and then describes how a synergy among model, landscape, and photographer produces something beyond the natural picture.[88] The photographer of the natural portrait will often not be able to remember what he did to fix the image of the vision floating on the ground-glass screen surrounded by shadow.

Henle linked the idea of the one bright-colored detail in a color image with a less explicit understanding that emphasizing some part of the body, often the eyes, made a portrait succeed in either black-and-white or color. He argued that a picture showing a perfectly sharp eye permitted a slight softness elsewhere in the face or body, and he suggested that such images might be routinely accomplished using the Franke and Heidecke close-up lenses, the Rolleinars, and focusing on the bridge of the nose between the eyes and then stopping down the aperture to increase depth of field.[89] The book was illustrated lavishly and almost entirely with pictures that readers had never seen reproduced elsewhere.

In "A Look at Glamour" they found nuance almost beyond measure. Henle distinguished among full-figure portraiture, fashion photography, and glamour photography, the last defined as the making of images of beautiful women "for no other reason than the pleasure of looking at them." A full-figure portrait existed as a record, and a fashion image existed to sell attire. Henle had pioneered much of the fashion aesthetic by then accepted as the norm—he invented the jarring juxtaposition of a gowned woman wading barefoot along the edge of a beach, something that *Town and Country* editors accepted with wariness until they watched its success—and he detailed how a beautiful woman who innately understood both clothing and photography usually became a top-ranked model very quickly. The glamour image existed for and in itself, however, and Henle noted that aside from family snapshots it proved "the most popular picture subject in the country." Reader-interest studies confirmed that women readers valued the images, especially on magazine covers.[90]

Fritz Henle's Guide to Rollei Photography appeared near the end of an era. Within ten years the anonymous glamour girl had been replaced by a "celebrity," generally a model or an actress, who had some real or manufactured biographical history useful in public-relations firms. In 1956 she needed appear only as a vision—in Henle's work, a genius loci.

Henle reproduced a number of glamour shots, all illustrating his philosophy that natural and casual attitudes produce more successful photographs than those with "strange or surprising" settings or poses, and that the low camera angles possible with the Rolleiflex often make compositions succeed. He suggested that the photographer try experiments "with a cooperative friend" and emphasize the model, rather than the background or props.[91] He directed reader attention to the low horizon lines in so many of his photographs, and in so many other glamour shots critics considered successful. In the end, he argued that some models triumphed in glamour photography because they understood something about visual power. They made the photograph work in part by making light surround themselves.

Such models radiate light.

Such models energize surrounding landscape.

Henle confirmed this argument by reproducing images of nude women. Today the book creates a frisson among undergraduates. Many of the images of children in the book are images of children nude, frolicking on Virgin Islands beaches or snuggled with their bikinied mothers. Many of what Henle categorized as glamour shots are nudes, often of his wife enjoying herself on the beach. The vast number of glamour shots made every year in the United States at that time featured clothed (though often very scantily clothed) women, simply because only very few women could pose nude and "free of every trace of self-consciousness" and had the place to do it. Henle decried the bulk of glamour shots, largely because they demeaned women and demeaned photography too. A woman confident in her skin, and with total confidence in her photographer as a person and an artist, ought to look good in little or nothing. Henle accepted a simple fact: a model and photographer might have to work together for a year or more in order for the relationship to click as smoothly as the Rolleiflex Compur shutter. "Once you have found the perfect model, the longer you continue to photograph her, the more likely you are to produce worthwhile pictures," he insisted. "You yourself must bring more to these sessions than a Rollei," he added. The photographer must consider the landscape, every feature of it, every detail of it, every least component, before determining to ask his model to pose in it. "What needs to be established is a common mood, an understanding of the emotional atmosphere which the pictures are to document." In the end, the right model (clothed or unclothed) needed no more direction than "Feel yourself as a woman. Be natural."[92] Glamour imagery, especially ones of women nude, involved something of women shaping power about them, making the landscape surround them, radiating light or some similar energy, in ways photographers recorded as best they could. Sometimes this was accidental, when cameras worked independent magic.

Henle suggested that most photographers of nudes might just as well use black-and-white film and process it themselves. "Most commercial photofinishers have a blanket rule forbidding the return of any figure studies sent to them for processing," he lamented. "While this may seem unreasonable in certain instances, it is a sound policy for the companies to follow." No color film processor wanted trouble with the United States Post Office, the ever-vigilant guardian of public morals.[93] The prudent amateur photographer either worked in monochrome or else chose Ektachrome film, which he processed himself, perhaps exactly as Eastman Kodak intended. If his girlfriend or wife enjoyed posing, he often produced over a few years images that far surpassed those appearing in pulp or fashion magazines.

Despite its introductory chapter, *Fritz Henle's Guide to Rollei Photography* addresses experienced photographers. In 1959 Henle and the editor of *Popular Photography*, H. M. Kinzer, published an elementary volume, *Photography for Everyone*, which addresses amateurs determined to move beyond the snapshot camera or already a bit frustrated with 35 mm photography. While it deals with the photography of children, the use of flash equipment, and photography at night, its underlying purpose is to assist the prosperous American anxious to make acceptable vacation photographs in both monochrome and color. Henle explains that "for the layman (that is, you who want to be neither a professional nor a serious amateur) technique is less important than approach, style, and the development of taste," and he introduces his entire argument in a brief section entitled "Visual Organization." *Photography for Everyone* implies that even well-educated readers lack the power to see composition and light: it many ways, it seconds Watkins's view that otherwise powerful, smart, competent people (especially men) often blunder when making photographs. It implies too that the same readers could not envision their vacations as events happening in a larger flow of time even as they happened. Much of the book aims at "the unsatisfied vacationer." Henle gently suggests that making improved photographs originates in more conscious looking around and far more conscious analysis of ongoing activity. Despite its disciplined, shop-theory approach to photography for nonphotographers, the book voices doubts about the ability of many amateurs to use a camera maturely.[94] They can imagine what they want to see, but cannot make it apparent on film when (and if) they do descry it.

Henle and Kinzer's *New Guide to Rollei Photography*, the book that makes sense of *Photography for Everyone*, appeared six years later. It consists mostly of articles Henle wrote over three years for *Popular Photography* but with many large, well-reproduced example images. Some of the book is tongue-in-cheek iconoclasm: Henle championed the square-format image over the 35 mm rectangle, and he routinely showed that the size of the medium-format image mattered, something that perhaps ended his short career as a sometime columnist. He extolled the virtues of the ground-glass viewfinder and the objects it so brilliantly displayed. He suggested all Rolleiflex photographers spend some time just wandering around looking into the dark, square-shaped black tube shielding the ground-glass image at its bottom. If they did so, they might escape the prison of the human eye, which continuously adapts and adjusts to varying light, scale, depth of field, color, and composition.

Henle championed too the medium-format twelve-exposure roll of film, telling readers to "try some eye-education exercises." He prescribed choosing a simple subject "that's not going to run away or change form while you shoot, and study it in the ground glass from many angles and distances"; then make twelve exposures, process the film, and bring the twelve contact printed images back to the subject and compare them. He dismissed attacks on his favorite camera as absurd. He did not back down. He knew the large size of the medium-format contact printed negatives made the experiment possible, and he knew too that Rolleiflex photographers looked down into the viewfinder with both eyes wide open. "What I'm talking about is something psychological, perhaps too subjective to apply generally," he concluded of such experiments. "But it is a feeling evolved from many years of peering into that little square of glass."[95] Something had changed in the transition from box camera to 35 mm photography, and perhaps it explained the growing frustration Henle addressed in *Photography for Everyone*. Cinema and television might have blunted the visual acuity of photography enthusiasts, but perhaps they simply had the wrong cameras—or cameras with very duplicitous viewfinders.[96]

Fritz Henle's Guide to Rollei Photography trumped *Popular Photography* and similar magazines. In its 1957 *Color Annual, Popular Photography* reproduced two of Henle's nudes, one in black-and-white, one in color. The editors suggested that the two large images facilitated direct comparison between monochrome and color in ways that advanced their moral (and political) concerns about the impact of color nudes and unwittingly displayed the depth-of-field power of the Rolleiflex.[97] The huge color enlargement showed grains of sand covering Marguerite Henle's stomach, elbow, knee, and right breast; the image emphasized the relaxed model in natural surroundings but renewed the enduring tension involving format.[98] Even during the three years Henle produced a column for *Popular Photography*, the magazine struggled with his tightening grip on readers of *Vogue, Town and Country*, and similar upscale magazines. By

1960 Henle had almost single-handedly engineered a subtle realignment of American attitudes toward a fast-evolving postwar German aesthetic juxtaposing the healthy body, often nude or nearly so, against incongruous extreme landscapes, machinery, or places where people routinely relaxed in the nude. In *Rolleigrafie* and his many books, Henle furthered a class-based aesthetic split that challenged *Popular Photography* editors. Not only did he champion an aesthetic of nudes and landscape far beyond the bounds of Hollywood and fashion magazine imagery, he insisted on the primacy of people making such images themselves as confidently as they made superb images of vacation locales.

Other photographers followed his lead. Irving Penn worked frequently in the Caribbean too, often for cosmetic manufacturers, and frequently depicted women swimming or relaxing nude in tropical waterfalls or in ocean shallows. *Popular Photography* saw his images as blurring the line between commercial and "creative" photography, and placed them "among the most remarkable figure studies done in a natural setting since the introduction of color photography."[99] Penn used a Rolleiflex too, and his work contributed to the deepening suspicion of many 35 mm photographers that Henle and other photographers of elites knew of places and behavior beyond ordinary middle-class metropolitan ones.[100] The new full-figure nudes displaced older World War II cheesecake imagery and made so-called boudoir photography appear sleazy; but an increasing number of photographers, both professionals and advanced amateurs, had decreasing access to the other lands where people played in their skins, and they condemned the new aesthetic as elitist.[101] The bulk of the "natural nudes" appearing in high-end magazines and in photography magazines were captured by Rolleiflex cameras, as *Rolleigrafie* and *Photo Technik* made clear. And the Rolleiflex cost far more than a 35 mm camera—far, far more.

The early 1970s were a revolutionary period in which photographers depicted scantily attired and nude women in a new way that both magazines scrutinized. "The new and very much up-to-date direction in the Bach studios is romance and a longing for far-off places," opined a 1971 *Photo Technik* article on the changes wrought by a second-generation owner of an established studio "in the high-class residential area of Grünwald in Munich." Eric Bach took his models to the Canaries, islands in the Indian Ocean, and anywhere else he might find the natural tropical settings in which the women became nereids or nymphs. *Photo Technik* pointed out what frustrated so many 35 mm photographers: a large part of his business involved record-album covers, whose square shape made his Rolleiflex the perfect camera. The models appeared sensibly attired (or not attired) in luxurious places, and his images caught an energy highly valued in Cold War Europe and elsewhere.[102] Two years after the magazine profiled him in an article entitled "White Slavery," clients around the world had become even more enamored of his work.

A year later, in "Quo Vadis: Photography of Nudes?," Adolf Gruber looked back over the changes since 1961, considered how abolition of the "commercial porno-photography laws" had affected commercial and artistic photography, and then mused on the attraction of the modern nudes. "Who can find anything erotic about a picture which shows a great deal less than many a model in a fashion photo?" Gruber maintained that clothes make the model exude sex. Nudes carry either an erotic or pornographic sexual charge or else none at all: they are essentially aesthetic, beautiful figures at the far borderlands of fashion photography who exemplify the human being in harmony with nature, as one with the natural environment, as radiating some sort of energy drawn from or enlivening the natural environment.[103] A new romanticism might be near, Gruber concluded, but until models asserted some authority little would change for the good. "They should not permit their bodies to be simply photographed, but must give thought to the pose and facial expression and, above all, support the photographer with charm."[104] Other experts even recommended that "inexperienced photographers" begin by photographing only the backs of nude women. The volatile cultural situation made frontal imagery subject to disaster, since the plethora of magazine images appearing after the abolition of obscenity laws might warp the thinking of young photographers.[105]

Amateurs trying to avoid making images akin to those in girlie magazines frequently blundered when they asked amateur models to pose in ways that revealed their faces. When the models turned they often became wooden, not so much embarrassed to be photographed nude as worried that their poses might be the "wrong" sort of nudity downscale magazines displayed.[106] Accomplished amateurs and professionals unfamiliar with creating nudes might remember that some poses tend to clothe the model in classical form, and the magazine frequently reminded readers of the nuances distinguishing nude women from women wearing only jewelry.[107] In the end, one *Photo Technik* author asserted, "If the state of nakedness of the human body, however beautiful it may be, exerts a purely erotic provocation, then either senility or sexual perversity must be assumed" to afflict the provoked.[108] If nudity did not equate with natural, then attention to human intervention in the natural environment, especially the biosphere, might be in for disaster. "It's like a glimpse of Paradise to see people move about in the open air freely and uninhibited, as they did thousands of years ago," Jozsef Nemeth explained to *Photo Technik* readers in 1965 of his photographs of nudes at the seashore.[109] A successful photographer understood the immediate cultural tension, but always remembered that he brought technology into the natural setting. Some photographers chose cameras and film types wisely, and produced images for clients (local and global) or for their models or for themselves.[110]

In 1965 *Photo Technik* began publishing the work of young photographers following Henle's precepts. The Swiss photographer Erhard Bertele wrangled an invitation to the privately owned La Maddalena archipelago in the Strait of Bonifacio between Corsica and Sardinia about the time the Bradfords sailed among it in the voyage they recounted in *The Wind Off the Island*. There he found sea-worn granite in such forms that in "civilized surroundings it could scarcely be distinguished from the work of modern sculptors," but it defied his effort to photograph it in color. Eventually he hit upon the idea of incorporating nude figures into the compositions, demonstrating both the "essential unity of man with nature" and the contrast between "the warm, living body and lifeless rock." He wanted to prove that photography might depict nudity in reality juxtaposed against the traditional forms in which artists typically render it. At first he tried to slightly abstract it with soft-focus lenses, coarse-grain film, and so on, but eventually he abandoned all such devices as old-fashioned, having found that "the erotic significance is determined largely only by the environment and by the pose and character of the model."[111] Over several years Bertele transitioned into underwater photography of nudes, all bereft of the masks, fins, and snorkels that would have destroyed the effect he sought of people merged with the sea that carved the rocks. His effort to combine sky, rock, and flesh, and in time water, succeeded in ways that the prescient editors of *Photo Technik* recognized as integral in a future focused on environmental issues. Twenty-nine years later France and Italy made the little-visited, almost uninhabited but ecologically important archipelago a world heritage site.[112]

Other experts had not only discerned the divisions Gruber articulated but had begun to delineate a new (and sometimes very naive) primitivism evolved from the "carefree poise of the model as well as the liberal view of the photographer" who found themselves genuinely a part of natural surroundings. The images originated in the abandonment of studio restrictions, especially the suddenly obsolescent front-projection sort of work that never perfectly simulated natural light. The experts valued the power Cable and others found in voodoo and other non-Western forces.[113] Whatever its origins and seeming primitivism, however, it appealed to affluent people wanting a new sort of portrait of themselves, often made outdoors, and often in the nude, but with an "amateur flair."[114]

While a handful of successful photographers emphasized the nexus of technology and the nude or nearly nude woman, especially in fashion photography, by 1978 their work had become much less visible.[115] At the same time, fashion photography involving nightgowns and lingerie had become increasingly difficult, since in outdoor settings the clothes tended to look ridiculous and in indoor ones they seemed pornography.[116] The woman in the bikini or the woman nude in a natural setting became the new genius loci in the dominant fashion photography as well as in full-figure portraiture, and in the work of many photographers who understood her as an avatar of a new environmentalism and as an emblem of female power.[117]

Conclusion

In the twilight of film photography, the view camera as container of phantasmagoria becomes a fading memory. Simple and efficient, digital cameras lack the capacity for creative accident that fused photography with fantasy.

"In the old days, long before anyone thought of speaking 'candid' and "photography' in the same breath, amateur photographers concerned themselves almost exclusively with 'views,'" mused Thomas H. Miller and Wyatt Brummitt, two Eastman Kodak Company employees who produced *This Is Photography: Its Means and Ends* in 1945. Writing at the end of the war, the writers understood that "the mood of the world in general and of photography in particular has changed," and that "the tempo is swift, our emotions are brittle, and we lean naturally toward irony and satire." In a chapter entitled "Land, Sea, and Sky" they suggested on behalf of their employer that "it is good for us to take time out, once in a while, and to prowl with our cameras, seeking out a little of natural beauty and serenity. We can use all we can find." Their book changed over the years, but through the 1963 edition it retained their advice. The Eastman Kodak Company understood the psychological need for calm contemplation of pastoral beauty and for making photographs along unfrequented rural paths and lanes. In such places photographers learned to descry light and color and the complexities of intricate cameras. Such sustained discovery proved useful elsewhere, especially in cities, at sea and alongshore, and indoors at night, under shifting artificial illumination.[1] Moreover, such places facilitated both the rare autonomous action of cameras and the posing of subjects away from censorious viewers.

Deliberate, contemplative photography in quiet rural landscape had become extremely important by 1945 to Eastman Kodak and other manufacturers of color transparency film learning the long-term marketing impacts of selling film with very narrow exposure latitude. Once exposed, not much can be done to adjust color transparency film.[2] Even color print film presented intractable problems, especially to a generation familiar with black-and-white film. Color, especially chrome film, meant that the photographer had to do everything right when making the image: it made snapshot and candid photography even more haphazard and often irritating and disappointing. But it rewarded photographers who took time with composition and exposure, who learned to integrate meditated understanding of landscape with and without the presence of subjects understood (however tacitly) as genii loci.

Fifteen years before Miller and Brummitt acknowledged the need for a bit of serene photography and for contemplating the personal, perceptual implications of Einstein-based physics, the editors of *Photo-Era* urged readers to find disused side roads winding through half-abandoned rural landscape. "Watch this same scenery for several weeks after an improved road goes through and you will find that everything in sight will be completely touristized, barbequed, and suburbanized," they warned of landscape "all spruced up for Sunday drivers and gas consumers," who make contemplative photography impossible. "The forgotten road which goes nowhere but which leads one everywhere" rewards the photographer anxious to immerse himself in possibility.[3] But in 1930 such roads had become hard to find. The editors of *Photo-Era* and other traditional magazines saw many photographers seduced by fast automobiles, fast lenses, 35 mm candid image–making effort, and Hollywood cinema, but above all by urban frenzy emblemized in high-speed film. Too few photographers explored the potential along overgrown rural paths meandering through regions most people avoided; too few photographers explored the overgrown roads and faraway meadows that Robert Frost and other poets knew as vital to discovery.

In 1936 William Mortensen averred that urban, media-driven frenzy had constricted photography. "The miniature camera has become the particular stamping ground of the *Popular Mechanics* graduates and the Boy Blacksmiths," he argued of "fundamentally magnificent" cameras "transformed by these lads into a super-Gadget, which is constantly giving birth to little gadgets." He claimed that children often made better images with a "two-dollar Brownie." His *Monsters and Madonnas* opens with a portrait made with an Eastman Kodak Hawkeye Brownie camera costing $1.39 and fitted with a 75-cent supplementary lens and Eastman Panchromatic roll film. The box camera made a medium-format negative, one Mortensen had processed at his local camera store. The large negative printed well, better than most he saw made in expensive 35 mm cameras held by hurried photographers unaware of everything from ambient light to the inner energy of their models.

Monsters and Madonnas explains that "the imagination works most readily with the material one enjoys," and suggests that men should photograph their girlfriends and wives outdoors, away from other people who have no right to see. It advances the argument Mortensen made two years earlier in *Venus and Vulcan,* a volume analyzing the juxtaposition of female model and machine-wielding photographer. "Learn about the art of photography not in camera clubs but in silence and solitude," it counsels; "seek the clean air of the wilderness" even if the first location is an interruption-free, secluded back yard.[4] Outdoors and out of the public view, the model and the contemplative photographer might create an intimate, symbiotic frisson that makes superb pictures. A model free of Hollywood-inspired poses and motifs may indeed create genuine glamour, making the landscape surround her in ways that transcend any cinema imagery, studio pinup, or fashion shot.

In many *Camera Craft* articles and in a series of books, Mortensen warned photographers about the perils of clothing and cosmetics. "The party frock, if you must have a picture of it, should be in front of a plain white wall, preferably indoors," he cautioned in his 1940 *Outdoor Portraiture*. He advised against "all fancy eyebrows, exotic eye-shadow and over-imaginative revamping of lip contours," and he stated bluntly that "an extremely white skin is inappropriate in an outdoor setting. A nude figure that is too white looks merely casually naked."[5] Clothed or unclothed, the model should appear a natural, integral part of the outdoor setting. Mortensen explicated a nascent human ecology, one distinct from artificiality: he inveighed against swimsuit tan lines marring the skin of a nude model, and he framed human ecology against limits of mechanical and optical technology and against outdated prudery. He wrote for health-conscious, open-minded, environmentally aware readers accustomed to private outdoor space where photography facilitated glamour. He wrote for photographers aware of European, especially German, landscape-with-figure thinking; often such photographers owned not only Rolleiflex cameras but the books and magazines and leaflets that accompanied them. And he wrote for readers who had seen for themselves that some women made landscape surround them, made visual magic happen that was beyond the craft of the photographer. Generally, such phenomena occurred in natural places, often ones more or less abandoned to artistic possibility.

Many such women either grew up in rural areas less influenced by Hollywood cinema or moved to them, seeking not only refuge from urban frenzy and artificiality but a more healthful, contemplative, ecologically sound way of living. In his 1938 book *The Culture of Cities,* Lewis Mumford remarked the way some adventurous people had begun thinking of their bodies as no longer "dualistically separated from mind." Mortensen angled his books at that cohort.[6] Even Eastman Kodak acknowledged in the late 1930s that farm women posed without thinking in ways urban and even suburban women did not.[7] Photographers struggling with the landscape–genii loci enterprise recognized that faerie and fantasy involved some new understanding of the body in place, the body as somehow natural.

In the Depression many hitherto well-off people fled cities for isolated rural places, many of them determined to live simply on the land while earning money through local or long-distance effort. Many wrote about their experiences, and among the themes linking the outpouring of books and magazine articles (including those in *Camera Craft* and other photography magazines) by and about them a quiet glamour figures largely. Away from the public eye, many of the incomers relaxed, made the abandoned landscape their personal theater, and embraced a photography far removed from the urban, rapid-fire 35 mm.

"One advantage of bathing on the lawn is that the water is so easy to get, and so easy to dispose of. Another is that one can splash and spill and pour with abandon," observed Charles Allen Smart in his 1938 report from rural America, *R.F.D.* "The most important is that it is such pure sensual fun to be naked and bathe in the open air, on the green grass, under the trees, with gentle airs, and slanting sunlight, or even moonlight, caressing our bodies."[8] Smart and his wife routinely swam nude at their nearby swimming hole. After a few days they no longer cared that people aboard infrequent trains might glimpse them. Nude or in homemade brief swimsuits, they enjoyed the sun, and the outdoors, and the expressive freedom of deserted rural places.[9]

In 1956 Clarence John Laughlin published a two-part *Art Photography* article explaining how few photographers reached a certain small population of wealthy, well-traveled people who disdained cinema and television and almost all magazines. The ill-defined cohort enjoyed visual philosophic complexity; it experienced genuine glamour as a powerful transformer of particular space, distinguished among costume and fashion and nudity and nakedness, and prized the rare photographs that opened on the "completely convincing and unified total impression" of momentary transcendence of place and person.[10] This Mortensen called "the inner world," the imaginative constructs that evolve from making rather than consuming.

Mortensen explained of draped and sometimes masked women standing inside ruined plantation houses that "the human figures in these photographs help to condense the feeling of ruin-haunted grandeur, of things lost." World War II had destroyed as much of mid-twentieth-century American culture as the Civil War had southern culture. Astute postwar Americans, Mortensen speculated, saw no salvation in mass media or in high-paced urban life, but instead looked well beyond such narrow confines.[11] "The human figure can be used photographically to wholly crystallize the feeling of a building—to project or intensify its innate character," he concluded. The figure simply had to be the right one for the space.[12]

But somehow the power did not work in cities. It worked best in places where long-vanished people had left behind traces of enterprise. Laughlin saw such traces as the detritus of plantation agriculture, but other photographers knew them as the stone walls of afforested New England or the shrinking meadows of rural Pennsylvania or the swimming holes of Ohio or Iowa or Washington.[13] In a way, the glamour partook of sorcery, magic involving the dead, or perhaps the departed. It required quiet and peacefulness, freedom from prying and censorious eyes, and relics of times before. And it required a specific frame.

The shop-theory basis of glamour photography involved the square image, typically the brilliant ground-glass image floating at the base of the view-surround well of the Rolleiflex medium-format camera. The casual dismissal of 35 mm photography after the late 1920s merits consideration, for it opens on the world of photographers who knew its rectangular format (and very small negative size) as one more tentacle of the Hollywood cinema monster. Hollywood and the New York fashion industry delighted in the rectangular image, the one horizontal in movie houses, the other vertical in magazines; advocates of square-format imagery directly contradicted the authority and standards of mass media even as they championed something different. As the medium-format (and large-format) camera became something quintessentially pastoral and exurban, its advocates subtly championed the quasi-abandoned rural landscape that so fixed the attention of Tolkien and Cornish and so many other fantasy writers and photographers intrigued by genuine glamour.

After the appearance of *The Hobbit*, a handful of readers, many of them children, found a way into modern faerie. The appearance of *The Lord of the Rings* roughly two decades later sparked the subsequent 1970s fantasy effort epitomized in Cooper's *The Dark Is Rising*. Despite the massive overburden of trash and moving-image adaptations, first-rate fantasy literature continues to focus on seeing outside ordinary, mass-media frames, especially the glimpsing of genuine glamour, the shaping or making of something special in ordinary space and structure. The best of it still aims at children of privilege whose tastes have already angled away from mass-media entertainment.[14] It addresses children who think they have been directed to think of themselves as special, or who suspect some children and adults are special, but who know that voicing such thoughts is unseemly in classrooms where equality and homogeneity are bywords.

In the dusk of film photography, fantasy literature of all sorts becomes more powerful and more poignant. Far more compact thematically than science fiction and vastly more likely to touch girls and women, it now shapes much of the imagery in fashion magazines and other upscale advertising media aimed largely at women. It emphasizes the peculiar radiance of some women, even if it never mentions Od specifically. It explains that the radiance cannot be purchased at the mall. It extols light and the noticing of it, and it centers on the places transformed by out-of-the-ordinary-light, the light that makes old alignment apparent to the discerning observer. This is the light that makes things happen.

Medium-format, square-framed photography harks back to the box cameras Eastman Kodak popularized as somehow touched by brownies. It is an older photography, one grounded in the expectation that cameras sometimes work on their own, and enlivened by a constant making and remaking of equipment. It is a more simple photography than the accessory-fixated 35 mm photography of the Depression and subsequent decades. Most Rolleiflex photographers still carry only a lens hood; their cameras are massive but their attachments are very few indeed. In the end, medium-format photographers expect to make a photograph using simple if splendid equipment. If they do not scorn the mass of accessories favored by 35 mm photographers they puzzle at it. More often than not, medium-format photographers think themselves superior to all others: they work with a simple camera that demands great skill.

Very often their large cameras evoke faint but discernible feelings of German photographic technology and prewar German aesthetics. This can be discomfiting. Sometimes students ask about the letters stamped on my older Rolleiflexes, and I explain that they stand for "Deutsche Reich Patent." I see eyes widen, then narrow. Older Rolleiflexes are indeed from another era, one that still troubles, and even the postwar models conjure wraiths of unease.[15]

Superiority links medium-format photography and the best modern fantasy literature. Tolkien, Cooper, Le Guin, and Pullman suggest that some people have skills superior to those of others, skills that might be honed but cannot be bought. Even Rowling's Harry Potter is born special. Such characters carry very little with them throughout their adventures and they adventure directly, not in some virtual, second- or third-hand way. In certain places their abilities grow strong and sometimes even visible to commoners. Many Rolleiflex photographers find the lack of accessories, especially the lack of interchangeable lenses, incomprehensible to 35 mm photographers and also to children and adults who know nothing of photography beyond electronic point-and-shoot cameras. The Rolleiflex camera itself and the distinctive bent-at-the-waist posture of its holder contribute to both curiosity and unease, while the typically slow pace of making the exposure often irritates bystanders who wonder what the photographer sees that they do not. Something secret, something almost alchemical suffuses the Rolleiflex photograph-making enterprise in a way that parallels the theme of so much first-rate fantasy literature. And it is secret, unless the Rolleiflex photographer invites a bystander to look down into the dark well shading the brilliant ground-glass viewing screen.

In so much fantasy writing, authors explore the significance of the special—particularly glamour, the visual magic one must see to know. A society tolerant of people with perfect pitch still fails to understand those with a good eye for its visual equivalent: light, color, composition, posture, clothing, and perhaps Od itself. Far too often, when the subject involves ancient alignments, old fields, or even belly buttons, indeed anything contemporary mass media avoids, those with good eyes become suspect in the eyes of those occluded by programming.

As film photography fades, as square-shape, medium-format film photography becomes an anachronism, the fantasy view grows stronger and fuses itself into the environmental movement. Some photographers discern this. Glamour can be the expensive, contrived look of the fashion magazines and Hollywood, but it can also be something free and natural in an overgrown, ruined place.

NOTES

Introduction

1. Academics dismiss the importance of the poetry of Robert Frost, for example, by pointing out that "New England is no longer rural." Such comments confuse undergraduates from rural New England and often upset them.

2. Frazier, *Cold Mountain,* 388–89, addresses the concept of living fully in a place over decades by reducing the scale of observation.

3. While important, the distinction lies beyond the scope of this book; see Effland, "When Rural Does Not Equal Agricultural."

4. The name dates to the 1840s. My students easily accept my raising hens; only when they realize I sometimes slaughter flocks do they become uncomfortable. Many have never killed an animal larger than an insect.

5. I have been unable to find any scholarship defining the division that occurred as television reception improved in rural and small-town regions after the middle 1950s.

6. In part, our interests developed from those of our fathers, who passed their Depression-era boyhood pastimes directly to us, sometimes with their toys or tools or sporting equipment.

7. The repair of antique box cameras often involves nothing more than re-attaching shutter springs.

8. W. S. Davis, "Photography in Fog," addresses some of the dangers.

9. "Photographing Your Own Playmate" is the sort of technical article that impressed me.

10. This is another distinction beyond the scope of this book, but one perhaps crucial in understanding the power of cinema and television over girls after about 1960 to 1965.

11. See, for example, Bischoff, Brown, and Richardson, *Personal Demon;* and Ball, *Mathemagics.*

12. My students formally studying photography still learn the necessity of good composition, but most others speak glibly of "fixing" images with Adobe Photoshop and other software.

13. Brown, *Da Vinci Code,* is a useful introduction to the new genre.

14. The graphic novel emerging from comic books proves a contradictory current, of course; see, for example, Gaiman et al., *Sandman.*

15. Chödrön, *When Things Fall Apart,* 146, offers a useful illustration.

16. See Vogel, Cagan, and Boatwright, *Design of Things to Come,* 88–90. Bookstores shelve works by Joshilyn Jackson away from the fantasy section too; see her *The Girl Who Stopped Swimming.*

17. Garreau, "Perfecting the Human," offers a useful introduction to the imminence of the imminent; see also Greenman, "Watson."

18. Salvatore, *Woods Out Back,* 16–17.

19. Nutting, *Photographic Art Secrets,* 5.

20. Stilgoe, *Landscape and Images,* 266–69.

21. See John Muller, "Landscapes," in *Prize-Winning Photography,* 46–51.

22. Crawford and Keiller, *Wessex from the Air,* 52.

23. Cooper, *Greenwitch,* addresses this; see esp. 57–58.

24. Sousa, "All in the Family."

25. T. Brown, *Way of the Scout.*

26. The creation of new life forms fixes undergraduate attention.

27. While some fantasy illustrators have websites, informal connections link

artists with authors and publishers. See Westfall, Slusser, and Plummer, *Unearthly Visions,* for an introduction.

28. Newton, *Pages from the Glossies.*

29. Leibovitz, "Let the Games Begin," welds fashion model imagery and photography of athletes in a way that makes the athletes supernatural. L. Collins, "Pixel Perfect," offers a popularized introduction to the shop-theory techniques of altering digital photographs of models and other celebrities.

30. For an exception, see Theweleit, *Männerphantasien.*

31. See, for example, Breward, *Fashion;* Calefato, *Clothed Body;* and Lehmann, *Tigersprung.* Lord, *Forever Barbie,* sometimes probes more deeply than recent scholarship.

32. Barry, *Complete Book,* emphasizes this view.

33. On the creation of avatars, see Bans, "Same Shit, Different World."

34. Mack, *Heart Religion in the British Enlightenment;* see also Hempton, "Enchantment and Disenchantment."

35. On the relation of vision and cameras, see Ericksenn, *Medium Format Photography,* 19–20.

36. Nutting, *Photographic Art Secrets,* 46–47.

37. I. Berger, "New Cameras Revive an Old Format."

38. Screen format deserves a monograph.

39. Almost no automobiles offer centerline steering wheels.

40. For an introduction, see Walser, *Golden Section.*

41. Heering, *Rolleiflex Book,* 16.

42. Adams, "Exposition," 73.

43. While Heering did not explicitly worry about the ability of language to carry his message, Mortensen did; see his "More About Projection Control," 31.

44. Friedberg, *Virtual Window,* esp. 129–30, 310, offers an excellent introduction to Edison-based aspect ratios; see also Heath, *Questions of Cinema,* 1–18.

45. Eisenstein, *Film Essays,* 48–49, 51, 50–51, 59, 53, 60.

46. Nutting argued for vertical images of landscape; see *Photographic Art Secrets,* 47.

47. Architectural theory may not apply to any cinema house built after about 1930; see Forty, *Words and Buildings,* 157–58.

48. See, for example, Schlobin, *Aesthetics.*

49. When a few friends thought the square old-fashioned, I enlarged and printed part of the negative in rectangular format.

50. Cooper, *Greenwitch,* 57–58.

51. The Rolleiflex lately figures in many Tokyo advertisements and billboards, photos of which have been sent to me by observant alumni who have not thought to gather proper bibliographical data.

52. Kelland, "Romance" (1930), makes clear that glamour perhaps subverted traditional American power and class structures. His is the earliest explicit mention I have found.

53. K. Burke, *Rhetoric of Motives,* 210; and Quick, "Your Summer Studio," 39; see also chap. 14 below.

54. For a 1941 comment on haze, see Brace, *Light on a Mountain,* 191.

55. Risk itself rewards scrutiny in a risk-adverse culture that understands the phrase "children at risk" as denoting children at risk of something bad, perhaps very bad, happening to them, not something spectacularly good; see Swiss Reinsurance Company, *Landscape of Risk.* See also Bempechat, *Against the Odds.*

56. On alternative presents, see Winterson, *Tanglewreck* (2006).

57. Fantasy may be a new component in the long tradition of social Darwinism; see Hofstadter, *Social Darwinism.*

58. Dating facets of glamour photography proves tricky, given the variation of images that come to hand. Certainly in the early 1920s some photographers knew glamour photography as distinct

from other genres, even though Hollywood studio photographers called corporate publicity work "glamour photography" from the 1920s onward. By 1940 magazines aimed at accomplished amateurs understood glamour imagery as distinct from corporate imagery intended to advertise anything, and by 1950 a handful of critics realized it as distinct, mysterious, and somehow subversive. It prospered as a genre into the early 1970s, then perhaps moved sideways, out of the line of feminist movement attack. The last is conjectural, since the late 1980s resurgence of interest in advanced amateur magazines (see below) implies that glamour photography had merely lost critical attention for ten to fifteen years.

59. Pullman, *Golden Compass*, 18–22.

60. The passage proves especially powerful when read against Berkeley's 1709 *New Theory of Vision*.

61. Elmendorf, *Lantern Slides,* offers an introduction to making the slides.

62. Students from independent schools often see a liking for digital projection as something that defines high-school students no longer familiar with better-quality projection.

63. The projector requires a projectionist, since it lacks a self-loading feature: the switch to 35 mm projectors originated in cost-cutting efforts in the early 1970s.

64. As early as 1927, Nutting remarked the out-of-fashion excellence of transparencies; see *Photographic Art Secrets,* 26.

65. One sees something similar in art galleries, when young people find a silver print hung next to an ink-jet one, know the superiority of the former, and know too they have little vocabulary to voice their understanding of difference.

66. Clarke, *Jonathan Strange,* 785.

67. The film scholar Linda Williams addresses this issue in "Discipline and Fun: *Psycho* and Postmodern Cinema," in Williams and Gledhill, *Reinventing Film Studies,* 352–78.

68. Personal communication from a scholar in the office adjacent to mine.

69. "As Good as It Gets," 37.

70. Handlin, *Truth in History,* 231, 235.

71. Bachelard, *Poetics of Space,* 33.

72. Amateur Internet pornographic video seems so extensive now that it may well put out of business for-profit makers of visual pornography: that young people volunteer to appear in amateur photography in such numbers makes difficult the task of faculty who condemn pornography.

1 Fantasy

1. Spence, *British Fairy Origins,* 2. See also R. Kirk, *Secret Commonwealth.*

2. Brontë, *Jane Eyre,* 96–97, 104.

3. Scott, *Demonology and Witchcraft,* 94–97. See also Repplier, *Books and Men,* 51–52.

4. Tolkien, *Tree and Leaf,* 10.

5. Kipling, *Plain Tales,* 144. See also his *Rewards and Fairies,* 87.

6. Spenser, *Poetical Works,* 400. See also C. Koch, "P. H. Oelman and the Feminine Ideal."

7. Spenser, *Poetical Works,* 149–50. On scrying, see Stilgoe, *Landscape and Images,* esp. 266–70.

8. Williams's book shaped much of my understanding of Spenser's poem. On Spenserian fantasy and visual imagination, see Bradner, *Edmund Spenser;* L. S. Johnson, *The Shepheardes Calendar;* and Alpers, *Edmund Spenser: A Critical Anthology.* See Thoer, "Photographing Glass."

9. On Massachusetts coast glass, see Irwin, *Story of Sandwich Glass;* and Lee, *Sandwich Glass.* For an example of winter evening window-glass reflection, see Whittier's poem "Snow-Bound" (1866), in *Poetical Works,* 288; Whittier includes "the old rhyme" to explain the "mimic flame." See also Frazier, *Cold Mountain,* 48–49.

10. Forbes, *Boston Book,* 67, associates the glass and seeing with "blue-blooded" New Englanders accustomed to visual distortion.

11. I date my change in thinking to the year 1988, when I realized that many well-educated, thoughtful women harbored deepening doubts about the long-term impact of academic feminism on the power of women in society.

12. The extreme class division implicit in print-media versus all other sorts of advertising lies beyond the scope of this book, but see the use of mirrors, glass, and water reflection in the Holiday 2007 issue of *Bal Harbour Magazine.*

13. Rodriguez, "It's All in the Frame."

14. Wittgenstein, *Philosophical Investigations,* 118–22, 190, and 205, 213.

15. On second sight, see R. Kirk, *Secret Commonwealth,* esp. 2–19.

16. Pearlman, *Rollei Manual* (1955), 125–27.

17. I have always heard this filter called by its German name, "Verlauf."

18. It is equally useful alongshore: coastal-zone photography involves awkward issues of lighting (glare, especially) within compositional ones. See W. S. Davis, "Sail Ho!"

19. The mere existence of the filter is unknown to many photographers, although graduated filters have been in use since the 1910s.

20. I have found no books that explain the plethora of images for sale in secondhand shops and on Internet auction sites.

21. Other illustrators exploring faerie skirt the same boundaries; see, for example, Royo, *Wild Sketches.*

22. P. Burke, *Popular Culture,* esp. 266–86.

23. In an age when electronic cameras immediately reveal to photographers the success or failure of a particular image-making effort, using a film camera itself seems risky to many, since the photographer must wait until he develops his film.

24. See, for example, Salvatore, *Woods Out Back.*

25. See Pedersen, *Glance at the History of Linguistics,* for one overview of the changes.

26. Tolkien, *Lord of the Rings,* 2:68.

27. See, for example, the explanation of the place-name Minas Morgul in *Lord of the Rings,* 1:321.

28. Tolkien, *Pictures;* and Hammond and Scull, *J. R. R. Tolkien.*

29. At least once, Tolkien suggested that he intended his books to work both philological and geographical magic; see *Lord of the Rings,* 1:307.

30. Tolkien, *Lord of the Rings,* 1:107

31. Tolkien, *Lord of the Rings,* 1:249–51, 274. See also 1:107.

32. Tolkien, *Hobbit,* 134, 232.

33. On the etymology of advertising, see Partridge, *Charm,* 29–31.

34. See esp. Shippey, "The Magic Art." On the place of "gifted" individuals in the 1970s, see esp. Frum, *How We Got Here,* esp. 188–28; and Kahn, George-Warren, and Dahl, *Rolling Stone,* esp. 54–58; B. Schulman, *The Seventies.*

35. For an introduction to Peake's work, see G. Smith, *Mervyn Peake;* Watney, *Mervyn Peake;* and Glancey, *Train,* 127.

36. See Gardiner-Scott, *Mervyn Peake,* for an introduction to Peake's envisioning.

37. Borrelli, "Fashion Thinks Ink," esp. 42. See also C. Hanson, "Metamorphosis of Tituba."

38. *The Encyclopedia of Fantasy* and D'Ammassa's *Encyclopedia of Fantasy and Horror Fiction* make a start.

39. See A. Moore, "Magic Afoot"; see also Davidson, "Folklore and Man's Past."

40. Le Guin, *Farthest Shore,* 44. See also Opie, "Tentacles of Tradition."

41. Post-shipwreck passage making perhaps demonstrates this most clearly; see Stilgoe, *Lifeboat,* 186–216. See also Nix, *Sabriel,* esp. 288–97.

42. See, for example, Sullaway, *Chasing Dreamtime,* esp. 207–304.

43. See, Vogel, Cagan, and Boatwright, *Design of Things to Come,* 87–104, 129–30.

44. On this phenomenon, see Baxandall, *Patterns of Intention.*

45. Pine and Gilmore, *Experience Economy*.

46. Le Guin, *Farthest Shore*, 92–93.

47. Bradley, *Warrior Woman*, 12–49.

48. Typically, academics understand art evolving from the imagination. Whimsy receives little attention.

49. Hawthorne, "Great Magician."

50. It still characterizes some; see the December 1990 issue of *Pinhole Journal*, devoted to "Still Life & Fantasy."

51. N. M. West, *Kodak and the Lens of Nostalgia*, esp. 86, 58, 35–40, 107–8.

52. I have been unable to learn whether "twelve-year-old child" really meant "eighth-grade child": oral tradition in much of the Midwest and South suggests that the firm gave cameras to children likely to attend high school.

53. See esp. Mees, *Photography*, 56.

54. Depression-era poverty may explain the way elderly people still speak of "wasting a picture" when a child or rare adult chooses to photograph something the old think unworthy of what they still think of as a frame of expensive film.

55. Kennedy, "Peter Pan," esp. 28–29.

56. McGonigal, "'Sumpmin' Has Gotta Be Done.'"

57. Only rarely do I encounter cell-phone photographers who have the slightest concept of the lenses fitted into phones.

58. March 14, 2006.

59. "Creating Heirlooms."

60. Crary, *Techniques of the Observer*, esp. 40, 63–64, 86. See also Bennet, Hoffman, and Prakash, *Observer Mechanics*.

61. Newton, *Opticks*, lix.

62. Newton, *Opticks*, 52–54.

63. Cornish, *Scenery and the Sense of Light*, is almost unknown today despite its precise arguments; Minnaert's *Light and Color*, much revised in many subsequent editions, remains in print.

64. The shriveling of shop theory perhaps explains not only Walter Benjamin's avoidance of the improperly fixed negative or photograph in his essay "The Work of Art in the Age of Mechanical Reproduction," in *Illuminations*, 217–51.

65. See, for example, D. E. Thomas, "Mirror Images"; and J. Walker, "Physics of the Pattern of Frost."

66. See, for example, Lewis H. Lapham's introduction to McLuhan, *Understanding Media*; and D. D. Hoffman, *Visual Intelligence*, esp. 139–71.

67. Lethem, "Brando's Last Stand," 100.

68. See, for example, McKay, *Theory and Practice of Photography*, 4.

69. See Gregg, *Experiments in Visual Science*, esp. 3–18, 56–59.

70. M. Warner, "Stolen Shadows," offers an introduction to the conflation of shadow and reflection.

71. Warner argues that only the death mask is equally strong in its assertion that the person himself or herself came in contact with the artist.

72. See, for example, the images in any issue of *Bal Harbour Magazine*; see also the Robert McGinnis cover art of Terrall, *Kill Now*.

73. I have been unable to confirm the rumor.

74. W. Eisner, *Comics and Sequential Art*.

75. In the past twelve years I have met not one undergraduate who has noticed such things, but I have met several elderly people learning to use computers who do wonder and receive no answers.

76. See, for example, Dawber, *Pixel Surgeons*; and Reichert, *Erotic History of Advertising*.

77. Foresta and Wood, *Secrets of the Dark Chamber*.

78. Young children play video games while sitting on the floor, looking up at the monitor: almost certainly, their position evolves from the characteristic siting of the horizon in so many games, especially *Tomb Raider*.

79. Halley, *Split Decisions*.

80. H. Newton, *Pages from the Glossies*, offers a useful introduction.

81. Johnson and Lennon, *Appearance and Power*. See also Williams, *Decoding*

Advertisements, esp. 138–51. Perhaps the last prefeminist study of media, fashion, and American concepts of beauty, Perutz's *Beyond the Looking Glass* uses the concept of the mirror explicitly (138–51).

82. Perutz, *Beyond the Looking Glass,* 26–27, 76–77, 148, 204–6, 237, 242.

83. Etcoff, *Survival of the Prettiest;* Craik, *Face of Fashion;* Bergler, *Fashion and the Unconscious;* König, *Menschheit auf dem Laufstag;* Müller, *Art and Fashion;* Fiorani, *Abitare il corpo;* and Kaiser, *Social Psychology of Clothing.* See also Paglia, *Sexual Personae.*

84. M. Mitchell, *Gone with the Wind,* 1.

85. Ekman and Friesen, *Unmasking the Face.*

86. Baym, "Melodramas of Beset Manhood."

87. The response of Harvard undergraduate woman to the decision figures in a book currently in hand.

88. For the past ten years, Diane Smith has edited the swimsuit issue of *Sports Illustrated.* Having a woman in charge of the issue perhaps deflects some feminist protest; see "Raphy's World."

89. The May 1993 issue of *Lighthouse: A Forum for Women and Men to Discuss Women's Issues* devoted to "Perceptions of Beauty" echoed concepts that undergraduate women (and a handful of men) had been speaking privately to me about since the middle 1980s.

90. M. Wilson, *Charm* (1928), 19–20, 22, 33–34.

91. Priestley, *Midnight on the Desert,* 178–79.

92. M. Wilson, *Charm* (1928), 46–47; see also M. Wilson, *I Found My Way,* esp. 125–64.

93. M. Wilson, *Charm* (1928), 103.

94. M. Wilson, *Woman You Want to Be,* 47. She did advise readers to wear (and enjoy wearing) "dainty underthings."

95. M. Wilson, *Woman You Want to Be,* 97, 80, 94.

96. M. Wilson, *Woman You Want to Be,* 39, 94.

97. Wilson turned her first book into an entire industry: she lectured, wrote magazine articles, answered mail (with a staff), and did private and small-group classes and courses, including ones focused on New York executive women (one of which featured ways to flag down a cab); see M. Wilson, *I Found My Way.*

98. M. Wilson, *Woman You Want to Be,* 261, 105, 100.

99. Joan Smith, *Different for Girls,* 63–76, approaches such thinking.

100. Nicholas and Anthony Bruno's article "Glamour," in *Prize-Winning Photography,* 52–57, offers a succinct summary of the change away from cosmetics and the way a confident model interested in her own ideas photographs especially well. See also Bernsohn and Bernsohn, "Photographer and the Model," esp. 231, 236.

101. Ray, *Avant-Garde Finds Andy Hardy,* 108.

102. Schoenfeld, *Look Great Naked.*

103. Wedding photographers must deal with formally attired women too, but usually ones wearing white and in daylight conditions.

104. See, for example, Gowland, *How to Photograph Women.*

105. W. C. White, "The Strapless." See also M. Harris, *Weegee's Secrets.*

106. D. Turner, "Glamour in Your Living Room."

107. On Valentine's Day 2007, snow turned to rain, falling temperatures froze slush and skimmed puddles, and faculty marveled at miniskirted, high-heeled undergraduate women, plastic bags taped around their shoes, carrying roses to their boyfriends nesting snug and dry in dormitory rooms.

108. Caldwell, "Pour That Girl a Drink."

109. "School Reading Scores Worsen."

110. Webb and Zito, "Portraits of Women"; Alpert, "Sensuality in the Cinema"; and Clark, "Black and White and Technicolor."

111. M. Wilson, *Charm* (1934), 119–30.

112. More than half of the time they refer to the photographs of their mothers and grandmothers as revealing "a side" of the person hitherto unknown to them.

113. See, for example, *Critical Landscape,* and esp. the preface by Jasper De Haan.

114. Many of my advanced students equate the end of the openness they identify with the growing financial insecurity of college-educated adults.

115. Yeats, *Celtic Twilight,* 66.

116. Gaiman, *Graveyard Book,* esp. 105–19.

2 Media

1. An informal code still rules the airwaves: on February 14, 2008, Jane Fonda used a vulgarity on the NBC show *Today;* she and the network immediately apologized. "We would do nothing to offend the audience," the *New York Daily News* quotes one NBC spokesman as saying.

2. For a general introduction to the role of Hollywood cinema in shaping middle-class perceptions of women's attire, see Gaines and Herzog, *Fabrications.*

3. Overseas radio broadcasting remains oddly unstudied as a shaper of American culture.

4. Radio, domestic and World Service alike, is absent from books analyzing the way "media" impact children and adults; see, for example, Greenfield, *Mind and Media.*

5. As early as 1950, Powdermaker, *Hollywood,* offered anthropological explanations of the uneasiness; see esp. 54–81. Twice in my high school years, schoolteachers explicitly stopped incipient classroom discussion of the code.

6. Stilgoe, *Alongshore,* 365–67.

7. Histories of swimwear emphasize public-realm apparel, and books emphasizing photographs of people in swimsuits tend to eschew any mention of private behavior; see, for example, *Swimsuits: 100 Years of Pictures.*

8. Starting in the late 1980s I began

hearing the expression, often said by women in store-bought, perfectly modest bikinis and maillots confronting circumstances changed by the appearance of a male, even a boy, not well known to them. While the expression implies that the suits are not clothes, it vexes me that I am unable to recall when I first heard it, and by whom. In the late 1960s and early 1970s, women said, "I'd better get a shirt," or words to that effect.

9. See, for example, Schwind, *Cape Cod Fisherman,* 48.

10. In 1968 I first heard the argument that nudity itself is sexless. The homemade suits perhaps made wearers more sexual creatures but not nearly as much as did slinky one-piece suits many women kept for social swimming.

11. Lindbergh, *Gift from the Sea,* 31. See also Pope, Phillips, and Olivardia, *Adonis Complex.*

12. Stilgoe, *Alongshore,* 334–67.

13. Some parents disagreed with the post–Benjamin Spock advice about child nudity.

14. By 1972 I knew that many parents feared LSD and other illegal drugs, but still had little understanding of the drugs or teenage drug use.

15. The term is the technical one for the fig leaf or leaves that cover male genitalia on statues; see Elster, *There's a Word for It,* 93. The fall 1976 *Daedalus* devoted an entire issue to the concept of adulthood; see especially K. S. Lynn, "Adulthood in American Literature"; and Goldstein, "On Being Adult." As late as 1983, the Study Group of New York found many parents and children utterly relaxed about family nudity; see its *Children and Sex,* esp. 40–55.

16. R. W. Lewis, "Those Swinging Beach Movies," esp. 82–84.

17. Goldstein, "On Being Adult." See also Friedenberg, *Vanishing Adolescent,* 181–89. In her 1949 short story "Moon Lake," Welty refers to the southern superstition that teenage girls who see a teenage boy nude will die old maids; see *Thirteen Stories,* 212.

18. Raucher, *Summer of '42,*" esp. 1–14.

19. Oakley, *Sex, Gender, and Society,* 100.

20. Craik, *Face of Fashion,* 147–50, offers an excellent analysis of a fashion revolution begun by women disconnected from cinema values and from fashion magazine dictates both.

21. People who are proud of, or at least not ashamed of, their bodies often tend to take very good care of them, something seemingly lost on public-school substance-abuse educators. It is possible that vitamin D forestalls breast cancer in women, something about which older people in my town have mused for years, especially women wondering why "sun bunnies" rarely seem to suffer from breast cancer.

22. J. Miller, "Stern Hedonism," emphasizes this.

23. Quoted in J. Miller, "Stern Hedonism," 142.

24. Hollander, *Sex and Suits,* offers the sharpest introduction to the business suit.

25. Morris, *The Naked Ape,* sharpened my interest in observing the human body.

26. Remarkably little scholarship exists concerning children (and adults from nontelevision locations) who simply dislike the medium; see, however, Bryant and Zillman, *Responding to the Screen.*

27. The age at which I first saw television puts me almost outside the limit McLuhan sets in his 1969 *Counter Blast* for the "multiple lifetimes" lived by television-watching children before they enter first grade. See also Gitlin, *Watching Television.*

28. See Rosenblatt, "Growing Up on Television," for a prescient 1976 view of the rapidity of the change.

29. For background on commercials, see Boddy, *Fifties Television;* and esp. Bella Thomas, "What the Poor Watch."

30. People who watched little or no television as very young children may be a discrete cohort nowadays: at least some popular critics think so; see, for example, Pearce, *Evolution's End,* 154–55, 164–72, 195–98. It is seductively easy to dismiss Pearce and his colleagues, but reading John Berger's *Ways of Seeing* knowing from the start that the book originated as a supplement to a BBC television series raises awkward issues about people who did not watch television as children.

31. By then I had read McLuhan and Fiore, *The Medium Is the Massage,* and had a glimpse of how book design might change.

32. Leff and Simmons, *The Dame in the Kimono,* 206–7.

33. In graduate school, office-hour conversation with senior professors revealed that some thought that visual media had begun to "rot" the traditional liberal arts reliance on the written word and logic.

34. By 1974 my friends and I remarked on the way lack of money deflected people into television watching.

35. By 1975 I realized that people who wore little took pride in their bodies, and often did not use illegal drugs or even drink beer.

36. Mortensen, *Monsters and Madonnas,* n.p.

37. Riis, "People's Institute," 856.

38. On the code, see Doherty, *Pre-Code Hollywood.*

39. Walsh, *Sin and Censorship,* esp. 9–67.

40. Ernst and Lorentz's 1930 *Censored* offers a contemporaneous view of the imminent impact of the proposed nationwide code.

41. Leff and Simmons, *Dame in the Kimono.*

42. Goldwyn, *Behind the Scenes,* esp. 15–29.

43. Brownlow, *Hollywood,* esp. 54–57.

44. David Wallace, *Lost Hollywood,* esp. 8–9.

45. On celebrity, see Rein, *High Visibility;* and Joan Smith, *Different for Girls.*

46. K. Fuller, *At the Picture Show,* 144–45.

47. Slide, *Aspects of American Film History* and *Early Women Directors;* see also Dixon, *Transparency of Spectacle,* 136.

48. A Hollywood industry eager for female readers complicates the otherwise strong argument of Mulvey, *Visual and Other Pleasures.*

49. See Charles Burke, "Black Country," *Best British Short Stories of 1923,* 58–66.

50. Bob Thomas, *Walt Disney,* 60–65.

51. Studlar, "'Perils of Pleasure.'"

52. Hollander, "Costume and Convention," 674–75. The book mentioned appeared as *Seeing through Clothes.*

53. In the early 1970s rural backyard private nudity hovered on the cusp of what many thought would be everyday beach nudity within a year or so, especially as store-bought bikinis grew briefer each summer.

54. Susan J. Douglas, "Amateur Operators," in Corn, *Imagining Tomorrow,* is especially astute on this subject; see esp. 50–56.

55. Arnheim, *Radio,* 235–37. See also D. Kahn and Whitehead, *Wireless Imagination.*

56. Reeves, *Power of Film Propaganda;* and Rentschler, *Ministry of Illusion,* offer two approaches to Nazi propaganda in terms of weighting the importance of radio; see also an earlier book, Zeman, *Nazi Propaganda.*

57. See D. Kahn, "Track Organology."

58. Film studies scholars rarely emphasize the growing power of radio-centered capitalization in the studio system era; see T. Schatz, *Genius of the System.*

59. Seldes, *Great Audience,* 21. See also K. Fuller, *At the Picture Show,* 16–57.

60. Huxley, *On the Margin,* 50–52, emphasizes the audience change.

61. Between 1918 and 1934 one of my great uncles did exit-interview research at Boston cinemas: his notes make up the chief source material for a book beyond this one and a book in progress.

62. Tomlinson, *Mingled Yarn,* 77–79, 83. See also Gerould, "Hollywood."

63. K. Fuller, *At the Picture Show,* 145–49.

64. Pitkin, "Crisis in the Movies."

65. "Should Children Go to the Movies?" See also Repplier, *Books and Men,* 64–93; A. E. Moore, "Shall We Banish the Fairies?"; and Chamberlin, "Shall We Let Our Children Fly?" Nutting, *Photographic Art Secrets,* loathed films for their poor photographic quality and content; see esp. 74–76.

66. Hollywood studios competed strongly with radio; see, for example, Paramount Pictures, "Magic Carpet." See also Knight, *Liveliest Art.*

67. Dunning, *On the Air,* offers an excellent starting point. This is the revised edition of his 1976 *Tune in Yesterday.*

68. Only extremely traditional and avocational farmers still broadcast seed: most farmers drill it.

69. W. Morris, *North toward Home,* 108–19.

70. See, for example, *Complete War of the Worlds.*

71. I have encountered no one who thought the news bulletins a trick or even wrong or partially wrong; on belief and disbelief, see Remmling, *Road to Suspicion.*

72. I now think they must have either read or known of Wiener's 1948 book, *Cybernetics.*

73. B. Jackson, "Führer Comes to Liechtenstein," is the closest I have found in print to their thinking.

74. Not until Shirer published his *Nightmare Years* did I find a narrative into which my friends' remarks fitted.

75. On Coughlin, see Athans, *Coughlin-Fahey Connection;* D. Warren, *Radio Priest;* and General Jewish Council, *Father Coughlin.* Coughlin started *Social Justice* in 1936. McLuhan, *Understanding Media,* 78–79.

76. World Committee, *Brown Network,* esp. 239–63.

77. Mencken, *American Language,* esp. 186, 22, 230–32: Mencken understood how rapidly American radio and sound films introduced Americanisms into British English; see 230.

78. See Subirats, *Antropofagia;* and Freyre, *Order and Progress.* On the Macfadden publishing empire, see esp. Fabian, "Making a Commodity of Truth."

79. It is difficult to trace such thinking, esp. in light of postwar Allied intentions of removing all collections of the Grimm folktales from Germany and mandating that every German radio receiver be equipped with World Service features; see, for an introduction, Grimm and Grimm, *Annotated Brothers Grimm,* esp. 409, 416–17.

80. Papini, *Storia di un' Amicizia,* 317–19.

81. Lyttelton translates Papini's expression as "the chattering classes"; see his "'Crisis of Bourgeois Society,'" 20.

82. Falasca-Zamponi, *Fascist Spectacle,* esp. 15–41, 120–25.

83. Zolla, *Eclipse of the Intellectual,* 202.

84. Macfadden may have been the consummate manipulator of serials, radio, and film in the first half of the twentieth century, but his far-right, sometimes protofascist angle of vision not only put off most intellectuals (librarians included—finding complete runs of his serials can be difficult) at the time but repulses contemporary young media historians who turn away from Macfadden "cosmographs" as prototypes of contemporary computer-altered imagery.

85. Stenhouse, *Cracker Hash,* 165.

86. R. Moore, *Candlemas Bay,* 295.

87. T. Jones, *Boyhood at Sea,* 108, 129.

88. See Allen, *Horrible Prettiness.*

89. Seldes, *Seven Lively Arts,* 36–37.

90. The book makes splendid reading against Fitzgerald's *The Great Gatsby,* published a year later.

91. Vasey, *World according to Hollywood,* esp. 122–57, offers a much later

analysis that confirms most of Seldes's assertions. Oddly enough, Vasey's book fails to cite Seldes.

92. Seldes, *Great Audience,* 103.

93. Galbraith's analysis dovetails with Seldes; see esp. his chapter "The Imperatives of Consumer Demand," *Affluent Society,* 139–51.

94. See H. Schiller, *Culture, Inc.* N. L. Chapman, *Comparative Media History,* acutely identifies the oddnesses of popularist media historians who see the 1940s and 1950s "as a defining epoch in terms of mass communication" but do not examine the larger frames (social, financing, etc.) that changed so dramatically at the time.

95. Punk music blossomed in a similar way against the strictures of so-called big-label recording; see P. J. Martin, *Sounds and Silence,* 252.

96. Walsh, *Sin and Censorship.*

97. Hobsbawm, *Age of Extremes,* 192, asserts that the twentieth century was "the century of the common people and dominated by the arts produced by and for them." He says little about the other people who recognized this early on and acted accordingly.

98. Burns, *It Came from Bob's Basement,* esp. 28–33.

99. Murrow, "Newsroom Resources."

100. Stanton, "Mass Media," n.p. This is a critical statement by an industry insider; essentially, it recognizes that television has no need to improve programming, since advertisers have no other venues anywhere near effectively reaching the mass of consumers. It also implies that those who view few films and little television are neither poor nor ill informed, but instead form a niche market upscale advertising reaches in nonbroadcast ways. Together with Murrow's speech, it suggests a fast-deepening class divide reflected in and exacerbated by television, and perhaps by film. By 1978 issues had become exceptionally clear; see Cole, *Television, the Book, and the Classroom,* especially in light of Durkin, *Children Who Read Early;* and

Lang and Lang, *Politics and Television,* which analyzes McCluhan's concepts. See also Arlen, *Living-Room War.*

101. Here see Mander, *Four Arguments,* esp. 29–53; and McKibben, *Age of Missing Information.* See also Noam, *Television in Europe;* and Gilmore, *Reading Becomes a Necessity of Life.*

102. Bertrand, *Race, Rock, and Elvis,* esp. 220–23.

103. McLuhan's incisive understanding of comic books in the context of broadcast media remains oddly unremarked; see *Understanding Media,* esp. 164–69.

104. See Shippey, *J. R. R. Tolkien,* for an introduction to the reception of Tolkien's *Lord of the Rings.*

105. Christakis et al., "Early Television Exposure."

106. Pullman, *Golden Compass,* 59.

107. Sinclair, *Uncanny Stories,* 228.

108. See, for example, Brumberg, *Body Project,* esp. 97–107; Rotundo, *American Manhood,* 221–25; Horwood, "'Girls Who Arouse'"; and Fass, *Damned and the Beautiful,* 4–6.

109. Priestley, *Midnight on the Desert,* 178.

110. See Valant, *Vintage Aircraft Nose Art.*

111. Basinger, *A Woman's View.*

112. Almost certainly, the "good girl" issue explains the reluctance of now-elderly women to speak of the photos their husbands still carry in their wallets.

113. Henle, *Figure Studies.*

114. Basch worked with a Rolleiflex camera identical to the one Henle used; see Basch, *Figure Study Photos,* 3.

115. Evening gown photography typically requires the model to wear makeup and the photographer to arrange sophisticated lighting: it is not something easily accomplished before dashing off to dinner or a charity ball. Most photographers and models chose the opposite end of the glamour structure involving little or no clothing.

116. My women students now ask regularly and frequently how fashion magazines "survived" the 1970s feminist moment. I say little, but suggest to the students that they spend several days reading all the 1970s issues of *Vanity Fair* and other magazines. Typically, students conclude that the magazines trusted visual images to overwhelm the printed word.

117. United States film historians remain reluctant to examine non-corporate-manufactured film.

118. On the films and their impact on swimming attire, see Stilgoe, *Alongshore,* 334–67.

119. Bocca, *Bikini Beach,* 29–32.

120. In the Caribbean the clash between European and American swimming attire proves worthwhile to study in detail.

121. I have been unable to find the colloquialism used before 2000; it may be connected with the warehouse industry jargon term for "distribution process."

122. Alvi, McInnes, and Smith, *Vice Guide to Sex and Drugs,* 159.

123. Linke, *German Bodies.*

124. In the 1950s male scuba divers wore suits briefer than contemporary competitive-swimming suits made by Speedo and other manufacturers. Images in books like Fontova's *Helldivers' Rodeo* (108) unnerve students who cannot "place" them in time and who associate very brief suits with gay men relaxing in the Caribbean.

125. Deresiewicz, "Love on Campus."

126. Altheide, "Impact of Television Formats."

127. See Debra Merskin, "Where Are the Clothes? The Pornographic Gaze in Mainstream American Fashion Advertising," in *Sex in Consumer Culture,* ed. Reichert and Lambiase, 199–217.

128. Bourdieu, *On Television,* offers a useful introduction to such views.

129. As an undergraduate a few years later I read Münsterberg's *Film.*

130. Only when I read Hollander's "Costume and Convention" in 1972 did I realize that others noticed details in films the way I did.

131. Aside from a handful of very poor immigrant students, only a few home-schooled undergraduates approach the precollege distancing from electronic mass media my friend and I so casually accepted.

132. Joan Didion's essay "In Hollywood" (1973) confirmed my suspicions that many people pay no attention to Hollywood; see her *White Album*, 153–67.

133. Christie implies that youth-oriented culture, especially that evident in music, might freight a new fascist era speeded by emotional response to oratory, lyrics, and music itself; see esp. *Passenger from Frankfurt*, 104–5, 144–45.

134. The phrase is Vasey's, *World according to Hollywood*, 3.

135. Authors focused on rural living repeatedly confirm my finding; see, for example, Barrette, *Countryman's Journal*, 19.

136. See, for example, Rice, *Blackwood Farm*, 138–39.

137. Eisenstein, "Montage and Architecture," 116.

3 Shop Theory

1. See Gottlieb's *Lost and Found in America;* and Lesy, "Fame and Fortune." See also Woodward, "Disturbing Photographs of Sally Mann."

2. Privacy seems to have been the chief motivation in keeping such images from albums.

3. The role of Polaroid "instant" photography as a precursor to digital photography lies outside the scope of this book.

4. Bernsohn and Bernsohn, "Photographer and the Model," 236.

5. D. A. Miller, *Place for Us,* 12.

6. The image size is roughly 26.5 × 26.5 mm; the square-format slides it made still startle my students when they appear among rectangular-shaped ones.

7. Rothschild, "Secret Life."

8. Gowland, "Underwater" and "Underwater Nudes."

9. B. C. Brown, "Available Light."

10. Schwalberg, "126 Moves Up to the Majors."

11. The dusty collections of the James included books on photography.

12. Growing up in an information-poor place does focus the young mind on what the environment provides.

13. The store was Ferranti-Dege in Harvard Square, immediately across the street from Widener Library. Its staff (many would-be artists or professional photographers working to support their careers), customers (many professional photographers), and owner, Anthony Ferranti (Harvard Class of 1955), provided me with a second university education.

14. Information flow before the Internet era often worked idiosyncratically: one Saturday in 1979, following a brief presentation of new products, a representative of a European film manufacturer handed me a booklet on Spanish glamour photography, and said he had been thinking about our conversation of a year before and thought the booklet might prove useful.

15. In retrospect, perhaps they thought that images might overwhelm words, and that my interest in photography, especially glamour photography, undermined the primacy of the graduate-school education on which we had all embarked.

16. H. Roberts and Yates, "Altair 8800 Minicomputer."

17. Ceruzzi, *History of Modern Computing,* 226.

18. Bruce, "Pinhole Photography," 40.

19. Nutting, *Photographic Art Secrets,* 28–29.

20. J. Parker, "Needleholing with Your Kodak."

21. The 1951 issue of *Photokinks* is especially eclectic, with articles ranging from box kite photography to figure studies to homemade studio lighting systems and contact printers. Almost all the articles assume readers familiar with woodworking tools, and sometimes machine tools.

22. Harvard Square newsstands retail about twenty different photography magazines each month, and for years I have browsed monthly.

23. *Rolleiflex 2.8C in Practical Use,* 24; for additional warnings, see Emanuel, *Rolleiflex Guide,* 44; A. Mannheim, *Rollei Way,* 216; and Pearlman, *Rollei Manual* (1953), 62–63.

24. Parents of young children often say that children cannot break a computer. When my students break their computers they feel somehow betrayed.

25. "How to Pose a Pretty Girl," esp. 62–63.

26. Thorek, "Paper Negative," esp. 28–29.

27. Mortensen, *Monsters and Madonnas,* esp. "Preparation."

28. Mortensen, *Outdoor Portraiture,* esp. 106–12; see also his *The Model,* esp. 215–16.

29. Mortensen and Dunham, *How to Pose the Model,* esp. 114–24.

30. Mortensen and Dunham, *How to Pose the Model,* 116.

31. Merrill, *Nudism.*

32. Mortensen, *Monsters and Madonnas.*

33. Slide, *Aspects of American Film History* and *Early Women Directors;* see also Dixon, *Transparency of Spectacle,* 136.

34. Such films required no lights, which saved much money and trouble.

35. Women who enjoy being photographed find male friends, boyfriends, and husbands devoted to glamour photography useful to have around.

36. See, for example, S. J. Douglas, *Inventing American Broadcasting.*

37. By 1922 Allen Chapman had published five novels in the Radio Boys series; see esp. *Radio Boys Trailing a Voice* for sustained mention of continuous technical innovation.

38. T. S. W. Lewis, *Empire of the Air,* esp. 56–79.

39. Brooks, *Letters and Leadership,* 32.

40. Disney, "Mickey Mouse and 16 mm."

41. Throughout the 1920s, RCA (and RKO) understood the need to acquire upstart competitors.

42. Short-wave radio circa 1935 mirrored today's Internet chat rooms and blogs.

43. Studlar, "'Perils of Pleasure.'"

44. The circa 2005 collapse of professional pornographic video making caused by technically proficient amateur-made videos posted on Internet websites offers a contemporary example of what 1920s Hollywood feared.

45. Disney, "Mickey Mouse and 16 mm," 473.

46. *Ciné Miniature* magazine advertising offers intriguing parallels to the development of 35 mm photography.

47. "Radio World's Fair," 283. See also J. E. Watkins, "What May Happen."

48. Burghard, "History of the Radio Club."

49. "Transmission of Pictures." It also heralds the stunning shift in Internet usage following the invention of the HyperText Markup Language (HTML).

50. See esp. Priestley, *Midnight on the Desert,* 182–84.

51. Chandler, Hikino, and Flycht, *Inventing the Electronic Century,* offers a useful starting point.

52. See Donaldson, "My Grandmother's Swing." Donaldson developed his first roll of film at age nine, in the blacked-out kitchen of a rural Arkansas house circa 1950. See also Hannah, "Photography."

53. Until the 1940s the company aimed its magazine *Popular Mechanics* at specialists, not at amateurs and do-it-yourselfers.

54. Manufacturing firms produced most of the literature. See, for example, Cleveland Twist Drill Company, *The Use and Care of Twist Drills;* Henry Disston & Sons, Inc., *Saw, Tool, and File Manual;* Gould & Eberhardt Co., *The Hobbing Method of Cutting Gear Teeth;* and Boston Gear Works, *Textbook on Spur Gears.*

55. Henry Ford Trade School,

Shop Theory. See also Amiss, *Shop Mathematics.*

56. I learn about some of this when alumni telephone me, often in muted excitement, to ask about citations to long-obsolescent technical processes that I assume have suddenly interested their high-tech employers; see Stilgoe, *Train Time,* esp. 2–9.

57. See Leese, "Shop Recipes."

58. See Snyder, "Market Place"; and Roy, "Focusing Device."

59. Hibbs, "Horizontal Enlarging Outfit," 419.

60. Hopkins, "Enlarging Your Miniature Enlarger."

61. Voigtländer, *100 Jahre Fotografie,* 7.

62. See "How Liquid Condensers Work" and "ABC's of Radio."

63. "Spotting Dynamic Speaker Ills"; and Carr, "Current Filters." See also Waltz, "Tom Thumb Radios."

64. "Amazing Cameras Built by Invalid."

65. "Studio Opened."

66. The magazine announced the success inside the January 1937 front cover.

67. "Mirror Gives Distance."

68. Pratt, "Taking Photos."

69. Mees, *Photography,* 108–46.

70. Martin, "Home Movies."

71. "Freak Movies."

72. Mok, "Talking Newspaper."

73. Seldes, *Great Audience,* 186–90, 192–207.

74. "Women's Noisy Dresses."

75. General Electric, "This Thing"; and R. W. Wood, "New Departure."

76. "Dazzling Spark."

77. Wailes, "Weird Lights."

78. W. E. Brown, "Neon Darkroom Light"; and "Direct Current Makes Neon Tube Flash."

79. "Low Voltage Current"; R. E. Martin, "Electric Shocks."

80. "Effect on Life"; and "Electric Tides."

81. Read, "Television Needs Cameramen."

82. See Laughlin, "Why?"

83. See Gowland, "Your Complete Power Workshop" and "How to Make a Desk."

84. Barthes, *Camera Lucida,* 10; see also 15. See also Jaeger, *Image Makers.*

85. Sontag, *On Photography,* 5–6, esp. the lines following the words "when we're shown a photograph," and 16, about photographs as "incitements to reverie"; and Barthes, *Camera Lucida,* 4–8.

86. See, for example, Fite, "Teleconverter."

87. Hannah, "Photography of the Nude," 162–63, 164.

88. S. Mann, *Deep South,* illustrates the extraordinary creativity of a great photographer working with equipment she has altered or built herself.

89. Branch, *Photographer's Build-It-Yourself Book.* Critics too frequently ignore the question Barthes admits is equally central to everything critics address: "How did the photographer make this image?" Evans, *Eye, Film, and Camera,* and Mortensen, *Pictorial Lighting* (1947 ed.), insisted the question lay at the heart of understanding changing notions of vision in modern society. Evans understood it in terms of television (18, 25).

90. Fast, *Body Language,* offers a popular introduction.

91. See *Guide to Fantasy Art Techniques,* esp. 8–44, for examples of the rebellion.

92. Bates, *Plastic Cameras.*

93. On the general technical background, including optics, see Greene, *Primitive Photography.*

94. The best introduction to Holga-based modification is A. Scott, *Holga.*

95. See especially Zollner, *Out of Focus.*

96. Chernewski and Chernewski, *How to Make Three Pinhole Cameras,* suggests that the revolt against digital image making includes many well-to-do photographers who have the funds and time to make large-format cameras producing images they compare against

those made with expensive, factory-built large-format cameras.

97. Szulakowska, *Alchemy of Light,* esp. 30–39.

98. See, for example, Peter Burke, *Popular Culture,* esp. 270–86. Burke argues explicitly that across northern Europe the "withdrawal of the upper classes" from emergent popular culture came later than it did in France and England, and explicitly includes Scotland as part of the north (278–79).

99. Following directions and diverging from them may be defining characteristics of knowledge elites. See Marty, "Knowledge Elites and Counter-Elites."

100. Here I follow the example of Leavis, *Common Pursuit,* esp. 188. See also Passow, *The Gifted and the Talented,* the 1979 yearbook of the National Society for the Study of Education. This volume is rarely cited by scholars intrigued by the 1970s origins of what is nowadays designated "the creative class."

101. After about 1920 this understanding guided much of the firm's advertising and much of the content of its magazine *Kodakery;* see, for example, "What's Wrong with These Pictures?"

102. Ewen, *All Consuming Images,* esp. 41–78, 98–101.

103. I have been unable to learn much about Eastman Kodak advertising to film studios at any time.

104. See, for example, Koszarski, *Evening's Entertainment.*

105. I base this conclusion on analysis of five decades of Eastman Kodak advertising and its annual reports to stockholders.

106. See Boddy, *Fifties Television.*

107. When I arrived at Harvard University in 1973 all of my older teachers remarked on such changes in preparation (and lack of preparation); all understood that speaking about this in public made administrators "uncomfortable."

108. See Gordon and Gordon, *Blight on the Ivy.* This remains a provocative and much-ignored book.

109. For a 1920s example of this, see Coolidge, *Building a Model Railroad.*

110. The Harvard Department of Visual and Environmental Studies teaches no courses in television. Despite official reasons, beginning with lack of resources, the reason discussed in senior faculty meetings in 1984 through 1986 and in 1992 and 1993 remains the fact that many concentrators have scant knowledge of the medium and no desire to study it. The student newspaper intermittently glimpses the divide; see, for example, "School Reading Scores Worsen."

111. Pope is quoted in Singhal, "Study Doubts," 6.

112. Pope et al., "Is Dissociative Amnesia?"

113. See N. L. Chapman, *Comparative Media History,* for a sustained analysis of the mass-culture appeal of United States cinema versus that of Denmark, Japan, and other countries.

114. See Barnouw, *History of Broadcasting,* for some background on the era when we evaluated the anthology.

115. T. J. Ross, *Film and the Liberal Arts.*

116. Stilgoe, *Outside Lies Magic,* 1–19, details a bit of what I do in the classroom.

117. See, for example, "Photography for Railroaders."

118. Personal conversation.

119. On railroad photography shop theory, see Shaughnessy, *Call of Trains.*

120. See, for example, Cushing, "Photograph's Debt to the Treetops"; and Stilgoe, *Landscape and Images,* 320–28.

121. Silverman, "Inside the Loop."

122. Jasper De Haan makes this point in the preface to Speaks, *Critical Landscape,* 9.

123. The woman to whom this book is dedicated.

124. Some girls wanted to become very good at sewing so they could make clothes that looked especially good on them; several I knew devoted much effort to making abbreviated swimsuits that stayed in place.

125. Lange, "Photographing the Familiar," 5.

126. I base this assumption on three decades of asking colleagues, especially ones I encounter at conferences, to make sketch maps (often of the location of nearby restaurants at which they have enjoyed a pleasant meal) or to make a photograph of something in a place.

127. The hypertext language protocols that made the web visual produced a wave of distaste among my colleagues, who already disliked the prospect of a web that empowered undergraduates wanting to write for wide audiences. Again and again, colleagues asked me, who will edit the web? As nearly as I could determine, they wanted to edit the writing of young people, and realized (if they did not so state) that the web would "mushroom." It did, and the hypertext language protocols made it visual.

128. Marchand, *Advertising the American Dream,* began to change this view; see, for example, Schutts, *Selling Modernity,* 2–4.

129. Taylor, "Iconophobia."

130. Wilderness does too, perhaps because they cannot talk to wilderness any more than they can talk to a machine.

131. C. James, *Book of Alternative Photographic Processes,* iv, xiv, 256–57. See also J. Wood, *Photographic Arts;* and S. Mann, *Deep South.*

132. Clerc, *Photography,* 239.

133. Lange, "Photographing the Familiar," 5.

134. Mees, *Photography,* 163–65. Litzel's *Darkroom Magic* appeared in a second, expanded edition in 1975; the second edition is especially strong in the uses of solarization. Amphoto Editorial Board, *Photographic Tricks,* emphasizes risk; see esp. 31.

135. Benjamin, "The Storyteller," in *Illuminations,* 107–8.

136. Cooper, *Greenwitch,* 20–21.

137. Much first-quality fantasy writing focuses on education, especially the ways adept children master differ-

ent ways of knowing typically taught by master teachers.

138. Now and then photographic shop-theory experts address such issues: see, for example, Hunter, Biver, and Fuqua, *Light,* esp. 3, where they state explicitly that their book is a sort of tool kit about technology, not aesthetics.

4 Brownies

1. Ralphson, *Boy Scout Camera Club,* 128–29, 207–9, 211–12.

2. Hawthorne, *Works,* 9:149, 280.

3. Hawthorne, *Works,* 9:211, 26, 109, 39.

4. Hawthorne, *Works,* 1:251–53, 3:489–91.

5. Hawthorne, *Works,* 3:115–17.

6. Emerson, *Journals,* 14:126, 127.

7. Stilgoe, *Landscape and Images,* 278–97.

8. See, for example, Greenough, et al., *On the Art of Fixing a Shadow,* esp. 127–55; Armstrong, *Fiction in the Age of Photography,* offers a brilliant explication of photography as shaper of fiction.

9. "Miniature Camera Work," esp. 177–80.

10. The parallels with contemporary software innovation accomplished by amateurs using personal computers lie beyond the scope of this book.

11. Black, "Amateur Photographer," 722, 723, 724.

12. "Miniature Camera Work," 179.

13. See, for example, Huntington, "The Camera Club of Cincinnati."

14. Eastman Kodak, *History of Kodak Cameras,* esp. 2–5.

15. Ralphson, *Boy Scout Camera Club,* 122.

16. Information gleaned from various Internet sites.

17. By way of comparison, between 1906 and 1912 a mid-line Singer household sewing machine retailed for about $40, according to figures compiled by the International Sewing Machine Collectors' Association (private communication).

18. Eastman Kodak, *Kodaks and Supplies.*

19. As early as 1912, experienced photographers had begun publishing articles in *Camera Craft* and other magazines reminding photographers of the capabilities of box cameras; see, for example, Walter, "Merits of the Box Camera." See also Eastman Kodak, "Snow Scenes."

20. Eastman Kodak explicitly suggested a more deliberate approach to photography; see its *How to Make Good Pictures.*

21. Ford and Steinorth, *You Press the Button.*

22. James, *Daemonologie,* 65.

23. H. F. Talbot fails to mention *brownie,* although he defines *goblin, ogre,* and *imp;* see his *English Etymologies,* 257, 11, 465, 39.

24. Ewing, *Brownies,* 10.

25. Stevenson, *Across the Plains,* 231, 230, and 227–28.

26. See Owen, *Place of Enchantment,* esp. 180, 206–8.

27. For a contemporaneous account of Brownies, see Campbell, *Superstitions of the Highlands,* 11–14.

28. P. Cox, "Origin of the 'Brownies.'"

29. Spence's *British Fairy Origins* and *The Fairy Tradition in Britain* offer a useful introduction to the general history of fairies. He argues in *British Fairy Origins,* 2–6, that brownies are among the oldest creatures of faerie, and primarily agricultural in focus.

30. P. Cox, "Brownies' Ride."

31. P. Cox, *Brownies,* 19–24.

32. P. Cox, "Brownies in February."

33. P. Cox, "Brownies in June."

34. P. Cox, "Brownies in August."

35. P. Cox, "Brownies" and "Brownies in October."

36. It is possible some American illustrators confused Scottish brownies with Cornish and Devon knockers, the latter diminutive tin miners wearing traditional mining hoods; see, for example, Froud and Lee, *Faeries.*

37. For an example of the Dickens-like city, see "The Fairy Ring," in Gruelle, *Friendly Fairies.*

38. The New England interiors prove jarring to any thoughtful reader; see "Granny Hawkins," in Gruelle, *My Very Own Fairy Stories.*

39. Most "fairy-tale" writers wallowed in medievalism; see, for example, Mrs. Valentine, *The Old, Old Fairy Tales.*

40. P. Cox, *Brownies and Other Stories,* esp. 4–19.

41. P. Cox, *Brownies in the Philippines.*

42. Banta struggled mightily to create characters as powerful as Cox's brownies.

43. See R. Doyle, *In Fairyland;* and M. R. James, "After Dark in the Playing Fields," in *Ghost Stories,* 619–25 (the story is definitely not one about ghosts). See also Silver, *Strange and Secret Peoples,* 157–67; and Owen, *Place of Enchantment,* 305n

44. Ruskin identified the division as early as 1868; see his *Old Road,* 171.

45. Gruelle, *My Very Own Fairy Stories.*

46. Kuznets, *When Toys Come Alive,* esp. 23, 56–57, 82–85, 90–90, 182. This is an extremely well researched, very provocative book.

47. P. Cox, *Juvenile Budget.* The vengeful goat is found in the story, "A Change in the Situation."

48. Eastman Kodak, *Book of the Brownies,* 3–4.

49. See, for example, the cover of Eastman Kodak, *Kodaks and Supplies,* and *Picture Taking and Picture Making,* 56–96.

50. The premium pages usually ran at the end of the magazines, following ordinary small-size advertising; see, for example, *Ladies' Home Journal,* July 1892, 35–36.

51. "Out-of-Door Girl with Camera," 9.

52. Hope, *Outdoor Girls,* 169, 98, 160.

53. See Repplier, *Books and Men,* esp. 1–32, 64–93.

54. J. E. West, "Boy Scouts Train," 29, 104.

55. The relationship endured for decades; see, for example, Boy Scouts of America, *Photography*, esp. ii–iv, 3–5.

56. C. King, *Conquering Corps Badge*, 231–36.

57. The fiction parallels actual incidents; see, for example, Marriott, *Spanish Holiday*, 213.

58. L. De Giberne Sieveking, "The Prophetic Camera," in *Best British Short Stories of 1923*, 267–78; quotation on 275.

59. Farjeon, "The Photograph," 638.

60. Howard Wandrei, "The God-Box," in *Strange Ports of Call*, 171–84; quotation on 180.

61. Basil Copper, "Camera Obscura," in *Alfred Hitchcock Presents*, 13–32; quotation on 24.

62. Malec, *Extrapolasis*, 147–58.

63. O. Davis, "Girl Bathing," in *Scent of Apples*, 96–117.

64. Bradbury, *Golden Apples*, 19, 185.

65. Buchan, *Watcher*, v, 159, 110–11, 207–8, 142.

66. Shippey, *Road to Middle Earth*, 177.

5 Od

1. N. M. West, *Kodak and the Lens of Nostalgia*, 20.

2. Here von Reichenbach perhaps followed the thinking of Thouvenel, *Mémoire physique*.

3. On von Reichenbach's career, see the entries in *Brockhaus Enzyklopädie*, 18:215; and *Allgemeine Deutsche Biographie*, 27:670–71.

4. By the late 1990s magnetism had become the focus of much brain disease research; see, for example, Cromie, "Magnetic Wand Changes a Brain."

5. Cross, *Burned-Over District*.

6. Leicht, *Wilhelm Conrad Rontgen;* Schedel, *Der Blick in den Menschen;* Glasser, *William Conrad Rontgen;* and Dry, *Curie*, offer a useful introduction to the discoveries and their intellectual contexts.

7. See, for example, Repplier, *Books and Men*, 33–63.

8. Ground-based experiments fascinate a coterie of ham radio operators: almost any operator knows of an associate investigating the phenomenon.

9. Rogers, "Rogers Underground Aerial," 39–40. I know about measuring earth-carried current from experiments conducted in my cornfield in the summer of 2006.

10. "Underground Wireless."

11. Stilgoe, "Design Standards," esp. 22–27.

12. Rogers, "Rogers Underground Aerial."

13. "Underground Wireless."

14. A. Lang, *Book of Dreams*, 56–62.

15. Crystal radio continues to have thousands of devotees. Fair Radio Sales of Lima, Ohio, still offers components and a booklet, *Experimental Crystal Set Receivers Book*, a compilation of articles and letters to the editor from magazines published in 1911 and 1912. See also K. E. Edwards, *Radios That Work for Free*.

16. "Wireless Fencing Receiver" is a useful introduction to willy-nilly experimentation.

17. See A. Chapman, *Radio Boys' First Wireless*, for an introduction to the successful series. The novel makes clear how inexpensive amateur radio was in relation to the photography Ralphson depicts.

18. Kinzie, *Crystal Radio*, offers a useful introduction. See also United States Bureau of Standards, *Construction and Operation of a Two-Circuit Radio*, a 1922 effort that demonstrates government understanding of the importance of non-electric-powered radio receivers.

19. Baum, *Master Key*, 7, 9, 10–11, 57–58, 120–24.

20. Baum, *American Fairy Tales*, 112–13. See also G. Brown, *American Fairy Tales*.

21. J. E. Watkins, "What May Happen," deals with "invisible light." This sort of *Ladies' Home Journal* article re-

wards scrutiny, since its highly technical specifics were aimed at a largely female audience.

22. Carpenter and Page, "Production of Fever"; "Haunted Restaurant"; "Electric Dangers"; Knudsen, "Remedies for Electrolysis." The work of Carpenter and Page proves eerily similar to contemporary research reported in *Nature* and the *Ecologist;* see, for example, Schulman, "Cancer Risks"; and Best, "Electromagnetic Cover-Up." Even in the late 1960s public-health scientists warned about microwave ovens; see Rothstein, et al., *Microwave Ovens,* a product of the United States Bureau of Radiological Health.

23. Russell, "What's Zapping You?"

24. Visual art in the borderlands of the visual rewards scrutiny; see M. Warner, *Inner Eye.*

25. Ashmole, *Theatrum Chemicum Brittannicum,* viii.

26. Szulakowska, *Alchemy of Light,* esp. 19–46.

27. In his 1955 story "The Adventure of a Photographer," Calvino uses the word *alchemy* explicitly to describe photographic darkroom work; see *Difficult Loves,* 124. Alchemy infuses much contemporary fantasy literature aimed at adolescents; see esp. Winterson, *Tanglewreck,* 374–77.

28. See, for example, Clulee, *John Dee's Natural Philosophy,* 39–74.

29. Peirce, *Values,* 255.

30. See, for example, N. R. Hanson, "Picture Theory of Meaning."

31. Maier, *Atalanta Fugiens.*

32. Szulakowska, *Alchemy of Light,* esp. 167–81.

33. C. G. Jung, *Collected Works,* 15:135.

34. Maier, *Atalanta Fugiens* (ed. Streich), 10.

35. By 1768 alchemy had become the pseudoscience prologue to chemistry it remains today, and almost all knowledge of the prospective stone had been lost; see *Encyclopedia Britannica,* 1st ed., s.v. "alchemy."

36. See, for example, F. S. Taylor, *Alchemists,* 170–75.

37. Atwood's *Suggestive Inquiry* sits at an unvisited intersection of the history of physical science (esp. chemistry), the history of psychology (esp. Freudian and Jungian thought), and the history of religion (esp. mysticism). It offers a solid if sometimes cryptic framework in which to understand Von Reichenbach's work and the early acceptance of photography in the contexts of either alchemy or "the black arts."

38. Jung, *Collected Works,* vols. 12 and 13.

39. Jung, *Collected Works,* 12:243; see also 245–68.

40. W. James, *Principles of Psychology,* 1:203.

41. W. James, *Principles of Psychology,* 1:203–6.

42. Heering, *Rolleiflex Book,* esp. 38–39, 60–61, 66–67, 68–69, 112–14, 66.

43. How his discoveries and hypotheses relate to the contemporary illness of electro hypersensitivity I have been unable to ascertain.

44. Browning, *Aurora Leigh.* It is useful to follow definitions of *od* through the Merriam-Webster dictionaries.

45. "Recent Observations on Earth Currents." This article demonstrates the incisiveness with which electrical engineers moved to study earth-current fluctuation seemingly produced by magnetic storms.

46. Von Reichenbach, *Der sensitive Mensch,* 89–92.

47. A. C. Doyle, *Essays on Photography,* 84–87.

48. Ives, "Japanese Magic Mirror."

49. A. C. Doyle, *Coming of the Fairies,* 3–19.

50. W. James, *Principles of Psychology,* 2:114–15, 123–25.

51. Galton, *Inquiries,* 57–64.

52. Galton, *Inquiries,* 70, 74–75.

53. Galton, *Inquiries,* 79–82, 82–104. I have taught students, all undergraduate women from the Massachusetts Institute

of Technology, with similar faculties: several do calculations because they visualize numbers in colors.

54. Galton, *Inquiries*, 114–15.

55. Galton, *Inquiries*, 127–28.

56. Galton, *Inquiries*, 79.

57. J. Wood, "Flaubert, Love, and Photography."

58. Rose, *Edwardian Temperament*, 6–9, 179–91.

59. Blondlot, *"N" Rays*, esp. 43–47.

60. Machen, *Tales of Horror*, 63–64, 369–70.

61. Nutting, *Photographic Art Secrets*, 68.

62. Temple, *Blue Ghost*, 30. Temple suggested, 33, that Hearn saw, at least at night, shadows lengthened by the extreme height of the tiny room in which his aunt locked him at night.

63. A. Lang, *Book of Dreams*, 57.

64. Owen, "'Borderland Forms,'" offers an excellent introduction to the Doyle effort, which continues to intrigue artists; see the novel by Szilagyi, *Photographing Fairies*.

65. See, for example, "Photography and Relativity." A. C. Doyle, *Coming of the Fairies*, 56.

66. A. C. Doyle, *Coming of the Fairies*, 9, 14, 23.

67. Hearn, *Spirit Photography*, esp. 19, 27–28.

68. I have been able to learn little about the Cameo, since the Houghton Company was destroyed by enemy action early in World War II. Camera collectors know of two models at least, one slightly more versatile than the other, but with a very slow (ca. f/7.7) lens. The cameras were not expensive in their era, and scarcely more accurate than a Brownie 2A.

69. A. C. Doyle, *Coming of the Fairies*, 160, 77.

70. Strand, "Photography," 252, 256–57.

71. Moholy-Nagy, "Light," 284.

72. On trees as communication systems and tree decimation caused by radar emissions, see Coats, *Living Energies*, 235–38.

73. S. E. White, *Road I Know*, 126–27, 97; see also his *Betty Book* and *Unobstructed Universe*.

74. S. E. White, *Road I Know*, 233, 186, 159–60, 168, 239. Now and then Betty (or her husband) described her creative force as something remarkably akin to Od, perhaps electrified; see 196.

75. Funk, *Widow's Mite*, vii. See also Stark, "The Color of 'the Damned Thing': The Occult as the Suprasensational," in *Haunted Dusk*, ed. Kerr, Crowley, and Crow, 211–27.

6 Ways

1. Belloc, *On Anything*, 30–37. See also Oppenheim, *Nicholas Goade*.

2. On the concept of wildering and wildered places (what Germans have called *ortsbewüstung* since the Black Death years), see Stilgoe, *Metropolitan Corridor*, 321–49.

3. S. Cooper, *Dark Is Rising*, 59, 60–61.

4. Darke, "Celebrating Natural Light," "Found Art," and "Sixty Seasons."

5. This is the version given by Tolkien in *Tree and Leaf*, 5; he first used it in a 1938 lecture (i). For another version, see "The Queen of Elfland's Nourice," in *Oxford Book of Ballads*, ed. Quiller-Couch, 241.

6. Grahame, *Wind in the Willows*, esp. 102–6: Milne, *Winnie-the-Pooh*, 67–72; Ransome, *Pigeon Post*, 101. On gypsies, see Ransome, *Swallows and Amazons*, 134–35.

7. Hudson, *Afoot in England*, 6, 66, 102–3, 232–33, 242–43.

8. By this time, many educated walkers had learned to listen for fragments of phrase indicating much older belief systems.

9. Belloc, *On Anything*, 31, addresses advertising-based travel.

10. Belloc, *Old Road*, 4–6, 74, 108–9.

11. Belloc, *Old Road*, 160, 140–41, 232–33, 280–81.

12. R. H. Cox, *Green Roads of England*, viii, 14–15, 96–99, 128.

13. H. James, *English Hours;* and Howells, *Certain Delightful English Towns.*

14. Shelley, *Untrodden English Ways;* and Murphy, *British Highways.*

15. See E. Thomas, *Icknield Way,* 100–103.

16. On quaintness, see Stilgoe, *Alongshore,* 295–33.

17. Murphy, *British Highways,* 3–4, 2, 5, 6–8, 34–36, 65, 102.

18. Grahame, *Wind in the Willows,* 94–95.

19. Dobson and Dobson, *English Ways,* 72–73, 86.

20. Grahame, *Wind in the Willows,* 134–35.

21. See Belloc's analysis of secluded places in *On Anything,* 30–37.

22. See, for example, A. C. Doyle, "Dry Plates on a Wet Moor," in *Essays on Photography,* 30–37 (first published in the November 1882 issue of the *British Journal of Photography*).

23. Helphand, "Bicycle Kodak."

24. Herlihy, *Bicycle,* esp. 225–30.

25. Early bicycles lacked springs and shock absorbers, except in saddles: vibration moved directly through frames to cameras. See, for example, D. G. Wilson, *Bicycling Science,* 16–46.

26. Murphy, *New England Highways,* reads as a near copy of his book on England.

27. For an early example of the shift, see Garrett, *Romance and Reality.*

28. On James, see M. Cox, *M. R. James.*

29. M. R. James, *Ghost Stories,* 533, 539–40, 541, 549–50, 551.

30. M. R. James, *Ghost Stories,* 547–48.

31. On the visual in James's work, especially regarding illustrators and illustrations, see M. Cox, *M. R. James,* 135–40.

32. W. James, *Principles of Psychology,* 2:212–14.

33. Elinor Mordaunt, "The Inspired 'Busman," in *Best British Short Stories of 1923,* 234–41, quotation on 239.

34. See Emily Hanson Obear, "Aunt Rebecca and the Idol," and Kathleen Field, "The Back Road," in *New England Short Stories,* 1:234–46 and 186–201, respectively.

35. Jewett, *Country of the Pointed Firs,* 136–38.

36. Clifton Johnson, *Highways of New England,* 92.

37. Clifton Johnson, *Highways of the South.* Johnson rarely explains how he arrives at any place, or what *byway* designates; see 31.

38. Murphy, *New England Highways,* 9, 17.

39. Machen, *Tales of Horror,* 63, 71–72, 317–18, 358, 348, 181, 113.

40. Machen, *Tales of Horror,* 345; and *Autobiography,* esp. 15–62.

41. Hearn, *Shadowings,* 213.

42. H. F. Talbot, *English Etymologies,* 197, 463–65.

43. Hearn, *Shadowings,* 213, 238–39, 214–15, 222.

44. See H. F. Talbot, *English Etymologies,* 35, on perspective. Talbot was one inventor of photography.

45. Clerc, *Photography,* 12–16; see also Moëssard.

46. Moëssard's *L'optique photographique* and *Étude des lentilles* offer an excellent introduction to a subject nowadays ignored by most photographers.

47. Reprinted in Stevens, *Nightmare and Other Tales,* 227–47.

48. Howard, *Black Stranger,* 264–65, 280, 288.

49. Stilgoe, *Metropolitan Corridor,* 313–33.

50. Lovecraft, *Colour Out of Space,* 7–10.

51. See, for example, Lovecraft, "The Moon Bog" (1921), in *Lurking Fear,* 81–89.

52. Lovecraft, *The Case of Charles Dexter Ward* (1928–29), demonstrates the shift.

53. Conrad, *Heart of Darkness,* 5, 3, 7.

54. Much fantasy fiction accepted the literary device of the insensitive wan-

derer blundering into something from the past, or before the past.

55. Belloc, *Old Road,* 9–10; see also 11–15.

56. As the old rural Yankeeism goes, it is one thing to know honey is sweet, and another to have tasted honey.

57. Belloc, *On Anything,* 31, 33.

58. Belloc, *On Anything,* 35–36. Here Belloc anticipates the role of the cinema in producing the simulacrum of visiting exotic places. He is one of the first observers to assign importance to the location, usually metropolitan, of reading, esp. of travel books. In *Old Junk,* 65–75, Tomlinson makes a similar point, focusing on travel books read late in the evening in cities, sometimes by candlelight.

59. Goodell, *Black Tavern Tales,* 53. See also Faulkner, *Absalom, Absalom!*

60. Lovecraft, *Colour Out of Space,* 89.

61. Lovecraft, *Colour Out of Space,* 114–115, 98.

62. Lovecraft, *Colour Out of Space,* 99–100, 96, 85, 89.

63. Lovecraft, *Horror in the Museum,* 97.

64. See, for example, Eaton, "The 'Good Roads' Delusion."

65. Tolkien, *Hobbit,* 43, 66.

66. Tolkien, *Tree and Leaf,* 37, 9–10.

67. On enchantment, see Partridge, *Charm of Words,* 86.

68. Minter, "Wilderness and Wise Province," offers a useful introduction to the ways ecosystem-focused scholars have recently interpreted Royce's thinking.

69. Royce, *Race Questions,* 73–74, 81–82.

70. Norton's *Why Preserve Natural Variety?* offers a useful example; see also Sagoff, *Economy of the Earth;* and Kegley, *Genuine Individuals.*

71. MacKaye, "Appalachian Trail" and "Project for an Appalachian Trail"; see also Spann, *Designing Modern America;* and Callicott, *In Defense of the Land Ethic.*

72. See, for example, MacKaye, "Ten-

nessee." Defining "community" preoccupied Royce in ways that champions of Dewey came to ignore; see J. E. Smith, *America's Philosophical Vision,* 139–52.

73. Royce, *Race Questions,* 48–49.

74. Only recently have scholars confronted issues of provinces; see esp. Dorman, *Revolt of the Provinces.*

75. Royce, *Race Questions,* 51–52, 53.

76. Royce, *Race Questions,* 77.

77. It seems to have shaped Southern Agrarian thinking; see *I'll Take My Stand;* and J. Gilbert and Brown, "Alternative Land Reform."

78. Royce, *Race Questions,* 153.

79. K. J. Parker, *Evil for Evil,* 385.

7 Light

1. A. Watkins, *Photography,* ii–iii, v–vi, viii.

2. For a modern introduction to the subject, see Gaunt, *Practical Exposure.* On British pictorial tradition in photography, see M. Weaver, *Photographic Art.*

3. Watkins, *Manual,* 34–35, 37.

4. Watkins, *Manual,* 21–24.

5. Watkins, *Manual,* 12, 54–55, 57.

6. Watkins, *Manual,* 43–45.

7. Watkins, *Manual,* 22, 43.

8. Watkins, *Manual,* 16–17, 59.

9. If they did not use a Watkins meter they used similar ones manufactured by his competitors.

10. Wondering how any photographer considering exposure settings might have responded to turn-of-the-century description of extraordinary light—say the descriptions of sunlight presaging the circular storm in Conrad's 1902 *Typhoon*—suggests the experiment of asking contemporary photographers to respond. "The sun, pale and without rays, poured down leaden heat in a strangely indecisive light" (20–21) produces wildly varying responses in terms of exposure setting and shutter speed.

11. Nutting, *Photographic Art Secrets,* 16–19, argues that the Bee and its competitors did not always prove accurate.

12. See A. F. Collins, *Amateur Photographer's Handbook,* 122–24.

13. Posographe, *Instructions,* 1.

14. The Posograph offers endless possibilities to the contemporary photographer experimenting with antique emulsions and homemade glass negatives.

15. "New Meter."

16. Watkins, *Old Straight Track,* 23, 14–14 .

17. Watkins, *Old Straight Track,* 74–75, 117, 81. By 1920 Stonehenge had become a focal point of deep-history narratives angled at the "forgotten" past; see Wells, *Outline of History,* 133–35.

18. A. Watkins, *Old Straight Track,* xv, xvii–xviii, 104–5, 189, 214–16, 220.

19. Many seem to have been Great War veterans walking off the intense stress of prolonged trench warfare.

20. Shippey, *Road to Middle Earth,* 32–33.

21. Maxwell, *Detective in Kent,* 3, 27–28.

22. Maxwell, *Detective in Kent,* 57–58.

23. Maxwell, *Detective in Kent,* 60, 72.

24. A. Watkins, *Old Straight Track,* 79; see also 75–78.

25. Spence, *British Fairy Origins,* 46–47.

26. J. G. Campbell, *Superstitions of the Highlands,* 11–15.

27. Teudt, *Germanische Heiligtümer,* esp. 9–15, 147–58.

28. Reuter, *Germanische Himmelskunde,* esp. 21–34.

29. L. M. Mann, *Craftsmen's Measures,* offers a useful starting point.

30. Reuter, *Der Himmel über den Germanen,* provides a useful introduction to the Nazi links.

31. See, for example, Crawford and Keiller, *Wessex from the Air,* 6.

32. Firth, *The Goat-Foot God,* 197–198.

33. Firth, *The Goat-Foot God,* 203–4.

34. Crawford, *Air Survey,* esp. 3–9.

35. A. Watkins, *Old Straight Track,* 222.

36. For general background on British aerial imagery, see Hauser, *Shadow Sites.*

37. Crawford quoted in Hauser, "Earth from the Air," 105, 114–15, 117, 120–21, 127, 129.

38. Crawford and Keiller, *Wessex from the Air,* 91, 95.

39. Crawford quoted in Hauser, "Earth from the Air," 116.

40. Beresford, *History on the Ground,* 13–14.

41. Pennick and Devereux, *Lines on the Landscape,* 47.

42. Way, *Air-Photo Interpretation,* esp. 2–6; see also Way, *Terrain Analysis.*

43. A. Watkins, *Old Straight Track,* 70, 192, 101, 22.

44. Pennick and Devereux, *Lines on the Landscape,* 23.

45. Hoskins, *Making of the English Landscape,* 32.

46. Hoskins, *English Landscapes,* 6.

47. W. Johnson, *Folk-Memory,* esp. x, 12–13, 54–69.

48. Hoskins, *English Landscapes,* 7.

49. Evans-Wentz, *Fairy Faith,* 33n.

50. On dowsing, see especially Jarricot, *La radiesthésie;* and Zorab, *Wichelroede en "Aardstralen."*

51. Knoblauch, *Die Welt,* esp. 9–33.

52. See Coats, *Living Energies,* esp. 287–93.

53. Jung, *Flying Saucers,* is one source of post-1965 fantasy writing energy.

54. See, for example, Unger, *Flying Saucers;* and Michie, *Flying Saucers.*

55. Price, *Gears from the Greeks.*

56. G. S. Hawkins's work profoundly affected undergraduate thinking about history and prehistory.

57. Thom's work raised significant issues involving visual mathematical calculations.

58. Suess, "Brittlecone Pine Calibration."

59. R. H. Cox, *Green Roads of England,* 96–111, offers an excellent overview of earlier ideas about sites as observatories; see also A. Watkins, *Old Straight Track,* 100–109.

60. Randerson, "Is There Anybody Out There?"

61. J. Mitchell, *New View over Atlantis,* 23–24. See also Underwood, *Pattern of the Past.*

62. J. Mitchell, *New View over Atlantis,* 84–85, 92–93. Cornish had already focused on the yew; see his *Churchyard Yew.*

63. See also J. Mitchell's *City of Revelation,* esp. 140–54.

64. Acupuncture is explicitly mentioned in Rubin and Krippner, *Kirlian Aura,* 181–87.

65. Rubin and Krippner, *Kirlian Aura,* esp. 17–23.

66. See, for example, two stories reported in the *Harvard Crimson:* Xianlin Li, "HMS Studies Stroke Treatment" (October 13, 2005); and Jacob M. Victor, "Professors Seek Alien Radio Waves" (October 27, 2006). Given the research conducted in Harvard University science departments, and the use of the word "aura" in papers concerning MRI imaging, it is difficult to blame undergraduates who see such research as a window opening on the Kirlian aura.

67. I listened to such casual arguments as late as 1979. Young archaeologists headed for tenure and fame now and then wondered if alignments might not reveal the location of sites not even suspected by senior faculty. After about 1984 such arguments moved underground, since they appeared to belittle Asian thinking regarding acupuncture and yoga.

68. See esp. Devereux and Thomson, *Ley Hunter's Companion;* and Fidler, *Ley Lines.* Pennick and Devereux's *Lines on the Landscape,* which appeared in 1989, contains a useful survey of the fringe-element material that obscured—and still obscures—much alignment research.

69. See Pennick and Devereux, *Lines on the Landscape,* 44–45; also Teudt, *Der himmel,* 48.

70. Devereux and Thomson, *Ley Hunter's Companion,* 10. Shoesmith, *Alfred Watkins,* ignores this phrase and its contexts.

71. Evans-Wentz, *Fairy Faith,* 35. Such thinking endures; see, for example, M. Talbot, *Holographic Universe,* 162–93.

72. Johnson, *Folk-Memory,* esp. 54–62; Johnson's arguments dovetailed perfectly with Evans-Wentz's *Fairy Faith.*

73. Petitpierre, *Exorcising Devils,* 45–48.

74. Morrison, *Pathways to the Gods.*

75. From what I can learn, chiefly by hearsay, alignment researchers typically enjoy their lunches more, especially in fair weather.

76. See, for example, Kenyon, *Forbidden History.*

77. Pratchett, *Interesting Times,* 8.

78. Pratchett's *Guards! Guards!* rewards close scrutiny from the viewpoint of an adolescent struggling to understand contemporary American and British affirmative-action issues.

79. Pratchett, *Truth,* 107–8.

80. One can trace the trust back to the 1970s, at least; see Margot Adler, *Drawing Down the Moon.*

81. In a way, they use close observation as the "prospective stone" that enhances seeing as Ashmole describes in the introduction to his 1652 *Theatrum Chemicum Britannicum.*

82. Aerial and other top-down photography often supports their hypotheses; see, for example, Crutchley, "Landscape of Salisbury Plain."

83. Kenyon, *Forbidden History,* 221–35.

84. The impact of spot-metering capabilities circa 1975 rewards any sustained inquiry.

85. While Baxandall, *Patterns of Intention,* scarcely mentions cameras, it nonetheless provides a useful way of examining the role of camera optics and light metering in the last third of the twentieth century.

86. See esp. Stephenson, "Meters and How to Use Them."

87. Holtzman, "Hints on Photographing." Even in 1938, however, meters had

begun distracting photographers from certain subjects; see "Tiny Exposure Meter."

88. As nearly as I can remember, by the summer of 1977 many photographers had given up photographing aerial fireworks. Frank Gohlke is one of the few contemporary photographers who routinely photographs lightning; see his *Landscapes from the Middle of the World*.

89. Deep cold indeed makes electric-operated cameras malfunction.

90. R. S. Harris, *Harris Memory Meter*.

91. For a similar view on the subject, see Mout, "Exposure Calculator"; and "Correct Exposure in an Instant."

92. Stephenson, "Meters and How to Use Them."

93. See, for example, Hunter, Biver, and Fuqua, *Light*.

94. Electronic cameras prove awkward in such shop-theory efforts, since switching their autoexposure systems to manual (or off) sometimes flummoxes other subcircuits (including auto focus).

95. Few electronic camera photographers seem to know how to switch their devices to "manual."

96. The narrow latitude of color transparency film requires very precise exposure, especially in deep shade, and perhaps makes the discovery of glamour more likely.

97. All this is different from the use of photography in finding evidence of the occult; see, for example, *Perfect Medium*.

98. Nutting, *Photographic Art Secrets*, 25; on seasonal variation in light in the northern hemisphere, see 19–20.

99. K. J. Parker, *Devices and Desires*, 434, 432.

8 Voodoo

1. Laughlin, *Personal Eye*, 123.
2. *Look at America*, 186–87.
3. Laughlin, "Era of Sentiment," 114.
4. "Camera's Selective Eye."
5. The Hollywood focus on eastern slavery tended to follow and presage the scholarly focus; see, for example, Cash, *Mind of the South*, 17–49; and W. R. Taylor, *Cavalier and Yankee*, esp. 280–304. See also Rubin and Jacobs, *South*, 11–28.

6. Laughlin, *Ghosts along the Mississippi*, plates 84, 87, 86.

7. Anderson, "New Orleans," 119, 121, 125.

8. "Southern Letters," 214–15.

9. Faulkner, "New Orleans," 106–7.

10. Asbury, *French Quarter*, 391–93, 433, 437–38, 442–43.

11. Asbury, *French Quarter*, 209–10. Semper idem, "*Blue Book*," 11–12, 13, 15–22.

12. The core legality of New Orleans prostitution can be found in New Orleans City Ordinance 3267, "Lewd Women," adopted March 10, 1857.

13. See, for example, MacDougall's chapter on the photography of Jean Audema, in *Corporeral Image*, 176–209.

14. See Lomax, *Mister Jelly Roll*, esp. 41–61; a major advantage of this book, published in 1946, is the direct connections made by its folklorist author.

15. Hearn, *Creole Sketches*, 78–81.

16. Hearn, *Inventing New Orleans*, 31–32.

17. Hearn, *Creole Sketches*, 3.

18. Hearn, *Creole Sketches*, 2, 4.

19. Hearn, "New Orleans in Carnival Garb."

20. On the cultural depths of Mardi Gras, see Gill, *Lords of Misrule*.

21. Hearn, *Creole Sketches*, 116, 117.

22. Hearn, *Inventing New Orleans*, xiv.

23. Cable, "The 'Haunted House,'" esp. 595–97.

24. Cable, *Grandissimes* (1898), 89, 263, 229–30, 167.

25. Cable, "Creole Slave Songs," 816–17.

26. Cable, "Creole Slave Songs," 815–21. See also his "Dance in the Place Congo."

27. See, for example, Cable, "1888: How I Got Them," "Francoise in Louisiana," and "The History of Alix De Morainville."

28. F. H. Smith, "White Umbrella in Mexico," 244.

29. Charles Barnard, "Something Electricity Is Doing," esp. 736–37.

30. De Kay, "Pagan Ireland," esp. 368–69.

31. Yeats's *Celtic Twilight* is contained in his *Mythologies*, 5–144.

32. O'Sullivan, *Twenty Years A-Growing*, v.

33. F. H. Smith, "White Umbrella in Mexico," 244–45.

34. It fit no class-divided intellectual framework either; see, for example, Repplier, *Books and Men,* esp. 53.

35. See Tong, "Pioneers of Mound Bayou." For a similar instance of the transformation of reporting about Caribbean blacks, see C. J. Post, "Little Paradise." By 1910 mainstream periodical authors had followed Cable in averting their attention from voodoo.

36. It is difficult to discern the reasons why so many post-1925 literary critics dismissed Cable's worth as genteel: much of it proves violent, erotic, and scandalous in its implications about turn-of-the-century United States culture.

37. See, for example, "New Orleans in Transition."

38. By 1930 the impact of Stoddard's *Rising Tide of Color* had begun to reshape much traditional southern understanding of white-black cultural division, largely by directing attention at the Caribbean basin and beyond.

39. Hearn, *Inventing New Orleans,* 45–46.

40. Hearn, *Inventing New Orleans,* 72–73.

41. Hearn, *Fantastics,* 23–24.

42. Denier, *Great Secret of Shadow Pantomimes,* offers a brief history of early nineteenth-century hand-shadow contriving. I am indebted to Margaret Ross for an introduction to these works. See also I. Fox, *Shadowgraphs;* and Casati, *Shadow Club.*

43. Howitt, *History of the Supernatural,* 213–17, offers an introduction to telluric forces.

44. E. O. P. Smith, *Shadow Land.*

45. Gardette, "Two Shadows," 494.

46. Darkness, however, remained fearsome for many; see "Psychology of Fear."

47. See, for example, E. O. P. Smith, *Shadow Land;* Stoichita, *Short History;* and M. Warner, *Phantasmagoria.*

48. In 1900 John Burroughs addressed such atmospheric qualities; see *Winter Sunshine,* esp. 7–12.

49. Hearn, *Fantastics,* 57–58, 147.

50. Hearn, *Fantastics,* 148, 166–67.

51. Hearn, *Fantastics,* 37–39.

52. Hearn, *Fantastics,* 169, 230. Now and then southern scholars understand such light and color as, in the words of Cash, *Mind of the South,* 58, "a sort of cosmic conspiracy against reality in favor of romance."

53. For an introduction to the Filipino deserters, see Espina, *Filipinos in New Orleans,* 27–43.

54. Hearn, *Inventing New Orleans,* 85–86, 87, 90.

55. Hearn's *Cuisine Créole* is far more than a cookbook.

56. On French colonial New Orleans, see Dawdy, *Building the Devil's Empire.*

57. Hurbon, *L'insurrection.* See also, Blancpain, *La colonie française.*

58. Coates, *Outlaw Years,* offers a useful introduction to the potential of slave revolt in the area between Louisiana and Natchez in the 1830s. This book appeared as a Literary Guild selection in 1930 and seems to have reawakened awareness of the potential of slave revolt along the Mississippi River.

59. Deive, *Los guerrilleros negroes.*

60. Quoted in Buel, *Metropolitan Life,* 528–30.

61. Quoted in Asbury, *French Quarter,* 281–82.

62. For an introduction to voodoo, see Davis, *Serpent and the Rainbow.*

63. On the "new South," see H. Thompson, *New South;* Grady, *What Might Be Termed;* Schurz, *New South;* and American Academy of Political and Social Science, *New South.*

64. Hyatt, *Hoodoo,* remains the most thorough work.

65. Information from informants on the back roads between New Orleans and Memphis, including West Memphis, Arkansas, between 1987 and 1996.

66. Hyatt, *Folklore.*

67. Lull, *Popular Music,* esp. 70–72.

68. See, for example, J. A. Hall, "Negro Conjuring and Tricking." For earlier work, see Norris, "Negro Superstitions"; and Skinner, *Myths and Legends.*

69. Stoddard's argument is a far more important one in mid-twentieth-century American culture than contemporary scholars recognize.

70. Puckett, *Folk Beliefs,* 167–203, esp. 187–90, 194, 196, 201.

71. One of the great contributions of Puckett's work is its emphasis on urban locales.

72. Huxley, *On the Margin,* 51–52.

73. Puckett, *Folk Beliefs,* 244–45.

74. Puckett, *Folk Beliefs,* 154.

75. Herskovits, *Myth of the Negro Past,* opens a portal on such thinking after 1920. See also E. B. White, *One Man's Meat,* 129, for a 1940 mention of the edginess of radio warfare.

76. McLuhan and Watson glimpsed some of this in their 1970 *From Cliché to Archetype,* 144–45; they saw jazz as having "mechanically extended the speech modes of the lower middle classes with image-acceptance."

77. Many connected jazz with venereal disease. In 1920, at the behest of the city council, the police chief of Lansing, Michigan, ruled that "no beating of drums to produce jazz effect will be allowed" in public dance halls in order to protect white women from sexually aroused men; see Brandt, *No Magic Bullet,* esp. 127. By 1930 many manufacturers of domestic products emphasized that a beautiful, interesting, modern home would keep children and teenagers from "the siren call of unknown places" harboring jazz; see, for example, "Fight This Competition." For allied subjects, see Potter, *War on Crime.*

78. It is useful to examine theater-card advertising of post-1955 films like *Hot Rod Gang* (1958) which explicitly linked wild and dangerous driving with "living to a wild rock n' roll beat." See also P. Burke, *Come In.*

79. I have been unable to learn how immigrants in New York and other cities understood voodoo and hoodoo.

80. Yellen, "Vamp of Savannah."

81. G. King, *New Orleans,* 348. King insisted that more than "the racial license of Africa" drove the behavior of the quadroon women: "the desire of distinction, to rise from a lower level to social equality with a superior race" drove them. King suggested that such a desire "was implanted in the hearts" of all women, not just the quadroon (347–48).

82. See, for example, Beaumont, "Black Country" (1954), in *Playboy Book of Horror,* 314–37.

83. See, for example, Hentoff, *Jazz Country;* Brubeck, "Jazz Perspective"; and D. G. Hoffman, "Jazz."

84. At least a handful of authors see Katrina-devastated New Orleans as likely to be only further marginalized; see, for example, Abrahams, et al., *Blues for New Orleans,* esp. 22–35.

85. Hearn, *Fantastics,* 114.

86. Hearn, *Gombo Zhèbes,* 16n.

87. Hearn, *Fantastics,* ii, 3.

88. On the angel of Mons, see Jarrett, *Sleep of Reason,* 5–6, 191.

89. His analysis almost perfectly elucidates Hearn's *Fantastics* visions.

90. Wright, "Mystery of Arthur Machen," 105–6.

91. The performance of African American dancers in Europe in the 1920s focused critical attention in Paris and Berlin, and perhaps influenced the editors; see, for example, Goll, "Die Neger."

92. See, for example, Dunsany, "Songs of Al Shaldamir."

93. Any contemporary reader must wonder if the entire episode is fictional. The rest of the book appears wholly factual.

94. Saxon, *Fabulous New Orleans,* 311, 318–19, 321.

95. King, *New Orleans,* 341. See also her *Creole Families of New Orleans.*

96. No full bibliography of Howard's writing yet exists; many of his stories appeared in short-lived pulp magazines.

97. Howard, *Black Stranger,* 233, 243–44.

98. Faulkner, *Absalom, Absalom!,* 17.

99. Hurston, *Mules and Men,* 229–304.

100. Barrie's introduction can be found in the 1898 ed. of Cable's *Grandissimes;* quotations on xii and xv.

101. Rigaud, *Secrets of Voodoo,* esp. 7–78.

102. Stern found Mead far more cautious and nuanced in her thinking than de Beauvoir. He bases his distinction chiefly on Mead's *Male and Female* and de Beauvoir's *Second Sex.*

103. K. Stern, *Flight from Woman,* 12–13, 14, 17–18, 24–25.

104. Her novels may originate in an early 1970s counterculture thinking of the sort Hackney identifies in "South as a Counterculture."

105. Rice, *Blackwood Farm,* 122, 119.

106. Laughlin, "Why?," 64–65.

9 Old Fields

1. I first crossed Valley Swamp in January 2007 with my dog. Deep, unfrozen springs deflected us and we were lost for some while, but at age fifty-eight I achieved a lifelong goal. I know only one other townsman, a man of eighty-four, who crossed it in 1934. Rumors of quicksand do much to keep away even ardent birders and others.

2. Now and then authors focused on New England rural living analyze such landscapes. Barrette, *Countryman's Journal,* studies one after 1960; see esp. 13–29.

3. Perhaps the affinity for such lonely ways (and being alone on them) is somehow genetic; see Hillerman, *Seldom Disappointed,* 50.

4. In his 1978 *Tracker,* Tom Brown described similar experiences in a single sentence: "Summer woods were always more than magical" (55).

5. Belloc, *On Anything,* 30–37. Belloc emphasizes the inability or unwillingness of urban dwellers and highway and railroad travelers to accept the extent of abandoned, unpeopled landscape near their homes and routes.

6. I dated some of the abandoned machinery by asking former owners.

7. Such analysis resulted from lazy days of exploration.

8. Bullet-ridden cars, while not uncommon, existed as mysteries only if their location seemed less than immediately understandable.

9. No records exist concerning the graveyard before my discovery.

10. Such learning made us different from city-raised children. See Brown, *Tracker,* for an introduction to a subject that still distinguishes wilderness- and rural-raised adults from those accustomed to sidewalks from birth.

11. Authors remembering small-town boyhoods sometimes remark similar interests; see, for example, Willie Morris, *North toward Home,* 29–30.

12. A. R. Edwards, *Old Coast Road.*

13. Duncan and Ware, *Cruising Guide,* 238.

14. Briggs, *History of Shipbuilding,* fascinated boys in the 1950s and 1960s.

15. *Look at America,* frontispiece and esp. 67–106. See also Stilgoe, *Metropolitan Corridor,* 335–45.

16. It figured in tattered short-story anthologies and other schoolroom books. There I found Ambrose Bierce's ghost story of northern Vermont, "Some Haunted Houses," and other tales involving the abandoned New England landscape; see Bierce, *Ghost and Horror Stories,* 74–75.

17. See Pickering, *Right Distance,* esp. 1–78, for parallel observations on the South: never did we encounter elderly men like the one Frye describes in *Uncle 'Lish.*

18. Perhaps they saw death too; see Geselbracht, "Ghosts of Andrew Wyeth."

19. For another, near parallel view, see Brown, *Tracker.*

20. Nutting's States Beautiful series emphasized states in the northeast quarter of the country.

21. Nutting, *Photographic Art Secrets,* esp. 86–89, 100–103, 108.

22. Wiebe's *Search for Order* appeared in 1967, the year I went to college. It helped convince me I should study history, not biology.

23. On groups transcending change, see Brands, *Reckless Decade.*

24. The proliferation of backyard pools following the perfection of the polio vaccine encouraged many children, especially girls, to bicycle to the homes of friends owning pools rather than to the estuary and swimming holes.

25. Dubos helped me realize the feeling in his *American Scholar* "Despairing Optimist" columns, some of which he reprinted in 1980 as *The Wooing of Earth.* Several years later, when I encountered R. S. Moore's *Cunning Alphabet,* I began to glimpse the deep background of what framed the thinking of the middle-aged, college-educated women.

26. Many of the authors addressing New England farm abandonment were women; see, for example, Ruth Moore, *Speak to the Winds,* 225–26.

27. When I encountered Miss Perry in John Casey's novel *Spartina,* I recognized the type.

28. Brooks, *New England,* 462–63.

29. Brooks, *Letters and Leadership,* 3.

30. Brooks, *New England,* 462–63, 465.

31. His thinking endures: see S. Jacobs, "A Woman, Her Men," for a 2006 *Boston Globe* front-page story of a female Dracula of the New Hampshire hills.

32. Stilgoe, *Metropolitan Corridor,* 312–33.

33. This thinking lasted into the Depression. See, for example, D. Hall, *String Too Short to Be Saved.*

34. Barron, *Those Who Stayed Behind,* esp. 4–26.

35. H. F. Wilson, *Hill Country,* examines the second phase of abandonment.

36. Stilgoe, *Borderland,* esp. 207–22.

37. Ammons, "Myth of Imperiled Whiteness," analyzes race imperilment precisely.

38. Lowell, *East Wind,* 88–89, 198–99, 61.

39. Rural selectmen pasted up wallpaper, applied paint, and otherwise masked sinister or obscene drawings in houses whose owners they could not contact; they did not burn down the houses for fear of legal liability. See Lincoln, *Cy Whittaker's Place,* for an introduction to the problem of the abandoned house and tax payments arriving from the far side of the world.

40. Lovecraft shared Field's thinking about imports into coastal New England; see his *Case of Charles Dexter Ward.*

41. The salve of second sight and the problems it poses for midwives are well known in British and European folklore; see Spence, *British Fairy Origins,* 19–20.

42. Field, *Points East,* 110, 111–25, 10–57. Lovecraft assumed the same; see his *Case of Charles Dexter Ward.*

43. In *Abandoned New England,* Paton utterly ignores Field and mentions Lowell only once, and then as a critic of Robert Frost.

44. Danbom, *Born in the Country,* makes a solid argument for the media shaping mass thought.

45. S. Cox, *Hooterville Handbook,* offers at least an introduction to the subject.

46. See Poffenberger, *Psychology in Advertising,* esp. 227–30, 328–38.

47. I have written on this subject at length; see Stilgoe, *Train Time,* esp. 43–86.

48. Lowell, *East Wind,* 190.

49. Stilgoe, *Landscape and Images,* 64–77.

50. Ellis, *Deterioration,* esp. 3, 9, 18, 16, 11.

51. Field, *Points East,* 113.

52. Henkel, *Weeds Used in Medicine,* still proves a useful introduction to traditional medical uses of common plants; see also her *American Medicinal Leaves and Herbs.*

53. Field, *Points East,* 119.

54. Snelling, *History and Practice,* 36–38, 114–16. The old "language of flowers" entranced me around the same time; see Stilgoe, *Borderland,* 33–37.

55. Only recently has a work appeared that at least frames their view; see Hoberman, *Yankee Moderns.*

56. Perry Miller's thinking influenced my thinking greatly in those years, especially his *The New England Mind* and *Errand into the Wilderness.*

57. Ammons, "Myth of Imperiled Whiteness," emphasizes race over sexuality, but introduces the sexual jealousy that lies beyond the scope of this book.

58. The role of post–World War II travel deserves a monograph akin to Fussell's *Abroad.*

59. On this, see Derleth, *Lonesome Places;* and Wilkins, *New England Nun,* esp. 215–33. Wilkins notes that "there is a higher congeniality than that of mutual understanding; there is that of need and supply" (232).

60. They trapped or shot sparrows, starlings, and other nonnative invasive birds, and dispatched rabbits and woodchucks too. Not for decades did I realize how much this activity put off people who discovered it.

61. I had a very poor idea of what a liberal arts education should concern, but I had read several books: Garrison's *Adventure of Learning in College* struck me as sensible, but McGrath's *Are Liberal Arts Colleges Becoming Professional Schools?* and Calvert's *Vocational Analysis of Male College Graduates in Liberal Arts* set me to thinking. After 1971, articles in the *American Scholar* shaped my musing about people who had earned a liberal arts degree and seemed quite happy and otherwise successful.

62. Baltzell, *Protestant Establishment,* alerted me to the ways secure social position enables people to experiment with edgy ideas and behavior.

63. My mother lacked a college education, but shared many of the cohort's traits. She knew most of them and enjoyed their company.

64. Didion, *White Album,* 111, 116, 113.

65. I have found no women's studies experts who study the cohort I introduce here.

66. Their comments about reformers hit me hard: I heard them in the context of Mann's *Yankee Reformers.*

67. My earliest memory of connecting the women with something transcending class involves Ronald Reagan's 1964 speech "Rendezvous with Destiny," on behalf of the candidacy of Barry Goldwater. I listened to it as part of a classroom assignment, and in the most inchoate way framed it in terms of what a handful of newcomer women had begun telling me.

68. By then I had read Mills's *Power Elite.*

69. Nabokov's *Lolita* struck many of my undergraduate friends as pornography, and a few others as a first-rate novel; my friends who watched a lot of television found the book pornographic.

70. Bonnefoy, *Mythologies,* 508.

71. Nereids belong to both classical and modern Greece, something many fantasy writers ignore; see Spence, *British Fairy Origins,* 140–41.

72. See Merivale, *Pan the Goat-God.*

73. Bonnefoy, *Mythologies,* 508.

74. In the 1980s my colleague Vlada Petric introduced me to his concept of hypnogogic cinema-provoked states, one component within a larger framework he called oneiric cinema: the isomorphism of film and dreams.

75. Tomlinson, *Pipe All Hands,* 124.

76. Tomlinson, *Out of Soundings,* 129–30.

77. Priestley, *Midnight on the Desert,* 178–81.

78. I stumbled repeatedly over the concept of assertiveness. I went to

college knowing the word connoted something positive, and five years later knew it as an epithet.

79. That wondering led me to write *Lifeboat.*

80. M. Fuller, *Woman in the Nineteenth Century,* 228.

81. Didion, *White Album,* 111.

82. This concept is Austin Warren's; see *New England Conscience,* esp. 190–93 and 208–11.

83. After 1955 the town poured money into its public schools. In the late 1970s its investment paid off in an unexpected way, attracting many families devoted to very high quality public schools, whose arrival forced up real estate values, in turn enabling greater property tax revenues, which the town applied to its public schools and to purchasing more and more land for conservation purposes.

84. Gaiman, *Neverwhere,* 131, 214.

85. The alley perhaps takes its name from Diagon Binoculars, made in Britain before World War II.

10 Imagers

1. Leighten, "Clarence John Laughlin," 51.

2. Hearn, *Spirit Photography,* 10–11.

3. Hearn, *Spirit Photography,* 16, 13.

4. Hearn, *Spirit Photography,* 18–19, 27, 31 (the newspaper essay appeared on November 14, 1875).

5. Greenough, et al., *On the Art,* 33, 38n.

6. Most photographers considered themselves craftsmen, not artists; see Snelling, *History and Practice.*

7. For an introduction to trick photography, see Amphoto Editorial Board, *Photographic Tricks;* and Litzel, *Darkroom Magic.* See also Croy, *Secrets of Trick Photography.*

8. Rabb, *Literature and Photography,* 8–9. See also Nadar, *Quand j'étais photographe;* and Wilkinson, *"Le cousin Pons."*

9. Rabb, *Literature and Photography,* 66–67.

10. Ford, *Story of Popular Photography,* esp. 42–128.

11. B. Shaw, *On Photography,* 11–22.

12. The image is reproduced in color in Ford, *Story of Popular Photography,* 75.

13. Shaw, *On Photography,* 24–25.

14. Shaw, *On Photography,* 25–26.

15. Shaw, *On Photography,* 101–2.

16. Shaw, *On Photography,* 103–6.

17. Shaw, *On Photography,* 28–29, 106.

18. Davidov, *Women's Camera Work,* 27.

19. Van Dyke notes that in 1934 she developed her panchromatic film negatives "in Meto-hydroquinone," a remark that suggests she had moved beyond Kodak developers; see "Photographs of Dorothea Lange," 467.

20. Van Dyke, "Photographs of Dorothea Lange," 464.

21. Dater, *Imogen Cunningham,* 47.

22. Dater, *Imogen Cunningham,* 44.

23. Quoted in Davidov, *Women's Camera Work,* 325 and 464n.

24. Cunningham, *Selected Texts,* 41–46. See also Berding, "Imogen Cunningham."

25. Cunningham, *Photographs;* the words are Margery Mann's, n.p. In 1932 Ansel Adams expressed his dislike of Cunningham's use of matte rather than glossy paper; see Lorenz, *Imogen Cunningham,* 64 n. 47.

26. Cunningham, *On the Body,* 31. Amy Rule claims that Cunningham began using a Rolleiflex in 1946; see Cunningham, *Selected Texts,* xv.

27. Edwards, "First Salon of Pure Photography," 420, 423.

28. Dater, *Imogen Cunningham,* 91.

29. Her father studied theosophy and was a free thinker; see Cunningham, *Selected Texts,* 2.

30. Quoted in Cunningham, *Selected Texts,* 6.

31. AE, *Candle of Vision,* 71, 28, 25, 32–33. AE found his visions to be most clear in the same sort of landscapes in which Cunningham worked with her nude models.

32. Pullman, *Golden Compass*, 343. Lord Asriel knows about radiation because he can photograph it, but Lyra can see it, and the witches fly nearly nude so they can feel it on their skin (331, 275). Lord Asriel prides himself on his meticulous laboratory technique and both disdains and envies Lyra's vision.

33. AE, *Candle of Vision*, 33.

34. Cunningham, *Photographs*, n.p.

35. Leighten, "Critical Attitudes," offers the only introduction to the subject I have found.

36. Leighten, "Clarence John Laughlin," 142, 143–44.

37. Leighten, "Clarence John Laughlin," 144. Laughlin worked in a bank, but apparently could not afford to buy a secondhand camera to mount permanently on his enlarger.

38. See, for example, Maxwell, "Vertical Photo Enlarger."

39. See, for example, Jourdan, "Two for a Quarter"; Porkorny, "Home-Made Mortensen Lighting Equipment"; and Grunwald, "Cocktail Shaker."

40. Lissaman, "Low-Cost Enlarging Camera," 82, 84, 96; see also Schlegel, "Inexpensive Enlarger."

41. Leighten, "Clarence John Laughlin," 144.

42. Enlargers also worked with candlelight and sunlight; see Collins, *Amateur Photographer's Handbook*, 257–60. See also Blumann, *Enlarging Manual*; and Haynes, *Projection Printing*.

43. For an introduction (with comparative photographs) to the differences produced by condenser and diffusion enlargers, see Eastman Kodak, *Professional Black-and-White Films*, esp. 21–24.

44. Collins, *Amateur Photographer's Handbook*, 260–67. See also W. Alexander, *Enlarging and Enlargers;* and Jordan, *Photographic Enlarging.*

45. See, for example, A. Adams, "My First Ten Weeks," 20. There is more about this in the following chapter.

46. See, for example, Ryder, "Speedier Ways." The device Ryder describes is extremely versatile as well as fast.

47. In the 1930s, then, Laughlin seems to have enjoyed idiosyncratic technical discoveries akin to those in which Watkins delighted a generation earlier.

48. Leighten, "Clarence John Laughlin," 144–45. For an example of mainstream imagery against which he competed, see S. M. Lynn, *New Orleans.*

49. Leighten, "Clarence John Laughlin," 145.

50. Almost never do I encounter a photography critic at all interested in analyzing the quality of light used in printing the negative, but I finder older photographers much intrigued. Perhaps the next generation will find delight in using antiquated, often shop-built photographic equipment.

51. Laughlin, *Ghosts along the Mississippi*, plate 78 caption.

52. Laughlin, *Ghosts along the Mississippi*, plate 98 caption.

53. See, for example, Laughlin, "American Fantastica" and "Images of the Lost."

54. "Land in the Lens," 19.

55. Laughlin, "Tree and the Camera."

56. Laughlin, "Gone Are the Years." See, for example, the shortened caption (58) in comparison with the original for plate 100, *The Final Bell.*

57. "Laughlin's Enigmatic Lost World," 46.

58. See Laughlin, "Surfaces in Design."

59. Laughlin, *Personal Eye*, i, ellipsis in the original. This volume includes all of the captions but reproduces none of the illustrations.

60. Laughlin, *Personal Eye* (captions), G-7, G-1, H-6, G-16, H-5.

61. See the quotations reproduced on the page facing the title page in Laughlin, *Personal Eye* (catalog).

62. Laughlin, *Personal Eye* (catalog), 5–6.

63. In Laughlin, *Personal Eye* (catalog), 5–6.

64. See, for example, Whitten, "Contemporary Patterns"; and Simpson, "Four Vodun Ceremonies." Such articles

appeared as part of a long folklore tradition; see, for example, Hurston, "Hoodoo in America," for a seminal article that shaped much Depression-era scholarship.

65. See, for example, "Sex in the Caribbean Equals Voodoo" (this article may not appear in every issue of *Sir!* magazine; pulp magazines may have appeared in variants within single issues).

66. O'Brien's "Voodoo Queen of New Orleans" shares many similarities with Cable's tales.

67. See, for example, Whitten, "Events and Statuses."

68. Laughlin, *Personal Eye* (catalog), 123.

69. Laughlin, *Personal Eye* (catalog), 124.

70. Laughlin, "American Fantastica," 48.

71. *Clarence John Laughlin* (Tucson, 1979), esp. 16–17; the words are Henry Holmes Smith's in "An Access of American Sensibility."

72. Sontag, *On Photography*, 67.

73. The Hallmark collection is routinely underestimated by photographic historians.

74. See also, Lawrence, "Clarence John Laughlin." *New Orleans and Its Living Past* appeared in an edition of 500 copies.

75. Issues of *Art Photography* now sell on Internet auction sites for up to $500 each; collectors of film star images find the magazine the only source of many photographs, especially nudes. On *Playboy* photography, see Edgren, *Playmate Book*.

76. For seven years I have been asking undergraduate and graduate students, colleagues, and friends to comment on the photographs in *Art Photography*.

77. Hattersley, *Photographic Lighting*, 235.

78. Laughlin, "Backgrounds and Models" (April), 32, 36; (May), 36, 38.

79. Laughlin, "Backgrounds and Models" (May), 34, 38.

80. See, for example, Mortensen's "Fallacies of 'Pure Photography.'"

81. Mortensen, *Texture Screen*. Biographical information on Mortensen is still scarce.

82. For contemporaneous biographical and critical information, see the 1958 documentary film directed by Richard J. Soltys and Earl Stone, *Monsters and Madonnas and the World of William Mortensen*.

83. Mortensen, "Fallacies of 'Pure Photography,'" 263.

84. Mortensen's distrust seems prescient when juxtaposed with contemporary point-and-shoot digital cameras that download images into software that automatically "quick fixes" them.

85. It is difficult to learn much about Mortensen's "followers": unlike other leading photographers, he organized no "group," not even among the graduates of his school. His books sold well, were often reprinted, and were frequently updated; they are almost unmentioned in Boni's bibliography, *Photographic Literature*.

86. Young, "Pictorialism for Beginners," esp. 182, 185.

87. It may be that his insistence on avoiding expensive cameras and accessories, and on practicing for years with one type of film, did not endear him to manufacturers of such items who advertised in photography journals.

88. Any analysis of *Camera Craft, Popular Photography, Minicam,* and other magazines photographers (and would-be photographers) read from the mid-1930s through 1960 suggests that many authors knew Mortensen's work and valued it; they did not necessarily value his choice of subject matter.

89. Mortensen was a prolific author, yet the Boni bibliography includes only four citations. See also Newhall, "Photography as Art."

90. Mortensen, *Outdoor Portraiture*, 9, 77.

91. Mortensen, *Flash in Modern Photography*, 36–37.

92. Mortensen, *Mortensen on the Negative*, 20–21.

93. Mortensen, "Notes on the Miniature Camera: Outdoor Portraiture," 10.

94. Mortensen, "Essay on Creative Pictorialism," 312. In this essay Mortensen elaborates on what both Lange and Cunningham detailed, that "emotion is an essential quality of pictures" (312).

95. Mortensen, "Fallacies of 'Pure Photography,'" 262.

96. Benjamin, "The Work of Art in the Age of Mechanical Reproduction," in *Illuminations*, 217–51.

97. See Litzel, *Darkroom Magic*, for an introduction to looking at photographs made in idiosyncratic, unique ways.

98. Palmer, "Spider Webs to Order," esp. 33.

99. The technique works with a so-called Yankee Eggbeater Drill, turned by hand. The ones made by the Millers Falls Company after 1900 enable the production of cobwebs in places far from electric outlets.

11 Rolleiflex

1. Retrospect makes me realize that early on I gave up making snapshots of birds and other fast-moving animals. Even box turtles grew impatient when posing.

2. A recent general introduction to medium-format photography and cameras is Ericksenn, *Medium Format Photography*; on squares, see esp. 3–58.

3. See Farber, "Concentric Circles."

4. For an introduction to recent thinking about such questions, see Boff, Kaufman, and Thomas, *Handbook of Perception*.

5. Maier, *Atalanta Fugiens*, 147.

6. The visualizing capacity may be what Blondlot identifies in *"N" Rays*.

7. An handful of scholars have examined the role of seeing in alchemy. Urszula Szulakowska presents an especially intriguing thesis in *The Alchemy of Light*, esp. 30–39; her thinking explains much about the underlying premise of Pullman's His Dark Materials series.

8. Few undergraduates at Boston University between 1967 and 1971 routinely carried cameras or used them at all frequently. I do not know why, but the expense of film, developing, and printing surely figured in student equations. Since the Kodak Duoflex II focused from three and a half feet to infinity, and particularly well between four and twelve feet, it served my glamour purposes well enough. As I told my friends now and then, I did not do scenery photography.

9. Setting a Duaflex II beside a computer monitor, facing the keyboard, grabs the eye of anyone glancing toward the monitor screen: in the finding lens the face of the user appears inverted and elongated, a reflection that vanishes as the user raises the camera near eye level.

10. Typical mirrors are rear-silvered; front-silvered mirrors, and those backed with black varnish and other materials, behave somewhat differently, but few contemporary Americans encounter them. I keep one in my office to arrest the attention of students.

11. D. E. Thomas, "Mirror Images."

12. The attachment is very rare and nowadays an expensive collector item.

13. Fixing a mirror at a thirty-three-degree angle to the optical axis of the lens enables photographers to diminish the blue of the sky by polarization and so accentuates white clouds: almost no one does this, and instead uses yellow filters (for black-and-white film), and so almost no one discovers that the mirror (usually one varnished black on its reverse side rather than silvered) tends not to double the seeming distance of faraway objects (like clouds). See Clerc, *Photography*, 81.

14. Cannavo, *Nomic Inference*, 40–42.

15. Lummer, *Contributions on Photographic Optics*, esp. 14–19 and 24–28. Lummer and others examined pinhole photography especially closely. See also Von Rohr, *Theorie und Geschichte*.

16. See Clerc, *Photography*, 27, 47; and *Focal Encyclopedia of Photography*, 247–49.

17. Nowadays even my youngest stu-

dents cannot explain, even to themselves, why older television sets have square picture tubes and new ones have rectangular screens.

18. See, for example, his *Poetical Impression of Natural Scenery,* esp. 36–49. Cornish worked in a modern aesthetic centered chiefly in Britain and in Germany; see, Endell, *Zauberland des Sichtbaren.*

19. Cornish, *Poetical Impression of Natural Scenery,* 54–55.

20. Cornish, *Scenery of England,* 72–73.

21. Schön, "Is the Camera a Third Eye?," offers a useful introduction to this issue.

22. Only Stonehenge struck Cornish as fitted to the "circular" skyline of Salisbury Plain. Ocean liners had become so long that their straight hulls tricked passengers into "straightening out" the horizon sailing-ship passengers understood as curved; see *Scenery of England,* 79.

23. Cornish, *Beauties of Scenery,* 60.

24. Cornish, *Scenery of England,* 21; see also 29–30 on the bulk of pine trees becoming "sufficient for the monochrome" in ways beyond the limitations of birches.

25. See esp. *Scenery of England,* 25.

26. The woods of Roke in Le Guin's *Wizard of Earthsea* represent perhaps the best-known such woods in fantasy fiction.

27. Nutting, *Photographic Art,* 20, 41, 48–49, 88, 18, 108–9.

28. A. Adams, "My First Ten Weeks," 17, 20, 14, 17–18, 20. Despite protestations to the contrary (esp. 20), Adams returned to working with large-format cameras.

29. The content and tone of *Leica Photography,* the in-house monthly magazine published from 1933 on by E. Leitz, Inc. for American readers reward analysis. Leitz definitely wanted Leica owners to feel elitist, economically and technically beyond other 35 mm camera users.

30. Leitz, "Cat's Eye Leica."

31. Zeiss Ikon, "Day or Night Contax."

32. Rogliatti, *Leica,* esp. 37–62; Pestalozzi, *Leica Amateur's Picture Book.*

33. Pepper, "Miniature Cameras," 268, 273.

34. Perhaps the best way to follow the introduction of particular cameras is to read a range of period photography magazines. Advertising campaigns varied by magazine, which suggests that magazines catered to different income levels, and that publishers now and then shifted their attention from one to another.

35. The Argus, especially the C-3 model, made excellent photographs, although its external geared focusing system irritated users. The camera is often found in junk shops and Internet auction sites for a few dollars, and often in good cosmetic and mechanical condition, suggesting users consigned it quickly to closet shelves.

36. Lahue and Bailey, *Glass, Brass, and Chrome,* esp. 273.

37. I use "miniature" here as Lahue and Bailey define the term, meaning essentially 35 mm cameras; see *Glass, Brass, and Chrome,* viii.

38. Apparently especially for use at sporting events and while skiing downhill; see Heering, *Rollei* (1935), 35–37.

39. The ground-glass accessory back once sold well, judging by the many I find for sale. Its existence forces anyone studying the photography of the Rolleiflex-equipped photographer to scrutinize images, especially portraits and landscapes.

40. Prochnow, *Voigtländer,* 421–440.

41. Deschin, *Rollei Photography,* 40.

42. The Fresnel screen seems to have been introduced by Eastman Kodak on its Kodak Reflex II twin-lens reflex camera. The history of American-built twin-lens reflex cameras is not yet written, and aside from studying magazine advertisements, the best way is to acquire cameras (and manuals), most of which sell inexpensively. The Argus Argoflex

of 1947 introduced features Francke and Heidecke copied within several years, but went out of production the following year.

43. Oceanside Camera Repair in Manhattan Beach, California, installs the so-called Maxwell screens in Rolleiflex cameras.

44. Deschin, *Rollei Photography*, 40–41.

45. Heering, *Rollei Book*, 17. The translation by Fred Willy Frerk seems to confuse "size" with "shape."

46. Heering, *Rolleiflex Book*, 15–16; and Heering, *Rollei Book*, 16–17.

47. Heering, *Rollei Book*, 16–20; and Heering, *Rolleiflex Book*, 18.

48. Deschin, *Rollei Photography*, 46.

49. Deschin, *Rollei Photography*, 47. Within a few years, Francke and Heidecke produced a set of metal masks for photographers using Rolleiflexes as 35 mm telephoto cameras. The mask sets are useful in demonstrating to contemporary skeptics the optical arguments Heering made in the early 1930s.

50. Deschin, *Rollei Photography*, 47.

51. For examples of many now-rare miniature cameras produced as early as 1933, see Central Camera Company, *Mail Order Catalogue #43*.

52. Deschin, *Making Pictures*, 37–38. See also Dutton, "Lenses for the Miniature Camera."

53. "Build It Yourself!" See also "Look—Better Pictures!"

54. R. L. Simon, *Miniature Photography*, 16–19.

55. "Miniature Camera Work," esp. 177, 183–85. For another view agreeing with that of the editors of the *New Photo-Miniature*, see Anderson, "Some Pictorial History."

56. R. L. Simon, *Miniature Photography*, 64. See also Wyble, "Selecting a Used Camera." On converting older cameras, see a useful shop-theory article, Post, "Miniature Negatives."

57. R. L. Simon, *Miniature Photography*, 12.

58. Ansel Adams, "The Expanding Photographic Universe," in Morgan and Lester, *Miniature Camera Work*, 74.

59. Fraprie, "Miniature Camera."

60. See "Leica: The Original" for an example of a time-payment plan advertisement.

61. "Miniature Camera Work," 185.

62. See the excellent chapter on color photography by Harris B. Tuttle, an Eastman Kodak expert, in Morgan and Lester, *Miniature Camera Work*, 89–109.

63. "Kodak Retina." In July, Eastman Kodak insisted the Retina was "for those with 'continental ideas' but 'domestic purses'"; see "Kodak Retina: Speedy." For the deepening confusion, see A. Palme, "What Camera?"

64. See, for example, Mannheim, *Retina Reflex Way*, esp. 11–13; and J. D. Cooper, *New Ultra-Miniature Photograph*, esp. 7–17, for interpretations of the changes in the decade before 1960.

65. "Important Research Work."

66. Tuttle, "Color Photography" (cited n. 61), esp. 89, 96, 97–98.

67. See, for example, Mannheim, *Retina Reflex Way*, 237.

68. C. F. Jacobs, "Getting Results with Color," summarizes exquisitely the problems photographers faced immediately. See also Henney, "How to Make Separation Negatives."

69. "Armour-Plated Ebner."

70. "Entirely New Type of Camera."

71. Mortensen, "About the Paper Negative," 409.

72. Mortensen, "Notes on the Miniature Camera" (August), 362–63; this is a successful argument for low-cost, simple cameras.

73. Mortensen, "Glorifying the American Snapshot," esp. 68.

74. R. W. Brown, "It's the Man."

75. R. Green, "Pictures vs. Snapshots," offers a glimpse at the efforts of *Popular Photography* to broaden its readership.

76. Purchasers and frequent users of Rolleiflexes (not always the same group)

prove hard to research. I have examined chiefly the railroad photography hobbyists, since I know the cohort through decades of railroad-related research; see, for example, Wilder, "Dana D. Goodwin"; and Reevy, "Artist of the Rail." The latter notes that one rail photography enthusiast, a physician, enjoyed the generous magazine payments made possible by the large negatives.

77. Perrett, "My Rolleiflex Camera," 319–20.

78. "Get 'Em on the Wing." This important advertisement emphasizes that a Rolleiflex can capture "gulls in flight," skiers, and ballet dancers, but it also emphasizes that 120-size film is economical and easily obtained. This is the earliest mention of 120-film availability I have found, which suggests that Kodak 620 film had begun pushing 120 film from the shelves of drugstores and other box camera–oriented dealers.

79. Sullivan, "My Greatest Money-Maker," 14, 11.

80. Men proved quite willing to carry cameras suspended from straps; see Bryan, "On a Trip," 28.

81. Jourdan, "Minicams versus Megacams," 138.

82. All but film historians tend to be ignorant of the many formats of cinema film preceding 35 mm; see, for example, "Film Gauges and Sound Tracks," an undated poster produced by the Moving Picture Society (London) (I have no further bibliographical information on this extremely informative graphic).

83. Anderson, "Some Pictorial History," 209.

84. A. Palme, "What Camera?," esp. 463–65.

85. Frazer, "Facts and Comments," esp. 706–7.

86. In the late 1930s few advertisements for 35 mm cameras depict tripods at all.

87. McManigal, "Good Old Tripod," 278, 280.

88. R. Green, "Pictures vs. Snapshots," esp. 14–15.

89. Don Wallace, "Snapshots Are Better."

90. "Faking Films in Hollywood" offers an excellent introduction to an interest that shaped the magazine; see also Ward, "Movie Mood Music."

91. Tajiri, "Well Equipped Lensman," offers a useful example of upscale understanding of camera choice.

92. Downes, "First Stop: Germany."

93. Lahue and Bailey, *Glass, Brass, and Chrome,* esp. 257–78.

94. "Made in West Germany." For camera prices, see advertisements, 3–37.

95. Eisendrath, "After 35mm. What?," esp. 36–37.

96. "Great Summer for Roll-Film Users."

97. As late as 1983 magazine editors counseled would-be submitters to use medium-format cameras, at the time remarking that used cameras could be bought for about fifty dollars; see, for example, Hundman, "Prototype Photography."

98. W. S. Davis, *Practical Amateur Photography* (rev. ed. 1939), might be one of the last general-interest photography books to deal with landscape photography from a distinctly New England viewpoint. On the framework in which Davis wrote, see Stilgoe, *Landscape and Images,* 298–308.

99. Eaton, *In Berkshire Fields,* esp. 159, 168.

100. Eaton, *Barn Doors and Byways,* 24–25, 220, 255, 224. Eaton's view is distinctly twentieth century, especially when compared to Robinson, *In New England Fields* (Robinson was blind); see esp. 118–19.

101. See also O'Brian, *Ionian Mission,* 257.

102. Eaton, *Barn Doors and Byways,* 18–19.

12 Tutorial

1. Jourdan, "Minicams versus Megacams," 138.

2. Reviewed in the March 1935 issue, 195.

3. Undergraduates invariably notice the tone and appearance of the magazine when directed to visit bound volumes: they call it "serious" or "scholarly" and then awkwardly mention its "classy" or "upscale" characteristics.

4. Sandwith, "Night London."

5. Terry, "Shooting the Burlesque," esp. 24.

6. F. A. Morgan, "Panorama Pictures," typifies the sort of article the magazine featured. Although it is difficult to ascertain, most of the nude women appear to have been the wives of the photographer-authors. See, for example, Hannah, "Admiration."

7. Reisman, "Photographic Nude."

8. H. G. Bailey, "Feet First," offers a cogent explication of the posing problem.

9. It is useful to compare its reproduced images with those in German annuals, especially *Deutsche Lichtbild*. Comparing the 1938 issues and the 1938 annual (the tenth in the series) proves especially revealing.

10. "Theory of Miniature Photography."

11. See, for example, Vickers, "Plea for the Metric System."

12. Advertising supported the mass-circulation magazine stance, see, for example, Universal Camera Corp., "Speed Camera of Tomorrow."

13. Minnaert, *Light and Color*, plate 48.

14. As fascism threatened to explode into war, a number of European intellectuals found some sanity and refuge away from newspapers, newsreels, radio, and politics. Minnnaert perhaps did so in the years before he joined the Dutch resistance.

15. Windisch, *New Photo School*, 11.

16. See Blumtritt, *Geschichte der Dresdner Kameraindustrie*. Collectors pay exorbitant sums for KW multi-colored folding cameras, but little is known about the rationale for manufacturing them in the 35 mm minicam era.

17. Burleigh Brooks Co., "Pilot Super."

18. Seventy years after manufacture, the meter on my Pilot Super still works accurately.

19. Central Camera Company, "Altiflex." For a general background on the Altiflex that offers many insights into the Dresden camera industry that produced the Pilot Super, see Heyde, *Altix;* and Hummel, *Spiegelreflexkameras aus Dresden*.

20. Central Camera Company, "Altiflex." See also Kirland, "Go to Guatemala." *Photography with the Rolleiflex* began suggesting Central America too; see, for example, Severin, "Mexico from a New Angle."

21. Rudloff, "'GP' Vertical Enlarger." In order to save money, the easel moved up and down below a fixed lens.

22. Thorek, "Paper Negative Process"; see also his *Creative Camera Art* and *Camera Art*.

23. For one example, see "Minicam Rolleiflex Salon."

24. After studying both French and German in junior high school, I chose to study German throughout high school, in part because it struck me as the language of photographers and camera makers.

25. With its Rolleinar close-up attachments (esp. Type 1 and Type 2), the Rolleiflex excelled at head-and-shoulder portraits too.

26. Heering, *Rolleiflex Book,* 67–68.

27. Heering, *Rolleiflex Book,* 84, 90.

28. Heering, *Rollei Book,* 144.

29. Heering, *Rollei Book* (1954), 138, 141.

30. Knopf published the folio; by the late 1930s it and other established firms had begun publishing books documenting nude women as attired naturally for the beach, pools, and other outdoor environments.

31. Lohse, *Miniature Camera,* esp. 14–15.

32. Lohse, *Miniature Camera,* 15. Retrospective surveys of popular Amer-

ican photography magazines published during World War II suggest that Lohse nearly singlehandedly created the "jumping girl" sort of image that vied with static pinup girl images for GI attention.

33. André De Dienes in Croy, *Photographic Portrait*, 83.

34. Croy, *Photographic Portrait*, esp. 72–79, 66–67, 83, 38.

35. Heering, *Rollei Book* (1954), 140–41.

36. The magazine stopped publication in World War II and began in a new format in 1963, titled *Rolleigrafie*.

37. Heering, *Rolleiflex* (1954), 5–17. It is difficult to examine many of the Rolleiflex imitations. One that deserves sustained scrutiny is the Lyraflex, made in wartime Japan for domestic use; it seems to have been a prototype for postwar models manufactured for export to the United States and perhaps to Latin America.

38. Mannheim, *Rollei Way*, 11–12; van Wadenoyen quoted on 94–95.

39. Montgomery Ward Company, *New 1957 Camera Shop*, 30–33.

40. On women photographers (not models, wives, and otherwise) in pants before WWII, see Stagg, "Woman's Place in Photography," esp. 26.

41. Deschin, *Rollei Photography*, 93, 96–97.

42. Pearlman, *Rollei Manual* (1955), 271, 272–73.

43. Pearlman, *Rollei Manual* (1955), 275, 281–83.

44. Pearlman, *Rollei Manual* (1955), esp. 213–16.

45. Pearlman, *Rollei Manual* (1960), 123, offers a useful example.

46. Pearlman, *Rollei Manual* (1960), esp. 119–26.

47. Pearlman *Rollei Manual* (1971), esp. 156–64, 198–211.

48. Pearlman, *Rollei Manual* (1953), 280; (1971), 204.

49. Pearlman, *Rollei Manual* (1953), 214.

50. Heering, *Das Rollei-Buch*, 170–84; the phrase is on 174 (my translation).

51. I have been unable to trace the flow of German-made cameras, let alone instruction manuals, through Army of Occupation and then NATO base post exchange sales. I first saw a copy of the 1963 edition of Heering's book circa 1970 but could not afford it at the time.

13 Chrome

1. On chartreuse in film chemistry, see Stilgoe, *Shallow-Water Dictionary*, 37–40.

2. Pearlman, *Rollei Manual* (1960), 309. The best introduction to the Rolleimarin remains the operator's manuals provided with the several variations of the accessory.

3. Hass's *Manta* offers a useful introduction to his work.

4. Hass, *Unter Korallen und Haien*.

5. Hass, *Unter Korallen und Haien*, appeared in 1941; Hass, *Fotojagd am Meeresgund*, appeared the next year.

6. English-only readers still rarely learn about the Axis use of underwater technology; see M. Jung, *Sabotage unter Wasser*, for an introduction.

7. It illuminates too the early history of scuba-based underwater photography; see esp. "Underwater Photography" and "World's Largest Underwater Photo." Moosleitner, "Underwater Photography," is an especially useful article about how scuba diving drove undersea photography.

8. See, for example, Dovala, "Gender Question."

9. Fontova, *Helldivers' Rodeo*, esp. 30, 27–34.

10. On Hass as spear fisherman, see Roberts, *Unnatural History*, 238.

11. Bradford, *Wind Off the Island*, 158–59, 154.

12. Millar, *Isabel and the Sea*, 149–50.

13. Bocca, *Bikini Beach*, 138–40.

14. On the history of the bikini as a prewar invention, see Stilgoe, *Alongshore*, 334–67.

15. Vilander, "Advertising on Naked Skin," 16, 20.

16. Heering, *Golden Book*, 8, 13.

17. This is not exactly true: a handful of entrants used the Franke and Heidecke stereoscopic camera: three won honorable mentions.

18. Windisch, "Colour Photography," 12.

19. It is useful to examine the magazine images against those appearing in *American Annual of Photography* at the same time: see especially the years from 1936 to 1941 (*American Annual of Photography* carried volume numbers: 1936 is vol. 50).

20. See, for example, "Short Distance Exposures," *Rollei Annual 1951*, 51–54; see also Willi Mutschlechner, "Cardinal Points of the Technique of Developing," *Rollei Annual 1952*, 26–36; and Michael Neumüller, "Colour Photography of Today," *Rollei Annual 1953*, 27–46.

21. Frintz Henle, photo in *Rollei Annual 1951*, 14.

22. Carlheinz Albrand, "Medikams on the Style of Vivid Photography," *Rollei Annual 1951*, 24–30. Albrand emphasizes that "it is not a question of light simply, but of the light accent" that partly describes the difference in what the two types of cameras accomplish.

23. Albrand, "Results of a Competition" (1952), 14, 15.

24. Albrand, "Results of a Competition" (1952), 13, 9, 15–16.

25. Albrand, "Results of a Competition" (1953), 7.

26. This meaning of the word *cool* may lie at the heart of McLuhan's understanding of the term in his *Understanding Media*.

27. *Rollei Annual 1953*, esp. 47, 55, 3–5.

28. It is useful to compare issues of *Photography Annual* with contemporaneous issues of the *British Journal of Photography Annual*, which began publishing in 1860: the British annual might have been one prototype of what *Popular Photography* created, but the American editors chose a different audience from that of their far more experienced British peers.

29. Burleigh Brooks, "Wherever You Turn."

30. *Modern Mermaid, Photography Annual 1952*, 87, 264.

31. *Nude at Noon, Photography Annual 1952*, 131, 268.

32. See chap. 14 on the girlie magazines. *Popular Photography* editors struggled hard to find a middle ground that neither offended many readers nor bored others.

33. See, for example, *Bathers*, in *Photography Annual 1953*, 87, 263.

34. *High Tension*, in *Photography Annual 1953*, 164, 271–72.

35. See, for example, *Informal Figure Study*, in *Photography Annual 1954*, 151, 244.

36. *Exuberance*, in *Photography Annual 1955*, 31, 228.

37. *Glamour*, in *Photography Annual 1956*, 86–99.

38. See, for example, *Philippe Halsman*, in *Photography Annual 1957*, 202–11.

39. See, for example, *Nude by the Window, Nude*, and *Bath Time*, in *Photography Annual 1958*, 66, 104, 105.

40. Crawford and Keiller, *Wessex from the Air*, 107.

41. Burleigh Brooks, "Rollei Gives You Color."

42. "Symposium on Color," 13.

43. I have found no contemporaneous studies of why large images often upset viewers willing to examine them in 8×10–inch format.

44. Downes, "Nude in Photography," 63.

45. On this, see Barthes, *Camera Lucida*, 57–58.

46. Downes, "Nude in Photography," 63.

47. On color pigments themselves, see Moreau-Vauthier, *La peinture;* see also Devoe & Raynolds Co., *Pigments*. On the semantics of color, see André, *Étude sur les termes de couleur.*

48. See "Dufaycolor Process."

49. See esp. Oringer, "Way-Out Film."

50. The 1951 edition exemplifies the strain of introducing photography to beginners who have purchased either black-and-white or color film for no specific reason; see esp. 53–66. It is best read along with Tydings, *Guide to Kodak Miniature Cameras,* published the same year; see esp. 98–101 on amateur reasons for preferring Kodachrome.

51. Eastman Kodak, *Data Book on Black-and-White,* 9, 2, 23.

52. Eastman Kodak, *Kodak Films* (1952), 36–37.

53. Du Pont de Nemours, *Photographic Films,* 53, 40, 5.

54. The educated general public acquires and loses interest in color in roughly fifty-year cycles; see Rood, *Modern Chromatics;* Brusatin, *History of Colors;* and Finlay, *Colour.*

55. Eastman Kodak, *Photography of Colored Objects,* 11, 45–47.

56. Von Reichenbach, *Der sensitive Mensch,* 404–9. See also Albers, *Interaction of Color.* Over decades of teaching I have found many students who are extremely unwilling to test their color acuteness, even for fun.

57. See, for example, Mees, *Photography,* 147–66. When he published his book, Mees was working as director of research and development at the Eastman Kodak Company.

58. Eastman Kodak, *Photography of Colored Objects,* 11, 8, 50, 59–60, 52.

59. A useful way of establishing baseline knowledge of different photographic opportunities and problems is to examine university-level textbooks: the best I have found for the immediate prewar era is Mack and Martin's 1939 *The Photographic Process,* which deals well with color photography (its frontispiece is by Edward Steichen, courtesy of Condé Nast Publications, Inc.).

60. Experimental color photography had existed for decades; see R. C. Bayley, "Pictorial Aspect of Photograph"; and J. Wood, *Art of the Autochrome.*

61. McKay's introduction to C. A. Nelson, *Natural Color Film,* 15.

62. C. A. Nelson, *Natural Color Film,* 117, 119.

63. Reproduced in C. A. Nelson, *Natural Color Film,* 117.

64. Dmitri, *Kodachrome,* 108–9, 48–49, 115–16.

65. Wolff, *My Experiences in Color Photography* (*Meine Erfahrungen*). The original German edition is rare and contains an opening statement by the Oberregierungsrat im Reichsministerium für Volkauflärung und Propaganda (the page is frequently found razored out in secondhand editions); photographs are also different from those reproduced in the first Swedish edition (*Mina erfarenheter i färg* [Stockholm: Gernandts, 1945]), which are different from those reproduced in the first American edition, 1948.

66. Wolff, *My Experiences in Color Photography,* 15–16.

67. Dmitri, *Kodachrome,* 10–11. Dmitri here followed Eastman Kodak instructions.

68. Eastman Kodak, *Photography with Kodachrome Professional Film,* 33. The publication goes well beyond Dmitri's chart by examining the role of over-illuminating the background when the subject wears light colors (34–35).

69. Fraprie, *Portrait Lighting,* 41.

70. Wolff, *My Experiences in Color Photography,* 12–13.

71. Heering, *Im Zauber der Farbe,* 7–17, 63–74, 80–81.

72. See, for example, Eastman Kodak, *Professional Photoguide,* esp. 16–18, which include the color-temperature balance dial that worked in ways prewar owners of dial exposure calculators found familiar (I surely did).

73. Eastman Kodak, *Color Photography,* 20.

74. Eastman Kodak, *Slides,* esp. 2–8.

75. Eastman Kodak, *Color Photography,* 17, 38.

76. Eastman Kodak, *Applied Color Photography,* 21.

77. Better Homes and Gardens, *Photography for Your Family,* 108–9, sug-

gests that beginners buy a Rolleiflex not only because the large viewfinder makes composing shots easier but because the large transparencies are "remarkably effective when projected."

78. By this time, the Eastman Kodak Company research effort appears to have paralleled that of Bell Laboratories. See D. Collins, *Story of Kodak*, for an overview of the history of the firm.

79. R. M. Evans, *Eye, Film, and Camera*, 49–50.

80. R. M. Evans, *Eye, Film, and Camera*, 50, 52–53.

81. R. M. Evans, *Eye, Film, and Camera*, 57–60.

82. R. M. Evans, *Eye, Film, and Camera*, 44–46, 73.

83. Eastman Kodak, "Why a Color," 1–2.

84. Red hair presented peculiar problems; see, for example, Petersen, *Playboy Redheads;* and H. Schatz, *Seeing Red.* On red hair in general, see Roach, *Roots of Desire.*

85. *Popular Photography Annual 1958*, 115, 227–28.

86. See, for example, the Ben Dalsheim image in *Rolleigrafie* (Winter 1964/65), 27.

87. Contemporary Barbie dolls lack the eyeliner and other makeup of the 1950s doll, which simulated a sophisticated beautiful woman; see Lord, *Forever Barbie.*

88. The post-1995 frisson in architecture just now attracts scrutiny; see, for example, McCown, *Colors.*

89. *Photography Annual 1968* carried chiefly 35 mm advertising and only one advertisement for GAF Anscochrome color 35 mm slide film; photographers made the bulk of its images with Leica and Nikon 35 mm cameras.

90. Karasek, "Colour and Reality," 15.

91. I first became aware of the distrust of Rolleiflex users circa 1975. Feminists equated the camera with the fashion imagery they thought demeaned all women. Nowadays scholars examining photographs of or by women typically miss the distrust simply because they routinely ignore the types of cameras any photographer used.

92. Sloane's 1967 *Colour* did much to sharpen my awareness of divisions between my friends who painted and those of us who did color photography. See also her *Visual Nature of Color.*

93. This became the research that led to remarks in my *Shallow-Water Dictionary,* 48–53, and subsequently in *Alongshore,* 101–30; see also my *Landscape and Images,* esp. 298–308.

14 Spirit

1. By the early 1950s French women entering bikini-design competitions often eschewed tops completely; see "Carnival in Nice."

2. Franke and Heidecke advertising proves intriguing here: after about 1934 the firm often depicted scantily clad women holding Rolleiflex cameras. See, for example, Burleigh Brooks, "Incomparable Rolleiflex."

3. See, for example, Gehman, "Lives of Suzy Parker"; and Bergquist, "Strange Case of Suzy Parker."

4. T. B. Morgan, "World's Most Beautiful Woman"; and "Girl Next Door."

5. Amory, "Celebrity Register."

6. On responses to the prudery, see "Adhesive Bras," and the next chapter.

7. See, for example, the 1952 "Carnival in Nice," in which the many of the prizewinning contestants dispensed with bikini tops before the competition.

8. Schläger, "Rollei Photography."

9. The editors honed this theme over many issues; see, for example, Trenker, "Comradeship with the Rolleiflex."

10. It appeared again as vol. 1. I have been unable to unravel the precise volume numbering of the various German or the American editions, and find it best to note the date of the issue.

11. *Camera Craft* ceased publication in 1942; after that year the magazines inaugurated in the 1930s triumphed, but no longer had to compete with journals

offering highly technical articles like those written by Mortensen.

12. Schmölke, "High Key Shot"; and Spitzing, "Special Photo Effects," esp. 34.

13. Emanuel, *All-in-One* (1973), 146–47.

14. Emanuel, *All-in-One* (1944), 128–29. In this edition Emanuel insisted that 35 mm color transparencies were too small "to be seen comfortably"; he also explained Eastman Kodak Kodacolor as a new product "not likely to be made available outside America during the war" (133).

15. Emanuel, *All-in-One* (1958), 163, 134–35.

16. For more on this, see the next chapter.

17. Sussman, *Amateur Photographer's Handbook* (1952), frontispiece and 354–55.

18. Sussman, *Amateur Photographer's Handbook* (1965), 357.

19. Sussman, *Amateur Photographer's Handbook* (1965), 329; (1973), 453.

20. By 1939 the German firm Voigtländer had begun emphasizing images of scantily clad women in its advertising; see, for example, its *100 Jahre Fotografie* and *Foto-Taschenbuch*. I have been unable to trace the details of the late 1930s shift in Voigtländer imagery, but it may be that Sussman attempted to create a counterimagery, perhaps one distinctly "American."

21. It is worth comparing the 1973 edition against GAF Corporation material explaining its ISO 500 high-speed color transparency film; see esp. "500 Color Slide Film."

22. Boucher, *Fundamentals of Photography*, esp. 231–55. Landscape views with multiple contrasting high-brilliance color components especially intrigued Boucher, who cared little about beauty but determined to help readers conquer the "variegated composition" problem Emanuel enunciated (see esp. 257).

23. Not until 1981 did Eastman Kodak produce a book that distinguished between black-and-white film and color

film approaches to beach, snow, and desert photography, including full-figure imagery. Unfortunately titled *Using Filters*, it deals explicitly with the ways light changes throughout the day and the ways the changes mislead photographers who fail to notice the changes as they work. Its full-color diagrams, especially those depicting color wheels surrounded by filters placed perpendicularly, elucidate the ways color filters function in both black-and-white and color photography of monochrome and colored objects.

24. As light changes from bluish-white to yellow in early afternoon, exactly as Windisch made clear, many photographers already making photographs fail to notice the changes. A similar result occurs when yellow or blue filters are placed over the lenses of projectors showing color transparencies. Unless the audience is alerted to the change, within seconds viewer eyes adjust for the tonal change, and viewers accept the projected colors as "true." See R. M. Evans, *Eye, Film, and Camera*, 119.

25. It made some suspect that Lohse published one in every thousand shots.

26. "How to Pose," 60.

27. "Bathing Suits," 64.

28. Professional photographers who acquired studios to do color film work soon realized that having once arranged lighting they might work all day not only in color but in black-and-white without compensating for changing levels of sunlight produced by the passage of time or changing weather.

29. See, for example, "Brief, Briefer, Briefest." Photographers working with male models confronted the same problem; see "Swim Trunks Get Briefer."

30. Heydemann, "On the Importance." This is a very good article that emphasizes the usefulness of the medium-format camera in close-up imagery. Gürtler, "My Birds"; Schmölke, "High Key Shot."

31. Swiridoff, "Architectural Photography"; Winkler, "In the Ice Fissures"; Alexander, "Nude."

32. Metrios, "Outdoor Portraits," 29.

33. "Expression Group."

34. Pawek, "Women in Front," 9.

35. Heering, "Glance Back."

36. Flöter, "Rollei and Fashion," 21, 24.

37. Frankl, "Colour-Subjective Picture Element," 12.

38. Harder, "Black Is Beautiful"; Birney, "Effect pour l'effet"; Caesar, "Nude."

39. See, for examples, the advertisements in back pages of the September 1969 issue. In the December 1969 issue readers learned how two of the advertisements had been made with Rolleiflex cameras; see Bach, "White Slavery."

40. After the summer of 1969, *Rolleigrafie* used its inside back cover to announce themes of forthcoming issues. In September 1969 it addressed the middle ground between bikinied women and nude women: women top free.

41. In a 1973 comment on an image of two nude women intertwined on a forest floor, the editors emphasized that "in France the theme of the nude is not regarded with quite so much tolerance as elsewhere. Many rules have to be strictly observed if the pictures is not be classified as pornography." But the editors may have wondered whether the image involved lesbian overtones, and they cautioned readers about the legal difficulties of double nude images; see "Double Nude Study."

42. Theis, "Advertising Photography," 23–24.

43. Sobek, "Manipulated Consumer," 44.

44. Bach, "White Slavery," 13–15; see also Fürst, "Staged Advertising Photography."

45. Vilander, *La Femme*. This 1967 volume demonstrates how a woman photographer working chiefly with female models created images that rejected cinematic and television standards. Vilander sometimes photographed herself nude with her Rolleiflex nestled between her breasts; see the last page of the book.

46. Joan Didion approached this issue in *White Album*, esp. 109–32, 153–67, 180–86.

47. Pawek, "Women in Front," 9.

48. Von Frankenberg, "Maidens, Men, and Motors"; Stengel, "Of Maids and Men"; see also Sommer, "Girls Make a Stand"; and K. H. Fischer, "Nude 69." *Figure Photography* began publishing in 1958; it offers one avenue into these issues.

49. Spoerl, "Naked and the Rollei," 19.

50. See, for example, Strelow, "Portrait Photography."

51. On this, see issues of *Grossbild Technic* after 1970.

52. "Videography: A New Medium?" demonstrates the prescience of *Photo Technik* editors, who saw it as potentially a far cheaper method of making projection-based photographs.

53. Bollen, "Black-and-White"; see also Schwille, "Beauty and Brilliance."

54. Giebelhausen, "Quick-Action Shot."

55. Schmölke, "Horrible."

56. "One Model plus One Hat"; and "Who's Afraid of Dragons?"

57. For an explicit statement about the split, see "Specialist versus All-Round Photographer."

58. Riemel, "Photography and Visual Perception."

59. Petit, "Are Pin-Ups to Be Taken Seriously?," 29, 26.

60. Ronzel, *Flowers*.

61. Freytag, "Is the Photographic Portrait?," 15.

62. Schrobsdorff, "Candid Outdoor Portraits," 17, 18.

63. See, for example, *Pollution of the Environment*.

64. "Means to an End."

65. Schrobsdorff, "Candid Outdoor Portraits," 18, 17.

66. Frieling, "Colour as a Mode of Expression," 36, 58.

67. Frieling, "Colour as a Mode of Expression," 58.

68. "Monika Wegler."

69. *Pollution of the Environment.*

70. See also another Wegler image, *Most Recent Tendency.*

71. "Many Are the Possibilities."

72. "Extreme Landscape."

73. His work follows that of Raba; see, for example, Raba, *Eva und Er,* one image of which appeared on the cover of the June 1970 issue of *Rolleigrafie.*

74. See, for example, Frederic, "J. Ronzel's Brainwaves." This article provides examples of both outdoor and front-projection images intended to appear outdoor made.

75. Harder, "Fotographie Professionell," offers a cogent introduction to the changes, and example images.

76. Henle, "Caribbean Island," 24, 28.

77. "Glamour by Sam Haskins," 58, 194.

78. Haskins, *Five Girls,* esp. 3–9; the book appeared a year later in Germany, in translation.

79. *Popular Photography* illustration rewards scrutiny: while the magazine championed 35 mm photography, it frequently used cover images made with medium- and large-format cameras; see, for example, the July 1962 cover by Jerrold Schatzberg and its description (2). How many readers noticed the pattern at the time proves impossible to answer now, but in high school I noticed that many covers came from photographers working with other than 35 mm cameras.

80. Downes, "Nude in Photography," 63.

81. As a very young man, Henle traveled widely before emigrating, working on assignments in Spain, the Near East, North Africa, China, and Japan. After he arrived in the United States he continued to travel, finding the deep South as much a separate region as any foreign country; see Winterry's introduction to *Fritz Henle's Rollei,* esp. 10–15.

82. Henle and Knapp, *The Caribbean,* esp. 169–86.

83. Henle, *Holiday in Europe,* esp. 7–8.

84. Henle, *Holiday in Europe,* 167–68.

85. He wrote articles for both *Modern Photography* and *Popular Photography.*

86. Winterry, in *Fritz Henle's Rollei,* 16.

87. Henle, *Figure Studies,* esp. 15–16, 18, 65–69.

88. *Fritz Henle's Guide,* 97, 100, 102.

89. *Fritz Henle's Guide,* 94–100. This technique spares the photographer the difficulty of focusing on one eye or the other as they move, however slightly.

90. *Fritz Henle's Guide,* 114, 115, 120.

91. *Fritz Henle's Guide,* 122–23.

92. *Fritz Henle's Guide,* 128–32.

93. *Fritz Henle's Guide,* 133.

94. Henle and Kinzer, *Photography for Everyone,* esp. 15, 14, 83–85.

95. Henle and Kinzer, *New Guide to Rollei Photography,* 104, 112.

96. On this, see, for example, Von Miserony, "From a Still Man"; and Meyer-Hanno, "Photography in Film and TV Studios."

97. Fashion magazine photograph reproduction involved the use of densitometers to measure the color-density range of the original transparency so that reproduction technicians could find the optimum contrast characteristics for the color separation printing process. The densitometer testing was far more easily and effectively accomplished with transparencies much larger than 35 mm ones; see, for example, Bluth, "Four Models."

98. The images are reproduced as part of the essay by Downes, "Nude in Photography," 64–65.

99. Penn, "Jamaican Idyll," 72, 75. See also Penn, *Still Life* and *Career in Photography.* For an introduction into the importance of fashion in his work, see Penn and Vreeland, *Inventive Paris Clothes.*

100. See, for example, Parks, "Two Fashion Photographs."

101. See next chapter.

102. "Records, Nudes and Travel," 30.

103. Gunter, "Photographic Nude."

104. A. Gruber, "Quo Vadis?," 32, 54.

105. "Nude" (*International Photo Technik*); and Sweet, "Women, Wonderful Women." See the demonstration images of nude women seemingly hailing taxicabs, etc., in Storr, "Versatility of Front Projection"; when done well, only astute viewers realized that the undressed women had been photographed in front of projected medium-format transparencies.

106. Weber, "Nude—Topical as Ever."

107. Schmölke, "Nude and Pose," offers a good introduction to such thinking. On nude but bejeweled women, see Petit, *Woman in Necklace.*

108. Schmölke, "Nude and Pose," 10.

109. Nemeth, *Glimpse.*

110. "Michael Barrington Martin" is an exceptionally cogent piece on the technology-into-nature issue.

111. Bertele, "Show of Nature."

112. In the same issue, the editors presented the work of the Danish photographer Eric Betting; see Betting, *Girl at Water's Edge.*

113. Handel, "Fashion Photography in Practice," 14. See also Weber, "Sandwiched Nudes."

114. Bollen, "Portrait Photography"; and "Nude with an Amateur Flair." At least some of the sitters preferred baring only their torsos.

115. See, for example, Hauck Werbestudios, *Moon Girl;* and Raba, *Three Girls in a Flask.*

116. Hallinan/FPG Inc., "Advertising for Nightgowns."

117. Berenson, *Passionate Sightseer,* emphasized that fourth-century Italian mosaics showed women wearing nothing "except a *soutien-gorge* and a *cache-sexe,* a combination of garments re-invented for the young women of recent years who pass their summers basking and baking on the beaches of Cannes and other Riviera resorts" (86).

Conclusion

1. Miller and Brummitt, *This Is Photography,* 190.

2. A roll can be "pushed" (developed at a rate different from usual), of course, but once processed, the film cannot be altered; the photographer has no print-the-negative chance as in working with print film.

3. "Side Roads."

4. Mortensen, *Monsters and Madonnas,* n.p.

5. Mortensen, *Outdoor Portraiture,* 114–16.

6. Mumford, *Culture of Cities,* 422. For an opposite viewpoint, see H. Morris, *Facts about Nudism.*

7. Legman, *Rationale of the Dirty Joke,* esp. 1–78.

8. Smart, *R.F.D.,* 191–96.

9. The experience of wealthy, well-educated people retreating to rural places in the Depression forms the core of a book in progress.

10. Laughlin, "Backgrounds and Models," 33–34.

11. Friends and former students long in the financial and securities industries assure me that the same or a similar cohort created novel investment instruments between about 1950 and 1960, then became extremely wealthy as other Americans invested in them.

12. Mortensen, *Outdoor Portraiture,* 4–5. See also Laughlin, "Backgrounds and Models" (April), 32–36; (May), 35–36.

13. See, for example, Hannah, "Photography of the Nude."

14. This now changes, of course; see Gaiman, *Neverwhere,* for an example of urban fantasy. On the other hand, urban-focused writers far from the fantasy genre acknowledge the importance of alignments, the work of Dion Fortune, and other material underlying fantasy fiction; see, for example, Crombie, *Finer End,* esp. 94–95.

15. A generation raised on Disney films starring Herbie the Volkswagen often discovers the deep history of that automobile with shock.

BIBLIOGRAPHY

Aaron, Daniel. "Trash, Classics and the Common Reader." *Texas Humanist* 6 (May/ June 1984), 41–43.

"ABC's of Radio." *Popular Science* 117 (October 1930), 71.

Ableman, Paul. *Anatomy of Nakedness.* London: Orbis, 1982.

Abrahams, Roger D., with Nick Spitzer, John F. Szwed, and Robert Farris Thompson. *Blues for New Orleans: Mardi Gras and America's Creole Soul.* Philadelphia: Univ. of Pennsylvania Press, 2006.

Adams, Ansel. "An Exposition of My Photographic Technique." *Camera Craft* 41 (February 1934), 72–79; (April 1934), 173–83.

——. *Letters and Images, 1916–1984.* Boston: New York Graphic Society, 1988.

——. "My First Ten Weeks with a Contax." *Camera Craft* 43 (January 1936), 14–20.

Adams, Edward C. L. *Congaree Sketches: Scenes from Negro Life in the Swamps of the Congaree.* Chapel Hill: Univ. of North Carolina Press, 1927.

"Adhesive Bras." *Life,* May 16, 1949, 109–10.

Adler, Margot. *Drawing Down the Moon: Witches, Druids, Goddess-Worshippers, and Other Pagans in America Today.* Boston: Beacon, 1979.

Adler, Mortimer J. *Adler's Philosophical Dictionary.* New York: Scribner, 1995.

"Advertising on Naked Skin." *Rolleigrafie* 6 (December 1969), 16–20.

AE. See Russell, George William.

Agfa Ansco, Inc. *Better Photography Made Easy.* Binghamton, N.Y.: Agfa Ansco, Inc., 1938.

"Agfacolor 80S Professional." *International Photo Technik* 22 (Winter 1976), 52–55.

Ahaaron, Itzhak, et al. "Beautiful Faces Have Variable Reward Value." *Neuron* 32 (November 8, 2001), 537–51.

Aiken, Nancy E. *The Biological Origins of Art.* Westport, Conn.: Praeger, 1998.

Albers, Josef. *Interaction of Color.* New Haven: Yale Univ. Press, 1963.

Albrand, Carlheinz. "Results of a Competition." *Rollei Annual.* Various years. Vienna: Hammer, 1952.

Alexander, Jules. *The Fair Sex: Classic Simplicity of the Feminine Form.* [Los Angeles?], ca. 1959.

Alexander, Leo. "Nude." *Rolleigrafie* 2 (December 1968), 28.

Alexander, William. *Enlarging and Enlargers of Today.* London: Fountain, 1941.

Allen, Robert C. *Horrible Prettiness: Burlesque and American Culture.* Chapel Hill: Univ. of North Carolina Press, 1991.

"All French and Fully Magnetized." *Night and Day* 8 (March 1955), 11–13.

Allgemeine Deutsche Biographie. Berlin: Duncker and Humblot, 1970.

Allingham, William. *Irish Songs and Poems.* London: Reeves & Turner, 1887.

Allyn, David. *Make Love, Not War: The Sexual Revolution: An Unfettered History.* Boston: Little, Brown, 2000.

Alpers, Paul J. *Edmund Spenser: A Critical Anthology.* Harmondsworth: Penguin, 1969.

Alpert, Hollis. "Sensuality in the Cinema." *Calendar,* American Film Institute Theater, December 7–January 23, 1975, n.p.

Altheide, David L. "The Impact of Television Formats on Social Policy." *Journal of Electronic Media* 35 (Winter 1991), 3–21.

Alvi, Suroosh, Gavin McInnes, and Shane Smith. *The Vice Guide to Sex and Drugs and Rock and Roll*. New York: Warner, 2002.

"Amazing Cameras Built by Invalid as a Hobby." *Popular Science* 131 (July 1937), 42–43.

American Academy of Political and Social Science. *The New South*. Philadelphia: AAPS, 1910.

Amiss, John M. *Shop Mathematics and Shop Theory*. New York: Harper, 1943.

Ammons, Elizabeth. "The Myth of Imperiled Whiteness and *Ethan Frome*." *New England Quarterly* 81 (March 2008), 5–33.

Amory, Cleveland. "Celebrity Register." *McCall's*, July 1963, 144.

"AMPAS Study Raises Red Flags on Digital Storage." *In Camera* 11 (January 2008), 36–37.

Amphoto Editorial Board. *Photographic Tricks Simplified*. Garden City, N.Y.: Amphoto, 1974.

Anderson, Paul L. "Some Pictorial History." *American Photography* 29 (April 1935), 199–214.

Anderson, Sherwood. "New Orleans, *The Double-Dealer*, and the Modern Movement in America." *Double-Dealer* 3 (March 1922), 119–26.

"And Not a Stitch on Underneath." *Life*, July 3, 1964, 45–48.

André, J. *Étude sur les termes de couleur dans la langue latine*. Paris: Klincksieck, 1949.

Apsler, Robert. "Effects of the Draft Lottery and a Laboratory Analogue on Attitudes." *Journal of Personality and Social Psychology* 24 (November 1972), 262–72.

Aragon, Ray. "What Is Done for the Rising Generation of Photographers?" *International Photo Technik* 11 (Winter 1965), 6.

Archer, Fred R. "Improve Your Landscapes." *Popular Photography* 5 (August 1939), 20–21, 84–86.

"Are Bikinis Getting Too Naughty?" *Frolic* 5 (June 1956), 30–36.

Arlen, Michael J. *Living-Room War*. New York: Viking, 1969.

"Armour-Plated Ebner." *American Photography* 29 (March 1935), adv. 5.

Armstrong, Nancy. *Fiction in the Age of Photography: The Legacy of British Realism*. Cambridge, Mass.: Harvard Univ. Press, 1999.

Arnheim, Rudolph. *Radio*. London: Faber & Faber, 1936.

Asbury, Herbert. *The French Quarter: An Informal History of the New Orleans Underworld*. New York: Knopf, 1936.

"As Good as It Gets." *In Camera* 10 (July 2007), 36–37.

Ashmole, Elias. *Theatrum Chemicum Britannicum: Containing Severall Poeticall Pieces of our Famous English Philosophers who have Written the Hermetique Mysteries in their Owne Ancient Language*. London: Nathaniel Brooke, 1652.

Athans, Mary Christine. *The Coughlin-Fahey Connection: Father Charles E. Coughlin, Father Denis Fahey C.S. Sp. and Religious Anti-Semitism in the United States, 1938–1954*. New York: Peter Long, 1991.

Atti del Convegno: La prospettiva rinascimentale-codificazioni e trasgressioni. Ed. Marisa Dalai Emiliani. Florence: Centro Di, 1980.

Atwood, Mary Anne. *A Suggestive Inquiry into the Hermetic Mystery with a Dissertation on the More Celebrated of the Alchemical Philosophers: Being an Attempt towards the Recovery of the Ancient Experiment of Nature*. [1850] Belfast: Tait, 1918.

Ault, J. P. *Ocean Magnetic and Electric Observations, 1915–1921*. Washington, D.C.: Carnegie Institution of Washington, Department of Terrestrial Magnetism, 1926.

A. W. Shaw Company. *Advertising: Selling Points and Copy Writing, How to Plan*

Campaigns and Judge Mediums, Tests, Layouts, Records, and Systems. Chicago: A. W. Shaw, 1914.

Azémar, Guy-Patrick, ed. *Ouvriers, ouvrières: Un continent morcelé et silencieux.* Paris: Editions Autrement, 1992.

Bach, Eric. "White Slavery: Sex times Sex." Rolleigrafie 6 (December 1969), 13–20.

Bachelard, Gaston. *The Poetics of Space.* [1958] Trans. Maria Jolas. Intro. John R. Stilgoe. Boston: Beacon, 1994.

Bächtold, Hans R. "Postcards: What Subjects?" *International Photo Technik* 22 (Spring 1976), 6–9.

Bailey, Hillary G. "Feet First." *American Photography* 29 (June 1935), 358–61.

Bailey, Peter. "Parasexuality and Glamour: The Victorian Barmaid as Cultural Prototype." *Gender and History* 18 (Summer 1990), 138–54.

Bakal, Carl. *How to Shoot for Glamour.* San Francisco: Camera Craft, 1955.

Baker, Edward Cecil. *Sir William Preece: Victorian Engineer Extraordinary.* London: Hutchinson, 1976.

Ball, Margaret. *Mathemagics.* Riverdale, N.Y.: Baen, 1996.

Baltzell, E. Digby. *Protestant Establishment: Aristocracy and Caste in America.* New York: Random House, 1964.

Bans, Lauren. "Same Shit, Different World." *Bitch: Feminist Response to Pop Culture,* no. 39 (Spring 2008), 56–62.

Banta, Nathaniel Moore. *Brownie Primer.* Chicago: Flanagan, 1905.

——. *The Brownies and the Goblins.* Chicago: [Flanagan?], n.d.

——. *Busy Little Brownies.* Chicago: Flanagan, 1923.

——. *Little Black Sambo.* Chicago: Flanagan, 1922.

——. *The Little Brown Man.* Chicago: Flanagan, 1923.

——. *Ten Little Brownie Men.* Chicago: Flanagan, 1922.

"Bare Look Is Everywhere." *Life,* July 28, 1972, 58–64.

Barleben, Karl A. "Ship's Photographer." *Leica Photography,* no. 33 (August 1935), 1–2.

Barnard, Charles. "Something Electricity Is Doing." *Century* 37 (March 1889), 736–41.

Barnouw, Erik. *A History of Broadcasting in the United States.* 2 vols. New York: Oxford Univ. Press, 1966, 1968.

Barrett, William. *The Illusion of Technique: A Search for Meaning in a Technological Civilization.* Garden City, N.Y.: Anchor, 1978.

Barrette, Roy. *A Countryman's Journal: Views of Life and Nature from a Maine Coastal Farm.* Chicago: Rand, McNally, 1981.

Barron, Hal S. *Those Who Stayed Behind: Rural Society in Nineteenth-Century New England.* New York: Cambridge Univ. Press, 1984.

Barry, Peter. *The Complete Book of Photographing Women.* New York: Crescent, 1984.

Barthes, Roland. *Camera Lucida: Reflections on Photography.* [1980] Trans. Richard Howard. New York: Hill and Wang, 1981.

Basch, Peter. "The Cooperation between Model and Photographer." *International Photo Technik* 19 (Winter 1973), 20–23.

——. *Figure Study Photos.* Greenwich, Conn.: Fawcett, 1961.

——. *Glamour Photography.* Greenwich, Conn.: Fawcett, 1956.

——. "Nude or Naked." *International Photo Technik* 18 (Summer 1972), 10–11, 47.

Basinger, Jeanine. *A Woman's View: How Hollywood Spoke to Women, 1930–1960.* New York: Knopf, 1993.

Bates, Michelle. *Plastic Cameras: Toying with Creativity.* Burlington, Mass.: Focal, 2007.

"Bathing Suits." *Photokinks* 4 (1951), 60–61.

"Bathing Suits, Beaches, and Boys." *Life,* February 1983, 84–90.

Battarbee, Keith J., ed. *Scholarship and Fantasy: Proceedings of the Tolkien Phenomenon.* Turku, Finland: Univ. of Turku Press, 1993.

Baudelaire, Charles. *The Painter of Modern Life and Other Essays.* Ed. Jonathan Mayne. London: Phaidon, 1965.

Baum, L. Frank. *American Fairy Tales: Stories of Astonishing Adventures of American Boys and Girls with the Fairies of Their Native Land.* Indianapolis: Bobbs-Merrill, 1908.

——. *The Master Key: An Electrical Fairy Tale Founded upon the Mysteries of Electricity and the Optimism of Its Devotees.* Indianapolis: Bowen-Merrill Co., 1901.

Baxandall, Michael. *Patterns of Intention: On the Historical Explanation of Pictures.* New Haven: Yale Univ. Press, 1985.

Bayley, R. Child. "The Pictorial Aspect of Photography in Colors." *Camera Work* 1 (January 1903), 42–46.

Bayley, Stephen. *Taste: The Secret Meaning of Things.* New York: Pantheon, 1991.

Baym, Nina. "Melodramas of Beset Manhood." *American Quarterly* 33 (Summer 1981), 123–39.

"Beach Pictures." *US Camera* 9 (March 1946), 42.

Beardsley, Aubrey. *Later Work.* [1912] New York: Dover, 1967.

——. *Under the Hill and Other Essays in Prose and Verse.* London: John Lane, 1928.

Beaton, M. C. *Death of a Gentle Lady.* New York: Hachette, 2008.

Beaupré, Marion de, Stéphane Baumet, and Ulf Poschardt, eds. *The Archaeology of Elegance, 1980–2000: Twenty Years of Fashion Photography.* Trans. Jeremy Gaines. New York: Rizzoli, 2002.

Beauvoir, Simone de. *Brigitte Bardot and the Lolita Syndrome.* [1959] Trans. Bernard Fretchman. London: Deutsch and Weidenfeld & Nicolson, 1960.

——. *The Second Sex.* [1949] Trans. H. M. Parshley. New York: Knopf, 1953.

Becker, Robert, and Gary Selden. *The Body Electric.* New York: Morrow, 1985.

Behrend, Michael. *A Forgotten Researcher: Ludovic McLellan Mann.* Cambridge: Institute of Geomantic Research, 1977.

"Believe It or Not." *American Photography* 29 (July 1935), adv. 7.

Belloc, Hilaire. *The Old Road.* London: Constable, 1904.

——. *On Anything.* New York: Dutton, 1910.

Bempechat, Janine. *Against the Odds: How "At Risk" Children Exceed Expectations.* San Francisco: Jossey-Bass, 1998.

Benjamin, Walter. *The Arcades Project.* [1982] Trans. Howard Eiland and Kevin McLaughlin. Cambridge, Mass.: Harvard Univ. Press, 1999.

——. *Charles Baudelaire: The Lyric Poet in the Era of High Capitalism.* Trans. Harry Zohn. London: Verso, 1973.

——. *Einbahnstrasse.* Berlin: Ernst Rowohlt, 1928.

——. *Illuminations.* Trans. Harry Zohn. Ed. Hannah Arendt. New York: Schocken, 1968.

——. *Reflections: Essays, Aphorisms, Autobiographical Writings.* Trans. Edmund Jephcott. New York: Schocken, 1986.

——. "Die Wiederkehr des Flaneurs." *Bauwelt* 58 (January 25, 1967), 87–89.

Ben-Joseph, Eran, and Terry S. Szold. *Regulating Place: Standards and the Shaping of Urban America.* New York: Routledge, 2005.

Bennet, Bruce M., Donald D. Hoffman, and Chetan Prakash. *Observer Mechanics: A Formal Theory of Perception.* San Diego: Academic Press, 1989.

Berding, Christina. "Imogen Cunningham and the Straight Approach." *Modern Photography* 15 (May 1951), 36–41, 96–98.

Berenson, Bernard. *The Passionate Sightseer: From the Diaries, 1947 to 1956.* Ed. Raymond Mortimer. London: Thames & Hudson, 1960.

Beresford, Maurice W. *History on the Ground: Six Studies in Maps and Landscapes.* London: Methuen, 1957.

Beresford, Maurice W., and J. K. S. St. Joseph. *Medieval England: An Aerial Survey.* Cambridge: Cambridge Univ. Press, 1958.

Berger, D. "Long-Distance Views." *Photography with Rolleiflex and Rolleicord* 14 (June 1939), 7.

Berger, Ivan. "New Cameras Revive an Old Format." *Popular Mechanics,* September 1976, 88.

Berger, John. *About Looking.* New York: Random House, 1980.

——. *Ways of Seeing.* London: Penguin, 1972.

Bergler, Edmund. *Fashion and the Unconscious.* [1953] Madison, Conn.: International Universities Press, 1987.

Bergquist, L. "Strange Case of Suzy Parker." *Look,* August 19, 1958, 26–30.

Berkeley, George. *A New Theory of Vision.* [1709] London: Dent, 1910.

Bernard, Christopher. "The Common Sense of Anonymity." *Sunshine & Health* 22 (May 1953), 13, 25.

Bernhard, Nancy E. *US Television News and Cold War Propaganda, 1947–1960.* Cambridge: Cambridge Univ. Press, 1999.

Bernofsky, Susan. *Foreign Words: Translator-Authors in the Age of Goethe.* Detroit: Wayne State Univ. Press, 2005.

Bernsohn, Al, and De Vera Bernsohn. "The Photographer and the Model." *Camera Craft* 47 (May 1940), 231–37.

Bernstein, J. M., ed. *The Culture Industry: Selected Essays on Mass Culture.* London: Routledge, 1991.

Bertele, Erhard. "A Show of Nature." *International Photo Technik* 11 (Summer 1965), 112–13.

Bertonati, Emilio. *Das experimentelle Photo in Deutschland, 1918–1940.* Munich: Galleria Dellevante, 1878.

Bertrand, Michael. *Race, Rock, and Elvis.* Urbana: Univ. of Illinois Press, 2000.

Bessel, Robert, ed. *Fascist Italy and Nazi Germany: Comparisons and Contrasts.* New York: Cambridge Univ. Press, 1996.

Best, Simon. "Electromagnetic Cover-Up." *Ecologist* 21 (January 1991), 33–38.

Beston, Henry. *Northern Farm: A Chronicle of Maine.* New York: Rinehart, 1948.

——. *The Outermost House: A Year of Life on The Great Beach of Cape Cod.* [1928] New York: Ballantine, 1971.

Better Homes and Gardens. *Photography for Your Family.* Des Moines: Meredith, 1964.

Betting, Eric. *Girl at Water's Edge. International Photo Technik* 11 (Summer 1965), 127.

Betty Anne Cregan. Yank, December 7, 1945, 20–21.

Biddlecombe, George. *The Art of Rigging.* Salem, Mass.: Marine Research Society, 1925.

Bierce, Ambrose. *Ghost and Horror Stories.* Ed. E. F. Bleiler. New York: Dover, 1964.

"Bikinis in the Backyard." *Saturday Evening Post,* June 20, 1964, 18–25.

Binns, Archie. *Backwater Voyage.* New York: Reynal & Hitchcock, 1934.

Birney, William. "Effet pour l'effet." *Rolleigrafie* 7 (March 1970), 32–37.

Bischoff, David, Rich Brown, and Linda Richardson. *A Personal Demon*. New York: Signet, 1985.

"Bizarre Beauties of *Barbarella*." *Playboy*, March 1968, 108–17.

Black, Alexander. "The Amateur Photographer." *Century* 34 (September 1887), 722–29.

Blancpain, François. *La colonie française de Saint-Domingue: De l'esclavage à l'indépendance*. Paris: Karthala, 2004.

Blaser, Werner. *West Meets East: Mies van der Rohe*. Basel: Birkhäser, 1996.

Blondot, R. *"N" Rays*. Trans. J. Garein. London: Longmans, 1905.

The Blue Book: A Bibliographical Attempt to Describe the Guide Books to the Houses of Ill Fame in New Orleans as They were Published There. Together with Some Pertinent and Illuminating Remarks Pertaining to the Establishments and Courtesans as Well as to Harlotry in General in New Orleans. [New Orleans?]: privately printed, 1936.

Blumann, Sigismund. *Enlarging Manual*. San Francisco: Photo Art, 1936.

Blumer, Herbert. *Movies and Conduct*. New York: Macmillan, 1933.

———. *Movies, Delinquency, and Crime*. New York: Macmillan, 1933.

Blumtritt, Herbert. *Geschichte der Dresdner Kameraindustrie*. Stuttgart: Lindemanns, 2000.

Bluth, Hans. "Four Models—One Unit." *International Photo Technik* 11 (Winter 1965), 10–13.

Board of Education (Great Britain). *Report on the Teaching of English in England*. London: H. M. Stationery Office, 1921.

Bocca, Geoffrey. *Bikini Beach; the Wicked Riviera as It Was and Is*. [1960] New York: McGraw-Hill, 1962.

Bocock, Robert. *Hegemony*. London: Tavistock, 1986.

Boddy, William. *Fifties Television: The Industry and Its Critics*. Urbana: Univ. of Illinois Press, 1990.

Boff, Kenneth R., Lloyd Kaufman, and James P. Thomas, eds. *Handbook of Perception and Human Performance*. 2 vols. New York: Wiley, 1986.

Bollen, Friedel. "Black-and-White: Problems in Colour Photography." *International Photo Technik* 17 (Fall 1971), 34–37.

———. "Portrait Photography Yesterday, Today, Tomorrow." *International Photo Technik* 18 (Fall 1972), 64–66.

"Bongo Beach." *Night and Day* 8 (March 1955), 19–22.

Boni, Albert, ed. *Photographic Literature: An International Bibliographic Guide to General & Specialized Literature on Photographic Processes; Techniques; Theory; Chemistry; Physics; Apparatus; Materials & Applications; Industry; History; Biography; Aesthetics; etc*. New York: Morgan & Morgan, 1962.

Bonnefoy, Yves. *Mythologies*. Trans. Gerald Honigsblum. Chicago: Univ. of Chicago Press, 1991.

Bookshelf for Boys and Girls: Things to Make and Things to Do. [1927] [Rev. ed.?] New York: University Society, 1971.

Boone, Andrew R. "Aladdins of Hollywood Create Realistic Effects for Movies." *Popular Science* 130 (January 1937), 30–31, 122.

Boonhower, Ray E., and John A. Bushemi. *One Shot: The World War II Photographs of John A. Bushemi*. Indianapolis: Indiana Historical Society, 2004.

Borrelli, Laird. "Fashion Thinks Ink." *Bal Harbour Magazine* 8 (Holiday 2007), 42–46.

Borrmann, Norbert. *Paul Schultze-Naumburg, 1869–1949: Maler, Publizist, Architekt:*

Vom Kulturreformer der Jahrhundertwende zum Kulturpolitiker im Dritten Reich.
Essen: Bacht, 1989.

Borsodi, Ralph. *Flight from the City: The Story of a New Way to Family Security.*
New York, Harper, 1933.

Bortsch, Hans. "Controlling the Contrast in Colour Reversal Film." *International
Photo Technik* 22 (Fall 1976), 57–58.

———. "Interdependence of Pictorial Information and Film Size." *International Photo
Technik* 17 (Fall 1971), 70–71.

———. "New Aspects of Colour Technology." *International Photo Technik* 22 (Spring
1976), 16–20; (Summer 1976), 22–27.

Bosanquet, Bernard. *The Philosophical Theory of the State.* London: Macmillan,
1899.

Boston Gear Works. *Textbook on Spur Gears.* 2nd ed. Quincy, Mass.: Boston Gear
Works, 1953.

Boucher, Anthony, ed. *Best from Fantasy and Science Fiction: 6th Series.* Garden City:
N.Y.: Doubleday, 1957.

Boucher, Geoff. "At Last, Lloyd's Time Has Come." *Los Angeles Times,* November
27, 2005.

Boucher, Paul E. *Fundamentals of Photography, with Laboratory Experiments.* 4th
ed. Princeton, N.J.: Van Nostrand, 1963.

Bourdieu, Pierre. *On Television.* London: Pluto Press, 1998.

Bowers, John. "The Porn Is Green." *Playboy,* July 1971, 78–83, 182–88.

Bowman, Constance, and Clara Marie Allen. *Slacks and Callouses.* New York: Longmans, 1944.

Bowman, John. "Brownie Landscapes." *US Camera* 9 (June 1946), 18–20.

Boy Scouts of America. *Photography.* New Brunswick, N.J.: Boy Scouts of America,
1957.

Brace, Gerald Warner. *Light on a Mountain.* New York: Putnam, 1941.

Bradbury, Ray. *The Golden Apples of the Sun.* Garden City, N.Y.: Doubleday, 1953.

———. "A Serious Search for Weird Worlds." *Life,* October 24, 1960, 116–18, 120,
123, 124, 126, 128, 130.

Bradford, Ernle. *The Wind Off the Island.* [1960] London: Grafton, 1988.

Bradley, Marion Zimmer. *Warrior Woman.* New York: Daw, 1985.

Bradner, Leicester. *Edmund Spenser and the Faerie Queen.* Chicago: Univ. of Chicago
Press, 1948.

Branch, Tom. *The Photographer's Built-It-Yourself Book.* New York: Amphoto, 1982.

Brands, H. W. *The Reckless Decade: America in the 1890s.* New York: St. Martins,
1995.

Brandt, Allan M. *No Magic Bullet: A Social History of Venereal Disease in the United
States since 1880.* [1985] Rev. ed. New York: Oxford Univ. Press, 1987.

Brecht, Bertolt. "Radio as a Means of Communication: A Talk on the Function of
Radio." Trans. Stuart Hood. *Screen* 20 (Winter 1979–80), 11–31.

Breward, Christopher. *Fashion.* New York: Oxford Univ. Press, 2003.

"Brief, Briefer, Briefest." *Time,* June 2, 1967, 49.

Brigance, W. Norwood. "Get Better Color Transparencies." *Popular Photography* 5
(August 1939), 59, 92–93.

Briggs, L. Vernon. *History of Shipbuilding on the North River.* Boston: Coburn, 1889.

Brockhaus Enzyklopädie. Mannheim: Brockhaus, 1992.

Bronowski, Jacob. "Technology and Culture in Education." *American Scholar* 41
(Spring 1972), 197–211.

Brontë, Charlotte. *Jane Eyre*. [1847] Reprint, New York: Hurst, 1899.

Brooks, Van Wyck. *From the Shadow of the Mountain*. New York: Dutton, 1961.

——. *Letters and Leadership*. New York: Huebsch, 1918.

——. *New England: Indian Summer, 1865–1915*. New York: Dutton, 1940.

Brown, Betty C. "Available Light." *Popular Photography* 62 (May 1968), 83.

Brown, Carlton. *Famous Photographers Tell How*. New York: Fawcett, 1955.

Brown, Carter. *The White Bikini*. New York: Signet, 1963.

Brown, Dan. *The Da Vinci Code: A Novel*. New York: Doubleday, 2003.

Brown, Garrett. *American Fairy Tales*. Saint Louis: Mulligan, 1911.

Brown, Robert W. "It's the Man Behind the Camera." *Popular Photography* 4 (May 1939), 23, 118–19.

Brown, Tom. *The Tracker*. New York: Berkeley, 1978.

——. *The Way of the Scout*. New York: Putnam's, 1997.

Brown, W. Edwards. "Neon Darkroom Light." *Popular Science* 133 (July 1938), 100.

"Brownie Landscapes." *US Camera* 9 (June 1946), 18–19.

Browning, Elizabeth Barrett. *Aurora Leigh*. Indianapolis: Clayton, 1909.

Brownlow, Kevin. *Hollywood: The Pioneers*. New York: Knopf, 1979.

Brubeck, Dave. "Jazz Perspective." *Perspectives USA* 15 (Spring 1956), 21–28.

Bruce, Arthur Loring. "Pinhole Photography for the Amateur." *St. Nicholas*, November 1910, 38–40.

Brumberg, Joan Jacobs. *The Body Project: An Intimate History of American Girls*. New York: Random House, 1997.

Brusatin, Manlio. *A History of Colors*. [1983] Trans. Robert H. Hopcke and Paul Schwartz. Boston: Shambhala, 1991.

Bryan, Julien. "On a Trip: Take More Pictures." *Popular Photography* 4 (January 1939), 28–29, 86–88.

Bryant, Jennings, and Dolf Zillmann, eds. *Responding to the Screen: Reception and Reaction Processes*. Hillsdale, N.J.: Lawrence Erlbaum, 1991.

Buchan, John. *The Watcher by the Threshold*. New York: Doran, 1918.

Buel, J. W. *Metropolitan Life Unveiled, or, The Mysteries and Miseries of America's Great Cities*. San Francisco: Abbington, 1882.

Buffalo Camera Club. *Fourth Annual Salon of Pictorial Photography*. Buffalo, N.Y.: Albright Art Gallery, 1923.

Bugliosi, Vincent. *And the Sea Will Tell*. New York: Norton, 1991.

"Build It Yourself." *Minicam* 1 (September 1937), 24–25.

Bullough, Edward. "'Physical Distance' as a Factor in Art and an Aesthetic Principle." *British Journal of Psychology* 5 (June 1912), 87–118.

Burghard, George E. "A History of the Radio Club of America, Inc." Radio Club of America, *Twenty-fifth Anniversary Year Book*. New York: RCA, 1934.

Burke, Kenneth. *A Rhetoric of Motives*. New York: Prentice-Hall, 1950.

Burke, Patrick. *Come In and Hear the Truth: Jazz and Race on 52nd Street*. Chicago: Univ. of Chicago Press, 2008.

Burke, Peter. *Popular Culture in Early Modern Europe*. New York: Harper & Row, 1978.

Burleigh Brooks Co., Inc. "Incomparable Rolleiflex." *Camera Craft* 42 (September 1935), n.p.

——. "Pilot Super." *Popular Photography* 5 (August 1939), 96.

——. "Rollei Gives You Color in All 3 Popular Sizes." In *Popular Photography Color Annual 1957*, 13. New York: Ziff-Davis, 1957.

——. *Rollei Price List and Fair Trade Schedule*. New York: Burleigh Brooks, 1953.

——. "Size Is Important." *US Camera* 24 (February 1961), 11.

———. "Touch of Magic." *US Camera* 24 (February 1961), 42.

Burns, Bob. *It Came from Bob's Basement: Exploring the Science Fiction and Monster Movie Archive of Bob Burns.* San Francisco: Chronicle, 2000.

Burrell, Angus, and Bennett A. Cerf, eds. *Bedside Book of Famous American Stories.* New York: Random House, 1939.

Burroughs, John. *Winter Sunshine.* Boston: Houghton, Mifflin, 1900.

Burroughs, William S. *The Ticket That Exploded.* New York: Grove Press, 1967.

Buszek, Maria Elena. *Pin-Up Grrrls: Feminism, Sexuality, Popular Culture.* Durham: Duke Univ. Press, 2006.

"Button-Pushers Have Become Tired." *International Photo Technik* 11 (Summer 1965), 162.

Cable, George Washington. "Creole Slave Songs." *Century* 31 (April 1886), 807–28.

———. "The Dance in the Place Congo." *Century* 31 (February 1886), 517–32.

———. *The Grandissimes: A Story of Creole Life.* New York: Scribner's, 1880. Also published with an introduction by J. M. Barrie(London: Hodder and Stoughton, 1898).

———. "The 'Haunted House' in Royal Street." *Century* 38 (August 1889), 590–601.

———. "Strange True Stories of Louisiana." *Century* 37 (November 1888), 110–16; (December 1888), 254–60; (January 1889), 358–67; (March 1889), 742–48.

Caesar, Hellmut. "Nude." *Rolleigrafie* 7 (March 1970), 15.

Caldwell, Lucy M. "Pour That Girl a Drink Already." *Harvard Crimson,* February 28, 2007, 10.

Caldwell, R. J. "Enjoy Your Summer." *Sunbathing for Health* 7 (June 1, 1953), 12–13, 32.

Calefato, Patrizia. *The Clothed Body.* Oxford: Berg, 2004.

Callicott, J. Baird. *In Defense of the Land Ethic.* Albany: State Univ. of New York Press, 1989.

Calvano, Tony. *Sin Kids.* New York: Nightstand, 1963.

Calvert, Robert. *Vocational Analysis of Male College Graduates in Liberal Arts.* Berkeley: Survey Research Center of the Univ. of California, 1967.

Calvino, Italo. *Difficult Loves.* San Diego: Harcourt, 1985.

"The Camera's Selective Eye." *Life,* October 24, 1960, 2.

Campbell, J. "Old Gods, Young Goddesses." *Sports Illustrated,* January 27, 1975, 30–35.

Campbell, John Gregorson. *Superstitions of the Highlands and Islands of Scotland.* Glasgow: MacLehose, 1900.

Cannavo, Salvator. *Nomic Inference: An Introduction to the Logic of Scientific Inquiry.* The Hague: Martinus Nijhoff, 1974.

"Cardboard Shield Aids in Focusing Camera." *Popular Science Monthly* 133 (July 1938), 100.

Carl Zeiss, Inc. "Zeiss Ikon." *Photo-Era* 66 (May 1931), n.p.

"Carnival in Nice." *Art Photography* 3 (May 1952), 20–21.

Carpenter, Charles M., and Albert B. Page. "The Production of Fever in Man by Short Wave Radio." *Science,* May 2, 1930, 450–52.

Carr, John. "Current Filters for A. C. Sets." *Popular Science* 116 (February 1930), 71.

Casati, Roberto. *The Shadow Club.* Trans. Abigail Asher. New York: Knopf, 2003.

Casey, John. *Spartina.* New York: Knopf, 1989.

Cash, W. J. *The Mind of the South.* [1941] Garden City, N.Y.: Doubleday Anchor, 1956.

Castel, Robert. *Les métamorphoses de la question sociale.* Paris: Flammarion, 1995.

Cather, Willa. *A Lost Lady.* [1923] New York: Random House, 1990.

Central Camera Company. "Altiflex." *Popular Photography* 5 (August 1939), 7.
——. *Mail Order Catalogue #43*. Chicago: Central Camera, 1933.
Ceruzzi, Paul E. *A History of Modern Computing*. Cambridge, Mass.: MIT Press, 2003.
Chamberlain, Clarence D. "Shall We Let Our Children Fly?" *Parents' Magazine* 5 (January 1930), 14–16, 41–42.
Chandler, Alfred D., Takashi Hikino, and Andrew Van Norden Flycht. *Inventing the Electronic Century*. New York: Free Press, 2001.
Chapman, Allen. *The Radio Boys' First Wireless*. New York: Grosset and Dunlap, 1922.
——. *The Radio Boys Trailing a Voice*. New York: Grosset & Dunlap, 1922.
Chapman, Nathan Lean. *Comparative Media History: Windows on the Sixties*. London: Tauris, 2000.
Charters, Werrett Wallace. *Motion Picture and Youth: A Summary*. New York: Macmillan, 1933.
Chase, Stuart. *Men and Machines*. New York: Macmillan, 1929.
Chauncey, George. *Gay New York: Gender, Urban Culture, and the Making of the Gay Male World, 1890–1940*. New York: Basic Books, 1994.
Cheever, John. *The Brigadier and the Golf Widow*. New York: Harper, 1964.
Chernewski, Anita, and Albert Chernewski. *How to Make Three Corrugated 8×10 Pinhole Cameras: Wide-Angle, Normal, and Telephoto*. New York: Pinhole Format Co., 2003.
Chödrön, Pema. *When Things Fall Apart: Heart Advice for Difficult Times*. Boston: Shambhala, 2000.
Christakis, Dimitri A., et al. "Early Television Exposure and Subsequent Attentional Problems in Children." *Pediatrics* 113 (April 2004), 708–15.
Christie, Agatha. *Murder with Mirrors*. New York: Dodd, Mead, 1952.
——. *Passenger from Frankfurt: An Extravaganza*. New York: Dodd, Mead, 1970.
"Cibachrome A Print System." *International Photo Technik* 23 (Fall 1976), 54–57.
Clark, George, and Daniel Timmons, eds. *J. R. R. Tolkien and His Literary Resonances: Views of Middle Earth*. Westport, Conn.: Greenwood Press, 2000.
Clark, Michael. "Black and White and Technicolor." *Calendar,* American Film Institute Theater, February 13–March 17, 1976, 6–8.
Clark, W. B. "The Serpent of Lust in the Southern Garden." *Southern Review* 10 (October 1974), 805–22.
Clarke, Susanna. *Jonathan Strange and Mr. Norrell*. New York: Bloomsbury, 2004.
Clement, Hal. *Space Lash*. New York: Dell, 1969.
Clerc, L. P. *Photography: Theory and Practice*. [1926] Trans. George E. Brown. London: Greenwood, 1930.
Cleveland Twist Drill Company. *The Use and Care of Twist Drills*. Cleveland: Cleveland Twist Drill Co., 1931.
Clulee, Nicholas H. *John Dee's Natural Philosophy: Between Science and Religion*. London: Routledge, 1988.
Coates, Robert M. *The Outlaw Years: The History of the Land Pirates of the Natchez Trace*. New York: Macaulay, 1930.
Coats, Callum. *Living Energies: Viktor Shauberger's Brilliant Work with Natural Energy Explained*. Bath: Gateway, 1995.
Coatsworth, Elizabeth. *Country Neighborhood*. New York: Macmillan, 1944.
Cohan, Phil. "Risque Business." *Air and Space* 5 (April/May 1990), 62–71.
Cohen, Lester. *The New York Graphic: The World's Zaniest Newspaper*. Philadelphia: Chilton, 1964.

Cohn, David L., and Clarence John Laughlin. *New Orleans and Its Living Past.* Boston: Houghton, Mifflin, 1941.

Cole, John Y., ed. *Television, the Book, and the Classroom: A Seminar.* Washington, D.C.: Library of Congress, 1978.

"Colette." *Calendar,* American Film Institute Theater, May 15–June 30, 1976, n.p.

Collins, Archie Frederick. *The Amateur Photographer's Handbook.* New York: Crowell, 1925.

Collins, Douglas. *The Story of Kodak.* New York: Abrams, 1990.

Collins, Lauren. "Pixel Perfect: Pascal Dangin's Virtual Reality." *New Yorker,* May 12, 2008, 94–103.

Collins, Max Allan. *For the Boys: The Racy Pin-Ups of World War II.* New York: Collectors, 2000.

"Colour Film and the Schwarzschild Effect." *International Photo Technik* 17 (Spring 1971), 77–78.

The Complete War of the Worlds: Mars' Invasion of Earth from H. G. Wells to Orson Welles. Ed. Brian Holmsten and Alex Lubertozzi. Naperville, Ill.: Sourcebooks MediaFusion, 2001.

Connolly, J. B. *Head Winds.* New York: Scribner's, 1916.

Conrad, Joseph. *Heart of Darkness.* [1899] Ed. Robert Kimbrough. New York: Norton, 1963.

——. *Typhoon.* [1902] Garden City, N.Y.: Doubleday, 1926.

Cook, Nick. *The Hunt for Zero Point: Inside the Classified World of Antigravity Technology.* New York: Broadway, 2002.

Coolidge, Albert Sprague. *Building a Model Railroad.* New York: Macmillan, 1929.

Cooper, Joseph D. *The New Ultra-Miniature Photography.* New York: Universal, 1958.

Cooper, Susan. *The Dark Is Rising.* New York: Simon & Schuster, 1973.

——. *Greenwitch.* New York: Aladdin, 1974.

Corn, Joseph J., ed. *Imagining Tomorrow: History, Technology, and the American Future.* Cambridge, Mass.: MIT Press, 1986.

Cornish, Vaughan. *The Beauties of Scenery: A Geographical Survey.* London: Muller, 1943.

——. *The Churchyard Yew and Immortality.* London: Muller, 1946.

——. *The Poetical Impression of Natural Scenery.* London: Sifton Praed, 1931.

——. *The Preservation of Our Scenery.* Cambridge: Cambridge Univ. Press, 1937.

——. *Scenery and the Sense of Sight.* Cambridge: Cambridge Univ. Press, 1935.

——. *The Scenery of England: A Study of Harmonious Grouping in Town and Country.* London: Council for the Preservation of Rural England, 1932.

——. *The Scenic Amenity of Great Britain.* Manchester: Geographical Association, 1934.

"Correct Exposure in an Instant!" *American Photography* 29 (July 1935), adv. 29.

Cortázar, Julio. *Blowup and Other Stories.* Trans. Paul Blackburn. [1978] New York: Pantheon, 1985.

Coursey, P. R. "Submarine Wireless." *Wireless World* 27 (November 1920), 15–18.

Cox, Michael. *M. R. James: An Informal Portrait.* New York: Oxford Univ. Press, 1983.

Cox, Palmer. "The Brownies." *Ladies' Home Journal,* November 1891, 12.

——. "The Brownies Aid the Nursery." *St. Nicholas,* November 1910, 60–63.

——. "The Brownies in August." *Ladies' Home Journal,* August 1892, 11.

——. "The Brownies in February." *Ladies' Home Journal,* February 1892, 11.

——. "The Brownies in June." *Ladies' Home Journal,* June 1892, 11.

———. "The Brownies in October." *Ladies' Home Journal*, June 1892, 11.

———. *The Brownies and Other Stories*. New York: Century, 1880.

———. *The Brownies in the Philippines*. New York: Century, 1904.

———. "The Brownies' Ride." *St. Nicholas*, February 1883, 263–66.

———. *The Brownies: Their Book*. New York: Century, 1887.

———. *Juvenile Budget: Containing Queer People with Paws, Claws, Wings, Stings, and Others Without Either: Goblins, Giants, Merrymen and Monarch: Stories of their Mischievous Pranks and Humorous Doings*. Chicago: Donohue, 1888.

———. *Nursery Rhymes from Olden Times*. Chicago: Monarch, 1898.

———. "The Origin of the 'Brownies.'" *Ladies' Home Journal*, November 1892, 35.

Cox, R. Hippisley. *The Green Roads of England*. London: Methuen, 1914.

Cox, Stephen. *The Hooterville Handbook: A Viewer's Guide to Green Acres*. New York: St. Martin's, 1989.

Craik, Jennifer. *The Face of Fashion: Cultural Studies in Fashion*. New York: Routledge, 1994.

Crary, Jonathan. *Techniques of the Observer: On Vision and Modernity in the Nineteenth Century*. Cambridge, Mass.: MIT Press, 1990.

Crass, Elizabeth. "Too Many Clothes." *Modern Sunbathing* 18 (February 1949), 4, 42.

Crawford, Osbert Guy Stanhope. *Air Survey and Archaeology*. Southampton: Ordnance Survey, 1924.

———. *The Eye Goddess*. New York: Macmillan, 1956.

Crawford, Osbert Guy Stanhope, and Alexander Keiller. *Wessex from the Air*. Oxford: Clarendon Press, 1928.

"Creating Heirlooms of Life Events on Film." *In Camera* 11 (January 2008), 22.

Crockett, Art. "Murder Wears a Bikini." *Off Beat Detective Story Magazine* 5 (July 1963), 5–54.

Crombie, Deborah. *A Finer End*. New York: Bantam, 2002.

Cromie, William J. "Magnetic Wand Changes a Brain." *Harvard University Gazette* 93 (March 19, 1998), 1, 6.

Cross, Whitney R. *The Burned-Over District: The Social and Intellectual History of Enthusiastic Religion in Western New York, 1800–1850*. Ithaca: Cornell Univ. Press, 1950.

Croy, Otto R. *Design by Photography: Step by Step*. New York: Focal, 1963.

———. *The Photographic Portrait*. Trans. F. L. Dash. [1957] New York: Amphoto, 1968.

———. *The Retina Way*. New York: Focal, 1953.

———. *Secrets of Trick Photography*. New York: American Photographic Publishing Co., 1937.

Crutchley, Simon. "The Landscape of Salisbury Plain, as Revealed by Aerial Photography." *Landscape* 2 (August 2001), 46–64.

Cunningham, Imogen. *On the Body*. Ed. Richard Lorenz. Boston: Little, Brown, 1998.

———. *Photographs*. Ed. Margery Mann. Seattle: Univ. of Washington Press, 1970.

———. *Selected Texts and Bibliography*. Ed. Amy Rule. Oxford: Clio, 1992.

Curtis, Joshua James. *Sunkissed: Sunwear and the Hollywood Beauty, 1930–1950*. Portland, Or.: Collectors, 2003.

Curtiss Candy Company. "The Goblins." *Life*, October 24, 1960, 68–69.

Cushing, Charles Phelps. "Photography's Debt to the Treetops." *Outing* 58 (June 1911), n.p.

Dabney, Virginia Bell. *Once There Was a Farm: A Country Childhood Remembered.* New York: Random, 1990.

D'Ammassa, Don. *Encyclopedia of Fantasy and Horror Fiction.* New York: Facts on File, 2006.

Danbom, David. *Born in the Country: A History of Rural America.* Baltimore: Johns Hopkins Univ. Press, 1995.

Darke, Rick. "Celebrating Natural Light in the Landscape." *Taunton's Fine Gardening* 64 (November/December 1998), 58–63.

——. "Found Art." *HGTV Ideas* 6 (July/August 1999), 20.

——. "Sixty Seasons on Red Clay Creek." *Journal of the Pennsylvania Horticultural Society* 86 (September/October 1998), 11–14.

Darvill, Timothy. *Prehistoric Britain from the Air: A Study of Space, Time, and Society.* Cambridge: Cambridge Univ. Press, 1996.

Dater, Judy. *Imogen Cunningham: A Portrait.* Boston: New York Graphic Society, 1979.

Davidov, Judith Fryer. *Women's Camera Work: Self/Body/Other in American Visual Culture.* Durham: Duke Univ. Press, 1998.

Davidson, H. R. Ellis. "Folklore and Man's Past." *Folklore* 74 (Winter 1963), 527–44.

Davis, Keith. *Clarence John Laughlin: Visionary Photographer.* Kansas City, Mo.: Hallmark Cards, 1990.

Davis, Larry. *Planes, Names and Dames.* 3 vols. Carollton, Tex.: Squadron, 1990.

Davis, Manton. *Statement of Manton Davis Representing Radio Corporation of America: Hearings Concerning Senate Bill 2783.* Washington, D.C.: GPO, 1920.

Davis, Olivia. *The Scent of Apples.* Boston: Houghton, Mifflin, 1972.

Davis, Wade. *The Serpent and the Rainbow.* London: Collins, 1986.

Davis, William S. "Photography in the Fog." *Camera Craft* 42 (June 1935), 288–93.

——. *Practical Amateur Photography.* [1923] 3rd ed. Garden City, N.Y.: Garden City Publishing Co., 1939.

——. "Sail Ho!" *Camera Craft* 42 (March 1935), 114–19.

Dawber, Martin. *Pixel Surgeons: Extreme Manipulations of the Figure in Photography.* London: Beazley, 2005.

Dawdy, Shannon Lee. *Building the Devil's Empire: French Colonial New Orleans.* Chicago: Univ. of Chicago Press, 2008.

"Dazzling Spark Takes Fastest Photos." *Popular Science* 122 (January 1933), 41.

Dean, Roger. *Views.* Limpsfield, U.K.: Dragon's Dream, 1975.

DeArmand, David W. "How to Take Better Pictures." *Calling All Girls* 3 (July–August 1944), 11–12, 54.

De Dienes, André. "Airborne." *Popular Photography Annual 1958,* 28.

——. "The Sun." *Figure Photography* 11 (1956?), 12–20.

Dee, John, *Heptarchia Mystica.* Ed. Robert Turner. Wellingborough, U.K.: Aquarian, 1986.

Deive, Carlos Esteban. *Los guerrilleros negroes.* Santo Domingo: Fundación Cultural, 1989.

De Kay, Charles. "Fairies and Druids of Ireland." *Century* 37 (February 1889), 590–99.

——. "Pagan Ireland." *Century* 37 (January 1889), 368–79.

Delany, Paul. *The Neo-Pagans: Friendship and Love in the Rupert Brooke Circle.* London: Macmillan, 1987.

Denier, Tony. *The Great Secret of Shadow Pantomimes.* New York: French, 1868.

De Plancy, J. Collin. *Dictionnaire infernal.* 5 vols. Paris: Mongie, 1825.

"Depth of Field: Fully Exploited." *International Photo Technik* 11 (Spring 1965), 130–32.

Deresiewicz, William. "Love on Campus." *American Scholar* 76 (Summer 2007), 36–46.

Derleth, August. *Lonesome Places.* Sauk City, Wis.: Arkham House, 1962.

——, ed. *Strange Ports of Call.* New York: Pellegrini, 1948.

de Sazo, Serge. "Nude." *Popular Photography Annual 1958,* 100.

Deschin, Jacob. *Making Pictures with the Miniature Camera.* New York: McGraw-Hill, 1937.

——. *Rollei Photography: Handbook of the Rolleiflex and Rolleicord Camera.* [1952] Rev. ed. San Francisco: Camera Craft, 1953.

Destré, Sabine. "The French Revolution—1968." *Evergreen Review* 12 (August 1968), 41–49.

Devereux, Paul, and Ian Thomson. *The Ley Hunter's Companion: Aligned Ancient Sites: A New Study with Field Guide and Maps.* London: Thames & Hudson, 1979.

Devoe & Raynolds Co., Inc. *Pigments Used in Artists' Oil Colors.* New York: Devoe & Raynolds, 1920.

DeVoto, Bernard. "Seed Corn and Mistletoe." *Harper's,* December 1936, 109–12.

Didion, Joan. *The White Album.* New York: Simon & Schuster, 1979.

Di Leonardo, Micaela. *Exotics at Home: Anthropologies, Others, American Modernity.* Chicago: Univ. of Chicago Press, 1998.

Dilworth, John B. "A Beginner and a Box Camera." *Popular Photography* 4 (February 1939), 54.

Dion, Karen, Ellen Berscheid, and Elaine Walster. "What Is Beautiful Is Good." *Journal of Personality and Social Psychology* 24 (December 1972), 285–90.

"Direct Current Makes Neon Tube Flash at Intervals." *Popular Science* 130 (January 1937), 56.

Disney, Walt. "Mickey Mouse and 16 mm." *Camera* 44 (June 1932), 472–73.

Dixon, Wheeler Winston. *The Transparency of Spectacle: Meditations on the Moving Image.* Albany: State Univ. of New York Press, 1998.

Dmitri, Ivan. *Kodachrome and How to Use It.* New York: Simon & Schuster, 1940.

Dobson, John, and Ruth Dobson. *English Ways and By-Ways.* New York: Scribner's, 1920.

Doherty, Thomas. *Pre-Code Hollywood: Sex, Immorality, and Insurrection in American Cinema, 1930–1934.* New York: Columbia Univ. Press, 1999.

Donahey, William, and Effie E. Baker. *The Teenie Weenies.* Chicago: Beckley-Caudy, 1917.

Donaldson, Robert. "My Grandmother's Swing." *Grassroots: The Journal of the Grant County (Ark.) Museum* 27 (December 2006), 2–6.

Doremus, Donald R. "Tubular Lamps Give Uniform Illumination for Photo Copying Stand." *Popular Science* 133 (July 1938), 80.

Dorman, Robert. *Revolt of the Provinces: The Regionalist Movement in America, 1920–1945.* Chapel Hill: Univ. of North Carolina Press, 1993.

Dorr, Robert F. *Fighting Colors: Glory Days of the U.S. Aircraft Markings.* Osceola, Wis.: Motorbooks, 1990.

"Double Box Speeds Up Photo Printing." *Popular Science* 133 (July 1938), 99.

"Double Nude Study." *International Photo Technik* 19 (Fall 1973), 2.

Douglas, Charlotte, ed. *The King of Time.* Cambridge, Mass.: Harvard Univ. Press, 1985.

Douglas, Susan J. *Inventing American Broadcasting.* Baltimore: Johns Hopkins Univ. Press, 1987.

Dovala, Joseph C. "The Gender Question: Does Sex Really Matter?" *Dive Training* 19 (May 2009), 42–52.

Downes, Bruce. "First Stop: Germany." *Popular Photography* 51 (July 1962), 32.

——. "The Nude in Photography: Is It Art?" *Popular Photography Color Annual 1957,* 62–71.

——. *Photography with the Ciro-Flex: A Basic Book on Twin-Lens Reflex Camera Technique.* New York: Photo Imex, 1950.

Doyle, Arthur Conan. *The Coming of the Fairies.* London: Hodder & Stoughton, 1922.

——. *Essays on Photography.* Ed. John Michael Gibson and Richard Lancelyn Green. London: Secker & Warburg, 1982.

Doyle, Richard. *In Fairyland: A Series of Pictures from the Elf-World.* London: Longmans, 1870.

Drake, St. Clair, and Horace R. Cayton. *Black Metropolis: A Study of Negro Life in a Northern City.* [1945] Rev. and enl. ed. Chicago: Univ. of Chicago Press, 1993.

Dresbach, Glenn Ward. "Mardi Gras Night—Panama." *Double-Dealer* 4 (July 1922), 19.

Dry, Sarah. *Curie.* London: Haus, 2003.

DuBay, Bill. "The Return of the Blood Red Queen." *Vampirella* 87 (May 1980), 5–35.

Dubos, René. *So Human an Animal.* New York: Scribner's, 1968.

——. *The Wooing of Earth.* New York: Scribner's, 1980.

"Dufaycolor Process." *Leica Photography,* no. 28 (March 1935), 1.

Duffy, Don, and Ed Finley. "A Lesson in Pin-Ups." *US Camera* 13 (November 1950), 49–51.

Duncan, Roger F., and John P. Ware. *A Cruising Guide to the New England Coast.* [1937] Rev. ed. New York: Dodd, Mead, 1968.

Dunlap, Orrin E. *Marconi: The Man and His Wireless.* [1937] London: Macmillan, 1971.

Dunning, John. *On the Air: The Encyclopedia of Old-Time Radio, 1925–1976.* New York: Oxford Univ. Press, 1998.

Dunsany, Lord. "Songs of Al Shaldamir." *Double-Dealer* 2 (December 1921), 56–60.

DuPont De Nemours & Co. *Photographic Films.* Wilmington, Del.: Du Pont De Nemours, 1952.

Durkin, Dolores. *Children Who Read Early.* New York: Teachers College Press, 1966.

Dutton, Laurence. "Lenses for the Miniature Camera." *Popular Photography* 4 (February 1939), 32–33, 86–87.

Eastman Kodak Company. *Applied Color Photography Indoors.* Rochester, N.Y.: Eastman Kodak Co., 1962.

——. *The Art of Portraits and the Nude.* New York: Kodak/Time-Life, 1983.

——. *The Book of the Brownies.* Rochester, N.Y.: Eastman Kodak Co., 1911.

——. *Brownies: To Help You Choose Your Camera.* New York: Eastman Kodak Co., 1940.

——. *Color Photography in the Studio.* Rochester, N.Y.: Eastman Kodak Co., 1950.

——. *Data Book on Black-and-White Kodak Films.* Rochester, N.Y.: Eastman Kodak Co., 1951.

——. *Ektachrome & Kodachrome: Professional Films.* Rochester, N.Y.: Eastman Kodak Co., 1947.

——. *History of Kodak Cameras.* Rochester, N.Y.: Eastman Kodak Co., 1999.

——. *How to Make Good Pictures: A Book for the Amateur Photographer.* Rochester, N.Y.: Eastman Kodak Co., [1914?].

——. *How to Make Good Pictures: A Guide for the Amateur Photographer.* 29th ed. Rochester, N.Y.: Eastman Kodak Co., 1952.

——. *Kodak Films.* Rochester, N.Y.: Eastman Kodak Co., 1943; 1951.

——. *The Kodak on the Farm.* Rochester, N.Y.: Eastman Kodak Co., 1908.

——. *Kodaks and Supplies.* Rochester, N.Y.: Eastman Kodak Co., 1915.

——. *Photography for Rural Young People.* Rochester, N.Y.: Eastman Kodak Co., 1939.

——. *The Photography of Colored Objects.* 14th ed., rev. Rochester, N.Y.: Eastman Kodak Co., 1938.

——. *Photography with Kodachrome Professional Film.* Rochester, N.Y.: Eastman Kodak Co., 1941.

——. *Picture Taking and Picture Making.* Rochester, N.Y.: Eastman Kodak Co., 1898.

——. *Processing Chemicals and Formulas.* Rochester, N.Y.: Eastman Kodak Co., 1954.

——. *Professional Black-and-White Films.* Rochester, N.Y.: Eastman Kodak Co., 1981.

——. *Professional Photoguide.* Rochester, N.Y.: Eastman Kodak Co., 1977.

——. *Slides.* Rochester, N.Y.: Eastman Kodak Co., 1941.

——. "Snow Scenes." *Camera Craft* 19 (February 1912), n.p.

——. *Using Filters.* Rochester, N.Y.: Eastman Kodak Co., 1981.

——. *Why a Color May Not Reproduce Correctly.* Rochester, N.Y.: Eastman Kodak Co., 1985.

Eaton, Walter Prichard. *Barn Doors and Byways.* Boston: Small, Maynard, 1913.

——. "The 'Good Roads' Delusion." *New York Sunday Herald,* March 27, 1932, 4–5, 31.

——. *Green Trails and Upland Pastures.* Garden City, N.Y.: Doubleday, 1917.

——. *In Berkshire Fields.* Boston: Wilde, 1926.

Eder, Josef Maria. *Ausführliches Handbuch der Photographie.* 4 vols. Halle: Knapp, 1892–1900.

Edgren, Gretchen. *The Playmate Book: Six Decades of Centerfolds.* Cologne: Taschen, 2005.

Edwards, Agnes Rothery. *The Old Coast Road from Boston to Plymouth.* Boston: Houghton, Mifflin, 1920.

Edwards, John Paul. "First Salon of Pure Photography." *Camera Craft* 42 (August 1935), 419–25.

——. "Group F:64." *Camera Craft* 42 (March 1935), 107–13.

Edwards, K. E. *Radios That Work for Free.* Belmont, Calif.: Hope & Allen, 1977.

"Effect on Life of Unseen Rays Is Studied at Berlin." *Popular Science* 117 (July 1930), 51.

Effland, Anne B. W. "When Rural Does Not Equal Agricultural." *Agricultural History* 74 (Summer 2000), 489–501.

Eisendrath, David B. "After 35mm. What?" *Popular Photography* 51 (July 1962), 35–37, 119–22.

Eisenstein, Sergei. *Film Essays and a Lecture.* Ed. Jay Leyda. Princeton: Princeton Univ. Press, 1970.

——. "Montage and Architecture." Ed. Yve-Alain Bois. Trans. Michael Glenny. *Assemblage* 10 (December 1989), 111–13.

Eisner, Lotte H. *The Haunted Screen: Expressionism in the German Cinema and the Influence of Max Reinhardt.* London: Thames & Hudson, 1969.

Eisner, Will. *Comics and Sequential Art.* Tamarac, Fla.: Poorhouse, 1985.

Eitel, Ernest John. *Feng-shui; Or, The Rudiments of Natural Science in China.* Hong Kong: Lane, Crawford, 1873.

Ekman, Paul, and Wallace V. Friesen. *Unmasking the Face: A Guide to Recognizing Emotions from Facial Clues.* Englewood Cliffs, N.J.: Prentice-Hall, 1975.

"Electric Dangers." *Literary Digest* 46 (March 1, 1913), 352–53.

"Electric Tides Flow High Above the Earth." *Popular Science* 116 (February 1930), 62.

Ellis, John. *The Deterioration of the Puritan Stock and its Causes.* New York: Author, 1884.

Elmendorf, Dwight Lathrop. *Lantern Slides: How to Make and Color Them.* New York: Anthony, 1897.

"Elron Terry Wraps." *Flair* 1 (May 1950), 8.

Elsden, Robin. "One Light Is Sufficient." *Art Photography* 7 (May 1956), 26–29.

Elster, Charles Harrington. *There's a Word for It: A Grandiloquent Guide to Life.* New York: Scribner, 1996.

Emanuel, W. D. *All-in-One Camera Book: The Easy Path to Good Photography.* 6th ed. London: Focal, 1944; 42nd ed., 1958; 70th ed., 1973.

———. *Rolleiflex Guide: How to Make Full Use of Your Rolleiflex.* New York: American Photographic, 1957.

Emerson, Ralph Waldo. *Journals.* Cambridge, Mass.: Harvard Univ. Press, 1909.

Encyclopedia of Fantasy. Ed. John Clute and John Grant. New York: St. Martin's, 1997.

Endell, August. *Zauberland des Sichtbaren.* Berlin: Verlag der Gartenschönheit, 1928.

"Enter Wong." *Life,* October 24, 1960, 55–60.

"Entirely New Type of Camera." *Popular Photography* 4 (February 1939), 68.

Ericksenn, Lief. *Medium Format Photography: A User's Guide to Equipment and Applications.* New York: Amphoto, 1991.

Ernst, Morris L., and Pare Lorentz. *Censored: The Private Life of the Movie.* New York: J. Cape and H. Smith, 1930.

Ernst, Robert. *Weakness Is a Crime: The Life of Bernarr Macfadden.* Syracuse: Syracuse Univ. Press, 1991.

Espina, Marina. *Filipinos in Louisiana.* New Orleans: Laborde, 1988.

Etcoff, Nancy. *Survival of the Prettiest: The Science of Beauty.* New York: Doubleday, 1999.

Ethell, Jeffry L. *The History of Aircraft Nose Art: World War I to Today.* Osceola, Wis.: Motorbooks, 1991.

Evans, John. *Adventures with Pinhole and Home-Made Cameras: From Tin Cans to Precision Engineering.* Mies, Switzerland: RotoVision, 2003.

Evans, Ralph M. *Eye, Film, and Camera in Color Photography.* New York: Wiley, 1959.

Evans-Wentz, W. Y. *The Fairy Faith in Celtic Countries.* [1911] Reprint, New York: Carol, 1994.

Ewen, Stuart. *All Consuming Images: The Politics of Style in Contemporary Culture.* New York: Basic Books, 1988.

Ewing, Juliana Horatia. *The Brownies and Other Tales.* London: Bell and Daldy, 1871.

"Expression Group: A Team of Young Rollei Photographers." *Rolleigrafie* 3 (March 1969), 28–33.

"Extreme Landscape." *International Photo Technik* 22 (Spring 1976), 46–51.

"Eye." *International Photo Technik* 18 (Autumn 1972), 28–29, 56.

Eyman, Scott. *Five American Cinematographers: Interviews with Karl Struss, Joseph Ruttenberg, James Wong Howe, Linwood Dunn, and William H. Clothier.* Metuchen, N.J.: Scarecrow, 1987.

———. *The Speed of Sound: Hollywood and the Talkie Revolution, 1926–1930.* New York: Simon & Shuster, 1997.

Fabian, Anne. "Making a Commodity of Truth: Speculations on the Career of Bernarr Macfadden." *American Literary History* 5 (Spring 1993), 51–76.

Fagin, N. Bryllion. "Sherwood Anderson and Our Anthropological Age." *Double-Dealer* 7 (January–February 1925), 91–98.

"Faking Films in Hollywood." *Popular Photography* 1 (August 1937), 26–28, 78–79.

Falasca-Zamponi, Simonetta. *Fascist Spectacle: The Aesthetics of Power in Mussolini's Italy.* Berkeley: Univ. of California Press, 1997.

Farber, Eduard. "Concentric Circles and Chemistry." *Smithsonian Journal of History* 2 (Spring 1967), 31–42.

Farjeon, J. Jefferson. "The Photograph." *Detective Fiction Weekly,* September 15, 1928, 632–38.

"Fashion Photography." *International Photo Technik* 11 (Winter 1965), 1.

Fass, Paula. *The Damned and the Beautiful: American Youth in the 1920s.* New York: Oxford Univ. Press, 1977.

Fast, Julius. *Body Language.* New York: Evans, 1970.

Faulkner, William. *Absalom, Absalom!* [1936] New York: Random House, 1964.

———. "New Orleans." *Double-Dealer* 7 (January–February 1925), 102–7.

Federal Communications Commission. *Report of Persons and Other Entities Holding Stock Interest In or Control Over More than One Standard Broadcast Station.* Washington, D.C.: GPO, 1940.

Feininger, Andreas. *Successful Color Photography* [1954] Rev. ed. Englewood Cliffs, N.J.: Prentice-Hall, 1966.

Feltovich, Nick, Richmond Harbaugh, and Ted To. "Too Cool for School? Signalling and Countersignalling." *RAND Journal of Economics* 33 (Winter 2002), 630–49.

Fidler, J. Havelock. *Ley Lines: Their Nature and Properties: A Dowser's Investigation.* Wellingborough, U.K.: Turnstone, 1983.

Field, Rachel. *Points East: Narratives of New England.* New York: Macmillan, 1930.

"Fight This Competition." *Saturday Evening Post,* September 13, 1930, 121.

"Figure Photography." *Art Photography* 3 (May 1952), 22–27.

Finlay, Victoria. *Colour.* London: Hodder, 2002.

Fiorani, Eleonora. *Abitare il corpo: La moda.* Milan: Lupetti, 2004

Firth, Violet Mary. *The Goat-Foot God.* [1936] London: Wyndam, 1976.

Fischer, K. H. "Nude 69." *Rolleigrafie* 3 (March 1969), 47.

Fischer, Otto. "Landscape as Symbol." *Landscape* 4 (Spring 1955), 24–33.

Fite, James. "The Teleconverter." *Mainline Modeler* 7 (April 1986), 70–73.

Fitzgerald, F. Scott. *The Great Gatsby.* New York: Scribner's, 1925.

Fleming, John Adam, ed. *Terrestrial Magnetism and Electricity.* New York: McGraw-Hill, 1939.

Flöter, Hubs. "The Rollei and Fashion." *Rolleigrafie* 5 (September 1969), 20–24.

Flusser, Vilém. *Towards a Philosophy of Photography.* [1983] Trans. Anthony Mathews. London: Reaktion, 2000.

Focal Encyclopedia of Photography. [1956] 2 vols. Rev. ed. New York: McGraw-Hill, 1965.

Fogu, Claudio. *The Historic Imaginary: Politics of History in Fascist Italy.* Toronto: Univ. of Toronto Press, 2003.

Fonssagrives, Fernand. "Menace in the Darkroom." *Glamour Photography* 1 (Fall 1954), 42–43.

Fontova, Humberto. *The Helldivers' Rodeo: A Deadly, Extreme, Scuba-Diving, Spear Fishing Adventure amid the Offshore Oil-Platforms in the Murky Waters of the Gulf of Mexico.* New York: Evans, 2001.

Forbes, Esther. *The Boston Book.* Boston: Houghton, Mifflin, 1947.

Ford, Colin. *The Story of Popular Photography.* London: National Museum of Photography, Film, and Television, 1989.

Ford, Colin, and Karl Steinorth, eds. *You Press the Button—We Do the Rest: The Birth of Snapshot Photography.* London: Nishen, 1988.

"Foreign Look." *Beauty Photography* 1 ([September?] 1957), 63–69.

Forest, Jean-Claude. "Barbarella 1." *Evergreen* 37 (September 1965), 35–44.

———. "Barbarella 2." *Evergreen* 38 (November 1965), 37–45.

———. *Barbarella.* [1964] Trans. Richard Seaver. New York: Grove Press, 1966.

Foresta, Merry A., and John Wood. *Secrets of the Dark Chamber: The Art of the American Daguerreotype.* Washington, D.C.: Smithsonian Institution, 1995.

Forty, Adrian. *Words and Buildings: A Vocabulary of Modern Architecture.* New York: Thames & Hudson, 2000.

Foster, Richard. *The Real Betty Page: The Truth about the Queen of Pinups.* Secaucus, N.J.: Carol Publishing, 1997.

Fox, Imro. *Shadowgraphs and How to Make Them.* New York: Martinka, 1900.

Fox, Stephen. *The Mirror Makers: A History of Advertising and Its Creators.* [1984] Rev. ed. Urbana: Univ. of Illinois Press, 1997.

Franke & Heidecke. *Rollei.* Braunschweig, F&H, 1951.

———. *Rolleiflex.* Braunschweig: F&H, 1937; 1951.

———. *Rolleiflex 2.8C in Practical Use.* Braunschweig: Franke & Heidecke, [1953?].

———. *Rolleiflex 3.5F and 2.8F.* Braunschweig: Franke & Heidecke, [1962?].

———. *Rollei-magic II.* Braunschweig: Franke & Heidecke, [1964?].

———. *Rolleimarin.* Braunschweig: Franke & Heidecke, 1954.

Frankl, Horst. "Colour-Subjective Picture Element." *Rolleigrafie* 8 (June 1970), 12–17.

Franks, Mary Anne. "Review of *Split Decisions.*" *Harvard Journal of Law and Gender* 30 (Winter 2007), 257–67.

Fraprie, Frank R. "The Miniature Camera." *American Photography* 29 (July 1939), 451–52.

———. *Portrait Lighting by Daylight and Artificial Light.* Boston: American Photographic Publishing, 1935.

Fraser, Kennedy. *The Fashionable Mind: Reflections on Fashion, 1970–1982.* Boston: Godine, 1981.

Fraser, Robert. "WBF: A Typical Ute." *Speedx* 67 (July 1978), 59–61.

Frazer, Perry D. "Facts and Comments." *American Photography* 29 (November 1935), 704–9.

Frazier, Charles. *Cold Mountain.* New York: Random House, 1997.

"Freak Movies Easy with New Amateur Camera." *Popular Science* 122 (June 1933), 23.

Frederic, A. "J. P. Ronzel's Brainwaves." *International Photo Technik* 11 (Spring 1965), 84–88.

Freedman, Rory, and Kim Barnouin. *Skinny Bitch.* Philadelphia: Running Press, 2005.

Freeland, Cynthia. *The Naked and the Undead.* Boulder, Colo.: Westview, 2000.

Freye, Paul. *Stolen Stripper. Yank,* 4 December 7, 1945, 9.

Freyre, Gilberto. *The Masters and the Slaves: A Study in the Development of Brazilian Civilization.* Trans. Samuel Putnam. New York: Knopf, 1946.

———. *New World in the Tropics: The Culture of Modern Brazil.* [1959] Rev. ed. Westport, Conn.: Greenwood, 1980.

———. *Order and Progress: Brazil from Monarchy to Republic.* Trans. Rod W. Horton. New York: Knopf, 1970.

Freytag, Heinrich. "Is the Photographic Portrait Still Up-to-Date?" *International Photo Technik* 11 (Fall 1971), 12–15, 60.

Friedan, Betty. *The Feminine Mystique.* New York: Norton, 1963.

Friedberg, Anne. *The Virtual Window: From Alberti to Microsoft.* Cambridge, Mass.: MIT Press, 2006.

Friedenberg, Edgar Z. *The Vanishing Adolescent.* Boston: Beacon, 1959.

Friedman, Lawrence Jacob. *The White Savage: Racial Fantasies in the Post-Bellum South.* Englewood Cliffs, N.J.: Prentice-Hall, 1970.

Frieling, H. "Colour as a Mode of Expression." *International Photo Technik* 11 (Winter 1971), 36–37, 57–58.

Froen, Carl. "Unloading Miniature Camera Roll Film." *Popular Science* 133 (August 1938), 86.

Frost, Robert. *Poetry.* Ed. Edward Connery Lathem. New York: Holt, Rinehart and Winston, 1969.

Froud, Brian, and Alan Lee. *Faeries.* New York: Abrams, 1978.

Frum, David. *How We Got Here: The 70's.* New York: Basic Books, 2000.

Frye, Ralph. *Uncle 'Lish.* New York: Knopf, 1945.

Fuller, Kathryn H. *At the Picture Show: Small-Town Audiences and the Creation of Movie Fan Culture.* Charlottesville: Univ. Press of Virginia, 1996.

Fuller (Ossoli), Margaret. *Woman in the Nineteenth Century and Kindred Papers.* Ed. Arthur B. Fuller. New York: Tribune, 1869.

Fuller, Roger. *Who Killed Beau Sparrow?* New York: Pocket Books, 1964.

Funk, Isaac K. *The Widow's Mite and Other Psychic Phenomena.* New York: Funk and Wagnalls, 1904.

Fürst, Peter H. "Staged Advertising Photography." *Rolleigrafie* 6 (December 1969), 26–29.

Fussell, Paul. *Abroad: British Literary Traveling between the Wars.* Oxford: Oxford Univ. Press, 1980.

Gabor, Mark. *Illustrated History of Girlie Magazines from National Police Gazette to the Present.* New York: Harmony, 1984.

GAF Corporation. "500 Color Slide Film." New York: GAF Corporation, 1972.

Gagliano, Anthony. *Straits of Fortune.* New York: HarperCollins, 2007.

Gaiman, Neil. *American Gods.* New York: Morrow, 2001.

———. "'The Annotated Brothers Grimm': Grimmer Than You Thought." *New York Times,* December 5, 2004, Sunday Book Review.

———. *The Graveyard Book.* New York: HarperCollins, 2008.

———. Neverwhere. Woodlands: BBC Books, 1996.

Gaiman, Neil, et al. *The Sandman: A Game of You.* New York: DC Comics, 1993.

Gaines, Jane, and Charlotte Herzog, eds. *Fabrications: Costume and the Female Body.* New York: Routledge, 1990.

Galbraith, John Kenneth. *The Affluent Society.* Boston: Houghton, Mifflin, 1958.

Galton, Francis. *Inquiries into Human Faculty.* London: Macmillan, 1883.

Gantenbein, Douglas. "Fade to Black: The Twilight of Film Photography." *Wall Street Journal,* March 14, 2006, 1.

Garbicz, Adam, and Jacek Klinowski. *Cinema: The Magic Vehicle.* 2 vols. New York: Schocken, 1983.

Gardette, Charles D. "The Two Shadows: An Outline Sketch." *Godey's Lady's Book and Magazine* 71 (December 1865), 494–99.

Gardiner-Scott, Tanya J. *Mervyn Peake: The Evolution of a Dark Romantic.* New York: Lang, 1989.

Garland, Hamlin. *The Shadow World.* New York: Harper & Brothers, 1908.

Garner, Philip. *Rube Goldberg: A Retrospective.* New York: Delilah, 1983.

Garreau, Joel. "Perfecting the Human." *Fortune,* May 30, 2005, 101–8.

Garrett, Edmund H. *Romance and Reality of the Puritan Coast.* Boston: Little, Brown, 1897.

Garrison, Roger H. *The Adventure of Learning in College: An Undergraduate Guide to Productive Study.* New York: Harper, 1959.

Garrity, Terry. *Sensuous Woman: The First How-To Book for the Female Who Wants to Be All Woman.* New York: Stuart, 1969.

Gaunt, Leonard. *Practical Exposure in Photography.* London: Focal, 1981.

Gay, Jan. *On Going Naked.* New York: Garden City Publishing Co., 1932.

Gehman, R. "Lives of Suzy Parker." *Cosmopolitan,* November 1959, 86–89.

General Electric. "This Thing Called Ultra-Violet." *Popular Science* 117 (October 1930), 18.

General Jewish Council. *Father Coughlin: His "Facts" and Arguments.* New York: General Jewish Council, 1939.

Genovese, Eugene D. *Roll Jordan Roll: The World the Slaves Made.* New York: Pantheon, 1974.

———. *The World the Slaveholders Made: Two Essays in Interpretation.* Middletown, Conn.: Wesleyan Univ. Press, 1988.

Genthe, Arnold. "Photographing the Dance." *Popular Photography* 4 (May 1939), 26–27, 117–18.

Gerould, Katherine Fullerton. "Hollywood: An American State of Mind." *Harper's,* May 1923, 689–96.

Geselbracht, Raymond H. "The Ghosts of Andrew Wyeth: The Meaning of Death in the Transcendental Myth of America." *New England Quarterly* 47 (March 1974), 13–29.

"Get 'Em on the Wing with a Rolleiflex." *Popular Photography* 4 (May 1939), 7.

Gewehr, A. "Large-Format Photography with Extra-Long Focal Lengths." *International Photo Technik* 22 (Spring 1976), 4–5.

Giebelhausen, Joachim. "Quick-Action Shot: True or Fake?" *International Photo Technik* 11 (Summer 1965), 202–3.

———. *School of Nude Photography.* Munich: Grossbild Technik, n.d.

Gilbert, Jess, and Steve Brown. "Alternative Land Reform Proposals in the 1930s: The Nashville Agrarians and the Southern Tenant Farmers' Union." *Agricultural History* 55 (October 1981), 351–69.

Gilbert, Michael. *The Night of the Twelfth.* Harmondsworth: Penguin, 1976.

Gill, James. *Lords of Misrule: Mardi Gras and the Politics of Race in New Orleans.* Jackson: Univ. Press of Mississippi, 1997.

Gilliver, Peter, Jeremy Marshall, and Edmund Weiner. *The Ring of Words: Tolkien and the Oxford English Dictionary.* Oxford: Oxford Univ. Press, 2006.

Gilmore, William J. *Reading Becomes a Necessity of Life: Material and Cultural Life in Rural New England, 1780–1835.* Knoxville: Univ. of Tennessee Press, 1989.

Ginzburg, Ralph. *An Unhurried View of Erotica.* New York: Helsman, 1958.

Girl. Yank, April 30, 1943, 17.

"Girl Next Door." *Newsweek,* June 6, 1960, 114–15.

"Girls, Sand, and Water." *Popular Photography* 13 (August 1943), 36–37, 88–89.

Gitlin, Tod, ed. *Watching Television.* New York: Pantheon, 1986.

"Glamour by Sam Haskins." *Photography Annual 1963,* 58–65, 194.

"Glamour Portraiture." *Glamour Photography* 1 (Fall 1954), 30–35.

"Glamour Studio." *Master Photography* 1 (Summer 1957), 26–35.

Glancey, Jonathan. *The Train: An Illustrated History.* London: Carlton, 2004.

Glasgow, Ellen. *The Miller of Old Church.* Garden City, N.Y.: Doubleday, 1911.

Glass Container Manufacturers Institute. "Because Glass Itself Is So Pure." *Life,* October 24, 1960, 61.

Glasser, Otto. *Wilhelm Conrad Rontgen and the Early History of the Roentgen Rays.* Springfield, Ill.: Thomas, 1934.

Godwin, Francis. *Nuncius Inanimatus.* [1638] Ed. Grant McColley. Northampton, Mass.: Smith College Studies in Modern Languages, 1937.

Godwin, Joscelyn. *Robert Fludd: Hermetic Philosopher and Surveyor of Two Worlds.* London: Thames & Hudson, 1979.

Gohlke, Frank. *Landscapes from the Middle of the World.* Chicago: Museum of Contemporary Photography, 1988.

Goldstein, Joseph. "On Being Adult and Being an Adult in Secular Law." *Daedalus* 105 (Fall 1976), 60–86.

Goldwyn, Samuel. *Behind the Scenes.* New York: Doran, 1923.

Goll, Ivan. "Die Neger erobern Europa." *Die Literarische Welt* 1 (January 15, 1926), 3–4.

Goodell, Charles L. *Black Tavern Tales: Stories of Old New England.* New York: Willis McDonald, 1932.

Goodenough, Elizabeth, and Andrea Immel, eds. *Under Fire: Childhood in the Shadow of War.* Detroit: Wayne State Univ. Press, 2008.

Goodrick-Clarke, Nicholas. *Die okkulten Wurzeln des Nationalsozialismus.* Graz: Stocker, 1997.

Gordon, Elizabeth. "What Climate Does to You and What You Can Do to Climate." *House Beautiful,* October 1949, 131.

Gordon, Richard E., and Katherine K. Gordon. *The Blight on the Ivy.* Englewood Cliffs, N.J.: Prentice-Hall, 1963.

Gottlieb, Leonard. *Lost and Found in America: The Homefront, Fall 1968: Family Photos during the Vietnam War.* Stockport, U.K.: Dewi Lewis, 2004.

Gould, Gene. "One Man Show: Beauty and Cornel Lucas." *Art Photography* 7 (April 1956), 1014, 50.

Gould & Eberhardt Co. *The Hobbing Method of Cutting Gear Teeth.* Irvington, N.J.: Gould & Eberhardt, 1951.

Gowland, Peter. "Beauty and the Beach." *American Photography* 42 (July 1948), 421–23.

———. "Gowland Goes Candid at the Beach." *Popular Photography* 57 (October 1965), 74–75.

———. "How to Make a Desk." *American Home* 48 (September 1952), 38–39.

———. *How to Photograph Women.* New York: Crown, 1953.

———. *The Secrets of Photographing Women.* New York: Crown, 1981.

———. "Switch on the Glamour." *Popular Photography* 71 (December 1972), 130–31.

———. "Underwater." *Popular Photography* 62 (May 1968), 80–83.

———. "Underwater Nudes." *Figure Photography* 11 [1955?], 60–67.

———. "Your Complete Power Workshop in One Machine." *American Home* 48 (July 1951), 40–41.

"Gowland's L.A. Scene." *Popular Photography* 62 (January 1968), 72, 130.

Grady, Henry Woodfin. *What Might Be Termed a Sequel to "Gone with the Wind."* Detroit: Weaver, 1937.

Grahame, Kenneth. *The Wind in the Willows.* [1908] New York: Macmillan, 1989.

Graves, Robert. "The Naked and the Nude." *New Yorker,* February 16, 1957, 16.

"Great Summer for Roll-Film Users." *Photo-Era* 66 (June 1931), 335.

Green, Ruzzie. "Pictures vs. Snapshots." *Popular Photography* 4 (May 1939), 14–14, 76–81.

Green, Simon R. *Drinking Midnight Wine.* London: Penguin, 2001.

Greenberg, Clement. "Avant-Garde and Kitsch." *Partisan Review* 6 (Fall 1939), 34–39.

——. "Towards a Newer Laocoon." *Partisan Review* 7 (July–August 1940), 296–310.

Greenberg, Jerry. *Underwater Photography Simplified.* Coral Gables: Seahawk, 1956.

Greene, Alan. *Primitive Photography.* Woburn, Mass.: Focal, 2001.

Greenfield, Patricia Marks. *Mind and Media: The Effects of Television, Video Games, and Computers.* Cambridge, Mass.: Harvard Univ. Press, 1984.

Greenman, Jamie E. "Watson Promotes Preventative Eugenics." *Harvard Crimson,* March 7, 2005, 1, 3.

Greenough, Sarah, et al., eds. *On the Art of Fixing a Shadow: One Hundred and Fifty Years of Photography.* Boston: Little, Brown, 1989.

Greenwood, Ed. *Silverfall: Tales of the Seven Sisters.* Renton, Wash.: TSR, 1999.

Gregg, James R. *Experiments in Visual Science for Home and School.* New York: Ronald, 1966.

Grimes, Martha. *The Winds of Change.* London: Penguin, 2004.

Grimm, Jacob, and Wilhelm Grimm. *The Annotated Brothers Grimm.* Trans. Maria Tatar. New York: Norton, 2004.

Gross, Kathleen Cotter. "The Courtesan." *Double-Dealer* 5 (January 1923), 37.

Grossman, Debbie. "Why We Love Sunsets and Other Cliches." *Popular Photography* 71 (August 2007), 58–62.

Gruber, Adolf. "Quo Vadis: Photography of Nudes?" *International Photo Technik* 18 (Winter 1972), 32–33, 54.

Gruber, Michael. *The Book of Air and Shadows.* New York: Harper, 2007.

Gruelle, Johnny. *Friendly Fairies.* Chicago: Volland, 1919.

——. *My Very Own Fairy Stories.* Chicago: Volland, 1917.

Grunwald, Robert. "Cocktail Shaker Makes Efficient Enlarger." *Popular Photography* 5 (September 1939), 61, 119.

Guide to Fantasy Art Techniques. Ed. Martyn Dean. Text by Chris Evans. New York: Arco, 1984.

Gunter, Joseph. "The Photographic Nude: How Far Should One Go with Abstraction?" *International Photo Technik* 18 (Fall 1972), 14, 50.

Gunther, Max. "How Manly Will Your Son Be?" *Coronet* 50 (October 1961), 70–75.

Gürtler, Hans. "My Birds, My Hobby." *Rolleigrafie* 1 (October 1968), 28–29.

Hackney, Sheldon. "The South as a Counterculture." *American Scholar* 42 (Spring 1973), 283–93.

Haist, Grant M. "Four Men and a Model." *Art Photography* 7 (May 1956), 22–25, 50.

Hajek-Halke, Heinz. *Experimentelle Fotografie.* Bonn: Athenäum Verlag, 1955.

——. *Der Grosse Unbekannte.* Gottingen: Steidl, 1997.

Halberstam, David. "Discovering Sex: The Story of the Men and Women Who in the 1950s Helped Create the Sexual Landscape We Inhabit Today." *American Heritage* 44 (May/June 1993), 39–58.

Hall, Donald. *String Too Short to Be Saved.* Boston: Godine, 1979.

Hall, Julien A. "Negro Conjuring and Tricking." *Journal of American Folklore* 10 (July–September 1897), 241–43.

Halley, Janet. *Split Decisions: How and Why to Take a Break from Feminism.* Princeton: Princeton Univ. Press, 2006.

Hallinan/FPG, Inc. "Advertising for Nightgowns." *International Photo Technik* 18 (Winter 1972), 58–59.

Hamilton, James. *Arthur Rackham: A Life with Illustration.* London: Pavilion, 1990.

Hamilton, Richard F. *Who Voted for Hitler?* Princeton: Princeton Univ. Press, 1982.

Hammond, Arthur, "The Miniature Camera." *American Photography* 29 (February 1929), 118–20.

Hammond, Wayne G., and Christina Scull. *J. R. R. Tolkien, Artist and Illustrator.* Boston: Houghton Mifflin, 1995.

Handel, Arnold. "Fashion Photography in Practice." *International Photo Technik* 22 (Spring 1976), 10–14.

Handlin, Oscar. *Truth in History.* Cambridge, Mass.: Harvard Univ. Press, 1979.

Hannah, Forman. "Admiration." *American Photography* 29 (October 1935), 615.

———. "Photography of the Nude." *Camera Craft* 42 (April 1935), 159–66.

Hanson, Chadwick. "The Metamorphosis of Tituba." *New England Quarterly* 47 (March 1974), 3–12.

Hanson, Eugene. "Get Your Models Wet." *Art Photography* 5 (August 1953), 4–8.

Hanson, Norwood Russell. "A Picture Theory of Meaning." In *The Nature and Function of Scientific Theories: Essays in Contemporary Science and Philosophy,* ed. Robert G. Colodny. Pittsburgh: Univ. of Pittsburgh Press, 1970.

Harder, Jochen. "Black Is Beautiful." *Rolleigrafie* 7 (March 1970), 1.

———. "Fotografie Professionell." *Rolleigrafie* 8 (June 1970), 30–31, 43–44.

Harper, Charles G. *The Exeter Road.* London: Chapman, 1899.

Harrigan, Pat, and Noah Wardrip-Fruin, eds. *Second Person: Role-Playing and Story in Games and Playable Media.* Cambridge, Mass.: MIT Press, 2007.

Harris, Joel Chandler. *Free Joe: Stories.* Savannah: Beehive, 1975.

Harris, Mel. *Weegee's Secrets of Shooting with Photoflash.* New York: Designers 3, 1953.

Harris, Robert S. *Harris Memory Meter.* Rochester, N.Y.: Memory Meter Co., 1980.

Hartley, L. P. "New Fiction." *Saturday Review,* January 11, 1930, 54–58.

Harvey, David. *The Condition of Postmodernity: An Enquiry into the Origins of Cultural Change.* Oxford: Blackwell, 1989.

Haskins, Sam. *Five Girls.* New York: Crown, 1962.

———. "Glamor." *Popular Photography Annual 1963,* 58–65.

Hass, Hans. *Fotojagd am Meeresgrund: Erlednis und Technik der unterwasser Fotografie.* Harburg: Heering-Verlag, 1942.

———. *Manta: Under the Red Sea with Spear and Camera.* Trans. James Cleugh. New York: Rand, McNally, 1953.

———. *Unter Korallen und Haien: Abenteurer in der Karibischen See.* Berlin: Deutschen Verlag, 1941.

Hastings, Scott E. *Goodbye Highland Yankee: Stories of a North Country Boyhood.* Chelsea, Vt.: Chelsea Green, 1988.

Hattersley, Ralph. *Photographic Lighting: Learning to See.* Englewood Cliffs, N.J.: Prentice-Hall, 1979.

Hauck Werbestudios. "Moon Girl." *International Photo Technik* 18 (Winter 1972), cover and 1.

"Haunted Restaurant." *Literary Digest* 78 (August 11, 1923), 25.

Hauser, Kitty. "The Earth from the Air." *Granta* 99 (Fall 2007), 101–29.
———. *Shadow Sites: Photography, Archaeology and the British Landscape, 1927–1955*. Oxford: Oxford Univ. Press, 2007.
Hausmann, Raoul. "Photomontage." *a bis z* 3 (May 1931), 61–62.
Hawkins, Gerald S. *Stonehenge Decoded*. Garden City, N.Y.: Doubleday, 1965.
Hawkins, N. *Hawkins' Mechanical Dictionary: A Cyclopedia of Words, Terms, Phrases and Data Used in the Mechanic Arts, Trades, and Sciences*. [1909] Almonte, Ont.: Algrove, 2007.
Hawthorne, Hildegard. "The Great Magician." *St. Nicholas*, February 1911, 356–58.
Hawthorne, Nathaniel. *Works*. Boston: Houghton, 1896.
Haynes, A. J. *Projection Printing with the Photometer*. New York: Haynes Products, 1939.
Hearn, Lafcadio. *Creole Sketches*. Ed. Charles Woodward Hutson. Boston: Houghton, Mifflin, 1931.
———. *La Cuisine Créole: A Collection of Culinary Recipes, From Leading Chefs and Noted Creole Housewives, Who Have Made New Orleans Famous for its Cuisine*. New York: Coleman, 1885.
———. *Fantastics and Other Fancies*. Ed. Charles Woodward Hutson. Boston: Houghton, Mifflin, 1914.
———. *Gombo Zhèbes: Little Book of Creole Proverbs, Selected from Six Creole Dialects*. New York: Coleman, 1885.
———. *Inventing New Orleans*. Ed. S. Frederick Starr. Jackson: Univ. Press of Mississippi, 2001.
———. "New Orleans in Carnival Garb." *Harper's Weekly*, February 24, 1883, 133.
———. "New Orleans Superstitions." *Harper's Weekly*, December 25, 1886, 843–44.
———. *Shadowings*. Boston: Little, Brown, 1919.
———. *Spirit Photography*. [1875] Los Angeles: John Murray, 1933.
Heath, Stephen. *Questions of Cinema*. London: Macmillan, 1981.
Hecht, David. "For Those Slow Exposures Make This 'Chain Pod.'" *U.S. Camera* 16 (September 1953), 78.
Heering, Walther. "A Glance Back into the Future of Photography." *Rolleigrafie* 5 (September 1969), 9–13.
———. *The Golden Book of the Rolleiflex*. Harzburg: Heering Verlag, 1936.
———, ed. *Im Zauber der Farbe: Ein Bildwerk der Farbenfotografie*. Harzburg: Heering Verlag, 1943.
———. *The Rollei Book*. 6th ed. Trans. Fred Willy Frerk. Vaduz, Liechtenstein: Heering Publications, 1954.
———. *Das Rollei-Buch*. Seebruck am Chiemsee: Heering-Verlag, 1963.
———. *The Rolleiflex Book*. [1934] Trans. John L. Baring. Boston: American Photographic Publishing, 1935.
———. *Das Rolleiflex Book*. Halle: Heering Verlag, 1933.
Held, Jean-François. "Mon week-end chez les nudists." *Le nouvel observateur*, August 14, 1967, 10–12, 26–29.
Hellmann, Harald. *The Best of American Girlie Magazines*. New York: Taschen, 1997.
Helphand, Kenneth I. "The Bicycle Kodak." *Environmental Review* 4 (Autumn 1981), 24–33.
Hempton, David N. "Enchantment and Disenchantment in the Evangelical Tradition." *Harvard Divinity Bulletin* 36 (Winter 2008), 39–54.
Henkel, Alice. *American Medicinal Leaves and Herbs*. Washington, D.C.: GPO, 1911.
———. *Weeds Used in Medicine*. Washington, D.C.: GPO, 1904.

Henle, Fritz. "Caribbean Island Paradise of Dreams." *Rolleigrafie* 8 (June 1970), 24–29.

———. *Figure Studies.* Intro. Jacquelyn Judge. New York: Studio, 1954. Rev. ed., New York: Viking, 1962.

———. *Fritz Henle's Guide to Rollei Photography.* New York: Studio/Crowell, 1956.

———. *Fritz Henle's Rollei: Photographs by Fritz Henle.* With text by Vivienne Tallal Winterry. New York: Hastings House, 1950.

———. *Holiday in Europe.* Text by Anne Fremantle, with an intro. by Patrick Dennis. New York: Viking, 1964.

Henle, Fritz, and H. M. Kinzer. *A New Guide to Rollei Photography.* New York: Viking, 1965.

———. *Photography for Everyone.* New York: Viking, 1959.

Henle, Fritz, and P. E. Knapp. *The Caribbean: A Journey with Pictures.* New York: Viking, 1957.

Henney, Keith. "How to Make Separation Negatives from Color Transparencies." *Popular Photography* 4 (January 1939), 20–21, 78–81.

Henry, William A. *In Defense of Elitism.* New York: Doubleday, 1994.

Henry Disston & Sons, Inc. *Saw, Tool, and File Manual.* Philadelphia: Henry Disston & Sons, [1929?].

Henry Ford Trade School. *Shop Theory.* New York: McGraw-Hill, 1942.

Hentoff, Nat. *Jazz Country.* New York: Harper, 1965.

Herlihy, David V. *Bicycle: The History.* New Haven: Yale Univ. Press, 2004.

Herskovits, Melville. *The Myth of the Negro Past.* New York: Harper, 1941.

Hess, Thomas B., and Linda Nochlin, eds. *Woman as Sex Object: Studies in Erotic Art, 1730–1970.* New York: Newsweek, 1972.

Hesse, Hermann. *Fairy Tales.* Trans. Jack Zipes. New York: Bantam, 1995.

Heyde, W. G. *Altix: Kamera für alle Tage.* Halle: Fotokinverlag, 1959.

Heydemann, Berndt. "On the Importance of Sharpness in Photography." *Rolleigrafie* 1 (October 1968), 16–21.

Heymann, Lionel. "The Art of Photographing the Nude." *Popular Photography* 1 (July 1937), 52–54.

Hibbs, Wyatt. "A Horizontal Enlarging Outfit." *American Photography* 29 (July 1935), 418–26.

"Hidden Motors Give Life to Prehistoric Monsters." *Popular Science* 122 (June 1933), 38.

Higgins, Jack. *East of Desolation.* [1968] London: Hodder, 1969.

"High Quality Negative Development." *Minicam* 1 (September 1937), 80–82.

Hiler, Hilaire. *From Nudity to Raiment: An Introduction to the Study of Costume.* New York: Weyhe, 1929.

Hillerman, Tony. *Seldom Disappointed: A Memoir.* New York: Harper Collins, 2001.

———. *Skeleton Man.* New York: HarperCollins, 2004.

Hines, Babbette. *Photobooth.* New York: Princeton Architectural Press, 2002.

Hitchcock, Alfred, comp. *Alfred Hitchcock Presents: Stories That Scared Even Me.* New York: Random House, 1967.

Hoberman, Michael. *Yankee Moderns: Folk Regional Identity in the Sawmill Valley of Western Massachusetts, 1890–1920.* Knoxville: Univ. of Tenn. Press, 2000.

Hobsbawm, Eric. *Age of Extremes: The Short Twentieth Century, 1914–1991.* Harmondsworth: Penguin, 1994.

Hoffman, Daniel G. "Jazz: The Survival of a Folk Art." *Perspectives USA* 15 (Spring 1956), 29–42.

Hoffman, Donald D. *Visual Intelligence: How We Create What We See*. New York: Norton, 1998.

Hoffman, Donald D., Bruce M. Bennett, and Chetan Prakash. *Observer Mechanics: A Formal Theory of Perception*. San Diego: Academic Press, 1989.

Hofstadter, Richard. *Social Darwinism in American Thought*. Boston: Beacon, 1955.

Hogan, George Francis. "Dynamic Symmetry for Photographers." *American Photography* 29 (August 1935), 476–80.

Hollahan, Eugene. "Sir Kenneth Clark's *The Nude*: Catalyst for Robert Grave's 'The Naked and the Nude'?" *Publications of the Modern Language Association* 87 (May 1972), 443–51.

Hollander, Anne. "Costume and Convention." *American Scholar* 42 (Autumn 1973), 671–75.

———. *Seeing through Clothes*. New York: Viking, 1978.

———. *Sex and Suits: The Evolution of Modern Dress*. New York: Knopf, 1994.

Holmes, Nancy. *The Dream Boats: The Beautiful People on Their Beautiful Yachts*. Englewood Cliffs, N.J.: Prentice-Hall, 1976.

Holtzman, Israel. "Hints on Photographing Aerial Fireworks." *Popular Science* 133 (July 1938), 100.

"Homosexuals in Revolt." *Life*, December 31, 1971, 62–73.

Honda Motor Co. "You Meet the Nicest People on a Honda." *Life*, July 3, 1964, inside front cover.

Hoover, F. Valentine. *Beefcake: The Muscle Magazines of America, 1950–1970*. Cologne: Taschen, 2002.

Hope, Laura Lee. *Outdoor Girls of Deepdale: Or, Camping and Tramping for Fun and Health*. New York: Grosset & Dunlap, 1913.

Hopkins, Mary E. "Enlarging Your Miniature Enlarger." *American Photography* 29 (July 1935), 454–55.

Horbach, Michael. *Gestern war der jüngste Tag*. Munich: [Andler?], 1960.

Horwood, Catherine. "'Girls Who Arouse Dangerous Passions': Women and Bathing, 1900–1939." *Women's History Review* 9 (2000), 653–73.

Hoskins, W. G. *English Landscapes*. London: British Broadcasting Corp., 1973.

———. *The Making of the English Landscape*. London: Hodder & Stoughton, 1955.

———. *One Man's England*. London: British Broadcasting Corp., 1978.

Howard, Robert E. *The Black Stranger and Other American Tales*. Ed. Steven Tompkins. Lincoln: Univ. of Nebraska Press, 2005.

"How Brief Can a Bathing Suit Get?" *Glamorous Models* 4 (June 1949), 2–37.

Howells, Richard. *Visual Culture*. Cambridge: Polity, 2003.

Howitt, William. *The History of the Supernatural in All Ages and Nations and in All Churches, Christian and Pagan, Demonstrating a Universal Faith*. Philadelphia: Lippincott, 1863.

"How Liquid Condensers Work." *Popular Science* 117 (October 1930), 71.

"How These Pictures Were Made." *US Camera* 14 (May 1951), 67–70.

"How to Pose a Pretty Girl." *Photokinks* 4 (1951), 60–64.

"How to Win Prizes." *Photography with Rolleiflex and Rolleicord* 14 (June 1939), 1.

Hudson, W. H. *Afoot in England*. London: Hutchinson, 1911.

Hughes, Langston, and Arna Bontemps, eds. *The Book of Negro Folklore*. New York: Dodd, Mead, 1958.

Hulbert, James Root. *Dictionaries: British and American*. [1955] London: Deutsch, 1968.

Hummel, Richard. *Spiegelreflexkameras aus Dresden*. Leipzig: Reintzsch, 1994.

Hundman, Robert L. "Prototype Photography." *Mainline Modeler* 4 (January 1983), 56–65.

Hunter, Fil, Steven Biver, and Paul Fuqua. *Light—Science and Magic: An Introduction to Photographic Lighting.* Boston: Focal Press, 2007.

Hunter, Phil. "Selecting a Model." *Art Photography* 7 (April 1956), 20–25, 44.

Huntington, Dwight W. "Camera Club of Cincinnati." *Century* 34 (September 1887), 729–32.

Hurbon, Laënnec. *L'insurrection des esclaves de Saint-Domingue.* Paris: Karthala, 2000.

Hurston, Zora Neale. *Folklore, Memoirs, and Other Writings.* Ed. Cheryl A. Wall. New York: Library of America, 1995.

———. "Hoodoo in America." *Journal of American Folklore* 44 (Summer 1931), 317–417.

———. *Mules and Men.* Philadelphia: Lippincott, 1935.

Huxley, Aldous. *On the Margin: Notes and Essays.* London: Chatto & Windus, 1923.

Hyatt, Harry Middleton. *Folklore for Adams County, Illinois.* New York: Hyatt Foundation, 1935.

———. *Hoodoo, Conjuration, Witchcraft, Rootwork: Beliefs Accepted by Many Negroes and White Persons.* 5 vols. [1935–39] Rev. ed. Hannibal, Mo.: Western Pub., 1970–.

I'll Take My Stand: The South and the Agrarian Tradition. Intro. Louis D. Rubin. [1930] New York: Harper & Row, 1962.

"Important Research Work." *American Photography* 29 (October 1939), 659.

International Game Developers Association. *Game Developer Demographics: An Exploration of Workforce Diversity.* [San Francisco?]: International Game Developers Association, 2005.

"An Invaluable Pamphlet." *Photo-Era* 64 (April 1930), 218–19.

Irwin, Frederick T. *The Story of Sandwich Glass and Glass Workers.* Manchester, N.H.: Granite, 1926.

"Is This Really the End for Phoebe?" *Evergreen Review* 11 (October 1967), 39

Ito, Masami. *Broadcasting in Japan.* London: Routledge, 1978.

"It's Too Late for Me and Archie to Change." *Life,* November 19, 1971, 62–70.

Ives, F. E. "The Japanese Magic Mirror." *Journal of the Franklin Institute* 125 (January 1888), 24–28.

Ivory, Melvin. "The Drug Store Finisher." *American Photography* 29 (February 1929), 84–88.

Jackson, Brinckerhoff. "A Führer Comes to Liechtenstein." *Harper's,* March 1935, 298–310.

Jackson, Harry G. *On a Fast Streamliner: Fun from New York to Frisco.* Chicago: T. W. Jackson, 1937.

Jackson, Joshilyn. *The Girl Who Stopped Swimming.* New York: Grand Central, 2008.

Jackson, Rosemary. *Fantasy: The Literature of Subversion.* London: Methuen, 1981.

Jacobs, Charles Fenno. "Getting Results with Color." *American Photography* 29 (September 1935), 560–64.

Jacobs, Raymond. "Ballet on 8th Avenue." *Art Photography* 7 (May 1956), 30–33.

Jacobs, Sally. "A Woman, Her Men, and a Mystery." *Boston Sunday Globe,* July 2, 2006, 1, A18.

Jaeger, Anne-Celine. *Image Makers, Image Takers.* London: Thames & Hudson, 2007.

James, Christopher. *The Book of Alternative Photographic Processes*. Albany: Delmar, 2002.

James, M. R. *Casting the Runes and Other Ghost Stories*. Ed. Michael Chabon. Oxford: Oxford Univ. Press, 2002.

———. *Ghost Stories*. London: Arnold, 1970.

James, William. *Principles of Psychology*. 2 vols. New York: Holt, 1890.

James I, King of England. *Daemongologie*. [1597] Ed. G. B. Harrison. 1924. Reprint, San Diego: Book Tree, 2002.

Jantzen Knitting Mills. "Sun-Suit." *Saturday Evening Post*, June 22, 1929, 98–99.

Jarrett, Derek. *The Sleep of Reason: Fantasy and Reality from the Victorian Age to the First World War*. London: Weidenfeld & Nicolson, 1988.

Jarricot, Jean. *La radiesthésie*. Paris: Grou-Radenez, 1959.

Jensen, Homer. "Will the Miniature Survive the Candid Camera Craze? Yes." *Popular Photography* 1 (August 1937), 33, 84–85.

Jewett, Sarah Orne. *The Country of the Pointed Firs*. [1896] Garden City, N.Y.: Doubleday, 1956.

Johnson, Caleb. "Lindbergh: How He Does It." *Popular Science* 112 (April 1928), 1–5.

Johnson, Clifton. *Highways and Byways of New England*. New York: Macmillan, 1915.

———. *Highways and Byways of the South*. New York: Macmillan, 1904.

Johnson, F. Roy. *Supernaturals: Among Carolina Folk and Their Neighbors*. Murfreesboro, N.C.: Johnson, 1974.

Johnson, George. "Automatic Switch Quiets Radio When Phone Is Used." *Popular Science Monthly* 122 (June 1933), 53.

Johnson, Kim K. P., and Sharron J. Lennon, eds. *Appearance and Power*. Oxford: Berg, 1999.

Johnson, Lynn Staley. *The Shepheardes Calendar: An Introduction*. University Park: Pennsylvania State Univ. Press, 1990.

Johnson, Stanley. "Midget All-Wave Receiver Easily Built at Low Cost." *Popular Science* 130 (January 1937), 58–59, 121.

Johnson, Walter. *Folk-Memory; or, The Continuity of British Archaeology*. Oxford: Clarendon Press, 1908.

Jones, Diana Wynne. *Howl's Moving Castle*. New York: Greenwillow, 1986.

Jones, Stephen. *Drifting: Being the Author's Account of His Voyages in Dooryards, Alleys, Bayous, Millraces, Swamps, Sumps, Rivers, Creeks, Canals, Lakes, Bays & Open Sewers about the Historic Lands of New Orleans, Valley of Swans, Cape May, Yorktown, Jamestown, Mystic, Noank, and Westerly, Rhode Island*. New York: Macmillan, 1971.

———. *Working Thin Waters: Conversations with Captain Lawrence H. Malloy, Jr.* Hanover, N.H.: Univ. Press of New England, 2001.

Jones, Tristan. *A Boyhood at Sea*. [1982] New York: Sheridan, 1996.

Jordan, Franklin Ingalls. *Photographic Enlarging*. Boston: American Photographic Publishing, 1945.

Joshi, S. T. *The Modern Weird Tale*. Jefferson, N.C.: McFarland, 2001.

Jourdan, Albert. "Minicams versus Megacams." *American Photography* 29 (March 1935), 133–38.

———. "Two for a Quarter Telephoto and Magnifying Lenses." *Camera Craft* 42 (June 1935), 272–81.

Jung, Carl Gustav. *Collected Works*. 15 vols. Princeton: Princeton Univ. Press, 1976.

Jung, Michael. *Sabotage unter Wasser.* Hamburg: Mittler, 2004.

Kahn, Ashley, Holly George-Warren, and Shawn Dahl, eds. *Rolling Stone: The Seventies.* Boston: Little, Brown, 1998.

Kahn, Douglas. "Track Organology," *October* 55 (Winter 1990), 67–78.

Kahn, Douglas, and Gregory Whitehead, eds. *Wireless Imagination: Sound, Radio, and the Avant-Garde.* Cambridge, Mass.: MIT Press, 1992.

Kaiser, Susan B. *The Social Psychology of Clothing: Symbolic Appearances in Context.* [1985] Rev. ed. New York: Macmillan, 1990.

Kaplan, Alice Yaeger. *Reproductions of Banality: Fascism, Literature, and French Intellectual Life.* Minneapolis: Univ. of Minnesota Press, 1986.

Kaplan, Richard. "Underwater Honeymoon." *Coronet* 50 (August 1961), 89–97.

Karasek, Hellmuth. "Colour and Reality." *German Photographic Annual 1963,* 10–18.

Karetzky, Stephen. *Reading Research and Librarianship: A History and Analysis.* Westport, Conn.: Greenwood, 1982.

Kearney, Paul W. "How to Photograph Pets." *Popular Photography* 1 (July 1937), 11–12, 77.

Kegley, Ann K. *Genuine Individuals and Genuine Communities: A Roycean Public Philosophy.* Nashville: Vanderbilt Univ. Press, 1997.

Kelland, Clarence Budington. "Romance." *Saturday Evening Post,* September 13, 1930, 6–7, 83–89.

Kendall, John S. "Lafcadio Hearn in New Orleans." *Double-Dealer* 3 (May 1922), 234–42; (June 1922), 313–22.

Kendrick, Walter. *The Secret Museum: Pornography in Modern Culture.* Berkeley: Univ. of California Press, 1996.

Kennedy, David. "A Peter Pan of the Camera." *Photo-Era* 68 (January 1932), 28–32.

Kennedy, Kathleen, and Sharon Ullman, eds. *Sexual Borderlands: Constructing an American Sexual Past.* Columbus: Ohio State Univ. Press, 2003.

Kennelly, Arthur E. *Wireless Telegraphy and Wireless Telephony.* New York: Moffatt, 1909.

Kent, Maxwell. *A Detective in Kent: Landscape Clues to Discovery of Lost Seas.* London: John Lane, 1929.

Kenyon, J. Douglas, ed. *Forbidden History: Prehistoric Technologies, Extraterrestrial Intervention, and the Suppressed Origins of Civilization.* Rochester, Vt.: Bear, 2005.

Keppler, Victor. "Color for the Amateur." *Popular Photography* 4 (February 1939), 10–11, 82–85.

Kerr, Howard, John W. Crowley, and Charles L. Crow, eds. *The Haunted Dusk: American Supernatural Fiction, 1820–1920.* Athens: Univ. of Georgia Press, 1983.

Kett, Joseph F. *Rites of Passage: Adolescence in America: 1790 to the Present.* New York: Basic Books, 1977.

Kheifets, Leeka, et al. "Public Health Impact of Extremely Low-Frequency Electromagnetic Fields." *Environmental Health Perspectives* 114 (June 2006), 1532–37.

Kidwell, Claudia B. *Women's Bathing and Swimming Costume in the United States.* Washington, D.C.: Smithsonian Institution Press, 1968.

Kidwell, Claudia B., and Margaret C. Christman. *Suiting Everyone: The Democratization of Clothing in America.* Washington, D.C.: Smithsonian Institution Press, 1974.

Kidwell, Claudia B., and Valier Steele, eds. *Men and Women: Dressing the Part.* Washington, D.C.: Smithsonian Institution Press, 1989.

Kiley, David. "Starbuck Retro Logo." *Business Week,* April 11, 2008, 89.

King, Charles. *Conquering Corps Badge and Other Stories.* Milwaukee: Rhoades, 1902.

King, Grace. *Creole Families of New Orleans*. New York: Macmillan, 1921.
———. *New Orleans: The Place and the People*. New Orleans: Graham, 1905.
King, Laurie R. *Touchstone*. New York: Random House, 2007.
Kinney, Jack. *Walt Disney and Assorted Other Characters: An Unauthorized Account of the Early Years at Disney*. New York: Harmony, 1988.
Kinnie, Wayne. "Little Ones Out of Big Ones." *Modern Sunbathing* 26 (April 1956), 18, 40.
Kinzie, Philip A. *Crystal Radio: History, Fundamentals, and Design*. New York: Xtal Set Society, 1996.
Kipling, Rudyard. *Plain Tales from the Hills*. [1888] London: Macmillan, 1904.
———. *Rewards and Fairies*. London: Macmillan, 1910.
Kircher, Athanasius. *Magnues sive de arte magnetica*. Rome: Grignani, 1641.
Kirk, Elizabeth D. "'I Would Rather Have Written in Elvish': Language, Fiction and *The Lord of the Rings*." *Novel* 5 (Fall 1971), 5–18.
Kirk, Robert. *Secret Commonwealth*. [1691] Edinburgh, 1815.
Kirland, Wallace W. "Go to Guatemala for Color." *Popular Photography* 5 (September 1939), 32–33, 92.
Klessig, L. W. *The ELF Odyssey: National Security versus Environmental Protection*. Boulder, Colo.: Westview, 1980.
Klitgaard, Robert E. *The Decline of the Best? An Analysis of the Relationships between Declining Enrollments, Ph.D. Production, and Research*. Cambridge, Mass.: Harvard Univ. Kennedy School of Government, 1979.
Knight, Arthur. *The Liveliest Art: A Panoramic History of the Movies*. New York: Macmillan, 1957.
Knoblauch, Hubert. *Die Welt der Wünschelrutengänger und Pendler: Erkundungen einer verborgenen Wirklichkeit*. Frankfurt: Campus, 1991.
Knowles, David, and J. K. S. St. Joseph. *Monastic Sites from the Air*. Cambridge: Cambridge Univ. Press, 1952.
Knowlton, Evelyn H. *Pepperell's Progress*. Cambridge, Mass.: Harvard Univ. Press, 1948.
Knudsen, A. A. "Remedies for Electrolysis." *Cassier's Magazine* 30 (August 1906), 337–42.
Koch, Adolf. "Die Wahrheit über die Berliner Gruppen für freie Körperkultur." *Junge Menschen* 5 (1924), 35–42.
Koch, Clarence. "P. H. Oelman and the Feminine Ideal." *Figure Photography* 11 [1956?], 40–44.
"Kodak Retina." *American Photography* 29 (August 1935), adv. 31.
"Kodak Retina: Speedy." *American Photography* 29 (July 1935), adv. 31.
König, René. *Menschheit auf dem Laufsteg: Die Mode im Zivilisationsprozess*. Munich: Carl Hanser, 1985.
Korman, Murray. "The Technique of Glamour Photography." *Camera Classic: The Magazine of Beauty* 1 (June 1939), 10–13, 59.
Koszarski, Richard. *An Evening's Entertainment: The Age of the Silent Feature Picture, 1915–1928*. Berkeley: Univ. of California Press, 1994.
Kuznets, Lois Rostow. *When Toys Come Alive: Narratives of Animation, Metamorphosis, and Development*. New Haven: Yale Univ. Press, 1994.
Labi, Nadya. "My Harlequin Novel." *Boston Sunday Globe*, July 16, 2006, E10.
Lahue, Kalton C., and Joseph A. Bailey. *Glass, Brass, and Chrome: The American 35mm Miniature Camera*. Norman: Univ. of Oklahoma Press, 1972.
Lambert, John S., ed. *New Prometheans: Readings for the Future*. New York: Harper & Row, 1973.

Lancaster, Bill. *The Department Store: A Social History.* Leicester: Leicester Univ. Press, 1995.

"Land in the Lens." *Flair* 1 (June 1950), 18–27.

"Landmark II: Equal Rights." *Life,* June 26, 1964, 4.

Lane, Alfred P. "Modernizing the Old Radio Set." *Popular Science* 116 (February 1930), 69.

———. "New Kit Sets for the Radio Builder." *Popular Science* 116 (January 1930), 68–69.

———. "New Tubes Increase Battery Set's Power." *Popular Science* 117 (October 1930), 72–73.

———. "Why Loudspeaker Foils Experts." *Popular Science* 117 (September 1930), 69.

Lane, Robert Edwards. *The Loss of Happiness in Market Democracies.* New Haven: Yale Univ. Press, 2000.

Lang, Andrew. *The Book of Dreams and Ghosts.* London: Longmans, Green, 1897.

Lang, Kurt, and Gladys Engel Lang. *Politics and Television.* Chicago: Quadrangle, 1968.

Langdon-Davies, John. *Lady Godiva: The Future of Nakedness.* New York: Harper, 1928.

Lange, Dorothea. "Photographing the Familiar." *Aperture* 1 (Summer 1952), 4–15.

Langer, Ellen J., Richard S. Bashner, and Benzion Chanowitz. "Decreasing Prejudice by Increasing Discrimination." *Journal of Pesonality and Social Psychology* 49 (Spring 1985), 113–20.

Langeweische, Wolfgang. "How to Fix Your Private Climate." *House Beautiful,* October 1949, 151.

Langlois, Judith H., et al. "Maxims or Myths of Beauty." *Psychological Bulletin* 126 (May 2000), 390–423.

Lasers and Light: Readings from Scientific American. San Francisco: Freeman, 1969.

Lash, Scott, and John Urry. *The End of Organized Capitalism.* Madison: Univ. of Wisconsin Press, 1988.

Laughlin, Clarence John. "American Fantastica." *Saturday Book* 26 (1966), 48–67.

———. "Backgrounds and Models." *Art Photography* 7 (April 1956), 32–35; (May 1956), 34–38, 47.

———. *Clarence John Laughlin.* Text by Henry Holmes Smith. Tucson: Center for Creative Photography, Univ. of Arizona, 1979.

———. *Clarence John Laughlin: The Personal Eye.* Philadelphia: Philadelphia Museum of Art, 1973. 61 pp., containing captions for the exhibition.

———. *Clarence John Laughlin: The Personal Eye.* Intro. Jonathan Williams. Stories by Lafcadio Hearn. Philadelphia: Philadelphia Museum of Art/Aperture, 1973. Exhibition catalog.

———. "The Era of Sentiment and Splendour." *Life,* October 24, 1960, 105–14.

———. *Ghosts along the Mississippi: An Essay in the Poetic Interpretation of Louisiana's Plantation Architecture.* [1948] New York: Bonanza, 1961.

———. "Gone Are the Years." *Coronet* 37 (March 1955), 51–58.

———. "Henry Moore and the Exploration of Space." *Figure Photography* 11 [1956?], 57.

———. "Images of the Lost." *British Journal of Photography Annual 1967.* London: Greenwood, 1967.

———. "Surfaces in Design." *Print* 12 (September/October 1958), 37–38.

———. "Surrealism in New Orleans." *Harper's Bazaar,* February 1941, 63–65, 113.

———. "The Tree and the Camera." *Saturday Book* 15 (1955), 197–204.

———. "Why?" *Modern Photography* 25 (August 1961), 60–65, 86–87.

Laughlin, Clarence John, and David L. Cohn. *New Orleans and Its Living Past.* Boston: Houghton, Mifflin, 1941.

"Laughlin's Enigmatic Lost World." *Photography Year 1975.* New York: Time-Life, 1975.

Laughton, Charles. *Tell Me a Story, an Anthology.* New York: McGraw-Hill, 1957.

Lauwers-Rech, Magda. *Nazi Germany and the American Germanists: A Study of Periodicals, 1930–1945.* New York: Lang, 1995.

Lawrence, D. H. *Studies in Classic American Literature.* New York: Viking, 1923.

Lawrence, John H. "Clarence John Laughlin: His First Book." *Historic New Orleans Collection Quarterly* 15 (Winter 1997), 8–9.

Lawrence, John H., and Patricia Brady, eds. *Haunter of Ruins: The Photography of Clarence John Laughlin.* Boston: Little, Brown, 1997.

Lea, Homer. *The Valor of Ignorance.* [1909] New York: Harper, 1942.

Leahy, Michael. "Naked in America." *Washington Post Magazine,* November 2, 2003, 16–21, 25–32.

Leather, John. *Clinker Boatbuilding.* London: Coles, 1973.

Leavis, Frank Raymond. *The Common Pursuit.* [1952] Harmondsworth: Penguin, 1962.

Lee, Ruth Webb. *Sandwich Glass: The History of the Boston & Sandwich Glass Company.* Framingham, Mass.: Author, 1939.

Leese, John S. "Shop Recipes." *Model Craftsman* 5 (March 1937), 35, 62.

Leff, Leonard J., and Jerold L. Simmons. *The Dame in the Kimono: Hollywood, Censorship, and the Production Code from the 1920s to the 1960s.* New York: Grove Weidenfeld, 1990.

Legman, Gershon. *The Horn Book: Studies in Erotic Folklore and Bibliography.* New Hyde Park, N.Y.: University Books, 1964.

———. *Rationale of the Dirty Joke: An Analysis of Sexual Humor.* 2 vols. New York: Grove, 1968–75.

Le Guin, Ursula K. *The Farthest Shore.* [1972] New York: Simon & Schuster, 2001.

Lehmann, Ulrich. *Tigersprung: Fashion in Modernity.* Cambridge, Mass.: MIT Press, 2000.

Leibovitz, Annie. "Let the Games Begin." *Vanity Fair,* May 1996, 125–59.

"Leica: The Original Miniature Camera." *Minicam* 1 (September 1937), 5.

Leicht, Hans Dieter. *Wilhelm Conrad Rontgen.* Munich: Ehrenwirth, 1994.

Leighten, Patricia. "Clarence John Laughlin: The Art and Thought of an American Surrealist." *History of Photography* 12 (April/June 1988), 129–46.

———. "Critical Attitudes toward Overtly Manipulated Photography in the 20th Century." Pts. 1 and 2. *Art Journal* 37 (Winter 1977/78), 133–38; (Summer 1978), 113–21.

Leith, Valery. *The Company of Glass.* New York: Random House, 1999.

Leitz, Inc. "Cat's Eye Leica." *American Photography* 29 (August 1935), adv. 7.

Leprohon, Pierre. *L'exotisme et le cinema: Les "chasseurs d'image" à la conquête du monde.* Paris: Susse, 1945.

Lesy, Michael. "Fame and Fortune: A Snapshot Chronicle." *Afterimage* 5 (October 1977), 17–18.

———. *Real Life: Louisville in the Twenties.* New York: Pantheon, 1976.

———. *Time Frame: The Meaning of Family Pictures.* New York: Pantheon, 1980.

———. *Wisconsin Death Trip.* New York: Pantheon, 1973.

Lethem, Jonathan. "Brando's Last Stand." *Rolling Stone,* May 18–June 1, 2006, 100.

Lewandowski, Gary, Arthur Aron, and Julie Gee. "Personality Goes a Long Way: The Malleability of Opposite-Sex Physical Attractiveness." *Personal Relationships* 14 (December 2007), 571–85.

Lewinski, Jorge. *The Naked and the Nude: A History of Nude Photography.* London: Guild, 1987.

Lewis, C. S. *The Screwtape Letters.* New York: Macmillan, 1961.

Lewis, Richard Warren. "Those Swinging Beach Movies." *Saturday Evening Post,* July 31, 1965, 83–87.

Lewis, Sinclair. *It Can't Happen Here.* New York: Collier, 1935.

Lewis, Thomas S. W. *Empire of the Air: The Men Who Made Radio.* New York: HarperCollins, 1991.

Liboff, A. R., et al. "Time Varying Magnetic Fields: Effect on DNA Synthesis." *Science,* February 24, 1984, 818–20.

"Life Spends a Day with Sidney Skolsky." *Life,* May 3, 1943, 102–5.

Lincoln, Joseph. *Cy Whittaker's Place.* New York: Grosset & Dunlap, 1908.

Lindbergh, Anne Morrow. *Gift from the Sea.* [1955] New York: Random House, 1975.

Lindsay, Vachel. *The Art of the Moving Picture.* New York: Macmillan, 1915.

———. *The Congo and Other Poems.* New York: Macmillan, 1915.

Link, Kelly. *Magic for Beginners.* New York: Harcourt, 2005.

Linke, Uli. *Blood and Nation: The European Aesthetics of Race.* Philadelphia: Univ. of Pennsylvania Press, 1999.

———. *German Bodies: Race and Representation after Hitler.* London: Routledge, 1999.

Lippard, Lucy. *Pop Art.* New York: Praeger, 1966.

Lissaman, Reginald O. "Low-Cost Enlarging Camera: Built to Suit Your Own Needs." *Popular Science* 130 (January 1937), 82, 84, 96.

Litzel, Otto. *Darkroom Magic.* [1967] Rev. ed. Garden City, N.Y.: Amphoto, 1975.

Loengard, John. "Fortress on 78th Street." *Life,* November 19, 1971, 24–37.

Lofton, Cripple Clarence. "I Don't Know." Chicago: Vocalion, 1935.

———. "Strut That Thing." Chicago: Vocalion, 1935.

Logan, Ian. *Classy Chassy.* New York: A & W Visual Library, 1977.

Lohse, Remie. "Beach." *Popular Photography* 5 (August 1939), 46–47.

———. *The Miniature Camera in Professional Hands.* New York: Studio, 1939.

———. "Rhythm and Repose." *Minicam* 1 (September 1937), 35.

———. *Rhythm and Repose.* New York: Knopf, 1937.

Lomax, Alan. *Mister Jelly Roll: The Fortunes of Jelly Roll Morton, New Orleans Creole and "Inventor of Jazz."* [1950] Berkeley: Univ. of California Press, 2001.

Longfellow, Henry Wadsworth. *Poetical Works.* London: Collins, 1899.

"'Longplay Holders' for the Rollei." *International Photo Technik* 11 (Summer 1965), 189.

"Look—Better Pictures!" *Popular Photography* 5 (August 1939), 75.

Look at America: The Country You Know, and Don't Know. By the editors of *Look.* Boston: Houghton Mifflin, 1946.

Lord, M. G. *Forever Barbie: The Unauthorized Biography of a Real Doll.* New York: Morrow, 1994.

Lorenz, Richard. *Imogen Cunningham: Ideas without End: A Life in Photographs.* San Francisco: Chronicle, 1993.

Lovecraft, H. P. *At the Mountains of Madness and Other Tales of Terror.* New York: Ballantine, 1971.

———. *The Case of Charles Dexter Ward.* [1927] New York: Ballantine, 1971.

———. *The Colour Out of Space.* New York: Harcourt, 1978.

———. *The Doom That Came to Sarnath.* New York: Ballantine, 1971.

———. *The Horror in the Museum and Other Revisions.* New York: Ballantine, 1971.

———. *The Lurking Fear and Other Stories*. New York: Ballantine, 1971.

———. *Supernatural Horror in Literature*. [1945] Reprint, New York: Dover, 1973.

———. *The Tomb and Other Tales*. New York: Ballantine, 1970.

Low, Archibald. *Wireless Possibilities*. London: Kegan Paul, 1924.

Lowell, Amy. *East Wind*. Boston: Houghton Mifflin, 1926.

"Low Voltage Current May Cause Death." *Popular Science* 117 (July 1930), 37.

Luchesi, Aldo. "Barbarella: The World's Wildest Comic Book Heroine." *Ace* 10 (January 1967), 10–13, 68–69.

Lull, James, ed. *Popular Music and Communication*. London: Sage, 1987.

Lummer, Otto. *Contributions to Photographic Optics*. Trans. Silvanus P. Thompson. London: Macmillan, 1900.

Lyell, Anne Morse. *Nonquitt: A Summer Album, 1872–1985*. South Dartmouth, Mass.: Barekneed Publishers, 1987.

Lyell, Elizabeth Barrett. "The Barekneed Rocks." *Inside Outers* [1985], n.p.

Lynch, Kevin. *The Image of the City*. Cambridge, Mass.: MIT Press, 1960.

Lynn, Kenneth S. "Adulthood in American Literature." *Daedalus* 105 (Fall 1976), 49–60.

Lynn, Stuart M. *New Orleans*. New York: Hastings House, 1949.

Lyttelton, Adrian. "The 'Crisis of Bourgeois Society' and the Origins of Fascism." In *Fascist Italy and Nazi Germany: Comparisons and Contrasts*, ed. Richard Bessel, 12–22. Cambridge and New York: Cambridge University Press, 1996.

MacDonald, John D. *The Empty Copper Sea*. New York: Fawcett, 1978.

MacDonald, Scott. *A Critical Cinema 4: Interviews with Independent Filmmakers*. Berkeley: Univ. of California Press, 2005.

MacDougall, David. *The Corporeal Image: Film, Ethnolgraphy, and the Senses*. Princeton: Princeton Univ. Press, 2006.

Macfadden, Johnnie Lee. *Barefoot in Eden: The Macfadden Plan for Health, Charm, and Long-Lasting Youth*. Englewood Cliffs, N.J.: Prentice-Hall, 1962.

Macfadden, Mary Williamson. *Dumbbells and Carrot Strips: The Story of Bernarr Macfadden*. New York: Holt, 1953.

Machen, Arthur. *Autobiography*. London: Garnstone, 1974.

———. *The Hill of Dreams*. London: Grant Richards, 1907.

———. *The Shining Pyramid*. [1895] New York: Juniper, n.d.

———. *Tales of Horror and the Supernatural*. London: Baker, 1949.

Mack, Julian Ellis, and Miles J. Martin. *The Photographic Process*. New York: McGraw-Hill, 1939.

Mack, Phyllis. *Heart Religion in the British Enlightment: Gender and Emotion in Early Methodism*. Cambridge: Cambridge Univ. Press, 2008.

Mackail, J. W. *Classical Studies*. London: Murray, 1926.

MacKaye, Benton. "Appalachian Trail: A Guide to the Study of Nature." *Scientific Monthly* 17 (April 1932), 45–58.

———. "An Appalachian Trail: A Project in Regional Planning." *Journal of the American Institute of Architects* 9 (May 1921), 123–57.

———. *The New Exploration: A Philosophy of Regional Planning*. New York: Harcourt, 1928.

———. *A Project for an Appalachian Trail*. New York: American Institute of Architects, [1923?].

——— "Tennessee: Seed of a National Plan." *Survey Graphic* 22 (May 1933), 251–54, 293.

"Made in West Germany." *Modern Photography* 22 (October 1958), 115–30.

Maier, Michael. *Atalanta Fugiens: An Edition of the Fugues, Emblems and Epigrams*.

Ed. Hildemarie Streich. Trans. Joscelyn Godwin. Grand Rapids, Mich.: Phanes, 1989. Originally published as *Atalanta Fugiens: Bronnen van een Alchbemistisch Emblemboek*, ed. Helena Maria Elisabeth De Jong (Utrecht: Schotanus & Jens, 1965).

Malec, Alexander. *Extrapolasis.* New York: Doubleday, 1967.

Mallet, Ethel M. *First Steps in Theosophy.* London: Lotus Journal, 1905.

Mallet, Paul Henri. *Northern Antiquities.* Edinburgh: Stewart, 1809.

Maltin, Leonard. *Behind the Camera: The Cinematographer's Art.* New York: Signet, 1971.

Mander, Jerry. *Four Arguments for the Elimination of Television.* New York: Quill, 1978.

Mann, Arthur. *Yankee Reformers in an Urban Age: Social Reform in Boston, 1880 to 1900.* Cambridge, Mass.: Harvard Univ. Press, 1954.

Mann, Ludovic MacLellan. *Craftsmen's Measures in Prehistoric Times.* Glasgow: Mann, 1930.

———. *Earliest Glasgow: A Temple of the Moon.* Glasgow: Mann Publishing, 1938.

Mann, Sally. *Deep South.* New York: Bulfinch, 2005.

Mann, Thomas. *Mario and the Magician* [1930]. Trans. H. T. Lowe-Porter. New York: Knopf, 1931.

Mannheim, Alec. *The Retina Reflex Way: The Retina Reflex Photographer's Companion.* London: Focal, 1960.

———. *The Rollei Way: The Rolleiflex and Rolleicord Photographer's Companion.* London: Focal Press, 1955.

Mannheim, L. A. *The Rollei Way: The Rolleiflex and Rolleicord Photographer's Companion.* New York: Focal, 1951.

"Many Are the Possibilities." *International Photo Technik* 17 (Winter 1971), 2.

Marchand, Roland. *Advertising the American Dream: Making Way for Modernity, 1920–1940.* Berkeley: Univ. of California Press, 1985.

"Married to an Understanding Man." *Night and Day* 8 (March 1955), 22–23.

Marriott, Charles. *A Spanish Holiday.* London: Methuen, 1908.

Martignette, Charles G., and Louis K. Meisel. *The Great American Pin-Up.* New York: Taschen, 1996.

Martií-Ibáñez, Félix. *All the Wonders We Seek.* New York: Potter, 1963.

Martin, Peter J. *Sounds and Silence: Themes in the Sociology of Music.* Manchester: Manchester Univ. Press, 1993.

Martin, Robert E. "Electric Shocks: Do They Really Kill?" *Popular Science* 133 (July 1938), 44–45, 101.

———. "Home Movies: The 1930 Family Album." *Popular Science* 116 (January 1930), 26–27, 130.

———. "Most Famous Puppets." *Popular Science* 122 (June 1933), 20–22, 95.

———. "Mystery Cell Aids Television." *Popular Science* 117 (August 1930), 15–17, 119.

Martinez, Mario. *Lady's Men: The Story of World War II's Mystery Bomber and Her Crew.* Annapolis: Naval Institute Press, 1999.

Marty, Martin E. "Knowledge Elites and Counter-Elites." *Daedalus* 103 (Fall 1974), 104–9.

Mason, Van Wyck. *The Hong Kong Airbase Murders.* New York: Grosset & Dunlap, 1937.

Masters, R. E. L. *The Hidden World of Erotica: Forbidden Sexual Behaviour and Morality.* London: Lyrebird, 1973.

Mawer, A., and F. M. Stenton, eds. *Introduction to the Survey of English Place-Names.* Cambridge: Cambridge Univ. Press, 1924.

Maxwell, Donald. *A Detective in Kent: Landscape Clues to the Discovery of Lost Seas.* London: John Lane, 1929.

Maxwell, E. "Vertical Photo Enlarger." *Popular Science* 119 (March 1932), 43–46.

Mayer, Emil. *A Manual of Bromoil & Transfer.* Trans. Joseph M. Bing. Boston: American Photographic Publishing, 1927.

McCarthy, Joe. *Hurricane!* New York: American Heritage, 1969.

McCown, James. *Colors: Architecture in Detail.* Ed. Oscar Riere Ojeda. Photography by Paul Warchol. Gloucester, Mass.: Rockport, 2004.

McDermid, Val. *The Grave Tattoo.* New York: St. Martin's Press, 2007.

McDonagh, Edward C. "The Discharged Serviceman and His Family." *American Journal of Sociology* 51 (March 1946), 451–54.

McDonagh, Edward C., and Louise McDonagh. "War Anxieties of Soldiers and Their Wives." *Social Forces* 24 (December 1946), 195–200.

McDowell, Ernest R. *The P-40 Kittyhawk at War.* New York: Arco, 1968.

McFee, William. *Sailors of Fortune.* Garden City, N.Y.: Doubleday, 1935.

McGonigal, J. F. "'Sumpin' Has Gotta Be Done.'" *Photo-Era* 68 (January 1932), 32–36.

McGrath, Earl J. *Are Liberal Arts Colleges Becoming Professional Schools?* New York: Teachers College, Columbia Univ., 1958.

McIlvin, Robert K. "Filter Facts for the Beginner." *Popular Photography* 6 (March 1940), 54–55, 90–92.

McKay, Herbert C. *The Theory and Practice of Photography: Fundamentals.* Theory and Practice of Photography, 1. New York: New York Institute of Photography, n.d.

McKibben, Bill. *The Age of Missing Information.* New York: Random House, 1992.

McLuhan, Marshall. *Counter Blast.* New York: Harcourt, 1969.

——. *Understanding Media: The Extensions of Man.* [1964] Ed. Lewis H. Lapham. Cambridge, Mass.: MIT Press, 1994.

McLuhan, Marshall, and Quentin Fiore, *The Medium Is the Massage: An Inventory of Effects.* New York: Bantam, 1967.

McLuhan, Marshall, and Wilfred Watson. *From Cliché to Archetype.* New York: Viking, 1970.

McManigal, J. W. "Good Old Tripod." *American Photography* 29 (May 1935), 278–80.

Mead, Margaret. *Coming of Age in Samoa.* New York: Blue Ribbon, 1928.

——. *Male and Female.* [1949] New York: Mentor, 1955.

"Means to an End: The Pros and Cons: Large Format, Medium Format, 35mm." *International Photo Technik* 19 (Fall 1973), 9.

Mees, C. E. Kenneth. "The Modern Era in Photography." *Popular Photography* 5 (August 1939), 14–16, 76, 78.

——. *Photography.* New York: Macmillan, 1937.

Mellor, David, ed. *Germany: The New Photography, 1927–1933.* London: Arts Council, 1978.

Mencken, H. L. "An American Idealist." *American Mercury* 7 (May 1930), 124–25.

——. *The American Language: An Inquiry into the Development of English in the United States.* [1919, 4th rev. ed.]. New York: Knopf, 1937.

Menzel, Donald Howard. *Flying Saucers.* Cambridge, Mass.: Harvard Univ. Press, 1953.

Merivale, Patricia. *Pan the Goat-God: His Myth in Modern Times.* Cambridge, Mass.: Harvard Univ. Press, 1969.

Merrill, Frances. *Among the Nudists.* New York: Knopf, 1931.

Merrill, Frances, and Mason Merrill. *Nudism Comes to America.* New York: Knopf, 1932.

Metrios, Heinrich. "Outdoor Portraits." *Rolleigrafie* 2 (December 1968), 28–31.

Meyer-Hanno, Georg. "Photography in Film and TV Studios." *International Photo Technik* 18 (Winter 1972), 26–27, 60.

Mezzerow, Milton, and Bernard Wolfe. *Really the Blues.* New York: Random House, 1946.

"Michael Barrington Martin." *International Photo Technik* 17 (Fall 1971), 74–77, 80.

Michal, Thomas. *Surrealism and Architecture.* London: Routledge, 2005.

Michel, Aimé. *Flying Saucers and the Straight-Line Mystery.* New York: Criterion, 1958.

Michie, Archibald. *Flying Saucers.* New York: Vantage, 1957.

Middlebrook, Diana Wood. *Anne Sexton: A Biography.* Boston: Houghton, Mifflin, 1991.

Migne, Jacques Paul. *Encyclopédie théologique . . . Dictionnaire des sciences occultes.* 2 vols. Paris: Ateliers Catholiques, 1846.

Milgram, Stanley. "The Experience of Living in Cities." *Science,* March 13, 1970, 1461–68.

Millar, George. *Isabel and The Sea.* [1948] New York: Hippocrene, 1983.

Millaurd, A. *La créole: Operette.* [1875] Paris: Choundens, 1935.

Miller, D. A. *Place for Us: Essay on the Broadway Musical.* Cambridge, Mass.: Harvard Univ. Press, 1998.

Miller, Jane. "Stern Hedonism: The Pleasure of Clothes." *Raritan* 15 (Fall 1995), 136–43.

Miller, Perry. *American Thought: Civil War to World War I.* New York: Rinehart, 1954.

———. *Errand into the Wilderness.* New York: Harper, 1956.

———. *Life of the Mind in America: From the Revolution to the Civil War.* New York: Harcourt, 1965.

———. *The New England Mind: The Seventeenth Century.* New York: Macmillan, 1939.

Miller, Thomas H., and Wyatt Brummitt. *This Is Photography: Its Means and Ends.* Garden City, N.Y.: Garden City Publishing Co., 1945; Garden City, N.Y.: Doubleday, 1963.

Mills, C. Wright. *The Power Elite.* New York: Oxford Univ. Press, 1956.

Mills, John. *Letters of a Radio-Engineer to His Son.* New York: Harcourt, 1922.

Milne, A. A. *Winnie-the-Pooh.* [1926] New York: Dutton, 1954.

Mingione, Enzo. *Fragmented Societies: A Sociology of Economic Life beyond the Market Paradigm.* Oxford: Blackwell, 1991.

"Miniature Camera Work." *New Photo-Miniature* 18 (September 1935), 177–206.

"Miniature Reflex or Medium Format." *International Phototechnik* 11 (Fall 1965), 234–35.

"Minicam Rolleiflex Salon." *Minicam* 2 (February 1939), 42–49.

Minnaert, M. G. J. *Light and Color in the Outdoors.* Trans. Len Seymour. [1937] Rev. ed. New York: Springer, 1974.

Minter, Ben A. "Wilderness and the Wise Province: Benton MacKaye's Pragmatic Vision." *Philosophy & Geography* 4 (August 2001), 185–202.

"Mirror Gives Distance to Movie." *Popular Science* 117 (October 1930), 61.

Mitchell, John. *City of Revelation.* London: David McKay, 1972.

———. *The Flying Saucer Vision.* London: Sidgwick, 1967.

———. *The View over Atlantis.* London: Sago, 1969.

——. *The New View over Atlantis*. New York: Harper & Row, 1983.

Mitchell, Margaret. *Gone with the Wind*. New York: Macmillan, 1936.

Mitchell, S. Weir. *Lectures on Diseases of the Nervous System, Especially in Women*. Philadelphia: Lea, 1881.

——. *Rest in the Treatment of Nervous Disorders*. New York: Putnam, 1875.

——. *Wear and Tear, or Hints for the Overworked*. Philadelphia: Lippincott, 1871.

Moeller, Susan D. *Shooting War: Photography and the American Experience of Combat*. New York: Basic Books, 1989.

Moëssard, Paul. *Étude des lentilles et objectifs photographiques*. Paris: Gauthier-Villars, 1889.

——. *L'optique photographique*. Paris: Gauthier-Villars, 1898.

Mohler, Marvin F. "Construction of a Miniature Enlarger." *American Photography* 29 (April 1935), 254–57.

Moholy-Nagy, László. "Light: A Medium of Plastic Express." *Broom: An International Magazine of the Arts* 4 (March 1923), 224–25, 240–41, 283–84.

Mok, Michel. "The Talking Newspaper." *Popular Science* 117 (August 1930), 53–55, 116.

Molloy, John T. *Dress for Success*. New York: Warner, 1975.

"Monika Wegler." *International Photo Tecknik* 19 (Summer 1973), 8.

Montgomery Ward Company. *New 1957 Camera Shop*. Chicago: Montgomery Ward Co., 1957.

Moore, Alan. "Magic Afoot." *Arthur* 4 (May 2003), 17–35.

Moore, Annie E. "Shall We Banish the Fairies?" *Parents' Magazine* 5 (February 1930), 29, 53.

Moore, Richard S. *That Cunning Alphabet: Melville's Aesthetics of Nature*. Amsterdam: Rodopi, 1982.

Moore, Ruth. *Candlemas Bay*. New York: Morrow, 1950.

——. *Speak to the Winds*. New York: Morrow, 1956.

Moore, William. *Masonic Temples: Freemasonry, Ritual Architecture, and Masculine Archetypes*. Knoxville: Univ. of Tennessee Press, 2006.

Moosleitner, Horst. "Underwater Photography in the Ideal Format." *International Photo Technik* 12 (Winter 1976), 34–39.

Moreau-Vauthier, Charles. *La peinture: Les divers procédés, les maladies des couleurs, les faux tableaux*. Paris: Hachette, 1913.

Morgan, F. Allan. "Panorama Pictures with the Rolleiflex." *American Photography* 29 (September 1935), 587–90.

Morgan, T. B. "World's Most Beautiful Woman." *Redbook,* August 1961, 38–39, 67–68.

Morgan, Thomas B. *Italian Physical Culture Demonstration*. New York: Macfadden, 1932.

Morgan, Willard D., Henry M. Lester, et al. *Leica Manual: A Manual for the Amateur and Professional Covering the Field of Miniature Camera Photography*. New York: Morgan and Lester, 1935.

——. *Leica Manual and Data Book*. New York: Morgan and Lester, 1955.

——. *Miniature Camera Work: Emphasizing the Entire Field of Photography with Modern Miniature Cameras*. New York: Morgan and Lester, 1938.

Morison, Samuel Eliot. *The Maritime History of Massachusetts, 1783–1860*. Cambridge, Mass.: Harvard Univ. Press, 1921.

Morris, Desmond. *Body Watching*. New York: Crown, 1985.

——. *The Naked Ape*. New York: McGraw-Hill, 1967.

Morris, Hugh. *Facts about Nudism*. New York: Padell, 1935.

Morris, Lydia. *Dangerous Classes: The Underclass and Social Citizenship.* New York: Routledge, 1993.

Morris, Willie. *North toward Home.* Boston: Houghton Mifflin, 1967.

Morrison, Tony. *Pathways to the Gods.* London: Michael Russell, 1978.

Morse, Samuel. "Conducting Power and Galvanic Power of the Earth." *Silliman's Journal* 35 (July 1839), 253–67.

Mortensen, William. "About the Paper Negative." *Camera Craft* 41 (September 1934), 409–17.

——. "Essay on Creative Pictorialism." *Camera Craft* 41 (July 1934), 309–15.

——. "Fallacies of 'Pure Photography.'" *Camera Craft* 41 (June 1934), 257–63.

——. *Flash in Modern Photography.* San Francisco: Camera Craft, 1947.

——. "Glorifying the American Snapshot." *Camera Craft* 42 (February 1935), 65–73.

——. *The Model: A Book on the Problems of Posing.* San Francisco: Camera Craft, 1948.

——. *Monsters and Madonnas: A Book of Methods.* San Francisco: Camera Craft, 1936.

——. "More about Projection Control." *Camera Craft* 41 (January 1934), 29–35.

——. *Mortensen on the Negative.* [1940] New York: Simon & Schuster, 1947.

——. *The New Projection Control.* [1940] San Francisco: Camera Craft, 1942.

——. "Notes on the Miniature Camera." *Camera Craft* 41 (August 1934), 359–67.

——. "Notes on the Miniature Camera: Outdoor Portraiture." *Camera Craft* 42 (January 1935), 3–9.

——. *Outdoor Portraiture.* San Francisco: Camera Craft, 1940.

——. *Pictorial Lighting.* San Francisco: Camera Craft, 1937; 2nd ed., 1947.

——. *Print Finishing.* San Francisco: Camera Craft, 1942.

——. *The Texture Screen.* Newport Beach: Jay Curtis Publications, 1954.

——. *Venus and Vulcan.* San Francisco: Camera Craft, 1934.

Mortensen, William, and George Dunham. *How to Pose the Model.* New York: Ziff-Davis, 1956.

"Most Photogenic TV Women." *US Camera* 14 (May 1951), 38–39.

Mout, L. W. "An Exposure Calculator." *American Photography* 29 (January 1935), 34–36.

Müller, Florence. *Art and Fashion.* Trans. Anne Rubin. London: Thames & Hudson, 2000.

Muller, Herbert J. "Education for the Future." *American Scholar* 41 (Summer 1972), 377–88.

Mulock, Miss. *The Adventures of a Brownie as Told to My Child.* Boston: Page, 1896.

Mulvey, Laura. *Visual and Other Pleasures.* Bloomington: Indiana Univ. Press, 1989.

Mumford, Lewis. *The Culture of Cities.* [1938] New York: Harcourt, 1970.

Münsterberg, Hugo. *The Photoplay: A Psychological Study.* New York: D. Appleton, 1916.

Murphy, Thomas D. *British Highways and Byways from a Motor Car.* Boston: Page, 1908.

——. *New England Highways and Byways from a Motor Car.* Boston: Page, 1924.

Murrow, Edward R. "Newsroom Resources." [Chicago?]: Radio-Television News Directors Association, n.d.

Nabokov, Vladimir. *Lolita.* New York: Random House, 1955.

Nadar, Félix. *Quand j'étais photographe.* Paris: Seuil, 1994.

Nasser, Driss. "Exotica: The Women of Other Countries." *International Photo Technik* 19 (Spring 1973), 62–64.

National Geographic Society. *Swimsuits: 100 Years of Pictures.* Washington, D.C.: National Geographic Society, 2002.

Naumann, Helmut. "Control of Foreground or Background Sharpness through Calculation." *International Photo Technik* 22 (Winter 1976), 22–23.

The Nazification of Art: Art, Design, Music, Architecture and Film in the Third Reich. Ed. Brandon Taylor and Wilfried van der Will. Winchester, N.H.: Winchester Press, 1990.

Nelson, Buck. *My Trip to Mars, the Moon, and Venus.* Mountain View, Mo.: Author, 1956.

Nelson, Clifford A. *Natural Color Film: What It Is and How to Use It: A Work Devoted to the Technique and Handling of "Kodachrome" in Motion Picture and Still Photography.* Intro. Herbert C. McKay. New York: Galleon, 1937.

Nelson, Romeo. "Gettin' Dirty Just Shakin' That Thing." Chicago: Vocalion, 1929.

Nemeth, Joszef. *Girl in Forest. International Photo Technik* 17 (Winter 1971), 78.

———. *Glimpse. International Photo Technik* 11 (Fall 1965), 157.

Nesmith, Jeff. "Biotech: When Treatment Becomes Enhancement." *Quincy (Mass.) Patriot Ledger,* June 17, 2006, 16.

Nevins, Allan. "What's the Matter with History?" *Saturday Review of Literature* 15 (February 4, 1939), 3–4, 16.

"New Budget-Priced Linhof Compact Enlarger." *International Photo Technik* 22 (Summer 1976), 37.

Newcombe, H. S. *The Twin-Lens Camera Companion.* New York: Focal, 1948.

New England Short Stories. 2 vols. Boston: Pomfret, 1934.

Newhall, Beaumont. *History of Photography from 1839 to the Present Day.* [1949] 5th ed. New York: Museum of Modern Art, 1982.

———. *Photography, 1839–1937.* New York: Museum of Modern Art, 1937.

———. "Photography as Art in America." *Perspectives USA* 15 (Spring 1956), 122–33.

Newhall, Nancy. *Ansel Adams: The Eloquent Light.* San Francisco: Sierra Club, 1964.

"New Meter." *Photo-Era* 56 (June 1931), n.p.

"New Movie Rage." *Night and Day* 11 (September 1959), 28–29.

"New Orleans in Transition." *New England Magazine* 36 (April 1907), 230–44.

"New Rolleiflex Camera." *Photo-Era* 63 (November 1929), 281–82.

Newton, Helmut. *Pages from the Glossies: Facsimiles, 1956–1998.* Zurich: Scalo, 1998.

Newton, Isaac. *Opticks.* [1730] Ed. I. Bernard Cohen. New York: Dover, 1952.

New York Institute of Photography. *The Theory and Practice of Photography.* 32 vols. New York: New York Institute of Photography, n.d.

"Next Business Generation." *Fortune,* August 1945, 185–90.

Nichols, John. "Double Box Speeds Up Photo Printing." *Popular Science* 133 (July 1938), 99.

Nichols, Nick. "Cartoons and Camera." *Art and Camera* 1 (July 1951), 35–37, 46.

The Nineteen Thirties: The Making of the "The New Man." Ed. Jean Clair. Ottawa: National Gallery of Canada, 2008.

Nix, Garth. *Sabriel.* New York: HarperCollins, 1995.

Noam, Eli. *Television in Europe.* New York: Oxford Univ. Press, 1991.

Nobile, Philip. "Incest: The Last Taboo." *Penthouse,* December 1977, 116–18, 126, 157–58.

Norris, Thaddeus. "Negro Superstitions." *Lippincott's Magazine* 6 (July 1870), 90–95.

Norton, Bryan G. *Why Preserve Natural Variety?* Princeton: Princeton Univ. Press, 1987.

"Nude." *International Photo Technik* 17 (Summer 1971), 12–13.

"Nude Look in Paree." *Frolic* 5 (June 1956), 37–40.

"Nude Look Takes Over: Exposed 67." *Saturday Evening Post,* June 3, 1967, 32–34.

"Nudes from Other Lands." *Art Photography* 5 (August 1953), 28–31.

"Nude with an Amateur Flair." *International Photo Technik* 22 (Winter 1976), 53–56.

Nutting, Wallace. *Massachusetts Beautiful.* Framingham, Mass.: Old America, 1923.

———. *Photographic Art Secrets.* New York: Dodd, Mead, 1927.

Oakley, Ann. *Sex, Gender, and Society.* New York: Harper, 1972.

O'Brian, Patrick. *The Ionian Mission.* New York: Norton, 1981.

O'Brien, Brian. "Voodoo Queen of New Orleans." *For Men Only* 3 (November 1956), 13–16, 58, 60–61.

O'Brien, Edward J., and John Cournos, eds. *Best British Short Stories of 1923.* Boston: Small, Maynard, 1923.

O'Donoghue, Michael. "The Adventures of Phoebe Zeitgeist: Lethal Women." *Evergreen Review* 11 (October 1967), 35–38.

———. "Binders Keepers." *Evergreen Review* 13 (January 1969), 33–40.

O'Leary, Michael D. "Disney Goes to War." *Air Classics* 32 (May 1996), 40–51.

"On a Taboo Subject." *Escapade* 8 (February 1963), 20–23, 67.

"One Model plus One Hat Equals Eight Exposures." *International Photo Technik* 11 (Spring 1965), 100–101.

Opie, Peter. "The Tentacles of Tradition." *Folklore* 74 (Winter 1963), 507–26.

Oppenheim, E. Phillips. *Nicholas Goade, Detective.* Boston: Little, Brown, 1929.

Oringer, Hal. "The Way-Out Film." *US Camera* 31 (September 1968), 56–57.

O'Sullivan, Maurice. *Twenty Years A-Growing.* Trans. Moya Llewelyn Davies and George Thomson. Introductory note by E. M. Forster. London: Oxford Univ. Press, 1933.

Otter, Chris. *The Victorian Eye: A Political History of Light and Vision in Britain, 1800–1910.* Chicago: Univ. of Chicago Press, 2008.

Ottman, Viktor. *Picturesque Germany.* Munich: Carl Gerber, 1922.

"Out-of-Door Girl with Camera." *Wohelo: A Magazine for Girls* 2 (May 1915), 7–9.

Owen, Alex. "'Borderland Forms': Arthur Conan Doyle, Albion's Daughters, and the Politics of the Cottingley Fairies." *History Workshop Journal* 38 (Autumn 1994), 49–85.

———. *The Place of Enchantment: British Occultism and the Culture of the Modern.* Chicago: Univ. of Chicago Press, 2004.

Packard, Winthrop. *Wild Pastures.* Boston: Small, Maynard, 1909.

Paglia, Camille. *Sexual Personae: Art and Decadence from Nefertiti to Emily Dickinson.* New York: Vintage, 1991.

Palme, A. "What Camera?" *American Photography* 29 (August 1935), 463–70.

Palmer, William A. "Spider Webs to Order." *Camera Craft* 42 (January 1935), 32–34.

Papini, Giovanni. *Storia di un' Amicizia.* Florence: Vallelcchi, 1966.

Paramount Pictures. "The Magic Carpet That Takes You Everywhere!" *Saturday Evening Post,* September 13, 1930, 55.

Parker, Ian. *Rollei T. L. R.: The History: The Complete Book on the Origins of Twin-Lens Photography.* Jersey, U.K.: Club Rollei, 1992.

Parker, John. "Needleholing with Your Kodak." *Camera* 44 (June 1932), 441–45.

Parker, K. J. *Devices and Desires.* London: London: Little, Brown, 2005.

———. *Evil for Evil.* London: Little, Brown, 2006.

Parks, Gordon. "Two Fashion Photographs." *Popular Photography Color Annual 1957,* 88–89.

Parmelee, Maurice. *Nudism in Modern Life: The New Gymnosophy.* Garden City, N.Y.: Garden City Publishing Co., 1931.

Parrish, Anne. *The Methodist Faun.* New York: Harper, 1929.

Partridge, Eric. *A Charm of Words.* New York: Macmillan, 1960.

Passow, A. Harry, ed. *The Gifted and the Talented: Their Education and Development: The Seventy-eighth Yearbook of the National Society for the Study of Education.* Chicago: Univ. of Chicago Press, 1979.

Paton, Priscilla. *Abandoned New England: Landscape in the Works of Homer, Frost, Hopper, Wyeth, and Bishop.* Hanover, N.H.: Univ. Press of New England, 2003.

Paugam, Serge. *La société française et ses pauvres.* Paris: Presses Univ. de France, 1993.

Pawek, Karl. "Women in Front of the Camera." *Rolleigrafie* 4 (June 1969), 32–34.

Peake, Mervyn. *Gormenghast.* [1967] New York: Random, 1976.

——. *Titus Groan.* [1946] New York: Random, 1977.

——. *Titus Alone.* [1959] New York: Random, 1976.

Pearce, Joseph Chilton. *Evolution's End: Claiming the Potential of Our Intelligence.* New York: Harper Collins, 1992.

Pearlman, Alec. *Rollei Handbook.* London: Fountain, 1954.

——. *Rollei Manual: The Complete Book of Twin-Lens Photography.* London: Fountain, 1953; 2nd ed., 1955; 3rd ed., 1957; 4th ed., 1960; 4th ed. rev., 1966; 5th ed., 1971.

Pearson, Ralph M. *How to See Modern Pictures.* [1925] New York: Dial, 1934.

Pedersen, Holger. *A Glance at the History of Linguistics with Particular Regard to the Historical Study of Phonology.* Trans. Caroline C. Henriksen. Philadelphia: Benjamin, 1983.

Peirce, Charles Sanders. *Values in a Universe of Chance: Selected Writings of Charles S. Peirce.* Ed. Philip P. Wiener. Garden City, N.Y.: Doubleday, 1958.

Penn, Irving. *A Career in Photography.* New York: Bulfinch, 1997.

——. "Jamaican Idyll." *Popular Photography Color Annual 1957,* 72–75.

——. *Still Life: Photographs, 1938–2000.* New York: Bulfinch, 2001.

Penn, Irving, and Diana Vreeland. *Inventive Paris Clothes, 1909–1939: A Photographic Essay.* New York: Viking, 1977.

Pennebaker, John Paul. "Lighting for Color." *Popular Photography* 5 (September 1939), 36–37, 88–90.

Pennick, Nigel, and Paul Devereux. *Lines on the Landscape: Leys and Other Linear Enigmas.* London: Robert Hale, 1989.

Penrose, Bert. "Glamour with a 35mm.: Why I Prefer the 35mm. for Glamour." *Glamour Girl Photography* 1 (December 1959), 24–26.

Pepper, H. Crowell. "Miniature Cameras." *Camera Craft* 43 (June 1936), 267–74.

Peretti, André. *Les contradictions de la culture et de la pédagogie.* Paris: Editions de l'Épi., 1969.

The Perfect Medium: Photography and the Occult. By Clément Chéroux, et al. New Haven: Yale Univ. Press, 2005.

Perrett, Antoinette. "My Rolleiflex Camera." *American Photography* 29 (May 1935), 319–20.

Perry, Thomas. *The Face Changers.* New York: Ballantine, 1998.

Person, Alfred. *Bildmässige Leica-photos durch Tontrennung nach dem Personverfahren.* Frankfurt: Bechhold, 1935.

Perutz, Kathrin. *Beyond the Looking Glass: America's Beauty Culture.* New York: Morrow, 1970.

Peskin, Hy. "Folies Bergére." *US Camera* 10 (July 1947), 22–23.

Pestalozzi, Rudolf. *Leica Amateur's Picture Book.* London: Fountain, 1935.

Petersen, James R. *Playboy Redheads.* San Francisco: Chronicle, 2005.

Petit, Gilbert. "Are Pin-Ups to Be Taken Seriously?" *International Photo Technik* 11 (Summer 1971), 26–29.

———. "Coloured Light in Colour Photography." *International Photo Technik* 11 (Spring 1965), 125–27.

———. *Woman in Necklace. International Photo Technik* 17 (Winter 1971), 74–75.

Petitpierre, Dom Robert. *Exorcising Devils.* London: Hale, 1976.

Pettejohn, Elizabeth. *Beauty and Art, 1750–2000.* New York: Oxford Univ. Press, 2005.

"Photographing Your Own Playmate." *Playboy* 5, June 1958, 35–45.

"Photography and Relativity." *Photo-Era* 66 (April 1931), 222.

Photography Annual. New York: Ziff-Davis, 1951–.

"Photography for Railroaders." *Railroad Model Craftsman* 26 (November 1957), 43–47; (December 1957), 46–48.

Photography Handbook. Greenwich, Conn.: Fawcett, 1950; 1959.

"Photography in Film and TV Studios." *International Photo Technik* 18 (Winter 1972), 26–27.

Piazza, Joseph. *Candid Photography.* Greenwich, Conn.: Fawcett, 1956.

Pickering, Samuel F. *The Right Distance.* Athens: Univ. of Georgia Press, 1987.

Pilkington, Ed. "I Am Creating Artificial Life, Declares U.S. Gene Pioneer." *Guardian,* October 6, 2007.

Pine, B. Joseph II, and James H. Gilmore. *The Experience Economy: Work Is Theatre and Every Business a Stage: Goods and Services Are No Longer Enough.* Boston: Harvard Business School Press, 1999.

Pinkus, Karen. *Bodily Regimes: Italian Advertising under Fascism.* Minneapolis: Univ. of Minnesota Press, 1995.

Piselli, Stefano, and Riccardo Morrachi and Marco Giovanni. *The Glamorous Betty Page Cult Model.* Florence: Glittering Images, 1991.

Pitkin, Walter B. "The Crisis in the Movies." *Parents' Magazine* 5 (February 1930), 8.

Playboy Book of Horror and the Supernatural. Chicago: Playboy, 1967.

Poe, Edgar Allan. *Complete Tales and Poems.* Ed. Hervey Allen. New York: Modern Library, 1938.

Poffenberger, Albert T. *Psychology in Advertising.* Chicago: Shaw, 1925.

Pokorny, V. "Home-Made Mortensen Lighting Equipment." *Camera Craft* 43 (May 1936), 219–22.

"Pollution of the Environment." *International Photo Technik* 19 (Spring 1973), 28–29.

Pope, Harrison G., Jr., M. B. Poliakoff, M. P. Parker, M. Boynes, and J. I. Hudson. "Is Dissociative Amnesia a Culture-Bound Syndrome? Findings from a Survey of Historical Literature." *Psychological Medicine* 37 (February 2007), 225–33.

Pope, Harrison G., Jr., Katharine A. Phillips, and Roberto Olivardia. *The Adonis Complex: The Secret Crisis of Male Body Obsession.* New York: Simon & Schuster, 2000.

Popular Mechanics. *Shop Notes: Easy Ways to Do Hard Things.* Chicago: Popular Mechanics, 1909.

Popular Photography Annual. New York: Ziff-Davis, various years.

Posographe. *Instructions.* Paris: Posographe, [1925?].

Post, Charles Johnson. "A Little Paradise in the Dutch West Indies." *Century* 79 (December 1909), 176–84.

Post, Gerald V. "Miniature Negatives from Any Hand Camera." *American Photography* 29 (May 1935), 321.

Post Reader of Fantasy and Science Fiction. New York: Popular Library, 1964.

"Post-War Jobs." *Army Times,* August 11, 1945, 10.

Potter, Claire Bond. *War on Crime: Bandits, G-Men, and the Politics of Mass Culture.* New Brunswick: Rutgers Univ. Press, 1998.

Powdermaker, Hortense. *Hollywood: The Dream Factory: An Anthropologist Looks at the Movie-Makers.* Boston: Little Brown, 1950.

Pratchett, Terry. *Guards! Guards!* London: Gollancz, 1997.

———. *Interesting Times.* New York: Harper Collins, 1994.

———. *The Truth.* New York: Harper Collins, 2000.

Pratt, J. G. "Taking Photos before an Open Fireplace." *Popular Science* 117 (October 1930), 131.

Price, Derek J. de Solla. *Gears from the Greeks: The Antikythera Mechanism: A Calendar Computer from ca. 80 B.C.* Philadelphia: American Philosophical Society, 1974.

Price, Jack. "Tamara." *Popular Photography* 4 (May 1939), 19.

Price, Ken. "The 498 Ranch." *Sunshine and Health* 27 (February 1958), 6–9.

Priestley, J. B. *Midnight on the Desert: Being an Excursion into Autobiography during a Winter in America, 1935–1936.* New York: Harper, 1937.

Prize-Winning Photography. Greenwich, Conn.: Fawcett, 1954.

Prochnow, Claus. *Rollei Report 2: Rollei-Werke Rollfilmkameras.* [1994] Stuttgart: Lindemanns Verlag, 2008.

———. *Voigtländer Report 2.* Braunschweig: Lindemanns, 2005.

Provenzo, Eugene F. *Video Kids: Making Sense of Nintendo.* Cambridge, Mass.: Harvard Univ. Press, 1991.

"Psychology of Fear." *Science,* October 15, 1886, 351–52.

Puckett, Newbell Niles. *Folk Beliefs of the Southern Negro.* Chapel Hill: Univ. of North Carolina Press, 1926.

Pullman, Philip. *The Golden Compass.* New York: Knopf, 1996.

Quick, Herman. "Your Summer Studio . . . the Beach." *Popular Photography* 27 (September 1950), 34–39, 92–96.

Quiller-Couch, Arthur, ed. *Oxford Book of Ballads, Chosen and Edited by Arthur Quiller-Couch.* Oxford: Clarendon Press, 1927.

Raba, Peter. *Eva und Er.* Munich: Münchener Stadmuseum, 1968.

———. "A Phantastic Journey." *International Photo Technik* 18 (Summer 1972), 18–19, 71.

———. *Three Girls in a Flask.* International Photo Technik 18 (Winter 1972), 71.

Rabb, Jane. M., ed. *Literature and Photography Interactions, 1840–1990: A Critical Anthology.* Albuquerque: Univ. of New Mexico Press, 1995.

Rackham, Arthur. *Book of Pictures.* New York: Century, 1913.

———. *A Fairy Book.* Garden City, N.Y.: Doubleday, 1923.

———. *The Land of Enchantment.* London: Cassell, 1907.

Radio Corporation of America. *33 Years of Pioneering and Progress in Radio and Television.* New York: RCA, 1953.

"Radio May Be Used to Speed Up Brain." *Popular Science* 117 (September 1930), 63.

"Radio Speeds Up Plant Growth." *Popular Science* 117 (August 1930), 47.

"Radio World's Fair." *Photo-Era* 63 (November 1929), 282–83.

Rainey, Gertrude "Ma." "Black Dust Blues." Chicago: Paramount, 1928.

Ralphson, G. Harvey. *The Boy Scout Camera Club, or, The Confessions of a Photograph*. Chicago: Donohue, 1913.

Randerson, James. "Is There Anybody Out There? How the Men from the Ministry Hid the Hunt for UFOs." *Guardian,* September 25, 2006.

Randolph, Van. *Unprintable Ozark Folksongs and Folklore*. Fayetteville: Univ. of Arkansas Press, 1992.

Rankin, Ian. *The Naming of the Dead*. New York: Little, Brown, 2006.

Ransome, Arthur. *Pigeon Post*. [1936] Rev. ed. Boston: Godine, 1983.

——. *Swallows and Amazons*. [1930] Boston: Godine, 1990.

"Raphy's World." *Picture* 12 (June 2007), 20–23.

Raucher, Herman. *Summer of '42*. New York: Allen, 1971.

Ray, Robert B. *The Avant-Garde Finds Andy Hardy*. Cambridge, Mass.: Harvard Univ. Press, 1995.

Read, Oliver. "Television Needs Cameramen." *Popular Photography* 4 (February 1939), 13, 80.

"Recent Observations on Earth Currents." *Electrical Engineer* 18 (August 1894), n.p.

"Records, Nudes and Travel." *International Photo Technik* 17 (Summer 1971), 30–31, 52.

Reef, Betty. "Pinups." *Popular Photography* 19 (May 1946), 46–48, 171–73.

Reeves, Nicholas. *The Power of Film Propaganda*. London: Cassell, 1999.

Reevy, Tony. "Artist of the Rail: Phil Hastings." *Railroad History,* no. 198 (Spring–Summer 2008), 66–78.

"Registering Apparatus for Earth Currents." *Science,* June 1883, 235–36.

Reichert, Tom. *The Erotic History of Advertising*. Amherst, N.Y.: Prometheus, 2006.

Reichert, Tom, and Jacqueline Lambiase, eds. *Sex in Consumer Culture: The Erotic Content of Media and Marketing*. Mahwah, N.J.: Lawrence Erlbaum, 2006.

Reilly, Rosa. "Do It with Your Box Camera." *Popular Photography* 1 (June 1937), 21–22.

Rein, Irving J. *High Visibility: The Making and Marketing of Professionals into Celebrities*. Lincolnwood, Ill.: NTC Group, 1997.

Reinemann, J. O. "Extra-Marital Relations with Fellow Employees in War Industry as a Factor in Disruption of Family Life." *American Sociological Review* 10 (June 1945), 389–403.

Reisman, Nora E. "The Photographic Nude." *American Photography* 29 (June 1935), 336–38.

Remmling, Gunter W. *Road to Suspicion: A Study of Modern Mentality and the Sociology of Knowledge*. New York: Appleton-Century-Crofts, 1967.

Renfrew, Colin. "Ancient Europe Is Older Than We Thought." *National Geographic,* November 1977, 615–27.

Rentschler, Eric. *The Ministry of Illusion: Nazi Cinema and Its Afterlife*. Cambridge, Mass.: Harvard Univ. Press, 1996.

Repplier, Agnes. *Books and Men*. Boston: Houghton, Mifflin, 1892.

Reuter, Otto Sigfrid. *Der Himmel über den Germanen*. Munich: NSDAP, 1937.

——. *Germanische Himmelskunde*. Munich: Lehmann, 1934.

"Revolution in Glamor." *Bold* 4 (May 1956), 20–24.

Rice, Anne O'Brien. *Blackwood Farm*. New York: Random House, 2002.

——. *The Feast of All Saints*. New York: Simon & Schuster, 1979.

——. *Interview with the Vampire*. New York: Knopf, 1976.

Richter, Joachim Burkhard. *Hans Ferdinand Massmann: Altdeustscher Patriotismus im 19. Jahrhundert*. Berlin: Walter de Gruyter, 1992.

Riemel, Manfred. "Photography and Visual Perception." *International Photo Technik* 11 (Fall 1965), 278–79.

Rigaud, Milo. *Secrets of Voodoo*. [1953] Trans. Robert B. Cross. New York: Arco, 1969.

Riis, Jacob A. "The People's Institute of New York." *Century* 79 (April 1910), 850–63.

Roach, Marion. *The Roots of Desire: The Myth, Meaning and Sexual Power of Red Hair.* New York: Bloomsbury, 2005.

Robbins, L. B. "Handy Aids for Radio Workers." *Popular Science* 130 (January 1937), 57.

Roberts, Callum. *The Unnatural History of the Sea*. Washington, D.C.: Island Press, 2007.

Roberts, H. Edward, and William Yates. "Altair 8800 Minicomputer." *Popular Electronics* 7 (January 1975), 33–40.

Roberts, Kenneth L. "Billboard-Dämmerung." *Saturday Evening Post,* September 6, 1930, 20–21, 153–58.

Robikoff, Dimitry, and Paul Cherney. *Underwater Photography.* New York: Chilton, 1949.

Robinson, Rowland E. *In New England Fields and Woods*. Boston: Houghton, Mifflin, 1896.

Rodriguez, Nestor. "It's All in the Frame." *In Camera* 3 (April 2007), 30–31.

Rogers, James Harris. "America's Greatest War Invention." *Electrical Experimenter* 6 (March 1919), 22–27.

——. "The Rogers Underground Aerial for Amateurs." *Electrical Experimenter* 6 (June 1919), 38–46.

Rogliatti, Gianni. *Leica: The First Sixty Years*. Hove, U.K.: Hove Camera Foto Books, 1982.

Rollei Annual. Vienna: Hammer, 1951–.

Rolling Stone: The Seventies. Ed. Ashley Kahn, Holly George-Warren, and Shawn Dahl. Boston: Little, Brown, 1998.

Rollins, Alice Wellington. "When Woods Are Green." *Scribner's Monthly,* September 1880.

Ronzel, Jean-Pierre. *Flowers. International Photo Technik* 11 (Fall 1971), 10.

Rood, Ogden N. *Modern Chromatics, with Applications to Art and Industry.* New York: Appleton, 1879.

Rose, Jonathan. *The Edwardian Temperament, 1895–1919*. Athens: Ohio Univ. Press, 1986.

Rosenblatt, Roger. "Growing Up on Television." *Daedalus* 105 (Fall 1976), 61–68.

Rosovsky, Henry. *The University: An Owner's Manual*. New York: Norton, 1990.

Ross, T. E. "The Ley Lines in North America." *American Dowser* 14 (August 1974), 7–13.

Ross, T. J., comp. *Film and the Liberal Arts*. New York: Holt, Rinehart and Winston, 1970.

Rothschild, Norman. "Peter Gowland: Glamor Is His Homework." *Popular Photography* 63 (December 1968), 132–35.

——. "Secret Life of an Instamatic Camera." *Popular Photography* 62 (May 1968), 80–81, 130.

Rothstein, Marvin, et al. *Microwave Ovens and the Public*. Washington, D.C.: GPO, 1969.

Rotundo, E. Anthony. *American Manhood: Transformations in Masculinity from the Revolution to the Modern Era*. New York: Basic Books, 1993.

Roy, L. M. A. "A Focusing Device for Your Miniature Camera." *American Photography* 29 (July 1935), 452–54.

Royce, Josiah. *Race Questions, Provincialism, and Other American Problems.* New York: Macmillan, 1908.

Royo, Luis. *Wild Sketches.* Madrid: Norma, 2006.

Rubin, Louis D., and Robert D. Jacobs, eds. *South: Modern Southern Literature in Its Cultural Setting.* Garden City, N.Y.: Doubleday, 1961.

Rudloff, Everett. "The 'GP' Vertical Enlarger." *Good Photography,* 1939, 84–89, 146.

Ruskin, John. *The Old Road.* London: Allen, 1899.

Russell, George William [AE]. *The Candle of Vision.* [1918] New Hyde Park, N.Y.: University Books, 1965.

Russell, James S. "What's Zapping You?" *Architectural Record* 179 (February 1991), 113.

Ryden, Kent C. *Landscape with Figures: Nature and Culture in New England.* Iowa City: Univ. of Iowa Press, 2001.

Ryder, Frederick D. "Speedier Ways to Make Photo Enlargements." *Popular Science* 126 (January 1935), 78, 82.

"Safety First in Movie Lessons." *Literary Digest* 54 (May 5, 1917), 1329.

Sagoff, Mark. *The Economy of the Earth: Philosophy, Law, and the Environment.* Cambridge: Cambridge Univ. Press, 1988.

Salmond, John. *My Eyes Set on Freedom: A History of the Civil Rights Movement, 1954–1968.* Chicago: Dee, 1997.

——. *Southern Struggles: The Southern Labor Movement and the Civil Rights Struggle.* Gainesville: Univ. of Florida Press, 2004.

Salvatore, R. A. *The Woods Out Back.* New York: Penguin, 1993.

Samerjan, Peter James. "Glamour in the Surf." *Art Photography* 6 (August 1954), 4–8, 48–50.

Sammond, Nicholas. *Babes in Toyland: Walt Disney and the Making of the American Child, 1930–1960.* Durham: Duke Univ. Press, 2005.

Samuels, Charles Thomas. "The Context of *A Clockwork Orange.*" *American Scholar* 41 (Summer 1972), 439–43.

"Sand, Surf and Sun." *Art Photography* 5 (August 1953), 20–23.

Sandwith, Francis. "Night London with a Minicam." *American Photography* 29 (September 1935), 586–87.

Sarnhoff, David. *To Regulate Radio Communication: Hearings before the Committee on Merchant Marine and Fisheries.* Washington, D.C.: GPO, 1927.

Sauers, Jim. "Delivery Trip for *Annie's Toy.*" *Messing About in Boats* 23 (February 1, 2006), 12–15.

Saxon, Lyle. *Fabulous New Orleans.* New York: Appleton-Century, 1939.

Saxon, Lyle, et al., eds. *Gumbo Ya-Ya.* Boston: Houghton Mifflin, 1945.

Scacheri, Mario. "Getting Weird Effects." *Popular Photography* 1 (August 1937), 13–4, 78.

Schatz, Howard. *Seeing Red: The Rapture of Redheads.* San Francisco: Pomegranate, 1993.

Schatz, Thomas. *The Genius of the System: Hollywood Filmmaking in the Studio Era.* New York: Pantheon, 1988.

Schedel, Angelika. *Der Blick in den Menschen: Wilhelm Conrad Rontgen und seine Zeit.* Munich: Urban, 1995.

Scheffauer, Herman George. "The Naked, the Nude, and the Undrest." *Double-Dealer* 4 (July 1922), 20–24.

Scheier, Peter. "Sao Paulo." *US Camera* 9 (June 1946), 26–28.

Schenck, Hilbert, and Henry Kendall. *Underwater Photography.* Cambridge, Md.: Cornell Maritime Press, 1957.

Schickel, Richard. *The Disney Version: The Life, Times, Art, and Commerce of Walt Disney.* New York: Simon & Schuster, 1985.

Schiller, Herbert. *Culture, Inc.: The Corporate Takeover of Public Expression.* New York: Oxford Univ. Press, 1989.

Schiller, Lawrence J. "Bikinis in the Backyard." *Saturday Evening Post,* June 20, 1964, 18–25.

Schläger, Rudolf. "Rollei Photography with the Older Models." *Rolleigrafie* 1 (Winter 1964/65), 49.

Schlegel, James R. "An Inexpensive Enlarger." *American Photography* 29 (March 1935), 162–66.

Schlobin, Roger C., ed. *The Aesthetics of Fantasy Literature and Art.* Notre Dame: Univ. of Notre Dame Press, 1982.

Schmölke, Werner. "High Key Shot." *Rolleigrafie* 1 (October 1968), 35.

———. "Horrible: But Charming Nevertheless." *International Photo Technik* 11 (Fall 1965), 276.

———. "Nude and Pose." *International Photo Technik* 19 (Spring 1973), 10–14.

Schoenfeld, Brad. *Look Great Naked.* Paramus, N.J.: Prentice Hall, 2001.

Schön, Walter. "Is the Camera a Third Eye?" *International Photo Technik* 17 (Summer 1971), 54–59.

"School Reading Scores Worsen." *Harvard Crimson,* February 28, 2007, 3.

Schrobsdorff, Joachim A. "Candid Outdoor Portraits." *International Photo Technik* 19 (Fall 1973), 16–19.

Schuller, Gunther. *Early Jazz: Its Roots and Musical Development.* New York: Oxford Univ. Press, 1968.

Schulman, Bruce. *The Seventies: The Great Shift in American Culture, Society, and Politics.* Cambridge, Mass.: Da Capo, 2001.

Schulman, Seth. "Cancer Risks Seen in Electro-Magnetic Fields." *Nature,* June 7, 1990, 463.

Schultze-Naumburg, Paul. *Die Gestaltung der Landschaft durch Menschen.* Munich: Callwey, 1917.

———. *Das Glück der Landschaft, von ihrem Verstehen und Geniessen.* Berlin: Engelhard, 1942.

———. *Heroisches Italien.* Munich: Bruckmann, 1938.

———. *Die Kultur des weiblichen Köpers als Grundlage der Frauenkleidung.* Leipzig: Diederich, 1902.

———. *Kunst aus Blut und Boden.* Leipzig: Seemann, 1934.

———. *Nordische Schönheit, ihr Wunschbild im Leben and in der Kunst.* Munich: Lehmann, 1937.

———. *Saaleck: Bilder von meinem Hause und Garten in der Thüringer Landschaft.* Berlin: Gartenschönheit, 1927.

———. *Der Studiengang des modernen Malers.* Leipzig, 1896.

Schurz, Carl. *The New South.* New York: American News, 1885.

Schutts, Jeff R. *Selling Modernity: Cultures of Advertising in Twentieth-Century Germany.* Durham: Duke Univ. Press, 2006.

Schwaber, Paul. "Women and Freud's Imagination." *American Scholar* 41 (Spring 1972), 224–37.

Schwalberg, Bob. "126 Moves Up to the Majors." *Popular Photography* 62 (June 1968), 58, 60, 62, 90–91.

Schwille, Dieter. "Beauty and Brilliance." *International Photo Technik* 19 (Spring 1973), 22–23.

Schwind, Phil. *Cape Cod Fisherman*. Camden, Me.: International Marine, 1974.

Scott, Adam. *Holga: The World through a Plastic Lens*. Vienna: Lomographic Society, 2006.

Scott, Walter. *Demonology and Witchcraft*. [1830] New York: Bell, 1970.

Scotti, R. A. *Sudden Sea: The Great Hurricane of 1938*. New York: Little, Brown, 2003.

Seaman, Al, and Connie Seaman. "So You Really Want to Be a Model." *Popular Photography* 1 (July 1937), 56–58.

"Secret of Better Colour Pictures." *International Photo Technik* 11 (Spring 1965), 96–99.

Seldes, Gilbert. *The Great Audience*. New York: Viking, 1950.

———. *The Public Arts*. New York: Simon & Schuster, 1956.

———. *The Seven Lively Arts*. [1924] Rev. ed. New York: Sagamore, 1957.

Semper idem. *The "Blue Book": A Bibliographical Attempt to Describe the Guide Books to the Houses of Ill Fame in New Orleans as They Were Published There*. [New Orleans?]: privately printed, 1936.

"Seven Hundred and Thirty Six Secrets to Instant Glamour." *Lucky Magazine* 7 (June 2007), 21–59.

"Seven Pictures in Seven Minutes." *Popular Photography* 18 (June 1946), 40–41.

Severin, Kurt. "Mexico from a New Angle." *Photography with the Rolleiflex and Rolleicord* 14 (June 1939), 4–6.

"Sex in the Caribbean Equals 'Voodoo.'" *Sir!* 11 (February 1954), 28–31.

Seznec, Jean. *The Survival of the Pagan Gods: The Mythological Tradition and Its Place in Renaissance Humanism and Art*. [1940] Trans. Barbara F. Sessions. New York: Pantheon, 1953.

Shaughnessy, Jim. *The Call of Trains*. Ed. Jeff Brouws. New York: Norton, 2008.

Shaw, Bernard. *On Photography*. Ed. Bill Jay and Margaret Moore. Salt Lake: Peregrine Smith, 1989.

Shaw, Walter J. "Home Enlarging at Low Cost." *American Photography* 29 (October 1935), 624–28.

Sheckell, Thomas O., and Fred P. Peel. *Nude Figure Photography*. New York: New York Institute of Photography, [1950?].

Shenkman, Rick. *Just How Stupid Are We? Facing the Truth about the American Voter*. New York: Basic Books, 2008.

Shepherd, J. *Tin Pan Alley*. London: Routledge, 1982.

Shields, Rob. *Places on the Margins*. London: Routledge, 1991.

Shippey, T. A. *J. R. R. Tolkien: Author of the Century*. Boston: Houghton Mifflin, 2000.

———. "The Magic Art and the Evolution of Words: Ursula Le Guin's Earthsea Trilogy." *Mosaic* 10 (Winter 1977), 147–63.

———. *The Road to Middle Earth: How J. R. R. Tolkien Created a New Mythology*. New York: Houghton Mifflin, 2003.

Shirer, William L. *The Nightmare Years, 1930 to 1940*. Boston: Little, Brown, 1984.

Shoesmith, Ron. *Alfred Watkins: A Herefordshire Man*. Little Logaston Woonton Almeley, U.K.: Logaston, 1990.

Shore, Stephen. *The Nature of Photographs*. Baltimore: Johns Hopkins Univ. Press, 1998.

"Should Children Go to the Movies?" *Parents' Magazine* 5 (February 1930), 14–16, 42–45.

"Side Roads." *Photo-Era* 64 (January 1930), 83.

Silver, Carole G. *Strange and Secret Peoples: Fairies and Victorian Consciousness.* New York: Oxford Univ. Press, 1999.

Silverman, Lee. "Inside the Loop: Computer Graphics with the Technological Highway." *Views: The Journal of Photography in New England* 5 (Summer 1984), 6–10.

Simon, Richard L. *Miniature Photography from One Amateur to Another.* New York: Simon & Schuster, 1937.

Simpson, George Eaton. "Four Vodun Ceremonies." *Journal of American Folklore* 59 (Spring 1946), 154–67.

Sims, Michael. *Adam's Navel: A Natural and Cultural History of the Human Form.* London: Penguin, 2003.

Sinclair, May. *Uncanny Stories.* New York: Macmillan, 1923.

Singhal, Anupriya. "Study Doubts Amnesia's Literary Memory." *Harvard Crimson,* February 28, 2007, 1, 6.

Sitney, P. Adams, ed. *Film Culture Reader.* New York: Praeger, 1970.

"Six-Format TLR." *Popular Photography* 62 (January 1968), 81.

Skinner, C. M. *Myths and Legends of Our Own Land.* 2 vols. Philadelphia: Lippincott, 1896.

Slide, Anthony. *Aspects of American Film History prior to 1920.* Metuchen, N.J.: Scarecrow, 1978.

———. *Early Women Directors.* New York: Da Capo, 1984.

Sloane, Patricia. *Colour: Basic Principles and New Directions.* London: Studio Vista, 1967.

———. *The Visual Nature of Color.* New York: Design Press, 1989.

"Smallest Linhof Camera." *International Photo Technik* 22 (Summer 1976), 37.

Smart, Charles Allen. *R.F.D.* New York: Norton, 1938.

Smith, Anthony. *The Shadow in the Cave.* London: Allen & Unwin, 1973.

Smith, Elizabeth Oakes Prince. *Shadow Land; or, The Seer.* New York: Fowlers and Wells, 1852.

Smith, F. Hopkinson. "A White Umbrella in Mexico." *Century* 37 (December 1889), 244–53.

Smith, Gordon. *Mervyn Peake: A Personal Memoir.* London: Gollancz, 1984.

Smith, Joan. *Different for Girls: How Culture Creates Women.* London: Chatto & Windus, 1997.

Smith, John E. *America's Philosophical Vision.* Chicago: Univ. of Chicago Press, 1992.

Smith, L. "Nudity Cult." *Sports Illustrated,* January 18, 1965, 34–39.

Snelling, Henry H. *The History and Practice of the Art of Photography.* [1849] Intro. Beaumont Newhall. Hastings-on-Hudson, N.Y.: Morgan & Morgan, 1970.

Snyder, H. Rossiter. "The Market Place." *American Photography* 29 (July 1935), 448–50.

Sobek, Goetz. "The Manipulated Consumer." *Rolleigrafie* 6 (December 1969), 41–45.

Soja, Edward W. *Postmodern Geographies: The Reassertion of Space in Critical Social Theory.* London: Verso, 1989.

Soltys, Richard J., and Earl Stone. *Monsters and Madonnas and the World of William Mortensen* (film). Hollywood: Soltys Productions, [1958?].

Sommer, Siegfried. "Girls Make a Stand." *Rolleigrafie* 4 (June 1969), 20–23.

Sontag, Susan. "Against Interpretation." *Evergreen Review* 8 (December 1964), 76–80, 93.

———. *On Photography.* New York: Farrar, Straus and Giroux, 1977.

———. *Under the Sign of Saturn.* New York: Farrar, Straus, 1980.

Sousa, Richard. "All in the Family." *Hoover Digest* 11 (Fall 2007), 39–42.

South, Thomas. *Early Magnetism in its Higher Relation to Humanity: As Viewed in the Poets and Prophets.* London: Bailliere, 1846.

"Southern Letters." *Double-Dealer* 1 (June 1921), 214–15.

Spann, Edward K. *Designing Modern America.* Columbus: Ohio State Univ. Press, 1996.

Speaks, Michael, ed. *Critical Landscape.* Rotterdam: 010 Publishers, 1996.

Spears, Jack. *Hollywood: The Golden Era.* New York: Castle, 1971.

"Specialist versus All-Round Photographer." *International Photo Technik* 11 (Spring 1971), 11.

"Speeding Up Your Film with Mercury Vapor." *Popular Science* 133 (August 1938), 86.

Spence, Lewis. *British Fairy Origins.* London: Watts, 1946.

——. *The Fairy Tradition in Britain.* London: Rider, 1948.

Spenser, Edmund. *Poetical Works.* Ed. J. C. Smith and E. De Selincourt. Oxford: Oxford Univ. Press, 1924.

The Spenser Encyclopedia. Ed. A. C. Hamilton. Toronto: Univ. of Toronto Press, 1990.

Spitzing, Günter. "Special Photo Effects." *Rolleigrafie* 1 (October 1968), 30–34.

"Splashy and Stylish." *Newsweek,* February 18, 1985, 90–91.

Spoerl, Alexander. "The Naked and the Rollei." *Rolleigrafie* 4 (June 1969), 18–19.

"Spotting Dynamic Speaker Ills." *Popular Science* 116 (February 1930), 70.

Squier, George. "Tree Telephony and Telegraphy." *Journal of the Franklin Institute,* June 1919.

Stagg, Mildred. "Jobs for Veterans." *Popular Photography* 13 (May 1946), 42–45, 132.

——. "Woman's Place in Photography." *Popular Photography* 5 (September 1939), 26–27, 78–80.

"Stalling for Time." *Calendar,* American Film Institute Theater, February 13–March 17, 1976, 23.

Stanley Rule and Level, Inc. "Father and Son Pals." *Popular Science* 116 (January 1930), 99.

Stanton, Frank. *Mass Media and Mass Culture.* Hanover, N.H.: Dartmouth College, 1963.

Stebbins, Hilda Brace. "Youth Needs Red-Blooded Books." *Parents' Magazine* 5 (August 1930), 19, 42–44.

Steinheil, C. A. *Über Telegraphie.* Munich: Akademie, 1838.

Stengel, Georg. "Of Maids and Men." *Rolleigrafie* 4 (June 1969), 26–27.

Stenhouse, J. R. *Cracker Hash.* London: Percival Marshall, 1955.

Stephenson, Henry Thew. "Meters and How to Use Them." *American Photography* 29 (June 1935), 338–42.

Stern, Bert. "The Last Sitting." *New York,* February 25, 2008, 45–53.

Stern, Karl. *The Flight from Woman.* New York: Farrar, Straus and Giroux, 1965.

Stern, Radu. *Against Fashion: Clothing as Art, 1850 to 1930.* Cambridge, Mass.: MIT Press, 2004.

Stevens, Francis. *The Nightmare and Other Tales of Dark Fantasy.* Ed. Gary Hoppenstand. Lincoln: Univ. of Nebraska Press, 2004.

Stevenson, Robert Louis. *Across the Plains with Other Memories and Essays.* Leipzig: Tauchnitz, 1892.

Steyer, James P. *The Other Parent: The Inside Story of the Media's Effect on Our Children.* New York: Atria Books, 2002.

Stilgoe, John. *Alongshore.* New Haven: Yale Univ. Press, 1994.

——. *Borderland: Origins of the American Suburb, 1820 to 1939*. New Haven: Yale Univ. Press, 1988.

——. "Cosmetics, Cosmos, and Woman-Skin." *New Observations*, no. 52 (November 1987), 2–5.

——. "Design Standards: Whose Meaning?" *Regulating Place: Standards and the Shaping of Urban America*. Ed. Eran Ben-Joseph and Terry S. Szold, 1–36. London: Routledge, 2005.

——. *Landscape and Images*. Charlottesville: Univ. of Virginia Press, 2005.

——. *Lifeboat: A History of Courage, Cravenness, and Survival at Sea*. Charlottesville: Univ. of Virginia Press, 2003.

——. *Metropolitan Corridor: Railroads and the American Scene*. New Haven: Yale Univ. Press, 1983.

——. *Outside Lies Magic: Regaining History and Awareness in Everyday Places*. New York: Walker, 1998.

——. *Shallow-Water Dictionary: A Grounding in Estuary English*. New York: Princeton Architectural Press, 1990.

Stoddard, John T. "College Composites." *Century* 35 (November 1887), 121–25.

Stoddard, Lothrop. *The Rising Tide of Color*. New York: Scribner's, 1922.

Stoichita, Victor I. *A Short History of the Shadow*. London: Reaktion, 1997.

Stone, Reuben A. "Low-Cost Enlarger-Printer." *Popular Photography* 4 (February 1939), 55–56.

Storr, Ignatius. "The Versatility of Front Projection." *International Photo Technik* 19 (Winter 1973), 10–13.

Strand, Paul. "Photography and the New God." *Broom: An International Magazine of the Arts* 3 (November 1922), 252–58.

Strelow, Liselotte. "Portrait Photography." *Rolleigrafie* 5 (September 1969), 16–19.

Strong, Dick, and Lance Sterling. "Frank Fleet and His Electronic Sex Machine: The Nude Intruder." *Evergreen* 65 (April 1969), 36–43.

"Studio Opened for Television." *Popular Science* 130 (January 1937), 17.

Study Group of New York. *Children and Sex: The Parents Speak*. New York: Facts on File, 1983.

Sturgis, Matthew. *Aubrey Beardsley: A Biography*. London: HarperCollins, 1998.

Suarès, J. C., ed. *Hollywood Drag*. Charlottesville, Va.: Thomasson-Grant, 1991.

Subirats, Rafael. *Antropofagia: El continente vacio*. Mexico City: Siglo Veintiuno, 1994.

Suess, Hans. "Brittlecone Pine Calibrations of the Radiocarbon Times Scale from 4100 to 1500 B.C." Monaco Symposium on Radio-Active Dating Methods of Low-Level Counting, March 2–10, 1967, *Proceedings*. Vienna: Atomic Energy Agency, 1967.

Sullaway, Neva. *Chasing Dreamtime: A Sea-Going Hitchhiker's Journey through Memory and Myth*. Castleton-on-Hudson, N.Y.: Brookview, 2005.

Sullivan, Mildred S. "My Greatest Money-Maker—a Rolleiflex." *Photo-Era* 63 (January 1932), 10–14.

Sussman, Aaron. *The Amateur Photographer's Handbook*. 4th ed. New York: Crowell, 1948; 5th ed. 1952; 7th ed., 1965; 8th ed., 1973.

Sussman, Julia, and Maureen Thomas. "Interactivity and Digital Environments: Design a Storymap for *Gormenghast Explore*." In *Virtual Storytelling: Using Virtual Reality Technologies for Storytelling*, ed. Gérard Subsol, 284–87. Proceedings of the Third International Conference, ICVS 2005, November 30–December 2. Strasbourg: Springer, 2006.

Sussner, Julia, Maureen Thomas, and Paul Richens. "Patterning Reconfigurable Narrative Interactive Cinema as Architectural Elevation within 3D Interactive Digital Environments." *Digital Creativity* 17 (Fall 2006), 243–56.

Sutton, Dave. "The Nude." *Art Photography* 5 (February 1954), 26–29.

Sweet, Ozzie. *My Camera Pays Off.* New York: American Photographic, 1958.

———. "Why Cheesecake Photography?" *US Camera* 16 (September 1953), 50–52.

———. "Women, Wonderful Women." *International Photo Technik* 17 (Winter 1971), 18–19, 50–51.

"Swimsuits." *Look,* June 2, 1964, 59–63.

Swimsuits: 100 Years of Pictures. Washington, D.C.: National Geographic Society, 2003.

"Swim Trunks Get Briefer." *Look,* January 12, 1954, 52–53.

Swiridoff, Paul. "Architectural Photography with the Rollei." *Rolleigrafie* 2 (December 1968), 10–15.

Swiss Reinsurance Company. *The Landscape of Risk.* Zurich: Swiss Reinsurance Co., 2006.

"Symposium on Color." *Popular Photography Color Annual 1957.* New York: Ziff-Davis, 1957.

Szilagyi, Steve. *Photographing Fairies.* New York: Ballantine, 1992.

Szulakowska, Urszula. *The Alchemy of Light: Geometry and Optics in Late Renaissance Alchemical Illustration.* Leiden: Brill, 2000.

Tajiri, Vincent T. "The Well Equipped Lensman." *Playboy,* June 1958, 31–34, 46, 62.

Talbot, H. Fox. *English Etymologies.* London: Murray, 1847.

Talbot, Michael. *The Holographic Universe.* New York: HarperCollins, 1991.

"Talk, Hear, SEE on This Phone: Two-Way Television . . . as an Engineering Stunt." *Popular Science* 117 (July 1930), 22, 123.

Tallant, Robert. *Voodoo in New Orleans.* New York: Macmillan, 1946.

Tamara, Tay. "Bikinis Will Be Worn." *Art Photography* 5 (August 1953), 9–13.

Tate, Allen. "William Blake." *Double-Dealer* 4 (July 1922), 28.

Taylor, F. Sherwood. *The Alchemists.* [1952] London: Paladin, 1976.

Taylor, Lucien. "Iconophobia: How Anthropology Lost It at the Movies." *Transition* 69 (Spring 1996), 64–87.

Taylor, William R. *Cavalier and Yankee: The Old South and American National Character.* New York: Braziller, 1961.

"Teaching with Talkies." *Photo-Era* 64 (April 1930), 218.

Temple, Jean. *Blue Ghost: A Study of Lafcadio Hearn.* [1931] New York: Haskell, 1974.

Terrall, Robert. *Kill Now, Pay Later.* [1960] New York: Dorchester, 2007.

Terrill, Merle. "Aluminum Plates Stiffen Light Wooden Tripod." *Popular Science* 133 (August 1938), 86.

Terry, Pat. "Shooting the Burlesque from the Center of Baldheaded Row." *Popular Photography* 1 (May 1937), 24–25.

Teudt, William. *Germanische Heiligtümer.* Jena: Diederichs, 1929.

Tey, Josephine. *To Love and Be Wise.* [1951] Ed. Robert Barnard. New York: Simon & Schuster, 1978.

Theis, Jürgen. "Advertising Photography: A Synthesis of Art and Craft." *Rolleigrafie* 6 (December 1969), 21–26.

"Theory of Miniature Photography." *American Photography* 29 (December 1935), 785–87.

Theweleit, Klaus. *Männerphantasien.* 2 vols. Frankfurt am Main: Rote-Stern, 1977–78.

Thoer, Heinz. "Photographing Glass." *International Photo Technik* 11 (Summer 1965), 123–24.

Thom, Alexander. *Megalithic Sites in Britain.* Oxford: Clarendon, 1967.

Thomas, Bella. "What the Poor Watch on TV." *Prospect* 40 (January 2003), 46–52.

Thomas, Bob. *Walt Disney: An American Original.* New York: Simon & Schuster, 1976.

Thomas, David Emil. "Mirror Images." *Scientific American,* December 1980, 206–28.

Thomas, Edward. *The Icknield Way.* New York: Dutton, 1913.

Thomas, Gordon, and Max Morgan Witts. *The Day the Bubble Burst.* Garden City, N.Y.: Doubleday, 1979.

Thompson, Basil. "The Swamp Spirit." *Double-Dealer* 6 (April 1924), 112–13.

———. "Timothy Spied a Goblin." *Double-Dealer* 6 (April 1924), 114.

Thompson, Holland. *The New South.* New Haven: Yale Univ. Press, 1919.

Thompson, Maurice. *Poems.* Boston: Houghton Mifflin, 1892.

———. "A Voodoo Prophecy." *Independent* 44 (January 21, 1892), 73.

Thompson, T. P. "The Renaissance of the Vieux Carré." *Double-Dealer* 3 (February 1922), 85–89.

Thompson, Thomas. "A Place in the Sun All Her Own." *Life,* March 29, 1968, 66–72.

Thorek, Max. *Camera Art as a Means of Self-Expression.* New York: Lippincott, 1947.

———. *Creative Camera Art.* Canton, Ohio: Fomo, 1937.

———. "Harlemesque." *Popular Photography* 1 (July 1937), 45.

———. "The Paper Negative Process Is Simple." *Good Photography* 2 (1939), 26–31, 140–42.

Thouvenel, Pierre. *Mémoire physique et médicinal, montrant des rapports evidens entre les phénomenes de la baguette divinatoire, du magnétisme et de l'électricité.* Paris, Didot, 1771.

Thulin, W. Bernard. "Miniature Camera." *American Photography* 29 (September 1935), 586–87.

"Tiny Exposure Meter Is Worn on the Wrist." *Popular Science* 133 (July 1938), 41.

"Toast to Bikinis." *Playboy,* June 1962, 56–64.

Todd, Charles. *A False Mirror.* New York: Harper Collins, 2007.

———. *A Fearsome Doubt.* New York: Random House, 2002.

———. *A Pale Horse.* New York: Harper Collins, 2008.

Tolkien, J. R. R. *The Hobbit: or, There and Back Again.* [1937] Boston: Houghton, Mifflin, 2001.

———. *The Lord of the Rings.* [1954–55, 1966]. Boston: Houghton, Mifflin, 2001.

———. *The Lost Road and Other Writings: Language and Legend before "The Lord of the Rings."* Ed. Christopher Tolkien. Boston: Houghton, Mifflin, 1987.

———. *The Monsters and the Critics, and Other Essays.* Ed. Christopher Tolkien. London: Allen & Unwin, 1983.

———. "The Name 'Nodens.'" In *Report on the Excavation of the Prehistoric, Roman, and Post-Roman Site in Lydney Park, Gloucestershire,* 132–37. Reports of the Research Committee of the Society of Antiquaries of London, 9. Oxford: Printed at the Univ. Press for the Society of Antiquaries, 1932.

———. "Philology: General Works." *Year's Work in English Studies* 5 (1924), 26–65.

———. *Pictures.* London: Allen & Unwin, 1979.

———. *The Road Goes Ever On: A Song Cycle.* London: Allen & Unwin, 1968.

———. *The Silmarillion.* [1977]. Ed. Christopher Tolkien. Boston: Houghton, Mifflin, 2001.

———. *Tree and Leaf.* Boston: Houghton, Mifflin, 1965.

Tomlinson, H. M. *Between the Lines.* Cambridge, Mass.: Harvard Univ. Press, 1930.

———. *A Mingled Yarn: Autobiographical Sketches*. [1925] New York: Bobbs-Merrill, 1953.

———. *Old Junk*. New York: Knopf, 1923.

———. *Out of Soundings*. London: Heineman, 1931.

———. *Pipe All Hands*. New York: Harper, 1937.

Tong, Hiram. "The Pioneers of Mound Bayou." *Century* 79 (January 1910), 390–400.

Trachtenberg, Alan. *Reading American Photographs: Images as History, Mathew Brady to Walker Evans*. New York: Hill & Wang, 1989.

"Transmission of Pictures by Wire and Radio." *Experimenter* 5 (May 1925), 24–27.

"Transparency or Colour Negative Film?" *International Photo Technik* 17 (Winter 1971), 76.

Trenker, Luis. "Comradeship with the Rolleiflex." *Rolleigrafie* 5 (September 1969), 25–29.

Trowbridge, John. "The Earth as Conductor of Electricity." *Proceedings, American Academy of Sciences* 16 (May 1880–June 1881), 46–63.

Turner, Dick. "Glamour in Your Living Room." *Art Photography* 5 (February 1954), 4–9.

Turner, Graeme. *Understanding Celebrity*. London and Thousand Oaks: Sage, 2004.

Tydings, Kenneth S. *Guide to Kodak Miniature Cameras*. New York: Greenberg, 1952.

Tyler, F. C. *The Geometrical Arrangement of Ancient Sites*. London: Simpkin Marshall, 1939.

Ulrich, Celeste. *The Social Matrix of Physical Education*. Westport, Conn.: Greenwood, 1968.

"Underwater Photography." *International Photo Technik* 11 (Spring 1971), 34–45, 58.

"Underground Wireless." *Electrical Experimenter* 6 (March 1919), 23–25.

Underwood, G. *The Pattern of the Past*. London: Museum Press, 1969.

Unger, Georg. *Flying Saucers*. East Grinstead, U.K.: New Knowledge, 1958.

United States Bureau of Standards. *Construction and Operation of a Two-Circuit Radio*. Washington, D.C.: GPO, 1922.

United States Navy. *Radio Theory and Shop Room Manual*. San Diego: United States Naval Training Center, [1930?].

United States Signal Office. *Elementary Principles of Radio Telegraphy and Telephony*. Washington, D.C.: GPO, 1918.

Universal Camera Corporation. "Speed Camera of Tomorrow." *Popular Photography* 5 (September 1939), 89.

Uzzell, Thomas H. "Will the Miniature Survive the Candid Camera Craze? No." *Popular Photography* 1 (August 1937), 32, 66, 82.

Valant, Gary M. *Vintage Aircraft Nose Art*. St. Paul: MBI Publishing, 1987.

Valentine, Mrs. *The Old, Old Fairy Tales*. New York: Allison, [1890?].

Van Dyke, Willard. "Photography of Dorothea Lange." *Camera Craft* 6 (June 1934), 67–73.

Van Kavelaar, Paul. *From Artillery to Air Corps*. Bennington, Vt.: Merriam, 2007.

Van Vechten, Carl. "The Later Work of Herman Melville." *Double-Dealer* 3 (January 1922), 9–20.

Vasey, Ruth. *The World according to Hollywood, 1918–1939*. Madison: Univ. of Wisconsin Press, 1997.

"Versatile Lens." *Photography Annual 1951*, 34.

Vickers, Frank. "A Plea for the Metric System." *Camera* 44 (June 1932), 447.

"Videography: A New Medium?" *International Photo Technik* 19 (Spring 1973), 10–11.

Vilander, Ica. "Advertising on Naked Skin." *Rolleigrafie* 6 (December 1969), 16–20.

———. *Akt Adonis*. Ed. Heinz Peter. Vienna: Gebundene Ausgabe, [1970?].

———. *Akt Apart*. Bonn: Eurapäischen Bucherei, [1967?].

———. *La Femme: Vue par une femme: Album de modèles*. Bonn: Hieronimi, 1967.

Vilander, Ica, et al. *Nudes 69*. New York: Lyle Stuart, 1968.

Virilio, Paul. *The Vision Machine*. Trans. Julie Rose. Bloomington: Indiana Univ. Press, 1994.

Vogel, Craig M., Jonathan Cagan, and Peter Boatwright. *The Design of Things to Come: How Ordinary People Create Extraordinary Products*. Upper Saddle River, N.J.: Wharton School Pub., 2005.

Voice of America. *Behavioral Science*. Washington, D.C.: Voice of America, [1965?].

Voigtländer. *Foto-Taschenbuch 1939*. Braunschweig: Voigtländer, 1939.

———. *100 Jahre Fotografie*. Braunschweig: Voigtländer, 1939.

Von Däniken, Erich. *Chariots of the Gods: Unsolved Mysteries of the Past*. New York: Putnam, 1968.

Von den Socken, Hans. "Large Scale." *Rolleigrafie* 4 (June 1969), 11–14.

Von Frankenberg, Richard. "Maidens, Men, and Motors." *Rolleigrafie* 4 (June 1969), 24–25.

Von Hofmann, Albert. *Das deutsche Land und die deutsche Geschichte*. Stuttgart: Deutsche Verlags, 1920.

Von Miserony, J. Hyzdal. "From a Still Man to a TV Camera Journalist." *International Photo Technik* 18 (Winter 1972), 27, 60–63.

Von Reichenbach, Karl Freiherr. *Le fluide des magnetiseuis*. Paris: Carre, 1891.

———. *Der sensitive Mensch und sein Verhalten zum Ode*. Leipzig: Altmann, 1910.

———. *Wer ist sensitive, wer nicht? Kurze Anleitung, sensitive Menschen mit Leichtigkeit zu finden*. Leipzig: Altmann, 1920.

Von Rohr, Moritz. *Theorie und Geschichte des photographischen Objektivs*. Berlin: Spring, 1899.

Wacquant, Loic J. D. "The Rise of Advanced Marginality: Notes on Its Nature and Implications." *Acta Sociologica* 39 (March 1996), 121–39.

Wailes, Raymond B. "Weird Lights and Cold Flame in Homes Tests with Phosphorus." *Popular Science* 133 (July 1938), 74–75, 102–3.

Walker, Jearl. "The Physics of the Patterns of Frost." *Scientific American*, December 1980, 231–32.

Walker, Randy. *More Painted Ladies*. West Chester, Pa.: Schiffer, 1994.

———. *Painted Ladies: Modern Military Aircraft Nose Art and Unusual Markings*. Atglen, Pa.: Schiffer, 1992.

Wallace, David. *Lost Hollywood*. New York: St. Martin's, 2001.

Wallace, Don. "Snapshots Are Better." *American Photography* 29 (November 1935), 682–84.

Wallop, Douglas. *Night Light*. New York: Norton, 1953.

Walmsley, Leo. *British Ports and Harbors*. London: William Collins, 1942.

Walser, Hans. *The Golden Section*. Trans. Peter Hilton. Washington, D.C.: Mathematical Association, 2001.

Walsh, Frank. *Sin and Censorship: The Catholic Church and the Motion Picture Industry*. New Haven: Yale Univ. Press, 1996.

Walter, Avery. "The Merits of the Box Camera." *Camera Craft* 19 (February 1912), 75–77.

Waltz, George H. "Tom Thumb Radios." *Popular Science* 122 (June 1933), 54–55.

Waples, Douglas. *People and Print: Social Aspects of Reading in the Depression*. Chicago: Univ. of Chicago Press, 1937.

Ward, Geoffrey C. *Jazz: A History of America's Music.* New York: Knopf, 2000.

Ward, William M. "Movie Mood Music." *Popular Photography* 15 (October 1944), 69–70, 76.

Warhol, Andy, and Pat Hackett. *POPism: The Warhol '60s.* New York: Harcourt, Brace, Jovanovich, 1980.

Warner, Marina. *From the Beast to the Blonde: On Fairy Tales and Their Tellers.* London: Chatto & Windus, 1994.

——. *The Inner Eye: Art beyond the Visible.* London: National Touring Exhibitions, 1996.

——. *Phantasmagoria: Spirit Visions, Metaphors, and Media into the Twenty-First Century.* Oxford: Oxford Univ. Press, 2006.

——. "Stolen Shadows, Lost Souls: Body and Soul in Photography." *Raritan* 15 (Fall 1995), 35–58.

Warner, Rex. *The Aerodrome.* London: Bodley Head, 1941.

Warren, Austin. *The New England Conscience.* Ann Arbor: Univ. of Michigan Press, 1966.

Warren, Donald. *Radio Priest: Charles Coughlin, the Father of Hate Radio.* New York: Free Press, 1996.

Warstat, Willi. "Die Photographie in der Werbekunst." *Deutscher Kamera-Almanach* 20 (Berlin: Roth, 1930), 85–98.

Watkins, Alfred. *Archaic Tracks round Cambridge.* Hereford, U.K.: Hereford Times, 1932.

——. *The Old Standing Crosses of Herefordshire.* London: Simpkin Marshall, 1930.

——. *The Old Straight Track: Its Mounds, Beacons, Moats, Sites, and Mark Stones.* London: Methuen, 1925.

——. *Photography: Its Principles and Applications.* New York: Van Nostrand, 1911.

——. *The Watkins Manual of Exposure and Development.* London: Houghton, 1902.

Watkins, John Elfreth. "What May Happen in the Next Hundred Years." *Ladies' Home Journal,* December 1900, 8.

Watney, John Basil. *Mervyn Peake.* London: Joseph; New York: St. Martin's, 1976.

Watson, Elkanah. *Men and Times of the Revolution.* Ed. Winslow C. Watson. New York: Dana, 1856.

Way, Douglas. *Air Photo Interpretation for Land Planning.* Cambridge, Mass.: Harvard Univ., Dept. of Landscape Architecture, 1968.

——. *Terrain Analysis: A Guide to Site Selection Using Aerial Photographic Interpretation.* Stroudsburg: Dowden, 1973.

Weaver, Mike. *The Photographic Art: Pictorial Traditions in Britain and America.* New York: Harper & Row, 1986.

Weaver, Herbert L. *Divining the Primary Sense: Unfamiliar Radiation in Nature, Art, and Science.* London: Routledge, 1978.

Webb, Michael, and Stephen Zito. "Portraits of Women." *Calendar,* American Film Institute Theater, 17 January 17–February 16, 1974, 2.

Weber, Ernst A. "The Nude—Topical as Ever." *International Photo Technik* 19 (Winter 1973), 32–35, 70.

——. "Sandwiched Nudes." *International Photo Technik* 17 (Winter 1971), 16–17.

Wedd, Tony. *Skyways and Landmarks.* Hull, U.K.: Author, 1972.

Wegler, Monika. *Most Recent Tendency. International Photo Techik* 19 (Spring 1973), 10–11.

Weithass, Herbert. "The Rollei Exposure Table." *Photography with Rolleiflex and Rolleicord* 14 (June 1939), 20.

Welch, Paul. "The 'Gay' World Takes to the City Streets." *Life,* June 26, 1964, 68–74.

Wells, H. G. *The Outline of History: Being a Plain History of Life and Mankind.* New York: Macmillan, 1920.

Welty, Eudora. *Thirteen Stories.* New York: Harcourt, 1970.

West, James E. "Boy Scouts Train 4,000,000 Photographers." *Popular Photography* 6 (March 1940), 28–29, 104–5.

West, Nancy Martha. *Kodak and the Lens of Nostalgia.* Charlottesville: Univ. of Virginia Press, 2000.

Westfall, Gary, George Slusser, and Kathleen Church Plummer, eds. *Unearthly Visions: Approaches to Science Fiction and Fantasy Art.* Westport, Conn.: Greenwood, 2002.

"What Are Other Photographers Doing?" *International Photo Technik* 11 (Summer 1971), 11.

"What's Wrong with These Pictures?" *New Photography,* April 1932, n.p.

Wheeler, Otis B. *The Literary Career of Maurice Thompson.* Baton Rouge: Louisiana State Univ. Press, 1965.

Wheelwright, Jane Hollister, and Lynda Wheelwright Schmidt. *The Long Shore.* San Francisco: Sierra Club, 1991.

"While Their Men Are Away." *Survey Mid-monthly* 81 (April 1945), 109–12.

White, E. B. *One Man's Meat.* [1942] Reprint, Gardiner, Me.: Tilbury, 1997.

White, Minor. *Be-ing without Clothes.* New York: Aperture, 1970.

White, Randy Wayne. *Dark Light.* New York: Putnam's, 2006.

White, Stewart Edward. *The Betty Book.* New York: Dutton, 1937.

———. *The Road I Know.* New York: Dutton, 1941.

———. *The Unobstructed Universe.* New York: Dutton, 1940.

White, William Chapman. "The Strapless." *Coronet* 38 (May 1955), 132–38.

"White Sandy Beaches." *Night and Day* 11 (September 1959), 24.

"White Slavery: Sex times Sex." *Rolleigrafie* 6 (December 1969), 12–13.

Whitten, Norman E. "Contemporary Patterns of Malign Occultism among Negroes in North America." *Journal of American Folklore* 75 (Fall 1962), 311–24.

———. "Events and Statuses Involved in a Pattern of Occult Behavior." *Research Previews* (Institute for Research in Social Science, Univ. of North Carolina) 8 (April 1961), 9–16.

Whittier, John Greenleaf. *Poetical Works.* Boston: Houghton, Mifflin, 1892.

"Who's Afraid of Dragons?" *International Photo Technik* 12 (Summer 1976), 28–29.

"Why Do Projected Transparencies Seem Sharper than Paper Prints?" *International Photo Technik* 11 (Fall 1971), 77–78.

Wiebe, Robert. *The Search for Order, 1877–1920.* New York: Hill & Wang, 1967.

Wiener, Norbert. *Cybernetics: Control and Communication in Animal and Machine.* Cambridge, Mass.: MIT Press, 1948.

Wilder, H. Arnold. "Dana D. Goodwin." *B&M Bulletin* 16 (Spring 1989), 2–9.

"Wildest, Wickedest Film Ever Made." *Screen Stories* 67 (February 1968), 50–53, 80.

Wilke, Hermann. *Dein "Ja" zum Leibe: Sinn und Gestaltung deutscher Leibeszucht.* Berlin: Wernitz, 1939.

Wilkins, Mary E. *A Humble Romance.* New York: Harper, 1887.

———. *A New England Nun and Other Stories.* New York: Harper, 1891.

———. *The People of Our Neighborhood.* New York: International Association of Newspapers and Authors, 1898.

Wilkinson, Lynn R. "*Le cousin Pons* and the Invention of Ideology." *Publications of the Modern Language Association* 107 (March 1992), 274–89.

"Will Movies Supplant the Teacher?" *Photo-Era* 64 (April 1930), 219.

Williams, Charles. *The Diamond Bikini.* [1956] London: Simon & Schuster, 1988.

Williams, Hari. *Marconi and His Wireless Stations in Wales.* Llanrwst: Gwasg Carreg Gwalch, 1999.

Williams, Judith. *Decoding Advertisements: Ideology and Meaning in Advertising.* New York: Marion Boyars, 1978.

Williams, Kathleen. *Spenser's Faerie Queen: The World of Glass.* London: Routledge & Kegan Paul, 1966.

Williams, Linda. *Hard Core: Power, Pleasure, and the "Frenzy of the Visible."* Berkeley: Univ. of California Press, 1999.

Williams, Linda, and Christine Gledhill, eds. *Reinventing Film Studies.* London: Arnold, 2000.

Williams, Oscar. "Painted Girls." *Double-Dealer* 3 (February 1922), 112.

Williams, Raymond. *Culture and Society, 1780–1950.* New York: Harper, 1966.

Wilson, David Gordon. *Bicycling Science.* 3rd ed. Cambridge, Mass.: MIT Press, 2004.

Wilson, Edmund. "Oo, Those Awful Orcs!" *Nation,* April 4, 1956, 312–14.

Wilson, Howard Fisher. *The Hill Country of Northern New England: Its Social and Economic History.* New York: Columbia Univ. Press, 1936.

Wilson, Liza. "Instant Pixie." *American Weekly,* October 8, 1961, 8–9.

Wilson, Margery. *Charm.* New York: Chimes, 1928; New York: Stokes, 1931.

——. *I Found My Way.* Philadelphia: Lippincott, 1956.

——. *The Woman You Want to Be: Complete Book of Charm.* Philadelphia: Lippincott, 1942.

Wilson, Timothy D. *Strangers to Ourselves: Discovering the Adaptive Unconscious.* Cambridge, Mass.: Harvard Univ. Press, 2002.

Windisch, Hans. "Colour Photography with the Rollei Camera." *Photography with the Rolleiflex and Rolleicord* 14 (June 1939), 8–13.

——. *The New Photo School.* Harzburg: Heering Verlag, 1938.

Winkler, Wolf-Jürgen. "In the Ice Fissures of the Bossons Glacier." *Rolleigrafie* 2 (December 1968), 32–35.

Winters, S. R. "Underground Radio Telegraph." *Popular Radio* 3 (May 1924), 490–92.

Winterson, Jeanette. *Tanglewreck.* London: Bloomsbury, 2006.

"Wireless Fencing for Receiving Radio Messages." *Popular Science* 100 (January 1922), 75.

Wittgenstein, Ludwig. *Philosophical Investigations.* [1949] Trans. G. E. M. Anscombe. New York: Macmillan, 1968.

Wittke, Carl Frederick. *German-Americans and the World War, with Special Emphasis on Ohio's German-Language Press.* Columbus: Ohio State Archaeological and Historical Society, 1936.

Wolff, Paul. *My Experiences in Color Photography.* Trans. Warner S. Victor. Intro. Jacob Deschin. New York: Grayson, 1948. Originally published as *Meine Erfahrungen Farbig* (Frankfurt am Main: Breidenstein, 1942).

"Women's Noisy Dresses Help Public Speakers." *Popular Science* 117 (September 1930), 62.

Wood, Clement. *Bernarr Macfadden: A Study in Success.* New York: Copeland, 1929.

Wood, John. *The Art of the Autochrome: The Birth of Color Photography.* Iowa City: Univ. of Iowa Press, 1993.

——. "Flaubert, Love, and Photography." *Southern Review* 30 (April 1994), 350–57.

——. *The Photographic Arts.* Iowa City: Univ. of Iowa Press, 1997.

Wood, Robert Williams. "A New Departure in Photography." *Century* 79 (February 1910), 565–72.

Woodrow, Nancy Mann. "The Fascination of Being Photographed and the Improvement in Photography." *Cosmopolitan* 35 (October 1903), 675–84.

Woodward, Richard B. "The Disturbing Photographs of Sally Mann." *New York Times Magazine*, September 27, 1992, 28–36, 52.

Worcester, J. A. "Amateur Phone Transmitter." *Popular Science* 126 (January 1935), 56–57, 106.

"Words and Phrases Invented and Used by the Army." *Word Study* 19 (April 1944), 1–6.

World Committee. *The Brown Network: The Activities of the Nazis in Foreign Countries.* New York: Knight, 1936.

"World's Largest Underwater Photo from Kodak." *International Photo Technik* 11 (Spring 1971), 48.

"World's Only 5 Format Camera." *Popular Photography* 51 (July 1962), 34.

Wormley, Stanton L. "Innovation with a Purpose: Barrett's Model 98 Bravo." *American Rifleman,* April 2009, 44–47, 78, 80–81.

Wright, Cuthbert. "The Mystery of Arthur Machen." *Double-Dealer* 5 (March–April 1923), 104–7; 6 (March 1924), 59–61.

Wyble, Eugene. "Selecting a Used Camera." *Popular Photography* 5 (August 1939), 31, 107–8.

Wynne, Edward A. *Growing Up Suburban.* Austin: Univ. of Texas Press, 1977.

Yeager, Bunny. *ABC's of Figure Photography.* Louisville: Whitestone, 1964.

———. *How to Photograph the Figure.* New York: Whitestone, 1963.

———. "Nude but Not Naked." *Modern Sunbathing* 26 (April 1956), 27–31.

Yeats, William Butler. *The Celtic Twilight.* [1893] London: Bullen, 1902.

———. *Mythologies.* New York: Collier, 1959.

Yellen, Jack. "The Vamp of Savannah." New York: Ager, Yellen & Bornstein, 1924.

Young, George Allen. "Pictorialism for Beginners." *Camera Craft* 43 (April 1936), 180–86.

Zeiss Ikon. "Day or Night Contax." *Camera Craft* 42 (August 1935), n.p.

Zeman, Zbynek. *Nazi Propaganda.* London: Oxford Univ. Press, 1973.

Zielinski, Sigfried. *Audiovisions: Cinema and Television as Entr'acts in History.* Trans. Gloria Custance. Amsterdam: Amsterdam Univ. Press, 1999.

Zolla, Elémire. *The Eclipse of the Intellectual.* [1956] Trans. Raymond Rosenthal. New York: Funk & Wagnalls, 1968.

Zollner, Manfred. *Out of Focus: Statt Autofocus.* Augsburg: Augustusverlag, 1997.

Zorab, G. *Wichelroede en "Aardstralen."* Amsterdam: Breughel, 1950.

Zwerdling, Alex. "The Mythographers and the Romantic Revival of Greek Myth." *Publications of the Modern Language Association* 79 (September 1964), 447–56.